Leisure and Life Satisfaction

Foundational Perspectives

Leisure and Life Satisfaction

Foundational Perspectives

THIRD EDITION

Christopher R. Edginton

UNIVERSITY OF NORTHERN IOWA

Debra J. Jordan

OKLAHOMA STATE UNIVERSITY

Donald G. DeGraaf

CALVIN COLLEGE

Susan R. Edginton

UNIVERSITY OF NORTHERN IOWA

Boston   Burr Ridge, IL   Dubuque, IA   Madison, WI   New York   San Francisco   St. Louis
Bangkok   Bogotá   Caracas   Kuala Lumpur   Lisbon   London   Madrid   Mexico City
Milan   Montreal   New Delhi   Santiago   Seoul   Singapore   Sydney   Taipei   Toronto

McGraw-Hill Higher Education

*A Division of The **McGraw-Hill** Companies*

LEISURE AND LIFE SATISFACTION: FOUNDATIONAL PERSPECTIVES
THIRD EDITION

Some ancillaries, including electronic and print components, may not be available to customers outside the United States.

This book is printed on acid-free paper.

1 2 3 4 5 6 7 8 9 0 QPF/QPF 0 9 8 7 6 5 4 3 2 1

ISBN 0-07-235397-X

Vice president and editor-in-chief: *Thalia Dorwick*
Executive editor: *Vicki Malinee*
Developmental editor: *Carlotta Seely*
Senior marketing manager: *Pamela S. Cooper*
Project manager: *Christine Walker*
Production supervisor: *Enboge Chong*
Coordinator of freelance design: *David W. Hash*
Cover design: *Tsela Barr*
Cover image: *©PhotoDisc*
Interior design: *The Publishing Services Group*
Supplement producer: *Jodi K. Banowetz*
Media technology producer: *Judi David*
Compositor: *Shepherd, Inc.*
Typeface: *10/12 Times Roman*
Printer: *Quebecor World Fairfield, PA*

Library of Congress Cataloging-in-Publication Data

Leisure and life satisfaction : foundational perspectives / Christopher R. Edginton . . . [et al.] — 3rd ed.
   p. cm.
   Includes bibliographical references and index.
   ISBN 0-07-235397-X
    1. Leisure—United States. 2. Leisure—Canada. 3. Leisure industry—United States. 4. Leisure industry—Canada. 5. Quality of life—United States. 6. Quality of life—Canada. I. Edginton, Christopher R.

GV14 .L394 2002
790'.01'3097—dc21

2001034513
CIP

www.mhhe.com

The third edition of *Leisure and Life Satisfaction* is dedicated in memory of Clifford James Edginton and Ruth May Edginton. Loving parents who dedicated their lives to ensure that their children were well cared for, educated, and loved. They will be missed.

—The Authors

CONTENTS

CONTENTS

Preface xii

PART 1
LEISURE IN TODAY'S SOCIETY 1

CHAPTER 1
LEISURE AND LIFE SATISFACTION 2

Introduction 2

Leisure: Toward the Twenty-First Century 3

Life Satisfaction 6

   Leisure and Its Relationship to Life Satisfaction 9

   Leisure and Life Satisfaction as Related to Age 10

   Work, Leisure, and Life Satisfaction 11

   Leisure, Satisfaction, and Community Well-Being 12

Lifestyle and Leisure 12

   Lifestyle Management 13

   Leisure, Organizations, and Life Satisfaction 15

What Motivates People to Pursue Leisure? 17

   Leisure Motives 18

Constraints to Leisure 23

Summary 26

Discussion Questions 27

References 27

CHAPTER 2
THE WORLD OF LEISURE, RECREATION, AND PLAY 30

Introduction 30

What Is Leisure? 31

   Factors Related to a Satisfying Leisure Experience 31

   Ways of Viewing Leisure 33

   Serious Leisure 39

   Work and Leisure 40

What Is Recreation? 42

   Recreation as a Social Instrument 43

What Is Play? 44

   Dimensions of Play 45

Summary 48

Discussion Questions 49

References 49

CHAPTER 3
LEISURE: A HISTORICAL PERSPECTIVE 51

Introduction 51

Why Do We Study History? 52

   Knowledge of Leisure Concepts 52

   Appreciation for the Foundations of the Profession 53

   Understanding People in History 53

   Knowledge of Significant Historical Events and Places 53

   Knowledge That Can Be Useful—Present and Future 54

   Understanding Our Place in History 54

The History of Leisure 54

   Leisure in Preliterate Societies 56

   Leisure in the Agricultural Era 57

   Leisure in the Industrial Era 66

The Technological or Information Era 86

Summary 90

Discussion Questions 90

References 90

CHAPTER 4
PHILOSOPHICAL AND CONCEPTUAL THEMES 92

Introduction 92

What Is Philosophy? 93

Philosophy and Circumstances 93

Building a Philosophical Attitude 93

Values and Philosophy 96

Values and Ethics 98

The Value in an Ethic of Care 100

Why Build a Philosophy of Leisure? 101

To Know Yourself as Well as Your Organization 102

To Clarify Relationships with Consumers/Clients 102

To Clarify Relationships within the Organization 104

To Clarify Relationships with Other Institutions 104

Building a Philosophy 105

Major Philosophies 105

Steps to Building a Philosophy 108

The Meaning of a Philosophy in a Leisure Service Organization 111

Summary 113

Discussion Questions 114

References 114

CHAPTER 5
MASS LEISURE 116

Introduction 116

Mass Leisure: Is There Time? 116

Mass Leisure: Common Elements 120

Increase in Discretionary Income 120

Change in Values 120

Improved Infrastructure Related to Physical and Natural Resources 121

Improved Technology 121

Mass Leisure: What Do People Do? 122

Social Activities as Mass Leisure 123

Sport as Mass Leisure 127

Cultural Activities as Mass Leisure 128

The Environment and Mass Leisure 130

Tourism as Mass Leisure 131

Mass Media and Leisure 134

Summary 139

Discussion Questions 140

References 140

CHAPTER 6
LEISURE AND THE LIFE CYCLE 142

Introduction 142

Leisure throughout the Life Cycle 142

Lifestyles 143

The Life Cycle 145

Stages of Human Development 145

Childhood and Leisure 148

Adolescence and Leisure 153

Adulthood and Leisure 158

Older Adults and Leisure 162

Summary 166

Discussion Questions 166

References 167

PART 2
DELIVERING LEISURE SERVICES 169

CHAPTER 7
DELIVERY OF LEISURE SERVICES: LOCAL GOVERNMENT 170

Introduction 170

Characteristics of Local Leisure Services Agencies 171

Goals and Functions 171

Resource Base 173

Characteristics of Professionals 175

Orientation to Customers 178

Types of Local Governments Providing Parks and Recreation Services 178

Types of Legislation 179

Municipal Government 180

County Government 181

Special Districts 184

Recreation Services as a Part of a School
District   187
Types of Services   187
Professional Roles and Opportunities   191
Career Opportunities in Public Parks
and Recreation   193
Challenges for the Future   194
Summary   201
Discussion Questions   201
References   202

CHAPTER 8
DELIVERY OF LEISURE SERVICES:
STATE GOVERNMENT   204

Introduction   204
Characteristics of State Leisure Services   205
Goals and Functions   205
Coordination with Federal and Local
Governments   206
Resource Base   207
Characteristics of Professionals   208
Types of Direct Recreation Resources and Services
Provided by States   209
Outdoor Recreation and Resources   210
Tourism Promotion   217
The Arts   219
Other State Services   222
Challenges for the Future   224
Summary   225
Discussion Questions   226
References   226

CHAPTER 9
DELIVERY OF LEISURE SERVICES:
FEDERAL GOVERNMENT   228

Introduction   228
Characteristics of Federal Leisure Service
Agencies   229
Goals and Functions   229
Resource Base   233
Characteristics of Professionals   234
Customer Orientation   234
Types of Federal Agencies: United States   235
U.S. Forest Service   236
The Bureau of Land Management   240
National Park Service   242
U.S. Fish and Wildlife Service   245
Bureau of Indian Affairs   245
U.S. Corps of Engineers   246
Tennessee Valley Authority   246
Bureau of Reclamation   248
Veterans' Administration   248
Morale, Welfare, and Recreation Services, U.S. Armed
Forces   249
National Endowment for the Arts   250
National Endowment for the Humanities   251
Types of Federal Agencies: Canada   252
Sports Canada   252
Parks Canada   253
Health Canada   256
Canadian Tourism Commission   259
Challenges for the Future   260
Summary   261
Discussion Questions   261
References   262

CHAPTER 10
DELIVERY OF LEISURE SERVICES:
NONPROFIT   263

Introduction   263
Characteristics of Private, Nonprofit Leisure Service
Organizations   264
Goals and Functions   267
Resource Base   270
Characteristics of Professionals   274
Types of Youth and Voluntary Nonprofit Leisure Service
Organizations   275
Youth Serving Organizations   276
Religious Organizations   283

Organizations Serving Special Populations 284

Relief Organizations 286

Social Service Organizations 287

Conservation Organizations 288

Service Clubs 288

Challenges for the Future 289

Summary 289

Discussion Questions 290

References 290

CHAPTER 11
DELIVERY OF LEISURE SERVICES: COMMERCIAL 292

Introduction 292

Characteristics of Commercial Leisure Services 292

Goals and Functions 293

Resource Base 293

Characteristics of Professionals/Owners 294

Orientation to Customers 294

Types of Business Ownership 296

Sole Proprietorship 296

Partnerships 297

Corporations 297

Types of Commercial Leisure Services 299

Travel and Tourism 299

Hospitality and Food Services 301

Leisure Products (Manufacturing) 303

Entertainment Services 304

Retail Outlets 307

Leisure Services in the Natural
Environment 308

Entrepreneurship, Opportunities, and Challenges 309

What Is Entrepreneurship? 309

Opportunities in the Commercial Leisure Services
Sector 311

Challenges to the Entrepreneur 315

Summary 316

Discussion Questions 316

References 317

CHAPTER 12
DELIVERY OF LEISURE SERVICES: THERAPEUTIC RECREATION 318

Introduction 318

The Emergence of Therapeutic Recreation as a Profession 319

The Need for Specialized Services 319

The Influx of Wounded Soldiers from the World Wars 320

Professional Organizations 322

Legislation 322

Characteristics of Therapeutic Recreation:
People with Disabilities Today 324

Barriers to Success in Leisure 327

Goals and Functions 328

Resource Base 331

Characteristics of Professionals 331

Types of Therapeutic Recreation Programs/Settings 332

Challenges for the Future 335

Dealing with Assistive Technology 336

Addressing New/Growing Social Problems 337

Summary 339

Discussion Questions 339

References 339

PART 3
ISSUES, TRENDS, AND PROFESSIONAL PRACTICE 341

CHAPTER 13
LEISURE PROGRAMMING: PROMOTING QUALITY SERVICES 342

Introduction 342

Promoting Quality and Value 343

Building a Commitment to Quality 344

Developing a Service Orientation 346

What Is a Service? A Product? 346

Organizing a Strategy to Provide Services 347

Programs: The Services of Leisure Service Organizations 354

Types of Programs 355

Factors Influencing Leisure Program Planning 356

The Process of Program Planning 359

Management Approaches to Programming 363

Roles of Leisure Programmers 364

   Direct-Service Roles 364

   Types of Direct-Service Leadership 366

Summary 368

Discussion Questions 369

References 369

CHAPTER 14
PROFESSIONAL CAREER DEVELOPMENT 371

Introduction 371

Common Elements of a Profession 371

   An Organized Body of Knowledge 372

   Organizations and Institutions that Exist to Transmit
      Professional Knowledge 372

   Creation of Professional Authority as a Result
      of Public Sanction 373

Ethics and the Leisure Service Profession 373

   Code of Ethics 373

   Commitment to Professional Ideals 374

Professional Associations 375

   Types of Professional Organizations 377

Pursuing a Professional Career: Key Elements 384

   Career Assessment and Exploration 385

   Education 386

   Professional Experience 387

   Networking 387

   Certifications 388

   Lifelong Education and Professional Development 389

   The Use of a Professional Portfolio 389

Summary 390

Discussion Questions 391

References 391

CHAPTER 15
LEISURE AND CULTURAL DIVERSITY 392

Introduction 392

Future Trends: A Dramatic Increase in Diversity 393

Diversity: Foundational Perspectives 394

   Culture 395

   Prejudice 397

   Discrimination 399

Dimensions of Diversity 399

   Primary Characteristics 400

   Secondary Characteristics 403

   Interaction of Primary/Secondary Characteristics 404

Cultural Sensitivity: Valuing Differences 404

   A Process for Valuing Differences 404

Implications of Diversity for Leisure Service
      Professionals 405

   Administrative Practices 406

   Diversity and Leadership 411

   Diversity Programming: Building Self-Esteem 415

   Program Design for Individuals with Disabilities 416

   Marketing Practices 417

   Other Considerations 417

Summary 417

Discussion Questions 418

References 418

CHAPTER 16
FUTURE TRENDS 420

Introduction 420

Social Trends and Leisure 421

   Population Shifts 421

   Changes in Social Roles 427

   Greater Equality in Sports and Athletics
      for Women 429

   Blurring of Public/Private Involvement in Leisure 429

   Increase in Diversity 430

Health Trends and Issues 432

   Changes in Physical Health 432

   Changes in Social Health 434

Environmental Concerns 436

   Development Versus Ecosystems 437

   Resource Depletion 438

   Environmental Degradation 438

Educational Issues 439

    Desegregation and Open Enrollment 440

    Decreased Support for Extracurricular Programs 440

    Increased Emphasis on Higher Education 441

Technological Influences 441

    Changes in Time Use 441

    Systems and Innovations/Services and Equipment 443

    Transportation 445

Economic Trends 446

    Changing Nature of Work 446

    Continued Growth of the Service Sector
        of Employment 447

Summary 448

Discussion Questions 448

References 449

Credits 451

Index 453

PREFACE

Leisure is an important force influencing and shaping the lives of North Americans. Increasingly, we seek leisure in our lives as a way of enhancing, extending, and sustaining the quality of our lives. Leisure is woven into the fabric of our society and culture. It is evident in a larger sense as we celebrate community life, and yet it is more frequently found in our day-to-day activities. We seek leisure as a way of uplifting the spirit, improving our well-being, and enhancing our relationships with others. Leisure is a powerful force that helps shape our own sense of self-worth, assists in the formulation and communication of values and norms, and aids us in improving the livability of our lives and our communities.

For many, leisure is a perfect gift. It provides an opportunity for reflection, relaxation, the acquisition and enhancement of knowledge and skill, and the expression of one's creative interests. Through leisure, individuals find opportunities to express themselves in ways that are not possible in life's other venues. Leisure provides freedom to pursue one's unfettered interests as well as freedom from those elements that can constrain the perfect being of that interest. Unfulfilled leisure also promotes boredom and anxiety. The challenge of leisure is to see its opportunities and, as a professional assisting others, to aid individuals in their quest for happiness and satisfaction through leisure. This is the theme of this book: promoting life satisfaction through leisure.

As we move into the twenty-first century, leisure is seen more and more as a commodity. As a society, we are increasingly focused on the consumption of leisure experiences. We have lost the value of leisure in building community life, promoting sociability, and linking individuals to one another as a way of fostering the common good. We are, in effect, losing the opportunity to experience leisure as a way of contributing to our understanding of our inner selves and each other. The commodification of leisure has moved us from its more liberating, creative, energizing, and individually and communally fulfilling state to one where we are dependent on more external enhancements to guide our sense of satisfaction and well-being.

The gift of leisure in its fullness is about promoting human happiness and satisfaction. Leisure professionals' work focuses on improving and enhancing the human condition. Such individuals create a sense of hope, underscoring the promise of greater life satisfaction through leisure. The underlying theme of *Leisure and Life Satisfaction* suggests that leisure is a powerful vehicle that is available to individuals to assist them in achieving these ends. The role of professionals is one of crafting leisure environments to assist individuals, groups of people, and whole communities in achieving a higher quality of life and a greater level of happiness and satisfaction.

Overview

The third edition of *Leisure and Life Satisfaction,* like its predecessor, provides a complete overview of many of the aspects of leisure, including: basic concepts, definitions, fundamentals, and terms; the organization and delivery of leisure services; and critical professional trends, issues, and future perspectives. *Leisure and Life Satisfaction* was written to assist individuals, especially those preparing themselves to serve as entry-level professionals, to understand the broad dimensions of the leisure phenomenon in North American society, the organization of the leisure industry in all sectors, and the issues influencing professional practice. In addition, this new edition of *Leisure and Life Satisfaction* provides up-to-date facts, statistics, and support materials. The text is written with a North American perspective to include examples from both Canada and the United States. Each chapter is enhanced with complementary features, called *Leisure Lines*. These exhibits illustrate key concepts as well as elements related to professional practice.

This edition of *Leisure and Life Satisfaction* is divided into three parts. Part 1 provides an overview of basic terms, concepts, and ideas related to leisure, recreation, and play. In addition, historical, philosophical, and ethical elements are presented. Part 1 also presents an overview of leisure and the life cycle and mass leisure. Part 2 offers a basic overview of organizations involved in the delivery of leisure services from a public, commercial, or nonprofit perspective. Part 3 focuses on providing information dealing with issues, trends, and elements affecting future professional practice.

New to this Edition

This new edition has been significantly revised and updated. The following list is a sampling of topics that are either new to this edition or greatly expanded since the last edition.

Chapter 1: Leisure and Life Satisfaction

- Expanded generational perspective
- Life satisfaction and happiness among North Americans
- A model for understanding the work of leisure service organizations
- Constraints to leisure

Chapter 2: The World of Leisure, Recreation, and Play

- Challenges defining leisure, recreation, and play
- Serious leisure
- Enhancements to research perspectives

Chapter 3: Leisure: A Historical Perspective

- History of the leisure movement
- Historical perspectives in travel and tourism
- Cultural pluralism
- How passion drives the work of professionals
- Historical insights into youth and voluntary organizations

Chapter 4: Philosophical and Conceptual Themes

- Developing a philosophical perspective to leisure
- New insights into philosophical positions held by early leaders
- New reflections on the play movement as a reform movement
- Philosophical perspectives regarding availability of free-time and enforced leisure

Chapter 5: Mass Leisure

- Hosteling International
- Concept of *More Work/Less Play*
- Work/leisure relationship
- Amount of free-time available to Americans
- Completely revised discussion of social activities as mass leisure
- North Americans and the out-of-doors
- Tourism as mass leisure
- Television as mass leisure

Chapter 6: Leisure and the Life Cycle

- Redefinition of "lifestyle"
- New framework for defining the Baby Boom generation
- Lifestyle factors and leisure
- Updated statistics

Chapter 7: Delivery of Leisure Services: Local Government

- Benefits approach to operating services
- Characteristics of local leisure services: goals and resource base
- Characteristics of professionals
- Professionals as servant leaders
- Career opportunities in parks and recreation
- Trends and issues facing parks and recreation

Chapter 8: Delivery of Leisure Services: State Government

- Updated statistical information on state park systems
- Trends impacting state parks
- Terms and guidelines for state park resources
- Terms and guidelines for trails

Chapter 9: Delivery of Leisure Services: Federal Government

- Federal achievements in leisure activities the last 50 years

- Snowmobiles in natural resource areas
- New statistical information on federal leisure activities
- Federal government's role in Canada
- Tourism in Canada

Chapter 10: Delivery of Leisure Services: Non-profit
- Importance of non-profit organizations in the twenty-first century
- Best managed non-profit organizations in America
- Partnerships and building collaborative relationships
- Updated statistics and factors
- New tables on types of non-profit organizations

Chapter 11: Delivery of Leisure Services: Commercial
- Disney's new adventures
- Swimming with dolphins
- Theme park attendance
- Hotel and lodging industry
- Analysis of personal consumption and leisure

Chapter 12: Delivery of Leisure Services: Therapeutic Recreation
- Characteristics of therapeutic recreation
- Certifying therapeutic recreation specialist
- Barriers and disabled persons
- National Therapeutic Recreation Society's philosophical statement
- Characteristics of professionals
- Dealing with assistive technology
- Additional examples from professional practice

Chapter 13: Leisure Programming: Promoting Quality Services
- Health and well-being
- Seniors and the computer superhighway
- Perspectives on sport and women
- Customer service
- Importance of programming as focal point of the field of leisure
- Strategies for promoting customer service
- Benefits-based programming

Chapter 14: Professional Career Development
- State parks and recreation societies and associations
- Updated information on professional societies
- Use of a professional portfolio

Chapter 15: Leisure and Cultural Diversity
- Women's individual choices in leisure
- Updated statistics and information
- Insights into types of cultures—surface and deep culture
- Updated definitions

Chapter 16: Future Trends
- World population growth
- Changing household composition
- Changing ethnic composition of America
- Surgeon General's Report on *Physical Activity and Health*
- Drug use and violence
- Leisure and the environment
- Life-style coaching

Successful Features

The following successful features are being continued in this new edition:

- *Introductions*—These opening paragraphs spark the reader's interest in the chapter topic and outline how the material will be presented.
- *Leisure Line boxes*—These boxes highlight timely topics of interest, such as creating balance in your life, the right to take risks, virtual leisure, and the fast-food lifestyle.
- *Tables, figures, and photographs*—The tables provide statistics and facts to complement the text. A variety of figures and photographs highlight leisure themes and activities.
- *Summaries*—The summary at the end of each chapter offers a capsule view of the content, reinforcing learning and providing an effective tool for review.
- *Discussion Questions*—These end-of-chapter questions provide a valuable way to review the content and a starting point for further learning and individual activities.

Ancillaries

Instructor's Manual and Test Bank
The Instructor's Manual and Test Bank to accompany *Leisure and Life Satisfaction* features learning objectives, key terms and concepts, chapter outlines, and teaching hints. The Test Bank portion consists of true/false, multiple-choice, and short essay questions.

Brownstone's Diploma/Exam IV Computerized Testing A Computerized Test Bank us available for use with this edition of *Leisure and Life Satisfaction*. Brownstone's Diploma Computerized Testing is the most flexible, powerful, easy-to-use electronic testing program available in higher education. The Diploma system allows the test maker to create a print version, an online version (to be delivered to a computer lab), or an internet version of each test. Diploma includes a built-in instructor gradebook, into which student rosters and files can generally be imported. Diploma is for Windows users, and the CD-ROM includes a separate testing program, Exam IV, for Macintosh users.

PowerWeb This edition of *Leisure and Life Satisfaction* has been packaged with PowerWeb, a valuable learning tool. Power Web is an easy-to-use online resource from McGraw-Hill that provides current articles, curriculum-based materials, weekly updates with assessment, informative and timely world news, related web links, research tools, student study tools, interactive tools, and more.

Access to PowerWeb also offers these resources:

- Study tips with self-quizzes
- Links to related sites
- Weekly updates
- Current news
- Daily newsfeed of related topics
- Web research guide

PowerWeb is a password-protected website. Your McGraw-Hill Sales Representative can guide you in creating a student package with PowerWeb. Preview this website at: www.dushkin.com/powerweb.

Acknowledgments

As with any project of this magnitude and scope, there are many individuals who contribute to its development and completion. We would like to thank several individuals for their contributions to the third edition of *Leisure and Life Satisfaction*. Our support staff at McGraw-Hill was instrumental in advancing the project by continuing their faith in our writing efforts and their belief that the market continues to be well-served by a comprehensive, well-written, well-documented textbook for entry-level professionals in the leisure services area. In particular, we would like to thank Vicki Malinee, Executive Editor, for her continued commitment to this project. Carlotta Seely, our Developmental Editor, was very professional, thorough, and supportive in assisting us with this project. Carlotta was excellent in her communications with us, helping to forge a reasonable and effective writing schedule. We appreciate greatly her strong leadership and value her attention and commitment to this effort. The Production staff, including Christine Walker, was instrumental in the completion of the project and in moving it to actual publication. Over the years, Pam Cooper has provided her excellent marketing skills to a variety of our projects and to this one in particular. We greatly value Pam's consistent work in an environment that is often turbulent.

Support staff at each of our institutions was very helpful and supportive in helping with manuscript preparation and production. Perhaps most important has been the work of Lynda Moore at the University of Northern Iowa. Lynda was responsible for compiling the work of all four authors and packaging the materials so that it was prepared for production. Lynda is a gentle person whose commitment to this project was unsurpassed. She exhibited a great deal of energy when necessary and patience as the project ebbed and flowed through its processes. In addition, Lynda was supported at the University of Northern Iowa by Yuet Mui Kong, Michelle McClelland, and Jongsun "Sunny" Wee, graduate assistants who were responsible for researching key ideas, facts, and statistics necessary to update many chapters of the document. All of these individuals were supportive and assistive in this project, and we greatly appreciate their contributions.

We would like to thank our colleagues at the University of Northern Iowa, Oklahoma State University, and Calvin College. The faculty and staff of the School of Health, Physical Education, and Leisure Services at the University of Northern Iowa are supportive and tolerant of our scholarly activities. At times our scholarly focus robs faculty of our support. The faculty and staff have been understanding and, in fact, cheered us along through this and many other projects. We would like to thank the Leisure Studies faculty at Oklahoma State University for their support during work on the project. We appreciate the faculty of Health, Physical Education, Recreation, and Sports at Calvin College for their support and understanding while this project was completed.

Reviewers

We would also like to thank the reviewers of the second edition, who offered many valuable suggestions for improvement that have helped to make this a better book:

Patricia Ardovino
University of Wisconsin-La Crosse

William A. Becker
Christopher Newport University

Steven Gray
California State University-Sacramento

Charles Hammersley
Northern Arizona University

Frank Hendrick
California Polytechnic State University

Richard D. MacNeil
University of Iowa

Jack Samuels
Montclair State University

Our family members and loved ones have provided environments that allowed us to pursue this type of extensive writing project. We would like to say a special note of thanks to Carole Edginton-Flack, Tom Flack, Hanna Flack, David Edginton, to Kathy, Isaac, and Rochelle DeGraaf, and to Sherril York. Carole and David have always been understanding of the value and importance of our professional writing activities. We appreciate their consistent interest in these endeavors. As they have matured, they have become actively involved in our professional efforts, contributing their extensive knowledge, skills, and insights, helping us shape our thinking, writing, and the ways in which we practice the profession. We also appreciate the Jordan family and their interest in and enthusiasm for the various writing projects in which Deb is involved. Both near and far, they have always "been there"—every step of the way. Isaac and Rochelle have also provided us with powerful reminders of the potential for our field to make a difference in the lives of those it serves. They remind us in their daily actions of the playful joys of our profession. Last, but certainly not least, we are inspired by the newest member of the Edginton family, our granddaughter Hanna. She has brought great joy and inspiration to our lives. With her birth, we were reminded of the hope that springs forward for each new generation.

Christopher R. Edginton
Debra J. Jordan
Donald G. DeGraaf
Susan R. Edginton

Leisure in Today's Society

Leisure provides opportunities for dynamic, challenging, and fulfilling life experiences.

CHAPTER 1

Leisure and Life Satisfaction

Leisure experiences promote greater life satisfaction. There are many benefits to be derived from leisure. Some experiences offer great challenges, others provide opportunities for reflection, introspection, and/or relaxation.

Introduction

Leisure is an important social, cultural, and economic force that has great influence on the happiness, well-being, and life satisfaction of all individuals. The idea that leisure promotes great life satisfaction, however, is not a new one. A number of ancient civilizations, including the Greeks, realized the importance and value of leisure and its role in life satisfaction. The Greek historian Herodotus notes, ". . . man [*sic*] is most nearly himself when he achieves the seriousness of a child at play." In the last 150 years, the growth of leisure in the public, private nonprofit, and commercial sectors reflects the ever increasing value that both Americans and Canadians place upon leisure.

This book, with leisure and its relationship to life satisfaction as its theme, presents historical and contemporary concepts of leisure, recreation, and play. It describes what people in the United States and Canada do in terms of their leisure pursuits, what motivates them, and what they value. The types of agencies and institutions providing leisure services are also discussed. The book has been written to assist students preparing for professional careers in the leisure service industry.

As leisure professionals, we are in the *life satisfaction* business. Our role in society helps to improve the quality of life of individuals through the provision of quality leisure opportunities, thus enhancing intellectual, social, physical, spiritual, and psychological well-being. This chapter focuses on defining and understanding the terms "leisure" and "life satisfaction." In addition, the chapter discusses why leisure is important in people's lives and presents the benefits derived from participation in leisure. Further, a discussion of constraints to participation in leisure and strategies to enhance life satisfaction are included.

Leisure: Toward the Twenty-First Century

In the twenty-first century, there will be tremendous changes in the way people live, the material bounty available, and the opportunities for leisure pursuits. In a 150-year period in Canada and the United States, society has been transformed from rural, agrarian cultures to urban, highly technical societies. Millions of inventions have dramatically changed the way we live our lives. One of the greatest gifts we have been given as a culture has been the gift of increased leisure for many.

Changes will impact work, play, family structures, and mental and physical well-being. We have witnessed in the past century dramatic increases in the amount of leisure available to Canadian and U.S. citizens, resulting in changed attitudes toward seeking leisure experiences. We have moved from a society harnessed by a work ethic that demanded toil fourteen to sixteen hours per day, six days a week, to one in which the average industrial worker works a five-day, less-than-forty-hour workweek. Meanwhile, attitudes toward play and leisure—once seen as frivolous, nonessential activities or, at best, amusements or diversions—have changed so that leisure is viewed as a central focus in life that helps individuals define their self-concept.

Godbey writes that although we think of society ". . . as being composed of individuals who have shared common experiences, in reality our society is made up of . . . distinct generational groupings" (Godbey, 1986, p. 1). Each of these generational groupings has been influenced by a host of historical and cultural values that have shaped and molded their perspective of leisure. This, in turn, has greatly influenced the extent to which these groupings have derived satisfaction from their leisure experiences. From a personal family perspective, we all have seen dramatic changes in terms of the way various family members perceived work and leisure. One of the authors reflects on leisure in the lives of his family members.

My Grandparents' View of Leisure. My grandparents viewed leisure and play *as being frivolous.* As gender roles of the era dictated, my grandfather worked hard to survive in order to achieve the "American Dream" for his family. He worked as a coal miner and for the railroads, and often toiled sixty to seventy hours per week to clothe, feed, and shelter the family. My grandmother fulfilled her expected roles as well. She worked in the home, cooking, cleaning, raising the family, and serving as a helpmate for my grandfather. All of these tasks were accomplished, of course, without the modern conveniences of today. My grandfather loved the out-of-doors and enjoyed tent camping with friends when he could pursue it—which was not very often. My grandmother engaged in quilting and canning. Leisure activities during my grandparents' era often were justified as being in *support of subsistence* or were *utilitarian in nature.* When my grandfather died at age ninety-seven, he had been retired for more than thirty years.

My Parents' View of Leisure. My parents were born in the early 1900s and were raised during the Great Depression. That event shaped their entire lives. Always concerned about pursuing financial security, they often would forgo the pleasures of everyday leisure opportunities to ensure their financial well-being. Interestingly, during his leisure time, my father enjoyed playing the stock market and engaging in real estate investments—both activities related to acquiring financial security. My mother primarily worked in the home, focusing on raising the family. My father served in World War II and subsequently worked as an engineer for an electronics firm in the Silicon Valley, California. Like my grandparents, both my mother and father worked extremely hard, but they placed emphasis on using their leisure time *to restore or refresh themselves to work* harder on the job. Every summer, my father initiated family vacations to Oregon. We camped and fished and toured, enjoying the scenery. On these trips, my parents engaged in activities sufficiently different from daily tasks so as to be restorative.

My Generation's View of Leisure. I graduated from high school four decades ago, about the time of the United States' heightened involvement in Vietnam. My generation's values differed vastly from those of my parents and grandparents. We did not pursue financial security or stability; we had

Time Is of the Essence

If asked about their free time, many Americans will talk and (often) complain that they are busier than ever before. They talk about the long hours spent at work, the time required for child raising and household chores, and of not getting enough sleep each day. In fact, many Americans can be heard bemoaning the fact that a day is *only* 24 hours long. In survey after survey of asking people about their free time, this holds true. People report that they are very busy doing lots of things. In fact, people are becoming "time stackers"—they do multiple tasks, stacking them one atop of the other.

New information is being published, however, that makes us wonder about the amount of time we *think* we have and the time we *really* have. In a recent issue of Newsweek (May 12, 1997) it was reported that people have more aggregate free time than they think they do (Peyser, 1997). In fact, Peyser talked about a new book titled *Time for Life,* in which leisure and time experts John Robinson and Geoffrey Godbey note that Americans have more free time now than they have had in the past 30 years—an average of 40 hours per week. This is due, in part, to many people retiring earlier in life and having fewer children later. Robinson and Godbey note that the increase in free time holds

true even for working parents. Two of the few groups that do not have additional time each week are those with more than four children under 18 years old and parents of very young children.

One reason for this new and somewhat controversial finding is that the research was conducted, not by asking people how busy they are, but by having 10,000 people keep detailed time diaries. They kept minute-by-minute track of what they were doing, when, and for how long. In this way, the researchers did not get inflated perceptions of busyness—they got the truth. Where does all the extra free time go? Some people spend more time watching television, while others spend more time with their children. Men are helping women more with household chores than they were thirty years ago—in 1965 women were doing five times as much housework as men; that gap has narrowed to twice as much.

Now what? If time is of the essence for you, perhaps keeping a detailed time diary of weekly activities would help to see where all that time goes. Are you really that busy or do you just think you are? When time flies, does it contribute to the quality of your life satisfacation? Are you really having fun?

it. I grew up, when compared with my parents, in an affluent era. It was also an era of immediacy—instant leisure entertainment in the form of television and electronic home entertainment. Educational opportunity and the pursuit of college degrees were readily available. I rode the crest of the baby boom generation. During this period of time, work was not necessarily the focus of life or one's time—leisure became a predominant shaper of culture. Many of my generation "*worked to play.*" We did not seek financial security; we sought greater enjoyment in life via leisure pursuits. As Kelly and Godbey (1992) note, the emphasis of this generation changed from "we" to "me."

My Children's View of Leisure. My son and daughter recently graduated from college. One has begun his professional work life, and the other continues in graduate school. They are both married, and their family life is an important determiner of their leisure. They have a different set of values toward their work and leisure than my grandparents, my parents, and I have had. They appear to view leisure as a right rather than a luxury, although they are not currently as economically affluent as the previous generation. They appear to be more status oriented. They are a part of today's "*just do it*" society, the "*work hard, play hard*" group (Patterson, 2000). Leisure in many respects is a commodity to them to consume; they have many leisure experiences, but I'm not sure they experience leisure (Harper and Hultsman, 1994). The outward symbols of their leisure participation are often used as measures of personal success and achievements. Individuals in this age group desire to have meaningful, creative, fulfilling lifestyles both on and off the job. This generation seeks opportunities for continuous growth, personal and physical development, and increased spiritual awareness.

My Grandchild's Play. Nearly four years ago, my granddaughter was born two and a half months premature. Although her early life was in question, she has grown into a robust child full of the exuberance that comes from one's young age. She is vibrant and curious to learn, to discover new and exciting elements of our world. I am constantly amazed at her intellectual curiosity and ability to seek meaning in the world she encounters. Her world is one of play. From her early life she has learned about the importance of leisure in promoting greater quality of life. She is playful and joyful and expresses great enthusiasm in the pursuit of her play activities. At times she lives in a fantasy world, as all children do. Her play objects give meaning to her life, symbolically and realistically. For her, her play is her work. It is serious business that she pursues. There is no question in my mind that her life is being shaped by her world of play. It is interesting to observe how culturally her play activities are defining her role in future society. She has begun to assimilate into her role as a female through her play activities. She likes to dress up, build, read (or be read to), sing, pretend, and be with other children. She is gregarious and outgoing, yet shy and reserved at the same time. Her play is central to her well-being. Her leisure life will be vastly different from the generations that have preceded her. I believe that her quality of life and the livability of the community setting in which she lives will be important features in her future.

In review, each of these generations has different expectations, values, and attitudes that shape and mold its leisure interests and pursuits (see figure 1.1). One generation more strongly values economic stability, whereas another views leisure as a status symbol. Current status symbols associated with leisure include involvement in fitness, the ownership of clothing endorsed by professional sports teams, and participation in activities such as skydiving. Each of these generations approaches leisure in different ways in order to enhance its life satisfaction.

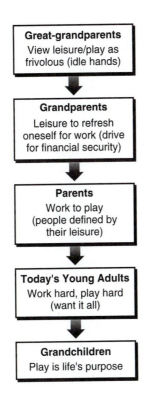

Figure 1.1

Generational views of leisure

For one generation, actual participation in leisure serves as an important yardstick in measuring life satisfaction and well-being; for another generation, leisure is an ideal that is to be pursued.

Although in the last 100 years society has developed in a way that contributes to individual material and spiritual well-being, we have also witnessed tragic wars and tumultuous devastation. In that time, more people have been killed in wars than in the entire history of humankind. On the other hand, conditions have given rise to opportunities for creative endeavors, intellectual developments, and opportunities for greater self-actualization. Today, people can use leisure to build life satisfaction and to enhance the well-being of individuals; it can serve as a positive force to enhance society and culture as a whole.

Life Satisfaction

A discussion of leisure and life satisfaction requires a working definition of terms. The next chapter presents a thorough discussion of the meanings and definitions of leisure, but for now we will define leisure as a *multidimensional construct in which one feels relatively free from constraints, has a feeling of positive affect, is motivated by internal forces, and allows the exercise of perceived competence.*

What is meant by life satisfaction? People often think of life satisfaction as *a sense of well-being, happiness, or quality of life* that is available to an individual (Shichman and Cooper, 1984). Happiness, morale, psychological well-being, and life adjustment are all indicators of the overall quality of our inner experience; ". . . happiness is often considered the extent to which we have positive attitudes and feelings about various aspects of our lives" (Russell, 1996, p. 38). To more precisely define life satisfaction or well-being is a complex and difficult task, as there are no universally accepted definitions. In fact, the question of life satisfaction or well-being is often a subjective, philosophical one, rather than one that can be stated in objective terms. Surveys can objectively measure the economic well-being of individuals, their mental and physical health, and other factors, but subjective measures are required to evaluate quantitative and qualitative factors that contribute to life satisfaction, such as one's spiritual well-being.

The literature concerning life satisfaction and well-being, while diverse, is primarily concerned with how and why people experience their lives in positive ways, including both intellectual factors and emotional reactions (Diener, 1984). Most of the literature has focused on terms such as happiness, satisfaction, morale, life satisfaction, well-being, and quality of life. In 1967, a review of the area of life satisfaction by Wilson suggests that the ". . . happy person emerges as a young, healthy, well-educated, well-paid, extroverted, optimistic, worry-free, religious, married person with high self-esteem, high job morale, [modest aspirations, of either sex], and of a wide range of intelligence" (p. 294). Myers (2000) reports that happy people are less self-focused, less hostile and abusive, and less vulnerable to disease. They also are more loving, forgiving, trusting, energetic, decisive, creative, sociable, and helpful. Positive emotions are conducive to sociability, optimistic goal-striving, even healthy immune systems (Weisse, 1992). It is interesting to note that an electronic search of *Psychological Abstracts* since 1887 turned up 8,072 articles on anger, 57,800 on anxiety, and 70,856 on depression, while only 851 abstracts mentioned joy, 2,958 happiness, and 5,701 life satisfaction (Myers, 2000).

Diener has suggested that definitions of happiness or well-being can be broken into three categories (1984, p. 543). These are as follows:

1. *External/Normative Criteria.* The value framework of one's culture or society will influence one's perception of life satisfaction or well-being. Normative definitions outline

what is desirable in the ideal state. For example, the Constitution of the United States defines many expectations related to life satisfaction, such as "life, liberty and the pursuit of happiness."

2. *Internal/Subjective Criteria.* One's personal assessment regarding what constitutes quality of life based upon one's own chosen criteria, and the degree to which these criteria are achieved, is a determinant of life satisfaction and well-being. For example, some individuals may desire to pursue leisure activities that enhance their social status or sense of self-esteem. Others may desire to pursue leisure activities that promote family togetherness or physical well-being.

3. *Internal/Emotional State.* Simply put, the degree to which one experiences pleasant emotions during life's activities can be used as a measure of life satisfaction. This is determined by the individual him/herself. During certain life activities, the individual may feel happy, content, creative, uplifted, socially rewarded, or spiritually moved, and these emotions may contribute to life satisfaction.

Diener goes on to suggest that all three of these measures should be combined for a total global assessment of life satisfaction. In other words, we should not only consider the external factors that influence a person's life satisfaction or well-being but also the internal ones. These measures help in identifying what constitutes quality of life for an individual and provide measures for determining quality of life.

More specifically, Csikszentmihalyi (1990) has focused on life satisfaction as related to involvement in specific life experiences, including those that can be defined as leisure. His paradigm is known as the concept of "flow." Flow is the experience that

. . . lifts the course of life to a different level. Alienation gives way to involvement, enjoyment replaces boredom, helplessness turns into a feeling of control, and psychic energy works to reinforce the sense of self, instead of being lost in the service of external goals. When experience is intrinsically rewarding life is justified in the present, instead of being held hostage to a hypothetical future gain. (Csikszentmihalyi, 1990, p. 69)

Flow can be viewed as that state of being between "boredom and anxiety," where the challenge of the activity matches the skills of the participant. If you were a soccer star playing with a group of novices, you would likely be bored. On the other hand, if you were a novice playing with a group of highly skilled players, you would be agitated and anxious. Flow is that experience where it all seems to come together; skills correspond to the level of play.

Csikszentmihalyi (1990) presents several elements of enjoyment or flow directly related to satisfaction. The elements of enjoyment are as follows:

1. *A Challenging Activity that Requires Skills.* As reported by participants, most optimal experiences occur within activity that is goal-directed, bounded by rules and requiring a certain level of skill. Csikszentmihalyi (1990) notes that skills and activity need not imply physical skill and activity alone. Reading requires skill and has a goal of completion; it could very well provide the stage for flow to occur.

2. *The Merging of Action and Awareness.* When all of a person's skills are necessary to deal with the activity at hand, that person becomes totally immersed in the activity. Distractions seem to fade away and the participant becomes one with the event. For example, a gymnast becomes so absorbed in the event that she is unaware of the noise of the crowd. People who experience this merging of action and awareness speak of being one with everything, losing touch with the world, and a feeling of being relaxed and energetic at the same time.

3. *Clear Goals and Feedback.* Optimal experiences result from clearly directed goals. The participant knows what to do, where to aim. In addition, constant feedback relates to those goals. In playing cards as one hand is lost and another dealt, players know the score. In playing a musical instrument a composer hears the tones and melodies and knows how the music relates to the goal of composing a new song.

4. *Concentration on the Task at Hand.* One aspect of the merging of action and awareness involves tremendous concentration on the task at hand. Those who experience flow often talk about such total immersion as to be able to forget the unpleasant tasks awaiting them. Omitting worries from conscious thought allows complete concentration on the activity. For example, you have been worrying about an uncompleted assignment, yet engage a friend in a game of tennis. During the tennis match you forget about the assignment as you concentrate on winning each point. You must concentrate to succeed in reaching your goals.

5. *The Paradox of Control.* Flow experiences involve a sense of personal control over one's destiny with regard to the activity of choice. Enjoyment comes from the sense of being skilled enough to eliminate or minimize risk of failure or injury; one exercises control by matching one's skill with the appropriate level of challenge. Competition related to martial arts always holds the risk of physical injury; however, competitors placed in classes with appropriate skill levels face little danger of injury.

6. *The Loss of Self-Consciousness.* Csikszentmihalyi (1990) talks about losing awareness of self in the flow experience. Being totally immersed in an activity, when concentration levels are high and action and awareness have merged, a person temporarily forgets about self as a being. This loss of self frequently accompanies a feeling of oneness with something else—the environment, the ball, other participants.

7. *The Transformation of Time.* The most commonly reported characteristic of flow or optimal experience is the change in perception of the passage of time. During the experience, people speak of time standing still, yet after the experience is over, time seems to have sped by. For example, all of us can remember at least one conversation we have had with another person when we had no idea how much time had passed—the conversation absorbed us, engaged our concentration, and gave us clear and continuous feedback.

Csikszentmihalyi (1990) suggests that all of these elements are present in a truly engrossing, enjoyable, and satisfying experience. Taken together, these factors help in identifying what constitutes quality-of-life experiences and provide measures for evaluating quality-of-life factors.

Leisure participation can affect and be affected by life satisfaction or well-being variables. Leisure, in fact, can be an important component contributing to the daily well-being of an individual. For example, on a day-to-day basis we all engage in mundane events and activities such as sleeping, eating, housework, and, for some, a monotonous work environment. These activities do not necessarily increase our pleasure, happiness, or well-being. As Reich and Zautra note, "if we do not do them, we do not necessarily feel worse, we simply do not increase our pleasure" (1983, p. 43). On the other hand, *leisure activities*—usually intrinsically motivated and often freely chosen—may provide more opportunities for pleasure, hence increased life satisfaction.

Are North Americans happy? Periodic studies by the National Opinion Research Center (Myers, 2000) report that nine out of ten individuals surveyed report that they are very happy, or pretty happy. Only one in ten indicate that they are not too happy. Further, individuals express great satisfaction with their life in general. Myers reports that eight of ten individuals in selected studies rate themselves more satisfied with life than dissatisfied. Likewise, some three-fourths of people say that they have felt excited, proud, or pleased at some point during the last few weeks; only a third indicate that they are lonely, bored, or depressed (Myers, 2000).

What do North Americans believe contributes to life satisfaction? Does money buy happiness? Does material gain influence life satisfaction, happiness, or well-being? Happiness tends to be lower among the very poor (Myers, 2000). Earning more money, however, does not necessarily improve one's happiness. Although, as Diener (2000) reports, individuals living in wealthy nations tend to be more satisfied with their lifestyles, in wealthy nations (United States, Canada, and Europe) the correlation between income and personal happiness is surprisingly weak (Inglehart, 1989). Interestingly, the more people strive for extrinsic goals such as monetary gain, the less robust is their well-being (Myers, 2000). What does produce happiness, life satisfaction, or well-being? The need to belong, close relationships, and friendships are all elements that contribute to greater happiness, life satisfaction, and well-being. Further, religiously active people also report higher levels of happiness (Inglehart, 1989).

If one views the benefits that may motivate individuals to participate in leisure found in table 1.1 (see p. 19), it is evident that many of the potential elements are focused on factors that influence happiness, life satisfaction, and well-being. For example, learning, exploration, being with friends, slowing down mentally, spiritual introspection, meeting people, and being with individuals with similar values are all factors that can promote greater life satisfaction. Leisure provides opportunities for individuals to find all of these ends.

Interestingly, ". . . most Americans now value their time on parity with money" as reported in one of the United Way of America's (1992, p. 21) series of environmental scan reports. This source reports that 65 percent of Americans are willing to give up pay in order to have more time off. Individuals are seeking ". . . more flexible hours, shorter work hours, increased vacation time, work at home arrangements and . . . job sharing" (United Way, 1992, p. 21). In a Time/CNN (1991) poll, seven of ten people surveyed indicated that they would like to ". . . slow down and live a more relaxed life, especially spending more time with their families." As indicated by those polled ". . . earning a living today requires so much effort that it is difficult to find time to enjoy life" (as cited in United Way, 1992, p. 22) (see figure 1.2).

A large number of identified variables contribute to life satisfaction or well-being. Some of the *subjective variables* include life satisfaction and its relationship to self-esteem, satisfaction with self, standard of living, family life, work, mental and physical health, community, mood, place of residence, physical attractiveness, and leisure. *Demographic variables* often studied and linked to life satisfaction and well-being include income, age, gender, race/ethnicity, employment, education, marriage, and family. When discussing *psychological dimensions* and life satisfaction, variables often include social contact, personality, creativity, and involvement in activities. All of these variables can be studied within the leisure experience itself. For example, one could view the relationship between life satisfaction, income, and leisure pursuits. The study of activities, for example, suggests that participation in leisure events, including hobbies and formal organizations, increases social contact, which, in turn, increases life satisfaction.

Leisure and Its Relationship to Life Satisfaction

A number of studies have focused on the topic of leisure and life satisfaction. Iso-Ahola (1980) reported that all of the studies he had reviewed showed a positive relationship between leisure and life satisfaction. Kelly and Godbey (1992) reported similar findings twelve years later. Leisure and life satisfaction consist of many elements. According to Kelly (1996), life satisfaction includes self-expression, companionship, integration, health, rest and relaxation, meeting new people, experiencing nature, and family relationships. Hull, Stewart, and Yi (1992) found that satisfaction is dynamic and that it fluctuates along experience patterns. People experience peaks in satisfaction, lulls in boredom, peaks in excitement, and peaks in relaxation. Leitner

Figure 1.2

Americans desire a slower pace of life.

Source: Data from Time/CNN, 1991, as appeared in What Lies Ahead: A Decade of Decision, *from the United Way of America, 1992. United Way Strategic Institute, Alexandria, VA.*

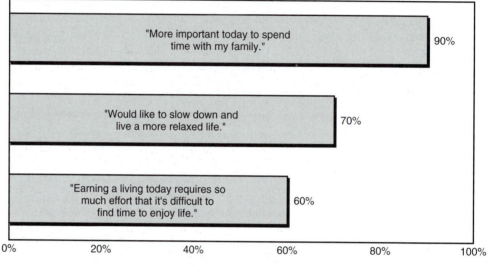

Americans Desire Slower Pace of Life
Pressure likely to increase for flexible and shorter work hours, work-at-home, and more vacation

"More important today to spend time with my family." 90%

"Would like to slow down and live a more relaxed life." 70%

"Earning a living today requires so much effort that it's difficult to find time to enjoy life." 60%

0%   20%   40%   60%   80%   100%

Percentage of those polled

and Leitner (1996, p. 26) report ". . . that leisure behavior is the most important or one of the most important determinants of life satisfaction and psychological well-being. . . ." They note that ". . . many studies support the assertion that leisure participation and life satisfaction are positively related to psychological well-being and life satisfaction" (Leitner and Leitner, 1996, p. 26).

Many studies conducted in the area of leisure and life satisfaction have focused primarily on the variable of age, with a special focus on older men and women. Studies also have explored the relationship between leisure activities and life satisfaction, and leisure and community well-being.

Leisure and Life Satisfaction as Related to Age

The relationship of life satisfaction, leisure, and age has been examined in a number of studies. Kelly, Steinkamp, and Kelly (1987) have suggested that in their later years men demonstrate a greater desire for companionship in their leisure than do women. The study also found that those kinds of leisure that provide satisfying interaction with other persons and those that require skill acquisition over a long period of time produced higher levels of life satisfaction than those that did not. When viewing leisure activities and their relationship to life satisfaction by age, the researchers found that (1) travel and cultural activities were most important to those forty-five to fifty-four years old; (2) social, cultural, and travel activities were most important to those fifty-five to sixty-four years old; (3) social and travel activities were most important to those sixty-five to seventy-four years old; and (4) home-based and family activities were most important to life satisfaction for those individuals seventy-five and older.

Kelly, Steinkamp, and Kelly (1987) also studied the relationship of social activity and leisure involvement to life satisfaction. They found a reduction in the level of leisure activity with age, although they noted that social activities and leisure activities related to family show the least decline. Leisure activities related to primary relationships with family and friends are usually maintained throughout later life. The findings are consistent with those of Gordon, Gaitz, and Scott (1976), who suggest that participation in seven leisure categories, many related to social entertaining and activities, is consistent throughout the life span. Sneegas (1986), studying life satisfaction of middle-aged and older adults and its relationship to perceived social competence, found that age was not related to social competence. She found one's perception of social competence affects the degree of leisure participation and leisure satisfaction, thereby influencing life satisfaction.

Riddick (1985) has also studied the relationship of life satisfaction to age. She found, in a national sample of men and women age sixty-five and over, that the strongest predictor of life satisfaction was involvement in leisure activities. For both males and females, she found that income and health problems impact participation in leisure activities and, hence, life satisfaction. As Bammel and Burris-Bammel (1996, p. 342) write, ". . . social participation has long been considered an important factor in determining the happiness, morale, well-being, and life satisfaction of elderly individuals." In 1990, Cutler and Hendricks reported similar results whereby engagement in activity was the determinant of life satisfaction.

Riddick (1986) also has studied leisure satisfaction among ten age groups, ranging from eighteen to sixty-five years old. She found that two factors—knowledge of leisure resources and leisure values—have significant influence on leisure satisfaction. Mobily, Lemke, Ostiguy, Woodard, Griffee, and Pickens (1993) found successful adaptation to the aging process depended largely on maintaining or enhancing one's competence and retaining a sense of self-determination. People with a large leisure repertoire were happiest. Kelly and Godbey (1992) agreed, indicating that a sense of worth, even productivity, and sharing oneself with others led to the greatest level of life satisfaction.

Work, Leisure, and Life Satisfaction

Are work and leisure linked to one another in such a way as to contribute to life satisfaction? Bergermaier, Borg, and Champoux (1984) tested three theories related to work, leisure, and life satisfaction. They postulated the following: (1) one's work might spill over into leisure and influence life satisfaction; (2) one might use leisure to compensate for a dissatisfying work experience or vice versa; or (3) there would be no relationship between work and leisure, and life satisfaction. Their research supports a "spillover" theory and "no-relationship" model in terms of the connection between work and non-work and life satisfaction. They suggest that there is little relationship between work and leisure, although work and leisure may spill over into one another, and this may affect life satisfaction. Controversy still exists as to the relationship of work, leisure, and life satisfaction, although many now view these aspects of life as multidimensional and extremely complex (Kelly and Godbey, 1992). For example, Siegenthaler and O'Dell (1997) report that individuals with greater knowledge about leisure and its benefits feel more positively about their leisure than those with less knowledge.

Several years ago Pierce (1980) suggested that certain dimensions provide satisfaction in both leisure and work environments, either separately or simultaneously. Four "satisfaction dimensions" were particularly significant—intimacy, relaxation, achievement, and power. In support of this multidimensionality, Kelly and Godbey (1992) indicated that people find both meaning and satisfaction in family, work, and leisure. They conclude that ". . . both work and leisure are too complex in motivations, styles, associations, and other factors to fit neatly into any circumscribed approach" (p. 133). Brown and Cashel (1995) have studied the relationship of job satisfaction and perceived amount of leisure and leisure satisfaction. They found that individuals participating in leisure activities that provided psychological rewards, social interaction, and/or were considered to be relaxing perceive themselves to have more leisure. In turn, they found that individuals with greater amounts of leisure have greater amounts of job satisfaction.

Leisure, Satisfaction, and Community Well-Being

Leisure also influences satisfaction in community life. Allen and Beattie (1984), seeking to understand what factors contribute to one's sense of community satisfaction, studied seven dimensions, including leisure. These researchers found that the economic dimension (how affluent the community was) was the most influential. The leisure dimension ranked fifth in importance; however, it was the best predictor of overall satisfaction with community life. Thus, participation in fulfilling leisure experiences appears to strongly influence individuals' perceptions of community well-being. In addition, the existence of leisure services aids in the economic development of a community.

In examining functions of leisure within a community, Kraus (1990) maintains that a primary function of leisure is to enrich the quality of life. The reduction of stress, emotional satisfaction, enjoyable social contacts, and feelings of achievement correspond closely to life satisfaction and directly relate to community well-being (Kraus, 1990). Leisure also contributes to personal development and makes a community a more attractive place to live. Each year popular periodicals publish a "best place to live" list, where the extent of leisure services available to community members is a primary consideration.

Life satisfaction and community well-being also increase as neighborhood ties are strengthened and intergroup and intergenerational relations improve (Kraus, 1990). When citizens share tasks, such as building a playground or a city beautification project, they enhance the quality of life for the entire community. Through leisure we can often move past the biases and prejudices—based on age, sex, mental or physical abilities, race/ethnicity, sexual orientation, or economic status—that we allow to interfere with relationships. The free flow of ideas and sharing through the medium of leisure benefits us all. Kelly and Godbey (1992) found that the most significant aspect of leisure is its ability to promote social bonding. Anything that supports a sense of family (loosely defined as close ties achieved through intense and ongoing relationships) will benefit the community.

Lifestyle and Leisure

One's lifestyle can greatly influence life satisfaction or well-being. *An optimal lifestyle is the integration and balance of the physical, mental, emotional, intellectual, social, and spiritual aspects of a person.* Each person strives to attain—and is capable of achieving—an optimal level of life satisfaction or well-being. Although levels of life satisfaction are often measured against external standards of appraisal, comparisons between individuals are usually not reliable. People have unique needs and pursue different levels of life satisfaction according to these needs.

While leisure influences lifestyle, it may not be the dominant factor in many people's lives; the focal point can be work, family, religion, social roles, societal commitments, or other factors. One's lifestyle is the sum total of all of these factors, some of which contribute greatly to life satisfaction and well-being, whereas others can detract. This is true for leisure as well. Leisure can contribute in a positive way to the maintenance of a healthy, vigorous lifestyle; on the other hand, it can detract from one's well-being in a significant manner.

Leisure services professionals have often failed to examine how leisure activities integrate with other factors that influence the lifestyles of individuals. The work of a leisure services professional, along with encouraging life satisfaction, should focus on facilitating both social (behavioral) and environmental (physical) conditions that help people achieve optimal lifestyles. This might involve the creation of activities or the development of areas and facilities. Further, it could also involve building a greater public awareness of the need for healthier, more satisfying lifestyles.

Lifestyle Management

How do the benefits sought in leisure experiences relate to the various programs that are directed toward enhancing optimal lifestyle behaviors? Figure 1.3 presents a model of lifestyle

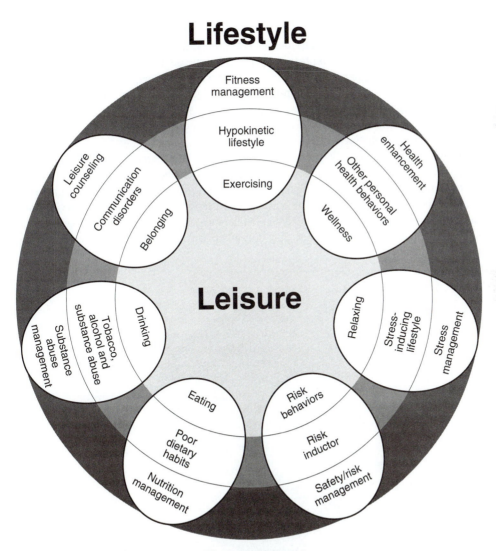

Figure 1.3

Lifestyle management

Source: After M. J. Ellis, C. R. Edginton, and D.R. Howard, Lifestyle and Health Promotion, *1985. Academy of Leisure Sciences, Dallas, TX.*

management developed by Ellis, Edginton, and Howard (1985). This model demonstrates some of the potential leisure activities in which people voluntarily engage. Some of these activities help to increase life satisfaction, whereas other activities have a negative impact. For example, eating for pleasure is one of the most popular leisure activities in many countries and cultures. This can be a positive use of leisure that optimizes life satisfaction by encouraging positive social relations in a relaxing atmosphere. On the other hand, eating to excess or eating the wrong kinds of foods can be detrimental to long-term life satisfaction.

It is interesting to note, and the model illustrates, that nearly all potential leisure experiences can have a great deal of impact—both positively and negatively—on the well-being of an individual. In addition, most of these experiences are directly tied to the work of leisure service organizations. Further, many of these activities can be initiated by an individual or carried out together with a leisure service organization, agency, or business.

Hull (1990) presents a three-dimensional representation of mood—a factor often considered to be integral to experiences of satisfaction. The two primary dimensions include pleasure and arousal. The third dimension, dominance, relates to feelings (e.g., anger, fear) one might experience when engaged in certain activities such as competitive sports or mountain climbing. As illustrated in figure 1.4, something that is sleepy and unpleasant would be boring; an experience that is arousing and unpleasant would result in stress; an arousing yet pleasant experience would be exciting, and a pleasant but sleepy experience would be relaxing. Obviously, moods, leisure, and life satisfaction are interrelated. Quality of life is generally measured and intuitively felt on a subjective scale; we base our decisions about our own quality of life on primarily intangible and highly personal factors.

Leisure serves as a central life force that the individual can shape to have either positive or negative consequences. Leisure joins work, family, religion, and other social contacts as another of the important variables that shape life. Leisure professionals should recognize the whole person and deal with individuals in a complete or holistic manner. Leisure services professionals in Hong Kong, for example, take a holistic approach to providing leisure services for young people. At their recreation centers, they not only provide leisure programs and activities

Figure 1.4
Factors that influence mood

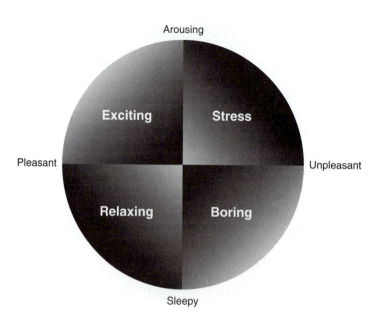

but also offer support for studying and homework, as well as opportunities for personal counseling. Leisure influences the behavior of people during much of their life, not only during their free time. Almost all of the behaviors represented in the model figure 1.3 require personal choice and are engaged in voluntarily. These are hallmarks of the leisure experience.

Leisure, Organizations, and Life Satisfaction

Why do leisure service organizations exist? What is their role in society? What is the relationship of these organizations to life satisfaction? From an ideal perspective, any organization exists to meet the needs of those it serves. Organizations, like individuals, however, also have needs—to be of service, to make a profit, or to shape or mold the character of individuals and/or society. Some leisure service organizations pursue a combination of all three of these ends.

In formulating a service strategy, a leisure service organization should work to develop mutually beneficial relationships where both the needs of the individuals it serves and its organizational needs are met. The organization must clearly focus upon its goals and simultaneously acknowledge the needs of individuals. A mutually beneficial relationship results when an organization commits itself to the needs of the individuals it serves and consciously pursues its goals. Focusing on individual needs and organizational goals at the same time serves as the most effective way of planning, organizing, and implementing services.

In promoting life satisfaction, via leisure experiences, leisure service organizations can engage in a number of roles. Some of these include the following:

1. *Awareness Building.* Leisure service organizations can help build awareness of different leisure opportunities. Awareness building can be as simple as providing interpretive information, or as complex as assisting individuals in understanding their attitudes, value states, and other factors influencing leisure participation. Awareness building helps people discover external resources that can assist them in achieving their full potential, and it can also help them learn more about themselves.

L e i s u r e   L i n e

Balancing Your Lifestyle

. . . In a *Time* magazine cover story entitled "Drowsy America," the director of Stanford University's sleep center concluded, "Most Americans no longer know what it feels like to be fully alert." Lacking a balance between work and play, responsibility and respite, "getting things done" can become an end-all. We function like *human doings* instead of *human beings*. We begin to link executing the items on our growing "to do" list with feelings of self-worth. As the list keeps growing longer, the lingering sense of more to do infiltrates our sense of self-acceptance.

. . . Nearly every aspect of American society has become more complex. . . . We are forging our own frenetic society. The good news is that the key to forging a more palatable existence can occur step by step. You, for example, *are whole and complete right now,* and you can achieve balance in your life.

You are not your position. You are not your tasks; they do not define you and they do not constrain you. You have the capacity to acknowledge that your life is finite; you cannot indiscriminately take in the daily deluge that your culture heaps on each of us and expect to feel anything but overwhelmed. It is time to make compassionate though difficult choices about what is best ignored, versus what merits your attention and action.

Source: Jeff Davidson, "Overworked Americans or Overwhelmed Americans?" *Public Management,* May, 1993.

2. *Transmission of Cultural Heritage.* Leisure service organizations play an important role in transmitting a society's culture. Games often serve to help children and youth prepare for their adult roles. Leisure activities also reinforce customs and rituals. For example, in the United States, the celebration of Kwanzaa (an African American celebration of community and life) as a ritual is done in connection with leisure events and activities. People often associate involvement in such activities with leisure pursuits.

3. *Knowledge and Skill Acquisition.* Leisure service organizations play an important role in helping individuals acquire knowledge and skills to participate in leisure; for many organizations it serves as a prime focus. Tennis classes, swim lessons, craft instruction, dance lessons, and gymnastics are just a few of the literally thousands of instructional programs that can be offered by leisure service organizations.

4. *Attitude and Character Formation.* A primary thrust of many leisure service organizations, especially those in the nonprofit private sector, is attitude and character formation. Leisure offers opportunities to teach sporting behaviors, fair play, teamwork, citizenship, social skills, and conflict resolution. Further, for the many organizations concerned with the spiritual and moral development of individuals, leisure becomes an important vehicle in which values can be shaped, molded, and influenced. It also provides opportunities for the creation of situations that foster discussion and formulation of beliefs.

5. *Fun.* Paul Haun once noted that ". . . fun is the steadfast goal of recreation, yet not its purpose" (1965, p. 18). Leisure provides a medium where people can pursue happiness and be playful, merry, joyful.

6. *Sensory Stimulation/Reduction.* Leisure also provides an opportunity for sensory stimulation or reduction. Leisure environments provide opportunities for our senses to be stimulated in terms of seeing, hearing, touching, tasting, and smelling. For example, walking on a nature trail can provide an individual with an opportunity to come into contact with new shapes, textures, sights, and smells. We can also choose to participate in leisure settings that reduce sensory stimulation and, in effect, relax us.

7. *Promotion of Social Skills/Interaction.* Many leisure activities occur in social occasions. They involve interaction among people, who often form groups. These types of leisure opportunities provide individuals with a chance to learn and practice their social skills. In addition, leisure provides opportunities for people to be with one another—to have contact with others. Perhaps it is this dimension of leisure that makes it such a powerful component in society. People want to be with other people, and leisure provides such opportunities.

8. *Promotion of Joy in Life.* Leisure activities and opportunities are often joyful experiences. Joy is pleasure, happiness, delight, rapture, and bliss. Leisure events or celebrations create opportunities for individuals who are brought closer together to share a common time of joy.

9. *Promotion of Psychological Well-Being.* Leisure service organizations also provide and promote activities that contribute to the psychological well-being of individuals and nurture the human spirit by enhancing stability, growth, health, self-esteem, self-confidence, and feelings of competence. Leisure leaders can build the self-confidence of individuals by encouraging them, equipping them with skills they need to successfully pursue activities, and rewarding their successes. Such action can contribute strongly to the psychological well-being of participants.

10. *Promotion of Creativity.* Leisure service organizations often provide opportunities that enable individuals to express or expand their creative abilities. These organizations provide opportunities for people to test their abilities, to extend their horizons, and to make new

and original contributions. To be creative means to be imaginative and inventive, and leisure is an excellent medium within which to explore one's creative potential.

11. *Providing Space for Enjoyment of Leisure.* Leisure services organizations often provide open spaces for play, reflection, contemplation, and communion and interaction with nature. Space to move openly and freely contributes to a variety of the previously mentioned factors such as psychological well-being, sensory stimulation/reduction, awareness building, and so forth. Parks, wilderness areas, and other leisure areas provide opportunities to get in touch not only with the natural environment but with ourselves.

12. *Providing Structures and Facilities for Enjoyment of Leisure.* Leisure service organizations construct and manage structures and facilities that enable the leisure experience. Theme parks, recreation centers, swimming pools, gymnasiums and fitness centers, ice rinks, bowling centers, theaters, and tennis and racquetball courts are examples of leisure structures and facilities.

Many types of leisure service organizations exist, including public agencies at the local, state, and federal levels, private nonprofit organizations, and commercial leisure service organizations. Each of these different types of organizations has unique goals, strategies for garnering resources, and different approaches to relating to their customer groupings. Some organizations emphasize more strongly one or more of the above roles, depending upon their organizational goals and values.

Edginton (2000) offers a useful framework to understand the importance of the work of leisure service organizations, as they relate to individual and community satisfaction. Using Frederick Hertzberg's "Theory of Motivation," which suggests that individual human needs can be placed on a continuum and divided into two types of needs—hygiene factors and motivators—Edginton writes:

> Hygiene factors refer to elements within the environment related to an individual's security, safety, and status. According to Hertzberg, hygiene factors do not motivate individuals. However, when they are not provided an individual becomes dissatisfied. On the other hand, motivators are factors that promote life satisfaction. The opportunity for people to achieve, have recognition, and be engaged in activities considered to be worthwhile to oneself and to society are all considered to be motivators. (p. 33)

Edginton suggests that these concepts can be applied to the opportunities that are made available by businesses, government agencies, and nonprofit organizations. Specifically, as noted in figure 1.5, Hertzberg's motivation/hygiene theory can be applied to government services. As one can see, viewing the model, government services such as fire, police, utilities, sewage treatments, and transportations systems are not motivators for people. On the other hand, recreation parks, cultural attractions, museums, festivals, events, heritage sites, and others give meaning to people, promote happiness, and hence contribute to greater life satisfaction.

What Motivates People to Pursue Leisure?

Why do people pursue leisure and leisure opportunities? The answer to this inquiry may produce as many different responses as there are individuals. People pursue leisure opportunities for different reasons and with different levels of intensity, depending upon the nature of their needs, values, and attitudes at any given time. Leisure can be pursued very intensely, as an end in itself, perhaps compensating for dissatisfaction in other areas of life, such as work. On the other hand, leisure may be pursued as an expression of status in society.

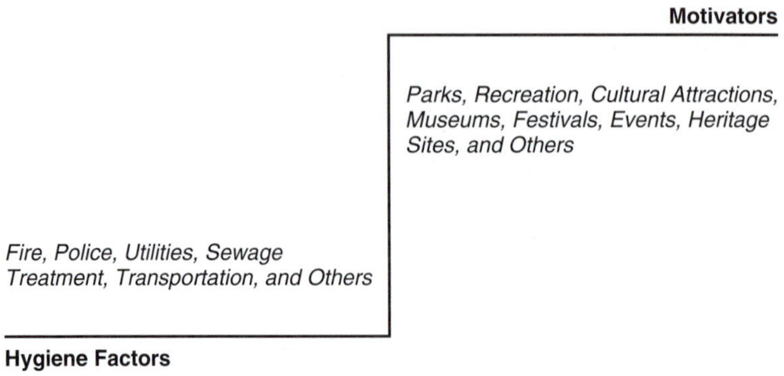

Figure 1.5

Life satisfaction:
What factors
move people?

*Data from
Edginton, C. R.
Community
Livability: A Model
for Iowa. In
Edginton, C. R.
(Ed.) (2000).
Enhancing the
Livability of Iowa
Communities: The
Role of Recreation,
Natural Resource
Development and
Tourism. Cedar
Falls, IA: The
University of
Northern Iowa,
29–41.*

Motivators

*Parks, Recreation, Cultural Attractions,
Museums, Festivals, Events, Heritage
Sites, and Others*

*Fire, Police, Utilities, Sewage
Treatment, Transportation, and Others*

Hygiene Factors

Schreyer (1986), in discussing motivation for participation in outdoor recreation, says that *individuals participate in leisure because it is a desirable, inherent value.* He notes, ". . . recreation is desirable: We all do it. Its value is inherent: Try to live without it" (p. 1). Schreyer suggests that all human behavior is goal-oriented and focused on trying to meet a need or needs. Leisure behavior is merely a subcomponent of human behavior. Just as we have needs that are fulfilled in other areas of our lives, leisure fulfills a need in a particular niche of our lives.

To maintain one's existence and subsistence, a person works, sleeps, or eats. These are necessary to maintain life. During one's leisure, goal-directed activity is not necessarily focused toward life maintenance activities. Leisure provides opportunities for expanding one's physical, social, intellectual, and spiritual needs. As Schreyer notes, leisure can be ". . . a nice, superficial and irrelevant way to pass the time . . . [or, leisure] . . . can be considered as playing an instrumental role in helping individuals fully complement the quality of their existence" (1986, p. 2).

Leisure Motives

Many factors motivate individuals to pursue leisure. These factors vary from person to person, depending upon their unique personalities, lifestyles, goals, and needs. Kraus (1994) indicates that many participants pursue leisure primarily for "fun" and "enjoyment." In reporting research conducted by Angier, Kraus notes the positive relationship of fun and enjoyment to quality of life. Driver and Brown (1986) have identified numerous factors that contribute to the motivation of individuals for leisure. Table 1.1 presents a composite list of factors, grouped into seventeen leisure experience preference domains, that might motivate individuals to pursue leisure. They are focused primarily toward outdoor recreation activities.

Tinsley, Teaff, and Colb (n.d.) present eight motivations identified as important to elderly individuals in pursuing leisure: (1) self-expression, (2) companionship, (3) sense of power/control, (4) security, (5) compensation, (6) service to others, (7) stimulation, and (8) solitude. This information reveals a vast number of factors that can potentially motivate individuals to participate in leisure. Some individuals seek risk-taking opportunities, whereas others seek risk reduction. Some individuals seek tranquillity and solitude; some desire interaction with people. Still further, some individuals seek stimulation where others seek to reduce the overloads that come as

TABLE

1.1 FACTORS THAT MAY MOTIVATE INDIVIDUALS TO PURSUE LEISURE

1. Enjoy Nature
   A. Scenery
   B. General Nature Experience
   C. Undeveloped Natural Area
2. Physical Fitness
3. Reduce Tension
   A. Tension Release
   B. Slow Down Mentally
   C. Escape Role Overloads
   D. Escape Daily Routine
4. Escape Noise and Crowds
   A. Tranquillity/Solitude
   B. Privacy
   C. Escape Crowds
   D. Escape Noise
   E. Isolation
5. Outdoor Learning
   A. General Learning
   B. Exploration
   C. Learn Geography of Area
   D. Learn About Nature
6. Share Similar Values
   A. Be With Friends
   B. Be With People Having Similar Values
7. Independence
   A. Independence
   B. Autonomy
   C. Being in Control

8. Family Kinship
9. Introspection
   A. Spiritual
   B. Personal Values
10. Be With Considerate People
11. Achievement Stimulation
    A. Reinforcing Self-Confidence/Self-Image
    B. Social Recognition
    C. Skill Development
    D. Competence Testing
    E. Seeking Excitement/Stimulation
    F. Self-Reliance
12. Physical Rest
13. Teach/Lead Others
    A. Teaching/Sharing Skills
    B. Leading Others
14. Risk Taking
15. Risk Reduction
    A. Risk Moderation
    B. Risk Prevention
16. Meet New People
    A. Meet New People
    B. Observe New People
17. Nostalgia

Source: Data from B. Driver and P. Brown, "Probable Personal Benefits of Outdoor Recreation" in *A Literature Review of the President's Commission on Americans Outdoors,* GPO, (1986) Washington, DC.

a result of work or family demands. Ibrahim and Cordes (1993) suggest that experiences that are intrinsically motivating can lead to happiness.

Driver and Brown (1986) also present a taxonomy of probable personal benefits that can be gained from leisure experiences in the out-of-doors, and Ibrahim and Cordes (1993) reported similar benefits. The results also apply to indoor leisure pursuits. The following factors may be strong motivators for pursuit of leisure opportunities:

1. *Personal Development.* The nature of the leisure experience is such that much of what motivates individuals to pursue leisure is personal. Leisure experiences can contribute to building self-concept, self-actualization, self-reliance, humility, and spiritual growth. They can also provide opportunities for values clarification and introspection, leadership opportunities, aesthetic enhancement, and learning. These all may be strong motivators influencing a person to participate in a given leisure activity or program.

2. *Social Bonding.* Leisure provides opportunities to have interactional needs met. As Driver and Brown (1986) indicate, social bonding increases the social cohesiveness of personal relationships and can take place in various forms. It can occur in primary groups such as the family or in groups that have been constructed to facilitate leisure experiences, such as teams, clubs, or instructional classes.

3. *Therapeutic Healing.* We live in a world of great stress, complexity, and demands. Many individuals need to escape or recover from the pressures or problems that arise in day-to-day living. Leisure provides opportunities for temporary escape from stress of work, family, interpersonal relationships, and others. Participation in positive, constructive forms of leisure provides an excellent alternative to negative forms of escape such as substance abuse.

4. *Physical Well-Being.* Human beings have a basic need for physical activity—to engage in fine and gross motor movement—so they often seek such activity during leisure participation. In fact, most scales of leisure pursuits show that among the highest rated are those associated with fitness or physical movement. For many people, active leisure pursuits provide the only alternative to the sedentary, work-oriented behaviors of a technological/information-based society.

5. *Stimulation.* Human beings are curious by nature. They constantly seek stimulation to satisfy their desire for newness or novelty, desire for exploration, and their need to relieve boredom and anxiety. Leisure pursuits provide an excellent medium within which new forms of stimulation can be introduced and experienced—observe the variety of stimulation provided by electronic home entertainment equipment, computers, and other technological developments that are available to people during their leisure.

6. *Freedom and Independence.* Some philosophers have argued that freedom and independence are necessary to nurture the human spirit. Because most leisure activities are noncompulsory, pursued on a voluntary basis, or freely chosen, a strong element of independence and freedom exists in such pursuits. Thus, the need to be free and independent can be nurtured, encouraged, and pursued through leisure. Leisure and freedom are often thought of in synonymous terms. There are few definitions that do not include "freedom" as a component of leisure.

7. *Nostalgia.* The need for reflection or for reflecting upon one's heritage or roots appears to be basic among all humans. Leisure often provides opportunities to learn about one's historical, cultural, and family heritage. As the philosopher Eric Hoffer once noted, when humankind was first freed from toiling in the soil and had the opportunity to think and explore, the first questions asked were "Where did we come from?" and "Why are we here?"

Although Driver and Brown (1986) framed their taxonomy in terms of probable personal benefits from leisure, such benefits only hold value for the individual in direct relationship to meeting needs. Thus, one could infer that the preceding benefits listed are, in fact, elements that motivate individuals to pursue leisure.

Other motives can be categorized differently. Rolston (1986), Cheek and Burch (1976), and others have suggested additional ways of defining needs that can be met as a result of participation in leisure experiences including psychological (self-concept, confidence, self-sufficiency, sensation-seeking, actualization, well-being, personal testing), sociological (comparison, group cooperation, respect for others, communication, behavior feedback, friendship, belonging), and physical needs (fitness, skills, strength, coordination, catharsis, exercise, and balance).

The Quest for Metaphors I: Carnival

Add up fickle and fashion, the need for bonkers "organizations," lots of tries and the matchless power of markets and what do you have? Among other things a clarion call for new imagery. . . . *How about [the organization as a] carnival?* Consider these attributes of carnivals:

- *Parts and wholes.* "The State Fair's next week." "The circus is coming to town." An image forms of the day with the kids at the Big Apple Circus last August or of a trip to Disneyland. That overall image (the whole) is central to our "purchase decision," yet we largely experience the parts—a ride, a concert, a horse show, the booth where you hurl baseballs at wooden milk bottles . . .
- *The "underpark."* Carnivals are about excitement and festivity. But we'll think twice about coming back if the portable toilets are dirty (or scarce), or if the parking is far away and overpriced. The "underpark" at Disney is the well-oiled, no nonsense, unheralded, unseen mechanism that permits the surface frenzy to proceed without a glitch.
- *Microeconomy.* A carnival is the ultimate marketplace. Fickle . . . customers make hundreds of choices each hour: to stop at this booth or even to skip that one. Carnival chiefs track booth/event attendance as carefully as retailers now track the hour-to-hour sales of each item off the shelf. They engage in a constant process of creation and destruction: removing a booth act that can't draw a crowd, refreshing an old favorite, pursuing exciting acts and new ideas.
- *Same/different.* The carnival boss, like the corporate boss, must address a prickly issue: Customers want "their" carnival the same, *and* they want it different. They want those clean toilets and their favorite rides/booths from last year. But they won't keep coming back unless they are regularly surprised by new offerings.
- *A moving target.* The excitement and frustration of creating/managing/maintaining a carnival is

that it won't stay put. Carnivals have a completely different character from one day to the next. Or one hour to the next—due to the weather, different crowds in the afternoon (mostly kids) and evening (mostly grown-ups), etc. Moreover, a carnival's personality changes when it moves from city to city and, of course, from year to year.

- *Low overhead, multi-entrepreneurial.* A bare bones staff of four (a chief [*sic*], an accountant, a computer ace, an administrative specialist), working out of a dinky, 200-square-foot, low rent space, may oversee a traveling carnival with 100 booths, 30 rides, 20 special events (which change from town to town), and an annual attendance in the millions. The carnival is the ultimate in "networked" or subcontracted events: Tents, toilets, and acts/booths are the work of entrepreneurs. Yet it all must add up, quirky day after quirky day, to a coherent whole.
- *The customer creates his or her own carnival (I call it "customerizing").* The carnival is a set of opportunities, a canvas on which the customer paints his or her own customized experience. If there are 5,000 customers tonight, they are painting 5,000 substantially different pictures.
- *Dynamism.* Say "carnival" and you think energy, surprise, buzz, fun. The mark of the carnival—and what makes it most different from a day at most offices—is its dynamism. Dynamism is its signature, the reason we go back. To create and maintain a carnival is never to get an inch away from dynamic imagery. As chief [*sic*], you must feel the dynamics in your fingertips, be guided by them in every decision.

. . . Today's global economic dance is no Strauss waltz. *It's break dancing accompanied by street rap.* The effective [organization] is much more like Carnival in Rio than a pyramid along the Nile. [The practical point for . . . leaders: Constantly using dynamic imagery, thinking of yourself as running a carnival.]

Cheek and Burch (1976) have suggested that numerous social benefits, including family cohesion and social interaction, are motivators. Allen (1990) has discussed the benefits of leisure to one's satisfaction with community life. Interestingly, he suggests that the relationship between leisure and community satisfaction is unclear and that there is a need for stronger theoretical and methodological procedures to help accurately reflect this dimension.

In discussing motives for participation in the natural environment, Rolston (1986) believes that outdoor recreational activities provide an extra dimension that indoor leisure activities do not. He notes, "one touched base with something greater . . ." (p. 9). He suggests that life support, aesthetics, natural history, philosophical, religious, scientific, and other topics can all be pursued in leisure experiences in the out-of-doors, a location that also enhances participation. Discussing philosophical and religious benefits in outdoor recreation experiences, he notes the following:

> Nature generates poetry, philosophy and religion and at its deepest educational capacity, Americans are awed and humbled by staring into the stormy surf or the midnight sky, by overlooking the canyon lands or by an overflight of migrating geese. If we must put it so, nature is a philosophical resource, as well as a scientific, recreational, aesthetic or economic one. Encounter with nature is the cradle of spirituality. The significance of nature is one of the richest assignments of the mind, and this requires detection, imagination, participation and decision. The great outdoors works on . . . [the] soul as well as the muscles and the body. (Rolston, 1986, p. 109)

Rolston's point is important in terms of understanding those factors that motivate individuals to participate in leisure. The wellspring of motivation occurs not only as a result of physical needs or even social needs, but also *spiritual needs.*

One's desire to participate in leisure may be either intrinsically or extrinsically driven, although most definitions of leisure suggest that leisure is pursued for its intrinsic rather than extrinsic value. Proposing a model to measure the individual differences in intrinsic motivation, Weissinger and Bandalos (1995) have identified the following components that contribute to an individual's motivation disposition:

L e i s u r e   L i n e

The Right to Risk

If we are to have any chance at happiness in this uncertain world, we must learn to embrace its insecurities, to give in to change, to celebrate the present moment. To do otherwise is to do battle with ourselves. We are as a wave moving forward to a distant shore. No matter how turbulent the sea, no matter how strong the urge to return to port, there is no turning back. Our happiness rests in our recognition of this fact of life and in our subsequent determination to enjoy the ride.

Source: Dustin, *The Wilderness Within*, p. 5, 1993.

The notion, then, that we human beings have "a right to risk" is misleading. We have no choice in the matter. There is nothing but risk. What we do have a choice in, however, is the way we deal with risks. We can delude ourselves, hide behind our fears, and pretend it just isn't so. Or we can confront the risks, announce our fears, and give it a go.

- **Self determination.** Self determination is characterized by awareness of internal needs, a strong desire to make free choices based on these needs. Persons high in this intrinsic motivation component usually want to feel in control of their leisure behavior and display a high degree of willfulness.
- **Competence.** Competence is characterized by attention to feedback that provides information about effectiveness, ability, and skill. Persons high in this intrinsic motivation component tend to seek out leisure behaviors that convey feedback about competence.
- **Commitment.** Commitment is characterized by a tendency toward deep involvement in, rather than detachment from, leisure behaviors. Persons high in this intrinsic motivation component tend to value leisure behaviors and feel dedicated to leisure in their lives.
- **Challenge.** Challenge is characterized by a tendency toward seeking leisure experiences that stretch one's limits and provide novel stimuli. Persons high in this intrinsic motivation component tend to select leisure behaviors that slightly exceed their skills and should perceive this state as challenging rather than adverse or threatening.

It is evident, in reviewing the literature, that a variety of factors can and do influence an individual's motivation to participate in a given leisure experience. For example, according to Ewert (1993) the outcomes of a leisure experience—that is, perception of success or failure—may impact on the individual's perception of underlying motives of participation in retrospect. He reports that climbers who failed to reach the goal of their climb placed higher levels of importance on disengagement, photography, wilderness, and scenery, whereas climbers who did reach the goal of their climb reported higher levels of importance for exhilaration, risk, and recognition.

Bergin (1992) studied the relationship between leisure activity, motivation, and academic achievement in high school students. This researcher found that leisure activity is a predictor of high school achievement and further notes that an in-school experience can be a motivating factor for continuing leisure interests outside of the school environment. Clough, Shepherd, and Maughan (1990) studied motives for participation in recreational running. Using six motivational categories—well-being, social, challenge, status, fitness/health, and addiction—they found that the prime motivations for running were challenge, health/fitness, and well-being.

Constraints to Leisure

If a major goal of leisure service professionals is to provide opportunities for satisfying life experiences, then it is necessary to recognize the constraints that prevent individuals from attaining satisfaction from and through their leisure. Constraints, those factors that intervene between the preference for an activity and participation in it (Henderson, Bialeschki, Shaw, and Freysinger, 1989, 1996), can come from many sources. Some constraints exist as a result of perceptions that individuals hold. For example, a perceived lack of the skill necessary to engage in a particular leisure activity may result in a constraint. Constraints may also be organizational in nature; programs and services provided by an agency may not be offered at a convenient time or location. As Kay and Jackson (1991, p. 32) write, ". . . for many providers, low participation levels among certain population subgroupings have long been regarded as self-evident proof of the existence of constraints which their organization should try to reduce." Environmental constraints relate to structural constraints within areas and facilities or the inaccessibility of natural areas.

Ellis and Rademacher define a constraint to leisure as ". . . *any factor which precludes or limits an individual's frequency, intensity, duration or quality of participation in recreation activities*" (1986, p. 33). The term "constraint" has been defined by Jackson (1988, p. 69) as ". . . a subset of reasons for not engaging in a particular behavior." He maintains that the term "constraint" is more appropriately used than that of "barrier." Jackson (1988, p. 203) notes that "the commonly-used word 'barriers' fails to capture the entire range of reasons for behaviors such as leisure nonparticipation, ceasing participation, etc." These factors can prevent individuals from successfully engaging in leisure experiences. Constraints include obstacles, limitations, impediments, restrictions, and other factors placed in front of individuals either by themselves or by the culture, society, or environment. These constraints prevent people from engaging in satisfying leisure experiences.

Constraints are not to be confused with limits that ensure order, safety, and stability, although some view many of society's rules and regulations as constraints to their freedom in leisure. For example, regulations limiting where people can use skateboards or in-line skates in public areas were likely developed for safety of pedestrians; to some avid in-line skaters, however, the restrictions appear to have been written simply to ruin their fun.

Freedom is usually considered a necessary part of the leisure experience. To facilitate freedom of thought, choice, and participation, it becomes necessary to understand the constraints that prevent people from successfully participating in leisure. Some of these constraints can be minimized or eliminated by the leisure professional; those constraints related to an individual participant's frame of reference are more difficult to influence or remove.

Jackson (1990) suggests two categories of constraints that can influence one's leisure participation. *Antecedent constraints* interfere or impact upon one's preferences for certain leisure activities. For instance, Kelly and Godbey (1992) interviewed older African Americans whose engagement in water-based activities (swimming and boating) was limited. Analysis indicated that during their childhood, neighborhood pools had been closed to children of color, resulting in an avoidance of water-based recreation for those interviewed and their children. Antecedent constraints might include incomplete knowledge of recreation and leisure opportunities, personal beliefs about entitlement to leisure, and "buying into" socially imposed gender roles.

Intervening constraints come between a preference for an activity and actual participation in it. Intervening constraints might include availability of recreation facilities, hours of operation, the ability to afford entrance and user fees, and safety of facilities. A number of authors have identified commonalties represented in a variety of studies conducted to identify constraints to leisure. In particular, Jackson (1993) and Hultsman (1995) identify six commonalties often associated with constraints to leisure participation as noted in various research studies. These include accessibility, social isolation, personal reasons, costs, time commitments, and facilities. Table 1.2 presents each of the six dimensions with descriptors to help define each of these terms.

According to Jackson (2000), the study of leisure constraints is important for a number of reasons. These are as follows:

- Barriers or obstacles exist to achieving a meaningful quality of life on both an individual and a societal basis.
- Access to and enjoyment of leisure are central to a high quality of life for individuals, and indirectly related to the quality of the society as a whole; therefore, leisure can play an important part in removing or alleviating these barriers.
- A wide range of barriers also may preclude people from achieving their leisure goals and realizing the full benefits of a high quality of leisure.
- Understanding the distribution of constraints in society, how they affect people's lives and leisure, and how people adapt to these constraints is a crucial task for leisure researchers.

TABLE

1.2   CONSTRAINTS COMPRISING SIX IDENTIFIABLE DIMENSIONS

Dimension	Constraints
Accessibility	Cost of transportation
	Lack of transportation
	No opportunity to participate near home
Social Isolation	Lack of knowledge about where to participate
	Difficulty in finding others with whom to participate
Personal Reasons	Lack of necessary skills
	Physically unable to participate
	Requires too much self-discipline
	Low energy level
	Lost interest in participating
Costs	Cost of equipment, materials, supplies
	Admission, rental fees, other charges for facilities or programs
Time Commitments	Work commitments
	Family commitments
	Lack of time due to other leisure activities
Facilities	Overcrowded recreation facilities or areas
	Recreation facilities/areas poorly maintained

From W. Hultsman, "Recognizing Patterns of Leisure Constraints: An Extension of the Exploration of Dimensionality" in *Journal of Leisure Research, 27*(3), p. 229, 1995. Reprinted by permission of National Park and Recreation Association, Alexandria, VA.

Numerous studies have focused on leisure constraints. A number of these, according to Jackson, have offered theoretical propositions and provided information regarding their practical implications (Goodale and Witt, 1989; Jackson, 1988, 1991; Jackson and Scott, 1999; McGuire and O'Leary, 1992; Searle and Jackson, 1985). Others have discussed the impact of constraints on individuals' lives (Crawford, Jackson, and Godbey, 1991; Henderson and Bialeschki, 1993; Jackson, Crawford, and Godbey, 1993).

Jackson (2000) effectively summarizes the following patterns regarding leisure constraints that have emerged over the past two decades from the studies just mentioned:

- Allowing for variations in the number, range, and content of the items included in a given study, a reasonably stable and replicable set of constraints "dimensions" has consistently emerged from a variety of studies. These dimensions typically include constraints related to the costs of participating, time commitments, the availability and quality of facilities, isolation (sometimes subdivided into social isolation and geographical isolation), and personal skills and abilities.
- No constraint is experienced with equal intensity by everyone, although time- and cost-related constraints rank among the most widely and intensely experienced inhibitors of the achievement of leisure goals and a balanced lifestyle.
- The experience of constraints varies among individuals and groups: no subgroup of the population is entirely free from constraints, and each group is characterized not only by varying intensities of the experience of each type of constraint, but also by a unique

combination of constraints. Thus, young people, relatively less constrained by time, are typically affected in their leisure by a lack of partners, opportunities, and costs. The transition to middle adulthood sees a decline in these types of constraints but a marked increase in time commitments, largely due to family and employment circumstances. Time- and cost-related constraints may decline in older adulthood, but problems of skills and isolation may become increasingly important.

- In addition to age, the effects of constraints are modified by other personal and social factors, such as family size and structure, gender, income, ethnicity, and race (Jackson and Rucks, 1995; Phillips, 1995; Scott and Munson, 1994; Stodolska, 1998).

Recently there has been a criticism of the leisure constraint research. Samdahl and Jekubovich (1997) have suggested that although this area of study was originally conceptualized as a way of understanding barriers to activity participation as well as helping professionals to understand the broader factors and influences that shape people's everyday leisure behaviors, research activities have stopped painfully short of a full explanation. As these authors explain, ". . . there is nothing in the constraints' theory to explain *why* some situations were viewed as constraints, or *why* some people were motivated to negotiate those constraints" (p. 49).

Summary

Leisure has been a means to promote greater life satisfaction throughout the history of humankind. In the last 100 years, leisure has increased in importance and value to society. Not only have we seen a rise in the amount of free time available to people, but we have also witnessed a qualitative and a quantitative growth of leisure programs and services. Leisure has become an important force, shaping not only individual values, but also collectively the values of U.S. and Canadian societies as a whole.

Life satisfaction and well-being are often linked to happiness and quality of life. Leisure and the presence of leisure opportunities have also been linked to life satisfaction and often identified as *flow*. Flow is the experience of matching skill with the challenges of the activity; it is reported as a natural "high." Nearly all studies report a positive relationship between leisure and life satisfaction. Life satisfaction and leisure are also related to community well-being, with leisure being an important factor when predicting community satisfaction.

Organizations providing leisure services play an important role in contributing to the life satisfaction of individuals. Not only do they serve those individuals toward whom their services are directed, but they often work actively to shape or mold the character of individuals and/or society. Leisure service organizations can be involved in a number of roles, including awareness building, transmission of cultural heritage, knowledge and skill acquisition, attitude and character formulation, fun, sensory stimulation/reduction, promotion of social skills/interaction, promotion of joy, promotion of psychological well-being, promotion of creativity, and provision of space as well as provision of structures and facilities for leisure.

A myriad of factors motivates individuals to participate in leisure. Leisure appears to be a desirable and inherent value. Reasons people pursue leisure, however, vary from individual to individual, community to community, and region to region. Some of the probable personal benefits from leisure include personal development, social bonding, therapeutic healing, mental and physical well-being, stimulation, freedom and independence, and nostalgia.

One of the major functions of any leisure service organization is to remove constraints to leisure—factors that preclude or limit an individual from participating satisfactorily in a leisure activity, event, program, or service. Constraints may be individual, cultural, or environmental. Some common constraints include lack of knowledge, previous negative experiences, work commitments, and socially imposed roles. Constraints often are greatly affected by demographic variables. For example, working married women with families may experience greater constraints to leisure than other groupings do within the population.

Discussion Questions

1. How does leisure relate to life satisfaction and well-being?
2. What does it mean to be in the life satisfaction business?
3. How do generational differences impact upon leisure value states, attitudes, and behaviors?
4. What is your generation's view of leisure versus that of your parents, grandparents, or great grandparents?
5. What does life satisfaction mean?
6. What motivates people to participate in leisure activities?
7. What benefits can result from leisure experience?
8. What roles do leisure service organizations play in the delivery of leisure services?
9. How do these organizational roles contribute to the life satisfaction and well-being of individuals?
10. Identify and provide examples of several constraints to leisure.

References

Allen, L. R. 1990. Benefits of leisure attributes to community satisfaction. *Journal of Leisure Research 22*(2), 183–196.

Allen, L. R., and R. Beattie. 1984. The role of leisure as an indicator of overall satisfaction with community life. *Journal of Leisure Research 16*(2), 99–109.

Bammell, G., and L. Burris-Bammel. 1996. *Leisure and Human Behavior.* Madison, WI: Brown & Benchmark.

Bergermaier, R., I. Borg, and J. Champoux. 1984. Structural relationships among facets of work, nonwork, and general well-being. *Work and Occupations 11*(2), 163–181.

Bergin, D. A. 1992. Leisure activity, motivation, and academic achievement in high school students. *Journal of Leisure Research 24*(3), 225–239.

Brown, K. A., and C. Cashel. 1995. Female elementary school teachers' job satisfaction, perceived amount of leisure, and leisure satisfaction. *Abstracts from the 1995 Symposium on Research Leisure 104.*

Cheek, N. H., and W. R. Burch. 1976. *The Social Organization of Leisure in Human Society.* New York: Harper and Row.

Clough, P., J. Shepherd, and R. Maughan. 1990. Motives for participation in recreational running. *Journal of Leisure Research 21*(4), 297–309.

Crawford, D. W., E. L. Jackson, and G. Godbey. 1991. A hierarchical model of leisure constraints. *Leisure Sciences 13,* 309–320.

Csikszentmihalyi, M. 1990. *Flow: The Psychology of Optimal Experience.* New York: HarperCollins.

Cutler, S., and J. Hendricks. 1990. Leisure and time use across the life course. Edited by R. Binstock and L. George, in *Handbook of Aging and the Social Sciences.* New York: Academic Press.

Davidson, J. "Overworked Americans or Overwhelmed Americans?" *Public Management,* May, 1993.

Diener, E. 1984. Subjective well-being. *Psychological Bulletin 95*(3), 543.

Diener, E. 2000. Subjective well-being: The science of happiness and a proposal for a national index. *American Psychologist 55*(1), 34–43.

Driver, B., and P. Brown. 1986. Probable personal benefits of outdoor recreation. In *A Literature Review of the President's Commission on Americans Outdoors,* Values, 63–70. Washington, DC: U.S. Government Printing Office.

Dustin, *The Wilderness Within,* p. 5, 1993.

Edginton, C. R. 2000. Community livability: A model for Iowa. Edited by C. R. Edginton, in *Enhancing the Livability of Iowa Communities: The Role of Recreation, Natural Resource Development and Tourism,* 29–41. Cedar Falls, IA: The University of Northern Iowa.

Ellis, G., and C. Rademacher. 1986. Barriers to recreation participation. In *A Literature Review of the President's Commission on Americans Outdoors,* Motivations, 33–50. Washington, DC: U.S. Government Printing Office.

Ellis, M. J., C. R. Edginton, and D. R. Howard. 1985. *Lifestyle and Health Promotion.* Academy of Leisure Sciences, Dallas, TX.

Ewert, A. 1993. Differences in the level of motivation based on trip outcome, experience level and group type. *Journal of Leisure Research 25*(4), 335–349.

Godbey, G. 1986. Societal trends and the impact on recreation and leisure. In *A Literature Review of the President's Commission on Americans Outdoors,* Demand, 1–8. Washington, DC: U.S. Government Printing Office.

Goodale, T. L., and P. A. Witt. 1989. Recreation non-participation and barriers to leisure. Edited by E. L. Jackson and T. L. Burton, in *Understanding Leisure and Recreation: Mapping the Past, Charting the Future* (421–449). State College, PA: Venture Publishing.

Gordon, C., C. Gaitz, and J. Scott. 1976. Leisure and lives: Personal expressivity across the life span. Edited by R. Binstock and E. Shanas, in *Handbook of Aging and the Social Sciences,* 310–341. New York: Van Nostrand-Reinhold Co.

Harper, W., and J. Hultsman. 1994. Whaling away at leisure. *Schole 9,* 41–52.

Haun, P. 1965. *Recreation: A Medical Viewpoint.* New York: Teacher's College Press.

Henderson, K. A., and M. D. Bialeschki. 1993. Exploring an expanded model of women's leisure constraints. *Journal of Applied Recreation Research 18,* 229–252.

Henderson, K., D. Bialeschki, S. Shaw, and V. Freysinger. 1989. *A Leisure of One's Own: A Feminist Perspective on Women's Leisure.* State College, PA: Venture Publishing.

Henderson, K., D. Bialeschki, S. Shaw, and V. Freysinger. 1996. *Both Gains and Gaps: Feminist Perspectives on Women's Leisure.* State College, PA: Venture Publishing.

Hull, R. B. 1990. Mood as a product of leisure: Causes and consequences. *Journal of Leisure Research 22*(2), 99–111.

Hull, R. B., W. P. Stewart, and Y. K. Yi. 1992. Experience patterns: Capturing the dynamic nature of a recreation experience. *Journal of Leisure Research 24*(3), 240–252.

Hultsman, W. 1995. Recognizing patterns of leisure constraints: An extension of the exploration of dimensionality. *Journal of Leisure Research 27*(3), 228–244.

Ibrahim, H., and K. Cordes. 1993. *Outdoor Recreation.* Dubuque, IA: Brown & Benchmark.

Inglehart, R. 1989. *Culture Shift in Advanced Industrial Society.* Princeton, NJ: Princeton University Press.

Iso-Ahola, S. 1980. *The Social Psychology of Leisure and Recreation.* Dubuque, IA: Wm. C. Brown.

Jackson, E. L. 1988. Leisure constraints: A survey of past research. *Leisure Sciences 10,* 203–215.

Jackson, E. L. 1990. Variations in the desire to begin a leisure activity: Evidence of antecedent constraints? *Journal of Leisure Research 22,* 55–70.

Jackson, E. L. 1991. Leisure constraints/constrained leisure: Special issue introduction. *Journal of Leisure Research 23,* 279–285, and *Leisure Sciences 13,* 273–278.

Jackson, E. L. 1993. Recognizing patterns of leisure constraints: Results from alternative analyses. *Journal of Leisure Research 25,* 129–149.

Jackson, E. L. 2000. Will research on leisure constraints still be relevant in the twenty-first century? *Journal of Leisure Research 32*(1), 62–68.

Jackson, E. L., D. W. Crawford, and G. Godbey. 1993. Negotiation of leisure constraints. *Leisure Sciences 15,* 1–11.

Jackson, E. L., and V. C. Rucks. 1995. Negotiation and leisure constraints by junior high and high school students: An exploratory study. *Journal of Leisure Research 27*(1), 85–105.

Jackson, E. L., and Scott, D. (1999). Constraints to leisure. Edited by E. L. Jackson and T. L. Burton, in *Leisure Studies: Prospects for the Twenty-First Century,* 299–321. State College, PA: Venture Publishing.

Kay, T., and G. Jackson. 1991. Leisure despite constraint: The impact of leisure constraints on leisure participation. *Journal of Leisure Research 23*(4), 301–313.

Kelly, J. R. 1996. *Leisure.* 3rd ed. Boston: Allyn and Bacon.

Kelly, J. R., and G. Godbey. 1992. *Sociology of Leisure.* State College, PA: Venture.

Kelly, J. R., M. Steinkamp, and J. Kelly. 1987. Later life satisfaction: Does leisure contribute? *Leisure Sciences 9,* 187–200.

Kraus, R. 1990. *Recreation and Leisure in Modern Society.* 4th ed. New York: HarperCollins.

Kraus, R. 1994. *Leisure in a Changing America.* New York: Macmillan.

Leitner, M. J., and S. F. Leitner. 1996. *Leisure Enhancement.* 2nd ed. New York: Haworth.

McGuire, F. A., and J. T. O'Leary. 1992. The implications of leisure constraint research for the delivery of leisure services. *Journal of Park and Recreation Administration 10,* 31–40.

Mobily K., J. Lemke, L. Ostiguy, R. Woodard, T. Griffee, and C. Pickens. 1993. Leisure repertoire in a sample of midwestern elderly: The case for exercise. *Journal of Leisure Research 25*(1), 84–99.

Myers, D. G. 2000. The funds, friends, and faith of happy people. *American Psychologist 55*(1), 56–67.

Patterson, M. E. 2000. Philosophy of science and leisure research. *Journal of Leisure Research 32*(1), 106–110.

Phillips, S. F. 1995. Race and leisure constraints. *Leisure Sciences 17,* 109–120.

Pierce, R. 1980. Dimensions of leisure I: Satisfactions. *Journal of Leisure Research 12*(1), 5–19.

Reich, J., and A. Zautra. 1983. Demands and desires in daily life: Some influences on well-being. *American Journal of Community Psychology 11*(1), 43.

Riddick, C. 1985. Life satisfaction determinants of older males and females. *Leisure Sciences 7*(1), 47–63.

Riddick, C. 1986. Leisure satisfaction precursors. *Journal of Leisure Research 18*(4), 259–265.

Rolston, H. 1986. Beyond recreational value: The greater outdoors preservation related and environmental benefits. In *A Literature Review of the President's Commission on Americans Outdoors,* Values, 103–113. Washington, DC: U.S. Government Printing Office.

Russell, R. V. 1996. Pastimes: *The Context of Contemporary Leisure.* Madison, WI: Brown & Benchmark.

Samdahl, D. M., and N. J. Jekubovich. 1997. A critique of leisure constraints: Comparative analyses and understandings. *Journal of Leisure Research 29*(4), 430–452.

Schreyer, R. 1986. Motivation for participation in outdoor recreation and barriers to that participation. In *A Literature Review of the President's Commission on Americans Outdoors,* Motivation, 1–8. Washington, DC: U.S. Government Printing Office.

Scott, D., and W. Munson. 1994. Perceived constraints to park usage among individuals with low incomes. *Journal of Park and Recreation Administration 12*(4), 79–96.

Searle, M. S., and E. L. Jackson. 1985. Recreation non-participation and barriers to participation: Considerations for the management of recreation delivery systems. *Journal of Park and Recreation Administration 3,* 23–26.

Shichman, S., and E. Cooper. 1984. Life satisfaction and sex role concept. *Sex Roles 11*(3/4), 227–240.

Siegenthaler, K. L., and O'Dell, I. 1997. Comparison of leisure attitude, leisure satisfaction and perceived freedom in leisure over the lifespan. *Abstracts from the 1997 Symposium on Leisure Research.*

Sneegas, J. 1986. Components of life satisfaction in middle and later life adults: Perceived social competence, leisure participation and leisure satisfaction. *Journal of Leisure Research 18*(4), 248–258.

Stodolska, M. 1998. Assimilation and leisure constraints: Dynamics of constraints in leisure immigrant populations. *Journal of Leisure Research, 30* (4), 521–555.

Tinsley, H., J. Teaff, and S. Colb. n.d. *The Need Satisfying Properties of Leisure Activities for the Elderly.* Southern Illinois University and Andrus Foundation.

United Way of America. 1992. *What Lies Ahead: A Decade of Decision.* Alexandria, VA: United Way Strategic Institute.

Weisse, C. S. 1992. Depression and immunocompetence: A review of the literature. *Psychological Bulletin 111,* 475–489.

Weissinger, E., and D. L. Bandalos. 1995. Development, reliability and validity of a scale to measure intrinsic motivation in leisure. *Journal of Leisure Research 27*(4), 379–400.

Wilson, W. 1967. Correlates of avowed happiness. *Psychological Bulletin 67,* 294–306.

CHAPTER 2

The World of Leisure, Recreation, and Play

Leisure, recreation, and play have different meanings for different people. This whitewater kayaker may be seeking risk in his leisure experiences.

Introduction

Leisure and life satisfaction are inextricably linked, yet their terminology is often difficult to define. Leisure, recreation, and play are difficult to define and measure because their meanings vary from individual to individual, community to community, and culture to culture. What constitutes leisure to one individual may not be the same to another. Furthermore, different communities perceive leisure in different ways, and terms may be culturally defined. For example, in the United States and Canada, leisure is usually associated with free time and often may be viewed as a commodity that is consumed. In India, adult leisure is reserved for special occasions such as birth, marriage, and religious festivals, while in old communist Russia, leisure was heavily controlled and viewed as ". . . time in which one regenerates for the real purpose of life—work" (Ibrahim, 1991, p. 111). In other countries, the language often offers no equivalent word for leisure. Rather, terms such as sport and culture, and recreation and sport are used to describe much of what North Americans view as leisure.

Why is it necessary to define these terms? Developing definitions and ways of measuring leisure, recreation, and play helps both the practicing leisure professional and those who study the leisure phenomenon. By defining and measuring these terms, we can more accurately predict the consequences and actions of our work as leisure professionals. As Edginton and Rossman (1988, p. viii) state, terms, definitions, and theories help leisure professionals ". . . understand our roles and responsibilities in providing service . . . [and] . . . help us define, explain, control, and ultimately predict the consequences of our intervention as professionals." The leisure professional can more accurately predict specific leisure benefits and deploy resources more effectively when terms are understood.

This chapter offers several definitions of leisure, recreation, and play. In addition, some of the more contemporary theories of leisure, recreation, and play will be presented. A discussion of how people make leisure choices and what people do in their leisure time will be included.

Finally, a discussion of the ways in which leisure contributes to various factors in our culture and society will be explored.

What Is Leisure?

Leisure is an elusive term—the meaning of which has been pursued by individuals for centuries. In ancient cultures, leisure was often viewed as the opposite of physical labor. Leisure provided the opportunity for individuals to think, to develop their spirituality, and to improve their physical culture. It was subject to the work rhythm of the seasons and was a way of freeing oneself from the toil of physical labor. It was viewed as a desired state of being and as a way of advancing civilization through intellectual, contemplative, and aesthetic activities. We now know leisure to be a component of lifestyle, another elusive concept in our search for life quality (Mannell and Klieber, 1997).

The term *leisure* is derived from the Latin word *licere,* to be free. The Greeks used the terms *scol, schole,* or *skole* to define leisure. These terms resulted in the Latin word *scola* and the English term *school. Schole,* according to Dare, Welton, and Coe (1987), can be thought of as a state or condition of being free from work. Barker (1946) has noted that the Greeks identified *schole* as an activity and differentiated the concept from work (occupation), recreation, and amusement. Barker wrote that *schole*

> is, therefore, contrasted not with activity, but with "occupation" (*ascholia*)—in other words with the sort of activity which is pursued not for its own sake (as the activity of leisure is), but for the sake of something else . . . it is also contrasted with, or distinguished from, "recreation" (*anapausis*) and "amusement" (*paidia*—"the sort of thing children do"). Amusement and recreation mean rest after occupation, and preparation for new occupation: they are thus both essentially connected with the idea of occupation. Leisure stands by itself, in its own independent right. Aristotle thus operates with three different notions; the notion of leisure; the notion of occupation; and the notion (in one sense intermediate between the two, but in another sense closer to the latter) of amusement and recreation. (pp. 323–324)

Contemporary society often views leisure as a way of bringing balance into one's life. Leisure is sought not only for the opportunity for relaxation, self-improvement, and cultural and family stability and interaction, but also for escape, novelty, complexity, adventure, excitement, and fantasy. In many societies, people use leisure as a way of counterbalancing stresses that result from living and working in a technologically oriented, competitive, rapidly changing society that requires attention to a high degree of stimulation in the form of information, media communications, and human interaction. In many societies, leisure has become many different things to different individuals. A definition of leisure often eludes agreement among leisure professionals and researchers.

Factors Related to a Satisfying Leisure Experience

In the past several decades, researchers studying leisure, such as Ellis (1973), Neulinger (1974, 1981), Csikszentmihalyi (1975), Iso-Ahola (1999), Kelly (1982), Unger (1984), Shaw (1985), Kleiber, Larson, and Csikszentmihalyi (1986), Gunter (1987), and Samdahl (1988, 1991), have identified a number of factors that help to identify and define the leisure experience. Some of these were touched upon in chapter one. A brief discussion of the four prevailing factors used to define the leisure experience—freedom, perceived competence, intrinsic motivation, and positive affect—follows:

> *Freedom.* The term *freedom,* or *perceived freedom,* is often used synonymously with the term *leisure.* Freedom implies that individuals have choice or perceive they have choice

Leisure and Culture

Benjamin Franklin (1784) once related an experience he had concerning how different cultures value different behaviors as follows:

At the treaty of Lancaster in Pennsylvania, anno 1744, between the Government of Virginia and the Six Nations, the commissioners from Virginia acquainted the Indians by a speech, that there was at Williamsburg a college with a fund for the education of Indian youth and that if the chiefs of the Six Nations would send down half a dozen of their sons to that college, the government would take care that they be well provided for, and instructed in all the learning of the white people.

The Indians' spokesperson replied thus:

. . . We are convinced . . that you mean to do us good by your proposal and we thank you heartily. But you, who are wise, must know that different nations have different conceptions of things; and you will not therefore take it amiss, if our ideas of this kind of education happens not to be the same with yours. We have had some experience of it; several of our young people were formerly brought up at the colleges of northern provinces; they were instructed in all your sciences; but, when they came back to us, they were bad runners, ignorant of every means of living in the woods, unable to bear either cold or hunger, knew neither how to build a cabin, take a deer, nor kill an enemy, spoke our language imperfectly, were therefore neither fit for hunters, warriors, nor counselors; they were totally good for nothing.

We are however not the less obligated by your offer, though we decline accepting it; and, to show our grateful sense of it, if the gentlemen of Virginia will send us a dozen of their sons, we will take care of their education, instruct them in all we know, and make men of them.

in the pursuit of a leisure experience. Freedom also suggests that an individual is free of the obligations that might arise from family, work, or home activities or of the constraints that may inhibit participation or involvement. Freedom is an abstraction that has been pursued by humankind consistently throughout history. To be free means to be able to act without the interference or control of another, to choose or to act in accordance with one's own will. Freedom also often implies the absence of external constraints or compulsions on an individual to act in a prescribed manner.

Perceived Competence. Perceived competence refers to the skills an individual believes he or she possesses that, in turn, relate to satisfying participation in leisure experiences. In other words, the perception of having skills and abilities necessary to successful participation leads to a satisfying leisure experience. It can be frustrating, anxiety-producing, or discouraging not to possess the required skills and abilities necessary to participate successfully in a leisure experience. Lack of skills, or lack of confidence in one's skills, can serve as a major constraint to participation or to fulfilling participation. For a successful leisure experience to occur, individuals must perceive themselves to have a degree of competence commensurate with the challenges of the intended leisure experience. This matching of skills and challenges is necessary for satisfying experiences. Whether or not this perception of competence is accurate or reality-based is irrelevant; the person's perception of competence while engaged in the experience is essential.

Intrinsic Motivation. A number of researchers have postulated that the leisure experience must be intrinsically satisfying and/or participation in leisure experiences must be intrinsically motivating. In other words, involvement in leisure pursuits often occurs because participants are moved from within and not because they are influenced by external factors. Mannell and Klieber (1997) note that intrinsic motivation is a major dimension of leisure. This motivation from within results in personal feelings of satisfaction, enjoyment, and gratification. In addition, intrinsic motivation is directly related to perceived competence. Iso-Ahola (1999) has noted, "People seek out activities that are likely to provide intrinsic rewards, of which a sense of competence is the most important" (p. 39).

Often, motivation by external factors reduces perceived freedom and, as a result, affects leisure participation. The engrossment or commitment that comes from being internally motivated and/or deriving internal satisfaction from a leisure experience is far more powerful than participation that results from external factors. Csikszentmihalyi (1975, 1990) refers to the concept of being totally engrossed in a leisure experience—where one's actions and intellect are completely synchronized—as "flow," or the "autotelic" experience. This level of engrossment, according to Csikszentmihalyi, produces its own reward and reinforcement.

Positive Affect. The fourth leisure-defining factor, the concept of positive affect, refers to the feelings individuals experience when they have some control or influence within the leisure process. This is sometimes referred to as a sense of choice, or self-determination (Iso-Ahola, 1999). This does not mean that individuals must be actively involved in planning or organizing the experience, but they must feel some degree of control as the experience unfolds.

Leisure professionals, when organizing programs and services, often plan for this type of input to occur by allowing freedom within structure. Programmers provide the participant with an opportunity to make decisions about some aspects of the experience by providing alternatives and choices. The leisure experience is dynamic; it is not static. Individuals play an important role in shaping the experience as they interact within an event, facility, or natural setting. Positive affect is produced by enhancing an individual's opportunity to ". . . play an active role in organizing their leisure experiences" (Rossman, 1988, p. 5).

All of the preceding variables are interrelated; they have in common an element of control. The greater the degree to which an individual perceives personal control in terms of feeling confident, shaping the leisure experience, feeling free from constraints and obligations, and feeling that the experience has personal relevance and meaning, the more satisfying and fulfilling the leisure experience. If an individual is not constrained and can participate in an activity, yet the activity does not provide opportunities for the individual to shape the experience, the leisure experience may be diminished. Thus, various factors are linked and related to one another and, in fact, may be mutually dependent on each other to produce the leisure experience.

Ways of Viewing Leisure

As indicated, leisure means different things to different people, resulting in a number of ways of viewing the concept of leisure. These approaches often depend on the perception of leisure in the minds of individuals, professionals, researchers, or, in an even broader perspective, society as a whole. Leisure does shape culture (and culture shapes leisure), and collective perceptions vary in terms of the value and importance of leisure, as well as the way it is ultimately defined. Today there are at least seven ways of looking at or defining leisure: leisure as time, as

Cruise Lines: Adventure Recreation?

Cruise lines are seeing a huge increase in younger vacationers. According to the Cruise Lines International Association, 72 percent of cruise goers are between the ages of twenty-five and fifty-nine. In addition, the adventure component of cruise ship vacations has increased tremendously. For example, Royal Caribbean International launched two new ships in 2000—they accommodate 3,100 passengers and are the length of three football fields. On board vacationers find rock-climbing walls, eighteen-hole computer golf courses, in-line skating, and ice rinks. Other cruise lines keep passenger numbers small as they turn to eco-conscious outdoor adventures. Temptress Adventure Cruises take 100 passengers at a time and involve them in eco-tourism trips to Costa Rica, Panama, and other Central American jungles.

Source: *USA Weekend,* January 12–14, 2001.

Figure 2.1

Definitions of leisure

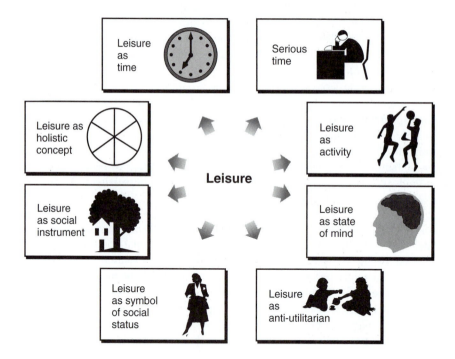

an activity, as a state of mind, as a symbol of social status, as a social instrument, as an anti-utilitarian concept, and as a part of a holistic process (see figure 2.1).

Leisure as Time Over the past century, one of the chief ways of viewing leisure was to perceive it as time—similar to work time, free time, and time to maintain bodily needs (i.e., sleep, eating, personal hygiene). Time, according to those advocating this approach of viewing life, can be divided into three segments—existence (work), subsistence (addressing physical needs), and discretionary (free or unobligated) time. Free or discretionary time is that time which is not obligated in terms of subsistence and existence activities; it is free for rest or a choice of activity. In this approach to defining leisure, Iso-Ahola (1999) notes, "In everyday usage of the language, people refer to all nonworking hours as free time. But as we know only a small portion of this time may indeed be free, free from obligations and free to do what one wants to do." The idea of viewing leisure as time occurred primarily as a result of the Industrial Revolution. During this period, lives were fragmented or segmented into work time and free time, where one's free time was used to rest and recuperate in order to go back to work (Juniu, 2000).

Kelly (1996) and Kraus (1990) maintain that leisure time can be viewed from two perspectives. The first views leisure as a product of residual time—time left over from other obligations. Such leisure time could occur as unplanned, unchosen leisure time. This type of time often produces casual, unstructured opportunities for leisure. The second perspective views leisure as discretionary time (Kelly, 1996), free from work and life-maintenance activities. Discretionary time implies that individuals have choice, autonomy, and freedom to exercise their will to experience leisure.

Leisure as an Activity   Another definition views leisure as a discrete set of activities. In this framework, leisure activities can be differentiated from other life activities, such as those that are work-oriented or involve life maintenance. This approach to defining leisure suggests that leisure and work/life-maintenance activities are not interrelated, but rather are each a unique and distinct set of functions. Dumazedier (1967) states that leisure can be viewed as an activity ". . . apart from obligations of work, family, and society—to which the individual turns at will for either relaxation, diversion, or broadening his [or her] knowledge and his [or her] spontaneous social participation, the free exercise of his [or her] creative capacity" (pp. 16–17).

This definition pays no attention to the concept of leisure as related to what happens within an individual's mind; rather, leisure is simply defined by categories of activity. This can be problematic because many activities serve dual purposes (e.g., cooking, walking; Kelly and Freysinger, 2000). As Kelly (1996, p. 19) writes, ". . . defining leisure simply as specified activities presents a strange paradox; almost no one actually defines leisure in that way in theory. There are no lists of activities that are said to encompass leisure." Kraus (1990) suggests that this view of leisure is closely aligned with that of recreation in that it involves the way free time is used. It is difficult, if not impossible, to list the myriad of activities in which one could participate during leisure. In addition, activities that some individuals consider to be leisure-oriented might be considered work-oriented by others. Thus, the line between leisure and work is not clear-cut but is subjective. Nonetheless, researchers and leisure professionals continue to use this definition of leisure as one of the bases for contemporary discussion of definitions of leisure.

Again, Kelly (1996) suggests that leisure as activity can be viewed from two unique perspectives. The first of these views the forms that leisure activities take, and numerous classification systems cluster leisure activities by their common components. Edginton, Hanson, Hudson, and Edginton (1998) suggest, for example, that areas of programming can be classified in the following ways: the arts; literary activities; self-improvement/education; sports, games, and athletics; aquatics; outdoor recreation; wellness; hobbies; social recreation; volunteer services; and travel and tourism. As DeGraaf, Jordan, and DeGraaf (1999) have written, "Classifying experiences that offer satisfying leisure and recreation experiences can be a difficult task. The possible categories are limitless and the means of classification often arbitrary" (p. 121). The second perspective views leisure activities in terms of their meaning. Such typologies focus on the benefits or outcomes of the activities. For example, MacKay and Crompton (1988) propose that leisure activities should be clustered in terms of such outcomes as relaxation, achievement, intimacy, power, or socialization.

Leisure as a State of Mind   This approach to defining leisure suggests that the leisure experience is a function of one's state of mind. In other words, leisure is a subjective attitude, an experience that is based on an individual's own perspective, feelings, values, and past life experiences. As Kelly writes (1996, p. 21), leisure ". . . is not distinguished by its form or location in time. Rather, from the experiential perspective, leisure is a mental condition that is located in the consciousness of the individual." This approach emphasizes what happens in a person's mind as he or she is engaged experientially.

Leisure has been referred to as not only a mental, but a spiritual attitude, ". . . a condition of the soul" (Pieper, 1963, p. 40). Authors subscribing to this perspective maintain that one can participate in activities that for all appearance seem to be leisure, but if the individual's attitude or mind-set is not positively open to the potential fullness of the experience, it may not result in leisure. While going on a vacation or holiday can provide the opportunity for leisure, many work roles are fulfilled while vacationing. A vacation can be full of stress, anxiety, and frustration if it holds too many of the negative aspects of work, or if one's mental mind-set is essentially negative. One family might go to Disneyland on vacation and have a wonderful leisure experience, virtually unaffected by minor inconveniences such as long lines. Another family may go to the same Disneyland theme park and on the same rides but be unable to attain a true leisure experience due to their tendency to focus on the negative aspects of the endeavor. Or the children may enjoy the experience, but the adults may not, having seen the attractions before. Different members of the family could experience the event differently in terms of the quality of the leisure experience depending upon their state of mind.

Russell (1996, p. 35) provides perspective to the discussion of leisure as a subjective attitude, and has suggested the following:

> Although the psychological condition of leisure suggests it is a matter of "feeling good," the connotation goes beyond this. Leisure is an entire way of being—an opportunity for building purpose into life—capable of providing opportunities for self-expression, self-achievement and self-actualization. Leisure is engaging in flights of imagination, developing talents, looking at things in new ways, and being ourselves.

Leisure as a Symbol of Social Status   From a historical perspective, leisure as a symbol of social status has existed since the beginning of agricultural civilizations. The evolution of the "leisure classes" emerged as a result of increased social organization, complexity, and functional differentiation of agricultural societies. Leisure as a symbol of social class was reflected in the writings of Thorsten Veblen in 1899 in his work, *Theory of the Leisure Class*. Veblen coined the term "conspicuous consumption" in his classic work of economic and sociological literature. He noted that ". . . as wealth accumulates, the leisure class develops further in function and structure and there arises a differentiation within the class[es]" (1899, p. 76). He suggests that the evolution of conspicuous expenditures, whether of goods, services, or human life, runs the obvious implication that in order "to effectively [maintain] . . . the consumer's good fame, it must be . . . wasteful" (Veblen, 1899, p. 96).

Today, people still use leisure as a way of claiming or demonstrating social status in society by virtue of the products and services that people consume or purchase. The brand name of an athletic shoe confers a certain social status on the owner of the shoe. Vacationing at Club Med provides a greater social status than camping at a state park. Nearly all forms of leisure appear to be a part of a conscious effort to align the leisure goods and services chosen with the status or image the consumer wishes to project. Leisure apparel provides a visible, external symbol of perceived status and values. Individuals consciously seek to present an image during their leisure that reflects their image of themselves and, often, what they desire to reflect to others. This is a form of social exhibition manifested by those in the higher social strata. The symbolic nature of leisure is one of "ostentation, luxury, pleasures, and squander" (Juniu, 2000, p. 70).

The downside of this phenomenon results when individuals make inordinate, inappropriate sacrifices in the quality of their daily lives in order to possess certain leisure status symbols. In addition, many leisure products and services can only reasonably be purchased by a certain segment of society, excluding others from participation. This raises issues of equity in the delivery of services and also promotes concern for the values that may be associated with some leisure purchases.

Another perspective of leisure as a symbol of social status is the value that is attached to having leisure. Today, many individuals seek more freedom, autonomy, and flexibility in both their leisure and their work. In addition, people desire meaningful and satisfying experiences in all aspects of life. In the information era, many professional workers have the opportunity for more flexible work hours, more concentrated, focused leisure experiences (referred to as time deepening) and, in general, more control over their creative potential and ability. Socioeconomic status influences this phenomenon; greater resources result in greater work flexibility. Great status is attached to individuals who work/play on their own terms and at their discretion; there is an understanding of associated social class. Such individuals often fuse their work and leisure lives in such a way as to take advantage of their creative potential. Our society is moving from a work-hard-play-hard orientation to attaching great status to an integrative, creative, flexible, and discretionary work-play lifestyle.

Leisure as a Social Instrument   Leisure can also be viewed as a social instrument (Murphy, 1974). From this perspective, leisure can be viewed as a way of enhancing individual or community life in ways that promote instrumental (useful) ends. Further, viewing leisure from this perspective also contains elements that see "free time" as having potentially negative or undesirable consequences. With this orientation, leisure would be controlled in order to promote social order and harmony within a given economic, political, or social framework or ideology. For example, the misuse of leisure time at the turn of the century was viewed as being detrimental to effectiveness at work. As Murphy (1974, p. 12) writes,

> In industrial society, leisure is separate from the rest of man's [*sic*] life. It has become, not a part of life, but a means to life—a thing of extrinsic value, useful only because it relaxes and restores the individual for work.

Today, misuse of leisure time has been linked to social disruption, poor health practices, and other issues. This approach to defining leisure has been criticized in that it has the potential to rob leisure of its spontaneity and freedom. As Leitner and Leitner (1996, p. 10) write, ". . . a drawback to this concept is that it can lead to a stressful attitude toward leisure, in which achievement during leisure activity is overemphasized. Leisure can become work-like in nature, approached with an emphasis on end results rather than as an experience in itself." Thus, as one can see, the idea that leisure is a social instrument has some drawbacks. However, in recent years, with a great emphasis on defining the social, economic, and other benefits of leisure, renewed emphasis on this approach of viewing leisure has gained value. The platitudes of leisure as promoting stress reduction, health, psychological well-being, human happiness, enhanced community life, and others are a part of the professional jargon of leisure.

Leisure as an Anti-Utilitarian Concept   The anti-utilitarian concept of leisure is not new. In *The Normal Course of Play* (1925), Lee suggests that the value of play is not tied to instrumental ends. He notes that ". . . the joy of play for its own sake is universally recognized. Play is above a mere instrument or means and, as a phase of life, it has its own justification" (p. 86). In a more contemporary context, Murphy (1974) has advanced the concept that leisure can be viewed from an anti-utilitarian perspective. That is, leisure need not serve any purpose and needs no justification. As Murphy (1974, p. 10) explains, "The social structure of the industrial society, governed by an economic principle of rationality, clashes with the emerging values of the culture, and anti-utilitarian, hedonistic, pleasure-seeking rationale based on openness, choice, flexibility, change and spontaneity." Quoting Charles Reich, Murphy (1974) further notes, that ". . . the anti-utilitarian philosophy, believing and doing what one wants to do rather than responding passively to outside pressures . . . provides an arena for fellowship, spontaneity, authenticity, and creativity" (p. 10).

The anti-utilitarian concept of leisure gained some interest among leisure theorists in the early 1970s as a way of explaining the emergence of a new leisure ethic evidenced in post-industrial society. This new leisure ethic was best reflected in the lifestyle of the countercultural movement of that period of time that rejected prevailing cultural norms and customs calling for a more open, spontaneous, and free society. Leitner and Leitner (1996, p. 10) suggest that this concept has several drawbacks. First, they note that ". . . anti-utilitarian view . . . is difficult to utilize in objectively quantifying leisure for research purposes." Another drawback, according to these authors, is that ". . . it can be used to justify leisure activities that are detrimental to health self-development" (p. 10).

Leisure as a Holistic Concept   The holistic concept of leisure, championed by Murphy (1981) and presented by other authors such as Neulinger (1974), Godbey (1981), Kraus (1984), and Kelly (1996), broadly suggests that all parts of a person's life have the potential for leisure. It integrates and combines many features of the preceding definitions with particular emphasis on individuals' ability to shape and control their own leisure destiny. As Murphy (1981) writes:

> The holistic concept of leisure is seen as a potentially synthesizing theoretical perspective in which elements of leisure are to be expressed in all aspects of human behavior—in work, play, education, and other social spheres. There is much debate as to whether the unique character of leisure, particularly as influenced by social organization of work can be effectively analyzed and operationalized because such a conceptual approach has not lent itself to either empirical testing or accurate prediction. (p. 34)

The holistic perspective suggests that leisure has the potential to be present in many forms of human endeavor (Kelly and Godbey, 1992). An individual might find the opportunity for leisure in work, church, school, or other settings that heretofore may have only focused on the potential for more specific, narrow outcomes. The holistic perspective forces examination of our work and other endeavors to determine whether they contain elements of leisure. It also raises the possibility that one's life cannot be fragmented into neatly organized and structured components.

Kelly (1990) offers a perspective on the holistic orientation, suggesting that leisure may be a realized action. He suggests the following:

> Leisure takes place in time. It is not defined by time or place, but it does not float off into an unrelated attitude or feeling. It is connected to the realities of identifiable spatial and temporal dimensions. Further, leisure has form. The forms are almost infinite in their variety, but it is possible to identify activity, be it contemplation or competition, in which leisure occurs. It is legitimate to study

these forms, not as leisure, but as the events in which leisure happens. Finally, leisure is experience. It involves perceptions of the actor—going into the experience, during it and coming out of it. Such perceptions are essential dimensions of the action. (pp. 22–23)

According to the holistic perspective, leisure addresses dimensions of time, activity, and experience. Kelly notes that leisure ". . . is a realized action" (1990, p. 23). To be considered leisure, an activity must have an outcome; something must have occurred to indicate that leisure has taken place—it is not solely a thought or attitude, but involves action. Even during contemplation, the formation of thoughts and ideas hold value for the individual.

Kraus (1990) also promotes the holistic view of leisure. He suggests that this perspective ". . . implies a lifestyle which is holistic, in the sense that one's view of life is not sharply fragmented into a number of spheres, such as family activities, religion, work, and free time. Instead, all such involvements are seen as part of a whole . . ." (p. 53). The holistic perspective of leisure, according to Kraus, finds the individual developing a lifestyle of enriching life experiences that promote a ". . . sense of being creative, involved, expressive and fully alive" (1984, p. 46). Linked to Murphy's definition stated earlier, this interpretation of the holistic concept emphasizes an integrated lifestyle in which opportunities to operate creatively, expressively, physically, and intellectually are found in all spheres of one's life and are not fragmented into subcategories such as sports and games, arts, work, leisure, and family life.

The holistic perspective to understanding leisure provides a broad basis for interpreting leisure. This integrative concept helps one to understand leisure in light of the nature of work and the contemporary technology of today's society. The information era has provided a different set of assumptions about the way people think and organize social institutions. The holistic perspective provides a fluid, organic approach to defining leisure that may be suited to the lifestyles emerging during this decade.

Serious Leisure

Stebbins has offered an alternative view to leisure, which seems to fit between how we understand leisure and how we understand work. He indicates that *serious leisure* is the "systematic pursuit of an amateur, hobbyist, or volunteer activity that participants find so substantial and interesting that, in the typical case, they launch themselves on a career centered on acquiring and expressing its special skills, knowledge, and experience" (1992, p. 3). This is commonly contrasted with *casual leisure,* which is leisure that is intrinsically rewarding and pleasurable, and requires no special training to enjoy it. According to Stebbins (1999), activities such as play, relaxation, passive and active entertainment, sociable conversation, and sensory pleasures are considered casual leisure.

Serious leisureists are defined by six distinctive qualities:

1. the need to persevere (often in the face of danger or fear);
2. finding a career in the endeavor;
3. a significant personal effort based on special knowledge, training, or skill;
4. durable benefits (self-actualization, self-enrichment, self-expression, renewal, social interaction, lasting physical products);
5. strong identification with their chosen pursuits; and
6. a unique ethos, or special social world, which arises when enthusiasts pursue their leisure experiences over the years (Stebbins, 1999).

As one might imagine, there are many examples of people engaged in serious leisure pursuits. They might include amateur photographers or astronomers, members of HOGs (Harley

Davidson motorcycle Owner Groups), career volunteers, and members of community bands and community garden clubs. Yoder (1997) notes that events such as tournament bass fishing are examples of how individuals can become involved in serious leisure pursuits.

Work and Leisure

A number of authors suggest that leisure and work are linked. The two major theories of linkage include the compensatory theory and the spillover theory. In the compensatory theory, leisure and work are linked "in the sense that leisure is used to compensate for the strains or demands of work" (Kraus, 1990, p. 56). Under this notion, people choose leisure activities that satisfy needs that they cannot satisfy at work. The spillover theory suggests that leisure activities are chosen that have similar characteristics as job-related activities (Mannell and Reid, 1999). In this case, individuals enjoy work so much it spills over into leisure (Kelly and Godbey, 1992). Other authors suggest that work and leisure are distinctly different concepts and are not interdependent. This is known as the neutrality approach (Mannell and Reid, 1999). However, from a historical perspective, a distinct relationship has existed between the concepts of work and leisure. Throughout the history of humankind, work has greatly shaped the lives of individuals. It has influenced fundamental values, customs, and norms, and it has defined, shaped, and molded cultures.

What is work? Humans have a large capacity for activity. When activity is organized and results in the creation of products or services and people are compensated (receive a paycheck), it is known as work. Typically, the activity must be socially necessary in that it makes a contribution to society (Kelly and Godbey, 1992). Concepts of work vary from culture to culture and range from agriculture to manufacturing to service delivery. Work often is defined as "purposeful effort." It is a job, an occupation, something that results from effort. Synonyms for work include "toil" and "labor." Antonyms for the term include "play," "leisure," "diversion," "pleasure," "fun," "amusement," "rest," and "relaxation." In other words, people often view work and leisure as opposites.

What is the relationship between work and leisure? Many people easily separate leisure from work, particularly those in monotonous, routinized jobs. Work is that which is done at the office, factory, or plant, while leisure is that which is done outside of the job. Many others, however, have difficulty distinguishing their work from leisure because they find work integrated into the whole of their lives (Kelly and Godbey, 1992). It is still true, however, that individuals often define their concepts of leisure based on their perceptions of work.

The lack of a clear distinction between work and leisure blurs our understanding of the precise nature and relationship of these two concepts. As has been written:

> Leisure and work mean different things to different people. Some people do not have enough discretionary time, some have too much. Some people seek to find satisfaction in their jobs, others seek it in leisure activities. Some define work as what we get paid for doing, but we also get paid for time not worked—vacations, holidays, coffee breaks. Moreover, the mobility of our labor force implies great discretionary choice. (Henneman, 1973, p. 23)

Thus, a paradox exists when trying to identify the exact relationship between work and leisure. Although some definitions may offer clear-cut distinctions between work and leisure, in reality, the nature of human perceptions and behavior blurs the difference. What is work to one person may be leisure to another, and vice versa. One person's toil may be another's pleasure.

Neulinger (1981) offers a way of distinguishing between leisure and non-leisure. He suggests that one can view the difference between leisure and non-leisure types of experiences

Figure 2.2

A paradigm of leisure: A psychological definition

Source: After J. Neulinger, "The Need for and the Implications of a Psychological Conception of Leisure" in The Ontario Psychologist, 8, *1976.*

Perceived Freedom

Freedom			Constraint		
Motivation			Motivation		
Intrinsic	Intrinsic and Extrinsic	Extrinsic	Extrinsic	Intrinsic and Extrinsic	Intrinsic
(1)	(2)	(3)	(4)	(5)	(6)
Pure Leisure	Leisure-Work	Leisure-Job	Pure Work	Work-Job	Pure Job

← ——————————— State of Mind ——————————— →

using *perceived freedom* as the primary distinguishing characteristic. As Russell (1996) notes in explaining Neulinger's work, perceived freedom means how much choice one feels in determining their own actions. Was it their choice (perceived freedom) or did they do it because they felt they had to (perceived constraint)? Neulinger uses the concept of *intrinsic/extrinsic motivation* to divide leisure and non-leisure categories. Intrinsic motivation comes from within an individual and the activity is chosen for its own sake; extrinsic motivation describes the motivation to do something as coming from outside of a person.

In Neulinger's model of leisure (see figure 2.2), there are six potential leisure or non-leisure experiences as follows:

- Pure Leisure → Perceived Freedom and Intrinsic Motivation
- Leisure-Work → Perceived Freedom and Extrinsic and Intrinsic Motivation
- Leisure-Job → Perceived Freedom and Extrinsic Motivation
- Pure Work → Perceived Constraint and Extrinsic Motivation
- Work-Job → Perceived Constraint and Extrinsic and Intrinsic Motivation
- Pure Job → Perceived Constraint and Intrinsic Motivation

Each of these categories represents a psychological state of mind that can be viewed as existing on a continuum. Each state of mind represents a different degree of potential for leisure to exist or not exist. Russell (1996, p. 91) suggests that ". . . what is important to realize about Neulinger's theoretical contribution is that the paradigm represents a psychological orientation with behavior attributed solely to self rather than to external forces."

L e i s u r e   L i n e

Faxing for Fast Food

Time is a commodity, and many admit to not having enough of it. How do we adjust? In many larger cities, one can speed up the lunch hour by faxing in meal requests to local restaurants. While this phenomenon has been in existence for many years, we now see it extending into fast-food restaurants as well. In downtown Phoenix, busy executives can fax in their lunch order to a local Burger King and pick up their lunch from an express lane a few minutes later.

What Is Recreation?

The term *recreation* is not as challenging to define as the term *leisure*. Professionals and researchers have used far more consistency in defining recreation. Recreation is often seen as *an activity that is engaged in during one's free time, is pleasurable, and which has socially redeeming qualities* (Kraus, 1990). Recreation involves an individual's participation in specific, wholesome, and voluntary activities. This is contrasted with leisure, which has no value orientation. By this we mean that participation in leisure or the leisure experience is neither good nor bad; the only value it holds is that which the individual places on it. Recreation participation, however, usually must result in constructive, positive, socially acceptable behaviors. This does not discount the often unhealthy and antisocial activities that some people undertake during their leisure. Kelly and Godbey (1992) noted that recreation is an "activity with social purposes and organization" (p. 20). Recreation is intended to be good for the people of a society in specific ways and is organized and supported to produce such results.

Two Latin terms provide the root for the word *recreation*. The first, *recreatio,* means "to refresh." The second, *recreare,* means "to restore." Thus, most dictionary definitions suggest that the term derives from concepts related to restoring or refreshing oneself. Synonyms for the term *recreation* include "relaxation," "amusement," "pleasure," "diversion," "pleasant," "create anew," "recreated," "refreshing," "reinvigorating," "refreshment," and "comfort." Other terms associated with recreation include *recreate, recreational,* and *recreative.*

Kraus (1984, 1990) provides one of the most complete analyses of the term *recreation* found in literature. He notes that over the past several decades most definitions of recreation include similar terms, and he suggests that there is a logical consistency between and among most definitions. Kraus' (1984, 1990) analysis includes the following elements as consistent terms found in most definitions of recreation:

1. Recreation is widely regarded as an activity in contrast to sheer idleness or complete rest.
2. Recreation may include an extremely wide range of activities. Activities may be engaged in briefly or in a sustained way, for single episodes or throughout one's lifetime.
3. Recreation is voluntary and does not occur because of outside pressures, compulsory or obligatory.
4. Recreation activities are socially redeeming, wholesome, and contribute to the development of society.
5. Recreation has the potential for many desirable outcomes—fun is the steadfast goal of recreation, yet not its purpose (Haun, 1965).
6. Recreation takes place during one's free time, although it is not so much the activity that one pursues, but rather the reason for engaging in it.

These elements suggest a vast range of activities and that recreation involves activity as contrasted to idleness. Furthermore, recreational activities may be pursued in short periods or may consume an individual's interest over an extended period of time. An important aspect of Kraus' analysis is that recreation activities are participated in on a voluntary basis; the individual must feel free to participate. Also, Kraus' analysis provides for a wide range of benefits or outcomes. One might engage in a variety of recreation behaviors including socializing behaviors, associative behaviors, competitive behaviors, risk-taking behaviors, exploratory behaviors, vicarious experiences, sensory stimulation, and physical expression (Kraus, 1990).

Recreation as a Social Instrument

From a recent historical perspective, recreation programs and services have been used as ways of promoting desirable social ends. During the Industrial Revolution, individuals had work time and free time. The misuse of free time was viewed as a social problem, and wholesome recreation activities became a tool to help alleviate or overcome concerns related to this problem. A host of social institutions were created to provide programs and services that were socially redeeming. In a sense, recreation was used to control certain classes of people (typically the working class), to support their productivity, and to keep them prepared for work. Laws outlawed unhealthy forms of recreation (gambling, drinking) and hours of operation for businesses were curtailed to encourage workers to get enough sleep to be ready for work the next day (Kelly and Godbey, 1992).

In discussing recreation as a social institution, Ibrahim (1991) suggests that mass leisure activities occur in industrial-urbanized societies. Such leisure includes what Ibrahim defines as recreative leisure; that is, purposeful leisure, distinguished from either contemplative activities or amusement. Kelly postulates that mass recreation occurred in Roman society as a way of diverting attention from problems of unemployment and social inequities (1996). It is interesting to note in reviewing historical literature from the leisure services field, one of the first textbooks written to provide professional training for individuals, *The Normal Course in Play,* states the following:

> Recreation, someone has said, is no longer merely desirable for our pleasure; it is physiologically necessary in order to retain normal equilibrium in the midst of the deadening monotony and the excess strain of the common life today, both in the city and country. (Lee, 1925, p. 15)

In 1917, Henry Curtis, writing in the book *The Play Movement and Its Significance,* discussed the need for institutionalized, wholesome recreation environments. He justified the sources of the need for such types of environments by stating the following:

> Nearly every parent and observer of children has seen that there has been little for children to do in the cities, and that in this time of idleness, the devil has found much for idle hands to do; that the children are an annoyance to their parents and the neighborhood and that they acquire many vicious habits during this unused time. . . . There has come a general, though dim, realization that if we would stem this tide, we must surround children with a different environment. (p. 8)

Curtis went on to suggest that there was a need to create institutionalized forms of play (recreation) to deal with this problem. It could be argued that this need still exists in contemporary society.

Over the past century in Canada and the United States, there has been an increased investment in recreation and park systems at the local, state, and federal levels of government. In addition, voluntary and/or youth-serving organizations, as well as nonprofit private and commercial leisure service organizations, have seen tremendous growth. No doubt this growth has occurred because of the importance of the use of recreation as an instrument of social reform or change.

Today, numerous institutions focus on providing recreation environments and/or using recreation activities or services as a way of promoting, teaching, and reinforcing organizational values. In fact, many recreation-oriented organizations have greatly influenced the shape and character of culture and values in the United States and Canada. For example, it is likely that three-fourths of the people who read this book will have been a member of a youth-serving organization such as the Boy Scouts, Girl Scouts, Girl Guides, YMCA, YWCA, YMHA, YWHA, Boys and Girls Clubs, and Camp Fire, Inc. These types of organizations provide a fundamental foundation of values that influence individuals throughout their lives. Such organizations have become important social institutions, using recreation activities, facilities, and other services to shape and guide the character of literally millions of young people.

What Is Play?

Like *leisure* and *recreation,* the term *play* is also complex and difficult to define. Like other human endeavors, it has great potential to nourish, enrich, and enhance life. Play has shaped the values, norms, and customs of all cultures; it is a major force in which all cultures participate. Play, like music, is universal. In every culture one can see people playing. In nearly every culture, some attention has been given to providing special environments in which to promote playful behavior. The universality of play links humankind in the same way that other shared experiences bind us to one another. Kraus (1990) defines play as follows:

> Play may be defined as a form of human or animal behavior, self-motivated and carried on for intrinsic purposes. It is generally pleasurable, and is often marked by elements of competition, exploration, and problem solving, and mimicry or role-taking. It may appear both in leisure and in work, and may be marked either by freedom and lack of structure, or by a set of rules and prescribed actions. (p. 41)

Mannell and Klieber (1997) suggest that play is nonliteral behavior and a transformation of reality—it is imaginative. In addition, it is intrinsically motivated, freely chosen, and actively engaging. It is a way for children to learn about the world around them and their place in it. Play is a mechanism for self-expression and enjoyment and shares many elements of leisure and recreation.

Throughout the history of humanity, play has served as a socializing force for its youth, as play transmits values, customs, traditions, and societal norms. Gender and other roles are often acted out in play environments and, as a result, our earliest notions of self-identity are formed in play environments. In preliterate societies, play rituals provided the major mechanisms used to pass information from one generation to the next. In more contemporary times, play activities are used for the same purpose of transmitting cultural values. Competition, cooperation, winning versus losing, preparation for adult roles, along with pursuit of happiness, pleasure, and joy and all cultural values are transmitted in play environments. As Winston Churchill noted, "The wars of England were won and lost on the playing fields of Eton."

Play is often viewed as frivolous rather than as a serious, important activity and is often considered acceptable only for children. Because many consider play to be the exclusive domain of children, an adult's ability to play is questioned. In reality, however, adults do play, although it is a complex, structured play and often laden with rules and regulations. Children often engage in spontaneous, uninhibited, joyful, and free play activity; however, adults seem more constrained. As a result, adults play but tend to identify play as recreation or leisure activity. Such activity is usually instrumental in nature (purposeful) and has benefits other than simply free play expression.

Dimensions of Play

According to the *Oxford English Dictionary,* the word *play* is derived from the Old English term *plegan,* meaning "to dance, to leap for joy, to rejoice and to be glad," as well as the term *plega,* which means "to exercise or occupy oneself, to busy oneself." Play often occurs in association with games, amusement, fun, freedom, diversion, sport, frolic, pleasure, joy, and delight.

Although many definitions of play have been offered during the last century, no real definitive or universally accepted theories have emerged. Recently, a number of empirically based theories, such as those advanced by Ellis (1973), Csikszentmihalyi (1975), and Levy (1978), have provided a basic foundation for the study of play. Theorists over the years have structured a number of theories to explain play behavior. For example, one of the earliest explanations of play during the industrial period was presented by the German poet Schiller in 1875. Schiller believed that people were only truly human when they were at play—when they engaged in creative activity for its own sake.

Today, nearly twenty theories of play can be identified. Because of the complexity of human behavior, however, it is difficult to develop a precise definition or theory of play. In the past several decades, renewed interest in the study of play has been evidenced by an increasing number of empirical or scientific investigations. Examination and acknowledgment of one or more theories of play can provide the leisure service professional with a foundation for practice. Professional practice must be guided by some theoretical underpinning; acknowledgment of a theory provides for direction, consistency, coordination of efforts, and, ultimately, evaluation of one's efforts. Some of the theories explaining play that have emerged over the past century include the following (see figure 2.3):

Surplus Energy Theory. The surplus energy theory of play (Schiller, 1875; Spencer, 1873) suggests that play occurs as a result of the excess energy available to people after their basic needs for survival are met. Spontaneous games of tag and running about with no apparent purpose meet this definition.

Recreation Theory. The recreation theory of play proposed by Lazarus in 1883 suggests that the need for play is created when fatigue occurs, as a result of misuse or overuse of one's body energy. Play acts in a restorative capacity, rejuvenating the fatigued individual. Thus, going jogging to restore oneself when fatigued serves as an example of this theory.

Contemplating values related to discretionary time

FRANK AND ERNEST reprinted by permission of Newspaper Enterprise Association, Inc.

Figure 2.3

Fifteen theories
of play

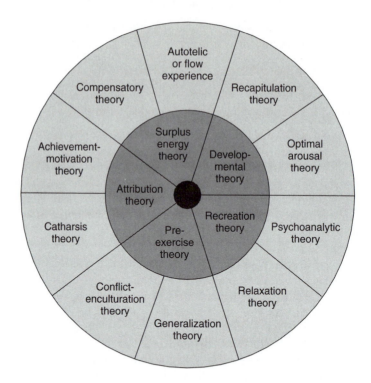

The preexercise theory, recapitulation theory, relaxation theory, catharsis theory, compensatory theory, psychoanalytic theory...

Preexercise Theory. The preexercise theory of play, proposed by Karl Groos in 1898, suggests that play is an instinct which is practiced as a result of inherited factors. This theory derived its conceptual base from and was strongly influenced by Charles Darwin. An example of this theory would be children playing family roles (pretending to be parents complete with teddy-bear children); it is believed this type of play is instinctual and prepares children for adult roles.

Recapitulation Theory. In the early 1900s, Hall proposed the recapitulation theory of play. He suggested that play essentially involves a recapturing or reenactment of the elements inherent in the development of humankind. Through play, children are thought to be enacting the lives of their ancestors (an evolutionary approach to understanding play).

Relaxation Theory. Patrick proposed an extension of the recreation theory of play, the relaxation theory, in 1916. This theory suggests that the need to play results from the need for relaxation. It is the opposite of the surplus energy theory.

Catharsis Theory. The catharsis theory of Carr and Claparede in the early 1900s suggests that play results from an individual's pent-up energies. Play, viewed as a release or safety valve, vents excess energies and emotions. The catharsis theory has an element of purging antisocial tendencies or urges.

Compensatory Theory. The compensatory theory of play, proposed by Reaney (1916) and Robinson (1920), suggests that play becomes a substitute outlet for desires and goals when other avenues to accomplish such goals are blocked. Play allows an individual to make up for unpleasant or unavailable experiences.

Psychoanalytic Theory. Proponents of the application of the psychoanalytic theory to play behavior include Waelder (1933), Peller (1952), and Erikson (1973). At the core of the psychoanalytic theory, memories, needs, and wishes can be deleted from an individual's *conscious* awareness; however, they will continue to be involved in the individual's behavioral repertoire. The relationship of this theory to play, therefore, involves the individual's use of play to react and respond to personal needs, desires, and wishes.

Developmental Theory. The developmental theory of play, advocated by Swiss child psychologist Piaget (1952, 1961), suggests that reality and play behavior are molded by the child to fit each stage of cognitive development. Toddlers play within their physical and intellectual abilities, five- to six-year-olds are more advanced in their play, and nine- to ten-year-olds even more advanced.

Generalization Theory. The generalization theory of play assumes that any learned play behavior will be generalized to other settings and behaviors by the participant (Witt and Bishop, 1970). This resembles the spillover effect (Kando and Summers, 1971), where enjoyable tasks at work spill over into one's play environment.

Attribution Theory. The attribution theory of play suggests that an individual's locus of control is a major determinant affecting the forms of play in which one is engaged. This theoretical proposition maintains that an individual exercising an internal locus of control will participate in forms of play behavior over which there is control and which has measurable outcomes of performance. On the other hand, individuals who are disposed to an external locus of control will select activities over which they have no control and for which they are not directly responsible.

Achievement-Motivation Theory. This theory of play was proposed by Levy (1978) building on the work of Atkinson (1964). The achievement-motivation theory suggests that play, like other life endeavors, involves the desire to strive, excel, master, and succeed. The theory incorporates risk-taking as an element in producing play-related outcomes in competitive situations. We tend to engage others who are more highly skilled than ourselves to increase our mastery and to continue to excel.

Optimal Arousal Theory. Ellis (1973) proposed the optimal arousal theory of play. He suggests that play elements include a combination of complexity, novelty, and dissonance. When individuals become bored, they seek stimulation in their environment. Thus, play occurs as an individual seeks stimulation from the surrounding environment.

The Autotelic or Flow Experience. Csikszentmihalyi (1975, 1990) offers an additional perspective on play by introducing the concept of the flow or autotelic experience. As discussed in chapter one, the individual who has entered into flow experiences a loss of ego and self-consciousness, engages in self-forgetfulness, is engaged in the transcendence of individuality, and loses an awareness of self. In this state, the individual is in control of his or her actions and of the environment. A person has no active awareness of control but is simply not worried by the possibility of the lack of control or failure. In this situation, one feels a sense of personal control or power. When one reaches this state, it is known as flow, and it occurs when the skill or mastery of the individual is equal to the challenge presented in the environment. Play is one environment in which flow can occur.

Conflict-Enculturation Theory. The conflict-enculturation theory of play suggests that play offers the participant an opportunity to experience and learn new behaviors in a safe environment (Sutton-Smith and Roberts, 1982). The individual can become involved in play situations and learn social and other skills with a minimum of emotional risk. This theory proposes that through play experiences the child is prepared for adult roles and trained to assume such abilities—cooperation, competition, ideals of fair play, and handling of intense feelings.

Kraus (1984) notes that play is ". . . a positive form of human experience or behavior . . . [although] . . . play may also have some less desirable connotations" (p. 34). In other words, if play is powerful enough to positively influence the individual, it also has the potential to affect people negatively from a physical or psychological standpoint. Kraus' (1984) comprehensive definition includes the following adapted elements:

1. Play is a form of behavior that is generally regarded as not being instrumental in purpose.
2. Play is often carried out in the spirit of pleasure and creative expression.
3. Play can be aimless, disorganized, and casual or highly structured or complex.
4. Play is commonly thought of as activity engaged in by children, but adults also play.
5. Play stems from an instinctive drive, although much play behavior is culturally learned.
6. Play is regarded as voluntary, pleasurable, and nonserious, although it may involve risk and intense commitment.
7. Play appears to be found in all cultures.
8. Play is linked to important social functions such as law, religion, warfare, art, and commerce.

Kraus' presentation of the elements of play points out the important social function of play in society. Play is simple, yet it is complex (Kelly and Godbey, 1992). It is pleasurable, nondirective, yet can be structured and highly organized. In most cultures, play is joyful, delightful, and pleasurable, although it can also be demanding, intense, and competitive. Play occurs instinctively, yet much of our play behavior is derived from cultural and societal norms, customs, and values. Without question, play has been used as a major vehicle to transmit cultural and societal values as reflected in activities that emphasize competition, cooperation, spontaneity, problem solving, and other outcomes.

Summary

Understanding the concepts of leisure, recreation, and play is fundamental to professional success and to life satisfaction. Leisure, recreation, and play are interwoven concepts, yet they also have their own unique definitional properties. Collectively, leisure, recreation, and play, all elements of human culture, meet many basic human needs and have served to shape, define, and provide meaning to human civilization.

In recent years, our understanding of leisure has been greatly advanced by the work of scientists and scholars studying this area. They have suggested that to experience leisure, certain properties must be in evidence. Four prevailing factors in the literature characterize the leisure experience—freedom, perceived competence, intrinsic motivation, and positive affect. Freedom implies choice, spontaneity, and being free from constraints that inhibit participation. Perceived competence refers to the skills that an individual believes he or she possesses that will contribute to successful participation. Intrinsic motivation refers to an individual's desire to participate in leisure experiences based on personal needs and desires, rather than external motivation. Positive affect refers to the need of an individual to control elements of the leisure experience once he or she is engaged in the process.

Leisure can be viewed from a number of different perspectives. Some theorists suggest that leisure is an element of time, whereas others have perceived it as a set of unique or discrete activities in which individuals participate. Still further, leisure has been defined as a state of mind—a subjective attitude—and as a symbol of social status. The most recent theoretical notion of leisure has been to perceive leisure as a holistic element, meaning that much of human activity has potential for leisure.

Recreation can be thought of as a wholesome activity in which individuals participate in their leisure time. Current definitions of recreation are fairly discrete; most definitions are set in the context of such factors as time, activity, and the social implications of such experiences. Recreation is a more commonly used and understood term among the general public than either leisure or play, although in business and commercial sectors the terms *leisure* or *entertainment* are often used to describe that segment of the field.

Play is an exceedingly interesting, yet diverse and difficult topic to identify. Although many think of play as the exclusive domain of children, it is not. Many theories have emerged to explain play, yet today it has no generally accepted explanation or definition. Play is universal; it occurs in all cultures and is often associated with pleasure, delight, and joy. It plays a major role in transmitting the values, culture, and traditions of a society. Leisure, recreation, work, and play all contribute to one's quality of life.

Discussion Questions

1. Why is it necessary to define leisure, recreation, and play?
2. What factors does a successful leisure experience require?
3. Define leisure from five different perspectives.
4. What is the relationship between work and leisure?
5. Define recreation. What are its defining elements?
6. Select three theories of play; compare and contrast them.
7. Create a collage on how the media views leisure, recreation, and play. How does this differ from the definitions presented in this chapter?
8. How do leisure, recreation, and play interact in your life?
9. Locate a professional in your community and learn about his or her definitions of leisure, recreation, and play.
10. Play is a universal human activity. Provide examples of play environments in your home, school, and community.

References

Atkinson, J. W. 1964. *An Introduction to Motivation.* Princeton, NJ: Van Nostrand.

Barker, E., trans. 1946. *The Politics of Aristotle.* London: Oxford University Press.

Carr, H. H. 1934. The survival value of play. *Investigation of Department of Psychology and Education.* The University of Colorado, 1902, as cited in Elmer D. Mitchell and Bernard S. Mason, *The Theory of Play,* p. 77. New York: Barnes.

Claparede, E. 1911. *Psychologie de l'Enfant et Pedagogie Experimentale,* translated by M. Louch and H. Holman. New York: Longmans, Green.

Csikszentmihalyi, M. 1975. *Beyond Boredom and Anxiety.* San Francisco: Jossey-Bass.

Csikszentmihalyi, M. 1990. *Flow: The Psychology of Optimal Experience.* San Francisco: Jossey-Bass.

Curtis, H. 1917. *The Play Movement and Its Significance.* New York: Macmillan.

Dare, B., G. Welton, and W. Coe. 1987. *Concepts of Leisure and Western Thought.* Dubuque, IA: Kendall Hunt.

DeGraaf, D., D. Jordan, and K. DeGraaf. 1999. *Programming for Parks, Recreation, and Leisure Services: A Servant Leadership Approach.* State College, PA: Venture.

Dumazedier, J. 1967. *Toward a Society of Leisure.* New York: Free Press.

Edginton, C. R., and J. R. Rossman. 1988. Leisure programming: Building a theoretical base. *Journal of Park and Recreation Administration 6*(4), viii.

Edginton, C. R., Hanson, C., Hudson, S., and Edginton, S., 1998. *Leisure programming: A service-centered and benefits approach.* WCBS/McGraw Hill: St. Louis.

Ellis, M. 1973. *Why People Play.* Englewood Cliffs, NJ: Prentice-Hall.

Erikson, E. H. 1973. Thought on the city for human development. *Ekistics 35*(29), 216–220.

Godbey, G. 1981. *Leisure in Your Life.* Philadelphia: Saunders.

Groos, K. 1901. *The Play of Man.* New York: Appleton.

Gunter, B. G. 1987. The leisure experience: Selected properties. *Journal of Leisure Research 19*(2), 115–130.

Hall, G. S. 1906. *Youth.* New York: Appleton.

Haun, P. 1965. *Recreation: A Medical Viewpoint.* New York: Teachers College Press.

Henneman, H. G. 1973. Work and non-work: Historical perspectives. Edited by M. D. Dunnett, in *Work and Non-work in the Year 2001.* Monterey, CA: Brooks/Cole.

Ibrahim, H. 1991. *Leisure and Society.* Dubuque, IA: Wm. C. Brown.

Iso-Ahola, S. 1999. Motivational foundations of leisure. Edited by E. Jackson and T. Burton, in *Leisure Studies: Prospects for the 21st Century.* State College, PA: Venture.

Juniu, S. 2000. Downshifting: Regaining the essence of leisure. *Journal of Leisure Research, 32*(1), 69–73.

Kando, T. M., and W. C. Summers. 1971. The impact of work on leisure: Toward a paradigm and research strategy. *Pacific Sociological Review 14,* 310–327.

Kelly, J. R. 1982. *Leisure.* Englewood Cliffs, NJ: Prentice-Hall.

Kelly, J. R. 1990. *Leisure.* 2d ed. Englewood Cliffs, NJ: Prentice-Hall.

Kelly, J. R. 1996. *Leisure.* 3d ed. Boston: Allyn & Bacon.

Kelly, J. R., and G. Godbey. 1992. *Sociology of Leisure.* State College, PA: Venture.

Kelly, J. R., and V. Freysinger. 2000. *21st Century Leisure: Current Issues.* Boston: Allyn & Bacon.

Kleiber, D., R. Larson, and M. Csikszentmihalyi. 1986. The experiences of leisure in adolescence. *Journal of Leisure Research 18,* 169–176.

Kraus, R. 1984. *Recreation and Leisure in Modern Society.* 3d ed. Glenview, IL: Scott, Foresman.

Kraus, R. 1990. *Recreation and Leisure in Modern Society.* 4th ed. New York: HarperCollins.

Lazarus, M. 1883. *About the Attractions of Play.* Berlin: Dummler.

Lee, J. 1925. *The Normal Course in Play.* New York: Barnes.

Leitner, M. J., and S. F. Leitner. 1996. *Leisure Enhancement.* 2d ed. New York: Haworth.

Levy, J. 1978. *Play Behavior.* New York: John Wiley.

MacKay, K. J., and J. L. Crompton. 1988. Alternative typologies for leisure programs. *Journal of Park and Recreation Administration 6*(4), 52–64.

Mannell, R., and D. Klieber. 1997. *A Social Psychology of Leisure.* State College, PA: Venture.

Mannell, R., and D. Reid. 1999. Work and leisure. Edited by E. Jackson and T. Burton, in *Leisure Studies: Prospects for the 21st Century.* State College, PA: Venture.

Murphy, J. F. 1974. *Concepts of Leisure.* Englewood Cliffs, NJ: Prentice-Hall.

Murphy, J. F. 1981. *Concepts of Leisure.* 2d ed. Englewood Cliffs, NJ: Prentice-Hall.

Neulinger, J. 1974. *The Psychology of Leisure.* Springfield, IL: Charles C Thomas.

Neulinger, J. 1981. *To Leisure: An Introduction.* Boston: Allyn & Bacon.

Patrick, G. T. W. 1916. *The Psychology of Relaxation.* Boston: Houghton Mifflin.

Peller, L. E. 1952. Models of children's play. *Mental Hygiene 36,* 66–83.

Piaget, J. 1952, 1961. *The Origins of Intelligence in Children.* New York: International University Press.

Piaget, J. 1952. *Play, Dreams and Imitation in Childhood,* translated by G. Cattegno and F. Hodgson. New York: W. W. Norton.

Pieper, J. 1963. *Leisure: The Basis of Culture.* New York: Random House.

Reaney, M. J. 1916. The psychology of the organized group game. *Psychological Review,* Mong., Sup. 4, 76.

Reich, C. 1970. *The Greening of America.* New York: Random House.

Robinson, E. S. 1920. The compensatory function of make-believe play. *Psychological Review, 27,* 429–439.

Rossman, J. R. 1988. Development of leisure programming theory. *Journal of Park and Recreation Administration 6*(4), 1–13.

Russell, R. V. 1996. *Pastimes: The Context of Contemporary Leisure.* Madison, WI: Brown and Benchmark.

Samdahl, D. M. 1988. A symbolic interactionist model of leisure: Theory and empirical support. *Leisure Sciences 10*(1), 27–29.

Samdahl, D. M. 1991. Measuring leisure: Categorical or interval? *Journal of Leisure Research, 23*(1), 87–94.

Schiller, F. V. 1875. *Essays Esthetical and Philosophical.* London: George Bell.

Shaw, S. M. 1985. The meaning of leisure in everyday life. *Leisure Sciences 7*(1), 1–24.

Spencer, H. 1873. *Principles of Psychology.* New York: Appleton.

Stebbins, R. 1992. *Amateurs, Professionals, and Serious Leisure.* Montreal, Quebec: McGill-Queen's University Press.

Stebbins, R. 1999. Serious leisure. Edited by E. Jackson and T. Burton, in *Leisure Studies: Prospects for the 21st Century.* State College, PA: Venture.

Sutton-Smith, B., and J. Roberts. 1982. Play, games, sports. Edited by H. Triandis and A. Heron, in *Handbook of Cross-Cultural Psychology: Developmental Psychology,* 425–443. Boston: Allyn & Bacon.

Unger, L. S. 1984. The effect of situational variables on the subjective leisure experience. *Leisure Sciences 6*(3), 291–312.

Veblen, T. B. 1899. *The Theory of the Leisure Class.* New York: Macmillan.

Waelder, R. 1933. The psychoanalytic theory of play. *Psychoanalytic Quarterly 2,* 208–224.

Witt, P. A., and D. W. Bishop. 1970. Situational antecedents to leisure behavior. *Journal of Leisure Research,* Winter, 2, 64–77.

Yoder, D. 1997. A model for commodity intensive serious leisure. *Journal of Leisure Research 29*(4), 407–429.

Leisure: A Historical Perspective

State parks are part of our early heritage. Here, a state park ranger in Iowa casually guides the observations of two young children.

Source: Department of Natural Resources, State of Iowa. Used by permission.

Introduction

Humankind has a natural curiosity as to why events occurred, how people became prominent and influential, how they lived, how they worked, and how they played. The study of history fosters understanding about what has occurred in the past and the factors that shaped the evolution of events, people, and activities. This is true for leisure just as it is for other areas of human history.

Studying history provides a view of the evolving concepts of leisure, what people have done during their leisure, and what institutions have emerged in order to meet people's leisure needs. Further, these can be tied to broader societal trends and events to show the relationships among them. Last, and perhaps even more fascinating, is to study about the individuals whose visionary leadership propelled the park and recreation movement forward.

What is history? It is *the record of important activities that have occurred in relation to an individual concept, person, institution, or geographical location* (such as a nation). Historians seek to describe what has happened—and try to determine the causes and effects of certain events and changes in people's behavior or thinking.

When historians engage in a review of past events or people, they are involved in historical research. *Historical research can be thought of as an orderly and systematic reconstruction of the past.* Such research is done in a rigorous fashion, objectively and often in relationship to the tenability of a set of research questions or a hypothesis statement. Historians use many resources to investigate the leisure area. Some of these historical sources include written laws, official records, diaries, letters, oral traditions (including eyewitness accounts of events), pictorial records, photographs, newspapers, physical remains, printed materials, and records from institutions and agencies. Even a review of textbooks can provide an understanding into the thinking taking place during a given period of time.

This chapter presents a short discussion of reasons to study history. It provides the reader with an understanding of the importance of a solid historical foundation in relation to leisure and the organized recreation movement in Canada and the United States. Next, it presents the history of leisure, from preliterate society to the information era. It also includes a discussion of the history of several of the early activities of the organized park and recreation movement and vignettes of early leaders of the movement.

Why Do We Study History?

Present understanding often stems from knowledge of the past. Some have said that those who ignore the lessons of history may be doomed to repeat its [history's] failures. Chief Justice Oliver Wendell Holmes noted, "to understand the todays, to talk about the tomorrows, I spent time in the yesterdays." A knowledge of history provides reference points from the past, which can be used to trace events and to make comparisons with other eras and cultures. It facilitates a sense of appreciation for those factors that have contributed to the present-day status of events and institutions. More specifically, a study of the history of leisure and of the organized park and recreation movement provides a knowledge of leisure concepts by which to develop an appreciation for the foundations of the profession, to understand the roles of people in history, to gain knowledge of historical events and places, and to understand our place in history. A discussion of these points follows (see figure 3.1, a creative approach to studying history).

Knowledge of Leisure Concepts

Perhaps the first and most important reason to study history is to understand the *evolution of concepts of leisure.* As forces in society have changed, influencing work, religion, and politics, so have leisure concepts evolved. In the industrial era, for example, clearly defined work time and free time occurred at regularly scheduled times. People were tied to a machine, a schedule, and a manager, and their life activities were regulated accordingly. Children and adults worked long hours established by company owners. Shopping, playing, and socializing were held to certain time periods as hours of operation for stores, taverns, and other establishments were heavily regulated by law. Today's information era offers more flexible work times, and attitudes toward work and leisure are more fluid. This has resulted in a blurring of the distinction between work and leisure; for some, work has become so interesting and rewarding that it could be considered a form of leisure activity. For many, however, work and leisure are still well segregated. Most of those who work have firmly established hours of work; leisure tends to be found only after work hours.

Figure 3.1

Multiple choice

PEANUTS reprinted by permission of United Feature Syndicate, Inc.

Appreciation for the Foundations of the Profession

The study of history also imparts knowledge regarding the *foundations of the leisure service profession,* its emergence, and the evolution of the provision of park and recreation services in the United States and Canada. It reveals social conditions that led to the establishment of agencies and institutions providing leisure services. Every organization has evolved because it met some societal need at some time and place in history, and it survives because it continues to change to meet present needs. These founding conditions are instrumental in the way a movement shapes itself and finds its place in history.

The modern park and recreation movement grew out of the need for social reforms that occurred during the Industrial Revolution in the mid-1800s in the United States. Urbanization, immigration, industrialization, child labor, poor sanitation, lack of open spaces, and other social and human conditions created a need for social reform. Early efforts aimed at providing proper play spaces for children, public baths, parks and other open spaces, and settlement houses were directed toward improving the human condition. The study of history provides an appreciation for the driving forces behind the creation of such areas, facilities, and other services.

Understanding People in History

History is a story about people and their actions and behaviors. Some of humankind's accomplishments have been noble, and some have not. A study of what people thought and did during various historical periods, however, can provide real understanding of how events were shaped. Many of the early leaders of the organized park and recreation movement had a deep commitment to social reform and to enhancing the dignity and welfare of people in Canada and the United States. This commitment extended to the notion that people should have access to natural environments to enable them to stay in touch with their rural pastoral roots.

Many of the early leaders of the park and recreation movement were leading thinkers whose concepts influenced a variety of fields. They gave birth not only to the park and recreation movement, but also to social welfare, city planning, landscape architecture, and youth serving organizations. As the radicals of their generation, they encouraged people to change and urged governments and businesses to become more responsive to human needs. Studying such individuals—their thoughts and actions—provides an appreciation and understanding of the development of the park and recreation movement and its relationship to and influence upon society.

Knowledge of Significant Historical Events and Places

Studying history enables people to gain knowledge about historical events and places. In addition, the study of history provides cause-and-effect information in order to trace the impact of events. Conversely, we can determine the factors that caused specific events to occur. We can examine historical events from economic, social, political, cultural, and other perspectives. Knowledge of events, coupled with the reasons they have occurred and their impact, provides critical insight into the historical evolution of the profession.

For example, the Playground Association of America, founded in 1906, held its first Play Congress in Chicago in 1907. Why Chicago? One of the reasons for selecting Chicago as the meeting site may have been the fact that between 1901 and 1903 the Chicago South Park District passed a $4 million bond issue to build field houses (gymnasiums and meeting rooms) and public baths (swimming pools). Four million dollars, when factored for inflation, is an enormous sum of money—more than $40 million today. In planning a conference for a newly emerging national organization, a likely location would be one that was on the cutting edge of the profession.

Knowledge That Can Be Useful— Present and Future

A study of history helps in decision making, both in the present and for the future. The history of the park and recreation profession, like the history of other professions, provides relevant information for the present and the future. Strategies used in the past to provide areas, facilities, and services have been both successful and unsuccessful. Studying these attempts can help in current planning efforts.

Tom Peters, writing in his book *Thriving on Chaos* (1987), notes that leaders of organizations must respect and acknowledge their heritage in designing visions for the future. Organizations have identifiable traditions, rituals, customs, and norms. These factors have historical bases that provide substance and meaning to the work of an organization or agency. To ignore these historically important factors actually denies or minimizes their contribution to the development of an organization or agency.

Understanding Our Place in History

It is vital that individuals, organizations, cities, and nations have an appreciation for their place in history. An understanding of how one's actions contribute in making history is to understand one's destiny and direction. This sense of history applies in terms of the world stage, on a national basis, or, perhaps more importantly, at the local community level where most leisure service professionals will operate.

When viewed in a global sense, history also grants a view of the differences and similarities among individuals, organizations, and movements in various cultures. People in different parts of the world have participated in similar movements that have occurred in response to social needs. For example, some developing nations, such as South Korea, are currently experiencing social movements that stress the need for increased leisure and social services similar to the movement in the United States in the mid- and late 1800s. Perhaps the social reform movements in these countries have been stimulated by many of the same forces of industrialization (urbanization and lack of open space) that stimulated the social reform movements (including park and recreation services) in Canada and the United States. By studying history and by making cross-cultural comparisons, one can detect patterns in the development of people, institutions, and nations.

The History of Leisure

In the broadest sense, the history of leisure should be viewed in the context of the history of humankind. Futurist Alvin Toffler (1982), writing in the book *The Third Wave,* suggests that recorded history emerged approximately 10,000 years ago. In general, historians have divided the history of humankind into four distinct periods. Thus, for the purposes of analyzing concepts of leisure, there are four distinct eras—precivilized or preliterate society, the agricultural era, the industrial era, and the technological era. John Naisbitt (1982), in his book *Megatrends,* refers to the technological era as the information era. Bell (1968), in the book *Toward the Year 2000,* refers to this period of time as the postindustrial era. Figure 3.2 portrays these four eras.

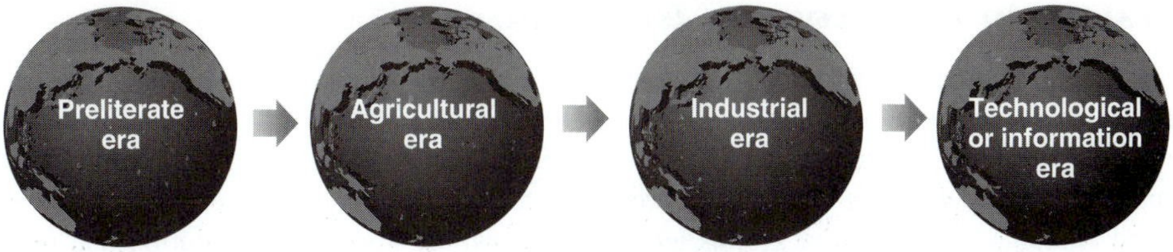

Figure 3.2
Four eras
of history

A brief description of each of the time periods is offered, followed by a more comprehensive discussion of each one.

1. *Preliterate society* existed prior to written history. As MacLean, Peterson, and Martin (1985) note, "We can only surmise which types of activities occupied humans before recorded history" (p. 30). They further note the struggle of preliterate times: Life in prehistoric times was a struggle for mere physical existence. In fact, the problems of daily survival are still a major concern in many parts of the world today. Yet, examples of the continuing search for a more enjoyable life through forms of recreation are evident. Wherever and whenever humans have existed, they have found some time for recreation.

2. The *agricultural era* began approximately 8,000 years ago, with the domestication of animals and crops and the establishment of civilization in Mesopotamia. Approximately 6,000 years ago, agricultural activity was initiated in Central America. Both of these events gave birth to the beginning of today's civilization.

3. The *industrial era* began in Europe, more specifically in Great Britain, in the 1700s and the early 1800s; it spread to the United States by the mid-1800s. The industrial era had both positive and negative consequences. First and foremost, it greatly improved the quality of life available to individuals. Inventions during this period led to newer and more efficient means of production that resulted in greater access to material goods and better transportation and communication systems. As previously mentioned, negative consequences of the industrial era—crowded conditions, child labor, poor sanitation, and other factors—resulted in the need for social reform.

4. The *technological or information era* began in the mid-1950s. The advent of computers and the changing nature of work in developed countries contributed to the evolution of this newer era. As a hallmark of this era, many more people work in service- and information-based industries in the United States and Canada today than in either manufacturing or agricultural occupations (Kelly and Godbey, 1992). The technological era has resulted in greater access to information and increased speed of transportation and communication.

Life in the information age has accelerated the rate of change in our world, thereby creating a common need to understand change. Godbey (1997) notes that while "technological change always runs ahead of the ability of the human race to understand or evaluate it prior to its introduction, today such change defies both our understanding and even our imagination" (p. 3). This environment has created unique opportunities for leisure service organizations that are able to understand the past as well as the changes that are taking place in our society and transform this knowledge to visualizing the future.

In each of these eras, people have conceptualized and engaged in leisure in different ways. The same has been the case with work and time. The ways in which people have enjoyed their leisure and/or the ways in which leisure has emerged as a social institution have varied during each of these historical periods.

Leisure in Preliterate Societies

In preliterate societies, survival was the main concern of life. Life was short and opportunistic. Much of what we know or understand about humankind before recorded history comes from one of two sources. The first source is the work of physical anthropologists, who have studied humankind in all periods of history. Anthropologists not only attempt to reconstruct the daily life and customs of prehistoric groups and populations but study their evolution and current practices as well.

The second source of anthropological information about preliterate people results from the study of primitive groups of people in the world today, such as the Tsaddi, discovered in a remote area of the Philippines more than a decade ago. These people apparently had never come into contact with modern civilization. By analyzing their environment, family life, religion, style of art, and dress, some broad assumptions made concerning their play and work behavior could indicate patterns of other preliterate groups. Discussing play in primitive cultures, MacLean, Peterson, and Martin (1985) write the following:

> . . . we strongly assume that children's play was essentially what it has always been. Children frolicked in streams and lakes; climbed trees; played with pets; planned mock battles against the enemy—both human and animal; and learned the art of survival. Times of rest for pre-historic peoples were filled with sewing, stringing beads, partaking in songs, chants, and dances; and telling stories and myths around the home fire. (p. 30)

The sharp distinction between work time and leisure time that emerged during the industrial era did not exist in preliterate days. In a sense, work and leisure activities were fused together. As Kraus (1990) writes, "Primitive people do not make a clear distinction between work and leisure that we tend to do in more technologically advanced societies . . . a primitive society has no precise separations; instead, work is customarily done when it is available or necessary and it is often fused with rites and customs that lend it variety and pleasure" (p. 114).

Clearly, it becomes difficult to distinguish between the work and play of primitive peoples. Play was often infused with ritual, transmitting the culture of preliterate societies from generation to generation. Numerous examples of activities now associated with leisure pastimes were a part of everyday life in preliterate society. Most of the leisure and play activities that existed during preliterate society related to the acquisition of survival skills, and included fishing, hunting, skiing, boating, swimming, horseback riding, combative activities, and arts and crafts (such as pottery, weaving, and leather work) (Kraus, 1990). Many of these activities served as the basis for the development of later civilizations. Today, for example, we do our hunting and gathering by proxy in that someone else grows, kills, cleans, packages, and sells meat and food goods to us. In our memories, however, we preserve ". . . the chase lingering in our joyful pursuit of anything weak or fugitive, and in the games of our children—even in the word *game*" (Durant, 1963, p. 7).

Interestingly, people in preliterate societies lived their lives primarily by life rhythms. When they were hungry, they hunted, fished, or gathered food; when they were joyful, they celebrated; and when they were tired, they slept. People moved at a natural pace depending upon their current state of need and natural conditions of the environment.

Much current knowledge about early historical cultures, such as the Egyptian culture, comes from the remains of their tombs or inscriptions. They had a well-developed class system with the lower classes engaging in athletics and physical sport while the upper classes were more sedentary and enjoyed being entertained (Kraus, 1984). Egyptian games included checkers and dice; children played with toys such as marbles, bouncing balls, ten pins and tops; they enjoyed wrestling contests, boxing matches, and bullfights (Kraus, 1984). At feasts and recre-

Figure 3.3

Ancient
Egyptians
singing and
playing musical
instruments

*Painted relief
from the tomb
of Nenkheftikai at
Sakkarah, Fifth
Dynasty. Photo by
Tor Eigeland/Black
Star*

ation functions, participants were anointed by attendants and were wreathed with flowers, feted with wines, and presented with gifts (Kraus, 1984). Figure 3.3 depicts ancient Egyptians engaging in leisure activity.

The Egyptians also enhanced outdoor spaces. Tomb paintings often depicted garden areas surrounding developments. Plantings provided an environment that protected individuals from the harshness of the climate. In preliterate times, gardens were established in and around the palaces and ziggurats of Mesopotamia. Among these, the Hanging Gardens of Babylon, referred to by Herodotus, were considered one of the seven wonders of the ancient world. The gardens, planted at a height of seventy-five feet, consisted of a variety of flowers and plants, including large and deep-rooted trees.

Leisure in the Agricultural Era

"The first form of culture was agriculture" (Durant, 1966, p. 2). Agriculture provided a stable supply of food, and when humankind began to labor in the soil, provided an opportunity for a long-term perspective on life. The development of agriculture enabled people to develop a sense of security resulting from a dependable food supply. With their energies no longer solely devoted to hunting or gathering enough food to survive, they could participate in other activities— activities that resulted in the advancement of civilization.

During the agricultural era, society established property rights for cultivation and farming. Prior to this no one person owned property; hunting or gathering occurred wherever food was found. As agriculture developed, so did the need for private property on which to produce crops. In order to protect and manage this property, a division of labor occurred. A ruling elite formed; government officials owned and managed the land; a military protected the land; and a peasant class farmed the land. A more complex form of social organization evolved than had been in place during preliterate society. For the first time in history, humankind produced a surplus of commodities, thus forming classes of people who were not involved directly in their production. Landowners, governmental officials, scribes, and artists were all supported by the efforts of others. These individuals became the *leisure class,* as contrasted with individuals in the *working class.*

For the people living during the agricultural era, the concept of time changed. Time became a regulatory dimension of life, and people tied their lives more closely to changes in the seasons. When it was time to plant, people planted; when it was time to harvest a crop, the harvest occurred. Leisure time and leisure activities became attached to these events, such as autumn harvest celebrations. When the harvest was in, the great celebrations included games, food, dancing, socializing, and rituals. Furthermore, strong evidence indicates that people had a great deal of leisure time during certain seasons of the year when field work was slow.

In many cultures, the new class of individuals not directly associated with the production of commodities met their responsibility to society in the development of civilization. They used their time and intellectual capabilities to enhance the economic well-being of their culture, to establish political organizations, to develop religions, and to pursue intellectual and artistic activities. The Greeks, in particular, used leisure to advance civilization. According to the Greeks, ". . . without a leisure class, there can be no standards of taste, no encouragement of the arts, no civilization. No man [*sic*] in a hurry is quite civilized" (Durant, 1966, p. 277).

Leisure in Ancient Greece   The Greeks believed that civilization advanced through the cultivation of the mind, body, and spirit. As a result, the Greeks, especially the Athenians, took great interest in a variety of activities linked to the development of civilization. These activities included writing, artistic endeavors, and athletics (Kraus, 1984). Children living in ancient Greek society participated in a variety of play pursuits.

> Babies have Terra Cotta rattles containing pebbles; girls keep house with their dolls; boys fight campaigns with toy soldiers and generals; nurses push children on swings or balance them on seesaws; boys and girls roll hoops, fly kites, spin tops, play hide and seek or blind man's bluff, or tug of war, and wage a hundred meter contest with pebbles, nuts, coins and balls. (Durant, 1966, p. 288)

School activities also prepared children for future leisure pursuits. Writing, reading, arithmetic, music, gymnastics, drawing, and painting were all part of the curriculum. Sports activities of youth served as a form of military preparation for males; they ran, hunted, wrestled, drove chariots, and hurled javelins (Kraus, 1984).

Perhaps the most influential Athenian philosopher recognizing the need for leisure was Aristotle, who believed in a balance between work and leisure. He suggested that individuals must learn to do both well, but leisure is to be preferred. Leisure, according to Aristotle, provides the opportunity for intellectual development, provides a way of relaxing the soul, and enhances enjoyment of life. Table 3.1 presents several practical aspects of the Greeks' leisure legacy that have stretched into today.

Leisure in Ancient Rome   Ancient Roman society was fascinating in terms of the leisure lifestyles of its citizens. Leisure pursuits and activities tended to be much more utilitarian than in Greek society. Although activities for the leisure or privileged classes provided entertainment, they were primarily directed toward maintaining the rigor of the young men of this militaristic society. As Rome adopted a more luxurious standard of living, leisure and spare time became a serious problem. A few members of the senatorial aristocracy exerted efforts to check the pleasure tendencies. One such leader was Cato the elder, who said "that a great man was accountable for every moment of his spare time as much as for every moment of his working day." According to Cato there were two charges that a man in prominent society must be careful to avoid. The first was self-indulgence and the second was idleness.

Wealthy Romans surrounded themselves with sculpture, painting, and other objects of art. By the fourth century A.D., Rome had more than 1,300 public swimming pools or baths (Durant, 1944). Baths became the social and athletic clubs of Roman citizens and for the leisure class, the daily routine of exercise, bathing, and eating was the usual order of the day. The baths were elaborate structures with pillars and walls of granite, and marble floors of mosaic and tile. Privately owned, the baths were erected by wealthy men as gifts to the city or were constructed from public funds. They were managed by people who leased them and charged fees for use.

TABLE

3.1   THE LEISURE LEGACY OF ANCIENT GREECE

Parks in Greece	• To the ancient Greek, trees—primarily olive trees—were a very sacred symbol. From the trees flowed the very lifeblood of the civilization. It is not surprising, then, that when the ancient Greeks were searching for a way of honoring fallen heroes, they would decorate tombs with trees, the very symbol of life. As time progressed, groves of trees dotted the landscape.
Olympic Games	• National festivals conducted every four years at Olympia to honor Zeus. Commenced in 776 B.C. and continued until the fifth century A.D. The games lasted five days.
	• All warring tribes were expected to observe a truce while the games were in progress—the truce of the gods.
	• Although women were not allowed in, in other respects the games were very democratic—noble and peasant competed on equal terms.
Greek Theater	• Began with elegy—poems reflecting on the disillusionment of life. Gradually replaced by the lyric, which was sung to music.
	• Tragic drama was the supreme literary achievement of the Greeks. Greek tragedy had as its theme the conflict between human and the universe. The purpose of Greek tragedies was not merely to depict suffering and interpret human actions but to purify the emotions of the audience by representing the triumphs of justice.
Greek Theater—Structure	• As impressive as the plays were the physical structures developed to house the dramas. Ancient Greek theaters were acoustically sound. Generally the stage was either built against a cliff or strategically placed in a round. Little modification of the basic structure has occurred today.
Greek Art	• The art of the Greeks also reflected their character and their view of the world. Architecture and sculpture embodied the idea of harmony, order, balance, and moderation.

Note: Beyond philosophy, the Greek legacy extends into recreation from both a programmatic and facility standpoint. Although Aristotle would not consider these items leisure, they have contributed to our "leisure legacy" in the modern sense.

Some of the larger bath houses became immense cultural centers that included libraries, lounges, art galleries, and dining rooms. The leisure activities in which wealthy male Roman citizens participated varied, as evidenced by the following:

> Baths were usually preceded by a vigorous workout, where individuals would run, jump, or play a ball game, using an object like a medicine ball. Following this, individuals were provided rooms for games like dice, chess, galleries of paintings and statues and areas where friends might sit and converse, libraries with reading rooms, and halls where a musician, poet might give a recital. (Durant, 1944, p. 375)

Entertainment in Rome was plentiful and inexpensive. Rome exhibited forms of leisure found in previous civilizations—gambling, reading, dancing, drinking, sports, and games were all part of the Roman way of life. In figure 3.4 young Roman women enjoy a gambling game. Recitations, lectures, concerts, mimes, plays, athletic contests, prize fights, chariot races, mortal combats of men with men or men with beasts, not-quite-sham naval battles on artificial lakes— never was a city so bountifully amused. Sports were popular. In Roman culture, sports were divided into three areas: hunting, riding, and competition of arms; boxing, wrestling, running, throwing the discus and javelin; weight lifting, trundling a hoop, and a great variety of ball

Figure 3.4

Young Roman
women playing a
gambling game

*Museo
Archeologico
Nazionale. Naples,
Italy. Scala/Art
Resource, NY*

games. In the fourth century A.D. there were twenty-nine libraries in Rome. These libraries seemed generally to have been in the vicinity of temples. They served the upper classes by lending books and scrolls for reading.

One of the most popular activities was the *circus maximus.* These chariot races were the center of attention of the community, and men gambled heavily on each of the five-mile chariot races that took place. The games concluded with the contests of animals and gladiators in the amphitheater-coliseum. The *circus maximus* also featured exhibitions of exotic animals from throughout the world. Approximately 2,000 feet long and 600 feet wide, the *circus maximus* accommodated about 385,000 people. Races were financed by the state or private individuals. Syndicates were identified by the colors the drivers wore. In the early days of the Republic, anyone could race, but in the later times "respectable" citizens did not participate. The race drivers were slaves.

The Roman Coliseum was the facility in which gladiators fought. The arena covered six acres and had walls 160 feet high; it could accommodate 90,000 spectators. Subterranean areas contained chambers for gladiators, dens for animals, and a maze of pipes to flood and drain the area for sea battles. Gladiators were mostly slaves, criminals, or captives. Originally the fights were small privately sponsored affairs. During the third century A.D. a mass of 500 pairs of men contested in a huge spectacle. Usually fighting continued until death was decided by the victor—"Thumbs up or thumbs down." The Nauchmacha was an amphitheater constructed to hold sea battles. In one event, four naval vessels fought a minibattle until all eventually were lost. One battle had 19,000 men fighting at once.

As in Greece the games began mainly as religious festivals to which were added festivals in honor of heroes, victories, and so on. At the time of the first emperor, ninety days were devoted to the games. Three hundred years later, there were twice as many days devoted to the games, plus special celebrations. At one time, seventeen of twenty-nine days in April were spent at the circus, amphitheater, or coliseum. The Greeks and Romans had differing views of leisure as related to the games. To the Greeks, the games were great events in which every person aspired to compete. The Romans, on the other hand, regarded the games as spectator entertainment.

Historians often depict the leisure pursuits of Romans as being hedonistic, vulgar, and corrupt. The maiming and butchering of individuals and animals have been viewed historically as obscene. The downfall of Rome has been linked with the inability of that culture to use its leisure in a positive and productive manner. When faced by the challenges of excesses of wealth, luxury, and time, the Romans responded by yielding to corruption and losing the simple virtues that had made them strong as a nation (Kraus, 1984).

Leisure and Christianity   The Christian faith has had a strong impact on attitudes and values toward work and leisure of Canadians and U.S. citizens. Early Christians believed that work was good for humankind and that idleness was not good. Work, framed in the context of being productive, provided a surplus of commodities to share with others. Thus, early Christians focused their activities on producing more in order to help those who had less and who needed charity.

This philosophy contrasted with that of early Catholic philosophers who had begun to distinguish between physical and intellectual labors. They perceived that they should engage in intellectual and spiritual activities while others engaged in physical labor. They believed that because a leisurely lifestyle allowed for prayer and contemplation, it was best for a priest. Early Catholic philosophers felt that work need not necessarily be emphasized when one's reward was realized in the life to come.

The Protestant Reformation, spearheaded by Martin Luther, changed the way Christians viewed work and, hence, play. Luther viewed work as being good and that God *calls* his people to their work or their vocation. His views reflected his belief that all callings are equally worthwhile in the eyes of God and individuals are not to seek material gains but to develop their own abilities to seek perfection. He maintained that religious work was not superior to other types of work. Work of any type was valued, whereas idleness was viewed as a sin. Luther's views supported a value system that promoted the desirability of work and thrift.

Whereas Luther fostered the Protestant Reformation, another reformer named John Calvin fostered the Protestant work ethic. Calvin built on Luther's sense of calling and further articulated that the purpose of work was to glorify God, not to accumulate wealth. "We are created for the express purpose of being in labor of various kinds, and that no sacrifice is more pleasing to God than when we apply ourselves diligently to our own callings, and endeavor to live in such a way as to contribute to the common good" (Calvin, as quoted in *An Engagement with God's World,* 1999, p. 7). Today many theologians have noted that proponents of capitalism used both Luther's and Calvin's idea of *calling,* and used it unjustly, to create a Protestant work ethic to supply the labor it needed to grow. This new Protestant work ethic not only encouraged hard work but also connected material blessings as a sign of God's approval. This Protestant work ethic is deeply embedded into North American culture today and in some ways has countered the development of a leisure ethic and influences the leisure-work guilt phenomenon experienced by many in society today.

Not all Christian philosophy suggests hard work, however. Numerous writings refer to the enjoyment of life and celebration of the harvest. As the church increasingly gained control over the affairs of the state with a corresponding merger of social, political, and religious beliefs, Sunday became an institutionalized day of prayer and leisure. Kraus (1984, 1990) notes that during the Middle Ages individuals may have had as many as 170 days off work per year, counting religious holidays and Sundays.

Leisure in the Middle Ages The Middle Ages in Western Europe linked ancient civilization with modern times; it spanned the years from A.D. 400 to A.D. 1500. The major civilizing force during the Middle Ages was the Christian Church. During this period of time, most areas of Western Europe were divided into feudal states. These feudal states saw a continued social and political hierarchy where large feudal states were managed by lords, and peasants worked the land in support of these individuals.

Spectacles in the form of religious pageants, political processions, tournaments, and festivals all formed a part of the revelry during the Middle Ages. In fact, during the Christmas season many towns appointed a "Lord of Misrule" to organize events. (Could this have been the first recreation leader?) Travel was possible, not only for merchants, but also for tourists who lodged at wayside inns. Minstrels, jugglers, exhibitions of exotic animals, and acrobats entertained as a part of circuses traveling among the villages. Figure 3.5 portrays a band of performers in the Middle Ages.

Class distinctions were evident during the Middle Ages, in terms of leisure pursuits as well as other activities. The male nobility engaged in such activities as hunting, jousting, falconry, skating, horse racing, archery, fishing, bowling, hockey, quoits, wrestling, boxing, tennis, and football. For example, hunting was regulated by strict game laws and was usually conducted in preserves set aside for the nobility. Sporting activities, often conducted in front of large crowds, became a leisure pursuit for spectators. Historical record of women's leisure is extremely limited. We do know that women were viewed as property of their fathers and, when they were

Figure 3.5

A band of performers during the Middle Ages

Detail from the Canterbury Psalter. Illuminated manuscript. 12 c, Trinity College Cambridge, England.

married, their husbands. We can only speculate that the mores of the times dictated work and leisure in the home focusing on servitude to one's husband and family. Figure 3.6 shows a group of individuals engaged in leisure activities in the late Middle Ages.

While many perceived the Middle Ages to be a harsh period because of the rigors of Christian morality, individuals did indeed enjoy themselves in their leisure. It was a period of merriment, marked by celebration—not a period, as historians have often described it, where rigorous codes of behavior squelched satisfying life experiences.

Leisure and the Renaissance   The Renaissance began in Italy about A.D. 1300 and lasted for approximately 300 years. The Renaissance, particularly notable because of advancements in the sciences and the arts, was a period of great intellectual activity and of great creative force. During the Renaissance, many changes in style in painting, sculpture, and architecture emerged.

The Renaissance saw the strict moral codes of the time held in contempt. Amusements such as dancing, conversation, and dramatic plays were often of a coarse nature and deliberately defied moral codes of the day. Records of the many leisure activities in which men participated during this period mention fencing, gambling, chess, bullfighting, horse racing, hunting, falconry, boxing, tennis, boating, and foot racing. People often walked or rode into the countryside to visit others and to view the scenery, and they enjoyed carnivals, processions, and festivals as in the Middle Ages. Women were sometimes allowed to accompany their husbands and fathers to these events. Figures 3.7 and 3.8 depict individuals of this period engaged in chess and a primitive form of tennis.

During the Renaissance period the arts flourished, with a revitalization of literature, architecture, sculpture, painting, music, and drama. Music concerts became an important leisure pastime available to women and all social classes. Artistic activities resulted in a creative frenzy that spawned such artists as Michelangelo, Raphael, Leonardo da Vinci, Titian, Bellini, and others. The Renaissance also saw the development of the first printing press in the mid-1400s in Germany, set up by Guttenberg.

Figure 3.6

Card playing in the late Middle Ages

THE CARD PLAYERS by Lucas van Leyden, Samuel B. Kress Collection, © 1994 National Gallery of Art, Washington, D.C.

Figure 3.7

Young people enjoying a game of chess

The Metropolitan Museum of Art, Bequest of Maitland Griggs, 1943. Maitland F. Griggs Collection (43.98.8).

Figure 3.8

Young woman of the Renaissance period playing an early form of tennis

Anonymous, LADY PLAYING BALL. Palazzo Borromeo. Milan, Italy. Scala/Art Resource, NY

Leisure in Colonial America   As Europe went through a great period of change in the 1500s and 1600s, it produced religious reformation and economic development. This reformation gave rise to the development of the theology of Martin Luther and economic expansion into what has become known as the United States and Canada. Protestant leaders in England emphasized family life, industriousness, participation in community activities, and education. These reformers fell into two categories: the Puritans, who sought to change the Church of England from within; and the Separatists, who wanted to separate from the Church of England.

In 1607, the Virginia Company of London received the charter for the establishment of an economically based settlement in what was then called the New World (present-day Canada and the United States). This economically based community established at Jamestown nearly met with collapse during its first decade of existence. Only 1,200 of the 8,000 people who immigrated to the Virginia-based colony between 1607 and 1625 remained alive after those ten years.

In 1608, a group of separatists left England for Holland. Displeased because their children were adopting the culture of Holland, they negotiated for passage on the Mayflower. In 1620, these Separatists, or Pilgrims, arrived at Plymouth Rock. In 1629, a group of Puritans in England organized the Massachusetts Bay Company. Moved by both economic and religious motives, they undertook a massive expedition in 1630. Between 1629 and 1640, a great exodus of Puritans left England; 25,000 individuals landed in New England. The Massachusetts Bay Colony, a religious colony, set the tone for leisure in the United States for years to come.

The original immigrants to the lands of Canada and the United States had little time to engage in leisure. The harshness of the environment and the need to survive placed great demands on them. To ensure that work was encouraged and idleness diminished, early Puritan leaders established strict regulations. "Religion provided the strongest moral sanction for every law suppressing amusements" (Dulles, 1965, p. 5).

One view of the Puritans was that they were legalistic and did not permit leisure. They valued frugality, hard work, self-discipline, and strict observance of civil and religious codes. They viewed play as the devil's handiwork and tried to legislate morality. For example, consider the following law from the colony of Massachusetts (presented in old English): "all men are ordered to work the whole day allowing convenient time for food and rest and that no person householder or other, shall spend his time idly or unprofitably under pain of such punishment as the Court shall think meet to inflict" (Records of the Court of Assistants of the Colony of the Massachusetts Bay 1633–1644, as quoted by Swanson and Spears, 1995, p. 46).

Although this view of the Puritans is widely held, Ryken (1994) presents an alternative view. According to Ryken, the original Puritan work ethic included in its basic principles that God calls people to work, that all legitimate work has dignity, that work can be stewardship to God and a service to self and humanity, and that work should be pursued in moderation and in deference to spiritual concerns. These ideas do not exclude leisure; they advocate balance in living a life to glorify God. Work and leisure give meaning to each other. Ryken goes on to verify that the Puritans were opposed to some types of recreation as well as keeping the Sabbath holy apart from pastimes. However, Puritans enjoyed such varied sports as fishing, hunting, bowling, reading, music, swimming, skating, and archery. Regarding recreation, a Puritan preacher said that Christians should "enjoy recreation as liberties, with thankfulness to God that allows these liberties to refresh themselves" (p. 41).

Virginia also enacted laws that restricted idleness. For example, in 1619 the Virginia Assembly decreed that any individual who was found idle could be made to work. It also prohibited gambling and regulated drinking and other amusements. Similar legal codes were established throughout the colonies.

Despite the harshness of the life of early colonists, leisure pursuits did emerge. Drinking, in particular, and meeting friends at the local tavern became commonplace for men. Women met in town centers while shopping or tending to other family needs. After the initial decades of Puritan influence, colonists generally sought to develop broader leisure pursuits. Such activities as animal baiting, country dances, music, sports, hunting, fishing, husking bees, skittles, horseback riding, tennis, cockfighting, dice, cards, and shuffleboard became popular. On the frontier, hunting, shooting matches, racing, pitching horseshoes, footraces, wrestling, card playing, horse racing, log rolling, and dancing all became important leisure pursuits. Traveling performers featured animal acts, acrobats, and dramatic readings. In addition, spiritual revivals on the frontier became important leisure events.

Although few specific organized activities related to the development of park and recreation services, several significant events occurred. The early colonists recognized the need for common open areas and subsequently established commons in Boston (in the United States) and in Halifax (in Canada). Initially, these commons primarily served as an area for common use by individuals in the community; use for leisure was incidental. In 1641, the Massachusetts Great Ponds Act was passed. This legislation decreed that all bodies of water over ten acres were open to the public for fishing and hunting. Further concern for environmental issues was seen in the establishment of squares and plazas by communities in Spanish colonies. Founders of Saint Augustine, Santa Fe, and San Diego brought with them the concept of open spaces as an integral part of town planning (Frye, 1980). In addition, in Savannah, Georgia, James Oglethorpe included open spaces as a part of his grand design for that community.

Leisure in the Industrial Era

The industrial era brought about sweeping changes, not only in Europe, but also in the United States. The new conditions brought about by industrialization changed the basic assumptions about the way people lived their lives. New conditions created new needs for political, economic, and social systems. The industrial era greatly improved the standard of living for many individuals, but, at the same time, greatly disrupted the social order for a period of time. During the agricultural era, less than 5 percent of the population lived in cities and towns. During the industrial era, that statistic changed dramatically.

The industrial era produced boom-and-bust economic cycles in the United States; it also produced mass waves of immigration and urbanization. Concentration of populations around economic concerns in urban areas created the need for social reform. Initially, social reform was undertaken by private philanthropists. Later, however, it required the support of government. Governmental intervention resulted in a social welfare philosophy. Through taxation, government redistributed income to help solve social problems in a variety of areas, including education, health, and leisure.

Class distinctions between men and women sharpened. Men went into the world of work (and worth) while women, essentially homebound, worked without pay. Middle-class women benefited from their husband's or father's financial success. They engaged in social activities, went to theaters and shows, and were entertained by diverse amusements. On the other hand, women from lower socioeconomic classes were forced to work in poor conditions and difficult circumstances out of economic necessity. This work, in addition to the housework and child care expected in the household, placed a double burden on women (Henderson et al., 1989, 1996).

During the Industrial Revolution, life became clock-driven; the clock regulated both work and play. Children and adults adjusted their work efforts to a schedule—not to personal desires, needs, and abilities. Thus, time was viewed differently than it had been viewed in the agricultural era. There was work time and there was free time. The misuse of free time came to be viewed as a social problem and the provision of wholesome productive leisure activities became an instrument of social reform.

The way in which work was organized also impacted general life satisfaction. Perhaps the great contribution of the Industrial Revolution involved the ability for mass production via the establishment of the division of labor and the creation of assembly lines. As work became more and more specialized, however, it robbed individuals of their sense of purpose. Not seeing a product to completion, people often found work to be tedious, boring, and monotonous. People began to look outside of their work environments for satisfaction. Leisure became a method for compensating for dissatisfying work experiences.

The commercialization of leisure made leisure more accessible to the general public, but it also brought bad influences for youth that many reformers thought needed to be addressed. Edwards writes in his book *Popular Amusements* (1915), ". . . the professional entertainer holds sway in every field from which he is not rigidly excluded, every field in which the rights of the amateur are not vigorously asserted. . . . A social disease has been spreading broadcast among us. . . . The disease of spectatoritis abounds in the land."

Excursion boats on Lake Michigan left Chicago with as many as 5,000 on board at a time. These boats carried unsupervised teenagers, and although they were billed as daytime outings, they often did not return until the early hours of the morning. "The Juvenile Protection Association . . . discovered that these boats were violating many laws. Gambling machines and devices of every sort were run openly upon the boats, liquor was sold to minors, while staterooms were rented over and over again throughout the night. These boats were largely patronized by young people who . . . became drunk and engaged in orgies" (Bowen, 1914).

In response to these conditions, several social movements were initiated by reformers. Many early movements and later institutions saw the use of recreation as a tool for furthering social, intellectual, and moral development.

Out of these conditions emerged women and men of great vision, energy, and drive. Such individuals as Jane Addams, Luther Gulick, Joseph Lee, John Muir, Henry Curtis, Stephen Mather, Gifford Pinchot, Frederick Law Olmstead, Theodore Roosevelt, Mabel Peters, Ernest Atwell, Jacob Riis, Juliette Lowe, and William D. Boyce made contributions to the development of new and innovative agencies and institutions to solve the emerging social problems of the industrial era (see table 3.2). This section of the text focuses on the development of some of the major movements that emerged and became institutionalized during this era.

Movements to Institutions   What is a movement? What is an institution? When does a movement become institutionalized? Many, if not all, of the strategies used to provide park and recreation services that emerged in the industrial era started out as the dream, idea, or vision of one or more people. The vision held by early leaders in Canada and the United States, in terms of providing meaningful leisure services, often met with public apathy, lack of financial support, and political opposition. Early leaders were often crusaders, zealots, or missionaries who championed their cause. Thus, the work of early leaders focused on the spearheading of a movement related to leisure.

A *movement* may be thought of as a crusade—a cause to which people become highly committed emotionally. A movement usually has a clear sense of direction that is well articulated by its leader or leaders and tied to a specific set of values and/or goals. Those involved in movements direct their energies toward attacking real problems—social, political, or otherwise. Movements often spawn more than political rhetoric and result in the actual creation and

TABLE

3.2   PIONEERS IN LEISURE SERVICES

Jane Addams (1860–1935)	Social reformer, founder of Hull House (1889), viewed as the creator of social welfare in America
Ernest T. Atwell (1842–1949)	Staff member National Recreation Association, pioneered programs for African Americans
Lord Robert Baden-Powell (1857–1941)	Founder of Boy Scouts (1909)
William D. Boyce (1858–1929)	Founder of Boy Scouts of America (1910)
W. P. Bowen (1864–1928)	Educator, author of *Theory of Organized Play Its Nature and Significance*
Samuel Bowles (1826–1878)	Advocate for the preservation of Niagara Falls, Adirondocks Forest, and Yosemite Valley
Neva L. Boyd (1876–1963)	Established training school for playground workers, Chicago, IL
Howard S. Braucher (1881–1949)	Executive Director of the National Recreation Association
Charles K. Brightbill (1910–1966)	Educator, author of *The Challenge of Leisure, Man and Leisure* (1960)
Virgil K. Brown (1883–1974)	Professional leader, Chicago, IL; first president, American Recreation Society
William Cullen Bryant (1794–1878)	Advocate for public parks in New York
George D. Butler (1894–1985)	Author, director of research National Recreation Association
Reynold Carlson (1901–1997)	Educator, author, leader in nature recreation, camping
Rachel Carson (1907–1964)	Author of *Silent Spring* (1962); raised environmental consciousness
George Catlin (1796–1872)	Author, painter, advocate for establishing national parks
Anna Botsford Comstock (1854–1930)	Environmentalist, author, *Handbook of Nature Study*
Abbie H. Condit (1883–1948)	Managing editor of *The Playground, Playground and Recreation, & Recreation*
Calvin Coolidge (1872–1933)	Established Presidents' Conference on Outdoor Recreation
E. Coulter (1871–1952)	Founder of the Big Brothers/Big Sisters of America in 1904
Robert Crawford (1906–1995)	Professional leader, Philadelphia, PA
Henry S. Curtis (1870–1954)	Author of *Education Through Play,* and *The Play Movement and Its Significance,* playground administrator; early leader Playground Association of America
John Dewey (1859–1952)	Educator advocating community use of schools
Walt Disney (1901–1966)	Innovator in theme parks, motion pictures
Gustavus C. Doane (1840–1892)	Spearheaded the movement to establish Yellowstone National Park
Charles E. Doell (1894–1983)	Park Administrator, Minneapolis, MN; author
Andrew Jackson Downing (1815–1852)	Early advocate of horticulture, editor of the *Horticulturist*
Summer F. Dudley (1854–1897)	Founder of Camp Dudley, the first YMCA camp in Newbugh, New York, in 1885
Foster Ray Dulles (1900–1970)	Author of *America Learns to Play: A History of Recreation* (1940)
Charles Eliot (1859–1897)	Metropolitan regional parks system, Boston, MA
Lottie (Charlotte) Gulick (1865–1928)	Cofounder of Camp Fire Girls
Luther H. Gulick (1865–1919)	First President Playground Association of America; cofounder of Camp Fire Girls
Frederick William Gunn (1816–1881)	Operated first camp, Gunnery Camp, New Hampshire
Kurt Hahn (1886–1974)	Founder of Outward Bound
Lee F. Hanmer (1871–1961)	Professional leader, Playground Association of America
Ferdinand V. Hayden (1829–1887)	Led scientific expedition in Yellowstone National Park
Cornelius Hedges (1831–1907)	Spearheaded the movement to establish Yellowstone National Park
C. Hanford Henderson (1861–1941)	Author, educator, proposed different patterns of camp activities
Ernst Hermann (1869–1943)	Pioneer in industrial recreation
Clark W. Hetherington (1870–1942)	Educator, prepared the normal course in play
Rev. George Hinckley (1853–1950)	Founder of first church camp
George Hjelte (1893–1979)	Professional leader Los Angeles, CA
Johan Huizinga (1872–1945)	Author of *Homo Ludens: A Study of the Play Element in Culture*

TABLE

3.2   PIONEERS IN LEISURE SERVICES, CONTINUED

L. P. Jacks (1860–1955)	Advocated education through recreation
Jens Jensen (1860–1951)	Promoted forest preserves in Chicago, IL
George E. Johnson (1862–1931)	Philosopher, educator, play leader; author of *Education by Plays and Games*
Robert Underwood Johnson (1853–1937)	Early wilderness enthusiast
Pierre L'Enfant (1754–1825)	Planner of Washington, DC, a vision of parks and pleasure grounds
Nathaniel P. Langford (1832–1911)	Spearheaded the movement to establish Yellowstone National Park
Joseph E. Lee (1862–1937)	Founder of recreation, philanthropist, author of *Play in Education* (1915)
Aldo Leopold (1886–1948)	Educator, conservationist, author of *Sand County Almanac* (1949)
Eugene T. Lies (1876–1954)	Early leader in recreation in the public schools
Juliette Gordon Lowe (1860–1927)	Founder of Girl Scouts in 1912
Otto T. Mallery (1880–1956)	Recreation Administrator, Philadelphia, PA
Robert Marshall (1901–1939)	Promoted wilderness preservation
Stephen T. Mather (1867–1930)	Founder of the National Park Service
Laura Mattoon (1873–1946)	Professional Association leader, advocate for camping for women and girls
John McLaren (1847–1943)	Landscape planner Golden Gate Park, San Francisco, CA
Herald D. Meyer (1842–1974)	Professional leader, educator, author
George L. Meylan (1873–1960)	Early YMCA camping leader
Horace Moses (1862–1947)	Founder of Junior Achievement in 1919
Robert Moses (1888–1981)	Park advocate, New York
William Penn Mott, Jr. (1909–1992)	Park Administrator, Director of National Park Service
John Muir (1838–1914)	Conservationist, founder Sierra Club
J. B. Nash (1886–1965)	Author of *Philosophy of Recreation and Leisure* (1960), educator, philosopher
Esther Neumeyer (1893–1975)	*Aspects* (1958)
Martin Neumeyer (1892–1978)	Authors of *Leisure and Recreation: A Study of Leisure and Recreation in Their Sociological*
Eugene Odum (1913–)	Founder and Pioneer of Ecosystem and Ecology—Father of Modern Ecology
James Oglethorpe (1696–1785)	Established plan with open spaces in Savannah, GA
Frederick Law Olmsted (1822–1903)	Founder of landscape architecture, Creator Central Park, NY
Sigurd Olson (1899–1982)	Philosopher, promoted wilderness preservation, author of numerous texts
Harry A. Overstreet (1875–1970)	Philosopher, author of *A Guide to Civilized Loafing* (1934), educator
George Amos Parker (1853–1926)	Founder, New England Association of Park Superintendents
Mabel Peters (1861–1914)	Early leader of playground movement in Canada
John A. Pettigrew (1844–1912)	First president, New England Association of Park Superintendents
Paul Petzoldt (1908–1999)	Founded the first Outward Bound school in the U.S., founded the National Outdoor Leadership school, cofounded the Wilderness Education Association
Gifford Pinchot (1865–1946)	Conservationist, leader of the U.S. Forest Service
Janet Pomeroy (1915–1988)	Professional leader, founder of Recreational Center for the Handicapped, Inc., San Francisco, CA, author
Clarence Rainwater (1884–1925)	Author of *The Play Movement in the United States: A Study in Community Recreation* (1922)
Jacob Riis (1849–1914)	Author of *Battle With the Slum,* first vice president Playground Association of America
Thomas E. Rivers (1892–1977)	International recreation leader
Theodore Roosevelt (1858–1919)	President advocating conservation
Charles R. Scott (1874–1954)	First president of the Camp Directors Association of America
Ernest Thompson Seton (1860–1946)	Founder of Woodcraft Indians
L. B. Sharp (1895–1963)	Educator, leader in outdoor education

3.2   PIONEERS IN LEISURE SERVICES, CONTINUED

Julian Smith (1900–1975)	Outdoor education leader
Ellen Gates Starr (1860–1940)	Co-founder of Hull House, Chicago, IL
Thomas Sullivan (1800–1859)	Founder of the Young Men's Christian Association in the United States (Boston) in 1851
Henry David Thoreau (1817–1862)	Nature advocate, author of *Walden* (1854), called for wilderness preservation
Ellen M. Tower (1848–1938)	Chaired committee that established sand gardens, Boston, MA
Pearl H. Vaughn (1914–1986)	African American recreation educator
Calvert Vaux (1824–1895)	Cocreator of Central Park plan *Greensward*
Thorstein B. Veblen (1857–1929)	Educator, author of *Theory of the Leisure Class*
William G. Vinal (1881–1976)	Early leader in nature recreation, naturalist, educator
Henry D. Washburn (1832–1871)	Spearheaded the movement to establish Yellowstone National Park
Lebert H. Weir (1878–1949)	Early author and park leader
George Williams (1821–1905)	Founder of the YMCA movement
Theodore Wirth (1863–1949)	Dean of park administrators in America
Marie E. Zakazewska (1829–1902)	Established sand gardens, Boston, MA

delivery of innovative services. For instance, the play movement resulted in the development and implementation of model playground programs.

As a movement becomes more and more accepted by the public, it becomes *institutionalized*. Its aims and objectives become widely supported by the public and its programs may be subsidized through tax dollars. Bureaucratic structures emerge and managers handle the functions of the movement. Often, the focus veers more toward the establishment of codified rules and procedures than toward the ideals of the movement. Further, as the workers within the institutions become more entrenched, they begin to think of themselves as belonging to a *profession*.

The creation of early institutions in the park and recreation movement is often referred to as the *Golden Era of the Parks and Recreation Movement* (1880–1920). One view of leaders during this time was that they were social reformers concerned with the plight of the urban poor, children, and immigrants. Financial support came mostly from philanthropists who felt a moral responsibility to help those less fortunate than themselves. These individuals were moved by ". . . an altruistic mission to create the civic ideal—to move urban populations toward a finer, purer, collective life" (Williams, Lankford, and DeGraaf, 1996, p. 1).

Another perspective of the development of the park and recreation movement suggests that it was a product of a class conflict. The movement, from this perspective, may be seen as a process of ". . . social control, often masquerading as social reform" (Williams, Lankford, and DeGraaf, 1996, p. 2). From this orientation, the park and recreation movement can be viewed as a way of promoting ". . . moral control . . . a more subtle and complex process that influenced behavior and molded character by consciously planning and transforming the urban environment . . . reforms were instituted by elites, generally local government leaders and business owners to inculcate values necessary for the growing commercial economy" (Williams, Lankford, and DeGraaf, 1996, p. 2).

During the 1920s more Americans were living in cities than in rural areas. Labor reform created more free time for workers as the five-day work week was created. New inventions, like the automobile, gave people increased mobility and made life easier. Women's roles changed dramat-

Did you know that the Civilian Conservation Corps . . .

- Restored 3,980 historical structures
- Spent 2,094,713 participant days razing undesirable structures and obliterations
- Spent 6,111,258.2 participant days in the operation of nurseries
- Built 63,246 buildings
- Built 800 state parks
- Built 7,622 impounding and large diversion dams
- Erected 405,037 signs, markers, and monuments
- Collected 13,634,415 pounds of hardwood seeds and 875,970 bushels of cones
- Developed 6,966.7 miles of wildlife streams
- Built 46,854 bridges
- Built 28,087.8 miles of foot and horse trails

- Spent 1,067,800 participant days on archaeological investigation
- Covered 13,099,701 acres in tree insect pest control
- Built 46,000 campground facilities
- Involved 225,000 World War I veterans
- Transplanted 44,927,339 trees and shrubs
- Built 32,148 wildlife shelters
- Spent 1,301,945 participant days on wildlife activities
- Built 395 bathhouses
- Built 38,550 vehicle bridges
- Spent 4,827,421 participant days surveying and mapping
- Built 204 lodges and museums
- Planted over 3 billion trees

Source: Data from the National Association of Civilian Conservation Corps, St. Louis, MO.

ically as they were given the vote and new careers were opened up to them. Faith in government was high and all levels of government became increasingly involved in recreation opportunities. The federal government became more involved in outdoor recreation and resource management, state governments opened more state parks, and local governments saw more government support for parks and programs than in earlier years. Institutions moved from serving only children to serving people of all ages, from the provision of facilities to the definition of standards for the use of leisure time, and from the satisfaction of individual interests to the meeting of group and community needs. The 1920s also brought about the beginnings of mass culture through the radio.

In the 1930s, the Depression brought unemployment and caused public funding for recreation programs to be cut just when the need for recreation was greatest, as people had an abundance of free time. Many new jobs were created in large federal work projects such as the Work Project Administration (WPA), which constructed recreation centers and parks in cities. At the same time the Civilian Conservation Corps (CCC) constructed recreation facilities on publicly owned lands such as state and federal parks.

Following War World II (1945–1959) there was an explosion of the middle class as an increased number of people were prosperous, and war goods production was switched to consumer goods. Opportunities for education became more abundant. Many educators began to be viewed as leaders in the parks and recreation field. Local public recreation and parks departments thrived. In addition, commercial recreation began to take off as Americans gained increasingly more disposable income.

A healthy economy and technological innovations continued to fuel growth in commercial recreation after World War II. The advancement of the car and the interstate highway system greatly expanded the areas accessible to American tourists. Electronic innovations generated a huge home entertainment industry of television, stereo, video recorders, and computers. Synthetic materials greatly improved sports and recreation equipment performance and durability (e.g., ski equipment, golf clubs, skateboards, windsurfing, and outdoor clothing).

For public recreation the period of 1960 to 1975 has been referred to as the *Zenith Era* of recreation. This was a time of great social change—civil and women's rights, the war in Vietnam, lifestyle changes, environmental movements, and economic inflation were contemporary issues. It was a time when Americans established the Great Society to address the social ills of the day. This time period was characterized by the rise of popular culture, as visual images through television opened the world to all U.S. and Canadian citizens. Increased government spending enabled the park and recreation profession to expand greatly.

Chubb and Chubb (1981), writing in the book *One Third of Our Time,* classify the 1960s as a time period of the second recreation revolution. Americans had high disposable incomes, high employment, and great aspirations. One reason that this time period has been called the Zenith Era of the recreation movement is the fact that immediately following it, funding for public programs dropped substantially as a result of property tax limitations. The events of the 1960s were a reaffirmation that the public valued the park and recreation movement. Great environmental gains were made in these years and in following years. America set aside vast amounts of land for wilderness and recreation during this time period and into the 1970s. Table 3.3 compares the Golden Era of recreation to the Zenith Era. As is evident from table 3.3 both periods were times of great social change, and change promotes opportunity.

Since the mid-1970s the park and recreation movement has been trying to deal with the shift society is experiencing from an industrial society to a postindustrial one. This uncertainty, although unsettling, presents the movement with great opportunities to urge the profession into a time of innovation. This window of opportunity or innovation may not be open long, however, so the time to act is now.

In current times, many of the same problems of poverty and the need for social reform still exist while additional problems (drugs, AIDS, homelessness, underemployment) are also being identified. Professionals must look to the underlying concepts that will govern postindustrial society and develop programs and institutions that can deal with the recreational needs of a changing society while still maintaining the proud history of the movement's past. Inherent in this process must be the reemergence of the passion that gripped early leaders in the Golden Era. As a movement becomes a profession, it becomes more institutionalized and it often loses some of its early passion. Rekindling this passion is a major challenge of the profession today.

A brief description of the early history of some of the major movements that emerged and became institutionalized during the industrial era follows, including movements to establish municipal, state, and national parks and to establish play areas for children.

Municipal Parks The creation of Central Park in New York City in the 1850s is generally acknowledged as the first public landscaped park established solely for leisure purposes. Major advocates of the park concept, William Cullen Bryant, editor of New York's *The Evening Post,* and Andrew Downing, editor of *The Horticulturist,* recommended strongly the establishment of public open areas in urban settings. In 1853, the city of New York passed legislation for what is now known as Central Park. In 1858, Frederick Law Olmsted and Calvert Vaux submitted the design of Central Park, entitled *Greensward.* Figure 3.9 depicts a map of Central Park in New York City as designed in the 1850s, and one as it appears today.

The work of Olmsted became instrumental in the development of parks, park systems, and city planning across the United States and in Canada. Central Park was developed to provide a pleasant contrast to the surrounding chaotic conditions of the city of New York. Although many attempts were made to amend the park plan, Olmsted sought to ensure the design's integrity and resigned from the project a number of times. Olmsted's principles of park design greatly influenced the park movement throughout the United States and Canada. He designed

TABLE

3.3 COMPARING THE GOLDEN AND ZENITH ERAS OF RECREATION IN THE UNITED STATES

Golden Era	Zenith Era
Background	
Seeing the needs of rapidly changing society and working to create social reform	The Great Society, national campaign against poverty, enjoying a high standard of living—Americans thought they could do it all. Rapid and radical change in recreation legislation, attitudes, and behavior
Great social change: immigration, social reform, urbanization, economic cycle of boom and bust, WWI, and Americans struggling with their role in the world	Period of great social change: civil and women's rights, the war in Vietnam, environmental movement, and economic inflation. America's role was to make the world safe for democracy; we were the "good guys"
Immigration saw the beginning of a pluralistic society	Great emphasis on civil rights and equality
Clash between agricultural wave and industrial wave was just finishing; Americans just beginning to deal with these changes	Start of the clash between industrial and postindustrial society; Americans just realizing these changes would take place
Concentration of people	
Urbanization in cities	Decay of many inner cities;
City slums were horrible places to live	new park districts developed as families moved from cities to suburbs
Suburbanization: concentration of people in suburbs	
Makeup of park and recreation departments	
Federal and local agency formation	Agencies became big bureaucratic organizations
Initially few public facilities were available; many large cities developed recreation facilities during this time	City parks and recreation centers become overused, under-maintained, and vandalized. Some federal money made available for renovations; often not used. States make use of federal funds
Great leaders dedicated to improving recreation opportunities that could be considered beneficial to the character and physical health of participants	Profession was institutionalized. Creation of National Recreation and Parks Association (NRPA)
Funding	
The idea of using substantial amounts of tax funds for the development of recreation was introduced. Philanthropic money was still relied upon to a great extent	Federal, state, and local governments were expected to fund all major projects—the great society. We could provide facilities and provision of recreation opportunities for all
Thrusts of the movement	
Concentrated on helping the urban disadvantaged	Recreation for all
Preservation and conservation of national resources began	In 1965 Congress, known as the Conservation Congress, passed 51 conservation bills

parks in New York, California, Connecticut, New Jersey, Massachusetts, Illinois, Pennsylvania, Michigan, Washington, DC, Rhode Island, Kentucky, Missouri, Wisconsin, and Quebec (Canada). The municipal park movement in the United States grew from one park in 1853 to a system in 1882, to 100 systems in 1889, and to 800 systems in 1902. By comparison there are more than 3,000 park systems today.

The modern development of parks and public squares in Canada can be traced to the city of Montreal in 1821, when the Place d'Armes Square was set aside for public use. In 1851, the Toronto City Council established a committee on Public Walks and Gardens. One of the first works of this committee was the development of a 287-acre military reserve for a pleasure and

Figure 3.9

(a) A map that
depicts the
original 1858
plan for New
York City's
Central Park,
and (b) as it is
today.

*Central Park
Conservancy*

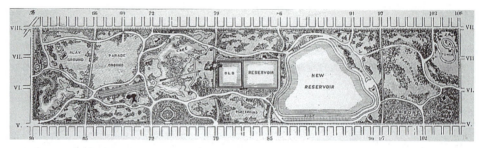

a.

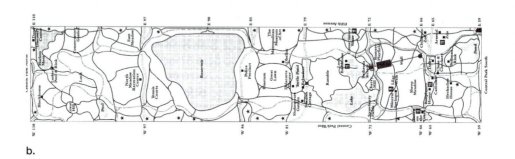

b.

recreation area for its citizens. Other parks founded in the 1880s included Mt. Royal Park, Montreal (Quebec), 1863; Victoria Park in London (Ontario), 1869; Stanley Park in Vancouver (British Columbia), 1886; Point Pleasant Park in Halifax (Nova Scotia), 1886; and Rockwood Park in St. John (New Brunswick), 1889.

The next important development in the local park movement in the United States was the establishment of a Metropolitan Park Commission in Boston, Massachusetts, in the 1890s. This park system was established under the leadership of a protégé of Olmsted, Charles Eliot. Eliot thought in broad terms. He felt that a park system for Boston should encompass the entire urban region, linking beaches, rivers, and other open spaces. The park system, developed as a result of Eliot's vision, brought thirty-six cities and communities together under a metropolitan district.

The establishment of the Cook County Forest Preserve District in Illinois paralleled the development of Boston's park system. This development, established under the visionary leadership of Jans Jensen, became a special district by popular vote in 1914. The Forest Preserve District emphasizes the preservation of natural forested areas and has created a green belt surrounding the city of Chicago.

Enabling legislation for the park function occurred first in the state of New Jersey in 1885. This legislation allowed for the establishment of individual municipal park systems, organized into one unified, countywide system. In the state of Illinois, in 1893, the Pleasure Driveway and Park District Act gave communities in unincorporated areas the opportunity to establish park systems. The importance of these two forms of legislation was that they encouraged the development of local park systems. Figure 3.10 outlines some of the important developments of the municipal park movement in the United States and Canada.

Frederick Law Olmsted, Sr. (1822–1903). Frederick Law Olmsted, Sr., known as the founder of landscape architecture in America, was a visionary leader with extraordinary personal accomplishments. He was a noted author, an adept administrator, an excellent engineer, and a man of political

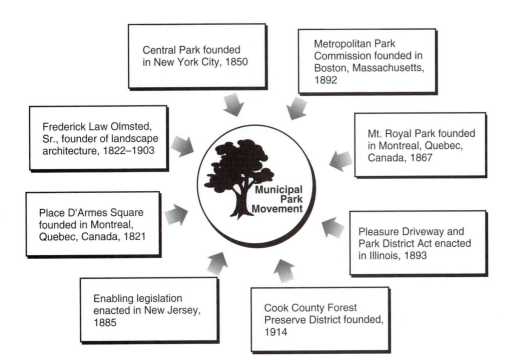

Figure 3.10

Major people and events influencing the municipal park movement in Canada and the United States

Central Park founded in New York City, 1850

Metropolitan Park Commission founded in Boston, Massachusetts, 1892

Frederick Law Olmsted, Sr., founder of landscape architecture, 1822–1903

Mt. Royal Park founded in Montreal, Quebec, Canada, 1867

Municipal Park Movement

Place D'Armes Square founded in Montreal, Quebec, Canada, 1821

Pleasure Driveway and Park District Act enacted in Illinois, 1893

Enabling legislation enacted in New Jersey, 1885

Cook County Forest Preserve District founded, 1914

Leisure Line

Yellowstone Park Legacy

The diary of Nathaniel P. Langford relates the specific origins of Yellowstone Park:

One member of our party suggested that if there could be secured by preemption a good title to two or three quarter sections of land opposite the lower fall of Yellowstone and extending down the river toward the canyon, they would eventually become a source of great profit to the owners. Another member of the party thought it would be more desirable to take up a quarter section of the land at the great Upper Geyser Basin, for the reason that the locality could be more easily reached by tourists and pleasure seekers. A third suggestion was that each member of the party preempt a claim, and in order that no one should have an advantage over the other, the whole should be thrown into a common pool for benefit of the entire party.

Mr. Hedges then said that he did not approve of any of these plans—that there ought to be no private ownership of any portion of that region, but that the whole of it ought to be set aside as a great national park and that each one of us ought to make an effort to make this accomplished.

Source: Lee, 1972, pp. 11–12.

and social conviction. "Olmsted believed implicitly that a close association with natural beauty was one of the most necessary elements of human life" (Fabos, Milde, and Weinmayr, 1968, p. 12). The scope and range of his projects were a testament to his genius. They include the design of urban parks, state and national parks, community design, regional planning, campus design, estate design, and urban design.

3.4 THE CREATION OF NATIONAL PARKS, 1872–1916

1872	(March 1)	Yellowstone, Montana-Wyoming-Idaho
1875	(March 3)	Mackinac Island, Michigan (ceded to Michigan, 1895)
1890	(September 25)	Sequoia, California
	(October 1)	Yosemite, California
	(October 1)	General Grant, California
1899	(March 22)	Mount Rainier, Washington
1902	(May 22)	Crater Lake, Oregon
1903	(January 9)	Wind Cave, South Dakota
1904	(April 27)	Sullys Hill, North Dakota (converted to Game Preserve, 1931)
1906	(June 29)	Platt, Oklahoma
1906	(June 29)	Mesa Verde, Colorado
1910	(May 11)	Glacier, Montana
1915	(January 26)	Rocky Mountain, Colorado
1916	(August 1)	Hawaii, Hawaii
1916	(August 9)	Lassen Volcanic, California
1916	(August 25)	Enabling Act to create a National Park Service

National Parks National parks are a unique contribution of the United States to the world. The first national park, Yellowstone National Park, was established on March 1, 1872, by the U.S. Congress. It was the first large-scale preservation of a land area as a park or wilderness concern. The establishment of Yellowstone, a social invention created to stem the exploitation of wilderness areas, acknowledged that natural resources were limited and that they needed to be preserved for future generations.

The national park concept sought to create permanent reserves of land for U.S. citizens. Although eighteen years passed between the creation of the first national park and the subsequent establishment of others, the national park concept became firmly entrenched as a U.S. institution. Table 3.4 presents a list of the early parks in the United States. The Antiquities Act of 1906 provided presidential power to claim and thus protect areas of scenic wonder and natural beauty. Many national monuments, established in this manner, later became a part of the National Park System. Figure 3.11 presents some key historical events in the development of national parks in the United States.

The national park concept rapidly transferred to countries outside of the United States. In 1887, the Ministry of the Interior of Canada set forth legislative steps to establish its first national park. A bill was introduced in the House of Commons to establish Banff National Park. The act, known as the Rocky Mountains Park Act, provided ". . . a tract of land reserved and set apart as a public park and pleasure ground for the benefit, advantage, and enjoyment of the people of Canada" (Lothian, 1977, p. 6).

> **Stephen T. Mather** (1867–1930). Stephen T. Mather was the first director of the National Park Service. A self-made millionaire with a deep love for the protection of natural resources, Mather became involved in the directorship when he wrote then Secretary of the Interior, Franklin Lane, to complain about the way in which the national parks were being managed. Lane wrote to Mather, "If you don't like the way the national parks are being run, come down to Washington and run them yourself"

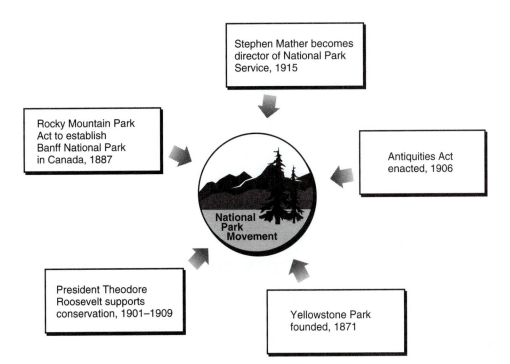

Figure 3.11

Major people and events influencing the national park movement in Canada and the United States

Stephen Mather becomes director of National Park Service, 1915

Rocky Mountain Park Act to establish Banff National Park in Canada, 1887

Antiquities Act enacted, 1906

National Park Movement

President Theodore Roosevelt supports conservation, 1901–1909

Yellowstone Park founded, 1871

(Runte, 1979, p. 101). Mather accepted the challenge and performed admirably. He secured legal authorization to manage the parks, established policies to manage the park service, worked to promote tourist activities to national parks, secured financial resources to manage the park systems, and, in general, helped to secure a much broader base of support for the work of the national park system.

State Parks The romantic and artistic efforts of poets, writers, artists, and explorers helped to plant the seeds of the state park movement, as well as the national park movement. Individuals such as George Catlin, James Fenimore Cooper, Ralph Waldo Emerson, and Henry David Thoreau all provided a philosophy of nature that awakened the consciousness of the public. The state park movement in the United States began in 1864, when Yosemite Valley and the Mariposa Big Tree Grove were ceded to the State of California to become state parks. Frederick Law Olmsted was involved in the development of a management plan for this program. Olmsted emphasized that the effort to secure Yosemite as a resort and recreation area was a testament to the advancement of civilization (Sax, 1987). Two decades passed, however, before additional developments at the state level occurred, when the State of New York set aside land in the Adirondacks as a forest preserve and set aside Niagara Falls as a state park in 1885.

Little happened with the state parks in the United States between 1885 and the 1920s. A few states—New York, Indiana, Wisconsin, California, and Connecticut—established what could be identified as state park systems. Newton (1971) reports that two significant factors influenced the development of state parks in the United States after this period of time. The first was the automobile. The automobile gave impetus to travel (as the precursor to what is now known as tourism) and provided people an opportunity to enjoy outdoor recreation resources. The second resulted from the work of Stephen T. Mather. Mather organized a general park conference. He encouraged the governors of each of the states to send representatives to this conference. Twenty-five states responded, with 200 representatives participating. The group was organized as the National Conference on State Parks.

Impetus for the development of state parks came in the 1930s from the federal government when it launched the submarginal land program and purchased many areas as "recreation demonstration areas." These areas were ultimately leased back to states and became part of their park systems. In addition, the newly organized Civilian Conservation Corps aided in the development of state park programs (see figures 3.12 and 3.13). The CCC helped expand the state parks systems from a handful of parks to a total of 1,346 in 1950 (Newton, 1971). Figure 3.14 portrays important historical events in the state park movement.

Figure 3.12

The Civilian Conservation Corps in Iowa

The Civilian Conservation Corps In Iowa

The Iowa Civilian Conservation Corps Museum

Backbone State Park
Dundee, Iowa 52038
(563)924-2527

John Muir (1838–1914). John Muir was a naturalist and one of the most eloquent authors advocating for the preservation of natural resources. His efforts led to the preservation of the Yosemite Valley area. Muir dedicated his life to the preservation of wildland and wilderness areas. His advocacy for preservation of natural resources often brought him into direct confrontation with both conservationists and developers.

Iowa received many benefits from the conservation efforts of Franklin Roosevelt. Backbone Park, as it stands today, is a result of the hard work put forth by the Civilian Conservation Corps (CCC).

While Company 1756 was busy building the dam to create the lake, Company 781 worked hard to prevent erosion. Trees were planted, and retaining walls were erected to hold the soil on the hills. In addition to work that conserved and preserved the natural beauty of the park, the corps installed telephone lines, firebreaks and sewage and irrigation systems.

Natural materials from the park were used in most projects. Limestone, timber and boulders can still be seen today in the bathhouse, boathouse, sundial, water fountains, bridges, trails, retaining walls and latrines that dot the park's landscape. In addition, the State Forest located near the north entrance to the park is a living reminder of the thousands of trees that were planted.

The CCC provided many intangible benefits, as well. Many of the camp members were young and away from home for the first time. Living, working and playing together instilled values that spurred many of them on to successful, productive lives. Many of the CCC members continued on as employees of the U.S. Forest Service or National Park Service.

Economically, times were hard, but the CCC camps provided a job, a chance for an education, an opportunity to learn a skill and time to have fun. Boxing and wrestling matches, ping-pong tournaments, orchestras, glee clubs, theatrical groups, science clubs and camp newspapers are some of the many activities that were enjoyed.

Designed By
Leslie E. Smith

 Printed on Recycled Paper

IOWA DEPARTMENT OF NATURAL RESOURCES
Wallace State Office Building
Des Moines, Iowa 50319

Figure 3.13

A Civilian Conservation Corps historical document

Camp SP-2
Company 1756
Dundee, Iowa

Camp SP-17
Company 781
Lamont, Iowa

Backbone State Park
Dundee, Iowa 52038
Telephone 563-924-2527

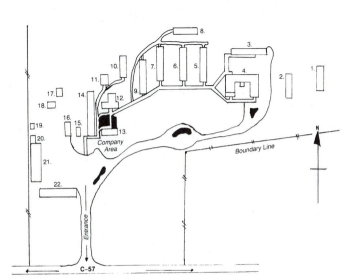

1. Barrack
2. Barrack
3. Latrine and Bath
4. Mess Hall and Kitchen
5. Barrack
6. Barrack
7. Barrack
8. Barrack
9. Barrack
10. Education Building
11. School
12. Hospital
13. Officers' Quarters
14. Headquarters Rec Hall
15. Telephone Office
16. Tools
17. Storage
18. Foreman's Quarters
19. Oil House
20. Blacksmith Shop
21. Army Repair Garage
22. Garage

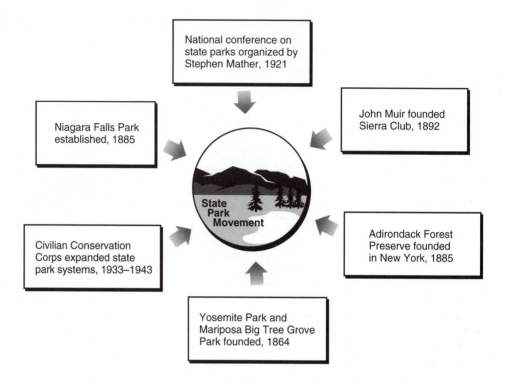

Figure 3.14

Major people and events influencing the state park movement in the United States

National conference on state parks organized by Stephen Mather, 1921

John Muir founded Sierra Club, 1892

Niagara Falls Park established, 1885

State Park Movement

Adirondack Forest Preserve founded in New York, 1885

Civilian Conservation Corps expanded state park systems, 1933–1943

Yosemite Park and Mariposa Big Tree Grove Park founded, 1864

The Play Movement The play movement in Canada and the United States began in response to child labor and crowded urban conditions. Figure 3.15 portrays important events and people that influenced the play movement in the United States. Early efforts at providing play environments for children drew inspiration from examples in Germany. Germans valued play and had systematized it as a part of their approach to education. Henry Curtis, writing in *The Play Movement and Its Significance,* in 1917, outlined five distinct and independent play movements in the United States.

1. *Play Spaces.* The first of these is what is ordinarily known as the play movement. It seeks to provide a place for play where children can go in their leisure time and be off the street and away from the evil influences they might encounter. Play spaces offer constructive leadership of trained directors as well.
2. *Play and Child Development.* The second play movement ". . . is built on the assumption that play is essential to the development of children and it must be furnished to every child every day" (p. 19). The focus of this type of play program is in the schools.
3. *Outdoor Play for Young Children.* This phase of the play movement ". . . consists of furnishing an adequate opportunity for outdoor life and play to children below school age. This must come through the facilities and yards of houses, in the interior courts of tenements, and by leaving an open park and playground in the center of all congested blocks" (p. 20).
4. *Public Recreation.* The movement for public recreation asserts that the ". . . development of recreation would mean the providing of social centers in the schools with public gymnasiums, dance halls, and swimming pools, either there or elsewhere, the municipalizing of the moving picture and the subsidizing of drama and the opera . . . the

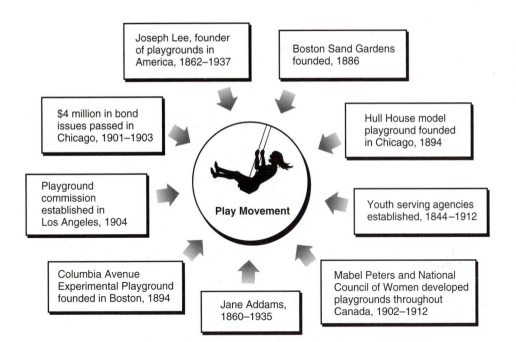

Figure 3.15

Major people and events influencing the play movement in Canada and the United States

Joseph Lee, founder of playgrounds in America, 1862–1937

Boston Sand Gardens founded, 1886

$4 million in bond issues passed in Chicago, 1901–1903

Hull House model playground founded in Chicago, 1894

Playground commission established in Los Angeles, 1904

Play Movement

Youth serving agencies established, 1844–1912

Columbia Avenue Experimental Playground founded in Boston, 1894

Jane Addams, 1860–1935

Mabel Peters and National Council of Women developed playgrounds throughout Canada, 1902–1912

organization of pageants and community celebrations, choral music . . . and the development of parks and amusement resorts" (p. 20).

5. *Spirit of Play.* The fifth movement is not a movement for the rebirth of play, but the spirit of play. For example, in the United States, we have become overmaterialized with our energies directed toward consumption of material goods—and have forgotten how to live. We must come to see the essential values in life, to work more moderately, to find more joy in our work.

What causes have contributed to the growth of the play movement in the United States and Canada? Joseph Lee (1925) has written in *The Normal Course in Play* that a number of causes contributed to the development of the play movement, including an appreciation of the value of play in the life of a child, prevailing social conditions (urbanization of population, child labor, juvenile delinquency, monotonous work), and commercial recreation. Most commercial recreation opportunities were viewed as passive. Figure 3.16 depicts Joseph Lee, founder of the playground movement in the United States.

In 1868, the city of Boston established an organized playground program as a part of one of its school yards. In 1886, Dr. Maria Zacharuski, following a visit to Germany, established a sand garden in Boston, sponsored by the Massachusetts Emergency and Hygiene Association. This is usually identified as the first supervised playground in the United States. By 1889, more than twenty-one playgrounds of this type had sprung up in Boston. Also, in 1886, the Charles Bank Outdoor Gymnasium opened. This park setting emphasized physical recreation facilities.

In Canada, the National Council of Women played an active role in the development of supervised playgrounds. The work of this organization, under the direction of Mabel Peters, encouraged the development of playgrounds in Montreal, Quebec, in 1902; in Halifax, Nova Scotia, in 1906; in St. Johns, New Brunswick, in 1906; in Toronto, Ontario, in 1908; in Hamilton, Ontario, in 1909; and in Vancouver, British Columbia, in 1912 (McFarland, 1970).

Figure 3.16

Joseph Lee,
founder of
playgrounds

*Courtesy of the
National Recreation
and Park
Association*

Hull House in Chicago and the Columbus Avenue Experimental Playground in Boston are two other noteworthy developments. In 1894, Jane Addams established a model playground adjacent to Hull House. Hull House was located in the midst of a crowded urban area heavily populated by immigrants and members of the struggling lower class. The Columbus Avenue Experimental Playground was established and financially supported by the philanthropist Joseph Lee. Lee became a noteworthy figure in the playground movement as the president of the Playground Association of America and contributed substantially to our understanding of play through his written work.

Recreation, or social, centers also emerged around the turn of the century. Initially, settlement houses, directed toward helping immigrants become familiar with the customs, norms, and language of the United States, served to provide social programs. Again, Hull House led the way. In the early 1900s, the Chicago South Park District initiated an innovative model program for the development of field houses and public baths. Between 1901 and 1903, this district passed two bond issues totaling $4 million. With these funds, the district constructed field houses or neighborhood center buildings with indoor gymnasiums, swimming pools, assembly halls, and smaller meeting rooms.

In 1904, the first instance of a separate playground commission was established within the city of Los Angeles. The first enabling legislation for municipal recreation occurred in 1915 in the state of New Jersey. Subsequently, municipal park and recreation functions have been historically linked together.

From this beginning, the play movement in Canada and the United States has evolved into a large, complex set of organizations, institutions, and businesses that not only respond to the play needs of individuals but also shape our culture as well as other cultures. The world is being saturated with the myths, fantasies, and dreams of the United States (Berstein, 1990). American play products—movies, records, books, theme parks, sports, cartoons, and television

Figure 3.17
Jane Addams,
founder of Hull
House in
Chicago
Bettmann Archive

shows—are merging as a driving cultural force around the world, and probably will remain so throughout the next century (Berstein, 1990).

Jane Addams (1860–1935). Jane Addams was a humanitarian who was closely associated with social work and made significant contributions to the play movement. She served as the first vice-president of the Playground Association of America and presented at the association's first Congress in 1907. Addams (see figure 3.17) developed a model playground at Hull House and strongly advocated for the rights of youth, particularly in poor, urban areas. She advocated for the eight-hour workday, child labor laws, and dignity for all.

Youth Serving and Voluntary Organizations Strongly aligned to the play movement, many youth serving organizations were established during the period of 1880 to 1920 to respond to such problems as unhealthy social conditions arising in big cities, decline in fitness in youth, and the need for moral education. Early goals of youth serving organizations included personality development, character development, social integration, development of new skills and interests, constructive use of leisure time, as well as physical health and spiritual growth. For example, consider the following excerpt from the Federal Charter of the Boy Scouts of America on June 15, 1916, by the U.S. Congress: "the purpose of the corporation shall be to promote, through organization and cooperation with other agencies, the ability of boys to do things for themselves and others, to train them in Scoutcraft, and to teach them patriotism, courage, self-reliance, and kindred virtues, using the methods which are now in common use by Boy Scouts."

Throughout their history, youth serving organizations have had an important impact on the development of youth and children. These organizations were often based on religious or educational goals as well as leisure ones. For example, the Young Men's Christian Association (YMCA) was founded by George Williams in 1844 in Great Britain. The first YMCA in the United States was established in Boston in 1851. The Young Women's Christian Association

First Recreation Center in the United States

Jane Addams and Ellen Gates Starr started Hull House in 1889 in an old mansion on Chicago's South Halsted Street. By 1910 Hull House had grown into an imposing complex of thirteen buildings that covered nearly a city block. Within this complex Addams and her staff offered programs in sports, crafts, cooking, citizenship training, dancing, theater, music, and photography. Hull House also served as a center for studying the urban experience and much public policy was created and advocated through the staff at Hull House. At its height of influence more than 9,000 people came weekly to Hull House to participate in its many activities. In many ways Hull House served as the first American community and recreation center.

Hull House established the first public gymnasium in 1893, and, a short time later, the first women's basketball team in the city was established. By the mid-1920s the Hull House gymnasium had been enlarged to include bathing facilities for the neighborhood. In 1925, it was reported that over 6,000 paid showers and 12,000 baths were taken in the gymnasium building.

Hull House also ran an after-school program in which numerous clubs and classes were offered each day after school. In the mid-1920s the average weekly attendance was about one thousand, with sixty-four clubs and classes in existence. A Boys Band was created and was one of the most prestigious activities of the Boy's Club within Hull House. It is reported that Benny Goodman was a member of this band in 1912.

The Hull House program also included a summer camp near Waukegan, Illinois, that looked over Lake Michigan. This camp became an increasingly popular place for activities and programs, and by the 1920s had become a second location for many Hull House activities.

Hull House programs were always responsive to the needs of nearby residents. As Jane Addams wrote: "The one thing to be dreaded in the settlement is that it lose its flexibility, its power of quick adaption, its readiness to change its methods as its environment may demand."

Source: From *The Many Faces of Hull House: The Photographs of Wallace Kirkland,* edited by Mary Ann Johnson, Urbana: University of Illinois Press, 1989.

(YWCA) was established shortly after this, also in Great Britain in 1855. The first YWCA in the United States was established in Boston in 1866. The YWCA organization, operating throughout the United States today, was founded in 1906.

The Young Men's Hebrew Association was first established in New York City in 1874, and another group was established in Philadelphia in 1875. The first Young Women's Hebrew Association was established in New York in 1902.

The Boys Club was established in 1860 in Hartford, Connecticut, but not until several decades later was a national organization combining Boys Clubs in several communities established. This occurred in 1906, when a national Boys Club organization was created. The first Girls Club was established in 1864 in Waterbury, Connecticut. These clubs currently exist as one national organization, the Boys and Girls Clubs of America.

A number of organizations have primary themes built on outdoor recreation activities. The Boy Scouts were founded in England in 1908 by Lord Robert Baden-Powell and brought to the United States by William D. Boyce in 1920. The forerunner of the Boy Scouts of America, the Woodcraft Indians, was established in 1902 by Ernest Thompson Seton. The Girl Scout program, preceded by the Girl Guides, was also initiated in England; it was brought to the United States in 1912 by Juliette Lowe. The Camp Fire organization was founded in 1910 by Dr. Luther H. Gulick and his wife, Charlotte Gulick, and incorporated in 1912.

One specific type of youth serving organization related to outdoor recreation was organized camping. The pioneers of organized camping were men and women with a vision of the impact of outdoor living experiences on the lives of girls and boys. Many of these pioneers saw camping as a healthy and educational antidote to the effects of urban life and industrialization as well as a "fun alternative" to a summer of idleness in the city. These early programs were geared to affluent families, were activity based, and were designed to help participants develop wholesome habits for life (Eells, 1986).

Whereas private independent camps developed around the strength and personality of individuals, agencies' camps developed as a part of the overall programs of larger church denominations and social service agencies. Church camps can be traced back to the early 1800s as believers gathered in outdoor frontier meetings for days at a time. Slowly, the needs of young people began to be addressed, and eventually the youth camp came into being (Mattson, 1983).

In addition to church camps, many national youth serving organizations (e.g., YMCAs, Boy Scouts, Girl Scouts, Camp Fire, 4-H, and the Boys and Girls Clubs) developed camping programs to complement the programs they offered in urban areas. Proponents of organized camping within large youth serving organizations saw the opportunity camps provided for children and youth to learn and practice the skills needed to sustain democracy. As one early camp director wrote, "in camp, poor and rich lads stripped to their swimming trunks as on an absolute equality; the best man wins. Courage, generosity, goodwill, honesty are the touchstones to success in camp" (Talbot, 1905). The YMCA was the first to integrate camping into its national program when Sumner Dudley began YMCA camping in 1885.

A third type of camp also developed in the late 1800s. These camps were related to the Fresh Air movement that started in the late 1800s out of a deep concern for the needs and conditions of the poor in inner-city slums and ghettos. The movement created vacation places in the country for needy children and families. The goal of the new program was to place city mothers and children with farm families or in small towns for ten days of good food and healthful outdoor living. Since willing farm families were hard to find, alternative plans were made to create Fresh Air camps. Many Fresh Air camps are still in existence today along with more than 8,500 other resident and day camp programs. These programs continue to be both agency and private and together serve more than 6 million children annually (American Camping Association, 1998).

Luther H. Gulick (1865–1918). Luther Halsey Gulick was an individual of multiple skills and talents. He was the first president of the Playground Association of America. Gulick was a physical education instructor, founder and president of Camp Fire Girls, and a noted writer and speaker for the play movement. He performed a leading role in founding the American Social Hygiene Association, the Boy Scouts of America, and the American Folk Dance Society. A highly energetic, enthusiastic and dynamic individual, his talent lay in the conceptualization of ideas that he would develop and institutionalize.

Although studying history cannot help recreational professionals predict the future, it can provide insights that help them make informed decisions in building their programs and organizations into the next century. The industrial era fostered many accomplishments. Leisure and work were clearly delineated, and the modern parks and recreation movement began. In reviewing the early history of this movement, several insights need to be highlighted as park and recreation professionals look to build programs in the future. These insights include the power of passion, the evolving nature of programs, and the benefits of inclusivity.

The Power of Passion Individuals who are passionate about their work with children and youth can make a difference in people's lives. Wilson (1981), in her book *Survival*

Skills for Managers, states that the world has plenty of talent (creativity) but lacks passion. She further quotes James Austin: "the best creative work represents passion fulfilled, whereas a neurosis may be thought of as passion thwarted. Enthusiasm is the elixir that pervades creativity, inspires it, frees it so that anything seems possible, and enlists others in the cause." This fact is reiterated in the words of Dr. Seuss (1971, p. 58) "Unless someone like you cares a whole awful lot, nothing is going to get better, it's not."

This fact has been modeled throughout the history of the parks and recreation movement. People who have been passionate about what they do have given us a legacy of institutions and programs that have made a difference in this world. Thus the greatest resource inherent to all organizations is the creativity and passion of its staff. While creativity and passion take many different forms and vary from individual to individual, key elements include open-mindedness, perseverance, collaboration, resourcefulness, and commitment.

The Evolving Nature of Programs   In examining the wide range of leisure service organizations that have developed over the last twenty-five years, Godbey (1997) notes that all successful leisure service organizations share three common characteristics. These characteristics include the desire to help people, an entrepreneurial spirit, and the ability to respond to the social needs of the times. Programs should be dynamic rather than static; they must grow and evolve. The evolving nature of recreation programs is a constant reminder of the need to understand local needs and the willingness to adapt to meet these needs. As the early social reformer Jane Addams wrote in 1893, "the one thing to be dreaded in the settlement (house movement) is that it lose its flexibility, its power of quick adaption, its readiness to change its methods as its environment may demand" (Addams, 1893, p. 22).

Inclusivity   In addition to evolving programs, the history of the recreation movement is a constant reminder to reach out to new groups of people in need of services. For example, organized camps started with serving just boys and later incorporated programs for girls, as well as people with disabilities and those who are economically disadvantaged. Today camp programs are still reaching out and trying to create more inclusive environments where children and youth can be integrated with others of different abilities and backgrounds. Likewise, other parks and recreation organizations have expanded programs to meet the new needs of emerging groups (i.e., younger children and older youth, single-parent families, nontraditional families, etc.). This drive to expand to include the needs of emerging groups is imperative as programs look to survive and thrive in the years ahead.

The Technological or Information Era

The technological, or information, era began in the mid-1950s in the United States and Canada and continues to the present. Enormous changes have occurred as industrialized society has given way to a new socioeconomic structure that emphasizes the creation and distribution of information and services. Two factors are usually attributed to the development of the technological or information era—the advent of the computer and a shift in the workforce. Computers have had a dramatic impact on the way people live. The growth of an electronic culture has created a dramatic transformation affecting the ability of people and organizations to process and use information (Bullaro and Edginton, 1986). Simply put, humankind is taking a quantum leap in the volume, speed, and versatility of the average person's use of information. In 1956, for the first time in U.S. and Canadian history, white-collar workers—technical, managerial, and clerical—

outnumbered blue-collar workers. Thus, the industrialized state gave way to a new society in which most individuals work with information rather than with the production of goods.

The information era is built on a different set of assumptions than the industrial era. As a result, it requires new ideas, new concepts, and new strategies to respond to the values that exist and that continue to emerge. Most of our existing leisure service delivery systems are based on "Industrial Revolution" assumptions; and these assumptions may no longer be relevant. As we shift from the industrial era to the information era, several factors have direct impact on leisure. Authors such as Bell, Toffler, and Naisbitt project a number of changes. Some of these follow:

Cultural Pluralism. Societies are becoming more diverse. For example, Dryfoos (1998) notes that in 1995 over two-thirds of teens (age fourteen to seventeen) were white and non-Hispanic, 15 percent were African American, 12 percent were of Hispanic origin, 4 percent were Asian, and less than 1 percent were Native American. By 2010, it is estimated that almost 40 percent of all youth will be non-white or Hispanic. Cultural infusion and a growing awareness of the recreation and leisure practices of Asians, Native peoples, those of African descent, Hispanics, and others will strongly influence the nature of leisure and recreation. Celebrations such as Cinco de Mayo, Kwanzaa, and other culturally relevant services will be found throughout our communities.

Urban versus Rural Society. Society will continue its shift from rural to urban areas; one study estimates that 80 percent of Americans will live in urban areas (Godbey, 1997). As a result, Godbey (1997) notes that the quality of urban life will be a critical variable to world peace and prosperity. Urban planners must continue to look for innovative ways to incorporate space for leisure as the density in urban areas continues to grow. For example, an urban society places much greater value on use of special buildings, rooms, entertainment, use of mass media, tolerance of individuality, more specialized goods, and involvement in leisure as a symbol of status. The increase in availability of electronic entertainment devices and home entertainment centers exemplifies this change.

Human Resources. Information-based societies place great value on human resources. Leisure becomes a process of assisting in the development of human resources— creativity, thinking, and positive human relations can be developed through leisure. Activities that encourage social interaction and use of cognitive skills will continue to be popular.

New Technology. New technology impacts leisure as well as other areas of society, including the structure of industry, the labor market, education, government, the family, and the cultural and psychological lives of individuals. In-line skates and jet skis are products of this new technology. Interactive television and the use of computers in generating visual images also demonstrate the infusion of technology into leisure and recreation alternatives.

Changing Demographics. Single-parent families, yuppies, flyers, evolving family structures, and other demographic changes influence leisure. Leisure service providers must be increasingly cognizant of the diverse market to meet the needs of their constituents.

Movement from Institutional Help to Self-Help. Self-help suggests that people can manage their own affairs effectively. This may result in less reliance on institutional and bureaucratic structures to provide leisure experiences and an increase in individually designed and sought-after experiences.

Spiritual and Personal Fulfillment. Greater emphasis is placed on personal fulfillment, spiritual fulfillment, and life satisfaction than in an industrial society. These will become a central concern of humankind. The search for spiritual meaning has huge implications for leisure and its use. Leisure has always been a medium for spiritual expression. "As the search for the spiritual intensifies, leisure activity may be based less around consumption and more around affirmation—affirming that life is good" (Godbey, 1997, p. 88).

Sophisticated Communications. Rapid communication via computers and satellites will enable new forms of leisure and a more socially and politically aware population. Interactive television, telephones that transmit live pictures, cellular phones from which one can send a fax, and the increase in use of fiber optics is transforming the nature of leisure and work.

Rapid Mobility. People can travel and move from one location to another quite rapidly. This affects leisure in dramatic ways, as travel and tourism continue to become more commonplace for the masses.

Changes in Perceptions of Leisure   Dramatic changes have occurred in perceptions of leisure during the technological or information era, with leisure increasingly viewed as an end in itself. Previous eras (especially the industrial era) viewed leisure instrumentally; that is, individual leisure was thought to be socially valuable. During the industrial era it was held that work time and leisure time were discrete. In the information era every life experience presents opportunities for leisure.

Environmental Services   One of the areas of greatest growth during the information era has been the increase in legislation and services related to the environment. Perhaps the most important factor influencing the growth of outdoor recreation services in the United States was the establishment of the Outdoor Recreation Resources Review Commission (ORRRC) in 1958. This commission made multiple recommendations leading to the expansion of outdoor recreation services at the federal, state, and local levels. A similar study—Canadian Outdoor Recreation Demands Study (CORDS), completed in the early 1970s—provided similar information for decision making in Canada.

In the 1960s, a federal Bureau of Outdoor Recreation was established in the United States to coordinate the work of various agencies. One of the most significant pieces of legislation passed was the Land and Water Conservation Fund Act in 1964. In the same year, the Wilderness Preservation Act was passed, and in 1968 the Wild and Scenic Rivers and National Trail System Act was established. Furthermore, the National Park System expanded dramatically through the acquisition of large tracts of land in Alaska in 1980. President Jimmy Carter authorized the Alaska National Interest Lands Conservation Act, tripling the size of the national preservation system. In 1986, President Ronald Reagan established a Commission on Americans Outdoors to encourage support for environmental issues. The report produced by this commission will be discussed in detail in a later chapter.

The increasing demand for outdoor recreation opportunities will create challenges for recreation professionals, but it also will create opportunities. People are interested in making a difference in the quality of our environment today. As a result, the parks and recreation profession has a wonderful opportunity. To make the most of this responsibility, Dustin, McAvoy,

Schultz (1995) advocate that parks and recreation professionals should serve as this society's environmental conscience and through the personal example of our lives demonstrate environmental wisdom in the conduct of our own lives.

Services for People with Disabilities Leisure services for people with disabilities also have expanded tremendously during the information era. Prior to the early 1950s, the historical development of services for the disabled could be traced to work of the American Red Cross in military hospitals and the development of recreation services in state hospitals and institutions. In the mid-1960s, the war in Vietnam and the human rights movement created new opportunities to fulfill the needs of persons with disabilities in a positive fashion.

Federal legislation has played an important role in expanding the public's awareness of the need for special services. Public Law 94–142, Education for All Handicapped Children Act, mandated equal rights for persons with disabilities and included therapeutic recreation services. In 1973, Section 504 of the Rehabilitation Services Act mandated that no discrimination could occur because of a disabling condition. Furthermore, a basic philosophical change occurred in the 1970s—services were deinstitutionalized and individuals were mainstreamed into community services. This resulted in an increased awareness of the need for local services for the disabled as a part of a community's offerings.

In the 1980s the influence of government in relation to services for those with disabilities lessened. Basically, this resulted in a number of strategies to finance the delivery of health-care services, including therapeutic recreation services for the disabled. Third-party (insurance) reimbursement systems have emerged and these, in turn, have created entrepreneurial opportunities for therapeutic recreation-service providers.

The 1990s saw a recommitment by the government to ensure that people with disabilities were treated fairly in all aspects of their lives. The Americans with Disabilities Act (ADA) of 1990 mandated fuller opportunities for persons with disabilities in community and educational services. The ADA is discussed more fully in other chapters of this book.

Travel and Tourism Tremendous changes have taken place since the early 1950s in the travel and tourism industry. Today, more people are mobile and travel opportunities are available to wider segments of the population than in past years. Tourism is now the world's largest composite industry with continued growth forecasted as we embarked in the twenty-first century. Tourism in the twenty-first century will likely continue to change; this is already evident as we see the number of options for tourists expanding. For example, eco-tourism options are increasing, according to the Stanford Research Institute; eco-tourism experienced 30 percent annual increases between 1990 and 1995 (Godbey, 1997). Furthermore, individuals continue to have more options in booking their own flights and setting up their own itineraries using the World Wide Web. These changes also are creating opportunities for many public parks and recreation departments as well as many private, nonprofit organizations (e.g., museums, nature centers, symphony orchestras) as they begin to recognize their role in tourism and seek to reposition themselves as sustainers and promoters of tourism.

Commercial Leisure Services The past several decades have seen tremendous growth in the area of commercial leisure services. One segment of the industry has provided a model for family leisure entertainment—family theme parks. The modern theme park can trace its origin to 1955 when Disneyland opened in Anaheim, California. Today, nearly every standard metropolitan area has a theme park. In four decades of operation, Disneyland increased its attendance from 3.8 million to 10 million visitors per year.

Leisure industries have become major contributors to the U. S. economy. Estimates reveal that in 1965, $58 billion was expended for leisure products; funds for leisure expenditures in the 1990s exceeded $430 billion. Televisions, radios, records, musical instruments, wheeled goods, toys, sports equipment, boats, and pleasure craft accounted for the majority of these sales. *Business Week* magazine ranked a composite of leisure-time industries seventeenth out of forty industries in the United States. Entrepreneurial activities in the commercial leisure field have resulted in a host of innovations from video home entertainment to leisure-related eating establishments featuring animatronics.

Summary

History may be thought of as the orderly and systematic reconstruction of the past. An analysis of the historical development of leisure can be useful for a number of reasons. By studying history, one gains knowledge of leisure concepts, an appreciation for the foundations of the profession, an understanding of the role of individuals in history, and knowledge of historical events and places. For professionals, the study of history fosters an understanding of the nature of life satisfaction and the impact of decision making, both in the present and for the future.

For the purposes of studying history and analyzing concepts of leisure, there are four distinct eras—preliterate society, the agricultural era, the industrial era, and the information era. During preliterate society, survival was the main concern, with few boundaries between work and leisure. During the agricultural era, division of labor created a leisure class.

The industrial era dramatically changed society's view of time, with a strong distinction between work time and leisure time. Many institutions were created during the Industrial Revolution, including parks, playgrounds, settlement houses, national parks, and youth serving organizations (e.g., Girl Scouts, Camp Fire, Inc., YMCA). The current information era, built on a different set of assumptions than the industrial era, requires a new set of strategies to meet people's needs.

Discussion Questions

1. What is history? What is historical research?
2. Why is the study of history useful to us as professionals?
3. The history of humankind can be divided into four distinct eras; what are they? How do the concepts of leisure vary within each era?
4. Compare and contrast leisure during the Middle Ages with leisure during the Renaissance.
5. Discuss how the concept of industriousness influenced early American colonials' perception of leisure.
6. Define a movement. Define an institution. When does a movement become institutionalized?
7. Identify four social reform movements leading to institutions during the industrial era.
8. Identify ten key leaders in the early organized park and recreation movement in Canada and the United States.
9. How does the information era differ from the industrial era?
10. List and discuss four new trends that have occurred in response to the information era.

References

Addams, J. 1893. The subjective necessity for social settlements: A new impulse to an old gospel. Edited by T. Y. Croswell, in *Philanthropy and Social Progress.* New York: Crowell.

American Camping Association. 1998. *ACA Fact Sheet.* Available at www.aca-camps.org/factsheet.htm.

Bell, D., ed. 1968. *Toward the Year 2000.* Boston: Houghton Mifflin.

Berstein, C. 1990. The leisure empire. *Time.* 136, 27.

Bowen, L. K. 1914. *Safeguards for City Youth at Work and at Play.* New York: Macmillan.

Bullaro, J., and C. Edginton. 1986. *Commercial Recreation: Managing for Profit, Service and Personal Satisfaction.* New York: Macmillan.

Chubb, M., and H. Chubb. 1981. *One Third of Our Time.* New York: John Wiley & Sons.

Curtis, H. 1917. *The Play Movement and Its Significance.* New York: Macmillan.

Dulles, F. 1965. *A History of Recreation: America Learns to Play.* New York: Simon & Schuster.

Durant, W. 1944. *The Story of Civilization: Part III Caesar and Christ.* New York: Simon & Schuster.

Durant, W. 1963. *The Story of Civilization: Part I Our Oriental Heritage.* New York: Simon & Schuster.

Durant, W. 1966. *The Story of Civilization: Part II The Life of Greece.* New York: Simon & Schuster.

Dryfoos, J. 1998. School-based health centers in the context of education reform. *Journal of School Health, 68*(10), 404–405.

Dustin, D., McAvoy, L., and Schultz, J. 1995. *Stewards of access, custodians of choice: A philosophical foundation for the park and recreation profession.* Champaign, IL: Sagamore.

Edwards, R. H. 1915. *Popular Amusements.* New York: Association Press.

Eells, E. 1986. *History of Organized Camping: The First 100 Years.* Martinsville, IN: American Camping Association.

Fabos, J., G. Milde, and V. Weinmayr. 1968. *Frederick Law Olmsted, Sr.* Amherst, MA: The University of Massachusetts Press.

Frye, V. 1980. Development of municipal parks and recreation. Edited by S. G. Lutzin, in *Managing Municipal Leisure Services.* International City Management Association.

Godbey, G. 1997. *Leisure and Leisure Services in the 21st Century.* State College, PA: Venture.

Henderson, K., D. Bialeschki, S. Shaw, and V. Freysinger. 1989. *A Leisure of One's Own: A Feminist Perspective on Women's Leisure.* State College, PA: Venture.

Henderson, K., D. Bialeschki, S. Shaw, and V. Freysinger. 1996. *Both Gains and Gaps: Feminist Perspectives on Women's Leisure.* State College, PA: Venture.

Johnson, M., ed. 1989. *The Many Faces of Hull House.* Chicago, IL: University of Illinois Press.

Kelly, J., and G. Godbey. 1992. *Sociology of Leisure.* State College, PA: Venture.

Kraus, R. 1984. *Recreation and Leisure in Modern Society.* 3d ed. Glenview, IL: Scott, Foresman.

Kraus, R. 1990. *Recreation and Leisure in Modern Society.* 4th ed. New York: HarperCollins.

Lee, J. 1925. *The Normal Course in Play.* New York: Barnes.

Lee, R. 1972. *Family Tree of the National Park System.* Philadelphia: Eastern National Park and Monument Association.

Lothian, W. 1977. *Extract from a history of Canada's national parks.* Parks Canada.

MacLean, J., J. Peterson, and D. Martin. 1985. *Recreation and Leisure: The Changing Scene.* 4th ed. New York: John Wiley and Sons.

Mattson, L. 1983. *The Camp Counselor: A Guidepost to Better Christian Camping.* Duluth, MN: Camping Guideposts.

McFarland, E. 1970. *The Development of Public Recreation in Canada.* Canada Parks and Recreation Association.

Naisbitt, J. 1982. *Megatrends.* New York: Warner Books.

Newton, N. 1971. *Design of the Land.* Cambridge, MA: The Belknap Press of Harvard University Press.

Olmsted, F. 1865. *The Yosemite Valley and the Mariposa Big Trees.*

Peters, T. 1987. *Thriving on Chaos.* New York: Alfred A. Knopf.

Runte, A. 1979. *National Parks: The American Experience.* Lincoln, NE: University of Nebraska Press.

Ryken, L. 1994. The Puritan ethic and Christian leisure for today. Edited by P. Heintzman, G. Van Andel, and T. Visker, in *Christianity and Leisure: Issues in a Pluralistic Society.* Sioux Center, IA: Dordt Press.

Sax, J. 1987. *Mountains without Handrails: Reflections on the National Parks.* Ann Arbor: University of Michigan Press.

Seuss, Dr. 1971. *The Lorax.* New York: Random House.

Staff. 1999. *An Engagement with God's World.* Grand Rapids, MI: Calvin College.

Swanson, R., and B. Spears. 1995. *History of Sports and Physical Education in the United States.* Boston, MA: WCB McGraw-Hill.

Talbot, W. T. 1905, May. Summer camp for boys. *The World's Work 6,* 174.

Toffler, A. 1982. *The Third Wave.* New York: William Morrow.

Williams, A., S. Lankford, and D. DeGraaf. 1996. A Presentation at the Leisure Research Symposium, Congress for Parks and Recreation, National Recreation and Park Association, Kansas City, MO.

Wilson, M. 1981. *Survival Skills for Managers.* Boulder, CO: Volunteer Management Associates.

CHAPTER 4

Philosophical and Conceptual Themes

Here, a woman painting in a garden is provided opportunites for creativity, self-expression, quiet thought, and reflection.

Introduction

A philosophy of leisure, so essential in guiding the work of a professional, provides understanding of direction, goals, and purpose. It provides a framework for action. Both individual and organizational philosophies reflect values, beliefs, priorities, and ideas about what is considered worth pursuing. In this light, philosophy has a direct relationship to perceived quality of life.

A philosophy, a highly practical tool in the hands of a leisure service professional, provides enduring stability and changes only marginally as the years pass. On the other hand, management techniques, types of programs, and types of areas and facilities change continuously. A philosophy provides vision and a core set of values that offer a long-term perspective. In addition, it provides a rationale for professional action, in contrast to the professional who operates without an underlying philosophy, in a vague, nondirected fashion.

A philosophy of leisure allows professionals to understand the "why" of their actions. To be successful as a professional, it is important not only to be a good technician but also to understand how one's professional actions have been influenced by underlying philosophical beliefs. Philosophy deals with the whys of our own beliefs as well as those of the organizations within which we work. For example, the Boys and Girls Club of America believes, philosophically, that their program shapes the character of young people in the United States by providing them with wholesome alternatives to life on the streets. This organization is built upon certain specific values, beliefs, and priorities. Its philosophy is directed toward providing educational, social, and recreational programs for children and young adults to build character, to train in responsibilities of community life, and to develop positive social skills. The Boys and Girls Club of America also cooperates and collaborates with various community groups with philosophies compatible with its own. Thus, Boys and Girls Club of America is often aligned philosophically with various religious, educational, civic, fraternal, business, and labor organizations, as well as corporations and professional associations.

This chapter has five major sections. The first section answers the question "What does the term philosophy mean?" The next section discusses the relationship of values and ethics. This is followed by a section examining why it is important to build a philosophy of leisure. The fourth section sets forth a process for developing a philosophy, and the last section discusses the role of philosophy in the work of an organization.

What Is Philosophy?

A *philosophy* may be thought of as a collection of *systematically defined values, beliefs, and preferences; its primary tool is reason.* A philosophy serves as a system that clarifies the values and principles used to guide and conduct one's professional life. It defines a set of beliefs that can be acted upon and which give meaning and direction to one's efforts.

Searle and Brayley (2000) help us to understand the importance of one's philosophy. They have written that one's philosophical approach ". . . influences how he or she conceptualizes leisure, recreation, play and so forth" (p. 49). And they note, ". . . we think of philosophy as denoting a set of basic values and attitudes toward life, the environment and society. It is a set of beliefs that guide our behavior" (p. 49).

A philosophy helps to determine priorities. It serves as a guide in dealing with the difficult questions that arise in everyday professional activities. It helps sort out what is important and what is not. Today, leisure service professionals face many problems and issues: overuse of resources, lack of funding, leisure awareness, and hedonism. These problems and issues, as well as others, require that the professional make decisions based on a set of core values. A philosophy can help to guide the professional in the assessment of these problems.

A philosophy is usually expressed as an abstract idea or set of constructs. These ideas or constructs, organized into a coherent framework, are called a philosophy of leisure or a philosophy of the management of leisure service organizations. While a professional's personal philosophy of leisure may not always be written, the philosophy used to manage leisure service organizations is imbedded in the vision or mission statement of the agency. The value of documenting an agency's philosophy lies in effective communication of its intentions to other individuals, groups, and organizations.

Philosophy and Circumstances

From where do philosophical ideas come? Philosophical beliefs derive from our society as well as from individual belief structures. Individual beliefs and cultural expectations constantly interact with one another to produce philosophical positions. As each life event occurs, philosophical ideas are engaged, challenged, affirmed, or in some way acted upon. In these interactions philosophy influences behavior and actions; life events have an influence upon our philosophical thought. Goodale and Godbey (1988) note ". . . there are numerous examples in history which provide clear indication of the interaction of philosophy and circumstances, some of which have and continue to have a direct bearing on our understanding of leisure" (p. 2).

Building a Philosophical Attitude

The park, recreation, and play movement was strongly motivated by a set of discrete values and principles at the turn of the century. In a study of the ethics of play, leisure, and recreation between 1900 and 1983, however, Sylvester (1987) observed that little research had been conducted on this subject. His research provides a descriptive map of the ethics of play, leisure, and recreation in the twentieth century. Sylvester analyzed more than eighty books, reports, articles, and monographs published between 1900 and 1983. Paraphrasing Sylvester, the following categories may be used to distinguish among philosophical approaches reported in these sources:

1. *Divine ends.* This philosophical approach suggests that play, leisure, or recreation is a part of God or a means of spiritual values of a religious, contemplative life.
2. *Happiness.* This approach includes creative work, personal happiness, spiritual balance, intellectual activity, spiritual freedom, harmonious living, and cultivation of the mind as ends of leisure, recreation, and play.
3. *Combination of work, play, love, and worship.* This philosophical approach finds a union of work, play, love, and worship. Basically, it perceives recreation as a means of revitalizing the individual.
4. *Self-actualization.* The self-actualization approach implies fulfillment or self-fulfillment through leisure.
5. *Play.* Play relates to play instincts or becomes a component of the ideal.
6. *Utopia.* Leisure play activities are an ends and a means leading to a utopian life according to this approach. Play and happiness are interrelated.
7. *No final end.* This approach views no grand end to play, leisure, or recreation, only personal ends or goals.
8. *Others.* Other philosophical approaches include life or knowledge, balance, character development, aesthetic appreciation, abundant living, joy, growth, personal freedom, well-being, and purposelessness.

As Sylvester (1987) notes, the most common end addressed by writers he studied in the twentieth century associated play, leisure, and recreation with divine ends. One quarter of the writers focusing on philosophical concerns of the leisure field associated values relating to play, leisure, and recreation to God, Christ, divine contemplation, and spiritual themes. The second most common end views play, leisure, and recreation in relationship to human happiness. These two categories account for 50 percent of the philosophical writings in the leisure service field from 1900 to 1983 (Sylvester, 1987).

Cooper (1999) has suggested that many questions can be probed from a philosophical perspective that are central to the question of understanding leisure. He writes: ". . . Most of us share a concept of leisure as free time, but there is considerable disagreement about which conception of this concept is best suited to guide theory" (Cooper, 1999, p. 3). He offers the following probing philosophical questions regarding leisure theory:

- Does unemployment count as free time, and hence leisure?
- How constraining can one's choice/situation be to leisure?
- Can one be at leisure while at work?
- Is the freedom of leisure the absence of causal determination, as an indeterminist philosopher might suggest?
- Is the freedom of leisure the freedom to exercise one's faculties as one wants, without care for the instrumental value of doing so?
- Does our clock-bound modern existence count as free time, or was true leisure available only in a past Golden Era, prior to the Industrial Revolution, when time for us was cyclical rather than linear, thanks to our being closer to the seasons and other aspects of nature (de Grazia, 1962)?
- Is the freedom of leisure more a reality for men than for women?
- Is our leisure distorted by class conflict? (p. 3)

Examination of these and other philosophical questions can help professionals discern their philosophy of leisure. To develop a philosophy of leisure one must probe such questions as an important first step in the process of clarifying one's ideas regarding leisure. Fundamentally, it is important to seek an understanding of the meaning of leisure for one's self in not only a personal context, but also a professional one. Still other important philosophical considerations can influence one's development. These may include framing a discussion regarding leisure by including such concepts as social justice, democracy, freedom, aesthetic appreciation, and others that give greater clarity and meaning to understanding one's concept of leisure.

Discussing the emergence of philosophical perspectives in the leisure service field, Murphy (1981, p. 2) suggests that the field ". . . has largely failed to provide the prospective educator and practitioner the opportunity to develop a meaningful, comprehensive interpretation of leisure because of a lack of significant guidelines". Ten years later, Fain (1991) suggests that "inquiry concerning the relationship between leisure and philosophy remains largely unconnected in both philosophy and leisure studies" (p. 16). In light of changes in social, cultural, and economic structures in the United States and Canada in recent years, one would expect changes in the philosophical approaches as well. As Fain (1991) notes, in recent years social circumstances have heavily influenced orientations to philosophies of leisure. Society tends to view leisure as an end in itself, as conceptually amoral, and as focusing on the value of exercising self-expression and satisfying individually determined needs.

It is interesting to note that the philosophical directions of the early play movement in America followed a reform pattern (Hunnicutt, 2000). Hunnicutt writes that a group of activists in the mainstream of America's Progressive movement provided powerful critiques of industrialization, urban society, and the excesses of capitalism. Their philosophical critiques suggested that modern life was alienating individuals and, with respect to leisure, Americans "were becoming passive in their free time, consuming rather than creating their amusements. 'Spectatoritis' was sweeping the land, alienating more and more people as fat, lazy, and quarrelsome bench-warmers" (p. 59). Hunnicutt (2000, p. 59) contends, "the best hope for men and women alienated at work was increasing leisure, leaders of our field were animated by inspiring vision of the mass, abundant leisure . . . leisure was opening astonishing new democratic vistas . . . [and] . . . with increasing leisure humans would be able to progress". These basic values or philosophical positions held by the early leaders of the movement strongly influenced their work in building the profession. Today, there is much debate about the availability of free time. Juliet Schor (1992), writing in *The Overworked American,* suggests that men and women who are employed full time are working longer hours. This is juxtaposed against the work of John Robinson and Geof Godbey (1997), writing in *Time for Life: The Surprising Ways Americans Use Their Time,* and Jeremy Rifkin's (1995) book *The End of Work,* which suggest increased free time, perhaps even enforced leisure.

The establishment and use of philosophical positions in the planning, organizing, and delivery of leisure services has been ambiguous in the United States and Canada in the past quarter of a century, with a few exceptions. For example, at the federal level of government in the United States, a strong commitment to preservation of natural resources guides the work of the National Park Service, and a strong orientation toward multiple use guides the work of the Forest Service. From a philosophical perspective, the work of local park and recreation agencies tends to be diffused, using varied means and seeking varied ends, depending upon local conditions. Far too often philosophical orientations at the local level of government are not articulated clearly, however, resulting in a lack of support, commitment, and direction for the work of these types of organizations. The work of youth serving agencies directed toward character development, citizenship, and other values (physical fitness, spiritual development) has provided a variety of philosophical orientations that meet this age group's needs. Today, some of these agencies are prospering, whereas others are seeking not only program redirection, but also philosophical reorientation.

The development of a clear and consistent philosophy regarding the purpose of work in the leisure services field is a demanding task. It requires considerable commitment to viewing alternatives and to debating the potential merits and outcomes of various philosophical approaches. All organizations are created for specific purposes. Like other organizations, leisure service organizations have goals; their goals are their reason for existence. Leisure service professionals must ask, "What goals are to be pursued?" "What human values within the leisure milieu are desirable and should be promoted?" and "What human experiences should be encouraged?" These questions require deliberation, analysis, and interaction with others. The development of an individual philosophy of leisure or a philosophy to manage a leisure service organization is the starting point for the work of a professional.

As one begins to examine her or his philosophical position, it becomes necessary to first review and articulate personal values as they interrelate with stated philosophies. Morality and ethics influence the world's systems—social, educational, leisure, work, religion, the military, the family, the environment, and others. In determining one's professional philosophical position and in articulating values, leisure service professionals question themselves: Do we promote competition over cooperation? Do we facilitate leisure experiences that might harm the environment? Are we passive about others' rights?

> A century ago, those interested in health, physical education, and recreation were among the nation's leaders—advocates, activists, and reformers campaigning for opportunities for children and youth and for a safe and healthy environment for us all. They cared about those to follow. We are their legatees, their beneficiaries. Unlike them, however, despite exceptions in some quarters and protestations from all, we no longer care about those to follow. Harsh words, but the evidence is persuasive. (Goodale, 1990, p. 27)

This reflection on the state of affairs in contemporary society challenges leisure service professionals to live responsibly in caring for future generations. All actions affect others, both today and tomorrow; no one lives in isolation. Making a choice today, no matter how minuscule, affects many others in future years.

Values and Philosophy

Most definitions of philosophy suggest that a philosophy reflects the values of the individual and/or organization. Just what are values? Edginton and Ford (1985) write that ". . . values are principles or guidelines that individuals regard as being important in life" (p. 178). As an ideal, a value has great usefulness or importance and affects all aspects of a person's life. Individuals and organizations operate based on an established set of ideals that govern their actions.

From a historical perspective, the park, recreation, and leisure service movement has pursued a number of specific values and principles. Some of these include the following:

1. *Preservation of natural resources.* To preserve natural resources suggests that land and water areas be maintained in a pristine or natural state for future generations.
2. *Conservation of natural resources.* Conservation of natural resources concerns the wise use of resources for multiple and compatible purposes. To conserve means to protect land and water resources while allowing compatible use of them for leisure and other activities.
3. *Wise use of leisure.* Much of the philosophical writing of the profession in the last decades focuses on using leisure for creative and spiritual development. Aristotle believed that wise

Enough Things

In an excerpt from her book *Finding Joy: 101 Ways to Free Your Spirit and Dance with Life,* Charlotte Davis Kasl writes the following:

There was a cartoon in the *New Yorker* portraying a man running toward the end of the rainbow only to see a pot of baked beans there. Whenever I think of striving for something I think of that image and realize its time to stop, breathe, and remember there's beauty in the ordinary.

Recently I visited a dear old friend. His sense of graciousness and ritual was as I remembered. . . . I sat at the table with the same green table cloth I had sat at 25 years before. I also saw the same bookshelves, the same tables, the same dishes, and the same couch as before. In a passing moment, a painful image flashed through my mind of the thousands of dollars I had spent on such items over the years and how little it mattered. How peaceful it was to be with him in this uncluttered home. I hold that image as I struggle to detach from wanting more things.

I went through a period of buying lots of pretty things in a compulsive way. I would buy something, and then after I had enjoyed it for a little while, I would start thinking about the next thing I would buy. One day a catalogue came in the mail with pictures of beautiful quilt covers and I started to fill out the order form. Then a part of me said, "No, stop." And as if I were led, I walked upstairs to my bedroom and sat down on my plain, natural cotton comforter and rubbed by hand over it. I said to myself, "Isn't this beautiful. It's mine, it's paid for, and it's restful. It is enough." Again and again I need to quell my restless mind and remind myself, *this is enough.*

So next time you sit down to a simple supper, crawl into a cozy bed, have a warm chat with a friend—imagine that you are at the end of the rainbow. This is it. This is life, and it's wonderful just in this moment.

Points to Ponder

- What ramifications does this quotation have for leisure experiences? Do you agree or disagree with the quotation? Explain your answer.
- How does this quotation support the theory that leisure is a state of mind? How can leisure professionals encourage this state of mind—encouraging people to enjoy the little things in life, to live in the present and make the most of their leisure time?
- Identify the philosophical orientation found within this quotation.

use of leisure was necessary in order to exercise the mind to promote intellectual thinking and advancement of civilization. This is known as the Aristotelian notion of leisure.

4. *Democracy, citizenship, and freedom of choice.* The assumption that freedom is essential to the leisure experience is fundamental to many concepts of play, leisure, and recreation (Sylvester, 1987). Organizations pursue this value in the creation of leisure services. The practice of democracy and promotion of patriotic values have been historically a function of institutions, particularly public institutions, in promoting leisure.

5. *Human happiness.* Human happiness, joy, fun, relaxation, pleasure, self-gratification, inner satisfaction, personal worth, and self-fulfillment are all values pursued within the leisure experience. Happiness and joy in life often occur through the act of engaging in freely chosen, meaningful leisure pursuits.

6. *Protection and promotion of human dignity.* Using leisure mediums to interact with people in a positive, constructive way—a value cherished by many leisure service organizations—promotes cooperation, respect for others, integrity, accessibility, and similar values.

7. *Personal growth.* One of the underlying values of leisure service organizations has involved promoting human growth and development. Organizations are often structured to encourage physical, intellectual, spiritual, social, and educational development.

8. *Leisure awareness.* Another value subscribed to by individuals and organizations has been the education of individuals to the availability of leisure opportunities. These values often provide the foundation for development of lifelong leisure skills.

9. *Leadership and moral character development.* Leisure professionals and organizations have long cultivated leadership skills and techniques and moral character development as important values. This is especially true in the creation of volunteer opportunities and in athletic clubs.

10. *Quality of life.* The creation of support networks to promote a hospitable living environment for individuals has constituted a major value. Professionals in the leisure field promote aesthetic opportunities (physical environment, beauty in community life), social opportunities (contact with others), psychological well-being (safety), and economic (tourism) components that, when present, assure a higher quality of life.

By no means are these the only values that are pursued by individuals or agencies providing leisure services. They do represent many of the major values, however, that have been pursued by the movement as a whole.

Values and Ethics

Whether a part of the major value movements identified above or personally desired, values are the underlying structures that shape and influence each person's ethics. Philosophies help to define values, and ethics are the exercise of those values. Values are not facts. They are principles and belief systems and tend to be enduring; that is, once they are learned, values tend to persist (Hitt, 1990). They serve as a foundation for a particular philosophical position one takes. This section deals with the role of values in defining self.

A values-free environment? Contrary to a belief held by many, a values-free or totally objective environment does not exist. People continually impart values, whether intentionally or unintentionally (Edginton and Edginton, 1993). What is or is not said, attitudes, and actions taken or left undone—these factors all communicate values. Values provide guidance to people's lives in two particular areas: (1) modes of conduct (behaviors), and (2) desired end-states (goals). Societies in the United States and Canada tend to attribute more worth to things that require the exercise of an ethical position—wrestling with the pros and cons of an issue.

Values shape individual lives. Hitt (1990) suggests that values shape personal lives, contribute to beliefs about the good life, provide direction, and give meaning to lives. Values determine what actions, thoughts, and attitudes constitute acceptable behavior for individuals and society. For instance, if a person values the rights of all living beings, environmental preservation and conservation might take precedence in that person's life with behaviors that could include recycling, planting only native plants in the backyard, watching nature shows, and becoming involved in local environmental groups. Seeing these behaviors, others might identify that individual as an environmentalist.

The need for value clarity. Individuals are bombarded with many different types of values every day—at school, on television, in church, at home, and in other activities. Certainly, MTV (Music Television) may impart different values than PBS (the Public Broadcasting System). Young people, as well as older people, can become confused by the avalanche of conflicting information regarding values. The following quotation from Raths, Harmon, and Simon, cited as a foundational concept in Purpel and Ryan (1976), serves as a base for discussion of moral education in the schools. It addresses the need for individuals to attain value clarity in order to function in a positive, productive manner.

Persons experiencing values confusion ". . . are often identifiable by idiosyncratic behavior patterns— apathy, flightiness, extreme uncertainty, and inconsistency; drift, overconformity, overdissension, and chronic posing, and frequently underachievement." On the other hand, those who have attained value clarity do not manifest these characteristics, but are "positive, purposeful, enthusiastic and proud." With this in mind, it is of paramount importance that each individual consider and clarify his/her values. (p. 153)

> *The good life.* Values contribute to basic beliefs about the good life and what constitutes life satisfaction. They serve as markers by which people measure levels of satisfaction. If a person believes that "the one who dies with the most toys wins," then accumulating material goods would be top priority. The need for more things would drive that person's decisions, actions, and search for fulfillment. If, on the other hand, an individual believes that life satisfaction comes from making others happy, then behaviors would be so directed. Volunteerism and an altruistic mind-set, giving to others, donating one's time and creativity, and being empathetic are manifestations of this values-based orientation.
>
> *Values as underlying structures.* Underlying values guide individuals in making choices. They affect a person's choice of food, friends, activities, language or dialect, clothing, and responses to others. A belief or values system influences whether hair is worn long or short, braided or loose. Values make the person, help to provide self-definition, and determine when one will stand or yield. Values also give meaning to life—people feel good about themselves when their thoughts, attitudes, and actions agree with their values.

Figure 4.1 shows a cartoon character who appears to be questioning his values. He appears to have highly valued winning, but after achieving his goal, he is disappointed and is now reconsidering that value.

Calvin and Hobbes   by Bill Watterson

Figure 4.1

Rethinking values related to winning

The Value in an Ethic of Care

The value exhibited in the comic strip is unsatisfactory in and of itself; people will want to examine the topic from alternative paradigms or worldviews. One paradigm views values and ethics issues from a rights and justice approach, which assumes one right answer that is fair and just for everyone. In leisure service organizations, this manifests in fairly cut-and-dried pronouncements through policies, regulations, and rules.

An ethic of care, on the other hand, considers values and ethics from a different view. It involves seeing and responding to needs, includes a sense of relationship, and takes care of issues while maintaining connections. A leisure services professional who follows the ethic of care would respond to moral and ethical issues and develop a personal philosophy out of caring and concern for others, and might not follow rules and policies exactly. As an example consider the following ethical dilemma:

A leisure service employee consistently arrives late to work. As the assistant director, the employee is scheduled to arrive at 8:00 A.M. each morning to open the recreation facility. Every day, however, he arrives between 8:15 and 8:30 A.M. Upon being questioned by the executive director about the consistent tardiness, the employee indicates that the responsibility for seeing off his young child for school each day rests with him; he cannot arrive at the center any earlier.

If one were to apply an ethic of rights and justice in dealing with this individual, the executive director might indicate that while she understood the dilemma, no one else received special consideration for family obligations, and if he could not arrive at work on time, perhaps he should rethink his position with the department. After all, it would not be fair to others.

Applying the ethic of care, the executive director and the assistant director would attempt to make arrangements to accommodate the employee's obligations at home. In an ethic of care, what is right is what maintains connections and relationships. An arrangement to open later or have someone else be responsible for opening the center would allow the assistant director to meet both his family and work obligations without compromising either. The relationship to family and work were both considered in the decision-making process.

Increasingly, an ethic of care orientation has entered the workplace. Shared management styles and tools such as Total Quality Management (TQM) use aspects of an ethic of care and

L e i s u r e   L i n e

What's the World Coming To?

To the editor:

Although I am only 12 years old I can tell poor sportsmanship when I see it. Not among young people like myself but among adults.

On June 16 our team was playing the Rockway team. With four minutes left to play and the score 1–0 in our favor a Rockway boy kicked the ball down the sideline. I and most people thought it went out, and the ref called it that way. Suddenly a Rockway father jumped out on the pitch and started hassling the ref. After a great deal of arguing the man hit the ref. When the ref walked away the man spit on him. After the game the man punched the ref again. He hassled the ref all the way to his car.

We have had many similar experiences and it ruins the game. It must be very frustrating for the referees who are only trying to do their best.

My friends and I play soccer for the fun of it, and we wonder, what is the world coming to?

Letter to the editor that appeared in the *Kitchener-Waterloo Record*, June 19, 1976.

have become established in business practices in manufacturing, technology, and human services. Treating employees like family members, sharing in the decision-making responsibilities, promoting a concern for others, and cooperative work teams all help to establish an ethic of care within an organizational structure. Understanding personal values and ethics aids in the development of a philosophy; now is the time to examine why it is important to build a personal philosophy of leisure.

Why Build a Philosophy of Leisure?

A number of important reasons exist to establish a personal philosophy of leisure as well as to understand the philosophies of leisure service organizations. From an individual perspective, having a personal philosophy of leisure provides a value structure upon which one might act. A personal philosophy presents a source of beliefs that guide an individual's behavior and professional actions.

A personal philosophy can serve as a strong sense of inspiration and encouragement to an individual. If one believes in an ideal strongly enough, it can encourage enthusiastic and committed behavior. When channeled toward an ideal, these types of behaviors can result in the creation of programs, services, organizations, and institutions that influence individuals, communities, and perhaps an entire society.

By knowing the philosophy of a leisure service organization, one can align his or her energies in a harmonious fashion with the work of that agency. When one's personal philosophy is consistent with the philosophy of the organization, harmony and congruence will likely exist. This can result in increased productivity and greater work satisfaction. On the other hand, if an individual's personal philosophy does not align with that of the organization, that individual might seek to influence the philosophy of the organization. Interestingly, ". . . one sign of a healthy organizational culture is congruence between the organization's statement of values and the daily behavior of its members" (Hitt, 1988, p. 86). Four major reasons for building a philosophy follow (see figure 4.2).

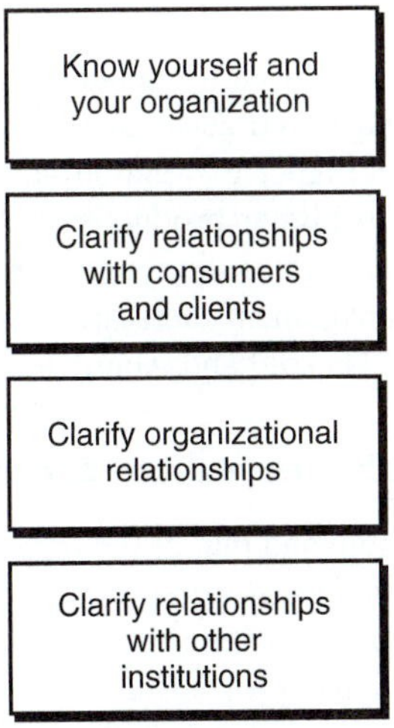

Know yourself and
your organization

Clarify relationships
with consumers
and clients

Clarify organizational
relationships

Clarify relationships
with other
institutions

Figure 4.2

Reasons for
building an
organizational
philosophy

To Know Yourself as Well as Your Organization

A personal philosophy of leisure helps to clarify important personal values regarding leisure. As Goodale and Godbey (1988, p. 2) write, "One of the uses of philosophy may be to help us understand ourselves and our circumstances and thereby reduce or at least better cope with our uncertainty and anxiety". The search for values forms a central theme throughout people's lives; individuals are confronted with major decisions about how they live. The way in which people have been socialized to certain values throughout their lives has a great impact on their responses to events and experiences. For example, if we have been socialized in our youth to value cooperation as contrasted with competition, this value will affect our personal philosophy and our leisure choices. If we value individual behavior versus teamwork, this, too, will have an impact.

One can examine personal beliefs by developing a personal philosophy of leisure. By focusing on what they consider important and articulating it, professionals begin to know themselves, their values, and what they believe. These values and beliefs, in turn, influence one's actions. If a person believes that the leisure experience is a spiritual or emotional one, that person will act differently than one who believes that the leisure experience is a frivolous expression of status in society. Perhaps the greatest challenge an individual has is to truly understand personal beliefs and values.

As mentioned, it is imperative to determine the value system of the organizations with which one interacts. All organizations have a set of guiding beliefs that influence their work. These guiding beliefs represent their philosophical underpinnings and as fundamental foundational statements, they rarely change. They are usually written broadly enough to incorporate a diverse number of situations that arise. Such beliefs, usually viewed as universal enduring truths, have broad appeal to both the individuals working within the organization and to the constituency served by the organization and society as a whole.

The vision statement of the Willamalane Park and Recreation District provides a good example of a set of guiding beliefs for a leisure service organization. This statement, written in an inspiring manner, appeals to individuals working within that system as well as to the public at large. It includes foundational beliefs, some of which suggest working as a partner, promoting happiness, growth, and well-being, and serving as a leader in the progressive development and care of attractive and hospitable places (see figure 4.3). Figure 4.4 presents the organization's brief mission statement.

Daily actions within an organization partly depend upon personal beliefs and values and partly upon understanding, knowledge, and acceptance of the guiding beliefs or values of the agency. As previously mentioned, a higher correlation between one's personal beliefs and the organization's beliefs contributes to higher productivity. Conversely, a low relationship between one's personal beliefs and the organization's goals results in poor organizational performance. This is referred to in the management literature as *goal interdependence* or *work alignment* (Jordan and Mertesdorf, 1994; Naisbitt and Aburdene, 1985).

To Clarify Relationships with Consumers/Clients

Understanding one's own value system and that of the organization provides a basis for interaction with consumers or clients. From a broad perspective, the leisure professional who operates from a particular value structure is in a position to influence the interaction that occurs with a client or consumer. A positive relationship of influence is mutually beneficial and satisfies the needs of the consumer in a manner consistent with the value structure of the organization. On

**Willamalane**
Park & Recreation District

Figure 4.3
Example of a
vision statement

Willamalane's Vision

Willamalane Park and Recreation District is a *partnership* of people dedicated to the happiness, growth, and well-being of the residents. This dynamic partnership will be committed to enhancing the quality of life in Springfield and will be a source of pride to everyone. The human spirit will be emphasized in all Willamalane does, resulting in superior services and an atmosphere of cooperation, openness, trust, and inventiveness.

Willamalane will be a *leader* in the progressive development and care of attractive and hospitable places where people may enrich their lives. Willamalane will always treasure our heritage and natural resources and will preserve and provide priceless open spaces for the children of the future.

Willamalane will be a *friend* who will offer unique opportunities for people of all ages and abilities to enjoy friendship and laughter, the beauty of nature, and a sense of well-being. With Willamalane, people will have the chance to experience the joy of learning and sharing, the thrill of adventure and discovery, and the pride of achievement and service.

Willamalane is dedicated to the *dreams* of its residents. Willamalane's tomorrows will be built on the dreams of today.

**Willamalane**
Park & Recreation District

Figure 4.4
Example of a
mission
statement

Mission Statement

"THE PURPOSE OF THE DISTRICT IS TO PROVIDE FOR THE PEOPLE'S PURSUIT OF HAPPINESS."

the other hand, the professional can use influence in inappropriate ways that are detrimental to consumers and the organization.

Organizational values help the consumer or client understand what services the organization will provide and from what perspective. Therefore, establishment of organizational values makes the work of the professional easier because it specifies the spheres of activity. Also, foundational statements or beliefs can provide information concerning specific consumer/client relations and deal with topics such as confidentiality, autonomy, degree of independence, service orientation, and openness to new ideas. The professional gains an advantage in knowing these values because they establish a code of ethics or behavior to guide professional practice.

To Clarify Relationships within the Organization

Knowledge of the guiding beliefs of an organization also can contribute to harmonious working relationships within the organization as a whole. Every organization has various components or units. Some of these components engage in work that could be defined as central to the mission of the organization, while others serve in a support capacity. Various units use various approaches to solving problems, managing resources, and conducting business. As long as all of the units pull toward the overriding, guiding beliefs and values of the organization, harmony will exist.

Often, leisure service organizations establish a set of policies and procedures based on guiding values and beliefs. These policies and beliefs usually translate values into practice. They help in making the daily decisions that guide organizational work. Shared values within an organization provide for a degree of internal consistency and allow for the work of an organization to become directed toward a common end.

To Clarify Relationships with Other Institutions

Knowledge of the guiding beliefs of an organization helps clarify interactions with other agencies and institutions. External relationships affect the success of an organization as much as internal ones. Externally communicated values and beliefs create a mental image of the quality, value, and caliber of professional efforts. For example, if a leisure service organization promotes such values as innovation, integrity, quality, service, teamwork, and community involvement, these will, in turn, influence others' perception of that organization.

L e i s u r e   L i n e

Nash's Hierarchy of Leisure Pursuits

In his book, *Philosophy of Recreation and Leisure* (1960), J. B. Nash has suggested that leisure is an age-old dream of humankind. He placed different kinds of recreation into a hierarchy on the basis of their potential value to the individual and society. Nash suggests that to use leisure intelligently and profitably is the most important test of a civilization. As he indicates, "the machine liberates, but for what? Does real happiness lie in achievement and the anticipation of the adventure or in rest and security?" Nash has suggested that people can use leisure in many different ways. Some contribute to society's well-being, whereas others do not. A little of each above zero, depending on work patterns, may be good, but too many activities low on the scale are dulling, and in the end progress and development of the individual and the group are slowed.

Some value statements directly relate to relationships with other agencies and emphasize values such as cooperation, communication, and coordination of services. Interestingly, organizations that are perceived to be successful and of great benefit to society often attract individuals and agencies who want to be aligned with them. A positive set of values or philosophy, backed by action, can result in the cultivation of highly positive attitudes toward the organization. For example, corporations that recognize their citizenship responsibilities and contribute to the development of the communities within which they operate tend to be more successful over the long term than those corporations that ignore broader societal values.

Building a Philosophy

Major Philosophies

A number of different philosophical constructs can be applied to leisure and may assist in developing a philosophy of leisure. Seven such philosophical constructs have general application to this discussion—perennialism, idealism, realism, experimentalism, existentialism, pragmatism, and humanism (see figure 4.5). These philosophies represent a broad spectrum of thinking that applies to understanding leisure as well as to the management of leisure service organizations. They present particular explanations as to the nature of truth and provide principles that can serve to guide the conduct of a professional. Individuals holding these various philosophical positions may have different views regarding the leisure experience and, as a result, create different approaches or methods for organizing services.

What a person believes affects that person's behavior. In the context of organizing leisure services, if one believes, for example, that a leisure service organization is focused on helping individuals develop their potential as human beings, one acts upon the philosophy of humanism.

Figure 4.5

Seven major philosophical constructs

On the other hand, when a leisure service organization, such as the YMCA, uses its progress to promote spiritual values, it acts upon the philosophy of perennialism. A discussion of each of these seven philosophical constructs follows.

Perennialism and Leisure As Sylvester (1987) reports, much of the philosophical literature written over the last eighty years presumes that play, leisure, or recreation is linked to spiritual values. Perennialism builds on the belief that life is constant and unchanging, and that eternal truths exist. Perennialists believe that the distinguishing characteristic of human beings is the ability to reason; therefore, life events should focus on developing rationality and discovering truth through study and divine inspiration.

A perennialist views leisure as an opportunity to bring individuals closer to God and to promote spiritual values. Play, leisure, and recreation are seen in the context of eternal truths presented in documents such as the Bible, the Koran, or the teachings of Buddha or Confucius. Reviewing the writings within such documents, leisure becomes a means or opportunity for celebration, harmony, union with God, joy, peace, revitalization, and contemplation. Many youth serving organizations are built upon philosophies emphasizing the philosophical position of perennialism. For example, in 1844, the Young Men's Christian Association (YMCA) was established for the purpose of ". . . influencing young men to spread the Redeemer's kingdom amongst those by whom they are surrounded" (Hopkins, 1951, p. 5).

Idealism and Leisure The philosophical construct of idealism builds upon the notion that some individuals act according to what they believe in, regardless of what people think or the consequences of their actions. Idealists value and attempt to adhere to fine ideals. They formulate and define their own individual ideals, which may or may not be reality based. Reality emerges from within the person's own mind. Zigler (1964) writes,

> Idealists believe, generally, that the mind (or spirit) as experienced by all men [*sic*] is basic and real. . . . One's own self is the immediate reality in his conscious experience; man is more than just a body; he possesses a soul. . . . Idealism holds that the world's order is due to a spiritual reality . . . man [should be] able to interpret his world accurately and as a part of the whole." (p. 196)

Idealists value consistency of ideas. To the idealist, values remain constant and unchanging and must be preserved. How would one use idealism to develop a philosophy of leisure? Idealists pursue specific values that they perceive to be reality itself, regardless of most practical limitations. The extent to which these values could be attained through leisure would depend upon the individual's ability to choose appropriate leisure experiences that promote or protect cherished values. From an idealist's perspective, many values are promoted through leisure services (e.g., preservation, conservation, quality of life). These ideals remain constant, represent the wisdom of the ages, and are worthy of pursuit. Leisure services supporting the idealistic philosophy might pursue activities such as promoting understanding and harmony among people of the world, promoting the ideal in nature, and other similar global themes.

Realism and Leisure Realism as a philosophy builds on works drawn from Aristotle. A realist is concerned with revealing the natural order of the world and of the universe. Realists hold that objects have an existence independent of human consciousness of them. A realist would be interested in what is real and practical rather than what is ideal or theoretical. Realists hold a different perception toward change than do either perennialists or idealists. They view change as a natural evolution that results in a perfection of order.

The realist sees the world as it is materially. As a result, the individual using realism as a philosophy in the context of a leisure service organization would use the leisure experience to learn about and define reality—to help people get in touch with the world. For the realist, goodness lies in the laws of nature and the natural order of the world and the universe. According to Zigler (1964), the realist sees play and work as distinct and sharply defined separate parts of life. The realist views leisure as a means to rejuvenate individuals to work more effectively.

Pragmatism and Leisure Pragmatism tests the value and truth of ideas by their practical consequences. Several American philosophers in the 1800s formulated this philosophy. Such individuals as William James, Charles Pierce, and John Dewey were proponents of this philosophy. They claimed that an idea only worked when actions based upon it produced results. Pragmatists view the world as constantly changing. Ideas must be tested through experience and are practical in nature.

Pragmatists believe that leisure should promote specific ends or specific observable, measurable results. Pragmatists maintain that if leisure services have true value they should produce practical, measurable results. For example, using a pragmatic approach, if a day camp staff surveyed its campers to determine the effects of the day camp experience on self-concept and the program intervention produced an increased level of positive self-concept in the campers, then this type of leisure experience promoted specific, measurable ends, supporting the pragmatist ideal.

Experimentalism and Leisure Experimentalism is a philosophy that suggests the world is ever changing. Like the pragmatist, the experimentalist is concerned with what works and what does not. Experimentalists seek to discover and expand the society and culture in which they live and to share these experiences with others. Leisure used as a medium by the experimentalist would help people explore different life experiences. Experimentalists encourage decisions to be made about the outcomes of leisure experiences in light of the consequences to the individual and to society as a whole.

Experimentalists see the role of leisure service organizations as emphasizing experiences. The leisure service leader would aid or consult with participants to help them discover and experience their world. They would be encouraged to test reality to determine what works in light of societal norms, customs, and values. Experimentalists openly accept change and shape the leisure experience in such a way as to improve upon the conditions of society and culture. Leisure programs would have a strong value component and would rely upon group cohesion, group problem solving, and group norms to shape individual behavior.

Existentialism and Leisure Existential philosophy developed in the 1800s from the works of Kierkegaard and Nietzche. Existentialism suggests that reality consists of living. Furthermore, existentialist philosophy suggests that individuals develop themselves and are responsible *only* to themselves for their behavior. For the existentialist, life is a world of existing, of personal choice, subjective choice, and freedom.

"Existentialists at play want no prescribed formations, no coach calling plays and destroying the players' 'authenticity,' and no crowd exhorting them to win at any cost" (Zigler, 1977, p. 200). Through leisure, participants guided by existentialism pursue unregimented experiences. The individual leisure experience focuses on developing or creating one's own rules. For the existentialist, change is constant and viewed as a natural and necessary phenomenon. Leisure service organizations based on existentialist philosophy would view themselves as existing to enable participants to define and pursue their own leisure means and ends. No attempt would be made to impose organizational values upon participants; rather, an attempt would be made to help individuals know themselves.

Humanism and Leisure   Humanism, as a philosophy, deals with the actions or thought processes that focus on human interests and values. More specifically, humanists suggest that humans are ". . . the supreme value in the universe and that human beings should, therefore, be concerned with human interests rather than . . . [with those of spiritual or divine beings, such as God]" (Murphy, 1981, p. 18). Humanism is concerned with the development of the potential of the individual. It focuses upon the promotion and protection of human dignity as well as cultivating the capabilities of the individual. Humanistic philosophy is contrary to perennialism. It does not espouse an eternal or universal set of means or ends. In addition, whereas perennialism speaks to the existence of a divine being, humanism does not.

Humanism has been actively applied to the leisure services field. In particular, Grey and Greben (1974) suggest that the park and recreation field ". . . adopt a humanistic ethic as the central value system of the movement" (p. 53). Murphy (1981) suggests that ". . . leisure provides each person with an opportunity to realize his or her full potential" (p. 19). He further indicates that through leisure individuals will have the opportunity to achieve joy, mastery, uniqueness, self-realization, and shared experience. Leisure serves as a wellspring for personal liberation and in this way can enable individuals to be personally autonomous, not only in their intellectual beliefs but in their aesthetic experiences, their romantic preferences, their moral tastes and values, and, ultimately, their development as human beings.

Steps to Building a Philosophy

The construction of a philosophy of leisure is no easy task. It involves examining information from a variety of sources and carefully analyzing this information with the knowledge gained about approaches to studying philosophy (see figure 4.6). A number of specific activities can be used to collect information for examination. Some of these involve reading, interviewing others, or studying the ideas found in existing leisure organizations. Still others involve taking a critical view of one's own ideas and values as well as identifying some of the major values that influence society as a whole. Specific steps that can be taken in the development of a philosophy of leisure include the following:

1. *Examine the historical philosophical foundations of the profession.* An important step in the process of developing a philosophy of leisure involves examining the historical foundations of the profession. A wide array of books, articles, and monographs written in the past century espouse various philosophies and serve as the foundation of current thinking today.

2. *Examine one's own personal values.* Development of a philosophy requires consideration of one's own personal values. For example, what do you value as a result of your own thinking, as well as the influence of your family, peers, education, religion, and community? What specifically about the field of leisure do you value or consider worthwhile? What events have shaped your values and philosophy? What has frustrated you or disillusioned you regarding leisure values? What has excited you about the field of leisure? What contributions do you think you can make to others and the leisure field based on your values and philosophy of leisure?

3. *Discuss with professionals their philosophy and values.* Professionals working in the field provide an excellent source of information concerning the philosophy and values of the field. Often, they have developed well-articulated values or philosophies that guide their

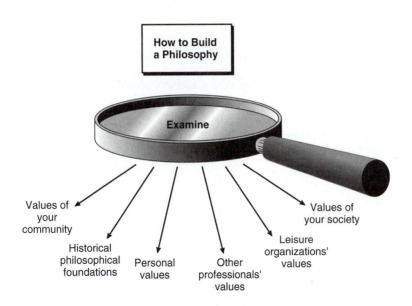

Figure 4.6

Building a leisure philosophy

How to Build a Philosophy

Examine

Values of your community

Historical philosophical foundations

Personal values

Other professionals' values

Leisure organizations' values

Values of your society

professional actions. Discussions with professionals from various subfields within the profession (i.e., youth serving agencies, federal agencies, commercial organizations, and community park and recreation centers) can provide valuable insight into the differences in philosophical orientation between agencies. Often asking professionals the question, "Why did you decide to become a part of this field?" opens communication and begins instructional dialogue.

4. *Examine the values of organizations delivering leisure services.* Organizations delivering leisure services often have explicit or expressed and implicit or implied values. The explicit, expressed values appear in mission statements, vision statements, goals and objectives, and policy and procedure documents. A review of these documents can provide valuable insight into the values of the leisure service organization. One agency promotes social interaction within a community, whereas another emphasizes the acquisition of land and water resources for preservation or conservation purposes. Implicit, implied values, often difficult to grasp, form the unwritten values of an organization. These can be learned by discussing values with several members of an organization to determine whether consistency exists between expressed and implied values and if there is consistency among several staff members, even if the values are only implied.

5. *Examine the values of the local community.* A person's local community consists of individuals, groups, and institutions, all of whom have values. Some communities are far more homogeneous than are others in the pursuit of a common set of values. Every community holds a set of common values, norms, and customs, however, that bind people together to produce community life. These values can have a great impact on how people live their lives and upon each person's values. Every community also has agencies within it, including leisure service agencies, that actively work to promote and cultivate certain values. Think of the influence upon the development of public character and morals by organizations and agencies such as senior centers, Girl Scouts, Camp Fire Boys and Girls, city parks and recreation departments, Special Olympics, 4–H, YMCA, or military recreation departments.

Anderson, N. 1985. *Work and Leisure.* New York: Glencoe Press.

Brightbill, C. K. 1960. *The Challenge of Leisure.* Englewood Cliffs, NJ: Prentice-Hall.

Brightbill, C. K. 1961. *Man and Leisure: A Philosophy of Recreation.* Englewood Cliffs, NJ: Prentice-Hall.

Dare, B., G. Welton, and W. Coe. 1987. *Concepts of Leisure in Western Thought: A Critical and Historical Analysis.* Dubuque, IA: Kendall/Hunt Publishing Co.

de Grazia, S. 1962. *Of Time, Work and Leisure.* Garden City, NY: Doubleday.

Driver, B. L., T. Dustin, T. Baltic, G. Elsner, and G. Peterson. 1996. *Nature and the Human Spirit.* State College, PA: Venture.

Dustin, D. L., L. H. McAvoy, and J. H. Schultz. 1995. *Stewards of Access/Custodians of Choice.* 2d ed. Champaign, IL: Sagamore.

Dumazedier, J. 1974. *Sociology of Leisure.* New York: Elsevier.

Fain, G., ed. 1991. *Leisure and Ethics: Reflections on the Philosophy of Leisure.* Reston, VA: American Alliance of Health, Physical Education, Recreation and Dance.

Godbey, G. 1990. *Leisure in Your Life.* 3d ed. State College, PA: Venture.

Goodale, T. L., and G. C. Godbey. 1988. *The Evolution of Leisure: Historical and Philosophical Perspectives.* State College, PA: Venture.

Goodale, T. L., and P. A. Witt, 1990. *Recreation and Leisure: Issues in an Era of Change.* 3d ed. State College, PA: Venture.

Grey, D., and S. Greben. 1974. Future perspectives. *Parks and Recreation Magazine* 9 (7), 26–33, 47–56.

Henderson, K., M. D. Bialeschki, S. Shaw, and V. Freysinger. 1996. *Both Gains and Gaps: Feminist Perspectives on Women's Leisure.* State College, PA: Venture.

Henderson, K., M. D. Bileschki, S. M. Shaw, and V. Freysinger, 1989. *A Leisure of One's Own.* State College, PA: Venture.

Huizinga, J. 1955. *Homo Ludens: A Study of the Play Element in Culture.* Boston: Beacon Press.

Kaplan, M. 1975. *Leisure: Theory and Policy.* New York: Wiley.

Kelly, J. 1987. *Freedom to Be.* New York: Macmillan.

Kimeldorf, M. 1994. *Serious Play.* Berkeley, CA: Ten Speed.

Lee, J. 1916. *Play in Education.* New York: Macmillan.

Lee, R. 1964. *Religion and Leisure in America.* Nashville, TN: Abingdon Press.

Leitner, M. J., and S. F. Leitner. 1996. *Leisure Enhancement.* New York: Haworth Press.

Levy, J. 1978. *Play Behavior.* New York: Wiley.

Lindner, S. B. 1970. *The Harried Leisure Class.* New York: Columbia University Press.

Murphy, J. 1981. *Concepts of Leisure.* Englewood Cliffs, NJ: Prentice-Hall.

Nash, J. B. 1965. *Recreation: Pertinent Readings.* Dubuque, IA: Wm. C. Brown.

Nash, J. B. 1981. *Philosophy of Recreation and Leisure.* Dubuque, IA: Wm. C. Brown.

Peiper, J. 1963. *Leisure: The Basis of Culture.* New York: Mentor-Omega Books.

Roberts, K. 1970. *Leisure.* London: Longman Group.

Rojek, C. 1985. *Capitalism and Leisure Theory.* New York: Travistock.

Russell, R. 1996. *Pastimes: The Context of Contemporary Leisure.* Madison, WI: Brown & Benchmark.

Shivers, J. S. 1981. *Leisure and Recreation Concepts: A Critical Analysis.* Boston, MA: Allyn & Bacon.

Staley, E. J., and N. P. Miller, eds. 1972. *Leisure and the Quality of Life.* Washington, DC: AAHPER.

Sutton-Smith, B., and D. Kelly-Byrne, eds. 1984. *The Masks of Play.* New York: Leisure Press.

Sylvester, C. 1987. The ethics of play, leisure and recreation in the twentieth century, 1900–1983. *Leisure Sciences 9,* 173–188.

Thoreau, H. D. 1910. *Walden.* Boston, MA: Houghton Mifflin.

Veblen, T. 1963. *The Theory of the Leisure Class. An Economic Study of Institutions.* New York: New American Library.

Wade, M., ed. 1985. *Constraints on Leisure.* Springfield, IL: Charles C. Thomas.

6. *Examine the values of society as a whole as they relate to leisure.* The United States and Canada are greatly influenced by the Judeo-Christian ethic, which permeates and influences our basic value structure. The Judeo-Christian ethic aligns hard work with righteousness, integrity, and morality. It also emphasizes other values such as love of fellow human beings and faith. Democratic institutions also provide a set of societal values; democracy implies freedom of choice. Other institutions that greatly influence values include work, school, the family, the national media, and the military.

A periodic review of one's philosophy can be beneficial, especially in light of the emergence of new knowledge and changing conditions within the environment. Professionals find it useful to write down ideas concerning values and philosophy throughout their careers. Often, a review of personal and professional philosophies and values serves to reinforce and recommit individuals to their original beliefs. Having a written philosophical statement and referring to it frequently provides a convenient guide and reference point for decision making. It enables the individual to stay focused on important values and not become sidetracked by peripheral or temporary issues.

The Meaning of a Philosophy in a Leisure Service Organization

The foundation of any leisure service organization is its philosophy. From an organizational perspective, a philosophy refers to the guiding concepts or premises upon which the organization builds. Organizational philosophies, also referred to as overarching or superordinate goals, provide significant meaning that the leisure service organization attempts to impart to its employees.

A philosophy is useful to a leisure service agency for a number of reasons. As mentioned, it provides an opportunity for decisions to be made on a consistent basis, with a set of values and ideals that remain relevant over a long period of time. In addition, a philosophy helps an organization define itself and its uniqueness. A leisure service organization cannot be all things to all people. It must identify its direction and its scope. Direction and scope mean defining what benefits the organization wants to address, what populations it seeks to serve, and what services it intends to provide. A carefully thought-out philosophy helps build consensus, coordination, and cooperation among individuals working within the organization.

Over a period of time, an organization develops a unique personality, based on the values and beliefs that have emerged within the organization. In general, the philosophy of a leisure service organization addresses three primary areas: (1) the goals and objectives of the organization; (2) the methods and procedures used within the organization to produce leisure services; and (3) the relationship that the organization develops with its constituents, the physical environment, and the community within which it operates.

As indicated, a philosophy provides direction to the organization and helps define its values and beliefs. Hitt (1988, p. 86) writes ". . . whether the values are explicit or implicit, they constitute the essence of the organization's management philosophy. Values are the soul of the organization." Leisure service organizations often develop management philosophies to guide the distribution of resources. The management philosophy found in figure 4.7 from the Willamalane Recreation and Park District illustrates the application of this concept.

What types of values do leisure service organizations pursue as a part of their management philosophy? Deppe (1986), examining trends and forces in the administrative environment affecting future managers, suggests that values have changed regarding the management of

Figure 4.7

Example of a
management
philosophy
statement

Philosophy Statements:

Service to district residents: Willamalane has a responsibility to promote superior
quality park and recreation facilities and services to the residents of our District,
services which promote personal and community growth, programs which recognize
and preserve personal and community integrity and positive self and community
image. We recognize that a superior product is the result of the effort of
professionally trained people united to meet our purpose who are sensitive to the
unique needs and hopes of our residents and who are aware of the ability of the
community to economically support our plans.

Place in the community: Willamalane consists of individual staff and residents who
have pride in our collective place in the community. We recognize the obligation to
be a good citizen in Springfield which means that our efforts will complement and
supplement already existing services. We will promote the responsibility of other
individuals and organizations to maximize their potential and acknowledge that our
efforts will not unnecessarily compete or duplicate the services of others.

Individual commitment: Willamalane is a team of individuals. We recognize and
encourage the diversity of our talents but understand that real strength and
effectiveness come from unity. True unity is much more than a blending of self-
interests; it results when values, ideals, and goals are shared. We recognize that we
share pride in our work, pride in our organization, knowledge that loyalty flows in
many directions and a belief that our power is strongest when shared. These beliefs
provide a basis for the future of Willamalane and all who depend on it.

leisure service organizations. For example, he notes that ". . . privatization of local park and
recreation departments calls for a new mission statement" (pp. 46–47). Deppe (1986) also
points out that administrators strongly disagree with the idea that the social welfare philosophy
is no longer fundamental to public parks and recreation. These two orientations are value-based
and provide direction to the work of agencies. While a need exists for local park and recreation
departments to continue to try to serve all of their clients, privatization places a much stronger
emphasis on assessing fees and charges in support of programs and services.

Edginton (1987), discussing the creation of organizational cultures in the leisure service
field, writes ". . . the culture of any leisure service organization is reflected in the norms, customs and values to which it is committed" (p. 7). He further notes that core organizational values can be tied to ethical concerns, relationship to customers and employees, and relationship to
the community. Core values, according to Edginton, can focus on quality, consistency, depend-
ability, integrity, safety, and value.

The following statement helps us understand why one's philosophical position is important
as a tool to guide one's professional efforts:

The philosophical position adopted by any particular leisure service professional or scholar will influence his or her conceptualization of leisure and leisure services. There have been a number of
views expressed over time and, more recently, there has been growing interest in studying philoso-

In America there has been no leisure time philosophy for the simple reason that up to this generation there has been no leisure. Our [ancestors] found the conquering of the wilderness a difficult task. There have been only three generations since the ox team was used.

Civilizations, in other days, paid dearly for the privilege of leisure. The great philosophers of Greece even went to the limit of justifying slavery because it gave leisure to the citizens. Greece had a philosophy for leisure; [but] America has despised it.

America has confused leisure with idleness . . . the reason for this has been quite simple. America's philosophy of success too often has been centered around quantitative things. One must make money—get on in the world. To get on in the world meant to be continuously at one's vocation. . . . Leisure has never been considered quite respectable.

Source: J. B. Nash, *The Philosophy of Recreation and Leisure*, 1960.

phy and leisure contextually. It is important for leisure service professionals and scholars to consider their philosophy because it contributes to the perspective they adopt and guides much of their behavior. For professionals, it is essential that they articulate their philosophy so employees and employers may better understand the goals they seek to achieve. (Searle and Brayley, 2000, p. 54)

Summary

The development of a philosophy of leisure in order to guide the work of the professional is essential. Likewise, the philosophy of a leisure service organization guides the work of the people within that agency. Philosophies, whether individual or organizational, provide a framework for action and an understanding of the purpose and reasons governing behavior and actions.

What is philosophy? Philosophy, in its original meaning, suggests the search for the wisdom and meaning of life. A philosophy may be thought of as a systematically defined set of values, beliefs, and preferences. A philosophy is usually expressed as an abstract idea or set of ideas.

There are numerous reasons to build a philosophy of leisure. First and foremost, a philosophy provides a value structure to guide action. A philosophy can also be a strong source of inspiration and encouragement. Knowledge of an organization's philosophy can help clarify the relationships one encounters working within an agency. More specifically, a philosophy can help individuals know themselves, know their organization and its expectations regarding relationships with customers, colleagues, and external institutions.

How do we build a philosophy? Those wishing to build a philosophy may pursue it from several different standpoints. Three basic approaches can be used—speculative, normative, and analytical. Furthermore, a number of different philosophical constructs can be applied to leisure, such as perennialism, idealism, realism, experimentalism, existentialism, pragmatism, and humanism.

The actual construction of a philosophy requires a number of steps. It involves examination, not only of one's personal values but also of the philosophy and values that have emerged within the leisure service profession itself. The development of a personal philosophy of leisure as well as acknowledgment of an organizational philosophy is an important step for the professional. By clarifying what one believes, one can better focus on certain goals and direct his or her behavior toward the achievement of those goals. A philosophy provides a reasoned framework within which to view leisure and the work of leisure service organizations.

Discussion Questions

1. What is meant by the term *philosophy?* What is meant when it is suggested that philosophy is a practical tool for the professional?
2. Why is the development of a personal philosophy important to the development of a professional?
3. Why is it important to understand the philosophy underlying leisure service organizations?
4. How do values, ethics, and philosophy relate with one another?
5. What discrete values and principles have philosophers pursued that offer insight into the leisure phenomenon during the twentieth century?
6. What foundational values of the leisure service movement exist in society today? List ten from the chapter, citing examples of how various leisure service organizations pursue them.
7. List the major reasons for building a philosophy. What process would you use to develop your own personal philosophy?
8. Briefly describe seven major philosophies.
9. Locate five different types of leisure service organizations in your community and categorize their philosophies, values, and beliefs.
10. Write down your personal philosophy of leisure so it is understandable to others.

References

Brightbill, C. 1961. *Man and Leisure: A Philosophy of Recreation.* Englewood Cliffs, NJ: Prentice-Hall.

Cooper, W. 1999. Some philosophical aspects of leisure theory. Edited by E. L. Jackson and T. L. Burton, in *Leisure Studies: Prospects for the 21st Century.* State College, PA: Venture.

de Grazia, S. 1962. *Of Time, Work and Leisure.* Garden City: Doubleday.

Deppe, T. 1986. New Federalism: The great federal switch and its impact upon municipal parks and recreation. *Journal of Parks and Recreation Administration 4*(1), 46–47.

Driver, B. L., D. Dustin, T. Baltic, G. Elsner, and G. Peterson. 1996. *Nature and the Human Spirit.* State College, PA: Venture.

Dustin, D., L. McAvoy, and J. Schultz. 1982. *Stewards of Access, Custodians of Choice: A Philosophical Foundation for the Park and Recreation Profession.* Minneapolis: Burgess.

Edginton, C. 1987. Creating an organizational structure. *Management Strategy 11*(1), 1+.

Edginton, C., and P. Ford. 1985. *Leadership in Recreation and Leisure Service Organizations.* New York: Macmillan.

Edginton, S. R., and C. R. Edginton. 1993. *Youth Programs.* Champaign, IL: Sagamore.

Fain, G., ed. 1991. *Leisure and Ethics: Reflections on the Philosophy of Leisure.* Reston, VA: American Alliance of Health, Physical Education, Recreation and Dance.

Godbey, G. 1990. *Leisure in Your Life.* 3d ed. State College, PA: Venture.

Goodale, T. 1990. Intergenerational inequities: The abuse and neglect of those to follow. *Leisure Today* 3–7 (October), in *Journal of Physical Education, Recreation, and Dance,* 27–31.

Goodale, T., and G. Godbey. 1988. *The Evolution of Leisure: Historical and Philosophical Perspectives.* State College, PA: Venture.

Goodale, T., and P. Witt. 1990. *Recreation and Leisure: Issues in an Era of Change.* 3d ed. State College, PA: Venture.

Grey, D., and S. Greben. 1974. Future perspectives. *Parks and Recreation Magazine 9*(7), 26–33, 47–56.

Henderson, K., D. Bialeschki, S. Shaw, and V. Freysinger. 1996. *Both Gains and Gaps: Feminist Perspectives on Women's Leisure.* State College, PA: Venture.

Hitt, W. 1988. *The Leader Manager.* Columbus: Battelle Press.

Hitt, W. 1990. *Ethics and Leadership.* Columbus: Battelle Press.

Hopkins, H. 1951. *History of the YMCA in North America.* New York: Association Press.

Huizinga, J. 1955. *Homo Ludens: A Study of the Play Element in Culture.* Boston: Beacon Press.

Hunnicutt, B. K. 2000. Our reform heritage: Recovering the vision of community leisure service. *Journal of Leisure Research 32*(1), 58–61.

Jordan, D., and J. Mertesdorf. 1994. The effects of goal interdependence between leisure service supervisors and employees. *Journal of Applied Recreation Research 19*(2), 101–116.

Kelly, J. 1987. *Freedom to Be.* New York: Macmillan.

Kimeldorf, M. 1994. *Serious Play.* Berkeley, CA: Ten Speed.

Leitner, M. J., and S. F. Leitner. 1996. *Leisure Enhancement.* New York: Haworth Press.

Murphy, J. F. 1981. *Concepts of Leisure.* 2d ed. Englewood Cliffs, NJ: Prentice-Hall.

Naisbitt, J., and P. Aburdene. 1985. *Reinventing the Corporation.* New York: Warner Books.

Nash, J. 1981. *Philosophy of Recreation and Leisure.* Dubuque, IA: Wm. C. Brown.

Pieper, J. 1963. *Leisure: The Basis of Culture.* New York: Random House.

Purpel, D., and F. Ryan. 1976. *Moral Education: It Comes with the Territory.* Berkeley, CA: McCutcheon.

Rifkin, J. 1995. *The End of Work.* New York: Putnam.

Robinson, J., and G. Godbey. 1997. *Time for Life: The Surprising Ways Americans Use Their Time.* University Park, PA: The Pennsylvania University Press.

Russell, R. 1996. *Pastimes: The Context of Contemporary Leisure.* Madison, WI: Brown & Benchmark.

Schor, J. 1992. *The Overworked American.* New York: Basic Books.

Searle, M. S., and R. E. Brayley. 2000. *Leisure Services in Canada: An Introduction.* 2d ed. State College, PA: Venture.

Sylvester, C. 1987. The ethics of play, leisure and recreation in the twentieth century, 1900–1983. *Leisure Sciences 9,* 173–188.

Zigler, E. 1964. *Philosophical Foundations for Physical, Health, and Recreation Education.* Englewood Cliffs, NJ: Prentice Hall.

Zigler, E. 1977. *Physical Education and Sport Philosophy.* Englewood Cliffs, NJ: Prentice Hall.

CHAPTER 5

Mass Leisure

Many leisure activities occur in group settings that produce opportunities for connecting with others and joyful social interaction.

Introduction

The Industrial Revolution, which began in the 1800s in the United States and Canada, increased the amount of leisure available to most individuals, giving them the opportunity to use it as an expression of their needs and lifestyles. Transformation of an industrial-based economy to one focused on the creation and dissemination of information has produced further opportunities for leisure. The pursuit of quality leisure experiences will continue to influence the culture and society of the United States and Canada.

Leisure both shapes and reflects culture. Although leisure involves personal time, society influences leisure behavior through its norms, values, and customs. As a result of this influence, various patterns of leisure behavior, referred to as *mass leisure,* have developed and evolved. Mass leisure is both fluid and dynamic and reflects the popular fads, trends, and interests of individuals in a culture. Similar to popular or mass culture, mass leisure consists largely of everyday activities, habits, beliefs, and tastes often shared by many people (Kando, 1980). Within popular culture, *mass leisure reflects the everyday, recreational activities of the majority of the population.* Godbey (1994) suggests that the United States is moving toward becoming a leisure democracy where more types of leisure activities are available to more people.

This chapter examines the phenomenon of mass leisure. It focuses on the concept of time and mass leisure, explaining what has led to the proliferation of mass leisure in this century and identifying some of the many forms that mass leisure can take.

Mass Leisure: Is There Time?

Historically, leisure has been tied to discretionary time, left over "after the practical necessities of life have been attended to" (May and Petgin, 1928, p. 3). Throughout the twentieth century people have sought to increase discretionary time for leisure. The number of work hours decreased greatly from the turn of the century until the mid-1960s. For example, it took approximately forty years, from 1919 to the 1960s, to reduce the workweek from forty-eight to forty hours. During this same time frame, numerous technological advances in the workplace, as well as appliances, such as dishwashers, microwaves, and washing machines, were developed. These trends led many sociologists in the early 1960s to predict the creation of a thirty-hour workweek, with a society based more on leisure and recreation than on work.

Yet, something happened along the way—a leisure society hasn't developed. In fact, the reverse seems to have occurred! A headline in a cover story from *Time* in the late 1980s read "How America Has Run Out of Time: Workers are weary, parents are frantic, and even children haven't a moment to spare: Leisure could be to the 1990s what money was to the 1980s." The article states that ". . . according to a Harris survey, the amount of leisure time enjoyed by the average American has shrunk 37 percent since 1973. Over the same period the average work week, including commuting, has jumped from under forty-one hours to nearly forty-seven hours. . . . Vacations have shortened to the point where they are frequently no more than weekends. And the Sabbath is for—what else?—shopping" (Gibbs, 1989, p. 58).

The most systematic approach to studying time use in the United States has been undertaken at the University of Maryland in the American's Use of Time Project. The findings of these studies contradict the Harris survey. Findings concerning the time use of individuals living in the United States came from a series of subjective questions taken over a period of time from 1965 to 1985. In these studies, participants responded to subjective questions about time use. In addition to recording all their activities on a single day, respondents were asked whether they "always," "sometimes," or "almost never" felt rushed to do things they have to do (Robinson, 1990a). From these studies, Robinson determined a number of interesting factors:

- Americans have more free time today than ever before. Men have forty hours of free time a week, and women have thirty-nine hours (Robinson, 1989; Spring, 1993).
- Increases in free time for women can be attributed to less household work, less time involved in child care, and a shorter workweek (Robinson, 1989).
- Unmarried people have more free time than married couples (Robinson, 1989).
- Most free time gains have occurred between 1965 and 1975 (Robinson, 1989). Between 1982 and 1988, the average workweek of an employed American increased by 1 hour to 43.8 hours (Cutler, 1990).
- People aged fifty-one to sixty-four have gained the most free time since 1965 (Robinson, 1989).
- For every extra hour of increased leisure time Americans have gained since 1965, they spend an extra hour watching television. Television takes up 38 percent of Americans' free time (Robinson, 1990b).
- Although Americans have more free time now than in the 1960s or 1970s, they report feeling frantic and rushed, especially those aged thirty-five to fifty-four (Robinson, 1990a). Individuals feel that they are in a "time crunch" (Robinson, 1991).
- Four out of ten Americans report cutting back on sleep to gain time. Nearly one-third of adults feel that they haven't accomplished what they set out to do in a typical day. More than one in four adults describe themselves as workaholics (Robinson, 1991).
- Americans value leisure time as highly as they value money (Robinson, 1991).
- A gap exists between the amount of free time that individuals have and the amount they desire (Robinson, 1991; Spring, 1993).

Robinson and Godbey (1997) note that since 1985 the workweek has shown virtually no change in the estimated hours worked per week, that television continues to play a large role in

More Work, Less Play

It's more work and less play for American kids. Children's free time is declining because of longer school hours, more studying, more day care, and more structured activities such as after-school sports, according to a recent report of the University of Michigan Institute for Social Research. The report said that children's free time accounted for 40 percent of their day in 1981, but only 30 percent in 1997. That means kids have less time for unstructured, creative play among or by themselves, free of direction or constant supervision by adults. Researchers say that much of the decline can be attributed to the increasing time squeeze among parents, especially working couples and single parents.

Points to Ponder

- In your opinion, is this a good or bad trend? What are the positives and negatives of unstructured, unsupervised, creative play?

Data from Staff. 1999, December/January. Odds n' ends. *Youth Today 8*(1), 51.

how we use our free time, that Canadian data mirror the U.S. data closely, and that the amount of free time has stayed close to the 1985 figures presented in the original Use of Time project. This information suggests that the amount of time available to Americans has increased. Yet Americans still feel rushed, frantic, and crunched in the use of time.

In her book *The Overworked American: The Unexpected Decline of Leisure,* Schor (1991) reports that in 1990 the average American owned and consumed more than twice as much as he or she did in 1948, but also had less free time. When surveyed, Americans report that they have approximately sixteen-and-a-half hours of leisure a week. This phenomenon of the evaporation of free time, referred to as time famine, may result from two distinct and sometimes related situations. The first situation finds people needing to work more hours or taking second jobs to support their families. One twenty-eight-year-old factory worker stated, "Either I can spend time with my family, or support them—not both" (Schor, 1991, p. 21).

The second situation finds that the desire for more leisure is distinctly secondary to the desire for more material goods. As de Grazia (1962) observed, what we want today are things; things cost money; money costs time. The increasing accumulation of goods also means spending more time in the consumption and maintenance of them. Consumption will become more commodity intensive, and people will attempt to speed up consumption since time is both limited and expensive in relation to things. International comparisons found that Americans spend more time shopping than any other group of people in the world.

Time famine is greater for women than it is for men, since working women still carry the bulk of the work within the family. Bammel and Bammel (1996) report that "women seem to feel that they are doing more in teaching and disciplining the children and taking care of the home than are their husbands" (p. 383). Many time-use studies back up this feeling as they indicate that women have less free time than men and that men spend more than twice the time as women in recreation (Bammel and Bammel, 1996).

With the increased use of computers and technology, where time is marked by the nanosecond, people's concept of time will likely change. In the future, will time be defined in human terms or in terms that machines have created? What does progress mean and how does it relate to the amount of things produced, distributed, and consumed or discarded? Is good health, which is almost assuredly related to happiness, related to the production of things, and, if so, how? Will people's lives slow down or speed up? While people may be happier if their pace of life slows down, is it possible for them to slow down?

How technology will change the work/leisure relationship was examined recently in an article entitled "The End of Leisure," which documents that today's average married couple labors a staggering 717 hours more each year than a working duo in 1969. Computers, cellular phones, palm pilots, and so on, that were to "free us from our desks have bound us to our jobs in ways unimaginable just a decade ago. They are electronic umbilical cords to the workplace" (Stein Wellner, 2000, p. 52). Does this all mean the end of leisure? Stein Wellner (2000) answers no, but it does signal a change in the way we view work and leisure. Today the lines between work and leisure are blurring. Today, Americans are taking work on vacation and surfing the Internet at work. "Rather than trying to isolate hours of the day that are completely free of work or slog through hours totally devoid of leisure, we're melding the two together" (Stein Wellner, 2000, p. 52).

Beyond society's view of time is its view of leisure. Perhaps people's definition of leisure will change from that of free time to that of leisure as a state of mind where satisfaction with time becomes a key component, and work and leisure can be fused. Thus, the issue becomes not one of satisfaction with work or leisure but with life's endeavors. Perhaps people will continue to combine activities as Robinson and Godbey (1997) explain in the concept of time deepening, which can occur in one of four ways. *Time deepening* involves "attempting to speed up a given activity, substituting a leisure activity that can be done more quickly for one that takes longer, doing more than one activity at once, or undertaking a leisure activity with more precise regard to time" (p. 39).

In studying the question of free time, Robinson and Godbey (1997) have identified a number of paradoxes: "Time devoted to work has declined, but Americans believe it has increased. The increases in free time have been largely devoted to more television viewing, even though that is a free-time activity that Americans rate low in terms of pleasure. They also spend little time doing the free-time activities they rate more pleasurable, such as socializing or playing sports" (p. 298). Despite these paradoxes and the differing opinions of such scholars as Schor and Robinson and Godbey, one bit of consensus seems to emerge: It will demand commitment, imagination, reflection, and discipline if we are going to take our free time and truly make it leisure.

In this process of truly claiming free time as leisure, it will be increasingly important to understand how leisure experiences are consumed, in that despite the perception or reality of decreasing amounts of leisure time in society, the consumption of leisure experiences continues to grow. The idea of consuming leisure experiences may be an important idea to grasp in understanding the concept of mass leisure. Individuals appear more concerned with the quality and quantity of their leisure experiences and tend to view their well-being from the standpoint of the experiences they have collected or consumed rather than the material possessions they may own. As Molitor (2000) states, "The new paradigm will emphasize experiences, instead of things. Leisure time dominance will usher in a host of new attitudes, outlooks, and activity preferences. As materialism wanes and experiences and self-development ascend, new business opportunities will grow by leaps and bounds. Responding to the dreams and hopes will evoke a dazzling profusion of new opportunities and entrepreneurial undertaking catering to every imaginable whim and fancy. Experiences, not things, are slated to become the focus of consumer interest. A dizzying array of incomparable choices will provide a dazzling array of pursuits suited to individual desires and needs of a growing leisure class. The new will replace the old" (pp. 15–16).

Mass Leisure: Common Elements

Throughout history, activities have emerged that could be classified as mass leisure. Examples of early forms of mass leisure include the circuses of the Roman empire and the playhouses of London in the thirteenth and fourteenth centuries. Not until the twentieth century, however, did mass leisure grow to epic proportions. This proliferation of mass leisure has resulted from a number of unique factors.

The daily use of leisure has been radically reshaped since the Second World War. Not only has technological change played a major role in this reshaping, so too have changing economic and social conditions as well as our value systems. The mass media, pleasure travel, outdoor recreation, and local institutions such as museums, botanical gardens, parks, and libraries all became an expected part of the leisure experience of millions of Americans. The post–World War II era was characterized by optimism, materialism, the emergence of a mass society, concern about quality of life and a variety of environmental and social issues, and a heightened belief in science and technology (Kelly and Godbey, 1992).

An increase in discretionary income, a change in values regarding mass leisure, improved infrastructure and technology, and an explosion of the amount of mass media to which people are exposed on a daily basis—these factors have all shaped the proliferation of mass leisure.

Increase in Discretionary Income

The period following World War II was an era of affluence in the United States and Canada. These countries were in an enviable position compared with many other countries. A period of rising income during the fifties and sixties produced a large middle class, unprecedented in the history of the world. As incomes expanded so did the opportunity for leisure, along with a great array of leisure choices. This relationship between income and leisure opportunity still exists today. To participate in most mass leisure activities requires some discretionary income that can be used for admissions, equipment, and travel.

Change in Values

To participate in mass leisure, individuals must value the experiences that exist within its realm. Traditionally, culture has been divided into popular or mass culture, and high culture. For many years, the activities categorized as mass culture were considered inferior to the activities that constitute high culture. According to Kando (1980), this elitist position was based on the assumption that a necessary inverse relationship exists between the quantity and the quality of leisure. The question for such purists becomes as follows:

> Is it possible to extend a higher civilization to the lower classes without debasing its standard and diluting its quality to the vanishing point? Is not every civilization bound to decay as soon as it begins to penetrate the masses . . . [the author answers] . . . the mass of men [sic] dislikes and always has disliked learning and art. It wishes to be distracted from life rather than to have it revealed; to be comforted by traditional truths, rather than to be upset by new ones. (Van den Haag, 1964, p. 55)

More writers have responded in recent years to this argument by highlighting the growth in the arts as well as the demonstrated ability of all people to enjoy all types of recreation. An increasingly educated populace has produced a greater number of people who enjoy cultural events and other traditional forms of high culture. At the same time, the popularity and participation in mass leisure activities continues to rise. This increase in participation accompanies increased acceptance, for the most part, of the leisure activities that are a part of mass culture.

De-Massification of the Media

Humans, of course, have always exchanged *symbolic images of reality.* That is what language is all about. It is what knowledge is based on. . . . The main producers of this imagery, until recently, were the major broadcast networks. Today, in the United States, where de-massification is most advanced, their power is plummeting.

Where ABC, NBC, and CBS once stood virtually alone, there are now *seventy-two* national services of various kinds, with more coming on line. . . . Recently four major companies banded together to deliver *108 channels* of standard, high-definition TV to American viewers. . . .

Asked what will happen to the Big Three, Al Burton, a top independent TV producer says, "Once upon a time there were three big radio networks too. Today hardly anyone even remembers they existed."

Data from Alvin Toffler, *Power Shift*, 1990.

The increased popularity of mass leisure also results from an important realization: popular culture reflects the society and the freedoms individuals enjoy—it is a rich expression of democracy (Brown, 1978). Thus, while popular culture has become legitimized and more accepted in this century, it carries with it great responsibility. "The study of popular culture [mass leisure], like that of other areas of human behavior, goes hand in hand with a search for solutions to human problems and a concern for the quality of human life" (Kando, 1980, p. 60).

Improved Infrastructure Related to Physical and Natural Resources

Federal, state, and local governments have encouraged mass leisure by helping to establish accessible environments for leisure activities. An improved highway system has greatly enabled access to mass leisure activities in the past three decades, as have improved technology and other factors. Continued efforts will ensure availability of leisure activities.

In addition, more natural areas are being opened to a wide variety of leisure pursuits. For example, the U.S. Forest Service (USFS) has committed itself to dedicating more of its budget to providing outdoor recreation experiences. The USFS now has more than 35,000 employees and a budget of more than 3 billion dollars. It provides a vast landscape for camping, fishing, hunting, boating, hiking, backpacking, and so on, especially in the western half of the United States. As the organization moves away from emphasizing timber production to maximizing the outdoor recreation opportunities within its borders it will continue to open up large natural areas for the enjoyment of a wide range of Americans (Robinson and Godbey, 1997).

Improved Technology

Technology impacts all aspects of leisure behavior. For example, consider how transportation has affected mobility and travel, mass media has influenced communication and information, credit cards have revolutionized shopping, and contraceptives have radically altered sexual behavior. In the coming decades the speed of innovation and new technologies will accelerate change. For example, the ongoing electronics revolution promises to continue to change our patterns of everyday life as the home becomes a multimedia center.

The continued infusion of new technology will greatly influence the nature of mass leisure activities of the future. Such technology will help meet the needs of people to seek novelty and new experiences in their lives and will assist many people in their quest for new adventures.

Increase in the Amount of Mass Media   Mass culture flourished in the twentieth century due in large part to the growth of mass media and, in particular, television. Television has served as the transmitter of both values and activities. According to Kelly and Godbey (1992) television has had a significant impact on the world in terms of leisure patterns. Following are leisure issues impacted by television.

- Television began to bring leisure home. Now the residence offers a variety of entertainment opportunities that are easy, accessible, and inexpensive.
- It has transformed images of play with its depictions of special locales, equipment, dress, associations, and activities that are available primarily throughout the market for a price.
- It has widened horizons by bringing the arts, sports, and travel possibilities into the home for both children and adults. For those unable to afford such possibilities, however, it may have widened the gap between the poor and those with discretionary income.
- It has reshaped leisure timetables with "prime-time" programming and offers special events at times once reserved for activities such as family interaction, religion, personal development in skills such as music, and even students' study.

Television will continue as a major vehicle for transmitting mass leisure activities and values. New technologies will use television as a medium to expand the individual viewing choices as well as to create new entertainment possibilities. This is particularly true as cable networks and direct TV increase individual choice in watching television.

Mass Leisure: What Do People Do?

What do people do in their leisure? Numerous studies have examined this question. In the United States, the leisure activities in which people most frequently participate include television watching, social visits, reading, social communication, hobbies, arts, crafts, dancing, sports and exercise, indoor games, relaxing (doing nothing), movies, music, hiking, hunting, fishing, and attending sport events and cultural activities (National Sporting Goods Association, 1995). In Canada, Searle and Brayley (2000) report that walking for pleasure, gardening, swimming, playing baseball, jogging, bowling, bicycling, dancing, home exercising, downhill skiing, jogging, and golfing are popular activities. Studies reported by these same authors in selective provinces including Alberta, Manitoba, and Ontario suggest that walking for pleasure, visiting friends, reading, bicycling, dining out, socializing, craft making, listening to music, listening to radio, gardening, shopping, watching television, attending a sporting event, spending time in the outdoors, swimming, hobbies, visiting museums, playing cards/games, sports and fitness, playing video games, traveling for pleasure, relaxation, camping, golfing, and hunting were popular activities.

To understand the various types of mass leisure (figure 5.1), this chapter examines the following broad categories of mass leisure behavior:

Social activities. These leisure experiences are carried out in a social context, often with other people.

Sports. This type of activity can be divided into two areas—active participation in any sport (either physically or mentally challenging) and spectator sports such as football, basketball, auto racing, and baseball.

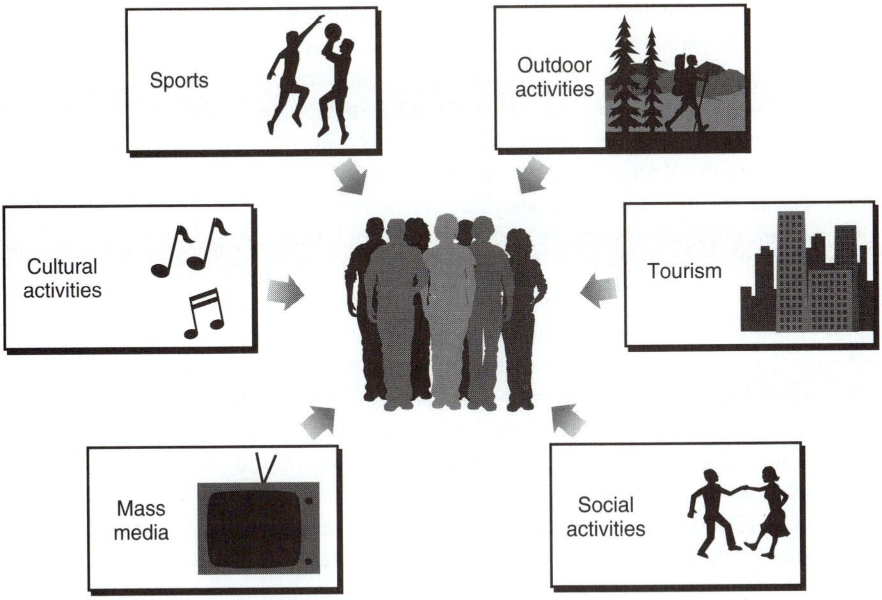

Figure 5.1

Types of mass leisure

Cultural activities. The diverse cultural area includes such activities and events as ballet, opera, classical music, art galleries, museums, and theater.

Outdoor activities (environmental). More broadly defined as outdoor recreation, these experiences involve any enjoyable leisure time activity pursued outdoors involving knowledge, use, or appreciation of natural resources.

Tourism activities. While not synonymous with recreation, tourism often includes recreation and leisure activity. "Tourism definitions usually include these components: travel from home; personal and business motivations; the expenditure of money; and many service businesses related to travel" (Gunn, 1986, p. 2).

Mass media. This realm of leisure activities includes time spent by people in front of the television as well as attending movies, listening to radio, or utilizing electronic equipment for entertainment, learning, and other forms of leisure.

Social Activities as Mass Leisure

Leisure can and usually is viewed within a social context. That is, most leisure activities involve some form of human interaction. Beyond the specific social interaction that can and does take place during leisure, the social fabric of our society helps to define our leisure behavior. Our society's norms, customs, and rituals greatly shape the very leisure activities in which we participate as well as how these activities are perceived and valued. Within this context, this section of the book examines how social capital is being lost in America, as well as how we can build social capital through leisure; the types of social activities in which Americans participate; and how values impact our view of social leisure.

Building the Social Capital Needed for Leisure and Life   Robert Putnam (2000), in his recent review of the "state of community" in America, writes about improving a sense of community by thinking in terms of developing the physical, human, and social capital of an area. Just as a new recreation center (physical capital) or an opportunity to gain new knowledge (human capital) can increase the livability of a community, so too do social contacts affect the livability of individuals and communities. Whereas *physical capital* refers to physical objects and *human capital* is linked to the properties of individuals, *social capital* refers to connections between individuals, networks, norms, and trust that enable participants to act together more effectively to pursue shared objectives. As a result of his work Putnam declares we are losing community and that our collective civic life is weakening. This loss of a sense of community is in part due to a decline in social capital.

This decline in social capital is documented by the downward trend of Americans participating in politics, civic organizations, religious organizations, and volunteer opportunities. According to Putnam (2000, p. 183), "during the first two thirds of this century Americans took a more and more active role in the social and political life of their communities—in churches and union halls, in bowling alleys and clubrooms, around committee tables and card tables and dinner tables. Year by year we gave more generously to charity, we pitched in more often in community projects, and we behaved in an increasingly trustworthy way toward one another. Then, mysteriously and more or less simultaneously, we began to do all those things less often."

Putnam (2000) attributes our loss of social capital to a variety of factors such as changing work patterns, urban sprawl, generational change, television, and other changes in technology. Regardless of the cause, the issue of social capital is an important issue for leisure service professionals, because one of the benefits of our programs and services is building social capital within communities. Leisure not only builds social capital but, as we have seen in chapter one, also contributes to one's sense of community satisfaction.

To be sure, the "state of community" or the level of social capital within a community is an elusive concept. It's much like the weather, hard to predict—but if you're a part of it, you can assess and determine the importance and degree of its influence. Leisure managers with great experience will attest that an uncommon but considerable benefit to a good leisure program is included in such items as social capital, community identity, and a sense of cohesiveness. As a result, as we move forward into the twenty-first century Putnam suggests that we look back to the Progressive era, which we discussed in chapter three as the beginning of the parks and recreation movement. Putnam argues that at the verge of the twentieth century the Progressive reformers faced a variety of similar problems related to social capital. In response, reformers diagnosed the problem and set to creating institutions, such as the Boy Scouts, public parks, recreation centers, organized camping, settlement houses, and the playground movement to address the problem. Today "we need a similar era of civic inventiveness to create a renewed set of institutions and channels for reinvigorating civic life that will fit the way we have come to live" (Putnam, 2000, p. 401).

Social Activities It is difficult to isolate specific social leisure, as almost all forms of leisure and recreation have a social dimension, which strongly affects the quality of the overall experience. For example, what we decide to do on a given night may be a function of schedules, finances, or location. First and foremost, however, is usually who we want to be with for the evening. Kelly and Godbey (1992) note the importance of leisure in the building of friendships and relationships: "In a social world in which workers seldom live in ethnic neighborhoods around the workplace with a thick network of interrelationships, many friendships are developed around leisure. Friends entertain and go out to eat together. They share cabins on vacations. Men fish together, teens water-ski together. Grandmothers share pictures together. Neighbors exchange tools and talk. What is surprising is that increasingly friendships are inaugurated and developed in leisure" (p. 215).

Mass Leisure . . . Global Leisure?

"The TV marketplace, internationally . . . is a real growth area," says Sam Roberts, an executive director at CBS News. *CBS Evening News* with Dan Rather . . . airs at 8:00 A.M. daily in Paris. The Japanese are watching Dan Rather, too, along with the *MacNeil/Leherer News Hour* and *Nightline* with Ted Koppel. Seventy-five percent of all imported television programs come from the United States. Most are not the news.

- *Dallas* is seen in 98 countries.
- In New Zealand 40 percent of television programming was American in 1986.
- Mickey Mouse and Donald Duck—their voices dubbed in Mandarin—are seen weekly in China.
- Australians are known to stay up until midnight to catch the *Today* show.
- *Sesame Street* was seen in 84 countries in 1989.

- *La Roue de la Fortune,* France's spin-off of the American *Wheel of Fortune,* is the hottest game show on French television.
- On Wednesday nights in Shanghai more than 70 percent of the television audience tunes in to catch Hunter, an American police show.

. . . "China is the last bastion," says Michael Jay Solomon of Lorimar Telepictures, which has a five-year agreement to provide all of Shanghai's non-Chinese television. "But it's scary because we're going to change the way these people think. . . . The potential of global television, along with the massive export of American television shows, raises many questions." . . . Will global television lead to . . . the homogenization of culture? Will it threaten differences that make individual countries interesting? Will it facilitate the tendency for powerful countries like the United States to impose their values upon Third World countries or, for that matter, on other developing nations?

In researching the social psychology of leisure, Samdahl (1992) suggests that most leisure experiences occur in casual, social settings. In other words, as people walk side by side, sit informally, "hang out" with friends who they trust and feel comfortable with, or interact quietly with their environment, opportunities for leisure emerge. It may be that although leisure is pervasive throughout our society, leisure experiences may well in fact find us, rather than the reverse. This implies that leisure, for most of us, "just occurs" and is not often characterized by special activities or events.

Leisure occurs in the minute-to-minute interactions of our daily living. An implication of this finding suggests that although leisure service programmers give great attention to planning, organizing, and implementing formal leisure activities, this type of leisure is relatively rare. Therefore, the challenge in programming is "to focus not only on the creation of the rare and exotic, but also facilitating and influencing the casual and 'just occurring' life events that have potential for leisure. This can be done by recognizing that the conditions of the leisure experience—perceived freedom, intrinsic motivation, and perceived competence—can be facilitated by programmers in a variety of life spaces" (Edginton, Hanson, Edginton, and Hudson, 1998, p. 5).

Social leisure activities have been identified as important categories of leisure interests by a number of authors in the literature (Ragheb and Beard, 1992). Yet it is hard to identify specific social activities beyond visiting with friends or talking on the telephone. The reason for this is clear: Social interaction is a component of almost all types of leisure, but it generally is associated with another activity such as playing cards, going to church, belonging to a fraternal organization, attending a sport or cultural event, going out for dinner, and so on.

Social Leisure: Value Laden or Value Free?   Viewing mass leisure in a social context allows the examination of widespread activities that are not embraced as a part of socially or legally acceptable behaviors. Such behaviors pervade society and compose a significant use of leisure in a social context by subcultures within society. A number of these behaviors are related to some kind of negative addiction on the part of the participant and can include drug use, abuse of alcohol, gambling, and sexual deviance.

Use of alcohol has long been a part of human history. It costs little to produce and has almost always been available to the masses. Within many traditional cultures its consumption served many purposes. Wine was used as a substitute for impure water while both beer and ale in medieval Europe served as a readily available source of nutrition. "In modern societies, however, the purposes of wine, beer and spirits have less to do with sanitation or nutrition than with socialization or intoxication" (Kelly and Godbey, 1992, p. 470).

Antisocial use of alcohol often centers around the binge drinker and those who drink with the sole intention of getting drunk. With such binge drinkers or drug users there is a process of socialization that takes place in a subculture that values such activities. Kelly and Godbey (1992) have noted that such socialization "teaches the novice to experience the activity as pleasurable. The use of alcohol, tobacco, LSD, and a variety of other drugs in not inherently pleasurable to the beginner, who without the positive reinforcement of the social group as well as instruction, would often find the experience negative" (p. 472).

The growth of gambling is also a concern for many people. Twenty years ago gambling was a contained activity in such places as Las Vegas, Nevada, or more recently Atlantic City, but in the last ten years, opportunities to gamble have grown tremendously. According to Molitor (2000), gambling is one of the fastest-growing segments of the entertainment industry. Legal revenues from gambling totaled more than $394 billion in 1993 and $650 billion in 1999, and they are projected to reach as high as $1.5 trillion in 2005. Today casinos are appearing on riverboats, Indian reservations, cruise ships, and even the Internet. Gambling in some form is allowed in forty-seven states, with Utah, Tennessee, and Hawaii being the only states where all types of gambling are illegal. Surveys reveal that 63 percent of all Americans engaged in some sort of gambling in 1998 (Molitor, 2000). As with alcohol use, the antisocial use of gambling often centers around the compulsive gambler, and as opportunities expand, so does the risk of financial devastation for the compulsive gambler.

Another dimension within the social context is sexual behavior. People's sexual behavior has changed greatly in the last several decades, and men and women stand on more equal ground when it comes to the consequences of being sexually active. Yet some sexual behavior is viewed as antisocial even though it prevails in pockets of the population. As Kelly (1996) observes, "despite ideologies of mutual decision, enjoyment and self determination, sexual intercourse is still defined as conquest by some. It becomes something less than leisure when the aims are winning a score, and the social prestige of success. Sexual activity is hardly relational leisure when one person becomes a trophy" (p. 391). This behavior was exposed in a group of high school athletes in California that nicknamed itself "the posse," which developed an elaborate scoring system for rating their various "conquests" with girls and women. Even after the group was exposed, many of the members of this group did not express remorse but in fact described their group with great pride.

When antisocial behavior emerges in leisure pursuits, it brings out many fundamental questions. These questions revolve around the values and morals we think should be espoused in leisure activities. Is there a universal set of values related to leisure? Should society try to identify those leisure activities it finds offensive and channel that energy into other "more acceptable" forms of leisure? Who should be making these decisions? By what process should these decisions be made? What should be the role of the leisure programmer in this process? Does the leisure programmer have a responsibility to serve the popular tastes for recreation or should leisure service programmers have allegiance to other personal or professional values?

Sport as Mass Leisure

Sports can mean different things to different people. Therefore, it is important to place some parameters on what is meant by sport and sports activities. Kelly (1996, p. 214) defines sport as an ". . . organized activity in which physical effort is related to that of others in some relative measurement of outcomes with accepted regularities and forms."

He further notes that

> . . . sport has a major place in modern society as an element of the economy, a spectacle with symbolic meanings, an arena of the development for the young and in the leisure lives of many individuals. Within these parameters sports can be active or passive, individual or team-oriented, as well as done for a variety of motives from fun to fitness. Thus, for some individuals sport is leisure (both passive and active); for others it is work, education or development. (p. 241)

This section of the chapter examines several selected spectator sports as well as favorite active sporting events of Canadian and U.S. citizens.

The desire to be spectators, to watch others involved in sporting contests, is evident all through human history. From the gladiators of the Roman Empire to the jousting of the Middle Ages to the popularity of boxing in the early part of the eighteenth century, people have enjoyed being spectators. The foundation of today's teams sports, however, can be traced to baseball, the American pastime. In 1876, the National League of Professional Baseball Clubs was formed. The American League was founded in 1899, the first World Series was held in 1903—and an American tradition was born.

During the twentieth century spectator sports have grown into a national obsession, with a tremendous growth of spectator sports at all levels of competition (professionals and amateurs—college, high school, and even youth leagues). Table 5.1 presents attendance figures for selected spectator sports for the years 1985 and 1997. The chart indicates professional baseball as the number one spectator sport in the United States followed by horse racing, football (combining college and professional), and basketball (combining college and professional).

One spectator sport not listed in table 5.1, auto racing, also draws large crowds. While automobile racing in Europe tends to remain an elite affair (formula-one racing), the United States Auto Club and National Association for Stock Car Racing events have become a true form of mass leisure (Kando, 1980). On any given weekend in the summer, hundreds of thousands of fans jam racetracks around the country. Large tracks such as those found in Indianapolis or Daytona can attract 400,000 fans in a weekend. Numerous spectator sports have flourished, at least for a time, in this century and include horse racing, bowling, golf, hockey, tennis, greyhound racing, track and field events, bicycling, and boxing.

The enormous growth in spectator sports has led to a concern about "spectatoritis." The twentieth century has also seen tremendous growth in sport *participation*, however. Over the last several decades, with the support of finances from the Land and Water Conservation Fund and other resources, a dramatic increase in the supply of leisure resources has occurred. This is reflected in the acquisition and development of parks, swimming pools, golf courses, ski slopes, stadiums, tennis and racquetball courts, and ice rinks. The continued emphasis on fitness and wellness in American and Canadian society should continue to encourage active participation in sports.

TABLE

5.1   ATTENDANCE FIGURES FOR SELECTED SPECTATOR SPORTS (1985–1997)

Sport	1985	1997
Horse racing	73,346	41,846
Baseball (professional)	47,742	64,921
Basketball		
Men's (college)	26,584	27,738
Women's (college)	2,072	6,734
Men's (professional)	11,534	21,677
Football		
College	34,952	36,858
Professional	14,058	Not Available
Greyhound racing	23,858	14,306
Hockey	11,621	15,701
Jai alai	4,722	2,125

Table 5.2 presents the total number of participants for a number of selected sports activities. Walking, swimming, bicycling, freshwater fishing, and bowling rank among the top activities in which Americans participate. The expenditures by sport listed in table 5.3 reflect the economic impact of involvement in sports.

Sport participation in Canada resembles that of the United States. Canadian cities have a variety of professional sports teams (e.g., Montreal Expos, Toronto Blue Jays, Edmonton Oilers, Montreal Canadians, as well as the Canadian Football League). Some differences in participation patterns emerge as Canadians are more likely to be involved in skating, hockey, skiing, and other winter sports. Canada also has a strong amateur and club tradition. For example, Sport Canada assists amateurs with expenses incurred through intensive training schedules. A second example of Canadian involvement with sport participation, the Fitness Canada program, works to reach youth, workers, and seniors.

Cultural Activities as Mass Leisure

Cultural activities, often seen as cultivation of the mind and spirit, historically have been referred to as *high culture*. In the past, the activities designated as high culture have rested in the domain of the wealthy and well-to-do and therefore consisted of activities in which only a few participated. A distinction traditionally made between mass culture and high culture defined high culture as ". . . recreational and cultural activities that are somehow more serious and more profound than mass and popular culture" (Kando, 1980, p. 143). This attitude is slowly changing, however, as the arts and other types of cultural experiences just mentioned have begun to appeal more to the masses. According to Naisbett and Aburdene (1990) in their book *Megatrends 2000,* the arts will gradually replace sports as society's primary leisure activity. "The 1990s will bring forth a modern renaissance in the visual arts, poetry, dance, theater, and music throughout the developed world. . . . The affluent information society has laid the economic groundwork for the renaissance, creating new patrons . . . [who are] educated, professional, and increasingly female. . . . Today's consumer is sophisticated enough to appreciate the arts and can pay the price of admission" (Naisbett and Aburdene, 1990, p. 63). This growth in the arts is reflected in table 5.4.

5.2 PARTICIPATION FIGURES FOR TOP TEN SPORT ACTIVITIES IN 1997

Sport	1993 (in millions)	1997 (in millions)
Exercise walking	64.4	76.2
Swimming	61.4	59.5
Exercising with equipment	34.9	47.8
Camping	42.7	46.6
Bicycle riding	47.9	45.1
Bowling	41.7	44.8
Fishing—freshwater	45.3	38.9
Billiards	N/A	36.9
Basketball	29.6	30.6
Hiking	N/A	28.3

N/A Not Available
Data from Data National Sporting Goods Association. 1999. *Statistical Abstacts of the United States.*

TABLE

5.3 SPORTING GOOD SALES BY PRODUCT CATEGORY 1980–1998

Sport	1980 (in millions)	1998 (in millions)
Athletic and sport clothing	10,130	12,412
Athletic and sport footwear	11,654	13,687
Athletic and sport equipment	11,964	18,225
Recreaton sport transport	14,502	22,171

Data from Data National Sporting Goods Association. 1999. *Statistical Abstacts of the United States.*

TABLE

5.4 AMERICA'S INCREASING INVOLVEMENT WITH THE ARTS

Performance Type	Attendance 1985 (in millions)	Attendance 1997 (in millions)
Broadway shows	7.3	10.6
Broadway road tours	8.2	18.0
Nonprofit professional theater	14.2	17.2
Opera	3.3	4.0
Symphony orchestra	24.0	31.9

Data from U.S. Bureau of the Census. 2000. *Statistical Abstacts of the United States.*

The Environment and Mass Leisure

In the last twenty years, outdoor recreation participation in the United States has increased. For example, in 1980 the U.S. Forest Service reported 233 million recreation visitor days. In 1996, this figure increased to more than 341 million visitor days (U.S. Bureau of the Census, 2000). In addition, the National Park Service registered over 275 million visitor days in 1997 (U.S. Bureau of the Census, 1999). By 2001, the number of visits registered by the National Park Service is expected to increase to nearly 300 million (Raymond, 2000). Nash (1982) reports on four major revolutions that have contributed to this increase in outdoor recreation.

First, a revolution in equipment that is lighter, stronger, and smaller than ever before allows people more access to remote areas. Furthermore, the invention of new equipment has created new sports such as windsurfing, snowboarding, and mountain biking.

The second major revolution has taken place in transportation. Pristine outdoor areas are reached more easily than ever before. People can fly from New York to Portland in a matter of hours, then drive another two hours and be on a glacier on Mount Hood where they can enjoy year-round snow skiing. As Nash (1982) points out, the bush plane is Alaska's covered wagon, and the helicopter has replaced horses as the preferred means of transportation.

The third major revolution revolves around the ease of accessing information about new areas. Pristine areas receive positive publicity and become world famous. It took John Muir a lifetime to learn about the Sierra Nevadas; this information can be gleaned in a matter of hours by reading guide books or viewing CD-ROM disks about northern California.

The fourth and final revolution involves an intellectual change in how people view the wilderness. As Nash (1982) notes, today's appreciation of wilderness and the outdoors represents one of the most remarkable intellectual revolutions in human history. Historically, humans have viewed wilderness and the outdoors as something to fear, something to tame in order to survive. Today, however, these areas are appreciated on a different level.

Further, interest in outdoor recreation results from a growing concern for environmental issues and the need to reconnect with our biological roots. Canadians and U.S. citizens have a long tradition of involvement with the outdoors, celebrating it in literature, music, and art. Highly valued, the outdoors is central to the quality of life in all communities across the United States and Canada.

> [Yet] . . . if there is a single word that describes Americans outdoors, it is diversity. We go outdoors for many reasons; to keep physically fit, for excitement, to have fun with family and friends; to get away from other people, to experience nature and to learn. Nearly 50 percent of Americans describe themselves as "outdoors people," and another 16 percent consider themselves a combination of indoors and out. It is a rare American who does not engage in some form of recreation outdoors. (PCAO, 1987, p. 17)

This author is reiterated by the fact that in 1999 only two in ten Americans did not participate in some form of outdoor recreation at some point in the year (Raymond, 2000). Although there still seems to be a number of different participation rates based on demographic variables like education level and ethnicity, there does seem to be something for everyone in the great outdoors. Today seniors, equipped with their good health, an abundance of free time, and hefty retirement accounts, are seeking out more outdoor opportunities such as elderhostel or organized camping. Environmentally conscious baby boomers are flocking to exotic adventure travel destinations. Gen-Xers have spurred the development of nontraditional outdoor activities and the recreation of new recreational sites for snowboarding, in-line skating, motocross, and telemark skiing (Raymond, 2000).

This growth in outdoor recreation participation is well documented. In 1987 the President's Council on Americans Outdoors submitted its report, *American Outdoors: The Legacy, The Challenge,* which was commissioned to review private and public outdoor recreation opportunities, policies, and programs and to make recommendations to ensure the future availability of outdoor recreation for the American people. Two of the trends identified were that pursuit of physically outdoor recreation will increase, especially in the area of high-risk adventure activities, and outdoor recreation will grow more diverse.

Priest and Gass (1999) have reiterated the findings of the President's Council on Americans Outdoors, especially noting the growth in adventure-based programs and activities. They cite the increasing number of participants and increased revenues from outdoor recreation participation and also note that many of the fastest-growing sports, such as rock climbing, surfing, and sailing, are adventure based. In addition, Priest and Gass (1999) cite the increase in artificial adventure environments that are being built throughout the United States and Canada. These facilities include wave pools, climbing walls, ski slopes, kayak roll tanks, and white-water canoe chutes. As technology continues to advance, it will be interesting to note what other "outdoor environments" will be simulated for pleasure.

Most people have a broad definition of outdoor recreation—it entails any activity that takes place outdoors (e.g., playing football and tennis, attending outdoor sports events, and visiting amusement parks). A more specific definition, however, is needed to differentiate outdoor recreation from such sports as football and tennis. In an attempt to create such a definition Carlson (1960) notes that outdoor recreation is any enjoyable leisure time activity pursued outdoors or indoors involving knowledge, use, or appreciation of natural resources. This definition best fits the fastest-growing area of outdoor recreation, outdoor adventure pursuits.

Outdoor adventure pursuits have been defined as "a variety of self-initiated activities utilizing an interaction with the natural environment, that contain elements of real or apparent danger, in which the outcome, while uncertain, can be influenced by the participant and circumstance" (Ewert, 1989, p. 6). Specific outdoor adventure pursuits include such activities as backpacking, white-water rafting, mountain biking, and rock climbing.

Americans' increasing participation in outdoor recreation, whether inside or outside, demonstrates the need to reconnect with the natural environment. As society becomes even more technical and advanced, this need will continue and will be met in a number of diverse outdoor activities—from fishing to white-water rafting, from hunting to outdoor photography, from sightseeing in one's car to backpacking in the wilderness.

Tourism as Mass Leisure

Whether it is a trip to a local museum or a trip around the world, most people have been or will be tourists at some point in their lifetime. In the later half of the twentieth century we saw tourism become the world's second-largest industry (behind the petroleum industry) with strong growth projected into the twenty-first century. Tourism has certainly become a major economic force in the United States, Canada, and the world. Consider the fact that world travel accounted for 11 percent of world GDP in 1997 and grew to 11.7 percent by 1999. Global tourism receipts doubled from $221 billion to $445 billion between 1992 and 1996. Globally, over 100 million new jobs are expected to be generated by the travel and tourism sector by 2010 (Molitar, 2000).

In the United States, travel and tourism rank among the top three economic activities in thirty-two states as of 1999. Global travelers are expected to double to 1 billion by 2010, and

Hostelling: Fulfilling the Promise of Travel

People have seen the world grow smaller in the twentieth century. Advances in transportation and communication have connected everyone in a global network. These advances, combined with increased discretionary income of people in the developed world, have led to an explosion in international travel in the last twenty years. However, much of the travel is predominantly a one-way exchange as Western tourists travel to developing countries in search of "exotic experiences." When one browses through travel brochures and magazines, it becomes apparent that developing countries are increasingly the destination point for planes and cruise lines. This phenomenon has caused many critics to claim that tourism has become another form of dependence, a kind of economic colonialism, which has a lasting effect on native cultures and traditions. Yet this description seems unfair, failing to give recognition to the opportunities that travel and tourism can present to promote global understanding. One must realize travel is only a medium that can be used for good or ill. The challenge to the tourism industry and the individual traveler is to promote travel, which strives to be equally beneficial to all members of the global community, and brings about the realization that all nations share a "cultural parity" or cultural equality within diversity.

One organization working to help promote travel as education is Hostelling International—American Youth Hostels (HI-AYH). For HI-AYH, hostelling is "a way of traveling that unlocks opportunity. It offers a chance to see the world—to experience people and places different from what we've known. The end result can be greater understanding of a country or a culture, a deeper appreciation of the world's diversity, or a new perspective on our own lives" (HI-AYH, 1999). HI-AYH is a part of the global network of Hostelling International, which makes travel possible by providing an expansive system of hostel facilities and programs. HI-AYH operates a network of hostels throughout the United States that are affordable, safe, and clean. Most important, however, is the fact that hostels are designed to foster interaction among guests. They include shared living space and common areas that give people from all over the world an opportunity to get to know one another.

HI-AYH hostels are often found in unique and historic settings such as San Francisco's Fort Mason, an old lifesaving station on Nantucket Island, Pigeon Point Lighthouse in California, and Bear's Den Hostel on the Appalachian Trail. Hostels also provide a wide range of educational programs. These programs help travelers learn more about cities and towns, histories, and cultures of the surrounding areas, providing them a sense of place. HI-AYH also offers a variety of programs for people in local communities. These programs range from travel seminars like "World Travel 101" and "Women Traveling Alone" to programs such as the Cultural Kitchen, which reaches out to local youth, helping them interact with travelers from around the world.

Although the mission of HI-AYH focuses on young people, hostels are open to and widely used by people of all ages. In choosing hostelling as the means by which they travel, these people make a conscious choice to travel in an alternative manner and support the aims of hostelling, which HI-AYH identifies as the following:

- Hostelling promotes world understanding—having a chance to see how people in other parts of the world live, and what's important to them can sometimes reshape a person's own values.
- Hostelling fosters discovery and learning.
- Hostelling supports community development.

Source: HI-AYH Annual Report, 1999.

expenditures are expected to top $1.6 trillion in that same year (Molitor, 2000). The United States ranked third behind France and Spain as the most visited country by international visitors. Revenues generated from international travelers in the United States are one of the true bright spots in the international trade accounts. The trade surplus generated by the travel and hospitality industry totaled more than $24 billion in 1998.

TABLE

5.5   Travel by U.S. Residents by Selected Trip Characteristics (1998)

Characteristic	Percentage of the Total Trips Taken in 1998 (%)
Visiting relatives and friends	48
Major purpose was entertainment	35
Pursued outdoor recreation interests	15
Involved motor transport only (car, bus)	83
Included air transport	13
Stayed in hotels and/or motels (with an average stay of 3.6 overnights per trip)	41

Data from: Molitar, 2000.

Tourism as mass leisure includes the activities in which people engage during their travels. People may travel to large metropolitan areas in search of cultural activities or major sporting events. Likewise, people may travel to rural areas for opportunities to participate in eco-tourism—outdoor recreation and adventure pursuits. Or people may simply travel to visit friends or family in a distance place. Table 5.5 presents a number of specific characteristics of American travelers in 1998. From these characteristics two major travel trends seem to have emerged. The first of these trends sees the vacation patterns of American families changing. Americans want weeklong or monthlong vacations; however, pressed-for-time people take shorter and more frequent vacations rather than one longer annual vacation (Molitar, 2000). During these vacations they are often seeking recreational activities closer to home. The second trend focuses on an emerging adventure tourism and eco-tourism markets.

As evidence of the growing demand of people to vacation closer to home, consider the amusement and theme park industry as well as the megaleisure complexes that are evolving. Although Disney is often regarded as the leader of the theme park industry, many smaller regional parks are springing up throughout the country. In 1998, Americans filled an estimated 900 million ride seats at some 450 amusement parks across the country (Gardyn and Fetto, 2000). Theme park revenues accounted for more than $6.1 billion in 1999 (Molitar, 2000). The rides at these parks grow bigger, faster, and more gravity-defying each year. As of May 2000, the Millennial Force roller coaster at Cedar Point amusement park in Sandusky, Ohio, is the world's tallest and fastest. This two-minute-plus ride climbs to 310 feet and plunges at a top speed of 92 mph.

With the continued emergence of technology, there is no limit of the type of entertainment complexes that may emerge. Consider Disney's latest park, DisneyQuest, in Chicago, Illinois. This complex fits more into the framework of a regional attraction and relies heavily on technology: "DisneyQuest is an indoor interactive park that combines the magic of Disney with the cutting edge immersive technologies such as virtual reality and real time 3-D. Spanning five floors DisneyQuest has four unique zones of entertainment bursting with attractions, rides and games" (Disney, 2000).

In addition to amusement parks, mega-multiuse leisure complexes are being built throughout the world—places like the Mall of America in Minneapolis, which includes shopping, an indoor amusement park (Camp Snoopy), Lego Land, an aquarium, restaurants, theaters, and comedy clubs. Year-round sports complexes are also expanding. Consider Gotcha Glacier, a facility situated in Anaheim, California, scheduled to open in 2001. The facility includes the first indoor snowboard and surf entertainment/sports attraction in America. Winter sports hosted include two snowboard halfpipes, beginner ski slopes, and an ice skating rink. Swimmers and surfers will be able to choose among six wave pools. These types of complexes attract people from throughout their region and in some cases develop a national reputation.

On the other end of the spectrum of humanmade theme parks and megafacilities, adventure tourism and eco-tourism are also continuing to expand at a rapid rate. These new industries are founded on the belief that travel is a form of education. For several decades, tourism has brought us closer to global (as well as national and regional) understanding and acceptance of various cultures. Not only does tourism stimulate economies and distribute wealth to less stable economies, it also encourages peace in this world. Tourism has been credited in part for the opening of China's borders, liberalizing Eastern Europe, and reducing international conflicts. When people from different cultures have the opportunity to meet one another and exchange ideas, inhibitions and misconceptions are destroyed (*Earth Journal,* 1993).

Although little consensus exists regarding exact definitions of adventure tourism and eco-tourism, these areas of the tourism industry encourage people of different cultures to interact and share common interests, such as concern for the environment or interest in a particular outdoor adventure pursuit. Adventure tourism (including eco-tourism) combines many of the trends of American society such as fitness, environmentalism, multiculturalism, and travel. In the last twenty years, adventure tourism has grown from a small segment of the travel industry to as much as one-fifth of the U.S. leisure travel market (Adler, Glick, King, Gorden, and Cohen, 1993).

Mass Media and Leisure

The media has a tremendous impact on the leisure behavior of U.S. and Canadian citizens. Television viewing, attendance at movies, listening to music, and other forms of mass media consume large blocks of leisure time of individuals. For example, adolescents, nine to eleven years of age, spend an average 21.5 hours per week watching television (U.S. Bureau of Economic Analysis, 1995). Not only does the mass media consume leisure time, it also greatly influences the leisure values of individuals. This section of the chapter discusses television viewing, movie attendance, and involvement with other forms of mass media.

Television Viewing as Mass Leisure   Television is by far the most popular of all American pastimes: Over 30 percent of free time is spent watching television, with Monday being the busiest viewing day (Spring, 1993). Robinson and Godbey (1997) report that Americans spend nearly three hours per day watching television, which was about 40 percent of the average American's free time in 1995, an increase of roughly one-third since 1965. Between 1965 and 1995 Americans gained an average of six hours a week in added leisure time, and we spent almost all six of those additional hours watching television. In short, Robinson and Godbey conclude, "Television is the 800-pound gorilla of leisure time" (p. 20). (See figure 5.2)

Americans are not alone in their television viewing. In fact, television is growing in popularity in almost every country on the globe. In countries where many families cannot afford their own television, people congregate in the houses of friends and viewing becomes a social experience. The people of the world spend upwards of 3.5 billion hours watching television every day (Kubey and Csikszentmihalyi, 1990).

Perhaps the most comprehensive study examining television and its effects on viewers was conducted by Kubey and Csikszentmihalyi in 1990. The results of the study, reported in their

Calvin and Hobbes

by Bill Watterson

Calvin and Hobbes

by Bill Watterson

book *Television and the Quality of Life: How Viewing Shapes Everyday Experiences,* were based on findings from 1,200 subjects in nine different studies conducted over the past thirteen years. These results are presented in table 5.6.

These results clearly indicate the power of television in people's lives and the need to use this medium widely. Kubey and Csikszentmihalyi (1990) suggest that schools must begin to accept some responsibility for helping students be astute television viewers and helping them use their leisure wisely. As Brightbill (1960) notes, "The future will belong not only to the educated man [*sic*] but to the man who is educated to use . . . leisure wisely" (p. 94). Clearly television can benefit people, but to optimize this benefit it must be used wisely.

The television habits of individuals reflect their values and interests in many ways. Table 5.7 provides a list of the most frequently viewed programs in the United States in 1998–1999. The top-ten television list reflects a mix of preferences—Americans like to watch thirty-minute situation comedies that require little, if any, thinking by the viewer, and they enjoy television dramas where complex social issues are raised, addressed, and resolved in less than an hour. The comedies, often highly predictable, are entertainment in the clearest sense of the word. In many ways these shows also shape people's views and influence their leisure choices. What values do the shows listed in table 5.7 transmit about leisure?

What values does television transmit about societies in Canada and the United States? Television is often seen as the reality of life rather than as fantasy. This can create problems when viewers begin to feel that their lives do not live up to the standards they see on television. False perceptions also can be detrimental on a global scale.

TABLE

5.6   TELEVISION AND ITS EFFECTS ON VIEWERS

- Viewers want television programs to be familiar and predictable, more so than unusual and stimulating—they prefer novelty in a safe context. Television is often designed to do the opposite of art, to reassure rather than excite.
- Roughly 90 percent of the time people choose to watch television because they want to do so.
- Americans watch television whenever they have the time, rather than because they want to watch a particular program.
- Nearly two-thirds of the time television is a secondary activity. Primary activities while viewing television include talking, eating, grooming, cleaning, doing chores, cooking, and reading.
- Men, on the average, watch slightly more television than women, and women's viewing tends to be slightly more active than men's. This is true partly because of a higher frequency of secondary activities accompanying television viewing for women, such as cooking and cleaning.
- In one sample it was found that Blacks tended to watch more television than Whites or Hispanics.
- Some findings suggest that education does not seem to influence how much television people watch; other findings suggest the opposite. More educated respondents did report a significantly greater "wish to do something else" beside watching television.
- "Television viewing is a passive and relaxing, low-concentration activity. When viewing television, people report feeling more passive and less challenged and alert, while simultaneously concentrating less and using fewer skills, than in almost any other daily activity except resting and doing nothing" (p. 171).
- "Television may both promote and be a hindrance to the quality of family life" (p. 172). Although heavier use of television seems to increase the time spent with other family members, the quality of this time is not high.
- Television viewing, often done in an attempt to avoid loneliness, can be used as a substitute for social interaction.
- After watching television, viewers tend to feel passive and less alert. "People reported feeling more passive, less alert, and experiencing somewhat more difficulty concentrating after television viewing than they did before viewing or after other activities" (p. 172).
- Satisfaction with television decreases the longer it is viewed. "The more people view the less they appear to enjoy it. Furthermore, the relaxing rewards only appear to occur during viewing and not afterwards. Viewing seems to provide relief from tension only temporarily" (p. 173).
- "Heavier viewers feel worse than light viewers generally, and particularly when alone or during unstructured time" (p. 173).

From R. Kubey and M. Csikszentmihalyi, *Television and the Quality of Life,* 1990. Copyright © 1990 Lawrence Erlbaum Associates, Inc., Hillsdale, NJ. Reprinted by permission.

    Enormous audiences around the world view programs such as *Friends, Baywatch,* and *Dallas; Dallas* has aired in more than ninety countries (Kubey and Csikszentmihalyi, 1990). They note that "at a 1988 international meeting of television program buyers and sellers in Cannes, one estimate set U.S. television program sales to Europe at $2.7 billion for 1992" (p. xi). MTV, an invention of the American media, powerfully shapes culture in Hong Kong as much as it does in the United States and Canada. MTV Hong Kong, a dynamic form of entertainment, integrates American mass leisure in the form of rock videos with rock videos produced in Hong Kong, China, Japan, and other Asian venues.

Movies and Mass Leisure   Big-screen cinema has a rich history in the United States and Canada. From the silent films at the beginning of the twentieth century to today's megahits, people hunger for the escape that only movies can provide. In the 1920s approximately seven to

TABLE

5.7 ENTERTAINMENT IN REVIEW

Top Ten Movies 1998	Top Ten Regularly Scheduled Television Programs (1998–1999)
Titanic	*E.R.*
Armageddon	*Friends*
Saving Private Ryan	*Frazier*
There's Something About Mary	*NFL Monday Night Football*
The Waterboy	*Jesse*
Dr. Dolittle	*Veronica's Closet*
Deep Impact	*60 Minutes*
Godzilla	*Touched by an Angel*
Rush Hour	*CBS Sunday Night Movie*
(Variety, Inc. 1999)	(Nielsen Media Research)

Top Ten All-Time Top Movie Money-Makers Through 1998	Top Ten Syndicated Television Programs (1998–1999)
Titanic (1997)	*Wheel of Fortune (M-F)*
Star Wars (1977)	*Jeopardy (M-F)*
E.T. The Extra-Terrestrial (1982)	*ESPN NFL Regular Season*
Jurassic Park (1993)	*Jerry Springer (M-F)*
Forrest Gump (1994)	*Judge Judy (M-F)*
The Lion King (1994)	*Friends (M-F)*
Return of the Jedi (1983)	*Oprah Winfrey Show (M-F)*
Independence Day (1996)	*Seinfeld (M-F)*
The Empire Strikes Back (1980)	*Entertainment Tonight*
Home Alone (1990)	*Buena Vista I*
(Variety, Inc. 1999)	(Nielsen Media Research)

Top Ten Video Cassette Rentals—1998	Top Ten All-Time Video Cassette Rentals Through 1998
Titanic	*Top Gun*
Air Force One	*Pretty Women*
Con Air	*The Little Mermaid*
Face/Off	*Home Alone*
As Good as It Gets	*Ghost*
My Best Friend's Wedding	*Cinderella*
Men in Black	*Beauty and the Beast*
The Devil's Advocate	*Lion King*
Armageddon	*Terminator 2: Judgment Day*
G.I. Jane	*Aladdin*
(Alexander & Associates)	(Alexander & Associates)

Data from *The World Almanac and Book of Facts*. 2000. Mahwah, NJ: World Almanac Books.

ten million people saw a movie every day. Dulles (1965) notes that by 1929 "weekly attendance jumped to an estimated 110 million—the equivalent of four-fifths of the entire population [of the United States] going to a show once a week throughout the entire year" (p. 299). The success of big-screen movies continued to rise until the early 1950s when television began to be mass produced.

With the creation of videos and the VCR, many people predicted the total demise of movie theaters. This, however, has not proven to be the case. Movie attendance steadily increased from 1975 to 1997. The Motion Picture Association of America reports that the number of theaters is increasing, with more than 32,000 movie theaters, 31,000 of which are walk-in; 1,000 are drive-ins. These figures represent an increase of over 100 percent since 1975. In 1997, Americans spent more than $6.3 billion at the box office, an increase of about 33 percent since 1990 (American Motion Picture Association, 1999).

Although Hollywood may never reach the peak it reached in the 1920s and 1930s, it is still a powerful force in people's lives and in the marketplace—its economic impact can be felt far from the box office itself. Through clever advance marketing, the 1996 hit *Independence Day* grossed $11 million dollars in its first twenty-four hours of showing. Another 1996 hit *Pocahontas* displays an example of the economic power of a megamovie. Sales from toys, t-shirts, and other related merchandise reached well into the upper millions. Partnerships with fast-food restaurants and other commercial ventures to use picture-related packaging and products both promote the movie and increase related sales and profits. Having weathered the onslaught of television and the home video market, Hollywood continues to prosper and will be a major shaper of many of the fads and trends of the United States and Canada in the decades to come.

Other Forms of Media and Mass Leisure Mass media includes several other mediums beyond those of television and movies. These additional mediums can be broken into two categories. The first, printed media, includes newspapers, magazines, comics, and books. The second category includes electronic forms of leisure such as radios, Nintendo, and other computer games.

The proliferation of mass media related to television, movies, and radio sometimes makes it easy to overlook the impact of printed material. Yet people are reading and writing as never before. In 1997, Americans spent more than $26 million on books (Book Industry Supply Group, 1999). A United Media study (1993) reported that newspapers are the most-favored reading material (67%), followed by books (25%) and magazines (19%). This seems consistent with a cross-cultural study completed almost two decades ago that found Americans spent on the average twenty-four minutes a day reading newspapers, five minutes a day reading books, and six minutes a day reading magazines (Ibrahim, 1991). Comic book collections also have made a surprisingly strong comeback in recent years.

Technology has created a number of other forms of mass leisure and changed how we participate in certain activities, such as listening to music. From eight-tracks and records to cassettes, compact disks, and videos, the music industry is rapidly changing. Today, compact disk sales comprise the fastest growing segment of the music industry. Sales between 1985 and 1994 show an increase in sales of compact disks, cassettes, and music videos, while the sale of vinyl records dropped tremendously (see table 5.8).

With the combination of computers and television, Nintendo and other video games have evolved. Computer games such as "Where in the World Is Carmen Sandiego?" are also growing in popularity. Many computer games combine education with recreation as participants gain computer skills along with new knowledge and insights.

5.8	TECHNOLOGY AND LEISURE	

Type	1997 (in millions)	Percent change from 1994
Compact disk	11,416	15.1
Cassette	1,419	8.2
Music videos	508	56.8
LP (vinyl records)	34	2.1

Data from U.S. Bureau of the Census. 1999. *Statistical Abstracts of the United States.* 119th ed. Washington, DC: U.S. Government Printing Office.

Future technological breakthroughs will continue to impact mass leisure. Initially, only a few can afford new technology, but as prices inevitably drop, participation and involvement increase. One of the newest and perhaps most far-reaching computer technologies, soon to be available en masse, is that of virtual reality. Virtual reality (VR) enables participants to experience "a through-the-looking-glass adventure in which they move freely in a three-dimensional space created by software" (Naisbitt, 1992, p. 7) by wearing fiber optic goggles and gloves, and sometimes earphones.

Application of this technology in entertainment includes an arcade where players can compete in video warfare, a Disneyland attraction entitled "Body Tours," a Universal Studio attraction entitled "Back to the Future," and virtual reality theaters in which the audience takes part in the video action. According to Naisbitt (1992), as computers become increasingly powerful, the development and use of virtual reality will accelerate. "VR probably will only begin to reach its full potential in the next 20 years, but within 30 years home VR systems could be as prevalent as television sets today" (p. 7).

Summary

In this chapter we have explored the concept of mass leisure and the activities in which the masses participate. As a shaper and a reflection of culture, leisure cannot be understood apart from the society in which it takes place. Although leisure is a personal matter, society encourages or discourages leisure behavior through its formal laws and regulations as well as through its unwritten values and traditions. As a result of this influence, various patterns of leisure behavior have developed and evolved. These patterns may be referred to as *mass leisure.* It is similar to popular or mass culture, which is defined as the most visible level of culture—the one found between the extremes of elite and folk culture. Within such popular culture, mass leisure is one facet of culture that reflects the everyday recreational activities of the majority of the population.

A number of factors have contributed to the proliferation of mass leisure in this century. First and foremost is the concept of time and mass leisure. Many people living in industrial societies today report a shortage of time, or "time famine," in their lives. People's views of time in the future will be critical to understanding leisure. Other factors influencing mass leisure that were identified in this chapter include an increase in discretionary income, the changing values of society toward mass leisure, improved infrastructure and technology, and the proliferation of the mass media.

The mass leisure activities explored in this chapter are diverse. These activities have been classified into several types of mass leisure that include *social activities*—done in a social context with other people;

sport activities, including both active participation and spectator sports; *cultural activities*—participating in the arts; *outdoor activities*—interacting with the outdoor environment (includes outdoor adventure pursuits); *tourism activities,* including all activities people do during their travels; and *mass media,* including television, movies, music, printed media, and so forth.

Many of these activities are overlapping. For example, a sporting event is also a social event. This overlap highlights the interconnectedness of leisure activities—one category of activities can have a direct impact on many other types of leisure behavior. This interconnectedness is reflective of the growing dependency upon connections among all aspects of our daily lives. The challenge to leisure service professionals is one of promoting cooperation and collaboration between and among service providers to more effectively meet the needs of the individual.

Discussion Questions

1. Define mass leisure. In what types of mass leisure do you participate?
2. What is the difference between mass culture and high culture? In your opinion, is one better than another? Explain your answer.
3. What four revolutions have contributed to the growth of outdoor recreation activities?
4. What is a leisure democracy? What implications does this concept have for studying mass leisure?
5. What is time famine? Is this phenomenon evident in your life? Do you think society is running out of time? What implications might time famine have for delivering leisure services in the future?
6. What future technological breakthroughs are you anticipating? What impact will this new technology have on leisure?
7. Identify some of the ways television impacts your personal leisure lifestyle. What are some of the positive and negative ways that television can affect leisure participation?
8. Choose a recent popular movie and discuss its influence on the leisure behavior and consumption patterns of Canadian and United States citizens.
9. Poll five of your friends as to the frequency and types of activities in which they are involved during their free time. How do the lists you generate compare to the activities listed in this chapter?
10. What forms of mass leisure might evolve in the future?

References

(1987). *Americans Outdoors: The legacy, the challenge with case studies.* Island Press.

Adler, J., D. Glick, P. King, J. Gorden, and A. Cohen. 1993. Been there, done that. *Time* (July 19), 42–49.

American Motion Picture Association. 1999. *Statistical Abstracts of the United States.* Washington, DC.

Bammel, G., and L. Bammel. 1996. *Leisure and Human Behavior.* Dubuque, IA: Wm. C. Brown.

Book Industry Supply Group. 1999. *Statistical Abstracts of the United States.* Washington, DC.

Brightbill, C. 1960. *The Challenge of Leisure.* Englewood Cliffs, NJ: Prentice-Hall.

Brown, R. 1978. Popular Culture, No. 4: Themes continue to be heard. *The Center Daily Times* (February 8).

Carlson, R. 1960, 1985. Outdoor recreation definition. Edited by N. T. Rillo, in *HPER* 542 Class Packet: Foundations Outdoor/Environmental Education. Indiana University: Unpublished Manuscript.

Cutler, B. 1990. Where does the free time go? *American Demographics* (November), 36–39.

de Grazia, 1962. *Of Time, Work and Leisure.* Garden City, NY: Anchor Books.

Disney. 2000. DisneyQuest website available at http://disney.go.com/DisneyQuest.

Dulles, F. 1965. *A History of Recreation: America Learns to Play.* New York: Appleton-Century-Crofts.

Earth Journal. 1993. *Earth Journal: Environmental Almanac and Resources Directory.* Boulder, CO: Buzzworm Books.

Edginton, C., C. Hanson, S. Edginton, and S. Hudson. 1998. *Leisure Programming: A Service Centered and Benefits Approach.* Boston, MA: WCB McGraw-Hill.

Ewert, A. 1989. *Outdoor Adventure Pursuits: Foundation, Models, and Theories.* Scottsdale, AZ: Publishing Horizons.

Famighetti, R., ed. 1995. *The World Almanac & Book of Facts 1996.* Mahwah, NJ: Funk & Wagnalls Corp.

Gardyn, R., and J. Fetto. 2000. Off the beaten path: Looking for a good time. *American Demographics* (July), 72.

Gibbs, N. 1989. How America has run out of time. *Time* (April 24), 58–67.

Godbey, G. 1994. *Leisure in Your Life: An Exploration.* State College, PA: Venture.

Gunn, C. 1986. Philosophical relationships: Conservation, recreation, leisure, and tourism. In *A Literature Review: The President's Commission on Americans Outdoors,* 1–9. Washington, DC: U.S. Government Printing Office.

Hostelling International—American Youth Hostels (HI-AYH). (1999). *Hostelling International—American Youth Hostels 1999 Annual Report.* Washington D.C. HI-AYH.

Ibrahim, H. 1991. *Leisure and Society.* Dubuque, IA: Wm. C. Brown.

Kando, T. 1980. *Leisure and Popular Culture in Transition.* St. Louis: Mosby.

Kelly, J., and G. Godbey. 1992. *The Sociology of Leisure.* State College, PA: Venture.

Kelly, J. 1996. *Leisure.* 3rd ed. Boston: Allyn and Bacon.

Kubey, R., and M. Csikszentmihalyi. 1990. *Television and the Quality of Life.* Hillsdale, NJ: Lawrence Erlbaum.

May, H., and D. Petgin. 1928. *Leisure and Its Uses.* New York: A. S. Barnes.

Molitor, G. T. 2000, May 3. *Here Comes 2015: The Onset of the Leisure Era.* Speech delivered at the Travel Business Roundtable Annual Meeting, Crystal City, Virginia.

Naisbitt, J. 1992. *Trends Newsletter.*

Naisbitt, J., and B. Aburdene. 1990. *Megatrends 2000.* New York: Morrow.

Nash, R. 1982. *Wilderness and the American Mind.* New Haven: Yale University Press.

National Sporting Goods Association. 1995. *Statistical Abstracts of the U.S. 1995.* 115th ed.

National Sporting Goods Association. 1999. *Statistical Abstracts of the United States.* Washington, DC.

President's Commission on Americans Outdoors (PCAO). 1987. *Americans Outdoors, the Legacy, the Challenge.* Washington D.C., Island Press.

Priest, S., and M. Gass. 1999. Future trends and issues in adventure programming. J. Miles and S. Priest, eds. in *Adventure Programming,* 473–478. State College, PA: Venture.

Putnam, R. 2000. *Bowling Alone: The Collapse and Revival of American Community.* New York: Simon & Schuster.

Ragheb M. and J. Beard. 1992. Measuring Leisure Interests. *Journal of Park and Recreation Administration, 10*(2), 1–13.

Raymond, J. 2000. Wild America. *American Demographics* (August), 54–58.

Recording Industry Association. 2000. *World Almanac and Book of Facts.* Mahway, NJ: World Almanac Books.

Robinson, J. P. 1989. Time's up. *American Demographics* (July), 33–35.

Robinson, J. P. 1990a. The time squeeze. *American Demographics* (February), 30–33.

Robinson, J. P. 1990b. The leisure pie. *American Demographics 12* (November), 39.

Robinson, J. P. 1991. Your money or your time. *American Demographics 13* (November), 22–26.

Robinson, J., and G. Godbey. 1997. *Time for Life: The Surprising Way Americans Spend Their Time.* University Park, PA: Pennsylvania State University Press.

Samdahl, D. 1992. Leisure in our lives: Enhancing the common leisure occasion. *Journal of Leisure Research 24*(1), 19–32.

Schor, J. 1991. *The Overworked American: The Unexpected Decline of Leisure.* New York: Basic Books.

Searle, M. S., and R. E. Brayley. 2000. *Leisure in Canada: An Introduction.* 2d ed. State College, PA: Venture.

Spring, J. 1993. Seven Days of Play. *American Demographics* (March), 50–53.

Stein Wellner, A. 2000. The end of leisure. *American Demographics* (July), 50–56.

U.S. Bureau of the Census. 2000. *Statistical Abstract of the United States.* Washington, DC: U.S. Government Printing Office.

U.S. Bureau of Economic Analysis. 1995. *Statistical Abstract of the United States 1995.* 115th ed. Washington, DC: U.S. Government Printing Office.

Van den Haag, E. 1964. A dissent from the consensual society. Edited by Norman Jacobs, in *Culture for the Millions? Mass Media in Modern Society,* 53–62. Boston: Beacon Books.

CHAPTER

Leisure and the Life Cycle

Leisure provides opportunities throughout the entire life span. Gardening is a significant activity among North Americans. Here, a man waters plants in his home greenhouse.

Introduction

How does the human life cycle relate to the concept of life satisfaction in leisure? Generally speaking, as individuals move through life, they grow, mature, gain wisdom and knowledge, and reflect leisure behaviors that result from their past experiences and development. As Erikson (1963) points out, the positive growth and development of individuals can lead to a life of fulfillment, characterized by trust, autonomy, initiative, industry, sense of identity, intimacy, and integrity. Successful leisure experiences can contribute to the positive growth and development of individuals.

According to Grey and Greben's benchmark article (1974), and underscored by the National Recreation and Park Association's Twenty-First Century Agenda (1992), the leisure movement in the United States must make the growth and development of participants a priority within its organizations and programs. Because it is freely chosen, the leisure experience can contribute in a unique way to growth and development throughout one's life. Yet during our lifetimes the activities we enjoy and participate in change. These changes are due in part to the process of development that is a part of the human experience.

This chapter addresses the life cycle and its relationship to leisure. It examines leisure throughout the life cycle, including a discussion of childhood, adolescence, adulthood, and older adulthood, and provides the reader with information regarding human development and its relationship to leisure.

Leisure throughout the Life Cycle

This section of the book discusses leisure and the life cycle along with a brief overview of the stages of human development and their relationship to leisure. This brief discussion provides a framework for understanding leisure and the life cycle in an overview of basic concepts and ideas related to the process of human development.

Lifestyles

Lifestyle is defined by *Webster's Encyclopedia Unabridged Dictionary* as "the habits, attitudes, tastes, moral standards, economic level, etc., that together constitute the mode of living of an individual or group." In addition to those demographic variables mentioned, lifestyle may also be influenced by other variables such as age, gender, social class, and more, including psychographic variables. Sessoms (1985) defines the term *lifestyle* as "a person's mode of expression." The outward manifestation of lifestyle includes such items as dress, speech patterns, language, activity selection, living situation, social relationships, and religion. Most sociologists agree that each dominant lifestyle has an integrated core of activities associated with it. Those who share a similar lifestyle tend to form subgroups that reinforce their individual choices and set their behavior priorities. These are often referred to as subcultures.

Lifestyles are dynamic and therefore may change during the course of a lifetime. For example, as a student moves from high school to college and then into the working world, lifestyle changes can accompany each stage. Yet other aspects of lifestyle (e.g., religion, ethnic, or racial background) may cut across many age groups or life stages. Even within a dominant lifestyle, such as being a student, subgroups may appear, such as athletic teams or fraternity and sorority members. Although these two groups may share many common characteristics of being college students, unique differences surface between them. These subgroups, or subcultures, have the potential of establishing the norms and defining the underlying values and common behaviors for each of the individuals in them.

For example, the baby boom generation has been talked about and studied for a number of years as a cohort that shares a common lifestyle. This generation encompasses those who were born between 1945 and 1963—the post–World War II years. In 1998, however, the American Association of Retired Persons (AARP) identified five distinct segments (subgroups) among the baby boom generation (AARP, 2000). People who represent each of these subgroups share more in common with one another than with those who represent other segments.

The Strugglers This subgroup constitutes 9 percent of the baby boom generation and is the lowest income group. It also has a large number of females (64 percent) in it. Those in this group find it difficult to save for retirement and have actually thought very little about it. A majority of Strugglers do not have an optimistic outlook about their later years.

The Anxious The people representing this group also have a sense of apprehension when looking ahead to their later years. This group comprises almost one quarter of the baby boom group (23 percent) and they have limited means. They expect to *have* to work into retirement years. Anxious group members also have a great concern with coverage for health care in later years.

The Enthusiasts Thirteen percent of baby boomers fall into this segment and include people who are eager to reach their retirement years. These people do not plan to work at all in retirement and envision plenty of money and plenty of time for recreation. Retirement is viewed as a time free from work.

The Self-Reliants The largest group of baby boomers (30 percent), Self-Reliants have the highest income and education levels of any group in this cohort. The 1 percent of people in

Welcome to Virtual Leisure . . .

The following newspaper article appeared in newspapers around the country in April, 1996. The article reports an interesting trend in which people surround themselves with lifestyle ornaments they do not or cannot use.

A young sales manager has a kitchen that would make Julia Child's mouth water. But all the appliances are dusty. A woman buys a baby grand piano. But no one in the household knows how to play. Urban dwellers behind the wheels of their Range Rovers navigate nothing more demanding than traffic jams. The vehicles are capable of trouncing the Outback. Witness a growing trend in which Americans surround themselves with lifestyle ornaments they do not or cannot use. They create a living tableau of leisure in which they do not participate. Welcome to virtual leisure.

We sink onto the couch and watch "This Old House," but the prospect of actually stripping 16 layers of paint makes many of us sweat. We lose ourselves in Martha Stewart's books but don't emulate her. What's going on? Seismic lifestyle shifts have changed the way we spend our free time, experts say. We also may be measuring our lives against the model of our parents. When we watch a crafts show without lifting a finger, we may be feeling nostalgia for the days when people made things with their hands, rather than putting things on a credit card.

When we watch "This Old House" or follow Martha Stewart's projects, "we're vicariously participating in the baking of cookies, the growing of a garden, or going to a workshop," says Steven Kelly, head of the Direct Marketing Institute at DePaul University. Norm Abrams, the how-to hero of "This Old House" and "The New Yankee Workshop" agrees. "There is no sweat. There's no dirt. There's no bills to pay. They can watch a piece of furniture come together at 'Yankee Workshop' and they feel at the end of the show they've participated in some way."

Many people escape into virtual leisure because they are dissatisfied, theorizes TV fishing guru Babe Winkelman. "Most people are not happy with their lives. They're not happy with what they do for a living. They're not happy with the environment they're raising their children in." His fans tell him: "We fish through you."

"We've grown accustomed to watching instead of doing," Kelly said. "Television allows an involvement with what is going on that wasn't previously there," said Dr. Sidney Weissman of Loyola University Medical Center. Instead of going out dancing on Friday, we often turn to passive leisure, surfing the Internet or watching a video. "I'm sure more Nordic Tracks function as coat racks rather than exercise equipment," Weissman said.

Points to Ponder

- Within this article is the concept of virtual leisure positive or negative?
- What concerns or opportunities does this article raise for leisure service professionals?

this segment who envision themselves working some during retirement years plan to do so because of interest and enjoyment they find in the work.

Today's Traditionalists One quarter of the baby boomer generation comprises this segment and is traditional in many attitudes. Traditionalists express a stronger sense of confidence than the other segments in government retirement programs (Social Security, Medicare). In addition, people in this group intend to work and rely on government programs during retirement years.

One thing is clear among all five baby boomer segments. Most of this generation plan to work for pay after retirement. This has a large impact on the provision of leisure services for the older population. The new seniors will be active well into their later years.

A Perspective on the Life Cycle

FRANK AND ERNEST reprinted by permission of Newspaper Enterprise Association, Inc.

The Life Cycle

Understanding leisure throughout the life cycle requires the realization that change is an integral part of life. This sort of developmental approach sees people as being in a constant state of becoming, changing, and developing by stages that are similar for most people. The concept of *stages* or *life stages* implies that life involves a series of connected stages, each influencing one another, but each being distinct (Sessoms, 1985). Education level, socioeconomic status, sex, and family status impact the nature of this cyclical process.

Within each life stage, age is not necessarily fixed as life stages overlap and vary widely in life situations. Life cycle does influence recreation and leisure choices. For instance, Kelly (1978, 1996) found that family life cycle proves to be a better indicator of participation in recreation than age. For example, the leisure activities of a twenty-five-year-old single person may well be different from a twenty-five-year-old married person with two children. Likewise, leisure patterns tend to rely more on the fact that a couple's children have left home than that the couple's age has advanced from forty to fifty years (Godbey, 1994). In these examples, parenthood plays a large part in leisure participation.

Other life cycle factors influence leisure participation. For instance, in your parents' and grandparents' generations, it was common for a person to complete grade school and either go to college or begin working. Between the ages of twenty and twenty-five, this individual would likely marry and continue to develop his or her work skills. Children would enter the family unit and this individual would remain with the same company for his or her entire work life. Today it is relatively common for a person to begin the same way (grade school, college, work), but then things change. Contemporary individuals are more likely to hold multiple jobs with multiple companies over the course of their work history, and it is not uncommon (particularly for men) to have two families—a first marriage with grown children and a second marriage with young children. One's participation in leisure is heavily affected by these types of cycles.

Stages of Human Development

The passage of individuals through various life stages involves all aspects of a person's development. According to Brill (n.d.), the five key aspects of human development are physical, social, emotional, intellectual, and spiritual. While many theories abound as to how people develop in each of these areas, one of the most accepted theories of personality development is Erikson's (1963) eight life stages (see table 6.1). Within each stage, individuals establish a new orientation to themselves and other people in their social world.

TABLE

6.1 ERIKSON'S LIFE STAGES

- **Infancy:**   **Trust versus Mistrust**

  Depending upon the quality of care received, the infant learns to trust the environment, to perceive it as orderly and predictable, or to be suspicious, fearful, and mistrusting.

- **Young Childhood:**   **Autonomy versus Doubt**

  The development of motor and mental abilities, and the opportunity to explore, encourage a sense of autonomy and independence. However, if the child is excessively criticized or limited in his/her exploration, it will lead to a sense of doubt over his/her adequacy and competency.

- **Middle Childhood:**   **Initiative versus Guilt**

  The manner in which adults respond to the child's self-initiated activities creates either a sense of freedom and initiative, or a sense of being an inept intruder in an adult world.

- **Late Childhood:**   **Industry versus Inferiority**

  The child has a concern for how things work and how they ought to operate, leading to a sense of industry in forming rules, organizing and ordering. However, if these efforts are rebuffed as silly, it may lead to a sense of inferiority. During this stage of development, outside influences begin to exert a greater influence on the child's development.

- **Adolescence:**   **Identity versus Role Confusion**

  The adolescent begins to develop the ability to see things from others' point of view. The youth must develop a sense of his or her own identity, as distinct from all others and personally acceptable, or he/she will be confused or settle on a "negative" identity, such as class clown.

- **Young Adulthood:**   **Intimacy versus Isolation**

  The consequences of the young adult's attempts at reaching out to make contact with others may result in a commitment to other persons or isolation from close personal relationships.

- **Middle Adulthood:**   **Generativity versus Self-Absorption**

  At this stage, one may become concerned about family, society, and future generations, or may become concerned with only material possessions and physical well-being.

- **Old Age:**   **Integrity versus Despair**

  One looks back at life with a sense of fulfillment and integrity, or despair, feeling that life has been misdirected.

From *Childhood and Society,* by Erik H. Erikson. Copyright 1950, © 1963 by W. W. Norton & Company, Inc., renewed © 1978, 1991 by Erik H. Erikson. Reprinted by permission of W. W. Norton & Company, Inc.

Each of the eight stages is characterized by a conflict that has two opposing outcomes. If the conflict is worked out in a constructive, satisfactory manner, the positive quality becomes part of the ego and enhances further healthy development (Salkind, 1985). If the conflict persists or is resolved unsatisfactorily, however, the negative quality is incorporated into the personality structure (Muuss, 1982). Table 6.1 presents each of these eight stages and the issues individuals must master within each level.

Erikson's eight stages serve as one model of life stages throughout the life cycle. Other researchers have developed their own stages. For example, Levinson (1978) identifies the following life stages: childhood, adolescence, early adulthood, middle adulthood, late adulthood, and old age.

Although the exact ages when people move from life stage to life stage may vary, most models of the human life cycle consist of three basic periods: preparation, establishment, and culmination. In the preparation period, learning and growing are the central tasks as young people prepare for adulthood. In establishment, individuals struggle with making a positive contribution to society and being accepted within a social group. In culmination, death is antici-pated and individuals seek ways to place their lives in perspective. With these thoughts in mind this section of the chapter focuses on the following life stages: childhood (more specifically middle and late childhood), adolescence, adulthood (more specifically early, middle, and late adulthood), and older adulthood.

Within these specific life stages, research on leisure behavior demonstrates two interesting tendencies. First, while individuals seek stability and the familiar at some points in their lives, they also seek novel leisure experiences at other times (see figure 6.1). Second, the number of daily leisure activities that make up a person's leisure repertoire steadily increases, reaching a peak during early adulthood before the number begins to decline as a person reaches old age (see figure 6.2). Thus, during early and middle adulthood, one has the most leisure activities available to them and typically seeks the most novelty.

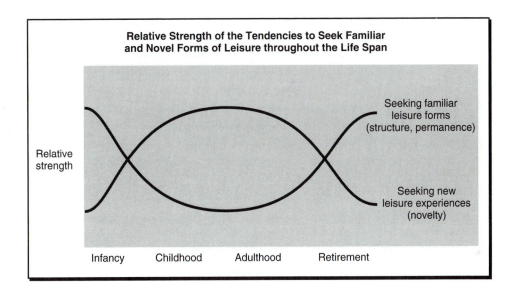

Figure 6.1
Leisure and the life span

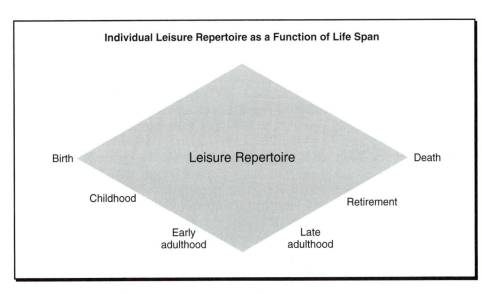

Figure 6.2
Relationship between leisure repertoire and life span

Childhood and Leisure

In many ways there has never been a better time to be a child than during this era. Children have opportunities, rights, and status that have never before been awarded to them collectively. Yet being a child in today's world can also bring more pressures and decisions than ever before—dealing with working parents, access to an almost overwhelming variety of information through mass media and the Internet, and many more choices—forcing many children to mature faster than ever. Play and leisure opportunities have a major role in the development process. Play and games are the main forms of leisure activity during the period from birth to adolescence.

Play does not have to be taught or justified during this period of life. Play is a self-motivated behavior; one cannot force a child to play. However, for the child play is serious business. In his research, Huizinga (1962) identified the following characteristics of play: voluntary, steps outside of ordinary life, limited in time and space, not serious but consuming for participants, bounded by rules, and promotes cultural values and as such is an important means of learning for younger children. Children have much to teach adults about play.

Hansel (1979) refers to young children as midget gurus of play in that gurus teach people profound truths. He noted that infants and young children can teach us some of the following principles:

Total immersion. No matter what children do, they do it completely and do not worry about any inhibitions. They have the ability to let life hug them.

Total concentration. Children concentrate on one thing and one thing only. The Greek word for worry is *merimnao,* which means literally to divide the mind. Watch children and you will notice how free they are from this problem that plagues society.

Ability to bounce back. Their spirit is indomitable. Children are able to bounce back from failure to try again and again.

Total honesty and expression. Children have a wonderful sense of spontaneity, and they tend to be completely open and honest with their feelings.

Children can teach a "sense of wonder and uninhibitedness, of gratitude and spontaneity, of unimpeded trust and freedom to change, of imagination and creativity. . . . Children can show people how to see everything as if it were for the first time and to share as if there were no end, how to smell, and taste and touch life" (Hansel, 1979, p. 78).

The period of childhood itself can be divided in many ways including infancy and toddlers (birth to three), preschool children (four- to five-year-olds), younger children (six- to eight-year-olds), and older children (nine- to twelve-year-olds). The play and leisure of infants, toddlers, and preschoolers is primarily home based, although with working parents, younger and younger children are being introduced to organized programs. In fact, in 1999 it was reported that 54 percent of all children from birth through third grade received child care on a regular basis from a nonfamily member (Forum on Child and Family and Statistics, 2000). With this rise in the participation of very young children, leisure programmers need to be aware that early and middle childhood are considered two of the greatest developmental periods of life. During this time children develop both fundamental locomotor skills and basic social skills.

Table 6.2 presents the developmental characteristics of younger children. During this time period, children expand their social world beyond their immediate family. The gender differences reported in earlier research may be lessened in the twenty-first century, as girls and boys participate in a wider variety of activities as society becomes more sensitive to gender inequalities. Within Erikson's (1963) framework, children should be encouraged to be self-directed in

6.2   DEVELOPMENTAL CHARACTERISTICS OF YOUNGER CHILDREN (AGES 6 TO 8)

Characteristics

- Beginning to become competitive
- Relatively short attention span; frustrate easily
- Involved in the magical world of play
- Desire to impress leaders and peers
- Social rules are important
- Play and learning are an integrated process
- Motor development proceeds downward from head and outward from the center of the body; hand and eye coordination are developing
- Pleasure is gained from achievement
- Show pride and affection for parents
- Social skills developing; developing a sense of humor; more thoughtful of others

Program Implications

- Specific programs to help children experience varied activities that encourage peer interaction and motor development. Leisure activities for this group tend to be found in the public and private nonprofit sectors.
- Play is particularly important for this age group. Play offers intrinsically rewarding experiences that help children gain competence in both problem solving and creativity. Play is an important means of learning and socialization.
- Programs should emphasize gross motor activities including throwing, climbing, and rolling, as well as provide high-energy activities alternated with periodic quiet activities. In the later stages of this age span, programs should introduce cooperative activities such as New Games.
- Programs tend to be more leader-directed. Staff need to be aware that they are role models for children, and they need to provide consistency and emphasize fairness.

Activities

- **Sports and Games:** Chasing games, singing games, individual games of skill (e.g., jacks), stunts, bike riding, and scavenger hunts. Some organized sports are introduced (e.g., baseball). Active hobbies (e.g., hiking, climbing) are often encouraged by parents.
- **Social:** Individuals are likely to interact with same-sex friends. Cliques are likely to form (e.g., treehouse club). Classes (e.g., karate, swimming, dancing), school, day camps—all foster socialization.
- **Miscellaneous:** Reading, board games, video games.

initiating activities. Public and school playgrounds become a focal point for many children during this period as the bulk of leisure activities for this group tends to be found in the public and private, nonprofit sectors (see table 6.3).

Leisure professionals should also be concerned with the physical fitness of youth. The most recent National Children and Youth Fitness Study found that, although most children are naturally active and fit until the age of ten, no more than 10 percent to 30 percent of adults participate in regular, vigorous exercise. In addition, the number of children today who are overweight doubled from 1970 to 1995 (Troiano, Flegal, Kuczmarski, Campbell, and Johnson, 1995). According to a study that examined data from 1989 to 1994, approximately 14 percent of children between the ages of six and eleven years old were overweight, and 11 percent of

TABLE

6.3 WHERE YOUNG CHILDREN PARTICIPATE IN RECREATION AND LEISURE ACTIVITIES

Location	Sponsorship	Percentage
Public parks and recreation departments	Public	65.3
Community-based sports teams or leagues	Public	31.9
Churches and other places of worship	Private nonprofit	24.3
Various health clubs and private spas	Commercial	18.9
Scouting groups	Private nonprofit	14.6
YMCAs and YWCAs	Private nonprofit	13.9
Farm clubs (4-H)	Private nonprofit	2.1

Note: The percentages total more than 100 because children could participate in more than one activity or program.
From J. Ross and R. Pate, a summary of findings of "The National Children and Youth Fitness Study" in *Journal of Physical Education, Recreation and Dance,* 51–56, 1987. Reprinted by permission.

those twelve to seventeen years of age were overweight (Forum on Child and Family Statistics, 2000). This is an increase of 6 percent from the mid-1980s. Further, the Surgeon General reports that 60 percent of Americans do not exercise regularly (U.S. Department of Health and Human Services, 1996). Many feel that current fitness efforts of physical education and leisure programs must improve in order to promote lifelong fitness.

Another area of potential development in leisure service organizations is that of youth sports. Often fraught with controversy because of the competitive nature of sport and athletics and the increase in sports-related violence, youth sports suggest more of a developmental orientation than in the past. Jordan (2001) suggests that youth sports should be implemented to enhance the emotional, physical, social, and educational well-being of children. Youth sports are also an opportunity for youth to be exposed to positive role models and healthy (drug- and tobacco-free) environments.

The lack of appropriate skills and the overemphasis on competition have driven many youth from sports programs. In fact, the number one reason youth play sports is to have fun (Ewing and Seefeldt, 1990). Contemporary youth sport programs operated by leisure service organizations recognize the importance of contributing to the growth of individuals at their own pace and consistent with their stages of development. They emphasize involvement in programs aligned to promote genuine opportunities for participation and skill development for everyone.

Youth sports produce a tremendous impact on the character and development of children. Consider the implications of Title IX legislation in the provision of youth sport programs for girls. Limited opportunities have given way to a full range of youth sport services available to girls that can contribute in significant ways to their development. Leisure service organizations can play an important role in providing such services with a philosophical commitment to the development and growth of the individual. An estimated 35 million children and adolescents participate in youth sport programs each year (DiFiori, 1999). Municipal park and recreation departments, Little League baseball, Pop Warner football, U.S. Ice Hockey Association, American Youth Soccer Organization, Boys and Girls Clubs, Girls Incorporated, Boy Scouts of America, YMCAs, YWCAs—all promote sport programs.

Build a Bear Workshop: When Best Friends Are Made

In St. Louis, Missouri, parents, children, and others can go to a local store and make their own teddy bear. Customers weave their way through colorful and exciting stations to make a personalized bear. First, one chooses the size and color of an unstuffed bear. The customer takes their bear and moves on to the stuffing machine where they can place a plastic heart in the bear and then help an employee hook the bear up to the stuffing machine. Once the bear has been stuffed, the customer moves on to the fluffing area where they help to fluff the bear to a desired level of softness and sew it shut. At the next station, the customer sits at a computer where they can name their bear and create and print out an "official" adoption certificate. No bear is complete without an outfit, of course, so at the next station the customer chooses from among hundreds of outfits in which to dress their bear. Finally, after paying the "adoption fee," the bear is ready to go home!

Some of the trends regarding youth sport programs follow:

- Participation in youth sport programs is highest in childhood (up to eleven years old) and young adulthood (eighteen to twenty-four years old) with a large decline in participation between the ages of twelve and seventeen years (National Sporting Goods Association, 2001).
- Younger children participate in sports to have fun, learn skills, and participate in a team atmosphere. Older children are more interested in competition (Carnegie Corporation, 1992).
- Financial support of school sports will continue to decrease, thus increasing the reliance upon municipal sports programs (Seefeldt, 1996).
- Many youth sport programs fail to integrate current knowledge of youth development principles into activities (National Alliance for Youth Sports, 2001).
- The need for volunteer assistance will continue to increase, although the threat of lawsuits will push youth sports programs to require certification of volunteer youth sport coaches (National Alliance for Youth Sports, 2001).
- Sports that permit the attainment of personal and individual styles of play will be increasingly popular; those that are highly regimented will decline (Seefeldt, 1996).
- Ethnic preferences will influence youth sports as sports like soccer, baseball, and basketball will continue to gain popularity while sports such as hockey, volleyball, racquetball, and swimming will decrease in popularity (Seefeldt, 1996).
- A gradual blending of youth sports for participants who are disabled and those who are able bodied will occur (National Alliance for Youth Sports, 2001).
- Boys are 1.5 times more likely to participate in youth sports than girls (Troiano et al., 1995).

The key to activities for infants and toddlers, as well as young children, involves offering a variety of appropriate activities that help them interact with peers in positive ways and assist in motor-skill development. Leisure service leaders should not push young children too intensely and should teach activities in a logical progression. DiFiori (1999) reports that 30 to 50 percent of all youth sport injuries are due to overuse. To minimize these types of injuries one should match physical abilities with the activity, allow adequate rest, teach and encourage complete conditioning, ensure the appropriate use of sports equipment and shoes, and monitor the social pressure applied by peers and adults on child athletes.

In the latter stages of childhood, life becomes more complex for children. Peers and school become increasingly important. Gender differences begin to become more pronounced, suggesting that males and females are learning social norms and values differently (Carlson, Uppal, and Prosser, 2000; Culp, 1998). Table 6.4 presents additional characteristics of this developmental stage. During this time, leisure continues to take place mainly in the public and private nonprofit sectors, although individuals begin to explore more school and commercially alternative opportunities.

Within Erikson's (1963) framework, youth throughout childhood need to achieve competency, a personal identity, and a feeling of closeness or intimacy with others within this process. As youth move through these stages, they ask and answer such questions as "Am I normal?" "Am I lovable?" "Am I competent?" "Am I loving to others?" As leisure professionals work with youth it is important to help them answer these questions with an emphatic yes.

TABLE

6.4 DEVELOPMENTAL CHARACTERISTICS OF OLDER CHILDREN (AGES 9 TO 12)

Characteristics

- Girls are approximately one year more mature than boys
- Fitness improves as individuals gain more stamina; realization of personal limits (through peer comparison) occurs
- New interests develop; competitiveness lessens
- Selective memory is engaged
- Creative imagination along with the development of abstract logical thinking exists
- Pride in traditions
- Responses to various situations are more in control, less impulsive
- Good sense of humor
- Role models are extremely important; children are easily influenced
- Closeness of peers, focus on "best" friends; some arguments; can conceal hurt feelings
- Importance of peers increases dramatically
- Onset of adolescence; often more self-conscious about their bodies at this stage

Program Implications

- Individuals are beginning to establish themselves outside the family unit. Individuals are also beginning to be interested in members of the other sex. Leisure organizations should give participants opportunities to develop specific skills and to socialize with peers. Leisure continues to take place mainly in the public and private nonprofit sectors; individuals begin to explore more school opportunities and commercial alternatives (e.g., movies).
- Programs should offer opportunities for gradual acceptance of additional responsibility.

Activities

- **Sports and Games:** Team games, hobbies (camping with parents, organizations), physical sports, initiatives, spectator sports.
- **Social:** Clubs, social activities (dances), hanging out at the mall with friends, music becoming more important.
- **Miscellaneous:** Movies, video games, reading.

During this time period, leisure professionals must be careful not to cater to some groups over others. Leisure organizations have sometimes been accused of sexism because they devoted more attention to males than females (Kelly, 1996). For example, almost twice as many boys as girls participate in sports teams and leagues. This may be partly due to cultural norms, but it might also relate to the opportunities presented to males and females. Likewise, as team sports become more important, many of those less skilled are left out. Dynamic leisure programs need to address the needs of all children, giving them equal opportunities to participate.

Being committed to helping children grow and develop through leisure demands that professionals ask and answer many of the questions raised by studies such as the National Children and Youth Fitness Study II (Ross and Pate, 1987) and the Surgeon General (U.S. Department of Health and Human Services, 1996). Questions raised by these studies include: As parents, teachers, and members of society at large, do we encourage children to be active enough? Do we use television too often to control behavior? Are we pushing the few too quickly into competitive sports to the near exclusion of the many? Do we offer children the right options? Do we set the right example by our own lifestyle? What needs to happen to foster an individual commitment in children to grow and develop through their leisure pursuits? What needs to happen to foster in children a commitment to lifetime fitness?

Adolescence and Leisure

The word *adolescence* comes from a Latin verb meaning "to grow into maturity." Thus, the period of adolescence is about the process of growing up. Table 6.5 presents some general characteristics of adolescence. In many ways, adolescence is a recent phenomenon, as modern society has altered the time whereby children participate fully in adult society. In the past, this transition came at an earlier age and resulted from some specific rite of passage into adulthood; today's adolescent experiences more time to become an adult. Yet this transition period can be difficult and confusing for adolescents—sometimes society expects them to act like adults, and other times encourages them to remain children. As a result, adolescents often seem to withdraw into their own separate society, drawing closer to their friends. In this context adolescents often develop their own taste in music, clothing, hairstyles, social concerns, language, and attitudes.

The adolescent's need to be a part of a group and to "fit in" contrasts with the need to establish his or her own identity. Erikson (1963) notes that adolescents must develop a sense of their own identity, as distinct from all others that is still personally acceptable, or they will be confused and settle on a negative identity such as "class clown" or engage in even more negative behavior such as drug abuse or becoming a gang member.

Basic Needs of Youth Various organizations, individuals, and groups have attempted to identify the basic needs of youth that must be met for them to develop into healthy and positive adults. Jaffe (1998) supports the ten basic needs of youth as defined by Pittman (1991) and Scales (1991). Figure 6.3 presents these factors. Leisure programs and services help meet these developmental needs as summarized here.

A need for positive social interaction. Youth want to belong and need opportunities to form positive social relationships with adults and peers. We do this through sports, fine arts clubs, classes, and drop-in programs.

A need for safety, structure, and clear limits. Expectations, structure, and boundaries are important for youth, so that they feel secure and also have a clear picture of the areas that they may or may not explore. Through the rules and guidelines we establish at our own agencies and organizations, youth come to know what is expected of them.

TABLE

6.5 DEVELOPMENTAL CHARACTERISTICS OF ADOLESCENCE (AGES 13 TO 21)

Characteristics

- Period of transition between childhood and adulthood
- Struggle over the lack of clearly defined role in society
- Search for personal identity and independence from parents
- Period of increasing freedom and access to resources
- Adolescents tend to be idealistic and egocentric
- Great confusion of values
- Affiliation and acceptance by peer group is of major importance
- Body experiences a number of internal biological changes as it begins to reach physical maturation
- Psychological reaction to bodily changes creates dissonance
- Interest in potential intimate relationships intensifies
- Have increased time for leisure

Program Implications

- Programs should provide opportunities for social interaction, development, and achievement as leisure experiences can provide the opportunity to establish relationships and desired independence. The majority of leisure opportunities take place in schools and the commercial sector. Some sports leagues are offered by public or private nonprofit organizations.
- Programs should help adolescents develop concepts of adequacy, self-respect, and self-confidence. Adolescents need a sense of who they are as they move from childhood to adulthood.
- Leisure service providers need to recognize that adolescents should be active and will be interested in trying out a wide range of activities; therefore, programs should offer variety and be sensitive to ongoing teenage fads. Areas for adolescents to safely "hang out" allow them to experiment with various roles and behaviors. Adolescent leisure provides a margin of freedom within institutionalized constraints.
- Programs can create opportunities for "rites of passage" into adulthood.

Activities

- **Sports:** Organized sports are very important. Greater emphasis should be placed on helping adolescents develop lifelong sport interests. Outdoor and adventure activities offer many adolescents opportunities for "rites of passage."
- **Social:** Music becomes important, dancing, places to "hang out" with friends, movies.
- **Miscellaneous:** Opportunities to help others, videos.

A need for belonging and meaningful involvement in family, school, and community. Youth have a desire to be a part of and to participate in activities related to their families, schools, and communities. Service projects and opportunities such as 4-H often provide this type of involvement.

A need for creative expression. Youth need opportunities to express to others who they are and how they feel. Music, writing, sports, cooking, and other activities help to achieve this goal.

A need for feeling self-worth/giving to others. Involvement in meaningful and worthwhile efforts related to larger goals is extremely important to youth. Volunteer efforts such as

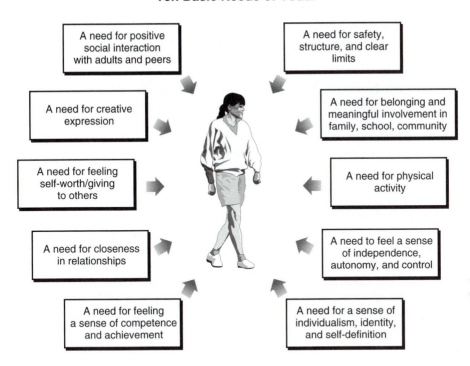

Ten Basic Needs of Youth

Figure 6.3

Needs that must be met for youth to grow into healthy adults

A need for positive social interaction with adults and peers

A need for safety, structure, and clear limits

A need for creative expression

A need for belonging and meaningful involvement in family, school, community

A need for feeling self-worth/giving to others

A need for physical activity

A need for closeness in relationships

A need to feel a sense of independence, autonomy, and control

A need for feeling a sense of competence and achievement

A need for a sense of individualism, identity, and self-definition

community clean-up projects and visiting elderly shut-ins are examples of leisure outreach programs that help youth experience this.

A need for physical activity. Youth have tremendous energy and require a great deal of physical activity and time for fun. Leaders provide these opportunities in almost every program and event they offer.

A need to feel a sense of independence, autonomy, and control. Youth have a desire to mature, to become more independent and to exert some control and influence over their lives. Youth-led groups (music, reading, sports, etc.) provide young people with opportunities for independence and leadership.

A need for closeness in relationships. Youth need opportunities to form close relationships with peers and adults. They also have a need for relationships with caring adult role models. Thus, it is important for leisure services leaders to reach out to youth and establish trusting relationships.

A need for feeling a sense of competence and achievement. It is important for youth to have opportunities to achieve success and to receive recognition. Awards for service, trophies for success, and handshakes for a job well done carry great meaning for young people.

A need for a sense of individualism, identity, and self-definition. Youth need to have opportunities to become individuals and to define their sense of identity and self-concept, based on positive input from others. Opportunities for personal expression, whether it be the clothing one wears, the language one uses, or the activities in which one engages are embedded in leisure opportunities for youth.

Leisure service programmers who provide services in a manner that allows youth to have input, involvement, and ownership; a sense of achievement and recognition; opportunities for creative expression and physical activity; and opportunities for social interaction will find that youth will seek to participate. Further, these youth will show evidence of benefits from their participation.

Youth Development: A Program Framework   As programmers identify and understand the needs of adolescents, a shift in delivering services to youth is being promoted. This shift toward a youth development approach encourages youth workers to see youth as resources to be developed rather than problems to be fixed. Whereas addressing the problems facing youth such as violence, substance abuse, and school failure is critical, it is not enough. Young people who are not on drugs, not dropouts, not in gangs, and not teen parents are viewed as "problem free," but are they prepared for work, for family, for citizenship? The commitment to prevention must be matched with an equal commitment to the promotion of positive personal and social development.

Youth development is an ongoing process in which young people are engaged and invested. Throughout this process, young people seek ways to meet their basic physical and social needs and to build the competencies and connections they need for survival and success. Youth development is multidimensional, can be viewed from a variety of perspectives, and is marked by the acquisition of a broad range of competencies and the demonstration of a full complement of connections to self, others, and the larger communities. With this in mind, Pittman and Wright (1991) note that there is no universally accepted definition of youth development, but rather it may be more profitable to focus on competencies that assist youth in their development.

Youth Development Competencies   In addition to these ten basic needs of youth, five basic areas of youth development objectives or *competencies* have been developed based on a review of the youth development factors that are seen as being important by youth-serving organizations (see figure 6.4). Five competencies that youth should acquire in order to be successful as adults, as adapted from Pittman (1991), Jaffe (1998), and Unger, Simon, Newman, and Montgomery (1998), include:

> *Health/physical competence.* Youth need to have good current health status and appropriate knowledge, attitudes, and behaviors to ensure future health (exercise, good diet, nutrition).

L e i s u r e   L i n e

Step on a Crack . . .

Mama says when she was a girl, kids said, "step on a crack, break your mother's back." I told her our old sidewalk is so cracked that mothers would be laid up day and night. My friends play a different game.

When people get killed on the street, the police draw an outline around him like they getting ready to play hopscotch. When they take the body away, they leave that outline behind like a ghost. We say, "step on the body line, be you next time." The macho boys lie down inside the outlines, but even they won't touch them. If you're a boy, it could definitely be you next time. Life and death they kiss too much.

Source: The Carnegie Foundation, 1992.

Personal/social competence. It is important that youth gain intrapersonal skills (ability to understand personal emotions, have self-discipline); interpersonal skills (ability to work with others, develop friendships and relationships through communication, cooperation, empathizing, negotiating); coping skills (ability to adapt, assume responsibility); and judgment skills (plan, make decisions, solve problems) to be successful in a rapidly changing world.

Cognitive/creative competence. Youth need to develop a broad base of knowledge, the ability to appreciate/participate in areas of creative expression, good oral and written language skills, problem-solving and analytical skills, and the ability to learn along with an interest in learning and achieving throughout the life cycle.

Vocational competence. It is important for youth to develop a broad understanding and awareness of vocational (and avocational) options and of the steps necessary to act on their choices to make adequate career preparations, and to understand the value and function of work and leisure.

Citizenship competencies (ethics and preparation). Youth need to understand their nation's and community's history and values, and desire to contribute to their nation and community. All of society benefits from young people meeting this competency.

**Five Competencies That Youth
Should Master to Become Successful Adults**

Figure 6.4

Five competencies that youth should master to become successful adults

Citizenship competence

• Understand nation/community history/values

Personal/social competence

• Understand personal emotions
• Develop friendships
• Self-discipline
• Coping skills
• Judgment skills

Cognitive/creative competence

• Broad base of knowledge
• Creative expression
• Language skills
• Interest in learning

Health/physical competence

• Food/current health knowledge/skills to ensure future well-being

Vocational competence

• Awareness of vocational/career options
• Understand value of work/leisure

As youth move toward mastering these competencies, they also progress in their feelings of achievement and self-esteem. Youth need to be good at something to feel good about themselves. Parks, recreation, and leisure opportunities facilitate this development of self-concept.

Leisure activities during youth can promote and maintain autonomy from parents while also strengthening the bond between friends. Leisure activities often provide opportunities for explicit learning about "forbidden" topics such as sexuality, tolerance for others, and a context where one can look back on youth with nostalgic sentimentality. Properly planned leisure options for adolescents can provide a margin of freedom within institutionalized constraints and can increase self-esteem. The social significance of leisure is great for adolescents. Leisure fosters opportunities for social contacts, development, and achievement.

Although adolescents comprise one of the most active groups in terms of leisure participation, they are also one of the most difficult groups to serve for public and private, nonprofit organizations. As public and private nonprofit organizations seek to better serve this group they should consider examining the success of the commercial sector in addressing the needs of adolescents. To meet their needs, programs and facilities should offer adolescents a safe place to hang out, places where teens can have the opportunity to establish sociosexual relationships, and desired independence. While programs should offer variety and be sensitive to changing teen fads, they need to invest in people who can build a relationship with teens. Many successful programs build on relationships with people whom teenagers feel they can trust and share confidences, rather than on activities or facilities.

Adulthood and Leisure

Adulthood is considered a period of establishment for most individuals; however, the establishment process does not happen overnight. For some, the transition to adulthood happens abruptly with a first full-time job or a move out on their own. For others, this transition is gradual as families continue to help children during early adulthood (e.g., helping with college tuition or helping young adults become established in their first residence). The period of adulthood, the longest period in life, spans from approximately age twenty to death. Therefore, rather than considering adulthood as a single period, it makes sense to envision it as several periods with different preoccupations, interests, and changing patterns of leisure. The periods examined within this chapter are early, middle, and late adulthood. The characteristics of each of these periods are presented in tables 6.6 through 6.8.

For most young adults, issues revolve more around socialization than work. Erikson (1963) identifies the major theme of early adulthood as the quest for intimacy and personal identity, where individuals work to establish independence from parents and build lives of their own. This identity development is related to both the personal identity (who am I?) as well as social identity (how do I fit into society?) (Kleiber, 1999). Two major changes that usually occur within this time period dramatically influence leisure pursuits. The first is marriage or choosing a partner, and the second is the addition of children.

Marriage or choosing a partner tends to be the first step in settling down and scaling back on the wilder aspects of leisure. Drinking and carousing with friends are often curtailed and the dating games of "cat and mouse" cease. However, Kelly (1996) indicates that the arrival of the first child makes the most significant changes in lifestyle and leisure behavior. This results from several factors, including the additional planning required to participate in leisure opportunities and the decrease in income that may occur if one parent (traditionally the female) quits paid employment to care for the baby. Following the arrival of the first child, leisure becomes much more home based as the family becomes the focus of

TABLE 6.6 CHARACTERISTICS OF EARLY ADULTHOOD (AGES 21 TO 30)

Characteristics

- Establishes autonomy from parents while still seeking to maintain some type of connection
- Builds life structure (marriage, family, friendships)
- Completes formal schooling, concern for occupation increases, emphasis is placed on success in a career
- Develops an identification with social institutions
- Develops the ability to be intimate and to make commitments
- Structures a dream of the future

Program Implications for Leisure Service Organizations

- Early in this stage recreation is commercial and school based. As people establish families and settle down, however, recreation tends to be more home based, especially when children are young and money is tight. Public recreation agencies can become important as families are established. Leisure activities with new couples and young families can encourage interactions and development of shared commitments to a new life together.
- This stage can be a time of new experiences; organizations should attempt to offer variety and opportunities to try new things.
- Opportunities for continued sociosexual contact and activity are still important as are activities which have a strong physical component.

Activities

- **Sports:** Outdoor pursuits (rock climbing, waterskiing, backpacking), team sports (softball, basketball, volleyball) still important, starting to make the transition to lifelong sports such as tennis and golf. Spectator sports are enjoyed.
- **Social Activities:** Movies, concerts, music, dancing, dating and courting, and bars.
- **Miscellaneous:** Shopping, television, and videos.

---

most leisure activities. Leisure is often used as a bonding experience for the development of family cohesion (Kleiber, 1999).

As individuals move into middle adulthood the focus shifts away from the issues of intimacy and establishment of a family to the establishment of a career. Levinson (1978) identifies two divergent themes of this settling-down period. One aspect of this period involves order, stability, security, and control. A second, contrasting element, is "making it": "This involves planning, striving, moving onward and upward, having an inner timetable that contains major goals and way stations by which they must be reached" (Levinson, 1978, p. 285). Many of those who fail to reach their professional goals turn to leisure as a way to find or add meaning to their lives. Many hobbies and avocations are begun or renewed at this life stage (Kleiber, 1999).

In the past, "making it" meant that the husband usually devoted time and attention to his occupation or profession while the wife's primary concern was for the family unit. These stereotypical roles have changed and continue to change as women pursue promising careers themselves, and men take a more active role in raising the family. As the desire to establish oneself in a career intensifies, leisure becomes an important outlet for achieving and maintaining marital and family stability and growth as well as maintaining individual emotional health.

6.7   CHARACTERISTICS OF MIDDLE ADULTHOOD (AGES 31 TO 50)

Characteristics

- Settling down, established in career and family
- Self-reflection of goals and decisions, can be a period of skepticism and self-questioning
- Adjustment to aging parents; often involves some type of care for parents
- Career development becomes a predominant concern as individuals seek to fulfill their earlier dreams
- Physical maturity peaks in the early thirties and then begins to decline
- Deadline decade—the halfway point of one's life brings with it the realization of one's own mortality; that there is a limited amount of time left to find fulfillment in life, which can lead to midlife crisis
- Divorce and career changes can happen frequently as people search for fulfillment
- As culture bearers, norms and values of culture are passed on to maturing children
- Involvement in civic and community organizations increases

Program Implications for Leisure Service Organizations

- Leisure pursuits are among the significant means of achieving family growth as well as individual emotional health. Leisure is found primarily in the commercial sector with some involvement in public and private, nonprofit sectors (especially with children). The most frequent leisure activities are home and family centered.
- Physical activities are needed as the body starts to decline. Physical activities can improve a person's general well-being as well as improve work performance.
- Leisure service organizations should not be bound by stereotypes of what this group of people want to do in their free time. A variety of experiences need to be offered in innovative ways (e.g., time schedules, settings, bundling of services) to meet the varied needs of individuals and family units during this stage of life.
- Activities begun in the early thirties determine the quality of subsequent life. Attention should be paid to making an orderly transition into lifetime sports and other activities that can be enjoyed throughout the rest of one's life.
- Emphasis should be placed on self-directed rather than leader-directed activities.

Activities

- **Sports:** Golf, tennis, swimming, bicycling, volleyball, bowling, and exercising. Involvement in team sports continues to diminish. Spectator sports, car camping, hunting, and fishing become prevalent.
- **Social:** Social interactions become more prevalent and socializing becomes more important than sexualizing. Traveling becomes feasible again. Trips and tours can be important leisure outlets.
- **Miscellaneous:** Gardening, hobbies, crafts, driving.

Physical activities and exercise are important to maintaining good health as individuals begin to realize their mortality during this time. When a person reaches his or her thirties, the realization comes that one's body will not last forever, and the need to take care of it becomes paramount. Lifelong sports become increasingly important as participation in team sports begins to decline slightly. This age period exhibits a greater tendency toward a consumer model of leisure behavior—planned vacations, buying a boat or recreational vehicle, dining out, and the like. As a result, leisure takes place more in the commercial sector with limited involvement in public and private, nonprofit organizations due to their children's participation.

Toward the end of middle adulthood, the mid to late forties, many individuals experience midlife transition. For some this becomes a midlife crisis, while for others it becomes a time to rethink priorities, evaluate life, and make subtle changes. This period sees a number of major

TABLE
6.8   CHARACTERISTICS OF LATE ADULTHOOD (AGES 51 TO 65)

Characteristics

- "Empty nest syndrome" encourages couples to reconnect with each other; adjusting to being grandparents
- Fulfillment or failure of life goals
- Search for meaning in past living and current life
- Concern with unmet needs of self
- Start of physical deterioration: bodies take longer to recover from exhaustion and show lack of endurance
- Transition from job to retirement: anxiety over loss of work role. Increase in concern over issues such as social security, health care, and leisure activities during retirement
- Shift from body to intellect
- Assume role of mentor
- Involvement continues to increase in professional organizations, service, civic, and social clubs as well as religious organizations

Program Implications for Leisure Service Organizations

- Leisure serves three basic functions during this time: acceptance, dispel personal despair, and give structure to increasing free time. Majority of leisure takes place in the commercial sector during this time period.
- In some instances this group has an increase in free time as children leave the home. Leisure programs and activities can encourage individuals in this age group to volunteer and share their expertise in a variety of ways.
- Programming should continue to take a self-directed focus rather than a leader-directed focus although individuals need to be informed about the leisure/recreation opportunities that are available to them and educated about the importance of developing meaningful leisure pursuits for retirement.

Activities

- **Sports:** Spectator sports, fishing, bowling, golf, tennis, walking, exercise, bicycling, swimming. For the majority, team sports have come to an end.
- **Social:** Increased group participation and socializing; involvement in social organizations often increases.
- **Miscellaneous:** Gardening, relaxing, reading, church related activities, picnics, hobbies, travel, and service to others.

---

life changes. Children leave home for college and other endeavors, the career pinnacle may be reached, physical endurance and flexibility begin to decline, and bodies take longer to recover from exertion.

The role of leisure during this stage varies from person to person. Kleiber (1999, p. 53) states, ". . . more free time and greater financial security often provide ideal conditions for self-expression in leisure at this time." Furthermore, Kelly (1987) indicates:

> Some look back, settle for where they have been and what they have become, and seek security and acceptance. Others want something more in the limited time remaining and prepare to make changes in their priorities and allocations. . . . Dignity may most often be sought in what is known and safe. Autonomy may be sought in some new context, investment, or enterprise. What is evident is that leisure may rise in salience as options in other roles are closed off. (p. 85)

According to Gorden and Gaitz (1976), leisure can serve three basic functions during this stage. First, it can bring acceptance from others, replacing the earlier focus on establishment and achievement. Second, developing meaningful leisure helps avoid personal despair, which

Erikson (1963) notes as a major problem of this life stage. Third, it structures time when people are beginning to reexperience more free time. Leisure continues to be commercially based and less home centered as decreasing financial responsibilities create more economic resources for leisure.

Leisure needs of adults vary; tables 6.6 to 6.8 present specific implications for leisure service professionals. However, some general considerations cut through the various stages of adulthood and should be considered in serving the leisure needs of this age group. These considerations include:

- Programs should be designed to encourage self-directed leisure behavior. Adults are generally more self-directed than at any other times in their lives. Their leisure behaviors are more likely to be self-motivated, experientially based, related to life tasks, focused on the present, and intrinsically motivated.
- Programs need to promote lifelong sports and activities as well as encourage new leisure behaviors early in adulthood. As evidenced in figure 6.2, people tend to seek less novelty and thus tend to participate in previously tried activities as they enter retirement. To ensure a varied leisure lifestyle during retirement, leisure service professionals should encourage new leisure pursuits throughout adulthood.
- A variety of experiences offered in innovative ways (e.g., time schedules, settings, bundling of services) will meet the varied needs of individuals and families during this stage of life. For example, Jackson and Scott (1999) and Lankford, DeGraaf, and Neal (1996) identify lack of time or conflicts with work schedules as major barriers to leisure participation. Innovative scheduling of programs could increase participation levels of adults in organized programs.

Older Adults and Leisure

Few days can cause so many people so much joy or so much anxiety as the day of their retirement. It is one of the milestones in life. It can signify freedom and the opportunity to pursue long-held dreams, or it can represent a feeling of uselessness, the beginning of the end. Growing old in a world infatuated with youth can be a frightening prospect to be sure, but many people also find retirement to be everything they have dreamed about and more. It is often perceived as time earned (through years of paid employment) to focus on one's self, one's family, and general happiness.

Older Americans comprise the most rapidly growing segment in the United States. Consider the following facts reported by the Administration on Aging (2000):

- In the United States, persons sixty-five years old or older represent approximately 13 percent of the population, about one in every eight Americans. In Canada, 11.8 percent of the population is over the age of sixty-five.
- By the year 2030, persons aged sixty-five or older are expected to represent 20 percent of the population.
- Eight out of ten persons over the age of sixty-five are women. Among the oldest old, there are 2.6 women for every man.
- Due to recent medical advancements the older population itself is getting older. The oldest old, aged eighty-five and older, are increasing at a faster rate than the total elderly population. In 1900, fewer than one in ten elderly persons was aged eighty-five or more. By 2045, the oldest old will represent one in five of the elderly.

The elderly, like other minority groups, fall victim to stereotyped images that are mainly based on misconceptions. Generally speaking, in Canada and the United States attitudes toward the elderly and the aging process are negative. Many believe that the elderly are sick, cognitively deficient, weak, and inactive. Thus, it is important to dispel some of the typical stereotypes of older people. See table 6.9 for many of the positive characteristics of old age.

Contrary to popular belief, only 4.3 percent of the 34.5 million U.S. citizens over sixty-five are confined to nursing homes and institutions. Fourteen percent of people aged sixty-five to sixty-nine need help with personal care such as eating, bathing, or toileting; 45 percent of people aged eighty-five and older need some degree of assistance (Administration on Aging, 2000). Over half of the elderly live with their spouses in independent households, usually in communities where they have roots; 31 percent live alone and only 13 percent live with their children. In addition, most older people are not poor and neglected. Although the number of elderly living at or below the poverty line (figure varies from 20 percent to 30 percent) is a major concern, the median net worth of older households in 1999 was $33,148, which was above the U.S. average of $32,000. Net worth was below $15,000 for 11.5 percent of the older households but was above $35,000 for 46.9 percent of this age group. In 1999, the United

TABLE

6.9 CHARACTERISTICS OF OLDER ADULTS (AGES 66+)

Characteristics

- Emphasis shifts from work to leisure: older adults want to stay active and feel good about themselves.
- Issues include integrity/integration vs. despair. In later stages of old age there is an attempt to maintain independence, self-direction, self-esteem, and self-concept.
- Life review and introspection occur during this stage.
- Coping with death, loss, and the prospect of widowhood.
- Physical health declines.
- Tendency to be alone increases.
- Decline in income; incomes often fixed.

Program Implications for Leisure Service Organizations

- The importance of leisure is most evident in offering seniors an identity and purpose for life. The majority of leisure takes place initially in the commercial sector. However, seniors increasingly turn back to public recreation programs. In the end the majority of leisure is home based.
- Meaningful integration is important for individuals in this stage. Opportunities should be created for intergenerational events as well as activities that encourage companionship and socializing.
- Meaningful and purposeful leisure is important rather than just trivial activities created to fill people's time. People want to feel needed; organizations can create opportunities for seniors to volunteer and share their skills and expertise.

Activities

- **Sports:** Spectator sports, golf, tennis, fishing, walking, bowling, swimming, bicycling.
- **Social:** Socializing with extended family and longtime friends, involvement in recreation centers, more activities are done alone. Many activities are centered around children and grandchildren.
- **Miscellaneous:** Gardening, relaxing, reading, church-related activities, picnics, television, hobbies, travel, museums, and board games and cards.

States recorded its lowest level of poverty among the elderly ever with only 9.7 percent of older Americans living below the poverty level (Administration on Aging, 2000).

Older people also continue to be valuable members of society. About 4 million (12 percent) of Americans sixty-five years and older were in the labor force in 1999. Nelson (2000) reported that in 1999, 40 percent of adults sixty-five and older either were working or intended to work for pay after retirement. AARP reports that eight in ten baby boomers say they plan to work at least part time during their retirement years. In addition, countless others are involved in volunteering with state and local organizations.

These statistics paint a far different picture of older people than is often envisioned. The elderly represent a vibrant aspect of society that cannot be ignored. Their leisure varies as well. The leisure patterns throughout life appear to set the course for leisure in old age as people tend to continue to participate in the same activities throughout their lives.

A study conducted by McGuire, Dottavio, and O'Leary (1987) suggested that there are two types of elderly: *Contractors* participate in 70 percent of their leisure activities before the age of twenty-one, and only 5 percent of their activities are learned after the age of fifty. *Expanders* continue to learn new activities throughout their lives, with 30 percent of leisure activities being learned after the age of fifty. McGuire et al. also found that contractors outnumber expanders almost two to one.

In terms of the impact of old age on leisure, Godbey (1997) notes that age is a false variable; it is other conditions that are sometimes, but not always, associated with growing older that more often cause changes in leisure behavior. The elderly are often more likely than others to live in urban areas, live on a fixed income, have health problems, and have low levels of education. These conditions, rather than old age, shape and limit leisure behavior. For example, a study by Godbey, Patterson, and Brown (1979) found that urban elderly who were poor and had low levels of formal education were considerably less likely to use public parks and recreation centers due to fear of crime than those with higher incomes and levels of education.

Some activities slow or disappear with some of the conditions of old age. For example, participation in leisure activities that involve high levels of physical exertion often decline. This is, in part, because of physically limiting conditions. For instance, the Administration on Aging (2000) reported that in 1999, 30 percent of people sixty-five to seventy-four years old indicated they had a chronic condition that limited them in their choice of activities; among those individuals older than seventy-five, this jumped to 50 percent. Yet Godbey et al. (1979) advocate keeping the elderly active in social roles for as long as possible. This theory, referred to as the *activity theory* and based on the belief that older people benefit from staying active, maintains that when the time comes to give up certain activities and relationships, it is important to find substitutes to replace those losses.

The opposite of the activity theory is the *theory of disengagement*. This theory views aging as a process of withdrawal of the individual from society in a pattern of voluntary reduction. According to Bammel and Bammel (1996), "this process of withdrawal replaces the equilibrium that existed between the individual and society in middle life with a new balance characterized by greater distance" (p. 341). Some feel that this greater distance helps both the individual and society as it reduces the psychological effect of death.

For leisure service organizations that are concerned about the growth and well-being of the individual, it seems appropriate to ascribe to the activity theory the caution that programs should offer worthwhile activities rather than time-fillers. Programming for this life stage should emphasize:

Retiring Where the Mariachis Play

In Mexico, a retired couple can live luxuriously on $1,500 a month.

Retiring to Mexico may seem like an exotic, bougainvillea-filled dream, yet 1 million Americans and Canadians, both retired and working, already live there. Increased trade under the NAFTA treaty, along with the reasonable cost of living, are likely to increase the number of Americans who choose retirement Mexico-style.

That's the hope of FONATUR, the National Trust Fund for the Development of Tourism in Mexico. The organization's objective is to draw tourists to Mexico and to convert some of them—70 percent of whom are American—into residents.

To make moving to Mexico enticing to natives of the United States and Canada, FONATUR develops residential communities such as Loreto, which is in Baja California Sur, 660 miles from the U.S. border. More than 700 Americans already call Loreto home, according to Jim Moore, president of the research firm Moore Diversified Services (MDS) of Fort Worth, Texas. MDS was hired by FONATUR to determine what influences Americans to move to Mexico.

Americans who move to Mexico typically first experience the country as tourists, Moore says. They often repeat their visits to Mexico and finally settle on a favorite area for permanent or semi-permanent residency.

The cost of living in Mexico is not as low for Americans as it was ten years ago, but the U.S. dollar still stretches farther in Mexico than it does in the 50 states. The low cost of health-care services available in Mexico also attracts nonnative residents, especially retirees. The country lacks some sophisticated treatments, however, and this discourages some potential residents, according to MDS's research. In addition, in-home healthcare and assisted-living arrangements need to be more readily available.

Frequent visitors to Mexico aren't the only ones who consider retiring there. South of the Border Tour & Travel of Petaluma, California, has seen strong demand for its "retire to Mexico" tours since it started the program in April 1994, says Loujean LaMalfa, the company's president. LaMalfa started the tours after she had difficulty getting information to plan her own retirement to Mexico.

South of the Border coordinates tours to the Guadalajara-Lake Chapala region in west-central Mexico, which is one of the three most popular areas for American retirees. Cuernavaca and San Miguel Allende are the other two. The Lake Chapala area—including Guadalajara and the smaller communities of Ajijic, Chapala Town, and Tlaquepaque—is home to 40,000 Americans.

The majority of those taking the retirement tour are already retired. Many have tried life-in-the-sun cities of Florida and Arizona and are dissatisfied. "By the time they sign up for the tour, they've done their homework. Now they want a first-hand look at life in Mexico," says South of the Border's LaMalfa. She tries to give that to tour participants by including dinners in private homes with longtime American retirees to Mexico.

Although many retirees are couples, life in Mexico is attractive to singles as well. A single person with a monthly income of $900 can live quite comfortably, while a couple with $1,500 a month will have no trouble leading a luxurious life. In the Lake Chapala region, attractively furnished two-bedroom apartments rent for about $500 a month. Buying a retirement home in Mexico is also well within the reach of many retirees. Houses sell for $40,000 to $65,000.

Choice. Individuals want to be able to decide on their own activities and their own level of participation. Drop-in senior centers that offer a wide variety of flexible programming often meet these needs.

Participant involvement. Recreation professionals must provide opportunities for seniors themselves to be involved in the planning process. Their voices must be solicited, heard, and acted upon.

Integrated rather than segregated activities. In today's fast-paced world, generations are often isolated from each other. As a result, the old fear the young, the young don't understand their elders, and society suffers growing tensions between generations. Leisure can provide a forum to bridge these gaps.

Being innovative. Leisure service organizations should not be bound by traditional rules and expectations when providing activities for older adults, but rather can modify traditional sports and games to facilitate seniors' involvement.

Being sensitive. Leisure service organizations must be sensitive to the needs of older adults, with barrier-free and accessible facilities. Equipment and facilities should be user-friendly with something for everyone.

Summary

A number of variables impact leisure throughout the life cycle. This chapter examined generational and environmental factors, level of education, culture, and lifestyle, followed by an overview of leisure throughout the life cycle. The use of a developmental approach emphasizes an attempt by leisure professionals to understand the life stages of participants and create programs to assist individuals in their growth and development. The concept of stages, or life stages, implies that life involves a series of connected stages, each influencing one another yet each being distinctive.

Leisure service organizations play an active role in offering programs and activities to the public. These organizations must be innovative and creative in programming for individuals throughout the life cycle—as the individual participant changes and evolves, so must programs. In designing play spaces for children or creating programs for children or adults, leisure service professionals should note the following:

> We must remember that our field is experimental, should be experimental and will not survive unless it continues to be experimental. It is not written in stone what a playground should look like, or that there should be playgrounds. Nor can we say what a park should look like, how and to whom leisure skills should be taught or who should teach them. As Cranz (1982) so wisely observed, many recreation and park professionals have developed the mistaken idea concomitant with professionalization that providing park and recreation services is a matter of technology when in reality it is a process of cultural discovery. Said another way, it is a process rather than a product. (Godbey, 1991, p. 5)

If leisure professionals can be innovative and responsive in meeting the recreational and developmental needs of the people served, then the future looks bright for the profession.

Discussion Questions

1. Explain the stages of human development as they relate to understanding a person's leisure lifestyle throughout life.
2. Interview one of your friends, your parents, your grandparents, or an older family member; ask them to discuss what leisure means to them. What activities do they remember doing as a child? Compare and contrast these different views of leisure. In the people you interviewed, how does generation affect their leisure pursuits and attitudes?
3. What environmental factors (as defined in this chapter) would affect leisure in your city, state, province, or region?
4. How does education level affect leisure participation? Why do you think this is the case?
5. Define the term *lifestyle.* What factors make up an individual's lifestyle?
6. In understanding leisure behavior, why is the concept of life stage more important than age?
7. When is a person's leisure repertoire the greatest and why?
8. Visit a playground and watch children play for thirty minutes. What changes would you make in the playground to better meet the needs of the children playing there?

9. Interview three teenagers. Discuss the role of leisure in their lives. What could leisure service organizations do to better meet their leisure needs?
10. What are the major considerations in serving the leisure needs of people in the various stages of adulthood?

References

AARP. 2000. AARP/Roper Baby Boomer Study. [available on-line at http://research.aarp.org/econ/boomer_seg_3.html].

Administration on Aging. 2000. Profile of Older Americans 2000. [available on-line at www.aoa.dhhs.gov].

Bammel, G., and L. Bammel. 1996. *Leisure and Human Behavior*. Dubuque, IA: Wm. C. Brown.

Brill, N. n.d. *Working with People: The Helping Process*. Philadelphia, PA: Lippincott.

Carlson, C., S. Uppal, and E. Prosser. 2000. Ethnic differences in processes contributing to the self-esteem of early adolescent girls. *The Journal of Early Adolescence 20*(10), 44–67.

Carnegie Corporation of New York. 1992. *A Matter of Time: Risk and Opportunity in the Non-School Hours*. New York: Carnegie Corporation.

Culp, R. 1998. Adolescent girls and outdoor recreation: A case study examining constraints and effective programming. *Journal of Leisure Research 30*(3), 356–379.

DiFiori. 1999. Overuse injuries in children and adolescents. *The Physician and Sportsmedicine, 27*(1), 22–27.

Erikson, E. 1963. *Childhood and Society*. New York: W. W. Norton.

Ewing, M., and V. Seefeldt. 1990. *American Youth and Sports Participation*. North Palm Beach, FL: Athletic Footwear Association.

Forum on Child and Family Statistics. 2000. Quality of life indicators. [available on-line at www.childstats.gov].

Godbey, G. 1991. Recreation and leisure in the 1990s: They are playing our song. *J. B. Nash Lecture*. Presented at the American Alliance of Health, Physical Education, Recreation and Dance National Convention, April 6. San Francisco, CA.

Godbey, G. 1994. *Leisure in Your Life: An Exploration*. State College, PA: Venture.

Godbey, G. 1997. *Leisure in the 21st Century*. State College, PA: Venture.

Godbey, G., P. Patterson, and W. Brown. 1979. *Crime and Fear of Crime Among the Elderly—Relationships to Leisure*. Washington, DC: American Association of Retired Persons.

Gorden, C., and C. Gaitz. 1976. Leisure and lives: Personal expressivity across the life span. Edited by R. Binstock and E. Shanas, in *Handbook of Aging and the Social Sciences,* 310–332. New York: Van Nostrand Reinhold.

Grey, D., and S. Greben. 1974. Future perspectives. *California Parks and Recreation* 11–19 (June–July).

Hansel, T. 1979. *When I Relax I Feel Guilty*. Elgin, IL: David Cook.

Huizinga, J. 1962. *Homo Ludens—A Study of the Play Element in Culture*. Boston, MA: Beacon Press.

Jaffe, M. 1998. *Adolescence*. New York: Wiley

Jackson, E., and D. Scott 1999. Constraints to leisure, in Jackson, E. and T. Burton (eds.), *Leisure Studies: Prospects for the Twenty-first Century*. State College, PA: Venture.

Jordan, D. 2001. (2d ed.) *Leadership in Leisure Services: Making a Difference*. State College, PA: Venture.

Kelly, J. 1978. Leisure styles and choices in three environments. *Pacific Sociological Review 21*(4), 187–207.

Kelly, J. 1987. *Freedom to Be: A New Sociology of Leisure*. New York: Macmillan.

Kelly, J. 1996. *Leisure*. 3d ed. Boston: Allyn & Bacon.

Kleiber, D. 1999. *A Dialectical Interpretation: Leisure Experience and Human Development*. New York: Basic Books.

Lankford, S., D. DeGraaf, and L. Neal. 1996. A comparison of barriers to leisure and sport satisfaction in the United States: Implications for Hong Kong. *Hong Kong Recreation Review 8* (January), 343–346.

Levinson, D. 1978. *The Seasons of a Man's Life*. New York: Knopf.

McGuire, F., A. Dottavio, and J. O'Leary. 1987. The relationship of early experiences to life leisure involvement. *Leisure Sciences 9*(1), 53–65.

Muuss, R. 1982. *Theories of Adolescence*. New York: Random House.

National Recreation and Park Association. 1992. The 21st century, part 1, park and recreation agenda. *Parks and Recreation* (July), 53–57.

National Sporting Goods Association. 2001. www.usga.org/public/articles/details

Nelson, P. 2000. An aging population: The challenges and the opportunities. *Journal of Family and Consumer Sciences, 92*(2), 10–11.

Pittman, K. J. 1991. *Promoting Youth Development: Strengthening the Role of Youth Serving Community Organizations*. New York: Center for Youth Development and Policy Research.

Pittman, K. J., and M. Wright. 1991. *A Rationale for Enhancing the Role of the Non-School Voluntary Sector in Youth Development.* New York: Center for Youth Development and Policy Research.

Ross, J., and R. Pate. 1987. A summary of findings of The National Children and Youth Fitness Study. *Journal of Physical Education, Recreation and Dance,* 51–56.

Salkind, N. 1985. *Theories of Human Development.* New York: Wiley.

Scales, P. 1991. *A Portrait of Young Adolescents in the 1990s.* Carborro, NC: Center for Early Adolescence.

Seefeldt, V. 1996. The future of youth sports in America. Edited by F. Smoll and R. Smith, in *Children and Youth in Sport: A Biopsychosocial Perspective.* Dubuque, IA: Brown & Benchmark.

Sessoms, H. D. 1985. Lifestyles and life cycles; A recreation programming approach. Edited by T. Goodale and P. Witt, in *Recreation and Leisure: Issues in an Era of Change,* 221–243.

Troiano, R., K. Flegal, R. Kuczmarski, S. Campbell, and C. Johnson. 1995. Overweight prevalence and trends for children and adolescents: The national health and nutrition examination surveys, 1963–1991. *Archives of Pediatrics and Adolescent Medicine 149* (October), 1011–1023.

Unger, J., T. Simon, T. Newman, and S. Montgomery. 1998. Early adolescent street youth: An overlooked population with unique problems and service needs. *Journal of Early Adolescence 18*(4), 325–348.

U.S. Department of Health and Human Services. 1996. *Physical Activity and Health: A Report of the Surgeon General.* Atlanta: CDC.

PART TWO

Delivering Leisure Services

The leisure service delivery system in North America involves local, state, and federal agencies, nonprofit organizations, and commercial businesses. Such agencies provide a vast array of programs and services.

CHAPTER 7

Delivery of Leisure Services: Local Government

Leisure activities and programs provide opportunities for families to enjoy one another. Here, a family hikes down a path in a local park.

Introduction

Evolving from needs created by the Industrial Revolution in the mid- and late-1800s in both Canada and the United States, the provision of local leisure services has contributed much to society. Local park and recreation and human service departments today provide a wide array of leisure activities, facilities, areas, and information. Organized and structured to meet specific community needs, such agencies vary tremendously in size, scope, and impact.

The term *local park and recreation services* refers to those public services that are provided at the subdivision of government with the closest relationship to the consumer. A local government can be a city, town, county, or other self-governed district. Such communities, usually incorporated, are granted powers via various types of laws to provide community services. Park and recreation services, from the turn of the century, have been considered to be an essential component of municipal services. Some of the services provided by local governmental agencies include police protection, fire protection, sewage, sanitation, community development, housing, protective inspection and regulation, public welfare, public works, corrections—and parks and recreation services.

This chapter explores a number of topics to help the reader gain a full understanding of and appreciation for the structure and processes of local park and recreation services. Initially, the characteristics of local park and recreation services are discussed, followed by a definition of the three types of governmental organizations within which park and recreation services are provided at the local level—municipal government, county government, and special districts. Further, a discussion of the types of services provided by local public park and recreation agencies—and professional roles and opportunities within them—is covered. Last, the current status and prospects for the future of this sector of the profession are reviewed.

Characteristics of Local Leisure Service Agencies

In terms of customer awareness, local park and recreation agencies are often perceived as the most obvious representation of the leisure service movement. People living in local communities relate, in a direct and tangible way, to their city's parks, swimming pools, playgrounds, community centers, and other leisure facilities and amenities. The availability of park and recreation services is often viewed as a strong determinant in the decisions made by large corporations to locate their businesses. As early as 1985 Naisbett and Aburdene noted in their book, *Re-inventing the Corporation,* that a major factor influencing the selection of an organization of an area in which to locate is the livability of the environment. Leisure amenities, as reflected in park and recreation opportunities, contribute significantly to the livability factor. This fact is reinforced by Kreck (2000), who cites A National League of Cities poll that found the most important qualities of a family-friendly city were, in order, education, community safety, recreation, and citizen involvement. Local park and recreation departments are often charged with increasing the quality of life of its citizens. This section presents a discussion of the goals, resource bases, orientation to customers, and other distinguishing characteristics of local leisure service agencies.

Goals and Functions

What are the goals of local park, and recreation agencies? In the broadest context, local park and recreation departments are primarily motivated by service to their customers. An organization categorized as a service provider has as its primary mission meeting the needs, wants, and desires of those target populations it serves. Individuals who provide public service are engaged in an activity for the general good—planning, organizing, staffing, and implementing activities that result in the provision of service to the general public.

Edginton (1978), Edginton and Neal (1983), Hastings (1984), and Howat and Edginton (1986) have conducted comprehensive studies of goals of local park and recreation departments. Over the past twenty years, these individuals have studied the goals of local park and recreation agencies in Australia, Canada, and the United States. The discussion here is limited to findings from Canada and the United States. In these studies, agency respondents rated fifty-nine goal statements in terms of actual or current importance and what the status of the goal should be in the future.

The major findings of these studies indicated strong concern for the maintenance of parks and other areas and facilities, along with general support for providing services to children, higher rankings for provision of services for seniors (in the United States), and higher rankings for providing services to people with special needs (in Canada). In both Canada and the United States "ensuring that their organizations received a fair share of the tax dollar" was ranked highly by directors. Concerns about securing fees and charges were more highly ranked in the United States than in Canada. Goal statements dealing with the realization of benefits or behaviors by participants were ranked low. The highest ranking item dealing with the realization of benefits by participants was to "enhance health and physical fitness" (Edginton, 1978).

Regarding the future level of importance of various goal statements, directors of local park and recreation departments ranked the following goals highly: (1) supplying adequate land for the future, (2) receiving a fair share of tax dollars, (3) effective management of staff, (4) long-range

Enriching City Life . . .

Enriching the lives of urban residents is an important component of local government. Recreation services play a key role in this enrichment in cities around the world. For example, in Hong Kong, a city of over 6 million people, municipal government has been divided into Urban and Regional Councils. The Leisure Service Branch of the Urban Council is responsible for the management and planning of leisure amenities in Hong Kong's most densely populated districts, Hong Kong Island and Kowloon.

The Urban Council manages 630 hectares (approximately 1,575 acres) of public open spaces and operates facilities that include 35 game halls, 30 natural turf soccer pitches, 6 artificial soccer pitches, 17 roller rinks, 30 jogging tracks, 128 tennis courts, 224 basketball courts, 121 volleyball courts, 137 squash courts, 234 badminton courts, 2 hockey grounds, 2 rugby grounds, 2 indoor and 2 outdoor stadiums, 274 children's playgrounds, 12 beaches, 13 swimming pool complexes, 803 parks and gardens (including a botanical garden), 4 aviaries, a zoo, and a holiday village. Due to constraints of limited space and to maximize the use of land for recreation, the latest trend is to build multipurpose leisure centers in multistory complexes that also incorporate community facilities, such as retail markets, restaurants, and libraries.

Throughout the New Territories and outlying islands of Hong Kong, various regional councils manage similar facilities to meet the recreation needs of residents. In addition, regional councils also manage several holiday camps that provide vacation opportunities for families throughout Hong Kong as well as provide opportunities for Hong Kong residents to explore the wonders of the Hong Kong countryside.

One such holiday camp is Tso Kung Tam Outdoor Recreation Center, which has a capacity of 240 resident campers as well as over 200 day campers at one time. Although the center is situated on only 7.21 hectares (approximately 18 acres), the camp has a wide range of indoor and outdoor facilities. In 1994–1995, more than 80,000 day and residential campers enjoyed the facilities. Average utilization rate of day camp facilities was over 90 percent, whereas the average utilization rate of residential camp facilities was close to 70 percent.

In addition to municipal facilities and programs, Hong Kong also has a substantial number of country parks that help to meet the recreation needs of Hong Kong residents. Although Hong Kong is regarded as one of the world's most densely populated cities, more than 70 percent of its 1,071 square kilometers is countryside. Much of this countryside has been set aside in 21 country parks that cover an area of 41,320 hectares. The government has established these parks to cater to the outdoor recreation needs of its residents while at the same time protecting the plant, wildlife, and scenic beauty of the countryside. Country parks have been designated in mountain areas, woodlands, and along the coast line. In addition to country parks, thirteen special areas have been designated for the purpose of conserving unique biological or scientific areas of interest.

Facilities at the parks include picnic areas, designated campsites, children's playgrounds, walking trails, rain shelters, nature trails, visitor centers, public toilets, and three long distance trails (100 km, 70 km, and 50 km). All facilities are built in harmony with the natural environment and can be enjoyed by all at no charge. Visitation to country parks has increased dramatically over the last ten years; in 1994 the park received more than 10 million visitors.

planning, and (5) maintaining parks, areas, and facilities. Goal statements receiving lower rankings included the following: (1) providing direct financial aid, (2) providing leisure-counseling programs, and (3) enhancing intellectual growth. Interestingly, "enabling" types of services (assisting/facilitating people to organize their *own* services) was ranked higher by directors in Canada than in the United States (Edginton, 1978). The reason for these differences may result from the difference in philosophy between park and recreation departments in the United States and Canada. Local recreation departments in Canada tend to empower citizens to create their own programs, while local departments in the United States tend to plan and develop programs and then offer them to the public.

In the late 1990s, local park and recreation departments (supported by the National Recreation and Parks Association [NRPA]) have turned to a benefits-based approach to meeting local goals and objectives. A benefits-based approach to park and recreation services involves identifying the benefits desired and realized by park, and recreation program participants, structuring opportunities to maximize benefit achievement, and assessing benefit achievement (Edginton and O'Neill, 1999). Jarvi (1993) states that public parks and recreation departments must "seek to discover the fundamental reason for the existence of our profession and be able to define it in the highly personal terms of those we serve. The key to our success as professionals will be found in the degree in which we can prove that we are relevant to the public we serve by being able to express what we do in terms that they can easily understand" (p. 16). A benefits-based approach encourages recreation providers to consider more of a medical model for explaining benefits in which managers understand the long-term benefits of participating in our programs. In this regard, benefits-based management (BBM) is turning out to be a major catalyst in helping dispel a popular myth: that recreation and leisure provide something of value but only as long as the pleasurable experience lasts. BBM moves the leisure profession forward a quantum leap by integrating within the concept that value which is added to people's lives following on-site recreation participation (Driver, Brown, and Peterson, 1991).

Fran Mainella, the NRPA president in 1997, accurately portrays the commitment to the benefits of parks and recreation as "much more than a campaign. It is a process, a philosophy and mindset that is critical to insure the future of the park and recreation movement" (NRPA, 1998). In implementing a benefits approach to delivering services, Edginton and O'Neill (1999) have identified three distinct components. The first is benefits awareness, which is an attempt to inform park and recreation professionals and the general public of the benefits of public parks and recreation programs. The second is benefits-based programming, which is programming using the benefits as the basis of programming, measuring them, and sharing the results. The third component of a benefits program is BBM, which is concerned with managing the benefits, especially marketing the benefits of the existing program to the public.

Resource Base

The resource base or revenue for municipal parks and recreation services is diverse and sometimes appears to be complex. Deppe (1983) writes that ". . . local units of government receive their revenue from two basic sources—local and external" (p. 18). The major source of local revenue has been, historically, property tax. External sources often include financial assistance from state and federal governments and other sources. The most comprehensive analysis of revenue types is a classification system developed by Hemphill. Hemphill (1985) suggests that there are four separate classifications of revenues available to public leisure service organizations—compulsory resources, earned income, contractual receipts, and financial assistance. Table 7.1 presents these classifications.

A brief description of each of these sources of revenue follows:

Compulsory resources. Some cash and noncash revenues occur, according to Hemphill (1985), as a result of the taxing and regulatory powers of a government agency.
According to Brayley and McLean (1999), government sources of income have changed dramatically since the late 1970s when California voters passed Proposition 13, which

TABLE

7.1   REVENUE CLASSIFICATIONS AND TYPES

Classifications and Types

I. Compulsory Resources
   A. Taxes
      1. property
      2. income
      3. sales
      4. franchise
   B. Special assessments
   C. Dedication ordinances/regulations
   D. Fines/penalties
II. Earned Income
   A. Fees and charges
      1. entrance fees
      2. admission fees
      3. rental fees
      4. user fees
      5. sales charges
      6. license/permit fees
      7. special service fees
   B. Investment interest
III. Contractual Receipts
   A. Land leases
   B. Facility rentals
   C. Operating concessions
   D. Lease concessions
   E. Lease, lease-backs
   F. Sale, lease-backs
IV. Financial Assistance
   A. Grants
      1. project
      2. block
   B. Entitlements
      1. specific
      2. general
   C. Special appropriations
   D. Current donations
   E. Planned gifts

From Stan A. Hemphill, "Revenue Management: Beginning with the Basics" in *Parks and Recreation, 20,* (12), December 1985, pp. 35–36. Reprinted by permission.

cut property taxes by almost 50 percent. Since this legislation governments have responded to the voter with massive tax cuts, which has forced public parks and recreation departments to be more creative in financing their programs. That said, Brayley and McLean (1999) still note that taxes continue to represent the largest single source of income for local governments.

Earned income. These cash revenues, realized through fees and charges, have become an increasingly important source of income for park and recreation agencies. Fees and

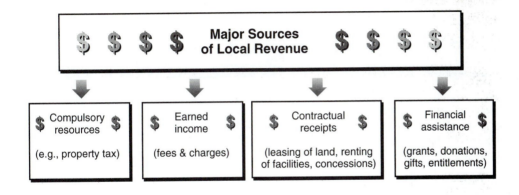

Figure 7.1

Major sources
of local revenue

charges are most often levied for program activities, rather than access to areas and
facilities.

Contractual receipts. These cash revenues accrue as a result of legal agreements between a
park and recreation agency and other parties and can include revenues from leasing
land, renting facilities, or concession operations at facilities. Public/private ventures
form an increasingly important way to create mutually beneficial ways of building cash
revenues for both parties.

Financial assistance. Brayley and McLean (1999) refer to this type of income as gratuitous
income. Some external funds come from grant sources, entitlement, donations, or other
gifts. This financial assistance is often solicited from foundations or individuals, or
gained from the acquisition of grants from various state or federal agencies and is
usually received without the expectation of a return (see figure 7.1).

In general, three types of local government strategies provide park and recreation services—
municipal, county, and special recreation district governments. A short presentation on the expenditures of these three types of governments for park and recreation services follows
in this section. In 1997, municipal governments in the United States expended more than
$10.7 billion for park and recreation services. This figure is down somewhat from the $13 billion spent in 1992 and represents approximately 3.9 percent of the total $274 billion spent for
all municipal services (U.S. Census Bureau, 1997a). Expenditures by county governments for
park and recreation services amounted to more than $3.9 billion for 1996–1997. This represents
1.9 percent of the total expenditures for county governments, which was over $198 billion
(U.S. Census Bureau, 1997b). Expenditures by special recreation districts' governments for
park and recreation services amounted to more than $2.1 billion in 1996–1997, which repre-
sents approximately 2.4 percent of the $52 billion of total expenditures for special districts'
government services (U.S. Census Bureau, 1997c). Note that the expenditures for special districts are less because this is not the most common form of organization for park and recreation
service in the United States.

Characteristics of Professionals

Occupational Outlook Handbook (2000) estimates that there were over 241,000 full-time recreation jobs in 1998. Of these year-round jobs, about half were located in park and recreation departments of municipal and county government. This number does not include seasonal hires
such as summer staff. Educational requirements for these jobs vary, however; for entry-level

NRPA Professional Code of Ethics

The National Recreation and Parks Association has provided leadership to the nation in fostering the expansion of recreation and parks. NRPA has stressed the value of recreation, both active and passive, for individual growth and development. Its members are dedicated to the common cause of assuring that people of all ages and abilities have the opportunity to find the most satisfying use of their leisure time and enjoy an improved quality of life.

The Association has consistently affirmed the importance of well-informed and professionally trained personnel to continually improve the administration of recreation and park programs. Members of NRPA are encouraged to support the efforts of the Association and profession by supporting state affiliate and national activities and by participating in continuing education opportunities, certification, and accreditation.

Membership of NRPA carries with it special responsibilities to the public at large, and to the specific communities and agencies in which recreation and park services are offered. As a member of the National Recreation and Park Association, I accept and agree to abide by the Code of Ethics and pledge myself to:

1. Adhere to the highest standards of integrity and honesty in all public and personal activities to inspire public confidence and trust.

2. Strive for personal and professional excellence and encourage the professional development of associates.

3. Strive for the highest standards of professional competence, fairness, impartiality, efficiency, effectiveness, and fiscal responsibility.

4. Avoid any interest or activity that is in conflict with the performance of job responsibilities.

5. Promote the public interest and avoid personal gain or profit from the performance of job duties and responsibilities.

6. Support equal employment opportunities.

Source: Busser, J. 1999. Human Resource Management. Edited by B. van der Smissen, M. Moiseichik, V. Hartenburg, and L. Twardzik, in *Management of Park and Recreation Agencies*. Ashburn, VA: National Recreation and Park Association, p. 558.

professional positions, a college degree is important, and many administrative positions in large public recreation systems require a graduate degree.

Certifications also are becoming increasingly important for professionals working in government agencies (e.g., municipal recreation departments). Certification is offered by the NRPA National Certification Board. The NRPA, along with its state chapters, offers certification as a "Certified Park and Recreation Professional" for those with a bachelor's degree in recreation, park resources, and leisure services from an NRPA/AALR accredited program with no less than two years full-time experience, and as an "Associate Park and Recreational Professional" for those possessing an associate's degree and no less than two years of experience.

In many ways, leisure professionals who work in government agencies see themselves as public servants promoting the common good through recreation spaces and programs. As with other individuals involved in public service, leisure professionals see themselves as altruistic, in that they are motivated primarily by service to others. Godbey (1997) identifies one of the three characteristics of successful leisure service organizations (whether public, nonprofit, or commercial) as having a service ethic.

In promoting such a service ethic, park and recreation professionals often have a strong commitment to maintain the dignity and worth of those whom they serve. In addition, many individuals in the park and recreation field also have a strong commitment to the preservation and

A Benefits Approach in Advocating for Public Parks and Recreation

It costs approximately $30,000 to incarcerate a juvenile offender for one year. If that money were available to the Park Department, we could: take him swimming twice a week for 24 weeks, and give him four tours of the zoo, plus lunch, and enroll him in 50 Community Center programs, and visit Oxley Nature Center twice, and let him play league softball for a season, tour the gardens at Woodward Park twice, and give him two weeks of tennis lessons, and enroll him in two weeks of day camp, and let him play three rounds of golf, and act in one play, and participate in one fishing clinic, and take a four-week pottery class, and play basketball for eight hours a week for 40 weeks after which we could return to you: $29,125 and one much happier kid. (Bob Jennings, Naturalist Oxley Nature Center on the subject of Youth at Risk from the Tulsa Park and Recreation Department Marketing Plan, 1997–1998)

Source: National Recreation and Parks Association. 1998. *Discover the Benefits.* Ashburn, VA: NRPA.

conservation of human resources. Connected with these types of values is having a high level of integrity. To support these types of values, the NRPA has developed and encourages its members to accept and promote a Professional Code of Ethics.

Beyond working to be a public servant, DeGraaf, Jordan, and DeGraaf (1998) urge park and recreation professionals to strive to be servant leaders in developing and implementing recreation programs. The term servant leadership was first coined in 1970 by Robert Greenleaf (1977) in an article entitled "The Servant as Leader." From this humble beginning, servant leadership is now in its third decade as a specific leadership and management approach. Spears (1995) has identified servant leadership as an approach that "attempts to simultaneously enhance the personal growth of workers and improve the quality and caring of our many institutions through a combination of teamwork and community, personal involvement in decision making and ethical and caring behavior" (p. 4). In describing the importance of servant leadership, Greenleaf (1977) states, "if a better society is to be built, one that is more just and more loving, one that provides greater creative opportunity for its people, then the most open course is to raise both the capacity to serve and the very performance as servant of existing major institutions by new regenerative forces operating within them" (p. 49).

In striving to become servant leaders and survive in today's workplace, Godbey (1997) has identified a number of personal strategies for those who will work in leisure services in the twenty-first century. These strategies, centered on being flexible and innovative in serving others, include the following:

- *Serve others.* An ethic of service will continue to distinguish leisure services in the public, private nonprofit, and commercial sectors. As a leisure services programmer the emphasis must always be on the people served and the benefits provided rather than the program itself.
- *Become an entrepreneur.* Entrepreneurs produce new ways of meeting needs, working to improve existing products and services, and responding to changing demographic conditions.
- *Seek continuous learning opportunities.* As the primary basis of the economy becomes knowledge, it becomes imperative that leisure service professionals stay current with the world around them through lifelong learning.

- *Become more flexible.* In a world of rapid and continuing change, the ability to adapt to changing circumstances is critical.
- *Call attention to the importance of what you do.* Leisure services professionals must believe in the power and potential of leisure programs to affect change in the lives of individuals and society. Leisure services are critical components of society, not just "frosting."

Orientation to Customers

Lappe and DuBois (1994), in their book *The Quickening of America: Rebuilding Our Nation, Remaking Our Lives,* put forth the idea that human service organizations (which include recreation and leisure) are moving away from simply providing services to creating a living democracy model whereby customers are viewed as partners in the planning process. Thus, community parks and recreation professionals must continue to build partnerships with customers—partnerships that link the professional and his or her skill with the needs, interests, and wants of the members of the community. This type of partnership focuses on solving common problems. Customers are viewed as clients; that is, they receive professional services and may participate in the problem-solving process.

To provide services, public park and recreation professionals tend to gather facts about problems and make decisions following the most rational course of action. In general, the population within the entire geographic boundary served by the park and recreation agency receives its services. Historically, a philosophy of providing the greatest good to the greatest number has prevailed. Because of limited organizational resources, however, park and recreation agencies have become more aware of the need to focus their activities on specific populations and services. Thus, they often apply marketing strategies to specific populations, such as children, people with disabilities, or older persons.

Park and recreation agencies increasingly are wed to the concept of quality. This is reflected in the use of such management strategies as Total Quality Management (TQM) and Continuous Quality Improvement (CQI). TQM focuses on the involvement of all organization members in the pursuit of quality as well as attention to the use of statistical measures as benchmarks, innovation, continuous improvement, anticipatory planning, and having a future orientation. With a commitment to quality, park and recreation professionals are increasingly seeking close communication with customers as reflected in an increase in the use of task forces, surveys, town meetings, and other ways of connecting with the consumer to improve quality.

Types of Local Governments Providing Park and Recreation Services

As mentioned, three basic types of local governments provide park and recreation services— municipal, county, and special district (see figure 7.2). All of these forms of government are close to the individuals served and also are characterized by their ability to be self-governed. Local park and recreation services derive their power from state government and must function within the laws established by it. Kraus and Curtis (1986) write,

> Under the American form of government, states have the authority to regulate governmental programs and various areas of human activity within their territories, except as limited by the federal Constitution or their own constitutions. This regulatory power is commonly known as "police power" and provides authorization to enact laws for the health, safety, morals, and general welfare of the citizens of each state. (p. 61)

Types of Legislation

The authority that states have given local governments to enable them to provide park and recreation services often occurs in the form of specific state statutes created to directly authorize the organization and implementation of such programs. Even without such specific legislation, local governments can operate park and recreation services by broadly exercising their police powers. Kraus and Curtis (2000) report five types of legislation (see figure 7.3) that have been created to assist in the establishment of local park and recreation services. They include the following:

Special park and recreation laws. These types of laws empower specific cities or communities to provide park and recreation services. In general, these laws set forth provisions for a governing structure, taxing powers, and methods and procedures to employ and supervise professional staff.

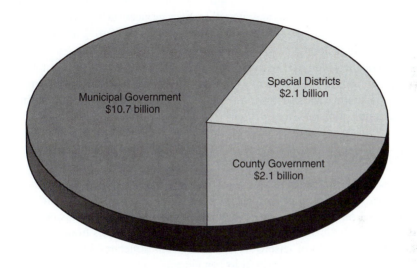

Figure 7.2

Expenditures for park and recreation services in the United States at the local level of government in 1997

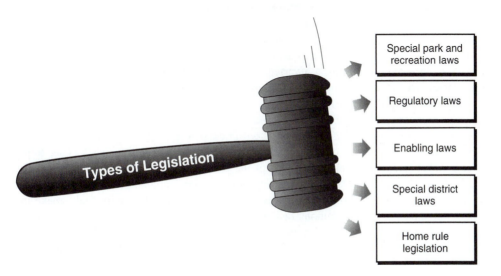

Figure 7.3

Types of legislation that can be used to establish local park and recreation services

Regulatory laws. Regulatory laws control or monitor park and recreation services in order to protect those individuals affected by such activities. Such regulatory laws affect the management of facilities such as swimming pools, ice rinks, or programs in which risk to the customer must be managed. Standards for sanitation of facilities also come under the heading of regulatory laws.

Enabling laws. The most important type of legislation impacting on park and recreation services is the enabling law. Enabling legislation specifies that a local branch of government can own, operate, or manage park and recreation services. Enabling legislation also usually provides for a governing body, spells out taxing powers, and so forth. Such state laws, usually written in a permissive fashion, provide communities the individual discretion to determine the size and scope of their services. Enabling legislation does not mandate the establishment of services, as do special park and recreation laws.

Special district laws. A large number of states have legislation that allows for the establishment of special single-purpose local units of government. This can involve park and recreation services as well as other services such as water, fire, electricity, and sewage. These types of laws provide guidelines for acquiring areas and facilities, and establishing programs, taxing powers, and governing structure.

Home rule legislation. Home rule legislation refers to the state statutes that provide local subdivisions of government with the ability to determine their own form of government. Communities that use this form of legislation often include park and recreation services as a part of their basic structure.

Municipal Government

A common form of organizing leisure services in Canada and the United States falls under the jurisdiction of a municipal government associated with a city or town. In this arrangement, park and recreation services become part of the community service offerings of the entire city government. A city, basically a self-governing unit, derives its powers from state or provincial government. The provision of leisure services within this structure, while not mandatory, is often provided by a community as a part of its complete package of services.

A municipal government can provide leisure services in a number of ways. The most common form is a combined parks and recreation department. In this organizational arrangement, the functions of park management and the creation and delivery of recreation activities merge under one administrative unit. It is also possible to have these two functions separate from one another. In some communities, a variety of leisure activities, including libraries, cultural arts, and other specialized facilities such as zoos or aquariums, may be combined into a human services or community services department.

Boards are often established to govern these various types of departments that provide leisure services. *Park and recreation boards* exist to provide input into decision-making processes by interested, knowledgeable, and informed citizens. Individuals serving on park and recreation boards represent the citizens of the community. The three basic types of park and recreation boards include *policy-making boards, semi-independent boards,* and *advisory boards.* Policy-making boards, composed of elected or appointed individuals, make independent judgments in an autonomous fashion concerning the direction of the organization. Semi-independent boards have partial rather than full decision-making power. These boards oversee a specific area of government, such as parks and recreation. Semi-independent boards may be ei-

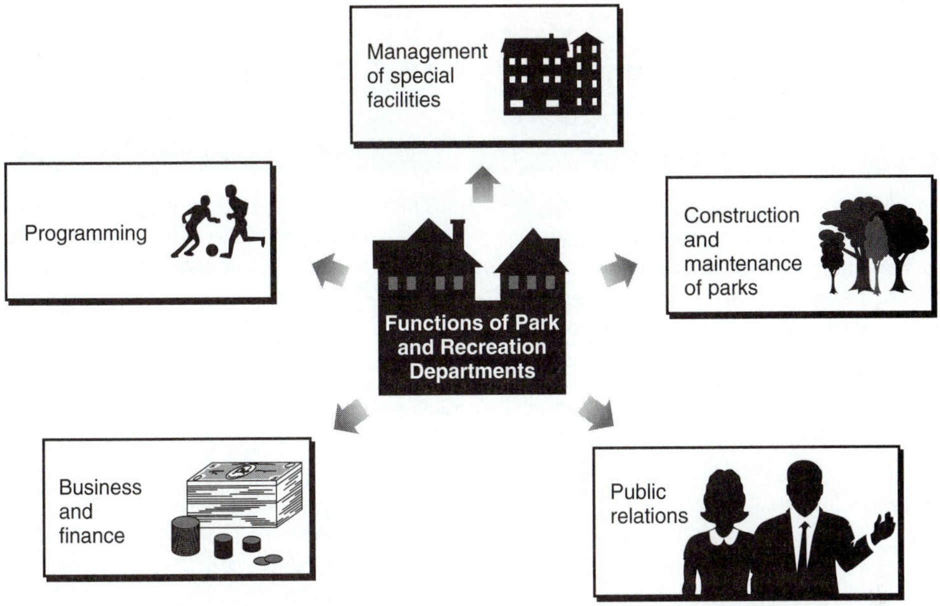

Figure 7.4

Major functions of combined parks and recreation departments

ther elected or appointed. Advisory boards or commissions, usually appointed by a mayor or governing body such as a city council, provide nonbinding advice to either one or both of these appointing authorities.

No specific organizational format for park and recreation services can be applied universally in any community. Each community will create an internal organizational structure for the delivery of park and recreation services that best suits its needs. In general, however, combined park and recreation departments often address several major functions. According to Rodney and Toalson (1981), they include the following: (1) recreation programming; (2) management of special facilities; (3) construction and maintenance of parks; (4) business and finance; and (5) public relations. These functions are also depicted in figure 7.4. Rodney and Toalson further note that a park department might be organized according to the following functions: (1) engineering; (2) horticulture; (3) forestry and street trees; (4) botanical gardens; and (5) park police.

The organizational chart for Albany, Oregon, is presented in figure 7.5. Albany, a community of slightly more than 25,000 inhabitants, has an outstanding park and recreation department and is noted for its excellence in innovative park design and recreation program development. This department's organizational structure addresses the functions related to parks as well as the functions related to recreation programming. Further, the park and recreation department is advised by a seven-member park and recreation advisory commission, whose primary function is to advise the director and the city council on matters pertaining to park and recreation services in the city of Albany.

County Government

County governments also provide park and recreation services. A county is the next political unit that exists below state government. Rodney and Toalson (1981) discuss the functions performed by counties.

The functions counties perform have become somewhat traditional and are similar in character. In most instances, counties build and maintain roads and bridges, care for the indigent, register land titles,

None of Twenty-Five Largest Cities Rates Five Stars in Report

The Trust for Public Land analyzed the park systems in the nation's twenty-five largest cities. Its ratings were based on fifteen factors, including percentage of parkland in each city and the availability of facilities such as pools, tennis courts, and recreation centers.

The cities were rated on a system of one to five stars against cities in the same population category. No cities received a five-star rating, which is the highest.

Four-Star Cities

Boston
Cincinnati
Minneapolis

Three-Star Cities

Chicago
Denver
New York
Phoenix
Portland, OR
San Diego
San Francisco
Seattle

Two-Star Cities

Atlanta
Baltimore
Dallas
Houston
Indianapolis
Kansas City
Los Angeles
Philadelphia
Pittsburgh
St. Louis
Tampa

One-Star Cities

Cleveland
Detriot
Miami

Source: Davis, K. 2000, August 10. 3 Cities Earn 4 Stars for Parks. *USA Today,* 3A.

preserve peace and administer justice, collect taxes and provide state and county elections . . . [In the 20th century,] however, county functions have become somewhat liberalized to include services of an urban nature such as parks, recreation, libraries, drainage, sewage control, and the like." (p. 197)

The development of county park systems occurred at the turn of the century in the United States. The first attempt to acquire lands that encompassed a broad area occurred in Boston in 1882. A metropolitan parks commission, established by the state legislature, encompassed thirty-six communities surrounding the city of Boston. The first actual system of parks established within a county occurred in Essex County, New Jersey.

What types of services do county park and recreation departments provide? Answers vary because counties vary in geographic size and density of population; however, a county park system usually provides services that are commensurate with the needs of its residents. In general, a county park system offers the following services:

1. Regional park and recreation areas and facilities that combine some of the resources of other park and recreation departments to create a unified system (e.g., the creation of a regional park system).

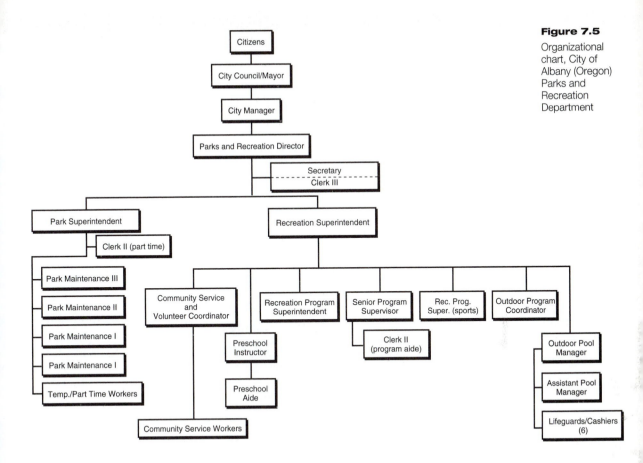

2. Unique or specialized parks and recreation areas and facilities that emphasize particular natural resources or other special features (e.g., a rodeo, fairgrounds, zoos).
3. Recreation program services that are difficult, if not impractical, to offer in urban areas (e.g., resident camping programs, yachting classes).
4. Specialized recreation services that require a broader base of support and population (e.g., programs for disabled populations).
5. Recreation program services that meet the general needs of the population of the county (especially in rural settings not served by incorporated communities).

County park and recreation departments also may provide informational services regarding the public leisure resources within their political jurisdiction. County governments can play an important role in advancing the park and recreation movement by coordinating various activities between and among individual city service providers. County governments can also serve to stimulate the development of public park and recreation services in incorporated cities and towns.

The managing authority established for county park and recreation departments across the United States varies and depends upon state legislation. In some cases, the highway department or a conservation department manages the county park and recreation board. In other cases, it functions as a separate department, managed by a policy-making or advisory board. Still further, the county park and recreation board can function under the management of an elected county commissioner.

The organizational chart from the Lane County (Oregon) Parks Division serves as an example of the structure of a county park and recreation system (figure 7.6). The Lane County Parks Division manages more than 5,000 acres of park land. County parks have been established in both urban and rural areas and vary from well-developed, well-manicured park areas to park sites that are in a natural state. Facilities include marinas, beaches, playgrounds, and camp sites.

The amount of funds spent for county park and recreation systems varies a great deal from state to state. Large populous states like California, however, tend to spend more on their county park systems than smaller, less populated states. In 1997, California spent the most for county parks and recreation services, followed by Florida, Maryland, New York, Arizona, and Wisconsin (U.S. Census Bureau, 1997b).

Special Districts

Another approach to organizing park and recreation services involves the creation of a special district. A special district is an autonomous, separate function of government having a particu-

Figure 7.6

Organizational chart, Lane County Parks Division

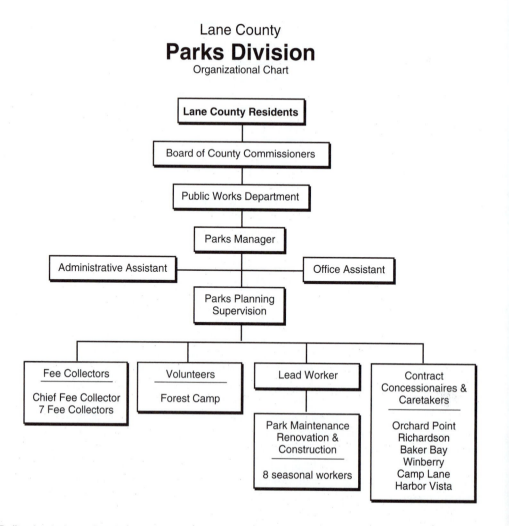

Lane County
Parks Division
Organizational Chart

- Lane County Residents
- Board of County Commissioners
- Public Works Department
- Parks Manager
  - Administrative Assistant
  - Office Assistant
- Parks Planning Supervision
  - Fee Collectors
    - Chief Fee Collector
    - 7 Fee Collectors
  - Volunteers
    - Forest Camp
  - Lead Worker
    - Park Maintenance Renovation & Construction
    - 8 seasonal workers
  - Contract Concessionaires & Caretakers
    - Orchard Point
    - Richardson
    - Baker Bay
    - Winberry
    - Camp Lane
    - Harbor Vista

lar purpose, in this case the provision of park and recreation services. The key terms are *separate* and *autonomous*. Special districts are created in such a way as to be independent of other government bodies. A park and recreation special district is a legally organized subdivision of a state. It derives its power as a legal entity from the state statutes that provide for its incorporation. In 1997, 1,253 special districts in the United States had been established for the specific purpose of providing park and recreation services, a 25 percent increase since 1987 when 1,002 special park and recreation districts existed (U.S. Census Bureau, 1997c).

Figure 7.7, an organizational chart for the Willamalane Park & Recreation District, Springfield, Oregon, has four major divisions: administrative services, leisure services, park services, and the office of the superintendent. The Willamalane Park and Recreation District operates a park system with 515 acres in thirty-four park sites. Special facilities include an indoor wave pool, fitness center, community center, and historic-cultural areas.

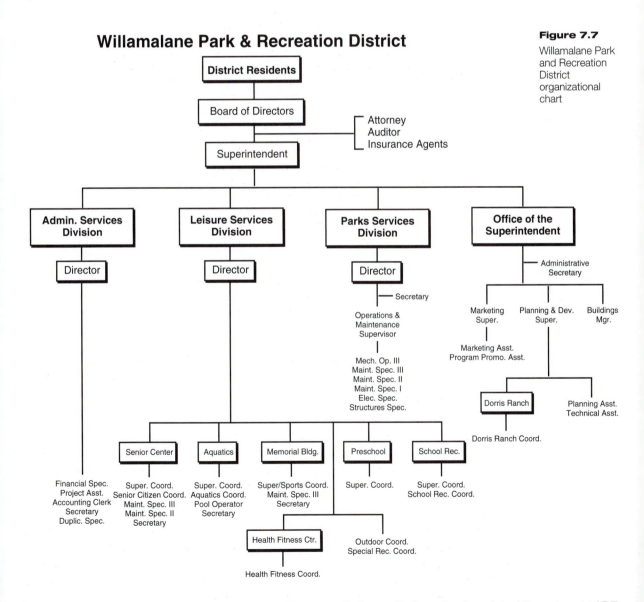

Willamalane Park & Recreation District

Figure 7.7

Willamalane Park and Recreation District organizational chart

Generally speaking, special park districts have several unique characteristics. They include the following: (1) existence as an organized entity with a resident population and defined geographic area; (2) governmental character as a separate legal governing body; and (3) substantial autonomy to provide a service (parks and recreation) and the taxing power to raise part of their own revenue (U.S. Census Bureau, 1997c).

In other words, a park and recreation special district represents a specific population in a defined geographic area. The district has a governing body—usually an elected board of directors. This board is empowered to acquire land, provide recreation programs, hire employees, and collect taxes and other revenues. A special district operates with autonomy in decision making and is not encumbered by political interference from other governmental decision-making bodies.

Special districts can be established to focus on the general functions of parks and recreation or they may be delimited to a more specific area (for example, a district established to focus on the preservation of wilderness areas, seashores, or other natural resources). Most park and recreation districts, however, serve urban or suburban community needs.

A special district has a great advantage in that the central work of the agency is focused primarily on parks and recreation. Within municipal governments, park and recreation departments compete with all other services for tax dollars and other revenues. Sometimes the competition in municipal government leads to a reduction of funds for park and recreation services. The disadvantage of special districts is their lack of access to other city resources, such as police protection and public works. All of these services must be provided by the district itself, or contracted for with other agencies.

Illinois, by far, leads all states in the number of organized special recreation districts with 360 special districts in existence (U.S. Census Bureau, 1997c). As a result, Illinois also leads all states in expenditures of special districts services in the United States. Other states that favor the special district system as demonstrated by the number of special recreation districts in existence are North Dakota (240 special districts), California (164), Ohio (94), Washington (61), and Pennsylvania (60) (U.S. Census Bureau, 1997c). Undoubtedly, the preference in these states for special district systems is due to the influence of early legislation in Illinois (in the late 1800s) influencing the establishment of the Illinois Park District Code.

An excellent example of the special district organizational arrangement is the West Suburban Special Recreation Association (WSSRA) in Franklin Park, Illinois. This cooperative extension of ten local park districts and one village came together in 1976 to create a special district to coordinate year-round recreation opportunities for individuals with special needs, disabilities, or handicapping conditions. By cooperating, the partner communities consolidate their resources and populations and hire staff who are trained to work with special populations (WSSRA, 1993).

WSSRA offers a variety of programs that reflect the mood and activities of the changing seasons and resemble programs offered by partner park districts and recreation districts. WSSRA strives to provide programs in centralized locations as close to home and school as possible. WSSRA does not own or operate any recreation facilities and therefore coordinates with local park and recreation districts, churches, schools, and other private facilities to offer their programs. This serves to enhance the special district's philosophy of assisting in the normalization and mainstreaming process (WSSRA, 1993).

In addition to public funds used to operate WSSRA, parents of children with disabilities who live in the service district formed a not-for-profit corporation, the West Suburban Special Recreation Foundation. This corporation is dedicated to raising funds to purchase recreation equipment and offer programs for the WSSRA.

Recreation Services as a Part of a School District

A school district is a special district and, although the provision of park and recreation services is not its primary function, a school district may assist in the provision of park and recreation services as a corollary function. From a historical perspective, use of schools for recreation services was viewed as being a desirable, practical approach. Thus, a number of states, particularly Wisconsin, California, New Jersey, and Michigan, established enabling legislation for schools to coordinate their efforts to provide leisure services.

Recently, the community education movement, organized within various school districts in the United States, has strongly embraced the pursuit of leisure activities as an important component of their activities. The community education movement, built on a concept that promotes the use of various resources in a community to meet community needs, focuses on facilitating communication and cooperation between and among individuals. Community education, a process that encourages community involvement, also organizes a service delivery system. Thus, focusing on the leisure needs of people, community educators have encouraged school systems to actively engage in problem-solving processes related to leisure as well as actually providing leisure services.

Community educators, although using the entire community or given neighborhood as their resource, often work within a particular school. This school facility becomes a primary resource base for promoting community activities and providing leisure services. School facilities have gymnasiums, classrooms, meeting rooms, art studios, and wood and metal shops, as well as playing and athletic fields. This resource base provides areas and facilities that can be used in programming activities and services.

Types of Services

Park and recreation systems at the local level of government provide a wide array of services. The innovation and ingenuity of area and facility planners and recreation programmers have resulted in the creation of many outstanding park and recreation services. The range of such services moves from traditional programs, such as youth sports leagues, to more highly sophisticated uses of technology, including the production of videocassettes from acquisition of leisure skills. Leisure services offered by local governments, while difficult to categorize, often fall into four general classifications: recreation activities, areas and facilities, information, and leadership.

Recreation Activities The category of recreation activities includes the creation and delivery of classes, leagues, drop-in programs, special events, outreach programs, and others. These programs can be provided in a variety of program areas, including sports, outdoor recreation, performing arts (dance, drama, music), arts, new arts (use of technology), travel and tourism, crafts, literary and self-improvement, hobbies, social recreation, and voluntary services.

A review of the Calgary, Alberta, Parks/Recreation Department, Division of Leisure Services shows that the department provided 361 direct programs during 1985, cosponsored 917, and initiated special events that focused on family- and child-related activities. Some special events included dance-alongs, bridge tournaments, badminton tournaments, volleyball tournaments, and a fitness round-up. Athletic services included a hockey school, tennis lessons, golf lessons, horse shows, soccer school, baseball school, and coaches and officials clinics.

Areas and Facilities   Recreation activities often depend on specific facilities. Hence, the planning and management of areas and facilities plays an important part in a well-designed program. A *facility* may be defined as a structure that provides for or houses a recreation service. For example, a community center is a recreation facility. An *area* may be defined as an open space or a piece of developed land that is used for recreation purposes.

People commonly associate a number of areas and facilities with parks and recreation—swimming pools, parks, ball fields, and playgrounds. Many of these traditional facilities are still present, yet new technologies and customer demand are adding a great deal of variety to park departments today. In the past ten years we have seen a number of trends manifest themselves in recreation space and facility design. These trends include more multiple-use facilities, creativity in creating new open space in cities using public/private cooperation, more linked linear trail systems, increased accessibility for people with disabilities, and environmental-friendly design (Kraus and Curtis, 2000). These trends are evident in some of the following innovative uses of both facilities and open space:

Aquatic facilities. In recent years leisure pools have begun to replace traditional pools that were created primarily for exercise and competitive swimming. Public agencies are following the lead of commercial aquatic water parks and creating pools that are more conducive to family recreation. For example, in Springfield, Oregon, the Willamalane Park and Recreation District built an indoor aquatic facility that offers guests a wave pool, water slides, hot tubs, waterfalls, a long narrow lap pool, wide spacious decks (both inside and outside), snack bars, and locker rooms. The facility also has high ceilings, skylights, indoor plants, and open space, creating the illusion of being outdoors.

Climbing walls. Indoor climbing walls are increasingly found as a part of the facilities provided by local park and recreation departments. Such structures effectively simulate outdoor environments, providing individuals access to one type of high adventure activity. Programs often include instructional programs as well as drop-in services. Climbing walls are usually built with several levels of difficulty and the ability to change climbing routes to promote interest and provide new challenges for participants.

Fitness centers. Americans' increased awareness of fitness has created a boom for fitness programs and equipment. Municipal governments are building new facilities and refitting old ones to provide accessible space and equipment for fitness programs for people of all ages and abilities. In conjunction with these programs, circuit training has developed. Between the early 1970s and 1990 more than 700 paracourses (that is, circuit training courses) were installed in parks, schools, and recreation centers (Kraus and Curtis, 2000).

Rails-to-trails corridors. In 1916, the United States boasted the largest rail system in the world with nearly 300,000 miles of steel connecting every large city and small town into a massive transportation network. Today, that impressive system has shrunk to less than 150,000 miles. As more than 2,000 miles of track are abandoned each year, unused corridors offer a perfect backbone for another type of transportation system—rails to trails (Rails to Trails Conservancy, 1993). Local governments are combining with state and federal governments, as well as the private sector, to create recreation resources of local, state, and federal significance. Other possibilities for creating new green space and parks include utilizing other transportation corridors such as highways and rivers. One northwest town has created a number of covered basketball courts by placing them under highway underpasses.

Ecological recovery sites. As the United States and Canada struggle with environmental problems such as water pollution, many new strategies are being developed. One wastewater treatment plan for small towns can create new park resources for many local park and recreation departments. Towns such as Union, Mississippi, and Haughton, Louisiana, use swamps and marshes to treat town sewage. These small-scale water-treatment areas can be practical and beautiful and provide new places for local parks. Although these plans may never replace large metropolitan sewage systems (to replace metropolitan Boston's current sewage treatment plant would require a thirty-nine-square-mile marsh), this may be a cost-effective way for small governments to deal with water-waste management as well as provide wildlife areas that could be used as parks (Burke, 1992).

Urban forestry projects. "Trees are not just a nicety, an amenity, something we can do without. In fact, they make our cities livable. . . . Trees are nature's janitor" (Haurwitz, 1992, p. 18). Yet, our urban forests are dying, and revitalizing them is imperative. The federal government provides some assistance to local government—the 1992 fiscal-year budget for urban forestry was $24 million. Municipal governments are also fighting to reverse the urban forest decline. Cities and towns can become a part of the Tree City USA program. To qualify for the program a city must spend at least $2 a resident on forestry. In return, the city receives a flag, a plaque, and technical reports on planting and maintaining trees. About 1,600 communities have enrolled in the program. In many cities this program is coordinated through the park and recreation department. Tree-planting projects offer municipal governments opportunities to build partnerships with volunteer groups and the private sector. For example, a local group of the Telephone Pioneers of America, a group of phone company retirees, planted over 15,000 seedlings in 1991. Such projects beautify existing open spaces as well as help combat environmental problems such as global warming.

National Program for Playground Safety. The National Program for Playground Safety is focused on assisting schools, park and recreation systems, child care centers, and other locations with information about playground safety. Operated at the University of Northern Iowa, the program has developed a national plan that includes four primary goals: (1) the design of age-appropriate playgrounds; (2) the provision of proper surfacing under and around playground equipment; (3) the provision of proper supervision on playgrounds; and (4) properly maintaining playgrounds. Information regarding this program's activities may be accessed by contacting the University of Northern Iowa, or at the website www.uni.edu/playground (see figure 7.8).

Information   Local governments also have a responsibility to provide public information concerning leisure pursuits. Most local park and recreation agencies disseminate information regarding their activities and resources and develop brochures emphasizing program offerings or focusing on unique facilities.

Some local park and recreation departments take an even more comprehensive approach to information dissemination, helping individuals become aware of available services throughout the entire community. Still further, a few parks and recreation departments have engaged in leisure education and leisure counseling. These two activities often aim at trying to influence the attitudes and behaviors of individuals. Some believe that cultivation of a positive leisure ethic and set of values contributes to a healthy lifestyle.

Figure 7.8

The National
Program for
Playground
Safety

The
National
Program for
Playground
Safety

Keep Your Children Safe

A parent's quick checklist*

Place this list in a prominent area of your home for quick reference. Then, before your children head out the door for the playground, check that:

Supervision is present, but strings and rope aren't

Adult presence is needed to watch for potential hazards, observe, intercede and facilitate play when necessary. Strings on clothing and ropes used for play can cause accidental strangulation if caught on equipment.

All children play on age-appropriate equipment

Preschoolers, ages 2–5, and children ages 5–12 are developmentally different and need different equipment located in separate areas to keep the playground safe and fun for all.

Falls to surface are cushioned

Nearly 70 percent of all playground injuries are related to falls to the surface. Acceptable surfaces include hardwood fiber/mulch, pea gravel, sand, and synthetic materials such as poured-in-place, rubber mats or tiles. Playground surfaces should not be concrete, asphalt, grass, blacktop, packed dirt or rocks.

Equipment is safe

Check to make sure the equipment is anchored safely in the ground, all equipment pieces are in good working order, S-hooks are entirely closed, bolts are not protruding, there are no exposed footings, etc. Safety checklists are available from the CPSC or the National Program for Playground Safety.

America's Playgrounds — Make them Safe

*This information was produced by the National Program for Playground Safety, University of Northern Iowa, Cedar Falls, Iowa 50614-0161, 800-554-PLAY, http:uni.edu/coe/playgrnd.

For example, one promotional brochure for recreation programs advertises "Tipi living." This program, sponsored by the Calgary, Alberta Parks/Recreation Department, helps individuals enjoy the outdoor environment and participate in winter outdoor pursuits (see figure 7.9).

Leadership Local park and recreation departments also provide leadership to communities. This leadership occurs not only in the form of instruction or supervision of recreation programs but also in a broader sense by helping communities to solve their leisure and social problems. Park and recreation personnel often play a key role in the identification and solution of

Figure 7.9

City of Calgary
brochure

community concerns. They bring to bear their expertise, knowledge, and experience to assist their community.

The leadership role played by professionals also includes promoting leisure values. In effect, the professional uses his or her expertise to influence community values concerning leisure. By promoting and interpreting the ideas and values of the leisure movement, professionals engage in leadership.

Professional Roles and Opportunities

Varied professional roles exist at the local level of government in the park and recreation area (see figure 7.10). In general, these professional roles can be divided into three classifications: direct service, supervisory, and administrative (Jordan, 2001).

Figure 7.10

Professional roles in the park and recreation field at the local level of government

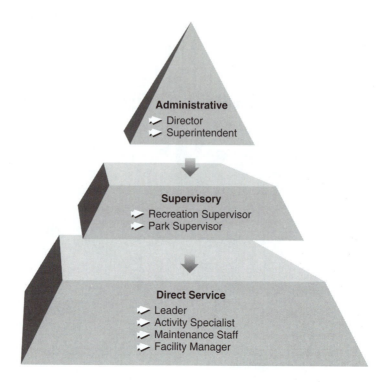

Direct service professional roles involve the leading of activities, provision of information, or the operation or maintenance of a special facility. The majority of positions at the local level of government carried out on a part-time or seasonal basis fall into the direct service category.

For example, a direct service provider in the position of a part-time or seasonal recreation leader would be involved in program leadership at a specific location such as a playground or community center. He or she would plan, organize, and lead groups in a variety of recreation activities. More specifically, the recreation leader might issue and collect equipment and supplies, teach recreation skills, perform simple maintenance tasks, and maintain records and activity reports.

Supervisory roles are middle-management functions within organizations. Park supervisors often manage a crew of workers or laborers, or maintain a cluster of areas or facilities. Recreation supervisors are employed for their specific knowledge of a program area or facility or for their general knowledge of recreation program development.

A recreation supervisor usually has primary responsibility for initiating and coordinating activity programs or managing a facility. In general, a recreation supervisor manages, oversees, and trains leaders and volunteers. She or he engages in such activities as planning programs with leaders, scheduling and coordinating activities, promoting and publicizing programs, and evaluating activities to determine whether they have met the needs of customers. The recreation supervisor is often called upon to speak publicly and to justify budget requests.

Another example of a supervisory role in the park and recreation field is that of a park supervisor. A park supervisor's work relates to the maintenance, construction, and landscaping of grounds and facilities and the supervision of work performed by semiskilled and unskilled personnel. In this role, a park supervisor would schedule jobs and work routines for maintenance, inspect areas to determine whether work met performance standards, and maintain basic time, material, and work records.

Administrative roles, held by the senior managers of park and recreation organizations, include division heads as well as the head executive officer. These individuals primarily engage in long-range planning, public relations, budget analysis and control, and the supervision and direction of personnel.

A director of parks and recreation, for example, holds an administrative role. The head executive officer of a park and recreation agency is sometimes referred to as the superintendent of parks and recreation or the general manager. A park and recreation director administers the program and supervises all personnel within the department, either indirectly or directly. He or she establishes a program for the recruitment and selection of staff and controls all expenditures directly or indirectly. The director engages in long-range planning and carries out established organizational policy. A director also works with the public and/or other public or private agencies to determine community needs.

Career Opportunities in Public Parks and Recreation

In the 1960s, experts predicted that a gap would occur between the supply of college-educated workers trained in the public parks and recreation field and the positions available in the field. By the late 1980s, this gap had closed as the supply of college-educated workers had exceeded demand (Dunn, 1986). This trend has continued as the *Occupational Outlook Handbook* (2000) indicates that competition will remain keen for career positions in recreation.

Three factors have contributed to a decline in the number of opportunities that are available in the public park and recreation sector today. First, there has been phenomenal growth in the number of colleges and universities offering professional education in the park and recreation area. In the early 1950s, only a handful offered these curricula throughout the United States. At one point, in the 1970s, more than 400 institutions offered degree programs in the park and recreation area. In 2000 the number of accredited bachelor's programs in parks and recreation was 100. Second, public support for public park and recreation services has shown a general decline, although more recent trends seem to indicate park and recreation departments are growing with funding coming from a wide variety of sources. The third factor influencing the decline in opportunities in the public park and recreation profession is the decrease in the movement of professionals within the field today as compared with past years. In the public sector, individuals extend their careers for long periods, resulting in little turnover and a lack of movement to new positions.

The future outlook for public (local) agencies is good however, as opportunities for recreation professionals is "expected to grow about as fast as the average for all occupations through 2008, as growing numbers of people spend more time and money on leisure services. Growth in these jobs will also stem from increased interest in fitness and health and the rising demand for recreational opportunities for older adults in senior centers and retirement communities. In particular, jobs will increase in social services as more recreation professionals are needed to develop and lead activity programs in senior centers, halfway houses, children's homes, and day-care programs for people with special needs" (*Occupational Outlook Handbook,* 2000, p. 60).

Individuals desiring a career in local government in the park and recreation field should follow several steps. First—and most essential—the student should attain a degree from an accredited institution in the park and recreation field. Second, individuals should seek paid seasonal, part-time, and voluntary opportunities in the park and recreation field. The more experience, the better, especially if it is diverse and of high quality. In addition, individuals should make an attempt to get acquainted with professionals in the field by joining professional associations or societies and attending conferences, meetings, and seminars. The key is to establish a network that will position the student prominently when opportunities are presented.

Challenges for the Future

Park and recreation professionals operating at the local level of government face many challenges. The rate of change in society is increasing. In the 1980s David Gray (1984) recognized this trend when he wrote,

> This is a time of great concern, uncertainty, ambivalence, and ambiguity in the recreation and park movement. It is a time of change. Change brings crisis and opportunity. In periods of rapid change, reforms are possible that could never be accomplished in periods of stability. Flexibility, recognition of opportunity, escape from pessimistic thinking, and leadership are required to respond to this period. (p. 47)

Change continues to be the norm as we begin the twenty-first century, and there is still a great deal of uncertainty for park and recreation professionals. The basic values and assumptions upon which the public park and recreation movement was built are being called into question. New approaches, strategies, and vehicles of service delivery will be required to meet emerging societal needs, as well as maintenance of the traditional values of the profession. This realization has led to a number of efforts to identify critical trends and issues in the field as well as to create an agenda for the profession in the future. The results of two such efforts are presented in table 7.2 and table 7.3.

Table 7.2 presents the results of two national conferences which convened leaders in the park and recreation field to identify the critical issues and trends in parks, recreation, and leisure services and to develop a professional agenda for the beginning of the twenty-first century. Table 7.3 presents the results of a Delphi study that elicited the opinions of thirty-six administrators and scholars from the American Academy for Park and Recreation Administration and Academy of Leisure Sciences. Participants were asked to determine the key trends and issues impacting local government recreation and park administration in the 1990s. The majority of the trends and issues presented in tables 7.3 and 7.4 are similar and still relevant in the first decade of the twenty-first century. The issues of financing and meeting the changing needs of customers while remaining true to the recreation field's social service mission are emphasized.

Innovative responses to specific trends and issues, as well as future needs and directions for public park and recreation departments, are the following:

- *Marketing Orientation.* Public parks and recreation programs are utilizing marketing techniques more to better respond to changing needs of those they serve. A marketing orientation requires a different way of thinking about the consumer than has been historically the case in the park and recreation field.
- *Fees and Charges.* Increasing public parks and recreation departments are using fees and charges to finance programs. In 1974–1975 self-generated funds constituted 14.2 percent of total expenditures on park and recreation services, but by 1987–1988 this had increased to 24 percent (Crompton and McGregor, 1994). In addition, a survey of sixty small towns in the midwest and west found that the most frequently reported revenue source for parks and recreation was fees and charges (Weissinger and Murphy, 1993).
- *Quality Services.* Assuring the quality of their programs is an important task for park and recreation departments, and many organizations are turning to the concept of Total Quality Management (TQM) to help ensure quality outcomes. In addition, accreditation of leisure professionals is another means of quality assurance.

TABLE

7.2 CRITICAL ISSUES AND TRENDS

- Change is the norm.
- There is a strong trend toward greater participation in the decision-making process by citizens and employees.
- The field of parks and recreation may be losing its mission orientation.
- Multicultural diversity will continue to grow rapidly.
- Substance abuse will continue as a major problem in society.
- The wellness movement will continue to grow.
- Success will depend on an organization's ability to build cooperative relationships and establish rewards and coalitions with other organizations.
- Lifelong learning will become a necessity.
- Success depends on quality of service.
- Tourism has emerged as one of the world's growing industries and an increasingly important part of leisure expression.
- The environment will increasingly become a focus of international concern.
- The mission of parks and recreation and leisure services is extremely broad and loosely defined.

Parks and Recreation Agenda

- Park and recreation professionals must be able and willing to identify, analyze, promote, and respond to changes in society.
- New leadership techniques will be required of park and recreation professionals to facilitate consensus building.
- Parks and recreation must return to its heritage of serving all the people. Renewed attention must be given to the poor and their impact on recreation and parks.
- Parks and recreation must find ways to celebrate the variety of cultures within the community.
- Park and recreation programs must provide other choices to the use of drugs and develop self-esteem in youth.
- Park, recreation, and leisure services must facilitate and identify directly with the growing wellness movement.
- Park and recreation organizations must work with other agencies building networks and coalitions to achieve success.
- Parks and recreation must make a commitment to continuing education and professional development.
- The success of parks and recreation will depend on the quality of service provided to all of the people served. It is essential to improve the image of the profession so that the relationship between recreation and parks programs and values and contemporary issues is clearly apparent.
- Parks and recreation must be involved in mutually beneficial partnerships with tourism.
- The park and recreation profession must take its rightful place as a leader in shaping environmental policy.
- The park and recreation profession must develop and articulate clearly defined mission statements, goals, and objectives for the field.

From T. Mobley and R. Toalson (Eds.), *Parks and Recreation in the 21st Century: Chapter 1,* 1992. National Park and Recreation Association, Arlington, VA. Reprinted by permission.

- *Building Partnerships.* Developing partnerships is one way of dealing with funding shortfalls. "Partnerships take many forms when it comes to protecting natural and cultural resources and providing recreation opportunities. Regardless of the form, they do have some common elements. These include a shared vision, shared risks, and shared benefits. Without this shared approach, the success of the partnership will be questionable" (Walters, 1992, p. 2). An example of a partnership with a local park and recreation

TABLE

7.3 KEY TRENDS AND ISSUES IMPACTING LOCAL GOVERNMENT RECREATION AND PARK ADMINISTRATION

Key Trends Ranked as Having Extreme or Great Impact on the Profession	Trend Implications
Deteriorating park and recreation infrastructure	Infrastructure deterioration, if left unchecked, would result in loss of use and support by citizens, and maintenance costs would increase.
Increasing crime	Increasing crime in communities and parks, if left unchecked, would result in loss of use and support by citizens, and security and enforcement costs would increase.
Declining park and recreation budgets relative to costs	Declining park and recreation budgets would lead to downsizing of park and recreation services and greater reliance on earned revenue.
Increasing competition for shrinking federal, state, and local tax resources	Increased competition for tax resources would result in taxes being reserved for essential government services, with parks and recreation services moving increasingly towards local support, fundraising and earned revenue generation and downsizing of services.
Massive public sector debt	Massive public debt would result in loss of revenue to debt servicing, with less tax monies available to government services.
Neglect of children	Neglect of children, if not acted upon, would result in behavior problems with future social and other implications. Park and recreation services, networking with other agencies, are likely to be drawn into a greater welfare role providing preventative programs.
Great cultural diversity: Growing influential minority populations	Greater cultural diversity would result in greater program and staff diversity, which would need to balance an integrative role with greater local control.
Greater difficulty in providing equal opportunity for leisure to all people	Greater difficulty in providing equal leisure opportunity, if left unchecked, would result in social unrest. Park and recreation services would be called upon to play a greater social service role.
Declining quality of life and livability of urban areas (insufficient city infrastructure)	Declining quality and livability of urban areas, if allowed to continue, would result in continued suburban drift by the middle classes, thereby reducing the available tax base and causing further decline. Park and recreation services would need to maintain a focus on urban areas to maintain the quality of life there.
Greater division between "haves" and "have nots"	Greater division between rich and poor would lead to further social unrest. Park and recreation services would play a vital community integration role with an increasing service focus on disadvantaged populations.
Increased public demand for participation, accountability, and productivity in government	Increased public demand for participation, accountability, and productivity would allow park and recreation services to increase opportunities for public involvement and demand greater skill of managers in communication, efficiency, and accounting.

Key Issues Ranked as Having Extreme or Great Impact on the Profession	Issue Implications
How to ensure adequate finances for capital development (land, open space, facilities, etc.)	Ensuring adequate finances for capital development would require the creation of greater citizen support, the exploration of other funding sources, and improving long-range planning.
What spending priorities should be set in the face of budget cuts when services are stretched too thin?	Spending priorities with a tight budget should focus on maintaining program quality over quantity, emphasize programs serving disadvantaged groups, and retain self-supporting programs.

How to make parks safe while maintaining visitor enjoyment	Parks should be made safe places by keeping them filled with programs and people, through a united community effort, and through attention to design and security.
How can parks and recreation strengthen its political position and shape the future through affecting state and federal policy?	Public parks and recreation services would best strengthen their political position and shape policy through attention to building local citizen and interorganizational constituencies (as should NRPA at the national level). A database indicating the benefits of parks, recreation, and leisure to community development and health is required, while professional education and training should ensure political skills.
How to compete successfully for funding against other community services (education, health, police)	The way to obtain funding in the face of competition from other community services is not to compete, but to work with other services. Maintaining visibility in the community and interpreting the benefits of parks, recreation, and leisure is recommended.
Should park and recreation services be managed more like a business?	Generally, park and recreation services should be managed more like a business in terms of efficiency, effectiveness, and marketing techniques, but without the profit motive. A balance would be required between taxed and earned revenues to ensure public welfare roles.
How to build on the wellness movement to promote alternative programs to drug abuse, antisocial behavior, etc.	Building on the wellness movement to promote alternate programs to drug abuse and antisocial behavior would best be achieved through networking with health and other community agencies, as well as through effective marketing of these programs.
How to make services more accessible to low income groups, single parents, and homeless people	Services would be made more accessible to low income groups and other disadvantaged populations through interorganizational networking, greater outreach, shifted hours of operation, and emphasis on programs assisting these populations.
How to increase local tax support	Local tax support would best be encouraged through having a database indicating the benefits of parks, recreation, and leisure services, and ensuring service visibility and public involvement.
How to build public trust and satisfy demands for accountability	Building public trust and satisfying demands for accountability would come from increasing the level of public involvement and being responsive to its input through greater communication and reporting via the media.
How to ensure investment in infrastructure maintenance and improvement (community pride)	Infrastructure maintenance and improvement would come through strong community involvement and a sense of true ownership, outlining the dangers of infrastructure decay and benefits of improvement, and through other funding methods such as enterprise funds.
How to foster coalition building and cooperation between service providers and related disciplines	Coalition building between related service providers should be fostered. Park and recreation administrators need to take the lead in bringing organizations and the community together for resource sharing and forming joint goals for community development and service.
How to develop public recognition that parks and recreation contribute to the health/well-being of society and counteracts the effects of disabilities	Developing public recognition that parks and recreation contribute to the health and well-being of society, while countering the effects of disabilities, would be achieved through universities and the NRPA. A supporting research database, a major public education campaign via the media utilizing citizen endorsement, and involvement with health organizations would aid in this effort.

department is Hostelling International's Chamounix Mansion, Philadelphia Hostel. The mission of hostelling is "to help all, especially the young, gain a greater understanding of the world and it people through hostelling" (see the Leisure Line box in chapter 5). The Philadelphia Hostel is situated in Fairmount Park in the Chamounix Mansion. Built in 1802, the Federal style mansion and surrounding property were taken over by the city in 1871 and incorporated into Fairmont Park, one of the largest urban parks in the nation. In 1954, the mansion stood desolate and the Parks Commission was contemplating demolition when a group of hostelling volunteers approached the Parks Commission with the idea of establishing a hostel in Philadelphia in the mansion. The Parks Commission agreed and provided funds to volunteers to help renovate the mansion. Over the last thirty years this hostel has been very successful. Today it has more than sixty beds for overnight guests and also serves as an active community center, hosting conferences, educational programs, young athletes attending sporting events, and much more (Krause, 1996).

- *Contracting Services.* Contracting and privatization are also becoming more commonplace as governments on all levels downsize. "Virtually anything and everything is up for grabs in the next decade" (Dickinson, 1996, p. 41). Eighty-three percent of city and county governments use private contractors to provide at least some form of service. Although core programs such as fire, police, and other social services (like recreation) are the least likely to be privatized, the possibility does exist as everyone continues to look for ways to shrink government and improve the quality of service.

- *Networking.* As public support in the form of tax revenues declines, park and recreation systems are generating revenue in other ways. Fees and charges generate considerable funds in support of park and recreation services. Park and recreation organizations are also working with other disciplines to find ways of sharing resources and problem-solving skills.

- *Diversity.* All demographic and census studies indicate that the population of the United States is becoming more multiracial and multicultural. African Americans, Hispanics, and to a lesser degree, Asian Americans are increasing in number (Kraus, 2000). This changing demographic picture will increasingly influence recreation and recreation resource demand. Park and recreation professionals will need to become increasingly aware of recreational preferences as well as to continue to develop programs that contribute to reducing racial tensions and discrimination and promoting respect for all groups in society (Kraus, 2000).

- *Inclusion.* Local park and recreation departments need to move to a more inclusive philosophy for delivering services to people with disabilities. Law mandates community park and recreation programs meet the needs of people with disabilities. This includes both integrating people with disabilities into traditional programming and providing specialized programs when necessary.

- *Child Care.* Increasingly, parks and recreation departments are creating child care programs that serve very young children. Furthermore, latchkey programs are being developed to serve the needs of children from the time they get out of school until their parents can pick them up.

- *Youth Development.* The youth development approach is a relatively new paradigm of research and service in dealing with children and adolescents. It is rapidly gaining acceptance as the preferred approach when dealing with young people by a large majority of youth-serving organizations (including local park and recreation departments). Although there is no universally accepted definition of youth development, it can be viewed as an orientation, which involves shifting away from concentrating on problems, toward concentrating on strengths. A youth development approach strives to create a wide variety of programs that build competencies and assets in youth and fosters opportunities for adults and youth to develop caring, long-term relationships (see table 7.4). In summary, youth development can be viewed as a multifaceted approach to working with youth whereby young people seek ways to meet their basic physical and social needs and to build a broad range of competencies making connections with themselves, others, and the larger community.

The move to a youth development approach in dealing with youth creates many opportunities for local park and recreation departments through the programs and services they offer to youth. To assist local park and recreation departments in implementing a youth development orientation in their programs, the National Recreation and Park Association has launched NRPA 2000, Urban Youth Initiative. The goals of this initiative include (1) increasing public awareness of recreation programs and activities and the benefits they provide, (2) broadening the knowledge of youth in regard to the field of recreation and the many opportunities it presents, and (3) implementing partnerships that provide programs in urban areas that will concentrate on building awareness, confidence, and self-esteem in youth (NRPA, n.d., Urban Youth Initiative).

An example of a local park and recreation department promoting youth development that embodies many of the characteristics put forth in table 7.4 is the city of Austin's "Get R.E.A.L. (Recreation, Education, Activities, Leader) Program." Since its inception in 1998, eight roving leaders and their assistants have gone into the city's neighborhoods to work with youth who are particularly vulnerable to gangs, drugs, violence, and alcohol. "Their overall goal is to be a beacon to guide kids into healthy lifestyles and help them make good choices for the future" (Baker and Witt, 2000, p. 87).

• *Developing Social Capital.* As mentioned in chapter 5, people today often feel isolated from their neighbors and feel that there has been a loss of community in recent years. This loss, described by Putnam (2000) as the loss of social capital, creates an opportunity for local parks and recreation departments. Putnam notes that in the past when America felt a loss of social capital, it was the parks and recreation movement that stepped in and created programs, facilities, and services, which helped bring Americans together again. Putnam's challenge to the park and recreation movement is this: "Let us find ways to ensure that by

TABLE

7.4 YOUTH DEVELOPMENT: A NEW PARADIGM IN WORKING WITH YOUTH

Old Paradigm		New Paradigm
Problems to be fixed	**View of Youth**	Resources to be developed
		Positive youth development
Structured paths	**Approach to Programming**	Creating multifaceted programs that develop competencies and build assets
Obedient doers	**Staff**	Staff develop relationships
Taskmasters, presiders		Leaders, enablers, and supporters
		Advocates
Youth come to programs	**Organization**	Programs go to youth

Source: DeGraaf, D., R. Ramsin, J. Gassman, and K. DeGraaf. in press.

2010 Americans will spend less leisure time sitting passively alone in front of a glowing screen [TV] and more time in active connection with our fellow citizens. . . . Henry Ward Beecher's advice a century ago to 'multiply picnics' is not entirely ridiculous today" (p. 410).

- *Open Space.* The recreation needs of an expanding population require new facilities and open space. Yet open space areas are becoming harder to find. For example, in the Chicago area it is projected that most of the remaining open space opportunities will be lost in the next twenty years (Westfall, 1991). One innovative response to providing open space is creating long linear parks that connect existing open space. Such greenways often follow rivers, power corridors, or old railway corridors. Another way for park and recreation departments to be innovative in developing open space is through partnering with both public and private organizations that are promoting many of the concepts of new urbanism.

- *New Urbanism.* In the early 1990s, a new architectural and urban design movement began to take shape and move into the mainstream. This movement has been identified as *new urbanism.* Katz (1994) feels this movement is relevant because it addresses many of the ills of our current sprawl development pattern while encouraging the building of social capital and community. According to Katz (1994, p. x), "If the New Urbanism can indeed be shown to deliver a higher, more sustainable quality of life to a majority of this nation's citizens, we can only hope that it will be embraced as the next paradigm for the shaping of American communities". The principles of new urbanism include examining both the neighborhood and the region as a whole and making the scale of neighborhoods more community friendly. A critical component of new urbanism is the concept of public space. Public space should be a primary consideration rather than a residual thought for neighborhoods. As urban planners contemplate how to apply the concepts of new urbanism in an effort to promote a sense of community, public park and recreation professionals have a wonderful opportunity to incorporate the key values of park and recreation programs. To this end, park and recreation professionals must learn more about the concepts of new urbanism and look for ways in which to partner with city planners as they move forward in encouraging the development of social capital and a sense of community in our towns and cities.

- *Documenting Benefits.* Documenting outcomes provided by programs is becoming common practice. Park and recreation professionals must be able to identify and substantiate the benefits of their programs and services. For example, for park and recreation departments to move beyond a fun and games approach to a youth development approach in working with youth, they must document and begin to understand how their programs impact youth. Caldwell (2000) reiterates this point and points out that if recreation services are not relevant to communities, and if the research that is conducted is not relevant, we may "go out of business."

The challenges and opportunities presented in this section will stretch park and recreation professionals in the next century to reach out and foster new partnerships with both the commercial and nonprofit sectors to forge a vision that will continue to address the quality of life issue for all Americans. In striving to meet these challenges of the twenty-first century, Hartsoe (n.d.), encourages professionals to keep in mind four central concepts that have fostered the growth of public parks and recreation over the last century:

1. Promoting the importance of parks and open spaces in creating a livable urban environment;

2. Stressing the need for positive recreation experiences for all citizens, particularly children and youth;
3. Emphasizing the essential role of recreation in improving individual health and well-being; and
4. Recognizing the central role that building strong local citizen support has had in developing successful park and recreation programs.

These types of responses provide insight for the future development of the public parks and recreation departments. The next several decades will be exciting and dynamic and will offer opportunities to redefine and reshape the very essence of the public parks and recreation movement.

Summary

Park and recreation services provided at the local level of government emerged as a result of social needs that occurred at the beginning of the Industrial Revolution in Canada and the United States. The phrase *local park and recreation services* refers to those public services that are provided at the subdivision of government that is closest to the customer. People view such services as important and necessary—and as a strong factor in the livability of an environment.

This chapter discussed the three basic subdivisions of government at the local level that provide park and recreation services—municipalities, counties, and special districts. Provision of park and recreation services under the jurisdiction of a municipal government is the most common form of organization. In this arrangement, services are offered as a part of the community service offerings of an entire city government. Counties, the subdivision of government just below state government, often provide park and recreation services in such a way as to link the resources of various cities, towns, and districts within their jurisdiction. Special park and recreation districts are autonomous and independent subdivisions of government. Their single focus on park and recreation services makes them an especially effective method for organizing services.

Individuals involved in professional positions in local park and recreation agencies often perceive themselves as working in partnership with the residents of their communities. They see themselves as service providers, as well as problem solvers, in identifying and analyzing community concerns. Individuals involved in public service also often see themselves as being altruistic. That is, they view themselves as being primarily motivated by service to others.

Professionals in local park and recreation agencies today face numerous challenges. The need to redefine basic values, adopt new management strategies, and seek innovative sources of funding make work opportunities in this area both exciting and challenging. Those individuals pursuing leadership, supervisory, and administrative roles in the local park and recreation area will often be rewarded with satisfying, stimulating, and creative professional opportunities.

Discussion Questions

1. Define the phrase *local park and recreation services.*
2. Identify sources of revenue for local park and recreation services.
3. Compare and contrast three types of governmental organizations providing park and recreation services at the local level.
4. Identify and define five types of legislation that can be used to establish local park and recreation services.
5. Identify five functions that may be performed by county park and recreation systems. Which do you believe is most important, and why?
6. Identify professional roles in the park and recreation field at the local level of government.
7. Discuss what you perceive as professional career opportunities in public parks and recreation.

8. Identify and discuss challenges facing professionals at the local level of government. How are they being addressed in your community?
9. Discuss how school districts are enabled to provide local park and recreation services.
10. What is the relationship of a local park and recreation agency to those whom it serves?

References

Baker, J., and P. Witt. 2000. Backstreet beacons: Austin's roving leaders. *Journal of Park and Recreation Administration 18*(1), 87–105.

Brayley, R., and D. McLean. 1999. *Managing Financial Resources in Sport and Leisure Service Organizations.* Champaign, IL: Sagamore.

Burke, W. 1992. A prophet of Eden. *Buzzworm 4*(2), 18–19.

Busser, J. 1999. Human resource management. Edited by B. van der Smissen, M. Moiseichik, V. Hartenburg, and L. Twardzik, in *Management of Park and Recreation Agencies.* Ashburn, VA: NRPA.

Caldwell, L. 2000. Beyond fun and games? Challenges to adopting a prevention and youth development approach to youth recreation. *Journal of Park and Recreation Management 18*(3), 1–18.

Crompton, J., and B. McGregor. 1994. Trends in the financing and staffing of local government park and recreation services. *Journal of Park and Recreation Administration 12*(3), 19–37.

DeGraaf, D., R. Ramsin, J. Gassman, and K. DeGraaf. in press. *Camp Counseling: A Staff Development Approach.* Dubuque, IA: Eddie Bowers.

DeGraaf, D., D. Jordan, and K. DeGraaf. 1998. *Programming for Parks, Recreation and Leisure Services: A Servant Leadership Approach.* State College, PA: Venture.

Deppe, T. 1983. *Management Strategies in Financing Parks and Recreation.* New York: Wiley.

Dickinson, R. 1996. The rush to sell off government. *American Demographics* (February), 41.

Driver, B., P. Brown, and G. Peterson. 1991. *Benefits of Leisure.* State College, PA: Venture.

Dunn, D. 1986. Professionalism and human resources. *Leisure Today—Journal of Physical Education, Recreation, and Dance* (October), 50–53.

Edginton, C. 1978. Organizational goals—what directors think they should be and are. *Recreation Canada 5*(36), 33–35, 39, 41.

Edginton, C., and L. Neal. 1983. Park and recreation directors' perceptions of organizational goals. *Journal of Park and Recreation Administration 1*(1), 39–49.

Edginton, C., and J. O'Neill. 1999. Program, services and events management. Edited by B. van der Smissen, M. Moiseichik, V. Hartenburg, and L. Twardzik, in *Management of Park and Recreation Agencies.* Ashburn, VA: NRPA.

Godbey, G. 1997. *Leisure and Leisure Services in the 21st Century.* State College, PA: Venture.

Gray, D. 1984. Managing our way to a preferred future. *Parks and Recreation 19*(5), 47–49.

Greenleaf, R. 1977. *Servant Leadership: A Journey into the Nature of Legitimate Power and Greatness.* New York: Paulist Press.

Hartsoe, C. n.d. A foundation for the future. *The Millenium Vision: Exploring the Future of Parks and Recreation.* A supplement to *Parks and Recreation,* 38–42.

Hastings, M. 1984. *A Comparison of Canadian Municipal Parks and Recreation Director's Perception of Organizational Goal Importance in 1976 and 1984,* unpublished doctoral dissertation, University of Oregon.

Haurwitz, R. 1992. Soothing the city soul. *Buzzworm 4*(5), 18–19.

Hemphill, S. 1985. Revenue management: Beginning with the basics. *Park and Recreation 20*(12), 35–36.

Howat, G., and C. Edginton. 1986. A study of the goals for Australian local government parks and recreation. *Australian Parks and Recreation 22*(4), 12–15.

Jarvi, C. 1993. Leadership to meet the demands of today's changing needs. Unpublished manuscript.

Jordan, D. 2001. *Leadership in Leisure Services: Making a Difference.* State College, PA: Venture.

Katz, P. 1994. *The New Urbanism: Toward an Architecture of Community.* New York: McGraw-Hill.

Kraus, R. 2000. *Leisure in a Changing America: Trends and Issues for the 21st Century.* Boston, MA: Allyn & Bacon.

Kraus, R., and J. Curtis. 1986. *Creative Management in Recreation, Parks and Leisure Services.* 4th ed. St. Louis: Times Mirror/Mosby.

Kraus, R., and J. Curtis. 2000. *Creative Management in Recreation, Parks, and Leisure Services.* 5th ed. Boston, MA: McGraw-Hill.

Krause, D. 1996. *Creative Partnerships: Private/Public Successes in Developing Hostels.* Washington, DC: Hostelling International—American Youth Hostels.

Kreck, C. 2000, January. Kid's-eye view of city's comprehensive plan: Looks at family issues. *Denver Post,* E. Z.

Lappe, F., and P. DuBois. 1994. *The Quickening of America: Rebuilding Our Nation, Remaking Our Lives.* San Francisco, CA: Jossey-Bass.

Mobley, T., and R. Toalson. 1992. *Parks and Recreation in the 21st Century: Part I.* Arlington, VA: NRPA.

Naisbitt, J., and P. Aburdene. 1985. *Re-inventing the Corporation.* New York: Warner Books.

NRPA. n.d. *NRPA 2000: Urban Youth Initiative.* Washington, DC: NRPA.

NRPA, 1998. *Discover the Benefits.* Ashburn, VA: NRPA.

Putnam, R. 2000. *Bowling Alone: The Collapse and Revival of American Community.* New York: Simon & Schuster.

Rails to Trails Conservancy. 1993. *Great Rail-Trails.* Washington, DC: Living Planet Press.

Rodney, L., and R. Toalson. 1981. *Administration of Recreation, Parks and Leisure Services.* 2d ed. New York: John Wiley and Sons.

Spears, L. 1995. Servant leadership and the Greenleaf legacy. Edited by L. Spear, in *Reflections on Leadership: How Robert K. Greenleaf's Theory of Servant Leadership Influenced Today's Top Management Thinkers,* pp. 1–16. New York: Wiley.

Staff. 2000. *Occupational Outlook Handbook.*

U.S. Census Bureau. 1997a. *1997 Census of Governments: Volume 4, Governments Finances—Finances of Municipal and Township Governments.* Washington, DC: U.S. Department of Commerce.

U.S. Census Bureau. 1997b. *1997 Census of Governments: Volume 4, Governments Finances—Finances of County Governments.* Washington, DC: U.S. Department of Commerce.

U.S. Census Bureau. 1997c. *1997 Census of Governments: Volume 4, Governments Finances—Finances of Special District Governments.* Washington, DC: U.S. Department of Commerce.

Walters, W. 1992. Partnerships in parks and preservation. *Trends 29*(2), 2.

Weissinger, E., and D. Murphy. 1993. A survey of fiscal conditions in small town public recreation departments from 1987 to 1991. *Journal of Park and Recreation Administration 11*(3), 61–71.

Westfall, R. 1991. Emerging trends at the state level. *Trends 28*(2), 39–42.

Whyte, D. 1992. Key trends and issues impacting local government recreation and park administration in the 1990s: A focus for strategic management and research. *Journal of Park and Recreation Administration 10*(3), 84–106.

WSSRA. 1993. *West Suburban Special Recreation Association.* Franklin Park, IL: West Suburban Special Recreation Association.

CHAPTER 8

Delivery of Leisure Services: State Government

State governments often provide natural resources such as lakes, parks, beaches, and historic and cultural areas.

Source: Department of Natural Resources, State of Iowa. Used by permission.

Introduction

Prior to the turn of the twentieth century the involvement of states in offering amenities for their residents was relatively simple. Services such as education, health, and welfare were the concerns of private agencies such as the church. With the coming of the Industrial Revolution and the concentration of people in larger urban areas, each state gradually accepted responsibility for providing specific services for its residents. Today, recreation has become an accepted and even expected service provided by individual states.

The basis for involvement by individual states in providing parks and recreation opportunities is found in the Tenth Amendment to the Constitution of the United States. This amendment, also known as the states rights amendment, was passed in 1925 and clarified the role of the state versus the federal government in providing services to its residents. The amendment states that "the powers not delegated to the United States by the Constitution, nor prohibited by it to the States, are reserved to the States respectively, or to the people." This amendment was originally regarded as the source of state powers in such areas as public education, welfare, and health services. As time progressed, states included recreation facilities and services as a part of their responsibility in meeting the needs of their residents.

The importance of state government in providing recreation facilities and programs is increasing. Many feel that federal programs have become "unmanageable, ineffective, costly, confusing, and unaccountable to the public" (Kraus, 1990, p. 226), and that states would do a better job of administering many programs, including recreation. Thus, this chapter examines the historical role of states in the provision of recreational facilities and services, current practices of states in the provision of recreational facilities and services, and future options of states in meeting residents' recreational needs.

Characteristics of State Leisure Services

This section of the chapter presents the characteristics of state and provincial governments as they pertain to leisure services. As Meyer and Brightbill (1950) stated nearly a half century ago, "State government is a foundation stone of the American way of life" (p. 1) and, "The aim and purpose of government should be to bring about the greatest good for the greatest number of people" (p. 2). Initially, the goals and functions of state government are discussed, followed by information concerning the resource base of state government. Finally, a review of the characteristics of professionals involved in the delivery of state and provincial government leisure services is presented.

Goals and Functions

The distinctions made between the functions of state government and the direct delivery of services are often difficult to understand. For the purpose of this chapter, however, the functions of state government revolve around the legislative process as well as the role state governments play in the coordination of services between federal, state, and local areas (see figure 8.1).

Legislation One important function of state and provincial governments is the creation of legislative acts in support of the provision of park and recreation services. Such legislation can directly impact the provision of services by state government. The state government also plays an important role in creating enabling legislation for local and municipal governments to establish and provide recreation and parks programs. Such enabling legislation provides city, county, and special-district governments with the specific authority to acquire property, employ personnel, or

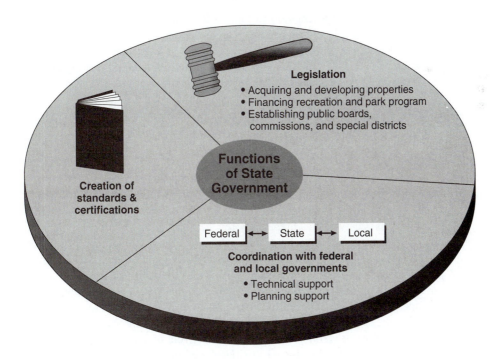

Figure 8.1

Roles and functions of state government

impose taxes to support recreation; it is generally granted to municipal governments by constitutional, statutory, or charter provision granted by the state legislature.

This type of legislation, often entitled *enabling legislation*, may range from simple authorization to fully detailed codes. According to Kraus (1990), enabling legislation can include such elements as the method of acquiring and developing properties, financing recreation and park programs, and establishing public boards, commissions, and special districts. Such legislation, as well as statutes and laws, vary from state to state as southern states like Florida do not need to be concerned with snow skiing or snowmobiling. Likewise, in states like Wyoming, issues about ocean beaches and saltwater fishing and boating are irrelevant.

Creation of Standards and Certifications The standards and regulations created by state governments to regulate many types of recreational providers also relate to the legislative process. For example, a commercial recreation provider, such as an organized camp, must adhere to the health and sanitation laws of the state. Likewise, the seating capacity for a sports event or a movie must conform to state or local laws and ordinances such as fire regulations. Other areas of regulatory laws include laws that specify facility standards, laws that ensure accessibility, and laws that regulate and/or prohibit certain types of recreation such as gambling or prostitution.

A growing number of states have also promoted and developed standards for recreation programs and leadership, influenced the development of new commercial recreation opportunities, and set up standards, certifications, and registration programs for specific positions in the field. For example, therapeutic recreation specialists are licensed in Georgia and Utah.

Coordination with Federal and Local Governments

The final report of the Outdoor Recreation Resources Review Commission (1962) encouraged states to assume the pivotal role of bridging the gap between federal and local services. At the beginning of the twenty-first century, this recommendation is even more timely. As government budgets on all levels shrink, due in many cases to citizen-initiated tax-cutting programs, it is increasingly important to coordinate existing services to avoid overlap and to stretch program dollars as far as they will go. Just as no governmental subdivision alone can clean up a polluted river or deal with such social issues as homelessness, the problems of recreation planning and programming must be approached in an integrated fashion. All levels of government need to be involved, and in many cases it appears that state governments are in the best position to fill this coordinating role.

State cooperation with the federal government has often centered around recreational planning. For example, through the Land and Water Conservation Fund Act of 1965, the federal government encouraged states to prepare an approved, comprehensive recreation plan. States that created such plans received matching funds for the acquisition and development of state recreation lands. The outgrowth of many of these planning efforts included proposals for wild and scenic rivers, historical preservation initiatives, and other grant proposals to improve both state and local recreation resources. In recent years, with the demise of the Land and Water Conservation Act, federal funds have diminished; however, many state governments are continuing this planning process in an effort to better coordinate resources for recreation. States also monitor federal resources and federal grants to expand recreation resources.

One of the first efforts at identifying the coordinating role of state government in promoting recreation and leisure on the local level was developed by Meyer and Brightbill (1950) in their book, *State Recreation.* These efforts can be summarized into two general areas, technical support and planning support. Technical support includes such things as assisting communities in organizing and improving local recreation systems, providing assistance in securing and improving local and state legislation and related legal recreation problems, providing research for good decision making as well as helping to prepare surveys and appraisals of statewide and specific recreation needs and conditions, and assisting in methods of financing and budgeting. Planning support includes such things as assisting in the preparation of long-range plans for recreation, creating a comprehensive recreation policy for the state, and investigating and helping meet recreation needs in special settings such as rural areas and state and local institutions.

Resource Base

State governments draw resources from a variety of sources to support the services they provide for their residents. An overview of revenues can be examined to highlight the specific revenue sources of leisure and recreation services. The more common methods of finance include the following:

Taxes. This type of financial resource comes from the general fund provided from tax revenues generated by state government. In general, these taxes occur as a result of levies against the income of individuals, corporations, or other units, as well as sales taxes from such commodities as gasoline, alcoholic beverages, tobacco, and other nondurable goods.

Fees and charges. Most state governments levy a fee or charge for exclusive use of an area or facilities. A good example of a fee is the levy charged an individual for the exclusive use of a campsite at a state park or forest for one or more nights. Another example of a fee or charge would be the levy required for entry into a specialized area such as a botanical garden, beach, marina, park, or other resource.

Federal funds. State governments use funds provided by the federal government to support acquisition and development of natural and other resources.

Endowments and trusts. State governments may receive gifts in the form of cash, natural resources, or other items of value. These may be placed in endowments or trusts that can be used to generate revenue in support of budgets of state governments. Most endowments or trusts specifically focus on maintenance, development, or acquisition of a specific resource.

Sales revenue from concessions and retail outlets. State governments can generate revenues from concessions on public lands. Sales of food, clothing, guides, books, pamphlets, and equipment may earn income for state government. Revenue is often also earned from the rental of equipment such as canoes, paddle boats, and beach umbrellas.

Table 8.1 represents information concerning the types and percentages of funds from each of the categories delineated. The majority of resources comes from taxes, followed by revenues generated from fees and charges. Like other leisure services provided by the government, state units increasingly generate revenues from sources other than taxes. As a result, those using the services of state governments often pay directly rather than having taxpayer-subsidized access to areas, facilities, and recreational programs and services.

For example, financing for state parks comes from a variety of sources. Wealthy individuals often help support state parks. In the United States, the federal government has in the past assisted in the acquisition of state park lands through the Land and Water Conservation Fund. Other means of financing both the acquisition and maintenance of park systems include state

8.1   REVENUE SOURCES OF STATE GOVERNMENT

Revenue Source	Amount (Millions of US $)	Percentage
Taxes—Includes:		
Property, personal income, corporation income, sales, and gross receipts	399,222	41.3
Charges and miscellaneous fees	120,752	13.5
Includes: parks and recreation fees	1,000	0.1
Interest earnings	28,621	3.0
Motor vehicles and operator licenses	13,848	1.4
Death and gifts	5,320	0.6
Sale of property	5,320	0.02
Special assessment	209	0.01

Source: U.S. Bureau of the Census, 1999. *Statistical Abstracts of the United States: 1999.* 119th ed. Washington DC: U.S. Government Printing Office.

and local taxes and bond issues. Financing continues to be a problem for many state park agencies. Park administrators attempt to meet this financial challenge in a variety of ways, such as charging more fees for using park facilities and developing facilities and programs that cater more to the needs of in-state residents. This means going beyond offering the traditional recreation activities to include a wider variety of income-producing sports and activities such as golf, conference centers, off-road vehicle races, and festivals.

Characteristics of Professionals

Ibrahim and Cordes (1993), discussing opportunities in outdoor recreation, note that many different types of positions are available. Some of the jobs include operating as foresters, forestry technicians, game wardens, naturalists, park rangers, range managers, and recreation specialists. In addition, state governments also employ therapeutic recreation specialists to work in hospitals and other institutions such as prisons. A growing number of state employees also work in travel and tourism. Thus, the type of work available in state government varies as it depends on the setting.

What skills, knowledge, and competencies do employees of state government need to be successful? This question is difficult to answer in a general way—the work setting varies from parks to hospitals to cultural arts facilities, such as museums and interpretive centers. A general model, however, would describe two types of required skills: *technical* and *interpersonal/human skills.* Although the technical skills required for positions vary, a partial list includes computer competencies, land-management skills, search and rescue skills, and administrative duties (e.g., understanding rules and regulations, risk management, the planning process, marketing, and evaluation procedures). A list of possible interpersonal skills includes working with people, interacting with the public (public relations skills), and communicating with and educating people on a variety of topics.

For example, the technical skills characteristic of a park ranger would include knowledge of biology, forestry, and park management. The interpersonal/human skills might involve the ability to teach, resolve conflicts between individuals, negotiate, and manage. There is a need for natural resource managers to be socially sensitive in dealing with customers and staff. The narrow focus of some individuals working in these positions often produces a "technical narrowness" that may result in a lack of creativity, innovation, and imagination in decision making.

Types of Direct Recreation Resources and Services Provided by States

States play an increasingly important role in providing direct recreation facilities and services. Collectively, the states spent more than $3.0 billion for park and recreation services and $12.3 billion for provisions of natural resources. When funds available from the National Endowment for Arts and the National Endowment for Humanities are included, the figure is increased by $19.1 million (U.S. Bureau of Census, 1999). Most of the funds for these two fund programs support partnership agreements, music, theatre, dance, media arts, and the visual arts. When all these funds are added together, one can see that a great deal of money is available for park and recreation services at the state level. Recreational programs and areas provided by state governments are well used by residents (see figure 8.2).

Furthermore, with the increasingly fast-paced lifestyles of most American families, vacation patterns are changing. People seek more frequent, shorter vacations rather than one longer vacation per year, with recreational opportunities closer to home (see figure 8.3). Findings of the President's Commission on Americans Outdoors (1987) indicate that states must prepare to meet the greater demands that will be placed on them in the years ahead. In providing recreation facilities and services, states should especially consider the following areas: outdoor recreation and resources, tourism promotion, promotion of the arts, and services for people with disabilities and other underserved groups.

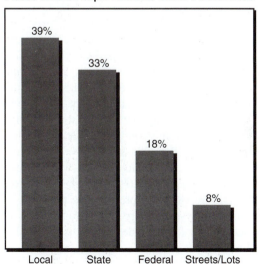

Places Where People Recreate Often: Public Areas

| Local | State | Federal | Streets/Lots |

39% — Local
33% — State
18% — Federal
8% — Streets/Lots

Figure 8.2

Use of recreation areas

Source: The President's Commission on Americans Outdoors, 1987, page 55.

Figure 8.3

Public area
visitation

*Source: The
President's
Commission on
Americans
Outdoors, 1987,
page 56.*

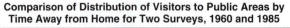

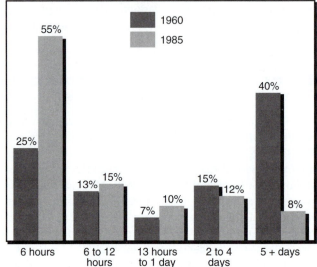

Comparison of Distribution of Visitors to Public Areas by Time Away from Home for Two Surveys, 1960 and 1985

Outdoor Recreation and Resources

States have long been involved in the management of outdoor resources. In the United States as early as 1626 the colony of Plymouth prohibited the cutting of timber on colony land without a permit. The Great Ponds Act of 1641 protected all freshwater bodies of water of more than ten acres, about 2,000 sites, and assured public access to these ponds. By 1776, twelve out of the thirteen states had enacted closed seasons on certain game. In 1872, New York established the Adirondack Forest Preserve. In 1885, the federal government placed Niagara Falls under the care of the state of New York as the State Reservation of Niagara. This action resulted because of the uncontrollable commercial development of the areas surrounding the falls. According to Knudson (1984), "It was difficult to see the falls because of all the hucksters and makeshift commercial shops that lined the sides of the scenic wonder" (p. 86).

Much of this early legislation related to subsistence hunting and fishing. Nonetheless, these early laws could be looked upon as the beginning of state involvement in protecting natural resources (Foss, 1968). Following the 1885 action of New York surrounding Niagara Falls, state legislation for recreation purposes increased dramatically. Today, states own approximately 6 percent of the total area of the United States (see figure 8.4). The bulk of state-owned land is found in the west (see table 8.2), primarily due to large state holdings in both Alaska and California. Management of state lands often varies due to the type of land being managed and the philosophy of the managing agency. Basic classifications of land are managed by different state agencies—state parks, state forests, and state fish and wildlife reserves (see table 8.3). The National Association of State Park Directors (NASPD) has provided definitions for the various areas operated by state agencies. These are presented in table 8.3. As the NASPD points out, "While all of the fifty state park systems share common attributes, they nevertheless vary considerably from state to state. . . . Common denominators . . . allow a useful degree of comparison" (NASPD, 2000).

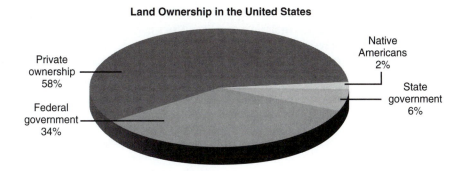

Land Ownership in the United States

Private ownership 58%

Federal government 34%

Native Americans 2%

State government 6%

Figure 8.4

Breakdown of U.S. land ownership

TABLE

8.2 STATE-OWNED LAND DISTRIBUTION BY REGION

Region	State-Owned Land (Acres)	State-Owned Land (%)	U.S. Population (%)
West	521,662,679.2 acres	92.6	22.2
North Central	17,403,322.6 acres	3.0	23.3
Northeast	2,239,133.6 acres	0.39	19.3
South	21,771,008.1 acres	3.8	35.2

Source: U.S. Bureau of the Census. 1999. *Statistical Abstracts of the United States: 1999.* 119th ed. Washington DC: U.S. Government Printing Office.

State Parks   The concept of land being owned by individual states for the enjoyment of its residents can be traced back to two events in the mid-1800s. The initial event centered around the federal government granting the territorial governor of the Arkansas Territory the right to hold the Arkansas Hot Springs from private ownership in 1832 (Ibrahim and Cordes, 1993). This tradition continued in 1864 with the designation of Yosemite as the country's first state park. At this time the state of California was awarded a land grant for acquiring ten square miles in Yosemite Valley for "public use, resort, and recreation." Although both Yosemite and the Arkansas Hot Springs eventually were given back to the federal government to become national parks in 1890 and 1921, the idea of state parks had been established.

State park legislation increased at the turn of the century. Minnesota developed Itasca State Park; New York developed the Adirondack Wilderness; and Illinois established Fort Massac State Park in 1903. The establishment of Fort Massac was of particular importance because it facilitated a 1909 legislature-appointed commission to investigate the best way to manage state parks. This commission led to the establishment of the Illinois Division of Parks and Memorials within the Department of Public Works and Buildings in 1919. That same year Indiana also established a Division of State Parks within the Department of Conservation (Jensen, 1995). Many state park systems have achieved a level of maturity. For example, Wisconsin's state park system, which was founded in 1900, recently celebrated its 100th year of service. Today, more than eighty-five parks, forests, recreation areas, and trails are managed under the direction of the unit serving over a million people annually (see figure 8.5).

8.3   TERMS AND GUIDELINES FOR DEFINING STATE PARK RESOURCES

Term	Definition
State parks	Areas containing a number of coordinated programs for the preservation of natural and/or cultural resources and provision of a variety of outdoor recreation activities supported by those resources.
State recreation areas	Areas where a clear emphasis is placed on the provision of opportunities for primarily active recreation activities.
State natural areas	Areas where a clear emphasis is placed on protection, management, and interpretation of natural resources or features.
State historical areas	Areas where a clear emphasis is placed on protection, management, and interpretation of historical and/or archaeological resources or features.
State environmental education sites	Areas used exclusively or primarily for conducting educational programs on environmental subjects, natural resources, conservation, etc.
State scientific areas	Areas set aside exclusively or primarily for scientific study, observation, and experimentation involving natural objects, processes, and interrelationships; any other allowable uses are secondary and incidental.
State forests	Areas that, while under the direct administrative supervision and control of the state parks agency, are identified separately from the state park system and distinguished from state park units by having primarily a forest management and/or timber production role rather than a natural area and/or provision of recreation role.
State fish/wildlife areas	Areas under the administrative supervision and control of the state parks agency that are identified and managed primarily for the propagation and recreational taking of fish and/or game ("fishing and/or hunting areas").
State trails	Linear areas outside any other unit of the state park system that provide primarily for trail-type recreational activities (hiking, cycling, horseback riding, etc.) and normally do not contain any land areas large enough to support non-trail activities.
Other specified areas	Areas other than the above, that are considered special or significant enough in a particular state to warrant separate identification and treatment.
Miscellaneous areas	Areas other than the above, that are not easily categorized or distinguished, or are not considered significant enough to warrant the specification of "everything else."

Source: The National Association of State Park Directors. 2000. *Definitions.* www.indiana.edu/~naspd/statistics/definitions.html

    When the National Park Service was established in 1916, its first director, Stephen Mather, saw the importance of the state park movement and promoted the idea strongly. In 1921 he organized the first National Conference on State Parks in Des Moines, Iowa. At this time only nineteen states had some type of state park or state forest system. The National Conference on State Parks became a permanent organization known today as the National Society for Park Resources (Ibrahim and Cordes, 1993).

    Mather believed state parks formed an important link in saving America's natural heritage. As director of the National Park Service, Mather knew that his fledgling agency could not protect all appropriate areas. "Mather saw state administration as an alternative to protecting some

Figure 8.5
Wisconsin State Parks celebrates its centennial

of the prize areas until he could gather political and financial support to bring them into the national park system" (Jensen, 1995, p. 125). Mather also hoped that state parks would bring outdoor recreation closer to the masses who were not able to visit many of the national parks that had been established in the western part of the United States.

The depression years brought greater cooperation between the states and the federal government. Many of the Civilian Conservation Corps (CCC) projects benefited state as well as federal parks through the building of trails and facilities. Following World War II, visits to state parks increased dramatically. State park systems tried to keep pace with demand. These efforts were aided by the Surplus Property Act of 1944 and amended in 1948, which allowed certain federal land to be converted to state parks and recreation areas. Other major legislation that helped the state park movement included the Recreation and Public Purposes Act of 1954 and the Land and Water Conservation Act of 1965.

Today, all fifty states have park systems in place. In 1997, these parks received a total of more than 783 million visitors; these visits generated more than $590 million. This compares with 1991 when parks received a total of 737 million visitors and generated $454 million in revenues. Table 8.4 presents the fifteen largest state park systems, as well as the number of people visiting these parks. Today's parks vary in many ways, including size, available facilities, the amount of development, types of administration, and financing. For example, in Oregon, the state's department of transportation administers the state park system, while in Michigan, state parks are administered by the Park Division of the Department of Natural Resources. Several factors enter into the many differences found in state park systems. These factors include historical events, political trends, intergovernmental relationships, and prevailing management concepts.

Yet state park lands also have many similarities. For example, land designated as state parks is mostly seen as intermediate areas, as contrasted to wild areas or municipal areas. This means that they are relatively close to large urban areas; provide activities such as picnicking, camping, swimming, hiking, fishing, and hunting; and are of medium size (hundreds to several thousand acres). Table 8.5 provides an overview of the type of state parks that exist in the United States today.

TABLE

8.4 THE FIFTEEN LARGEST STATE PARK SYSTEMS

State	Acreage (1,000)	Rank by Acreage	Number of Visitors (1,000)	Rank by Number of Visitors
Alaska	3,389	1	4,055	37
California	1,356	2	115,741	1
Texas	629	3	21,818	10
Maine	587	4	1,963	45
Florida	511	5	13,741	45
Colorado	401	6	40,391	5
Illinois	348	7	11,767	21
New Jersey	334	8	14,570	15
New York	308	9	67,006	2
Maryland	292	10	10,559	23
Pennsylvania	283	11	34,387	7
Massachusetts	277	12	13,169	19
Michigan	266	13	23,416	9
Washington	263	14	48,539	4
Minnesota	247	15	8,331	27

Source: U.S. Bureau of the Census. 1999. *Statistical Abstracts of the United States: 1999.* 119th ed. Washington DC: U.S. Government Printing Office.

State Forests   Whereas the management philosophy of state parks is one of preservation, state forests operate under a multiple-use approach. Initially, when state forests were acquired, the major thrust was to protect land from erosion, to develop areas for timber, and to provide experimental and demonstration areas. The outdoor recreation potential of these areas was not considered until after World War II. Today the management priorities of state forests vary from state to state due to such factors as type and abundance of forest land and the philosophy of the state government as to how state forests should be used. Typically, the management of state forests includes some combination of the following concerns: outdoor recreation, natural resource management (e.g., timber management), watershed, and fish and wildlife management. According to the National Association of State Foresters, twenty-eight of the forty-seven state forest administrative agencies or departments have specific recreation departments, whereas the remaining states handle recreation in conjunction with their other duties (Jones, 1992).

With the exception of Kansas, Nebraska, and Oklahoma, all states have some type of state forest system. These systems are usually administered by an independent state agency (e.g., Department of Forestry). According to Jensen (1985) the best state forest systems appear in the eastern, southern, and midwestern states with high-quality forests and small amounts of federal forested lands. States in the Great Plains or the Southwest tend to have small systems because of the relatively small amounts of forested land.

Activities that take place in state forests typically include hunting, fishing, boating, camping, hiking, nature study, bird watching, rock climbing, horseback riding, and mountain biking. As a general rule, recreational facilities in state forests tend to be less developed than counter-

TABLE

8.5   TYPES OF STATE PARK AREAS

Types	Number
Parks	1,906
Natural areas	336
Recreation areas	754
Historic areas	551
Water-use areas	548
Environmental education areas	19
Trail systems	23
Miscellaneous areas	314
Total number of areas	4,451

Source: C. Jensen, *Outdoor Recreation in America.* 2d ed. 1995.

part areas in state parks. For example, campsites are more primitive than in state parks and do not include as many conveniences, such as showers or water and sewer hookups.

In the future, the amount of land included in state forests will not likely increase or decrease a great deal as states do not wish to lose control of the lands they already have and there will be little opportunity to expand. Outdoor recreation will become increasingly important in state forests as people search for less-crowded areas that are still close to large urban areas. This increased demand may result in an improvement of recreation resources in state forests in the future.

State Fish and Wildlife Agencies   States have a long history dating back to before the Revolutionary War of being involved in the management of fish and wildlife populations. Today each of the fifty states has created a separate department or a major division within a department to administer a program of fish and wildlife management. One of the reasons for the importance of managing hunting and fishing resources within each state is the economic importance of fishing and hunting for state economies. In addition to licenses, expenditures by anglers, hunters, and other wildlife enthusiasts have significant economic impact throughout the country (see table 8.6).

Although many state fish and wildlife agencies manage some specific areas, their responsibilities extend well beyond the boundaries of their land holdings. For example, because wildlife is considered to be a resource of the state (unless it is endangered or crosses state lines), wildlife on federal lands is still managed by each state's fish and wildlife agency. According to Jensen (1995), the major responsibilities of these agencies include the following:

- *Issuing licenses* for hunting, fishing, and trapping, and enforcing the laws and regulations pertaining to these activities. The income generated from the selling of these licenses is reinvested into propagating, protecting, and distributing game fish, birds, and animals.
- *Managing a variety of wildlife areas,* including reserves, sanctuaries, game farms, hatcheries, and special shooting grounds.
- *Assisting landowners,* both private and public, with habitat management.

Hunting and fishing are still the primary recreational activities that take place on land managed by state fish and wildlife agencies. A number of nonconsumptive recreational pursuits are becoming increasingly popular, also (e.g., such as camping, hiking, and photography). With

TABLE

8.6	1996 WILDLIFE-ASSOCIATED RECREATION EXPENDITURES

	Fishing	Hunting	Primary Nonconsumptive
Numbers of participants (thousands)	35,246	13,875	62,888
Percentage of the general population	13	5.3	24
Activity days (millions)	626	257	NA
Total expenditures (millions of US $)	37,797	20,613	29,288
Food and lodging	5,990	2,512	5,352
Transportation	3,730	1,780	2,943
Other trip costs	5,661	864	1,150
Licenses, stamps, tags, and permits	3,242	4,185	3,132
Equipment	5,309	5,519	8,230
Auxiliary equipment	1,037	1,233	858
Special equipment	12,828	4,521	7,564

Source: U.S. Bureau of the Census. 1999. *Statistical Abstracts of the United States: 1999.* 119th ed. Washington, DC: U.S. Government Printing Office.

more users now enjoying state fish and wildlife areas, a number of additional pressures make it difficult for fish and wildlife managers. These pressures include the following:

Increasing user conflicts between noncomplementary forms of recreation users. For example, hiking and hunting cannot be done in the same area because of the inherent danger of a hiker getting shot. These types of conflicts increase as the number of recreationists increase in a variety of leisure pursuits.

Decreasing resource base for wildlife habitat places greater hardships on the remaining areas available for wildlife. The majority of habitat is being lost in the private sector, and, as a result, more hunting and fishing participants use public lands. This increase in the number of users presents challenges to fish and wildlife managers. Specifically, managers must face the dilution of the hunting and fishing experience caused by the inability of the fish and wildlife base to meet the expectations of the increasing number of hunters and anglers (Jensen, 1985).

The times have changed. People no longer live in a world of surplus, and with the recent technological and communication advances the decisions of resource managers are highly scrutinized. People are more involved with decisions, and more interest groups want to be a part of the decision-making process.

Trail Systems   In the past several decades there has been a tremendous expansion at the state level of trail systems. State governments are often involved in providing support funds to local governments. For example, the State of Iowa has made a great investment for the development and construction of trails. The General Assembly of the State of Iowa has made funds available through the Rebuild Iowa Infrastructure Fund. In the past decade, over $40 million has been invested in the development of recreational trails. Table 8.7 provides a definition of the various types of trails. These types of trails could be developed on a local, regional, or even statewide basis. Again, they are often done with state support.

8.7 TERMS AND GUIDELINES FOR TRAILS

Term	Definition
Backcountry Trails	Backcountry trails, sometimes called "single-track" or primitive trails, are generally unsurfaced natural routes that range from narrow treadways to carefully planned and elaborately constructed (but natural-looking) thoroughfares. Attention to slopes and effective drainage is essential for the long-term stability of this type of trail.
Recreational Greenways	A greenway is any linear open-space area along a natural corridor (riverfront, stream valley, ridgeline) or overland along a converted railroad right-of-way, canal, or scenic road (Little, 1991). As such, a greenway may or may not include a trail. A "recreational greenway" is a linear open space that contains a trail(s). Although a greenway trail can take any form, the term generally refers to a high-standard paved trial that accommodates multiple users.
Multiple-Use Recreation Trails	"Multiple-use recreation trails" or "multiuse trails" are generic terms for what many people call trails or greenways. These trails are built to high standards, are usually ten feet wide, asphalt or concrete paved, and designed for many types of use. Bicycling, walking, running, in-line skating, and other nonmotorized uses are typical on multi-use trails, and they are frequently very heavily used.
Rail-Trails	Rail-trails are trails constructed on abandoned railroad corridors converted to recreational use or "railbanked" for possible future rail use. They can be very short to hundreds of miles long. Typically surfaced in crushed stone or paved, their moderate grades make rail-trails popular with bicyclists, walkers, and others. Currently, there are more than 700 rail-trails totaling nearly 10,000 miles. With thousands of miles of rail corridor being abandoned every year, rail-trails offer tremendous potential for new trail opportunities. In fact, progress is being made on a coast-to-coast rail-trail.
Water Trails	Many people consider any corridor of open water used for recreational travel or string of lakes connected by portage to be a water trail. Camping accessibility by water along the route makes multiday travel possible. Canoeing, kayaking, and, in some areas, personal watercraft use are all popular ways to enjoy water trails.

Source: R. L. Moore and D. T. Ross. 1998, January. Trails and recreation greenways: Corridors of benefits. *Parks and Recreation,* 69–75.

An interesting example of a nonprofit organization that promotes the securing of areas for trails is the Rails-to-Trails Conservancy. The RTC is involved in securing multipurpose public paths that have been created from previous railroad passageways. This organization reports that since the 1960s throughout the United States almost 11,000 miles of rail-trails have been set aside. These types of developments promote environmental stewardship, tourism, and heritage management (see figure 8.6). This organization has acquired more than 650 miles of trails since 1993. Its goal is to find public agencies to own and manage these trails for public use.

Tourism Promotion

Figuratively, people saw the world grow smaller in the twentieth century. Advances in transportation and communication have created a global network. These advances, combined with increased discretionary income of people in the developed world, have led to an explosion in

Figure 8.6

The Rails-to-Trails Conservancy promotes conservation activities.

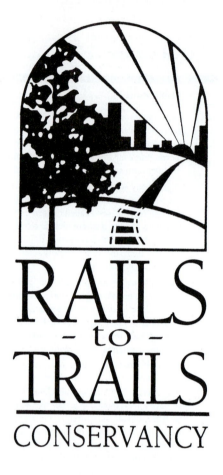

international and domestic travel in the last twenty years. Tourism ranks only behind oil as the world's second largest industry according to the United Nation's affiliated World Tourism Organization, which forecasts that tourism will become the world's most important global activity. States have seen the importance of promoting their lands as a potential tourist destination. Every state is actively involved in the development of tourist attractions and the promotion of tourism. "From the state's point of view there are two good reasons for promoting tourism: increased revenue from taxes and more jobs for the state's residents" (Jensen, 1995, p. 127).

In 1997, Americans spent more than $386 billion on domestic travel in the United States (U.S. Bureau of Census, 1999). This compares with the $323 billion that Americans spent in 1993 (U.S. Bureau of Census, 1995). Foreign visitors spent an additional $73 million in 1997. This can be compared with $29 million in 1988 (U.S. Bureau of Census, 1999). Interestingly, the top cities and states visited by overseas visitors are found in table 8.8. As one can see when viewing this table, the city most visited by overseas visitors is New York City, followed by Los Angeles and then Miami. California, Florida, and New York received the bulk of overseas travelers. These states combined have 73 percent of the market share for overseas visitors. The tax revenues alone from this industry are immense, generating $13.6, $8.9, and $2.7 billion for federal, state, and local treasuries, respectively (Ibrahim and Cordes, 1993). Although the private sector provides the majority of these jobs, state governments support the travel and tourism industry by promoting their state throughout the country (see table 8.9).

TABLE
8.8   TOP STATES AND CITIES VISITED BY OVERSEAS TRAVELERS

States	Cities
California	New York City
Florida	Los Angeles
New York	Miami
Hawaii	San Francisco
Nevada	Orlando
Guam	Oahu/Honolulu
Massachusetts	Las Vegas
Illinois	Washington, D.C.
Texas	Boston
Arizona	Chicago

Source: U.S. Bureau of the Census. 1999. *Statistical Abstracts of the United States: 1999.* 119th ed. Washington, DC: U.S. Government Printing Office.

The "war" to entice visitors as well as lure in-state residents to stay at home is increasing. Full-page advertisements in travel magazines, television ads, travel brochures, and magazines are all evidence of the increase in state budgets to promote tourism. Researchers are finding that leisure pursuits and outdoor recreation opportunities are an essential component of tourism. Ebberson (1983) found that opportunities to participate in certain activities were more important than a particular destination for vacationers.

Several states have a separate department of tourism while other states have agencies in larger departments. For example, the Texas Travel Information Center is a part of the State Department of Highways and Public Transportation. In addition to having one main office, many states also have regional offices to facilitate the dissemination of travel information. States vary greatly in what they emphasize to potential visitors. Whereas Florida might market its beaches and warm climate in the winter, South Carolina highlights its "Southern hospitality" and Virginia capitalizes on its colonial history and Civil War involvement. Each state's emphasis differs as each tries to capture potential visitors and market its uniqueness. This is mainly dictated by geography, culture, and history; however, different states have also established different marketing techniques and target markets for their advertising. One aspect of the "Say Yes to Michigan" campaign is geared to Chicago residents who are looking to get out of the big city on weekends.

The Arts

According to Kreisberg (1979), state agencies for the arts are a relatively recent phenomenon; most have developed since 1965 in response to the legislation that created the National Endowment for the Arts. The Congressional Declaration of Purpose of this legislation stated, "It is necessary and appropriate for the federal government to complement, assist and add to programs for the advancement of the humanities and arts by local, state, regional, and private agencies and their organizations" (Kreisberg, 1979, p. 180). State governments responded to this legislation by creating their own state agencies that could tap federal funds for the promotion of the arts.

TABLE

8.9   1996 DOMESTIC TRAVEL EXPENDITURES

State	Expenditures (Millions of U.S. Dollars)	Share (Percentage)	Rank
California	50,215	13.0	1
Florida	33,360	8.6	2
Texas	24,669	6.4	3
New York	23,158	6.0	4
Illinois	16,945	4.4	5
Nevada	15,492	4.0	6
New Jersey	12,494	3.2	7
Pennsylvania	11,937	3.1	8
Georgia	11,199	2.9	9
Virginia	10,545	2.7	10
Ohio	10,528	2.7	11
North Carolina	9,724	2.5	12
Michigan	8,958	2.3	13
Massachusetts	8,569	2.2	14
Tennessee	8,172	2.1	15

Source: Data from U.S. Bureau of the Census. 1999. *Statistical Abstracts of the United States: 1999.* 119th ed. Washington, DC: U.S. Government Printing Office.

A state agency for the arts exists in each of the fifty United States. The makeup and responsibility of these agencies differ from state to state. All state art agencies, however, administer certain federal programs and support the arts within their state. Most of the support provided by state art agencies takes the form of grants-in-aid to arts institutions, community arts agencies, production organizations, schools, and, in some cases, individuals (see table 8.10 and figure 8.7). State art agencies also provide technical assistance (e.g., workshops and seminars on topics such as fundraising) to arts programs and institutions within their state.

In many ways, the role of individual state governments is that of an enabler as the majority of direct services involving the arts and recreation will be carried out at the local level by public development agencies, private developers, arts organizations, municipal parks and recreation offices, nonprofit organizations, and commercial entrepreneurs. Yet, as pointed out by Peene and Shanahan (1990), states can make a significant contribution to linking arts and other recreation amenities to economic development in both supporting and leading roles. The starting point is to acknowledge the role that the arts and other recreation amenities can have in the economic development of an individual state.

Assuming that those involved with the planning of the arts and state economic development can see the benefits of collaboration, opportunities exist to strengthen the performance of development programs through systematically including cultural and recreational resources. Drawing from Peene and Shanahan (1990), each state can benefit from doing at least some of the following, especially with regard to the arts:

- Incorporate information about art programs, cultural events, recreation resources, and other quality-of-life amenities when it tries to recruit new businesses. This information should be as prevalent as information provided about schools, taxes, and utility rates.

8.10 ARTS AND HUMANITIES—SELECTED FEDERAL AID PROGRAMS: 1975 TO 1997 (IN MILLIONS OF DOLLARS)

Type of Fund and Program	1975	1980	1985	1990	1992	1993	1994	1995	1996	1997
National Endowment for the Arts										
Funds available[1]	86.9	188.1	171.7	170.8	163.0	159.7	158.1	152.1	86.9	98.4
Program appropriation	67.3	97.0	118.7	124.3	123.0	120.0	116.3	109.0	63.5	65.8
Matching funds[2]	7.5	42.9	29.5	32.4	30.3	27.4	29.4	28.5	17.2	16.8
Grants awarded (number)	3,071	5,505	4,801	4,475	4,229	4,096	3,843	3,685	1,751	1,098
Funds obligated[3]	81.7	166.4	149.4	157.6	154.6	148.4	145.2	147.9	75.3	94.4
Partnership agreements	14.9	13.6	24.4	26.1	37.0	42.0	40.7	39.2	25.9	30.0
Music	14.7	22.1	15.3	16.5	14.9	12.4	10.9	10.9	5.4	(X)
Museums	10.8	11.2	11.9	12.1	11.1	9.9	9.4	9.0	3.8	(X)
Theater	6.4	8.4	10.6	10.6	9.4	8.3	8.8	7.3	5.2	(X)
Dance	6.1	8.0	9.0	9.6	8.2	7.9	7.6	7.1	4.2	(X)
Media arts	5.4	8.4	9.9	13.9	12.0	10.2	10.9	8.9	3.0	(X)
Challenge[4]	(X)	50.8	20.7	19.7	13.8	11.7	9.6	21.1	4.0	(X)
Visual arts	1.0	7.3	6.2	5.9	5.6	5.1	4.8	4.4	1.2	(X)
Other	2.8	36.6	41.3	43.1	42.7	40.9	42.5	40.0	22.6	(X)
National Endowment for the Humanities										
Funds available	13.0	186.2	125.6	140.6	156.5	158.5	157.9	151.4	93.1	93.9
Program appropriation	6.1	100.3	95.2	114.2	131.2	131.9	131.4	125.7	77.2	80.0
Matching funds	2.0	38.4	30.4	26.3	25.2	26.5	26.5	25.7	15.9	13.9
Grants awarded (number)	542	2,917	2,241	2,195	2,199	2,197	1,881	1,871	815	900
Funds obligated	10.5	185.5	125.7	141.0	159.1	160.3	159.0	151.8	93.4	94.8
Education programs	4.2	18.3	17.9	16.3	20.0	20.8	19.6	19.2	13.5	10.5
State programs	(X)	26.0	24.4	29.6	31.8	32.4	32.2	32.0	29.0	29.5
Research grants	2.0	32.0	24.4	22.5	25.3	23.7	23.4	22.2	5.1	8.5
Fellowship programs	1.7	18.0	15.3	15.3	17.4	18.9	17.7	16.5	5.1	5.6
Challenge	(X)	53.5	19.6	14.6	12.4	14.2	14.4	13.8	9.9	9.9
Public programs	(X)	(X)	24.1	25.4	27.0	26.7	27.5	25.8	12.5	12.6
Preservation and access	(X)	(X)	(X)	17.5	25.1	23.5	24.1	22.2	18.3	18.2
National Capital Arts and Cultural Affairs Program	(X)	(X)	(X)	(X)	(X)	(X)	(X)	(X)	(X)	(X)
Other	31.8	37.7	(X)	(X)	(X)	(X)	(X)	(X)	(X)	(X)

X Not applicable.

[1]Includes other funds, not shown separately. Excludes administrative funds. Gifts are included in 1980; excluded thereafter.

[2]Represents federal funds obligated only upon receipt or certification by endowment of matching nonfederal gifts.

[3]Includes obligations for new grants, supplemental awards on previous years' grants, and program contracts. Beginning with 1997 data, the grant-making structure changed from discipline-based categories to thematic ones.

[4]Program designed to stimulate new sources and higher levels of giving to institutions for the purpose of guaranteeing long-term stability and financial independence. Program requires a match of at least three private dollars to each federal dollar. Funds for challenge grants are not allocated by program area because they are awarded on a grant-by-grant basis.

Sources: U.S. *National Endowment for the Arts, Annual Report;* and U.S. *National Endowment for the Humanities, Annual Report.*

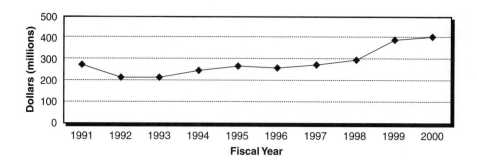

Figure 8.7

Legislative
appropriations
for the arts
1991–1998

*Source data from
National Assembly
of State Arts
Agencies.
www.nasa-
arts.org/new/nasaa/
nasaanews/leg
update00.shtml*

- Treat support for art institutions as opportunities to strengthen the state's investment climate.
- Make art institutions and art-related businesses eligible for state development financing programs.
- Encourage sound economic assessments before taking on major art projects, cultural event projects, or recreation projects that have economic development objectives.
- Involve artists in the planning and implementation of programs.
- Establish programs for strengthening the management of art institutions, as well as cultural events and recreation resources and programs.

Building on elements such as these can generate significant economic development for individual states as well as strengthen relationships between diverse areas within the state government. In many instances this will help states build the kind of partnerships discussed throughout this chapter.

Other State Services

Beyond the services mentioned in the preceding sections, state governments also provide a number of other services to their residents. The exact mix of services varies from state to state as governing bodies struggle to identify specific funding priorities for their state budgets. Yet many states recognize the provision of recreation programs as a legitimate responsibility. Some of the other major programs and facilities operated by state governments include the following:

Correctional institutions. Therapeutic recreation and other leisure services form an important component of correctional institutions operated by states. For example, the State of Iowa operates a correctional institution—Iowa Medical and Classification Center—that employs several certified therapeutic recreation specialists. Programs include social activities, physical recreation, table games, small-group interaction, leisure education programs, and other activities.

State hospitals and institutions. State governments often provide a full range of hospital services to persons with disabilities, including those under psychiatric treatment, the developmentally disabled, persons with visual and hearing impairments, and others. Such hospitals and institutions often provide a full range of recreation and leisure services. These programs include such therapies as assertiveness training, leisure education, leisure skill development, socialization activities, and physical activities. Diverse job opportunities exist in this area of therapeutic recreation. For example, the State of Iowa hires certified therapeutic recreation specialists to work at such places as the Mental Health Institute in Independence, Woodward State Hospital in Woodward, and the Iowa Braille and Sightsaving School at Vinton.

Care and activity centers. State governments often establish standards and the licensing of care and activity centers for older individuals. Few state governments provide direct-care facilities; rather, they emphasize regulatory activities and the creation of standards in support of quality care. In addition, state and federal governments provide funds to local and county governments to create support services to older individuals, keeping them in their homes as long as possible to avoid the expenses of institutionalized care.

Substance-abuse and chemical-dependency rehabilitation programs. State governments also support substance-abuse and chemical-dependency rehabilitation programs. Such efforts vary from direct involvement in state institutions, such as prisons and mental health facilities, to providing financial subsidies, regulatory legislation, and other forms of support to governmental, nonprofit, and private organizations.

Museums. State and provincial governments in both the United States and Canada operate museums. Such facilities often develop along historical, cultural, natural history, or other themes, such as science, technology, and art. An outstanding example of a provincially supported museum is the Royal Ontario Museum (ROM) located in Toronto, Ontario. This facility provides historical, cultural, and other information concerning important factors in the development of Ontario and Canada.

Fairgrounds. Perhaps one of the most popular programs throughout the United States is the annual state fair. Such programs often take place using land and facilities operated by state government. Programs include exhibits, shows, displays, and amusements. Well-developed state fairgrounds are often used on a year-round basis for sporting events, flea markets, fairs, exhibitions, conferences, revivals, and other activities.

Cultural programs and facilities. State governments also provide direct and indirect support for the organization of cultural and historical events, programs, and activities. Such programs can take diverse forms—from a reenactment of an important historical event to the promotion of art exhibits and performing arts activities. State governments also provide support to local governments and nonprofit organizations by providing funding to seed activities such as theater groups, community events, and others. In Ontario, funds from provincial government lotteries can be directly committed to leisure-oriented cultural and historical pursuits.

In addition to these direct services, most state governments have at least one state-supported institution of higher education that offers programs in recreation and park administration as

Leisure Line

Budget Cut Opportunities

For some reason the philosophy in the public sector is, "When funds are cut, there's no other way but to cut services." But in my opinion, sometimes the best opportunities come because you're forced by budget cuts to find new ways to do things.

Source: David Osborn and Ted Goebler.

well as tourism development. These programs support the state by providing qualified entry-level professionals. They also offer various state agencies technical assistance, interns, and professional growth opportunities such as conferences, workshops, and results of research focused on recreation.

Challenges for the Future

State governments face immense challenges in the twenty-first century. As the federal government continues to downsize, states must pick up the slack; yet most states face financial crises of their own. For most states the question is not whether they view many social and human services (including leisure and recreation) as important, but rather how to finance and pay for these services.

State funding for parks and recreation is changing. In the past, agencies had considerably more control over how they spent their appropriations. In the 1990s, agencies found that elected officials set agency funding priorities. Westfall (1991) indicates elected officials tend to favor new development projects over land acquisition, facility rehabilitation, natural resource protection and site operation, and maintenance. Each new development places increased demand on already-stressed agency operating resources and creates future rehabilitation needs. Agencies must now package and sell basic, less visible funding needs to state legislatures.

McLean, Hurd, Beggs, and Chavez (2000) have suggested that numerous trends are affecting state parks. Some of these include the following: (1) During the 1990s, state parks were models of slow growth (this was representative of the political tenor of the times—that of reduced or no government); (2) distribution of acreage and areas is not consistent with population distribution; (3) visitation is the most dramatic variable, often a result of weather and sometimes politics; (4) state support for state parks has, at best, been neutral, with few additional dollars being made available; (5) bond monies are becoming more available; and (6) legislatures, in some cases, are increasing operating funds.

Many states are cutting back on staff. In an effort to replace staff, agencies use technology as well as volunteers. For example, interactive computer information devices now orient many visitors to park resources and programs. Likewise, volunteers greet and help visitors in the campground host program. In this program private citizens (often retirees) serve as campground hosts in various state parks and forests. This often entails answering questions and dealing with minor problems in exchange for free camping from a week to several months.

States also use public-private partnerships to promote tourism and generate revenue. In Illinois, the state's first public-private resort was created in 1989 at Eagle Creek State Park. This privately developed resort includes a 130-room inn and an eighteen-hole championship golf course on Lake Shelbyville in central Illinois. The Illinois Department of Conservation contributed a cash incentive and infrastructure improvements to the venture, which was primarily financed and developed by the private sector (Westfall, 1991). Other possible partnerships include American Youth Hostels, which convert old buildings in public parks to provide low-cost travel accommodations. Hiking clubs help to maintain trails; local snowmobile clubs work with private landowners to develop trails and resting huts. In return, the snowmobile community has been instrumental in legislation providing liability protection for landowners. States need to find ways to create similar partnerships to increase recreation opportunities for their residents.

States also use fees and charges to finance their recreation programs. For example, in California, visitor and concession fees totaled $7.3 million in 1981; the fee target a decade later was ten times as high: $79.5 million (Myers, 1992). In response to many of these trends, agencies within each state cooperate with one another to develop a plan of action for the coming decade. Managers in outdoor recreation resources in Oregon, for example, created a list of priorities at

8.11 PRIORITIES OF OUTDOOR RECREATION RESOURCE MANAGERS IN OREGON

- *Create an outdoor ethic in individuals.*
  "For the past 100 years, especially the last 25, we have emphasized the role of government in conservation and have given little attention to the individual. We have not developed a land ethic in the minds and hearts of citizens in a manner and scale that complements public programs" (President's Commission on Americans Outdoors [PCAO], 1987, p. 83). According to the PCAO (1987) "an outdoor ethic means personal involvement in the outdoors as an essential part of life. It means a sense of appreciation for an obligation toward the air, land, water, and living things of the earth" (p. 81). For many, the best way for creating such an outdoor ethic involves increasing the amount of environmental education in all levels of the school curriculum.

- *Create a state-dedicated trust.*
  Such a trust would help resource agencies purchase land and open space to meet the outdoor recreation needs of future generations. This trust fund could be set up similarly to the Land and Water Conservation Fund, which helped states acquire land and build facilities for outdoor recreation.

- *Create a state recreation information clearinghouse.*
  A clearinghouse would allow resource managers from a variety of agencies to cooperate in meeting the outdoor recreation needs of state residents.

- *Increase coordinated efforts concerning wildlife habitats.*
  Due to the increasing demands on wildlife habitat, agencies must work together to meet future demands and create more opportunities for nonconsumptive use of wildlife such as nature study and tracking for photography purposes.

- *Encourage public/private partnerships.*
  The key to successful partnerships is to match resources to achieve mutual goals. Partnerships can be encouraged between government agencies and the private sector or between nonprofit organizations.

- *Plan and budget for renovation and maintenance.*
  In the past century, Americans have invested heavily in public recreation facilities. A large portion of this investment took place in the 1930s, 1940s, and 1950s. These facilities now need major renovation and maintenance. The recreation infrastructure is aging, and agencies must find innovative ways to renovate and maintain areas and facilities.

- *Encourage volunteer participation.*
  For many state recreation agencies volunteers remain an untapped resource, which could greatly improve services to state residents. In a successfully run volunteer program, the campground host program developed by state parks, volunteers help manage state parks during the peak summer season.

- *Determine recreation needs of the public periodically.*
  To meet the recreational needs of residents and visitors, managers must identify and understand what those needs are. This could take the form of a recreational needs survey completed on a five- or ten-year cycle.

Source: The 2nd Annual Oregonian's Outdoor Conference, 1987, Salem, Oregon.

the second Oregon Outdoor Conference. These priorities, which parallel the recommendations of the President's Commission on Americans Outdoors, are presented in table 8.11.

Summary

In many ways state involvement in recreation mirrors that of the federal government. States, responsible for vast amounts of public land, also serve as facilitators and enablers for local governments. The role of state governments in providing recreation for its citizens is increasing. More state and local involvement in recreation planning and program implementation encourages a more participatory approach to governments and allows local citizens to meet local and regional needs. This chapter discussed both the functions and direct services provided by individual state governments. Functions of state governments include drafting legislation, coordinating with both federal and local governments (especially in the planning process), and encouraging and creating standards for the field. Direct-service delivery for states revolves primarily around outdoor recreation resources while other direct services include tourism development, the promotion of the arts, and meeting the needs of such citizen groups as senior citizens, people incarcerated or institutionalized, and people with physical and mental disabilities.

Many state functions and services discussed in this chapter are interrelated. For example, the arts or outdoor recreation resources can play a role in tourism promotion. These functions and services also connect to other aspects of the state, such as economic development. Therefore, recreation agencies and organizations (or any other state agency) cannot be isolationists and expect to survive. Recreation agencies and organizations on both state and local levels must strive to create innovative partnerships within other aspects of government and the private sector to create multifaceted approaches to improving people's quality of life.

Discussion Questions

1. What is enabling legislation? What does it allow state governments to do?
2. Do you agree or disagree that states or provinces should take on greater responsibility in planning for the recreational needs of their citizens?
3. Identify a specific recreation business in your area and interview the owner. Identify all laws and standards that this business must adhere to in your state or province (specific to recreation). How does the owner of the business feel about the amount of state or provincial regulation? Should there be more or less regulation from his/her point of view?
4. What environmental issues are specific to your state or province? How do these issues affect the management of state or provincial land for outdoor recreation?
5. Find your state's or province's outdoor recreation plan in your school or local library. What are the management priorities of your state or province regarding outdoor recreation?
6. Identify the recreation resources (natural resources, cultural resources, festivals, and special events) that make your state or province unique. How are these resources marketed to entice both in-state or in-province and out-of-state or out-of-province visitors?
7. Identify one specific government partnership that is taking place in your state or province. What does the partnership entail?
8. Locate a leisure services professional working in state or provincial government and ask him or her to describe the technical and interpersonal skills required for his or her position.
9. What roles do state and provincial governments play that are not handled by either municipal or federal governments?
10. What are the skills needed to work in direct service at the state or provincial level? Evaluate your own skills in these areas.

References

Ebberson, A. 1983. Why people travel. *Journal of Physical Education, Recreation, and Dance—Leisure Today 54*(4), 53–54.

Foss, P. 1968. *Recreation: Conservation in the United States, a Documentary History.* New York: Chelsea House.

Ibrahim, H., and K. Cordes. 1993. *Outdoor Recreation.* Madison, WI: Brown & Benchmark.

Jensen, C. 1985. *Outdoor Recreation in America.* Minneapolis, MN: Burgess.

Jensen, C. 1995. *Outdoor Recreation in America.* 2d ed. Champaign, IL: Human Kinetics.

Jones, J. 1992. *The United States Outdoor Atlas and Recreation Guide.* New York: Houghton.

Knudson, D. 1984. *Outdoor Recreation.* New York: Macmillan.

Kraus, R. 1990. *Recreation and Leisure in Modern Society.* 4th ed. New York: HarperCollins.

Kreisberg, L. 1979. *Local Government and the Arts.* New York: American Council for the Arts.

McLean, D. D., A. Hurd, B. Beggs, and D. Chavez. 2000. *Trends in State Park Operations.* http://php.indiana.edu

Meyer, H., and C. Brightbill. 1950. *State Recreation: Organization and Administration.* New York: A. S. Baines.

Myers, P. 1992. Testimony before the subcommittee on energy and the environment. *Crisis in State and Local Recreation and Fiscal Year 1993 Budget for LWCF and UPARR.* Washington, DC: U.S. Government Printing Office.

The National Association of State Park Directors. 2000. *Definitions.* www.indiana.edu/~naspd/statistics/definitions.html

Outdoor Recreation Resources Review Commission. 1962. *Outdoor Recreation for America: A Report to the President and to the Congress.* Washington, DC: U.S. Government Printing Office.

Peene, L., and J. Shanahan. 1990. The role of the arts in state and local economic development. Edited by W. T. Pound, in *Economic Impact of the Arts: A Sourcebook.* Washington, DC: National Conference of State Legislatures.

President's Commission on Americans Outdoors. 1987. *Americans Outdoors: The Legacy, the Challenge.* Washington, DC: Island Press.

U.S. Bureau of the Census. 1995. *Statistical Abstracts of the United States: 1995.* 115th ed. Washington, DC: U.S. Government Printing Office.

U.S. Bureau of the Census. 1999. *Statistical Abstracts of the United States: 1999.* 119th ed. Washington, DC: U.S. Government Printing Office.

Westfall, R. 1991. Emerging trends at the state level. *Trends* 28(2), 39–42.

Delivery of Leisure Services: Federal Government

Federal lands and other resources provide opportunities for many different types of leisure experiences. In North America, our natural resources abound. Here, a family resting during a hike pauses for a reflective moment.

Introduction

The United States and Canada are blessed with many unique natural land areas. Federal agencies administer most of these areas and have as a primary and secondary goal the provision of parks, recreation, and/or cultural services. Both the United States and Canada have majestic environmental areas that draw tourists from around the world. One need only think of Yosemite Valley, the geysers of Yellowstone, and the vistas of the Grand Canyon (in the United States) or the serenity and majesty of Lake Louise in Banff National Park (Canada) to appreciate this heritage of natural resources.

From a historical perspective, the United States has acquired more than 1,837,770,000 acres of land and water as a part of its public domain. The majority of this land and water was acquired between 1781 and 1867, with additional small acquisitions at the close of the 1800s and the beginning of the 1900s. Canada is the world's second-largest country in land size. These land masses provide the basis for many leisure opportunities and have resulted in the creation of a large number of federal agencies and institutions to manage parks and recreation services.

This chapter reviews the involvement of the federal governments of the United States and Canada in the provision of parks, recreation, and cultural services. The number and types of areas, facilities, and services are diverse and do not lend themselves to a clean classification system. Some of the agencies discussed have the provision of parks and recreation services as a primary objective. Other agencies must contend with a variety of objectives under one administrative umbrella. Still other federal agencies provide recreation services in support of their primary mission. For example, the National Park Service's primary objective is to maintain preserves for the purpose of recreation, tourism, and preservation. The U.S. Forest Service has multiple objectives including timber management, watershed management, fish and wildlife management, range management, and recreation. Branches of the U.S. Armed Forces provide Morale, Welfare and Recreation Services in support of their primary mission of defense.

Characteristics of Federal Leisure Service Agencies

Kraus (1990) writes that more than ninety federal agencies, bureaus, commissions, and/or councils provide parks, recreation, and leisure services at the federal level of government. He suggests that the more than 300 federal programs have had little coordination or otherwise centralized planning. This involvement of the federal government has grown steadily since the late 1800s.

Goals and Functions

What are the goals and functions of federal agencies? The large number of federal agencies makes it difficult to specify the goals of the federal government with respect to leisure services. Nonetheless, Kraus (1990) identifies the following eight basic functions of the federal government in relation to parks, recreation, and leisure services (see figure 9.1):

1. *Direct management of outdoor recreation resources.* The federal government owns approximately 34 percent of the total land area in the United States; much of this land is used for a variety of outdoor pursuits. Thus, the federal government plays an immense role in providing outdoor recreation opportunities. Campgrounds, forests, parks, artificial and natural lakes, and other geographic areas come under the direct stewardship of the federal government and are managed by such agencies as the National Park Service, U.S. Forest Service, Bureau of Land Management, U.S. Fish and Wildlife Service, Tennessee Valley Authority, and the U.S. Corps of Engineers.

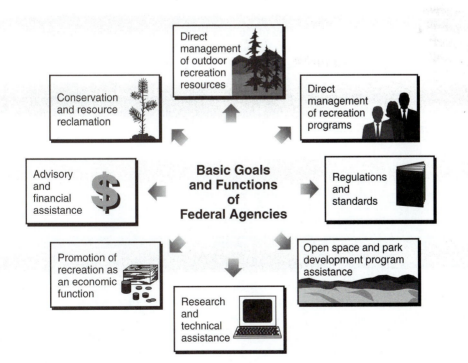

Figure 9.1

Eight basic functions of federal agencies related to leisure services

2. *Conservation and resource reclamation.* The federal government is involved in restoring land and water resources that have been damaged or destroyed and in conserving natural resources, including environmental management and wildlife conservation.

3. *Assistance to open space and park development programs.* During the past several decades, the federal government provided funds to state and local governments to acquire and develop park and recreation resources. The most significant legislation was that of the 1965 Land and Water Conservation Fund Act. One of the priorities for the use of this fund, the rails-to-trails movement, transforms old railroad corridors into new walking and biking greenways.

4. *Direct management of recreation programs.* Several federal agencies provide recreation programs directly to participants. These include activities provided by the Veterans' Administration, National Park Service, U.S. Armed Forces, and others. Many of these programs will be discussed later in this chapter.

5. *Advisory and financial assistance.* The federal government provides technical advice to community agencies and rural environments as well as leadership in the coordination of national recreation policy. From a historical perspective, the cooperative extension services in various states have provided this type of information and have been supported by federal funds.

Leadership direction for national recreation policy appears in such efforts as the National Outdoor Recreation Plans. Special federal commissions also have played major roles in shaping national policy. For example, three presidential commissions, examining the nation's outdoor recreation policy, were created in the 1900s. In 1924, President Calvin Coolidge initiated the first commission that dealt with outdoor recreation resources. Among other things, a National Conference on Outdoor Recreation resulted.

In 1958, the U.S. Congress appointed representatives to the Outdoor Recreation Resources Review Commission (ORRRC). This commission produced a twenty-eight-volume report that recommended major federal involvement in the outdoor recreation area. President John F. Kennedy presented the report to Congress, endorsing its findings. His endorsement encouraged a number of developments, including the establishment of the federal coordinating agency (Bureau of Outdoor Recreation) and funding program for outdoor recreation resources (Land and Water Conservation Act).

In 1985, President Ronald Reagan established a commission, the President's Commission on Americans Outdoors (PCAO), to review existing public outdoor recreation programs and opportunities provided by the federal government, state and local governments, and private organizations and entities. Table 9.1 presents an overview of the findings and suggestions of this commission.

L e i s u r e   L i n e

Best Intentions . . .

. . . Estimated annual numbers of through hikers: starts and finishes

	Start	Finish
Appalachian Trail (2,158 miles)	1,200 to 1,500	180 to 225
Continental Divide Trail (3,000 miles)	6 to 8	2 to 3
Pacific Crest Trail (2,600 miles)	75 to 100	12 to 24

Source: Staff, "Best Intentions" in *Backpacker*, p. 17, June 1996.

TABLE

9.1   FINDINGS AND SUGGESTIONS OF THE PRESIDENT'S COMMISSION ON AMERICANS OUTDOORS

Purpose:

To create a comprehensive governmental appraisal of the nation's outdoor recreation policy and to examine the roles that government and the private sector should play in protecting outdoor recreation resources and meeting anticipated outdoor recreation needs.

Participants:

The Commission, composed of fifteen members including two senators, three representatives, one governor, one mayor, and several conservationists and leaders from the private sector, heard testimony from more than 1,000 Americans in eighteen hearings in every region of the United States. Ideas, concerns, and hopes for the future were shared. Findings and suggestions are presented in the book, *Americans Outdoors: The Legacy, the Challenge.*

Selected Findings:

- Americans place a high value on the outdoors. More than anything else, the Commission found a love for the land and a shared conviction that it is our legacy and our future.
- Outdoor recreation provides significant social, economic, and environmental benefits.
- Quality of the outdoor estate remains precarious. Americans are losing open space as well as wild and free-flowing rivers. Competition for available lands and waters is increasing.
- The quality of recreation services delivery is inadequate. Funding poses a problem, as do liability concerns. Inadequate funding for staff, development of facilities, and maintenance limits recreation use on public lands.

Suggestions:

- *Light a prairie fire of local action.* People on the local level know what their needs are. Grassroots efforts can make communities attractive places to live, work, and play, with maintained open spaces.
- *Develop an outdoor ethic.* Every American must develop a sense of ownership of the outdoors and a commitment to maintaining outdoor opportunities for the future. The nation needs an aware, sensitive, and activated outdoor constituency.
- *Establish education programs about the outdoors.* Local school systems should establish outdoor education programs to encourage appreciation of the outdoors—the 4 R's: Reading, 'Riting, 'Rithmatic, and Resources.
- *Create an Outdoors Corps.* Groups of youth and individuals of all ages should be encouraged to dedicate a portion of their lives to the stewardship of natural resources.
- *Create greenways.* Greenways, corridors of open space linking public and private lands and waterways, can put recreation open space within a short walk of everyone's residence. A network of scenic byways, including roadways and thoroughfares, should be established.
- *Develop innovative funding and management strategies.* Public-private partnerships should be encouraged, realizing the vital role that can be played by volunteers; innovative strategies including fees and charges, a dedicated trust, and other mechanisms should be established to fund future outdoor recreation development.
- *Protect endangered resources.* Protecting 2,000 rivers by the year 2000, as well as expending greater effort to protect wetlands and shorelines and providing for the recreation of people in large urban areas where open space is scarce, must be a priority.
- *Enforce environmental laws.* Outdoor recreation depends on healthy resources, and Americans must diligently protect the environment.
- *Improve the quality of services.* The quality of areas and programs can be improved.
- *Protect our investment.* A systematic plan of renovation and replacement for recreation facilities should be in place.
- *Develop better leadership.* Well-trained professional staff must be developed and educated.
- *Create a clearinghouse of information on the outdoors.* Informational material must be made available.

Source: The President's Commission on Americans Outdoors (PCAO). 1987. *Americans Outdoors: The Legacy, The Challenge.* Washington, DC: Island Press.

In addition to coordination of policy and performing various advisory functions, the federal government also provides state and local governments, as well as nonprofit organizations, with financial assistance. Often this assistance takes the forms of grants. Two examples include the National Endowment for the Arts and the Administration on Aging. The National Endowment for the Arts provides grants to individuals and organizations to promote the arts; the Administration on Aging provides funds for demonstration projects that meet the needs of seniors in unique ways and help older Americans avoid institutionalization.

6. *Promotion of recreation as an economic function.* Numerous examples exist of the federal government's involvement in promotion of recreation, leisure, and park concerns. Some of the federal agencies operating in this arena focus on the promotion of tourist attractions and opportunities for international tourists. The United States attracts large numbers of international tourists, and their economic impact is growing. In 1997, international tourists spent more than $94 million in the United States (U.S. Bureau of Census, 1999). This compares with 1988 when international tourists spent $38 million, and there was a deficit between the total travel expenditures of Americans abroad and receipts from foreign visitors. The federal government also helps to provide outdoor recreation opportunities that can generate significant economic opportunities. In 1996, wildlife-associated recreation expenditures totaled $87.5 million (U.S. Bureau of Census, 1999). This compares with 1991 when expenditures totaled approximately $54 million (U.S. Bureau of Census, 1993).

7. *Research and technical assistance.* The federal government supports a wide variety of research, especially in the area of outdoor recreation. Some of the research, in turn, is applied and is available in the form of direct technical assistance to businesses and other levels of government. Other research projects of the federal government include examining the recreation needs of special populations as well as examining the recreation resources available to inner-city youth.

8. *Regulations and standards.* The regulatory activities of the federal government have influenced ". . . pollution control, watershed production, and environmental quality" (Kraus, 1990, p. 212). In addition, legislation has impacted upon services for individuals who are disabled and physically challenged. For example, the Americans with Disabilities Act (ADA) signed in 1990 by President Bush prohibits discrimination against people with disabilities in employment and in public services, public and private transportation, public accommodations, and telecommunications services. This legislation has tremendous implications for leisure service organizations as it mandates equal opportunity and access to recreation opportunities for persons with disabilities.

L e i s u r e   L i n e

Ethnicity and the Great Outdoors

A recent survey on outdoor recreation patterns revealed that only 4 percent of frequent backpackers are African American, while Hispanics make up 19 percent, and whites just over 70 percent.

Source: Staff, "Changing the Face of Backpacking" in *Backpacker,* p. 16, May 1996.

Resource Base

The resource base or revenue for federal parks, recreation, and cultural services comes primarily from two sources. The first includes revenues that are made available through appropriated funds from the Congress of the United States. In general, these revenues are subject to executive approval, although they are legislatively mandated. In addition, federal agencies can collect revenues in support of services. These "nonappropriated funds" are often locally generated fees and charges at specific sites, and many agencies are able to keep these funds in direct support of their areas, programs, and services.

In the United States, approximately $2.2 billion is expended yearly at the federal level for parks and recreation (U.S. Bureau of Census, 1999). If funds dedicated to the category of natural resources are included, the total amount is $41.2 billion (U.S. Bureau of the Census, 1999).

Funding for the National Park Service provides an illustration of appropriations from Congress, as well as revenues generated from other sources, such as operations. In 1997, approximately $23 billion was available for park operations; of this amount $6 billion came from federal appropriations and the remainder from other sources such as fees and charges. It is interesting to note that revenues in 1990 available for park operations were $13 billion. Table 9.2 reports expenditures as well as funds available.

TABLE

9.2 NATIONAL PARK SERVICE EXPENDITURES

Item	1995 (Millions of US $)	1990 (Millions of US $)	1997 (Millions of US $)
Expenditures reported	848.1	986.1	1,473.0
Salaries and wages	369.4	459.1	683.0
Improvements, maintenance	127.4	160.0	236.0
Construction	84.7	108.5	188.0
Other	266.6	258.5	356.0
Funds available	1,248.2	1,505.5	2,301.0
Appropriations	821.6	1,052.5	1,625.0
Other	426.6	453.0	676.0
Revenues from operations	50.6	78.6	174.2
Recreation visits	263.4	258.7	275.3
Parks	50.0	57.7	65.3
Monuments	15.9	23.9	24.1
Historical sites	61.9	57.5	63.0
Parkways	40.0	29.1	30.9
Recreation areas	49.4	47.2	52.6
Seashores	25.3	23.3	20.3
Capital parks	8.3	7.5	6.1
Other areas	12.6	12.5	11.3

Source: The U.S. Bureau of the Census. 1999. *Statistical Abstracts of the United States: 1999.* 119th ed. Washington, DC: U.S. Government Printing Office.

Characteristics of Professionals

The types and numbers of employees working for given federal agencies vary tremendously. Due to the large number of classifications, it is not possible to include a list of all of them in this chapter. In general, however, employment in the federal system involves qualifying for a GS (Government Service) ranking. Individuals with a bachelor's degree in the parks and recreation field often enter federal service as a GS 7 ranking under the federal civil service system.

For specific information about examinations for positions with the federal government, one can contact the nearest Federal Job Information Center. Some Federal Job Information Centers also provide information concerning jobs in other governmental jurisdictions. There is a Federal Job Information Center in most major cities and in every state of the United States. Most permanent positions in the federal government are filled by an employment list of eligible candidates. This employment list is usually established as a result of some type of competitive review; some reviews require a written examination, whereas others do not. An individual interested in applying for a specific type of position should obtain and review the relevant position announcement from the local Federal Job Information Center. The position announcement includes the education, experience, and skill-level requirements for individual jobs.

Customer Orientation

The customer orientation of employees of the federal government is termed a *public servant* orientation. To be a public servant means to be *in the service of the public.* A public servant is one who holds the public's trust. He or she has the responsibility to act on behalf of and in the interest of the public's welfare. Public servants do not work to earn a profit but rather to provide a service that is of value to society.

As an example, the mission statement of Community, Family, and Soldier Support Command-Korea outlines this federal organization's basic values and customer orientation. The mission statement indicates that its members will provide quality service in support of the mission of the military at a fair value to their customers. They pledge integrity and honesty in their dealings with customers. Furthermore, they point out the types of interactions that are desirable between themselves as public servants and their customers, suggesting that people be treated with respect and in a courteous manner (see figure 9.2).

Another example illustrates the public servant orientation of government employees. The U.S. Forest Service's pamphlet, *People Serving People* (n.d.), discusses the work of the U.S. Forest Service and points out that

> . . . the Forest Service, by definition, is devoted to serving the American public. . . . In order for the public's wants and needs to be known, sensitivity and responsiveness are required on our part. . . . Our public service attitude is communicated both directly and indirectly. For example, how available are forest service personnel to the public? Can someone be reached and information be obtained most of the time? In the forest, does the public feel safe and relatively protected by the presence of law enforcement staff? Is there a feedback system through which the public may indicate their desires or responses to existing services? All of these impressions convey to the public our role. Are we serving the public?

As Gifford Pinchot, founder of the U.S. Forest Service and the first native-born American to complete graduate training in forestry, indicated ". . . a public official is there to serve the public and not run them" (*People Serving People,* n.d.).

Figure 9.2

Service ethic

*Source:
Community, Family,
and Soldier
Support
Command-Korea,
Eighth United
States Army.*

Service Ethic

As a member of the Community, Family, and Soldier Support Command-Korea and in the spirit
of the highest standards of service and business responsibility

We Hereby Pledge to:

Programs Offered	Provide value in all the morale, welfare, and recreation programs we offer our patrons.
Service	Maintain courteous, attentive, and efficient service in a pleasant atmosphere and maintain a professional attitude at all times.
Clean Facilities	Meet and maintain all prescribed standards of sanitation service and remain constantly aware of our responsibility to our patrons.
Community Responsibility	Earn the respect of the military community and contribute to command and community life by supporting the programs that enhance the quality of life in the military community.
Fair Trade Practices	Operate with integrity in all operations and engage in fair and open competition based on truthful representation of services offered.
MWR Program Development	Contribute through dedicated service to our patrons toward the growth and development of better morale, welfare, and recreation programs.
Profit	Maintain the ability to earn a reasonable profit so that facilities can be renovated and value to our patrons can continue to be a primary objective.

Types of Federal Agencies: United States

This section discusses major federal agencies providing parks, recreation, and cultural services in
the United States. These agencies fall into the following groups: land-managing agencies, reservoir
providers, and other major agencies providing direct services or support to parks and recreation.

The total area of the United States, including land and water masses, is 3.7 billion acres
(U.S. Bureau of Census, 1999), of which the federal government manages 563 million acres, or
23.8 percent, of the land area. A few agencies manage the majority of this federal land. These
agencies include the U.S. Forest Service (part of the Department of Agriculture), and the Bureau of Land Management, National Park Service, U.S. Fish and Wildlife Service, and Bureau
of Indian Affairs (which are all divisions within the Department of the Interior).

In addition to managing land areas, the federal government also manages a number of large
reservoirs and, as a result, has become the nation's largest provider of inland water recreation
opportunities. The importance of these recreation opportunities is heightened by the fact that

Figure 9.3

Major federal
agencies
providing parks,
recreation, and
cultural services

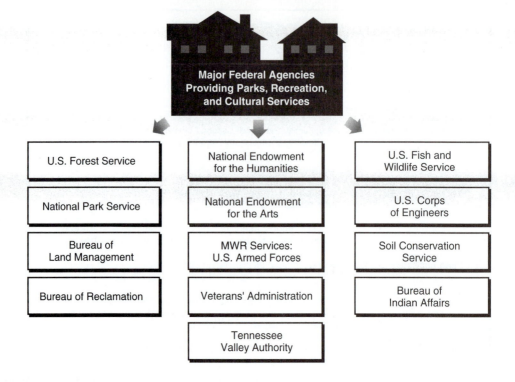

many of these reservoir areas are close to large cities in the northeast, southeast, and south, whereas the majority of federally owned land is located in the western half of the United States. Three agencies within the federal government—the U.S. Corps of Engineers, Tennessee Valley Authority, and the Bureau of Reclamation—manage the majority of these water resources.

A number of additional agencies and programs within the federal government provide services in specific ways. These agencies include the work of the Veterans' Administration in the area of therapeutic recreation as well as the involvement of the Morale, Welfare, and Recreation Services of the U.S. Armed Forces, the National Endowment for the Arts, and the National Endowment for the Humanities (see figure 9.3).

U.S. Forest Service

In 1891, Congress was authorized by the President of the United States to establish forest preserves from forest and range lands in the public domain. These forest preserves were subsequently organized for the intent of protection and management as national forests. In 1905, the management of national forests was transferred to the U.S. Department of Agriculture, and what is known today as the U.S. Forest Service was established. Today, the Forest Service is the largest and most diverse agency in the U.S. Department of Agriculture, employing more than 30,000 permanent full-time and seasonal employees. It is America's largest conservation organization.

Today, the United States has 156 national forests and grasslands and eighteen land utilization projects, located in forty-four states, Puerto Rico, and the Virgin Islands. Figure 9.4 presents the distribution of these resources across the United States.

The underlying philosophy of the Forest Service is conservation. Conservation suggests wise use of resources. It also suggests that resources are renewable (e.g., timber) and can be

Top Fifty Federal Achievements of Last Fifty Years

The federal government's fifty greatest achievements of the last fifty years:

1. Rebuild Europe after World War II.
2. Expand the right to vote.
3. Promote equal access to public accommodations.
4. Reduce disease.
5. Reduce workplace discrimination.
6. Ensure safe food, water.
7. Strengthen the nation's highway system.
8. Increase older American's access to health care.
9. Reduce the federal budget.
10. Promote financial security in retirement.
11. Improve water quality.
12. Support veterans' readjustment and training.
13. Promote scientific and technological research.
14. Contain communism.
15. Improve air quality.
16. Enhance workplace safety.
17. Strengthen the national defense.
18. Reduce hunger and improve nutrition.
19. Increase access to postsecondary education.
20. Enhance consumer protection.
21. Expand foreign markets for U.S. goods.
22. Increase the stability of financial institutions and markets.
23. Increase arms control and disarmament.
24. Protect the wilderness.
25. Promote space exploration.
26. Protect endangered species.
27. Reduce exposure to hazardous waste.
28. Enhance the nation's health care infrastructure.
29. Maintain stability in the Persian Gulf.
30. Expand home ownership.
31. Increase international economic development.
32. Ensure an adequate energy supply.
33. Strengthen the nation's airways system.
34. Increase low-income families' access to health care.
35. Improve elementary and secondary education.
36. Reduce crime.
37. Advance human rights and provide humanitarian relief.
38. Make government more transparent to the public.
39. Stabilize agricultural prices.
40. Provide assistance for the working poor.
41. Improve government performance.
42. Reform welfare.
43. Expand job training and placement.
44. Increase market competition.
45. Increase the supply of low-income housing.
46. Develop and renew impoverished communities.
47. Improve mass transportation.
48. Reform taxes.
49. Control immigration.
50. Devolve responsibility to the states.

Source: *The Washington Post* as cited in the *Waterloo-Cedar Falls Courier*, Thursday, December 28, 2000, C-7.

managed in such a way as to protect the values associated with them. Gifford Pinchot, Chief Forester of the Forest Service from 1898 to 1910, noted ". . . conservation of natural resources . . . is the key to the safety and prosperity of the American people and of all the people of the world for all time to come" (U.S. Forest Service, 1970, p. 1). A motto of the Forest Service (1986) is "caring for the land . . . serving the people."

The conservation mandate includes the idea of managing the land for multiple uses. The Multiple-Use Sustained Yield Act of 1960 identified the five primary uses of national forest

Figure 9.4

U.S. National
Forest Service
Reserves

*Source: Data from
the U.S. National
Forest Service
Reserve, Natural
Resources and
Environment, U.S.
Department of
Agriculture.*

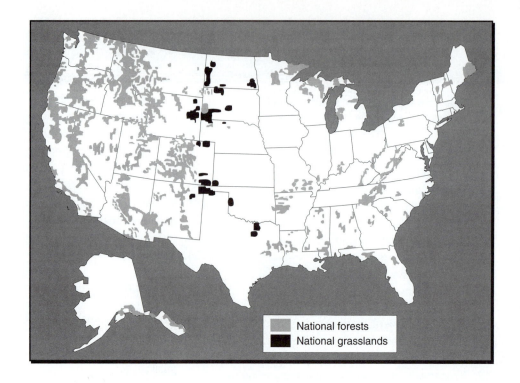

land as outdoor recreation, watershed protection, grazing, timber production, and the propagation of fish and wildlife. Although these five basic uses are supposedly of equal importance, any one of them may be emphasized over the others in a particular area. For example, within wilderness areas outdoor recreation, watershed, and the propagation of fish and wildlife would be emphasized while timber cutting might be forbidden.

The Forest Service provides more outdoor recreation resources than any other federal agency in the U.S. government—the natural resources found in national forests provide a focal point for many outdoor recreation activities. For example, the Forest Service administers more than 120,000 miles of hiking and riding trails (Jensen, 1995). In addition, it maintains more than 10,000 recreational sites, including campgrounds, picnic areas, ski areas, and boat ramps. The combined capacity of all recreation areas administered by the Forest Service exceeds 1.5 million people at any given time. In 1996, the Forest Service played to more than 341 million recreation visitor days (a visitor day is the recreational use of National Forest that aggregates twelve visitor hours) (U.S. Bureau of Census, 1999). This compares with 1980 when there were 233 million visitor days. Table 9.3 presents a list of recreation activities and the number of recreation visitor days in 1996. The Forest Service has also been active in the creation and management of wilderness areas, including the first one established in 1924—the Gila Wilderness Area in New Mexico. Today the Forest Service manages more than 32 million acres of wilderness lands.

In the area of outdoor recreation, the Forest Service has three primary roles (U.S. Forest Service, 1983):

1. *Management, protection, and use of the national forest system.* This involves care of the lands and water areas that provide opportunities for recreation experiences and related services.

TABLE

9.3 NATIONAL FOREST RECREATION USE

Recreation Activities	Visitor Days (in millions)
Mechanized travel and viewing scenery	122
Camping, picnicking, and swimming	87
Hiking, horseback riding, and water travel	33
Winter sports	19
Hunting	19
Resorts, cabins, and organization camps	17
Fishing	18
Nature studies	3
Other	20

Source: U.S. Bureau of the Census 1999. *Statistical Abstracts of the United States: 1999.* 119 ed. Washington, DC: U.S. Government Printing Office.

2. *Cooperation.* The Forest Service works with private interests and other governmental agencies to share its knowledge, resources, and capabilities to improve the delivery of recreation services.
3. *Research.* The Forest Service conducts research to improve opportunities for quality outdoor recreation experiences.

The U.S. Forest Service further clarified its role in providing for outdoor recreation until the year 2000 in its National Recreation Strategy. This strategy serves as the conceptual framework aimed at finding creative and imaginative ways to take advantage of outdoor recreation opportunities in the national forests by working with people. The ultimate goal of the strategy—to promote customer satisfaction with more high-quality recreation services—involves forging partnerships with state and local government as well as private enterprise, and developing the professionalism of recreation staff by creating standards and challenging career paths.

One unique partnership, developed in Atlanta, Georgia, is *The Urban Tree House: A Tree for All Reasons.* This project brought together a variety of partners including the U.S. Forest Service, Department of Parks, Recreation and Cultural Affairs from the city of Atlanta, North Carolina A & T University, Clark Atlanta University, Georgia Pacific, and others to create a project to bring an understanding of forestry concepts and careers to inner-city children. The structure, located in a city park and built around a large water oak, consists of a shelter surrounded by seventy feet of deck. The deck, in the shape of the continental United States, has been painted and routed to show state boundaries and major geographical features. A separate deck in the shape of Alaska serves as a stage for educational and entertainment programs, and an abundance of native vegetation is planted around the facility. "The first of its kind in the United States, it is a pilot for a nationwide network of tree houses conceived by Forest Service researchers to link urban populations with nearby National Forests" (U.S. Forest Service, 1993).

Partnerships between the U.S. Forest Service and the private sector date back to 1871. An example of a partnership is one existing between the U.S. Forest Service and the Hoodoo Ski Area in the Dechutes National Forest. The private sector operates campground concessions and ski areas on U.S. Forest Service land. This partnership, as well as others, has resulted in providing high-quality recreational experiences through improved and expanded facilities and excellent guest service (see figure 9.5).

The Bureau of Land Management

The Bureau of Land Management (BLM), created in 1946 as a part of the Department of Interior, has as its primary responsibility the management of lands within the original public domain. Lands within the public domain are those areas to which the public has right of ownership, rather than individuals. Although large parcels of land have been transferred or sold from the public domain to homesteaders, railroad corporations, in support of common schools, and otherwise dispersed, today the BLM manages an enormous portion of the United States—more

Figure 9.5

An example of partnerships with the U.S. Forest Service

Source: Data from U.S. Forest Service, Department of Agriculture.

"Partnerships In Action"

than 341 million acres. Most of this area is in the western portion of the United States. Figure 9.6 shows the distribution of lands under the jurisdiction of the BLM.

Like the U.S. Forest Service, the BLM uses the principles of multiple use and sustained yield to manage its land holdings. The Federal Land Policy and Management Act of 1976 mandates the BLM to manage its land in accordance with the multiple-use and sustained yield concept. Much of the land managed by the BLM is arid or semiarid and found in the southwest; however, the BLM also manages large land areas in Alaska and the Pacific Northwest. According to Ibrahim and Cordes (1993), the BLM manages national conservation areas, a national recreation area, about 2,000 miles of the Wild and Scenic River System, approximately 1,700 miles of national trails, 25 wilderness areas, and more than 470 developed recreation sites in eight states.

The BLM's primary function in the area of recreation is to provide outdoor recreation opportunities to the public, particularly those not provided by other public or private entities. Its secondary goals include protecting resources, maintaining visitor health and safety, and helping resolve conflicts between users involving recreation resources. In general, the BLM provides resource-dependent types of outdoor recreation. It focuses on the provision of such activities as fishing, hunting, rock hounding, and other resource-dependent activities. The BLM also invests in the creation of special or more intensely managed recreation areas, such as recreation assistance facilities and visitor assistance programs like campgrounds, picnic sites, sanitation facilities, trails, and information displays. The BLM is involved in the management of such areas as San Pedro Riparian Natural Conservation Area, Gila Box Riparian Natural Conservation Area, Aravaipa Creek Wilderness Area, and other riparian areas.

In a parallel initiative to the U.S. Forest Service's National Recreation Strategy, the BLM strives to meet the increasing demand for its recreation resources. The plan, entitled *Recreation 2000: A Strategic Plan,* sets forth the BLM's commitment to the management of outdoor

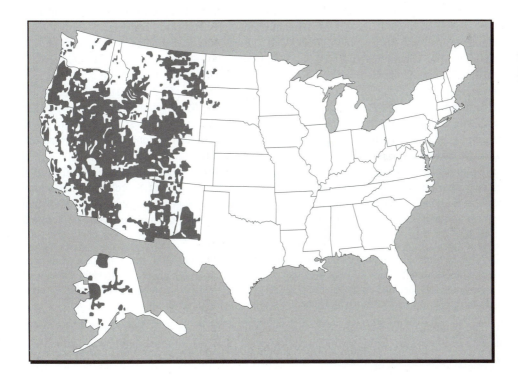

Figure 9.6

Areas under the jurisdiction of the Bureau of Land Management

Source: Data from the Department of the Interior.

recreation resources on public lands and presents a revitalized approach to managing outdoor recreation resources as one of the principal multiple uses of public land. Similar to the approach of the Forest Service's National Recreation Strategy, the plan calls for maintaining diversity and resource protection, enhancing and expanding facilities and maintenance efforts, developing tourism and interpretation services, promoting partnerships, increasing fees and charges, and implementing a professional development program for recreation and resource management specialists.

National Park Service

The National Park Service was founded as a part of the Department of Interior in 1916. Some areas administered by the National Park Service, however, predate the actual creation of this integrated administrative unit. For example, the first national memorial, Montgomery Monument, was established in 1776. The first national park in the United States, and the world, was established in 1872 when Yellowstone was set aside as a "pleasuring grounds" of unique geographic character for future generations (Lee, 1972). When the National Park Service was established in 1916, its responsibilities were set forth as follows:

> . . . to conserve the scenery and natural and historic objects and the wildlife therein, and to provide for the enjoyment of the same in such a manner and by such a means as will leave them unimpaired for enjoyment for future generations. (Lee, 1972, p. 6)

Through the National Park Service, an incredibly diverse system of parks, monuments, historical sites, and recreation areas has been established for the enjoyment and education of the citizens of the United States. The National Park Service administers more than 360 individual pieces of property. Within its charge, the National Park Service administers national parks (e.g., Yellowstone and Yosemite); national preserves (e.g., Big Cypress and Glacier Bay); national reserves (e.g., City of the Rocks, Idaho); national monuments (e.g., Casa Grande and Death Valley); national historic sites (e.g., Abraham Lincoln's Birthplace and Martin Luther King's Birthplace); national historic parks (e.g., Valley Forge and San Francisco Maritime); national memorials (e.g., Lincoln Memorial and J.F.K. Center for Performing Arts); national recreation areas (e.g., Lake Mead), national seashores (e.g., Assateague Island and Padre Island); national lake shores (e.g., Indiana Dunes); national military parks (e.g., Gettysburg); national wild and scenic riverways (e.g., Rio Grande); national rivers (e.g., Mississippi River); parkways (e.g., Natchez Trace); national battlefield parks (e.g., Manassas); national scenic trails (e.g., Appalachian); international historic sites (e.g., Saint Croix Island); national battlefield sites (e.g., Brices Cross Roads); and others (e.g., National Capital Parks and National Mall).

National Park Service operations are guided by the philosophy of preservation of resources. That philosophy is embedded in a 1918 letter written from Secretary of the Interior, Franklin K. Lane, to the first director of the National Park Service, Stephen T. Mather. Lane, suggesting that a policy be developed to guide the work of the National Park Service, wrote the following:

> . . . the National Parks must be maintained in absolutely unimpaired form for the use of future generations as well as those of our own time; they are set apart for the use, observation, health, and pleasure of the people; and that national interest must dictate all decisions affecting public or private enterprise in the parks. (Albright, Dickenson, and Mott, 1987, p. 18)

The National Park Service still maintains this philosophy of preservation, although this mandate becomes increasingly strained as the parks play host to more and more visitors. In the

Wyoming Parks to Stop Snowmobiles

If you've ever dreamed of riding a snowmobile over hill and dale in Yellowstone or Grand Teton National Park, you've got only this winter and the next two to live out that dream.

After studying the issue since 1993, the National Park Service (NPS) recently decided that individual snowmobile use in those Wyoming parks will be phased out by the winter of 2003–2004. The reason: They're noisy, polluting, and don't fit in with the park's mandate.

The NPS study concluded that "snowmobile use in these parks so adversely affects air quality, wildlife, natural soundscapes, and the enjoyment of other visitors that the resources and values of these parks are impaired." As individual snowmobile use is cut back, the National Park Service will encourage and license more private operators of snow coaches, larger vehicles that carry more people and operate more quietly. Also affected by the decision are the John D. Rockefeller Jr. Memorial Parkway and some adjacent areas.

The rule-making process requires a period of public comment, but this is the plan:

- Winter 2000–2001: No cap on snowmobile use, but most over-snow motorized travel will be prohibited from 11 P.M. to 6 A.M.

- Winter 2001–2002: Snowmobile use numbers would be set for all three park units at levels not to exceed the seven-year average for peak days. Most over-snow motorized travel would be prohibited from 9 P.M. to 8 A.M.
- Winter 2002–2003: The number of snowmobiles admitted at some entrances to Yellowstone would be reduced 50 percent and maintained at existing levels at other entrances. Snowmobiles in Yellowstone would have to be accompanied by an NPS-permitted guide and travel in groups of no more than eleven (including the guide). Snowmobile use would be eliminated in Grand Teton except on one trail and access routes to adjacent properties. Snowcoach operations would be expanded.
- Winter 2003–2004: Most over-snow motorized visitor travel in the three park units would be by NPS-managed snowcoach only.
- The full park service decision can be found on the Web at www.nps.gov/planning.

Source: *The Philadelphia Inquirer* as cited in the *Waterloo-Cedar Falls Courier,* Friday, December 29, 2000.

twenty-first century, park officials will continue to face the challenges of finding the correct balance between preserving national treasures and making them available for the enjoyment of the American people.

In addition to its direct service responsibilities, the National Park Service also administers a number of other federal programs. Many of these responsibilities require a great deal of coordination among many of the land-managing agencies of the federal government. For example, in managing the National Wilderness Preservation System, the National Park Service must work with a number of agencies. The Wilderness Preservation System, created by the 1964 Wilderness Act, defines wilderness in the following way: "A wilderness, in contrast with those areas where man [*sic*] and his works dominate the landscape, is hereby recognized as an area where the earth and community of life are untrammeled by man, where man himself is a visitor and does not remain" (The Wilderness Act, 1964). More than 474 wilderness units total nearly 91 million acres. Special attention to coordinating wilderness policy is needed as wilderness areas face a variety of high-priority issues. Cordell, Bergstrom, Hartmenn, and English (1990) identified the following issues for wilderness in the United States:

Allocation. Issues range from debating the appropriate size of wilderness to what types of ecosystems should be represented within the system.

Nontraditional wilderness. The issue is whether the National Wilderness Preservation System should be expanded to include aquatic and underground wilderness units (e.g., caverns).

Wilderness degradation. Can wilderness areas be protected from such natural phenomena as global environmental problems or human-imposed phenomena such as aircraft overflights or the introduction to exotic plant and animal species?

International cooperation. Can global cooperation be assured to protect areas of global significance such as the Everglades or portions of the Amazon rain forest?

Management coordination. Can management coordination and consistency between agencies with different management philosophies be assured?

Funding and training. Federal land-managing agencies are traditionally understaffed and underfinanced. Can resources for proper management be acquired?

Education. How can wilderness managers instill an outdoor ethic in the general public?

In addition to the Wilderness Preservation System, the National Park System administers the state portion of the Land and Water Conservation Fund, maintains the Nationwide Outdoor

Leisure Line

Hetch Hetchy Valley: The First Environmental Battleground

Within the boundaries of Yosemite National Park lies the Hetch Hetchy Valley, which resembles the more famous Yosemite Valley. In the early part of the twentieth century this valley achieved national prominence as the nation decided the fate of the valley itself. The issue was whether the Tuolumne River should be dammed to create a reservoir to provide the people of San Francisco with drinking water. The valley, with its high walls and narrow entrance, made a perfect site for such a reservoir. As part of the National Park System, however, the valley was supposed to be managed in its natural state. The debate over the fate of the valley was led by two men: Gifford Pinchot and John Muir.

Gifford Pinchot, the first director of the United States Forest Service, was a conservationist who believed that America's resources must be managed to . . . "provide the greatest good for the greatest number in the long run." Pinchot strongly advocated damming the valley to provide water for the people of San Francisco.

John Muir, a famous naturalist and the first president of the Sierra Club, was a preservationist. He believed that the valley should remain in its natural state and should not be dammed.

After more than a ten-year struggle, Congress authorized the building of the reservoir in August, 1913. Most legislators said they appreciated the value of unspoiled nature but did not feel justified in voting against progress.

A footnote to this struggle appeared in 1987 when the Secretary of the Interior, Donald Hodell, proposed the "undamming" of the Tuolomne River and the restoration of the valley to ease the overcrowding being felt in Yosemite Valley. Although this proposal will probably never come about, it does demonstrate the need to be cautious in developing areas that could one day serve as valuable recreational resources.

Recreation Plan, provides parks and recreation technical services, assists states in the development of comprehensive outdoor recreation planning, plans for the National Wild and Scenic River System, administers the National Trails System, and maintains the National Register of Historic Places, Historic American Building Survey, and the Historic American Engineering Record.

U.S. Fish and Wildlife Service

The U.S. Fish and Wildlife Service is responsible for conserving, protecting, and enhancing fish and wildlife and their habitats for the continuing benefit of humanity. The service was preceded by the Bureau of Fisheries established in 1871 and the Bureau of Biological Survey established in 1885. These two bureaus transferred their functions to the Department of the Interior in 1939 and were redesignated as the U.S. Fish and Wildlife Service in 1940. In 1956, the Fish and Wildlife Act created the U.S. Fish and Wildlife Service and established within it two bureaus—the Bureau of Commercial Fisheries and the Bureau of Sports Fisheries and Wildlife.

The U.S. Fish and Wildlife Service is responsible for protecting endangered species, migratory birds, marine mammals, and inland sports fisheries. The Service engages in research activities and is involved in the development of an environmental stewardship ethic. It is a preservation- and conservation-oriented organization that provides leadership in the protection and improvement of land and water resources. In addition, the Service improves and maintains fish and wildlife resources and manages the Wildlife Refuge System. The Wildlife Refuge System of the Forest Service is managed from the standpoint of the conservation ethic. These vitally important areas provide habitat for approximately sixty endangered species as well as hundreds of birds and other animals.

From a recreation perspective, the U.S. Fish and Wildlife Service provides opportunities for hunters and anglers in the form of stable sources of fish and game, as well as providing opportunities for activities such as photography, bird watching, animal tracking, and wildlife study. Interpretive services, increasingly made available at wildlife refuges, are being widely used. Estimates suggest that approximately 27 million visits are made annually to wildlife refuges. The majority of individuals attending these refuges engage in sightseeing activities (65%) as opposed to hunting or fishing (35%). This demand for nonconsumptive forms of recreation within wildlife refuges creates a challenge for wildlife managers. As in the national parks, fish and wildlife managers strive to meet the challenge of tourists by providing more extensive outdoor experiences while protecting the wildlife for which the refuges were created.

Bureau of Indian Affairs

The Bureau of Indian Affairs, created as a part of the War Department in 1924, was later transferred to the Department of the Interior in 1949. Tribal lands in the United States now exceed 50 million acres. The Bureau of Indian Affairs assists native peoples in organizing and implementing programs to assist in their advancement. Often, the development of recreation resources, tourist attractions, and other leisure amenities offer opportunities for economic development.

Estimates show more than 800,000 visitor days spent fishing on Indian reservations and 300,000 visitor days spent hunting on Indian reservations. Total recreation visitations are estimated at over 3 million visitor days per year. Many Indian reservations have unique resources including lakes, rivers, mountains, and other natural areas. A number of tribes operate campgrounds, tourist resorts, hotels, and other recreation facilities that are based on these natural resources.

U.S. Corps of Engineers

The U.S. Corps of Engineers was established in the earliest days of the United States as part of the Continental Army. In the early years, army engineers blazed trails for westward migration and cleared waterways and harbors for commerce. Today the Corps' duties include many of these same tasks as well as flood control, hydropower production, fish and wildlife management, and outdoor recreation. In the mid-1990s, the U.S. Corps of Engineers provided recreation opportunities for over 600 million day use visitors on 461 lakes and other projects (Jensen, 1995).

The U.S. Corps of Engineers manages approximately 11 million acres of land and water, with water resources as its main outdoor recreation resource. Such water resources provide opportunities for sailing, swimming, windsurfing, waterskiing, fishing, scuba diving, and pleasure boating. Many of the lakes developed by the Corps of Engineers for flood control, hydroelectric power, navigation, or other uses also serve outdoor recreation purposes. Eighty percent of these developments are within a fifty-mile radius of Standard Metropolitan Statistical Areas (cities with large populations).

The Corps provides access to the waterways and projects it manages and also provides natural resource amenities to complement them (e.g., campgrounds, marinas, picnic areas, parks, and sanitation facilities). Often, such land and water resources developed by the Corps of Engineers are leased to other public agencies for development and management. An illustration of this type of cooperative arrangement can be seen at Fern Ridge Reservoir, located west of Eugene, Oregon. Fern Ridge Reservoir not only protects the southern part of the Willamette Valley from flooding, but in cooperation with the Corps, has been the focus of several parks and recreation developments undertaken by public and nonprofit private organizations. Specifically, Lane County operates a major park facility in the area, and the Eugene Yacht Club provides a marina facility.

The recreation resource management orientation of the Corps encourages sustained public use, while maintaining the integrity of the natural resources. Recreation resource management, according to the Corps, suggests not only a natural resources ethic, but a people-oriented program of recreation services. The Corps of Engineers has developed a classification system to manage its water resources. This system not only helps protect the natural environment, but also encourages public use of facilities.

> To ensure sound management practices, the Corps has devised a land classification system which designates areas according to the primary use and types of management needed; these designations include natural areas, fish and wildlife management areas, and recreation areas with public facilities. Different types of public facilities and activity areas are separated by distance and natural barriers to maintain the recreation values of the resource, aid in management, and create the least possible conflict with other project purposes such as flood control, hydroelectric power production, navigation, and water supply. (U.S. Corps of Engineers, 1982, p. 6)

This classification system is managed through the employment of a group of professional managers, including people trained not only in biology, engineering, and forestry but also in outdoor recreation.

Tennessee Valley Authority

The Tennessee Valley Authority (TVA) is a public corporation that was established by an act of Congress in 1933. Basically, the TVA is an electric power program that is financially self-sufficient. The TVA constructed a system of dams on the Tennessee River for flood regulation,

Living History Programs

The Homeplace—1850

Living History programs, such as Civil War reenactments and living history farms, provide a first hand experience with the past. This form of educational experience is becoming more popular as a leisure opportunity both for the participants and those who come to watch and interact. Consider The Homeplace program in place at Land Between the Lakes.

Visitors to The Homeplace—1850 can go back in time to a nineteenth-century working farm. Dressed in period clothing, interpreters carry out the daily and seasonal work of the farm. The men can be found tending livestock, working the field, cutting wood, or doing any one of a number of other chores. The women might be preparing a meal on the cook stove or open hearth, spinning, gardening, quilting, or carrying out other domestic activities.

As visitors walk the farm at their leisure, they can see a single-crib cabin, double-crib house, ox barn, springhouse, and other buildings. Each of the buildings was restored and furnished to re-create a mid-nineteenth-century farm of the "between the rivers" region. Even the garden, fields, and patches are planted with crops and vegetables representative of those produced here in the 1850s.

Daily programs vary with the season but typically include activities such as buttermaking, fall plowing, tobacco firing, breadmaking, spinning, dyeing, weaving, and oxen working. During each of the demonstration programs, interpreters explain equipment used, techniques and processes, and importance to the culture.

Throughout the year (March through November), several special events take place at The Homeplace—1850, including an 1850-style wedding and Independence Day celebration. Several festivals, such as the Apple Festival, are also incorporated into the daily lives of the staff at The Homeplace.

Source: Tennessee Valley Authority (n.d.), *A Guide to Land Between the Lakes,* Tennessee Valley Authority, Golden Pond, Kentucky.

navigation, and hydroelectric power. The project also provided opportunities for outdoor recreation. In fact, TVA recognized the potential economic benefits of developing recreation resources in the 1930s and has worked to encourage a wide variety of outdoor recreation facilities and opportunities in the Tennessee Valley.

TVA projects have resulted in the creation of more than 500,000 acres of water resources and 11,000 miles of shoreline. These resources attract more than 70 million visitors for recreation purposes each year. The TVA emphasizes access to its resources and, as a result, features 500 public access points and more than 120 state, county, and municipal parks on the shores of TVA lakes, along with numerous private resorts, marinas, and boating facilities. The TVA has set aside a large number of natural areas for ecological study and annually conducts research and development programs in forestry, fish and game, and watershed protection.

In the western part of Kentucky and Tennessee, the TVA operates a national demonstration program known as the Land Between the Lakes. This program combines TVA's interest in outdoor recreation, environmental education, and natural resource management. The Land Between the Lakes program is situated between two of the largest human-made reservoirs in the United States—Lake Kentucky and Lake Barkley. This area consists of 170,000 acres of land, and the reservoirs include about 300 miles of shoreline.

The Land Between the Lakes program uses a multiple-use concept to promote both recreational and educational values. It is being developed as a public use area, where recreation can be enjoyed and people can gain a greater appreciation of the need for conservation principles and values. Activities in the Land Between the Lakes program include camping, fishing, hiking, horseback riding, hunting, nature study, and environmental education. Facilities include campsites, swimming areas, boat ramps, sanitation facilities, trails, an environmental education center, and an 1850s living history farm. In 1991, Land Between the Lakes was named the world's 300th biosphere reserve as part of the United Nations Educational, Scientific, and Cultural Organization's Man and the Biosphere program.

Bureau of Reclamation

In 1902, Congress passed the Reclamation Act, authorizing the Secretary of the Interior to establish a reclamation program to supply water to the semiarid lands of seventeen contiguous states in the western portion of the United States. As a result of this action, the Reclamation Service was established within the U.S. Geological Survey. Later, separated from that unit, in 1923 it was renamed the Bureau of Reclamation. The growth of the Bureau of Reclamation was directly tied to the expansion of population in the western United States. As the population grew in the West, so did the need for water resources. The Bureau's mission also expanded, and today it is not only responsible for providing water resources but also for the generation of hydroelectric power, river regulation, flood control, outdoor recreation, and the enhancement and management of fish and wildlife habitats.

Today, "the mission of the Bureau of Reclamation is to manage, develop, and protect water and related resources in an environmental and economically sound manner in the interest of the American public. The agency's program emphasis is on water conservation and reuse, environmental protection and restoration, and expansion of its customer base beyond agricultural interests to include rural and urban water users, Native American tribes, the environmental community, and recreationists." (Bureau of Reclamation, 2001)

The Bureau of Reclamation operates more than 600 reservoirs and dams, nearly sixteen miles of canals and some fifty-eight hydroelectric power plants in seventeen western states. Although, recreation pursuits were not an original part of the mission of the Bureau of Reclamation, in 1965 the Federal Water Projects Recreation Act provided statutory authority for the planning and construction of recreation areas and facilities. The majority of recreation areas within the land area of the Bureau of Reclamation are managed, however, by other governmental agencies such as the National Park Service, U.S. Forest Service, and local, state, or county government agencies. These agencies provide a variety of predominantly water-based recreational opportunities. Support facilities often include campsites, picnic areas, sightseeing areas, sanitation facilities, marinas, and boat ramps. More than 80 million visitors participate in water-based recreation activities at the more than 300 reservoirs developed by Bureau of Reclamation. Almost 200 of these recreation areas are managed by nonfederal entities such as state and county park and recreation systems. Still others are managed by federal agencies including the National Park Service and the U.S. Forest Service. The Bureau of Reclamation also seeks partnerships with nonprofit organizations to sponsor events and works with concessionaires to operate facilities and services such as marinas, campgrounds, swimming beaches, and golf courses.

Veterans' Administration

The Veterans' Administration, established by executive order in 1930, operates 150 medical centers, 39 domiciliaries, 391 outpatient community and outreach clinics, and 131 nursing home care units. The Veterans' Administration initiated the idea of recreation therapy and is the largest employer of recreation therapists in the federal government. Recreation therapists in Veterans' Administration hospitals use a variety of ways to treat individuals who are physically, mentally, emotionally, or socially ill or disabled. The Veterans' Administration uses recreation therapy as a means to improve the quality of participants' lives and to help facilitate their reentry into the community.

Programs focus on meeting the needs of a variety of veteran patient population groups, including those involved in cardiac rehabilitation, spinal cord injuries, drug and alcohol abuse, general medical and surgical conditions, chronic illness, psychiatrics, and geriatrics. Activities offered as a part of a typical recreation therapy program include games, sports, arts and crafts, music therapy, dance therapy, psychodrama, outdoor recreation, social activities, special events, leisure counseling, and community reentry.

In describing the functions of a recreation therapist, the Veterans' Administration notes several key job roles, including the following:

1. *Rehabilitation.* The recreation therapist functions as a member of the medical team, has knowledge of the illness and problems of the physically, mentally, emotionally, and developmentally disabled and the geriatric patient; works with the team and prepares the patient for community reentry.
2. *Education.* The therapist provides education and counseling in coping with leisure time, particularly with regard to a patient returning to life in the community.
3. *Implementation.* Working with patients to develop an individualized treatment plan, the recreation therapist implements and organizes this plan, modifying activities when appropriate, and evaluates the success of a program for each individual patient.

In describing the treatment program of the Veterans' Administration Medical Center in Portland, Oregon, the Medical Center Director writes,

Programs shall provide professional, rehabilitative, educational, and self-directed participation programs and services. These programs and services will enable hospitalized veterans to eliminate barriers to leisure, develop leisure skills and attitudes, and optimize leisure involvement to enhance the veterans' quality of life in the hospital and the community. . . . The primary function of recreation therapists shall be the assessment, interdisciplinary treatment planning, treatment intervention, and program implementation, and evaluation of patients. (Bell, 1984, p. 9)

The Veterans' Administration provides services to nearly 2.5 million individuals registering 27.5 million visits annually. The recreation therapy function has been transformed from its early image of diversionary fun and games to one of serious therapy and treatment.

Morale, Welfare, and Recreation Services, U.S. Armed Forces

The United States military has control over large preserves of land that are used for recreation purposes for military personnel and their dependents. Each branch of the armed services—the U.S. Army, the U.S. Air Force, the U.S. Marine Corps, and the U.S. Navy—have well-developed recreation areas, facilities, and programs. Furthermore, some of these areas and facilities are open to the public to pursue recreational interests. Each branch of the services refers to its units in a slightly different way. For example, the U.S. Marine Corps refers to its units as "Community Services," the U.S. Navy refers to its organizations as "Morale, Welfare, and Recreation Departments," the U.S. Army refers to its units as "Community and Family Support" and the U.S. Air Force refers to its units as "Service Squadrons." In this section we refer to all these units collectively as Morale, Welfare, and Recreation.

Morale, Welfare, and Recreation (MWR) activities provided by various branches of the armed forces offer a variety of social, recreational, and welfare activities, programs, and services. Morale, Welfare, and Recreation services can include management of such facilities as arts and crafts centers, bowling centers, entertainment programs, golf courses, libraries, outdoor recreation programs, multipurpose recreation centers, sport programs, and child and youth activities. MWR services also include the management of clubs, newspapers, museums, skeet and trap ranges, skating rinks, gift shops, snack bars, and music and theater programs. Military bases may be viewed as small American communities that offer all the recreation amenities of a small city in the United States.

Policies and procedures for the implementation of MWR programs vary by service (Army, Marines, Navy, or Air force). For example, the U.S. Navy's policy is designed to promote/provide a well-rounded recreation program to ensure the mental and physical well-being of its personnel. The recreation program of the navy is designed to assist in attaining and sustaining a high level of morale among navy personnel and their families. The navy does not use an absolute set of standards for each installation's recreation programs. On the other hand, the U.S. Army is very specific in its written policies and procedures for operating MWR programs and services. U.S. Army programs are operated, maintained, and funded as an integral part of the quality of life of the Department of Army. Objectives of the Army MWR program follow:

1. Maintain among personnel a high level of esprit de corps, job proficiency, military effectiveness, and educational attainment.
2. Promote and maintain the mental and physical fitness and well-being of Department of Army personnel, primarily active duty personnel.
3. Encourage Department of Army personnel to use their time constructively and creatively by taking part in programs that help develop and maintain motivation, talent, and skills that will help them discharge their duties as responsible citizens.
4. Aid in recruitment and retention by making service with the army an attractive career.
5. Assist military personnel in adjusting from civilian life to the military environment upon entry into the service.
6. Assist in providing a community support environment to Department of Army personnel and their families. This is most important when military sponsors are on unaccompanied tours or maneuvers or involved in armed conflicts.
7. Create a vital self-sustaining military community.
8. Provide programs that appeal to soldiers as members of their units.
9. Increase combat readiness and effectiveness (Department of the Army, 1988).

The organizational chart presented in figure 9.7 represents the services and staffing patterns of the Morale, Welfare, and Recreation Department, U.S. Naval Fleet Activities, Yokosuka, Japan. The organizational chart presents the various activities provided by this unit. They range from provision of a newspaper, *The Seahawk,* to a myriad of recreation services including clubs, child support, community centers, tours and ticketing, youth activities, hobby clubs, fitness programs, bowling, aquatic services, and others.

National Endowment for the Arts

The arts play an important part in the leisure domain. The National Endowment for the Arts has as a goal, the fostering of professional excellence for the arts in the United States. The endowment has been established to help nurture and sustain the arts and develop a climate in which the arts may flourish. The goals of the National Endowment for the Arts are the following:

1. To foster individual creativity and excellence;
2. To foster institutional creativity and excellence;

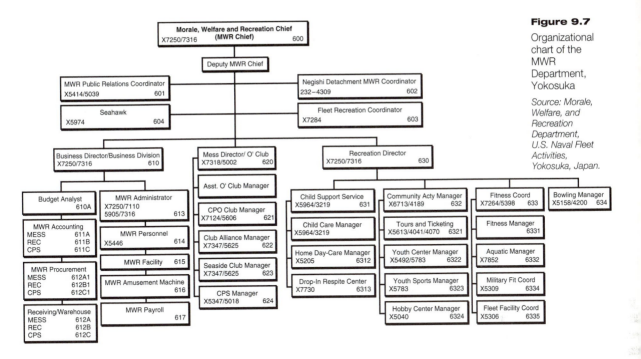

Figure 9.7

Organizational chart of the MWR Department, Yokosuka

Source: Morale, Welfare, and Recreation Department, U.S. Naval Fleet Activities, Yokosuka, Japan.

3. To preserve the artistic birthright of present and future generations of Americans by supporting survival of the best of all art forms that reflect the American heritage in its full range of ethnic and cultural diversity;

4. To ensure that all Americans have a true opportunity to make an informed, educated choice to have the arts of high quality touch their lives; and

5. To provide leadership on behalf of the arts.

The majority of funds spent by this agency provide endowments to specific projects, artists, programs, and museums. The funds for the National Endowment have grown rapidly in the last several decades. In 1997, the National Endowment for the Arts disbursed more than $98.4 million to 1,098 projects (U.S. Bureau of Census, 1999). This is a drastic reduction when compared with 1980 when $188 million was disbursed to 5,500 projects with the largest amount coming between 1995 and 1996. These funds have made an important contribution to the arts in the United States by bringing an awareness to Americans of the importance of art in their lives.

National Endowment for the Humanities

This independent agency, established by Congress in 1965, supports research, education, and public programs in the humanities. The term *humanities* refers to the study of language; linguistics; literature; history; jurisprudence; philosophy; archaeology; comparative religion; ethics; the history, criticism, and theory of the arts; and the portions of the social sciences that have humanistic content. The Endowment provides grants to help increase understanding and appreciation of the humanities. In 1997, the National Endowment for the Humanities had $94 million available to disburse and awarded 900 grants. Again, when compared with 1980 this is a dramatic reduction in projects supported where $186 million was previously available and supported over 2,900 projects. Many of the projects supported by the endowment are leisure related, including museums, libraries, public agencies, and nonprofit organizations.

Types of Federal Agencies: Canada

The federal government in Canada has addressed the need to allocate resources at the federal level to enable the development and management of recreation and leisure resources. A number of federal agencies directly organize and implement services related to recreation. Searle and Brayley (2000) have written that there are numerous federal departments that have direct or indirect responsibilities for promoting concerns related to recreation, leisure, and/or the environment. Among these are Health Canada (Fitness, Active Living), Canadian Heritage (Parks Canada, Sports Canada, CBC, National Arts Centre, National Gallery of Canada, National Museum of Science and Technology, Canadian Museum of Nature, Telefilm Canada, Canadian Council for the Arts, National Film Board, Canadian Radio-Television and Telecommunications Commission), Industry of Canada, the Department of External Affairs (e.g., international youth exchanges), and Natural Resources Canada (Canadian Forest Service). We briefly highlight three units—Sports Canada, Parks Canada, Health Canada, —and the Canadian Tourism Commission.

Sports Canada

A branch of the Department of Canadian Heritage, Sports Canada is focused on supporting the achievement of high-performance excellence and the development of the Canadian sport system. As such, Sports Canada is dedicated to strengthening the unique contribution that sport makes to Canadian identity, culture, and society. Sports Canada has two divisions. One is involved in the organization of sport programs and the other in the implementation of sport policy. Some of the objectives of Sports Canada include the following:

- *High-performance athletes and coaches.* Enhance the ability of Canadian athletes to excel at the highest international levels through fair and ethical means.
- *Sport system development.* Work with key partners to enhance coordination and integration to advance the Canadian sport system.
- *Strategic positioning.* Advance the broader federal government objectives through sport, position sport in the federal government agenda, and promote the contribution of sport to Canadian society.
- *Access and equity.* Increase access and equity in sport for targeted underrepresented groups.

Sports Canada operates several programs including: (1) National Sport Centres; (2) National Sport Organization and Multi-Sport/Multi-Service Organization Support Program; (3) Athlete Assistance Program; (4) Hosting Support Programs; (5) Domestic Sport Program; and (6) Canada's Doping Control Program. For example, Sports Canada operates several national sport centers including ones operating in Calgary, Winnipeg, Montreal, Victoria, Vancouver, Toronto, and in the Atlantic region. Social policy related to sport has been promulgated in the areas of women and sport, doping, language, and, in general, a national policy for the country dealing with the topic of sport.

Statistics Canada has reported the following:

- The most popular sports in Canada are hockey, downhill skiing, and swimming.
- 4.4 million individuals participate regularly in organized or club sports.

- 3.2 million individuals participate regularly in competition or tournament sports.
- 11 million individuals participate regularly in organized school sports.
- 3.2 million individuals belong to an amateur sport club or organization.
- 840,000 individuals serve as amateur sport coaches.
- 630,000 individuals serve as amateur sport umpires or referees.
- 1.9 million individuals serve as amateur sport volunteers.
- British Columbia (53%) and Quebec (49%) have the largest regional amateur sport participation rates among Canadians aged 15 years or more, while Newfoundland (36%) has the lowest.
- The greater the Canadian household income and educational attainment, the greater the amateur sport participation rates.
- The participation of parents in amateur sport increases the likelihood that their children will also participate. Amateur sport participation among youth increases the likelihood that they will continue to participate as adults. (Statistics Canada, 1999)

Parks Canada

Parks Canada has a broad mandate that includes responsibility for national historic sites, federal heritage buildings, heritage railway stations, national marine conservation areas, world heritage sites, heritage river systems, biosphere reserves, Ramsar sites, and, of course, the extensive national park system (Searle and Brayley, 2000). Canada's national park system began with the preservation of Banff National Park in Alberta in 1887. The dedication clause for the Act setting aside this park (known as the Rocky Mountains Park Act) states the following:

> The said tract of land is hereby reserved and set apart as a public park and pleasuring ground for benefit, advantage, and enjoyment of the people of Canada, subject to the provisions of this Act and of the regulations herein mentioned, and shall be known as the Rocky Mountains Park of Canada. (Lothian, 1977, p. 6)

In 1887, the Canadian Pacific Railway began construction on Banff Springs Hotel. The hotel and a bath house, containing two plunge baths and ten tubs supplied with water from nearby hot springs, were completed and opened in 1888. Canadian park historian, W. Lothian, writes, "Canada's first national park owed its creation to farsighted legislators who realized that the natural phenomenon in the midst of scenic magnificence should be preserved and administered as a public rather than private enterprise" (Lothian, 1977, p. 1).

The park system is organized into thirty-nine natural regions. Each region displays a particular combination of Canada's geography, landforms, wildlife, and vegetation (Searle and Brayley, 2000). Currently there are thirty-nine national parks and national park reserves (see table 9.4). Current plans call for national parks in each of the regions; to complete this plan, fourteen new additional areas will need to be established. When the system is completed, it will cover slightly more than 3% of Canada's land mass area.

The park system is extremely diverse, reflecting the character and nature of Canada. A majority of the parks, however, are located in the western portion of Canada. For example, Northern Yukon National Park is a wilderness refuge for caribou and other wildlife. The national park system provides numerous opportunities for leisure activities and attracts millions of visitors on a year-round basis. Some of the activities in which visitors participate include camping, sightseeing, hiking, mountain climbing, swimming, fishing, the study of natural history, skiing, and snow shoeing (see figure 9.8).

TABLE

9.4   CANADIAN NATIONAL PARKS, NATIONAL PARK RESERVES, AND NATIONAL MARINE CONSERVATION AREAS

Parks, Reserves, and Conservation Areas	Description
Aulavik National Park	Over 12,000 km² of arctic wilderness on Banks Island
Auyuittuq National Park	Baffin Island landscapes containing northern extremity of Canadian Shield
Banff National Park	UNESCO World Heritage Site and Canada's first National Park (1885)
Bruce Peninsula National Park	Landscapes including the northern end of the Niagara Escarpment
Cape Breton Highlands National Park	Home to Cabot Trail, a land blessed with spectacular cliffs
Elk Island National Park	Alberta plains oasis for rare and endangered species
Ellesmere Island National Park	Some of the most remote, fragile, rugged, and northerly lands in North America
Fathom Five National Marine Park	The spectacular underwater of the Niagara escarpment in Georgian Bay
Forillon National Park	The "Jewel of the Gaspé" where land meets sea
Fundy National Park	Atlantic's sanctuary with world's highest tides
Georgian Bay Islands National Park	Captivating islands representing Lake Huron's landscape
Glacier National Park	British Columbia's lush interior rainforest and permanent glaciers
Grasslands National Park	Saskatchewan's rare prairie grasses, dinosaur fossils, and badlands
Gros Morne National Park	UNESCO World Heritage Site amid Newfoundland's wild natural beauty
Gwaii Haanas National Marine Conservation Area Reserve	Haïda culture and coastal rainforest of the Queen Charlotte Islands
Gwaii Haanas National Park Reserve	This rich natural and cultural environment protects 138 of the Queen Charlotte Islands
Ivvavik National Park	Calving ground for the porcupine caribou herd
Jasper National Park	UNESCO World Heritage Site and glacial jewel of the Rockies
Kejimkujik National Park	Nova Scotia's inland of historic canoe routes and portages
Kluane National Park and Reserve	Yukon's UNESCO World Heritage Site contains Canada's highest peak
Kootenay National Park	UNESCO World Heritage Site featuring the famous Radium Hot Springs
Kouchibouguac National Park	Intricate Acadian blend of coastal and inland habitats
La Mauricie National Park	Lakes winding through forested hills for canoe and portage activities
Mingan Archipelago National Park	A reserve consisting of a string of islands carved out by wind and sea
Mount Revelstoke National Park	Rainforest of 1,000-year-old cedars and spectacular mountains
Nahanni National Park Reserve	Northwest Territories' UNESCO World Heritage Site
Pacific Rim National Park Reserve	Pacific Coast Mountains make up this marine and forest environment
Point Pelee National Park	Most southern point in Canada
Prince Albert National Park	Protects slice of northern coniferous forest and wildlife
Prince Edward Island National Park	A protected area with spectacular coast
Pukaskwa National Park	Canadian Shield's ancient landscape on Lake Superior's north shore
Quttinirpaaq National Park	Some of the most remote, fragile, rugged, and northerly lands in North America
Riding Mountain National Park	Protected "island" area in the Manitoba Escarpment
Saguenay—St. Lawrence Marine Park	A rich diversity of marine life: whales, seals, plants, and birds of all kinds
Sirmilik National Park	Northern Baffin Island landscapes containing Eastern Arctic Lowlands and Lancaster Sound
St. Lawrence Islands National Park	Canada's smallest national park located in Ontario
Terra Nova National Park	Remnants of Eastern Newfoundland's Ancient Appalachian Mountains

TABLE

9.4   CONTINUED

Parks, Reserves, and Conservation Areas	Description
Tuktut Nogait National Park	Calving ground for the Bluenose caribou herd
Vuntut National Park	Northern Yukon's unique non-glaciated landscape
Wapusk National Park	One of the largest polar bear denning areas in the world
Waterton Lakes National Park	International Peace Park; where the Rocky Mountains meet the prairie
Wood Buffalo National Park	UNESCO World Heritage Site larger than Switzerland, with herds of bisons
Yoho National Park	UNESCO World Heritage Site in the Rocky Mountains

Source: Data from http://parkscanada.pch.gc.ca/parks/alphap2e.htm

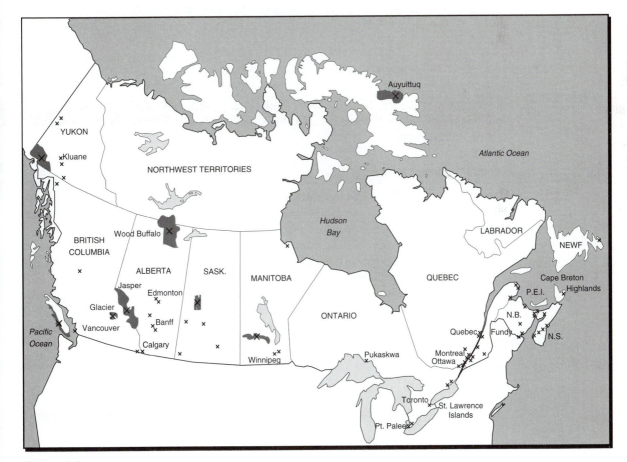

Figure 9.8

Map of the Canadian national park system, including national parks and historical parks

Source: Parks Canada Information Division.

Parks Canada administers more than 100 historical sites and over 1,000 plaques and monuments at significant sites. Canada's first designated historic park, Fort Anne in Nova Scotia, was established in 1917. Sites selected for designation are done so on the basis of their cultural, social, political, economic, military, or architectural importance. For example, some historical sites in Newfoundland are based at ancient Indian burial grounds. Other historical sites reflect the early exploration of Canada and its explorers' struggles with the land. In addition, Parks Canada also administers the country's heritage river system.

The Canadian Heritage River System (CHRS) is a joint program between the federal government and several provinces and territories. This program provides national recognition for many of Canada's scenic and important rivers. The program helps ensure the "long-term management and preservation of their national, historical, and recreational values" (Searle and Brayley, 2000, p. 199). Some examples of protected rivers included the Artic Red River, the Churchill River, and the St. Croix River. Parks Canada is involved in the management of migratory bird sanctuaries and national wildlife areas. The Canadian Wildlife Act provides for the management of such areas with compatible other uses.

Parks Canada also manages heritage canals and rivers. Canals today, maintained as examples of early engineering technology in Canada, are often used for recreational purposes as well. The Rideau Canal, built in 1832 to connect Ottawa and Kingston, is preserved today as a scenic waterway. Heritage rivers include those waterways that are free flowing and maintained in that state.

The capital of Canada, Ottawa, is administered by the National Capital Parks Commission. This body has an important role in conserving and developing space for outdoor recreation in and around the Ottawa-Hull metropolitan area. Primarily, the National Capital Parks Commission manages a large park, Gatineau Park (similar to a national park), a system of scenic driveways, bike paths, and a greenbelt. It also maintains the longest outdoor skating rink in the world on Rideau Canal.

Health Canada

In 1961, the Canadian federal governments involvement in the area of fitness and sport was established with the passage of the Fitness and Amateur Sport Act. This act was directed toward promoting fitness and amateur sport in Canada and provided for the authority of the Ministry to enter into grants and provincial cost sharing for the creation of the National Advisory Council on Fitness and Amateur Sport. In June 1993, responsibilities of Sports Canada were transferred to the Department of Canadian Heritage.

Health Canada is strongly responsible for promoting fitness and what is known as active living. Its basic mission is to encourage the health of Canadians through promotion and prevention activities; it supports the health system through research (see www.hc-sc.gc.ca/). This unit of government has identified several specific roles as follows:

- Promote policy development on issues related to health
- Encourage research and information dissemination, especially as it relates to health promotion and prevention
- Develop collaborative activities with other governmental, nongovernmental organizations, and businesses
- Promote and encourage active living

Searle and Brayley (2000) have noted that in this latter role, Health Canada has a strong commitment to encouraging Canadians to be fit and physically active. As such, Health Canada hopes to achieve the following goals as it relates to active living: (1) to encourage and assist all Canadians to adopt active living through enhanced awareness about the benefits and opportunities of being physically active; (2) to influence the provision of positive social and physical environments and opportunities that facilitate the integration of physical activity into daily life, and that are accessible to and equitable for all Canadians, and (3) to establish partnerships with other agencies across levels and sectors and encourage collaborative action for active living in Canada. (see www.hc-sc.gc.ca/)

Active Living Canada   Active Living Canada (ACL) is a nonprofit organization which receives much of its funding from Health Canada. Its board of directors is made up of individuals from many health, fitness, and recreation organizations throughout the country. These organizations work in partnership collaborating to promote healthy active lifestyles. For example, Active Living Canada works to build partnerships among agencies and institutions that are interested in promoting health and active living. The Coalition for Active Living is one such group of organizations working together to promote healthy, active living among all Canadians, enhance quality of life, and reduce the risk of illness associated with sedentary lifestyles. Some of the organizations participating in this are found in table 9.5.

TABLE

9.5   CANADIAN COALITION FOR ACTIVE LIVING PARTNERS

Agency	Description
Active Living Alliance for Canadians with a Disability	Promotes inclusion and active living for Canadians with a disability.
Active Living Coalition for Older Adults	Encourages older Canadians to maintain and enhance their well-being and independence through a lifestyle that embraces daily physical activities.
Active Ontario	Supports the work of physical activity leaders in Ontario.
Alberta Community Development	Plays an important role in assisting communities, whether they are places or groups of citizens sharing a common goal, in achieving a high quality of life for Albertans.
Canadian Association for the Advancement of Women and Sport and Physical Activity	Works in partnership with Sports Canada and with Canada's sport and active living communities to achieve gender equity in the sport community.
Canadian Fitness and Lifestyle Research Institute	Enhances the well-being of Canadians through research and communication of information about physically active lifestyles to the public and private sectors.
Canadian Intramural Recreation Association	Mission is to encourage, promote, and develop active living, healthy lifestyles, and personal growth through intramural and recreation programs within the educational community.
Canadian Nurses Association	Advances the quality of nursing in the interest of the public. Toward this end, it promotes high standards of practice, education, research, and administration.
Canadian Parks/Recreation Association	Dedicated to the enhancement of quality community leisure services, lifestyles, and environment for all Canadians through the efforts of its members and allies in advocacy, education, information sharing, policy development, and national initiatives.

—continued

9.5 CONCLUDED

Agency	Description
Canadian Recreational Canoeing Association	Coordinates the efforts of ten provincial and three territorial associations, and 2.3 million recreational paddlers involved in noncompetitive canoeing and kayaking.
Canadian Society for Exercise Physiology	Promotes the generation, synthesis, transfer, and application of knowledge and research related to exercise physiology (encompassing physical activity, fitness, health, and human performance).
Coaching Association of Canada	A not-for-profit organization with the mission to establish education, training, and ethical standards for coaches in Canada.
College of Family Physicians of Canada	The national medical association, which supports family physicians in providing high-quality health care to their patients.
Go for Green	Encourages Canadians to pursue healthy, outdoor physical activities that protect, enhance, or restore the environment.
Health Work and Wellness Institute of Canada	Created to promote the concept of workplace wellness.
Heart and Stroke Foundation of Canada	Mission is to further the study, prevention, and reduction of disability and death from heart disease and stroke through research, education, and the promotion of healthy lifestyles.
Lifesaving Society	Serves all Canadians by providing information and skills that promote safety in, on, and around water.
National Fitness Leadership Advisory Council	NFLAC is a Canadian collective/partnership dedicated to collaboratively developing, promoting, and recognizing the use of national guidelines and standards for fitness leadership and certification, leading to improved quality and safety.
ParticipACTION	Aim is to provide practical and authoritative advice, resources, and interactive components to encourage healthy physically active lifestyles.
Recreation and Parks Association of the Yukon	A group of individuals committed to empowering Yukon's people and their communities to adopt healthy lifestyles.
Recreation Connections Manitoba	Shares the benefits of recreation and is dedicated to the development and support of recreation professionals, practitioners, and volunteers who enhance the health and wellness of all Manitobans.
Recreation Nova Scotia	Promotes the values and benefits of recreation and leisure.
Régie régionale de la santé et des services sociaux de la Montérégie	RRSSSM contribut à l'amélioration de l'état de santé et de bien-être des Montérégiens en leur assurant l'accessibilité et la qualité des services tout en tenant compte des particularités locales et régionales de l'ensemble de son territoire.
Region of Ottawa-Carleton Health Department	Works to protect an individual's health through information and services.
Saskatoon District Health	One of Canada's few comprehensive, fully integrated health service networks.
YWCA of/du Canada	A movement of women, girls, and their families in all of Canada's cultural, racial, religious, and ethnic diversity.

Source: http://parkscanada.pch.gc.ca/parks/alphap2e.htm

Canadian Tourism Commission

The Canadian Tourism Commission (CTC) was established in 1995. The purpose of this organization is to deliver world-class culture and leisure experiences on a year-round basis while preserving Canada's clean, safe, and natural environments. The CTC was established to take advantage of the growth of tourism throughout the world. Organized as a public/private partnership, the CTC is industry driven and market focused. The Commission is dedicated to promoting the tourism industry by:

- marketing Canada as a desirable travel destination, and
- providing timely and accurate information to the Canadian tourism industry in its decision making.

The government of Canada funds the CTC. Funds provided by the government are matched by private industry. As Searle and Brayley (2000, p. 86) note, "the main thrusts of the Commission are to position Canada as a desirable destination to both international and domestic travelers, and to provide timely and accurate information to the tourism industry to assist in decision making." Table 9.6 presents information regarding tourists' expenditures in Canada.

TABLE

9.6 EXPENDITURES BY VISITORS TO CANADA, TOP FIFTEEN COUNTRIES OF ORIGIN

Country of Origin	Spending in Canada (C$ millions)	Trips	Nights Spent (Thousands)
United States	7,149	15,180	58,471
United Kingdom	883	780	8,725
Japan	572	516	3,192
Germany	481	392	5,158
France	465	414	4,895
Taiwan	227	155	2,628
Australia	194	152	1,835
Switzerland	141	101	1,299
South Korea	136	99	819
Mexico	130	127	1,126
Hong Kong	128	134	1,198
Netherlands	125	121	1,609
Italy	108	111	1,257
Israel	58	62	569
India	47	62	808

Source: Statistics Canada. 1999. *Culture, Tourism and the Centre for Education Statistics.*

Challenges for the Future

Federal agencies in Canada and the United States face many challenges. Decade by decade, the demand for services provided by the federal government in this area has increased dramatically. Massive governmental programs will positively impact upon the environment and increase outdoor recreation resources. The future holds numerous challenges, however. They include the following:

Decrease in the level of funding. The federal funding in the United States is a challenge in terms of continued provision of services. Agencies must find innovative strategies to finance services or they will be forced to cut back. In addition, more interagency coordination will be required to determine the most appropriate and cost-effective use of federal resources. As a result, partnerships are being encouraged on a federal level. For example, the National Park Service has more than 400 agreements with private businesses, nonprofit groups, individuals, and other public bodies (PCAO, 1987). Land trusts can help government agencies on all levels to protect lands with open space, recreation, or ecological significance. According to the PCAO, in 1959 just over fifty land trusts were established in twenty-six states. "In 1985, a total of 535 local land trusts have been instrumental in preserving over 700,000 acres of our natural heritage" (p. 190). These efforts must be encouraged and expanded to create more entrepreneurial activities.

Continue the Land and Water Conservation Fund. The success of the Land and Water Fund has been documented in this chapter. Efforts must be made to sustain such a trust for the acquisition and development of outdoor recreation resources. In addition to land acquisition and development, funds for maintaining existing resources and facilities must be assured.

Competition over the use of resources. There is competition for the same resources. Environmental concerns often conflict directly with the need for economic development. Even various types of recreation use create conflict (e.g., snowmobilers often conflict with cross country skiers). With new technology generating new outdoor pursuits such as windsurfing, these conflicts will increase. Resolution of these conflicts will become a responsibility of federal agencies and the courts.

Overuse of resources. The demand for selected outdoor recreation resources challenges basic preservation-conservation precepts. There is a need to find strategies to control use of resources to ensure their preservation for future generations.

Lack of consistency in the political environment. The federal government must develop consistency in its approach to managing the environment on a long-term basis. Changing political conditions often challenge long-term strategies. A strong environmental ethic needs to become a part of the political agenda in America and Canada. This includes educating people about the need for such an agenda. In many ways urban dwellers have lost their connection with the land. They have a strong idea that they want to preserve land, yet they are also the biggest consumers in the world. For example, American urbanites want to preserve free-flowing rivers, but they also like to water their lawns, wash their cars, and clean the driveway. In many ways Americans have created a paradox of preservation—people want to both preserve and use the resources as they wish. Resource managers are being asked to provide both resources (e.g., timber, oil, minerals, and grazing land) and amenities (e.g., clean air and water, places for outdoor recreation, wildlife refuges, and wilderness areas). Collectively, U.S. citizens and Canadians must develop a sustainable lifestyle both for themselves and for the millions of people still aspiring to a better way of life in developing countries.

Consumptive vs. nonconsumptive recreation pursuits. In light of the paradox of preservation, what kind of activities should recreational professionals provide for individuals? Dustin, in his article, "Recreational Limits in a World of Ethics" (1984), raises the question: "Should park and recreation professionals serve popular tastes for recreation or should they try to elevate them?" To Dustin the answer is clear: "We have a responsibility not only to educate recreationists but to encourage them to recreate in a way that reflects a more sensitive, a more caring attitude toward the earth" (p. 50). As recreational professionals face global environmental problems and the overuse of resources, the question of how to elevate recreation tastes without impeding personal freedom will become even more critical.

Accessibility issues. The Americans with Disabilities Act forces federal managers to make accessibility for people with disabilities a priority. The accessibility issue continues to be a financial strain for many federal managers.

These challenges and others stretch the mental, physical, and financial resources of future managers of federal agencies. The future of federally managed leisure programs and services hinges upon the ability of present and future managers to effectively resolve these and other emerging concerns.

Summary

The federal governments in both the United States and Canada play a vital role in the provision of parks, recreation, leisure, and cultural services. Both Canada and the United States have unique natural areas that provide opportunities for leisure services, especially outdoor recreation. Both countries are large geographically and have small populations compared with their land mass. As a result, they have had the opportunity to set aside large tracts of land for preservation and conservation purposes.

Numerous federal agencies in the United States provide parks, recreation, and leisure services. Some of the larger agencies are the U.S. Forest Service, the National Park Service, the Bureau of Land Management, the U.S. Fish and Wildlife Service, the U.S. Corps of Engineers, the Bureau of Reclamation, and the Tennessee Valley Authority. These agencies manage the land and water resources that fall within public domain. Other federal agencies that provide people-oriented recreation programs include the Veterans' Administration, the *U.S. Armed Forces,* the National Endowment for the Arts, and the National Endowment for the Humanities.

In Canada, agencies that focus their attention on the provision of parks, recreation, and leisure services include ones provided by several ministries and units within these jurisdictions. Some of the more prominent ones include Health Canada (Fitness, Active Living), Canadian Heritage (Parks Canada, Sports Canada, CBC, National Arts Centre, National Gallery of Canada, National Museum of Science and Technology, Canadian Museum of Nature, Telefilm Canada, Canadian Council for the Arts, National Film Board, Canadian Radio-Television and Telecommunications Commission), Industry of Canada, The Department of External Affairs (e.g., international youth exchanges), and Natural Resources Canada (Canadian Forest Service). We briefly highlighted three units, Sports Canada, and Parks Canada, Health Canada, and the Canadian Tourism Commission. These agencies administer a vast array of land and water resources, historical and cultural sites, and programs that emphasize sport and active healthy living.

Discussion Questions

1. What are the goals and functions of federal agencies?
2. Explain the fiscal resource base of federal agencies. What is the difference between appropriated and nonappropriated funds?

3. Discuss what you feel is the customer orientation of employees working for the federal government.
4. Identify three presidential commissions that have influenced the development of outdoor recreation resources in the United States.
5. Identify five federal agencies in the United States providing outdoor recreation services.
6. What is the difference between the philosophy of conservation and the philosophy of preservation?
7. What does multiple-use of resources imply? How does this affect the management of land and water resources managed by the federal government?
8. Discuss the role of federal agencies in Canada in providing recreation, parks, and leisure services.
9. Identify and discuss future challenges to the management of federal land and water agencies in the United States and Canada.
10. Contact a federal agency mentioned in this chapter to determine its current operating and capital budget, as well as current status of services.

References

Albright, H., R. Dickenson, and W. Mott. 1987. *National Park Service: The Story Behind the Scenery.* Las Vegas, NV: K.C. Publications.

Bell, B. 1984. *Medical Center Memorandum 117* (August 28), 9.

Bureau of Land Management. 1988. *Recreation 2000: BLM National Outdoor Strategy.* Washington, DC: U.S. Government Printing Office.

Bureau of Reclamation. 2001. www.usbr.gov/main/what/index.html

Cordell, H., L. Bergstrom, L. Hartmenn, and D. English. 1990. *An Analysis of the Outdoor Recreation and Wilderness Situation in the United States: 1989–2040.* Fort Collins, CO: U.S. Department of Agriculture Forest Service General Technical Report.

Department of the Army. 1988. *The Administration of Army Morale, Welfare, and Recreation Activities and Nonappropriated Fund Instrumentalities.* Army Regulation 215-1, 7. Washington, DC: Department of the Army.

Dustin, D. 1984. Recreation limits in a world of ethics. *Parks and Recreation 57* (March), 49–51.

Ibrahim, H., and K. Cordes. 1993. *Outdoor Recreation.* Madison, WI: Brown & Benchmark.

Jensen, C. 1995. *Outdoor Recreation in America.* 5th ed. Champaign, IL: Human Kinetics.

Kraus, R. 1990. *Recreation and Leisure in Modern Society.* 4th ed. New York: HarperCollins.

Land Letter. 1991. The Land and Water Conservation Fund. *Land Letter* (September 20), 1–6.

Lee, R. 1972. *Family Tree of National Park System.* Philadelphia, PA: Eastern National Park and Monument Association.

Little, C. 1991. *Greenways for America.* Baltimore: The Johns Hopkins Univeristy Press, 237.

Lothian, W. 1977. *Extract from a History of Canada's National Parks.* Vol. 1, 9. Parks Canada.

President's Commission on Americans Outdoors (PCAO). 1987. *Americans Outdoors: The Legacy, the Challenge.* Washington, DC: Island Press.

Searle, M. S., and R. E. Brayley. 2000. *Leisure Services in Canada: An Introduction.* 2nd ed. State College, PA: Venture.

Staff. 1992. *Canada Year Book.* Ottawa: Information Canada.

Statistics Canada. 1999. *Culture, Tourism, and the Centre for Education Statistics.*

U.S. Bureau of the Census, 1999. *Statistical Abstract of the United States 1999,* 119th ed. Washington, DC: U.S. Government Printing Office.

U.S. Corps of Engineers. 1982. *1980–1981 Statistical Summary of the U.S. Corps of Engineers,* 6.

U.S. Forest Service. 1970. *Forest Service Objectives and Policy Guidelines.* U.S. Department of Agriculture, Forest Service, U.S. Government Printing Office.

U.S. Forest Service. 1983. *What the Forest Service Does.* (Pamphlet FS-20). U.S. Department of Agriculture, Forest Service.

U.S. Forest Service. 1986. *The USDA Forest Service.* (Pamphlet FS-402). Washington, DC: U.S. Department of Agriculture, Forest Service.I

U.S. Forest Service. 1993. *The Urban Tree House—A Tree for All Reasons.* (Pamphlet). Washington, DC: U.S. Department of Agriculture, Forest Service.

U.S. Forest Service. n.d. *People Serving People.* (Pamphlet) U.S. Department of Agriculture, Forest Service.

Wilderness Society. 1984. *The Wilderness Act Handbook.* The Wilderness Society.

Delivery of Leisure Services: Nonprofit

Private, nonprofit organizations often provide leisure programs that promote youth development. Such programs have strong educational components as well as providing opportunities for fun and enjoyment.

Introduction

Nonprofit leisure service organizations form a large and important segment of the leisure service industry. Nonprofit organizations provide a wide variety of programs and services. Such organizations pursue multiple goals, including the character development of individuals, the pursuit of worthwhile leisure experiences, and the development of community interest. Drucker (1999, p. 9) has written that the greatest growth among organizations will be among nonprofit organizations. He has suggested, ". . . as far as we can predict the growth sector of the 21st century in developed countries . . . is likely to be the nonprofit sector."

Oleck notes that "far more Americans now participate in the activities on nonprofit organizations than those of profit-seeking organizations" (1988, p. 2). Again, Drucker (1999) suggests that a growing number of individuals will seek opportunities to develop parallel careers and/or retire early. He feels that many individuals doing so will be drawn into nonprofit organizations. Many individuals will become "social entrepreneurs" developing nonprofit enterprises to "keep on doing what they have been doing all along, though they spend less and less of their time on it . . . they start another, and usually nonprofit activity" (Drucker, 1999, p. 191).

Nonprofit leisure service organizations in the United States and Canada have great impact—consider nonprofit organizations that provide leisure services as a primary and/or secondary purpose. Churches, clubs, golf courses, fraternal organizations, sport groups, hobby clubs, condominiums, museums, social service organizations, hospitals, and many other types of associations can, and do, plan, organize, and deliver leisure services. The outgrowth of nonprofit leisure service organizations is a natural extension of the attitudes that Canadians and U.S. citizens hold toward volunteerism and community involvement.

Americans of all ages, all stations of life, and all types of dispositions are forever forming associations . . . religious, moral, serious, futile, very general and very limited, immensely large and very minute. . . . Americans combine great individualism with an attitude toward community action that knows no counterpart in the world. Altruistic volunteerism . . . runs throughout all of the history of nonprofit enterprise and community service of the American "nation of joiners." (Oleck, 1988, p. 1)

Steckel and Lehman (1997) have explored the work of nonprofit organizations. They have found many to be the best managed and operated organizations in the United States when compared with businesses or government agencies. Describing why viewing the best managed nonprofit organizations can be valuable for professionals, they have suggested the following:

- There are admirable organizations worthy of consideration, ones that promote the highest caliber of standards for charitable activity regardless of their geographic location, mission, or size. Many of these are run like the world's most respected corporations: efficiently, creatively, and with a clear vision for the future.
- There are fresh concepts about the roles nonprofit organizations should play in American society, including ideas for sustainable earned-income generation, employee benefits and incentives, and innovative leadership styles.
- There are insights shared by Americans active in the nonprofit world that can encourage better understanding of the organizations to which we contribute our time and money. These individuals suggest questions we can ask that make us a better-educated constituency for charities working in our communities. (Steckel and Lehman, 1997)

It is evident that nonprofit organizations play an important role in North American society. Further, it is evident that their influence will increase in the immediate decades to come.

This chapter explores the work of nonprofit organizations delivering leisure services and discusses the characteristics of these types of organizations, including their goals, resource bases, and other distinguishing characteristics. Of particular importance will be a discussion of nonprofit organizations that deliver youth and voluntary services; several different types of nonprofit youth and voluntary service organizations have provided the historical backbone for leisure services to children and youth, as well as adults, in the United States and Canada.

Characteristics of Private, Nonprofit Leisure Service Organizations

Nonprofit leisure service organizations share a number of distinguishing features. In general, nonprofit organizations follow guidelines that have been established by state statutes and laws to provide for their existence. According to Wolf (1990), the ". . . term *nonprofit organization* refers to those legally constituted nongovernmental entities, incorporated under state law as charitable or not-for-profit corporations that have been set up to serve some public purpose and are tax exempt" (p. 6). In other words, nonprofit organizations are legal entities that promote, in some way, a public service orientation or mission. Nonprofit organizations have three basic characteristics. First, they are designated, specifically, as nonprofit entities when established. Second, a nonprofit organization may not divide its assets among its members, officers, or directors. Third, nonprofits may only pursue those activities that they have been established to promote.

There are many different types of nonprofit organizations. The National Taxonomy of Exempt Entities (NTEE) provides a classification system for identifying nonprofit organizations. This classification system identifies twenty-six different types of nonprofit organizations. The system enables organizations to be sorted by major purpose, program focus, and the primary beneficiary of the organization. Many of the types of organizations in the classification system are related to leisure, recreation, the environment, youth services, and other concerns that are indirectly related to the aforementioned (see table 10.1).

What are the distinguishing characteristics of nonprofit organizations? How do they differ from business and government organizations? Perhaps the best way to identify the distinguishing characteristics is to point out the differences between nonprofit and profit and government organizations. A nonprofit organization does not earn a profit that is returned to its owners or members, and it often receives its primary financial support from charitable contributions, donations, and user fees. Government organizations rely on taxes and fees; profit-oriented or commercial organizations rely primarily on charges paid by customers for services.

TABLE

10.1 CLASSIFICATIONS OF NONPROFIT ORGANIZATIONS

Type of Organization

Arts, Culture, Humanities

Educational Institutions and Related Activities

Environmental Quality, Protection, and Beautification

Animal-Related

Health: General and Rehabilitative

Mental Health Crisis Intervention

Diseases, Disorders, Medical Disciplines

Medical Research

Crime, Legal-Related

Employment, Job-Related

Food, Agriculture, and Nutrition

Housing, Shelter

Public Safety, Disaster Preparedness, and Relief

Recreation, Sports, Leisure, Athletics

Youth Development

Human Services: Multipurpose and Other

International Foreign Affairs and National Security

Civil Rights, Social Action, Advocacy

Community Improvement, Capacity Building

Philanthropy, Voluntarism, and Grantmaking Foundations

Science and Technology Research Institutes, Services

Social Science Research Institutes, Services

Public, Society Benefit: Multipurpose and Other

Religion-Related, Spiritual Development

Mutual Membership Benefit Organizations, Other

Unknown (Not Yet Classified)

Source: National Taxonomy of Exempt Entities. *National Center for Charitable Statistics.* (As cited in Hodgkinson, V., and Weitzman, M. (1996). (1996–1997) Nonprofit Almanac: Dimensions of the independent sector. San Francisco: Jossey-Bass.

Some of the distinguishing characteristics of nonprofit organizations are reflected in the following:

1. *Altruistic.* Most nonprofit organizations operate with altruistic motives. In fact, most nonprofit organizations' dominant themes are focused on altruistic, ethical, moral, or social values (Oleck, 1988).

2. *Public service mission.* According to Wolf (1990), an essential characteristic of a nonprofit organization is that it has a public service mission. In other words, nonprofits have the public interest at heart. Mason (1996) writes that nonprofit organizations hold different values than government or profit-oriented organizations. Some of the core values found in nonprofit organizations include *accountability, caring, citizenship, excellence, fairness, honesty, integrity, loyalty, promise-keeping, respect, fidelity, democracy, frugality, pluralism, stewardship, volunteerism, prudence, proportion, contextualism, consensus, community, openness, noblesse oblige (obligation to community) charity, service,* and *others.*

3. *Tax-exempt.* Nonprofit organizations are organized according to Internal Revenue Service guidelines that enable them to be tax-exempt. Section 501 (c) and 501 (d) provide exemptions for organizations from federal taxation. These types of organizations must meet the criteria of performing a service of social value, rather than promoting private ends (profit).

4. *Governance.* The governance structure of nonprofit organizations is established in such a way as to preclude self-interest and private financial gain (Wolf, 1990).

Mason (1996) suggests that there is a wide range of nonprofit organizations. In defining nonprofit organizations, he suggests that they can be distinguished by comparing and contrasting them to business and governmental organizations. As he notes, ". . . the primary goal of business is to be instrumental in making money. The goal of government is to be instrumental in governing. Nonprofits take their generic name not from their goals, but from the fact that distributing profits is not one of their goals" (p. 32).

Mason defines a nonprofit as an organization that is ". . . *usually self governed by local representative boards that achieve compliance by normative means rather than an exchange of wages for work or by coercion, or supported by contributions for member or public benefit and have instrumental and/or expressive purposes*" (p. 31). Mason views nonprofits on a continuum, along the expressive and instrumental dimensions, as follows.

- *Expressive.* Both the stated purposes and activities of purely expressive organizations involve the doing of the action itself. Examples are chess clubs, fraternities, and garden clubs.
- *Expressive-instrumental.* Expressive-instrumental organizations combine the purposes and activities of organizations at the extreme ends of the present continuum, but overt expressive values predominate. Examples are civic clubs and charismatic congregations.
- *Instrumental-expressive.* Instrumental-expressive organizations combine the purposes and activities of organizations at the extreme ends of the present continuum, but instrumental production activities predominate. Examples are hospital auxiliaries, parent-teacher associations, and the Literacy Volunteers of America.
- *Instrumental.* The purposes and activities of the purely instrumental nonprofit organization focus on producing something of value for people outside of the organization, and any expressive aspect is incidental or distractive. Examples are nursing homes, private schools, and hospices.

One of the key factors influencing the work of nonprofit organizations in the provision of leisure services is the reliance on the use of volunteers for the delivery of services. Many non-profit leisure service organizations depend on volunteers to serve as board members, supervisors, and leaders in the delivery of services. Take, for example, youth sports programs. Such programs require coaches, scorekeepers, officials, fundraisers, and individuals in other positions in order to ensure their success. Most, if not all, nonprofit youth service organizations depend on volunteer leadership to organize programs, conduct meetings, plan special events, and, in general, ensure the continued management and maintenance of the organization. Thus, an additional distinguishing characteristic of many nonprofit leisure service organizations is reliance on volunteers.

Goals and Functions

Nonprofit organizations often serve different groupings, often with divergent needs. Oleck (1988) suggests three basic orientations that nonprofit organizations take:

Public benefit. Nonprofit organizations can be organized to promote the public welfare. In general, this type of organization appeals to a wide variety of individuals. Although these organizations may have a specific focus (such as a specific age group, philosophy, and character development), their general purpose is to promote the common good. Organizations such as hospitals, museums, and schools often fit into this category.

Mutual benefit. Organizations formed to serve a more exclusive group of individuals for mutual benefit defines this category. Fraternal clubs, hobby groups, art associations/guilds, and the like are examples of these types of nonprofit associations. In general, these organizations promote the welfare of their constituents.

Private benefit. Organizations can form as nonprofit units for private benefit, such as golf clubs, swim and tennis associations, and others. These organizations promote an exclusive use of an area, facility, or service, or provide opportunities for a group of people to interact with one another for the exclusive benefit of that group. Numerous private, nonprofit leisure service organizations have formed to promote the interests of a more select group of individuals.

The benefit structure of a given nonprofit organization impacts its goals, programs, and membership.

What are the goals of nonprofit leisure service organizations? The answer to this question is as varied as the nature of the organization. Like public leisure service organizations, nonprofit organizations primarily promote the interests of those they serve. Their primary mission is *not* to make a profit, but, rather, to serve society in such a way as to promote the general welfare. Some nonprofit organizations have broadly defined goals such as promoting the development of youth, whereas others, more specifically focused, direct their work toward the provision of a specific program, facility, or area that benefits a more narrowly focused group of individuals.

The goals of nonprofit organizations are often difficult to measure or quantify. In the commercial sector, an organization's financial status is a quantitative measure stated in profit or loss. The measurement of the goals of nonprofit organizations creates a greater challenge. Nonprofit organizations often state their goals in terms of promoting "quality of life," "enhancing the general welfare," "pursuing excellence," "promoting equity," and other statements that are difficult to quantify. The greatest challenge to nonprofit organizations lies in the development

Increasing Opportunities for Service for Youth

While no state and only a small percentage of districts as of 1990 required community service for high school graduation, the climate is largely working to promote that eventual development. Service and opportunities for community connection, as noted earlier, are among the key recommendations in practically all the blue-ribbon commission reports on "at-risk" youth, and the National and Community Service Act was signed into law in late 1990. The $125 million program, the only one of dozens of service bills that included young adolescents as eligible participants, would stimulate a host of service efforts around the country. The more we can encourage this service, apparently, the better: a Gallup survey reported that teenagers fourteen to seventeen are not only volunteering slightly more than adults (58% to 54%), but that 69% of those whose schools encouraged service actually volunteered, versus just 44% in schools where service was not especially encouraged.

There are endless examples of how we can provide as well as promote caring and a sense of community among young people. The following is just a sampling of the many efforts being conducted across the country.

- The Magic Me program in Baltimore pairs at-risk middle-grade youth with nursing home residents (for the school year).
- In the Valued Youth Partnership in San Antonio, the Coca-Cola Company and the Intercultural Development Research Association are serving a primarily Mexican American population through a mentoring initiative. Seventh and ninth graders, as well as high school students, are given extra help to sharpen their math and reading skills and then work, at minimum wage, at a nearby elementary school with younger Latino students. Instead of an expected dropout rate of 45% among these youth, only 4% of the tutors have dropped out of school.
- The principal of the Challenger Middle School in Colorado Springs created HUGSS—Help Us Grow Through Service and Smiles. The school of 900 is divided into nine academic teams, with each team adopting a community agency for school year service projects. The academic curriculum is realistically woven around these community service experiences.
- In Alaska, many of the Governor's Commission on Children and Youth recommendations that resulted in new funding were developed from the testimony of young people from around the state, including ten- to fifteen-year-olds, and the Commission awarded $30,000 in funds to youth-designed and -led prevention programs in junior and senior high schools.
- In Washington, high school seniors who have been through the Governor's Summer Citizenship School work with at-risk middle school students and their teachers/advisors to design and conduct community leadership projects that run throughout the school year.
- The Lutheran Brotherhood has developed a social studies program, Speak for Yourself, that encourages seventh and eighth graders across the nation to reflect on current issues and then share their opinions with government leaders.
- Now in a number of communities, the Early Adolescent Helper Program works with schools to place ten- to fifteen-year-olds in service settings such as Head Start or senior citizen centers. The program has documented the positive effects on Head Start children, and its success has led to its expansion as the National Center for Service Learning in Early Adolescence.
- In Detroit, young adolescents are caring for each other in Twelve Together, a program of the Metropolitan Detroit Youth Foundation. Hundreds of at-risk ninth graders are organized into peer helping groups of a dozen each who, with adult volunteers, hold thirty meetings during the school year, including one parent reception and six monthly academic forums. Peer counseling occurs in the offices of businesses that have adopted each group. Four years later, the graduation rate of these Twelve Together youth is 12% to 16% higher than that of control groups.

Increasing Opportunities for Service for Youth—concluded

- The Teen Outreach Program of the Association of Junior Leagues combines curriculum-based life-skills instruction for seventh to twelfth graders with volunteer community service. A study of its impact across thirty-five sites showed that although program participants entered the program with more problems than comparison youths, they exited with fewer problems, such as involvement in a pregnancy, school course failure, or suspension from school.
- The Indiana Black Expo, Inc., designs programs that empower adolescents to help themselves, including holding Youth Empowerment Summits on economics, politics, African American culture, education, and the entertainment industry, and Youth Financial Literacy Workshops aimed ultimately at helping Indiana's youths create their own Youth Credit Union.

- The Children's Museum in Boston has an Early Adolescent Program for nine- to fifteen-year-olds, including adolescent-designed exhibits, a Youth Advisory Board, and after-school and Friday evening free workshops on rap music and recording, video improvisation, fitness, job opportunities for young artists, and much more.
- There are numerous KidsPlaces around the country. These boards of eleven- to fifteen-year-olds examine the conditions of growing up in those communities and make recommendations to the community leaders about how to improve the communities. For example, Minneapolis is setting its children's agenda through a communitywide City's Children: 2007 initiative. In May 1990, the Seattle KidsPlace hosted a national gathering of scores of these city- and state-based children's efforts.

Nonprofits: America's Largest Employer

Few people are aware that the nonprofit sector is by far America's largest employer. Every other adult—a total of *80 million-plus* people—works as a volunteer, giving an average of nearly five hours each week to one or several nonprofit organizations.

This is equal to 10 million full-time jobs. Were volunteers paid, their wages, even at minimum rate, would amount to some $10 billion, or 5 percent of GNP (Gross National Product).

Source: Peter F. Drucker, *Managing for the Future: The 1990s and Beyond,* 1992.

of goals that have clarity, purpose, and focus. Such clarity provides an opportunity to nonprofit organizations to clearly articulate and measure the benefit structures which they pursue.

An example of the goals of a nonprofit organization is that of Girls, Incorporated. This organization, dedicated to assisting girls to develop themselves as individuals, has a broad mission statement that promotes the general welfare of its targeted population. Its mission statement is found in table 10.2.

Obviously, the goals of Girls, Incorporated are broad in nature. Overcoming discrimination, developing self-sufficiency, advocating for girls, and focusing on the specific needs of girls provide a level of specificity in this statement that offers direction to the organization.

TABLE

10.2	MISSION STATEMENT: GIRLS, INCORPORATED

The mission of Girls, Incorporated is to assist affiliates in meeting the needs of girls in their communities; to help girls and young women overcome the effects of discrimination and to develop their capacity to be self-sufficient, responsible citizens; and to serve as a vigorous advocate for girls, focusing attention on their special needs.

Source: Girls, Incorporated, New York, NY. Reprinted by permission.

TABLE

10.3	MISSION STATEMENT: BIG BROTHERS/BIG SISTERS

Big Brothers/Big Sisters is a universally recognized youth development force that empowers children to reach their potential through supported dynamic mentoring relationships.

Source: Big Brothers/Big Sisters of America, Philadelphia, PA. Reprinted by permission.

Another example of a goal statement is that of the Big Brothers/Big Sisters program. The Big Brothers/Big Sisters organization provides stable role models to children on an individual basis. Its mission statement is direct, focusing on promoting the welfare of children. Table 10.3 presents the mission statement. This mission statement focuses on defining the benefits to be derived from participation in the Big Brothers/Big Sisters program.

Resource Base

The resource base for nonprofit leisure service organizations is as diverse and complex as it is for other types of organizations. Depending on the philosophy and nature of the nonprofit organization, resources are sought both externally and internally, with an attempt to generate programs and services that produce revenues. Resources found in the "support" category are derived from contributions made by individuals, corporations, foundations, and the government (see figure 10.1). The "revenue" category shows income from membership fees, interest, dividends, and funds from special events.

In general, a number of revenue sources are available to nonprofit organizations, including the following:

Membership fees. Often, nonprofit leisure service organizations charge a basic membership fee for participating in the organization. For example, summer memberships at a midwestern YMCA range from $41 for basic services for children to $669 for a full family membership. Figure 10.2 presents information regarding the membership fee structure for a family YMCA. Included is a discussion of membership information describing types of membership services available.

Program fees and tuition. Program fees/tuition are the charges assessed for participation in a specific program. For example, a member of the Family YMCA of Black Hawk County may elect to participate in the summer day camp program. Fees for this program are $65 per week and $75 for nonmembers. Program fees may vary depending on the cost required to produce a given program.

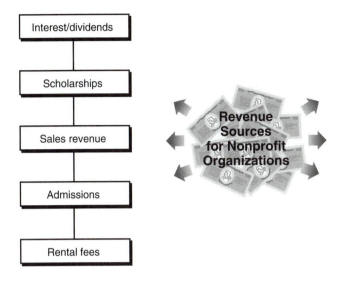

| Interest/dividends |
| Scholarships |
| Sales revenue |
| Admissions |
| Rental fees |

Revenue Sources for Nonprofit Organizations

| Membership fees |
| Program fees/tuition |
| Government grants |
| Corporate gifts |
| Donations |
| Foundation grants |

Figure 10.1

Revenue sources available to nonprofit organizations

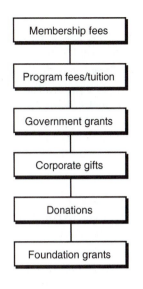

YMCA
We build strong kids,
strong families, strong communities.

Figure 10.2

Fee structure, Blackhawk County YMCA, Waterloo, Iowa

Family YMCA of Black Hawk County
Membership Rates for 2000

Membership Types	Full Pay Start-Up	Autochecking	Autochecking Start-Up	30/60 Day	30/60 Day Start-Up
8 and Under	$41.00	NA	NA	NA	NA
Youth 7–12	$72.00	$8.00	$16.00	NA	NA
Youth 13–18	$84.00	$9.00	$18.00	NA	NA
College	$117.00	NA	NA	NA	NA
Basic	$318.00	$26.46	$76.92	$98.00	$122.00
Fitness Center	$436.00	$36.33	$96.66	$137.33	$161.34
1 Parent Basic	$370.00	$29.83	$95.66	$111.34	$147.34
1 Parent FC Family	$488.00	$39.66	$115.32	$150.67	$186.67
H/W Basic	$427.00	$34.62	$105.24	$130.34	$166.34
H/W Basic/FC	$536.00	$43.63	$123.28	$166.67	$202.67
H/W FC	$633.00	$51.78	$139.56	$199.00	$235.00
Basic Family	$469.00	$38.05	$112.10	$144.33	$180.33
Basic/FC Family	$582.00	$47.49	$130.98	$182.00	$218.00
FC Family	$669.00	$54.79	$145.58	$211.00	$247.00
60+	$115.00	$10.58	$33.16	NA	NA
60+ Couple	$162.00	$14.02	$46.04	NA	NA

Start-up costs include a one-time Joiners Fee of $24 (Individual) or $36 (Family).
Start-up costs for 60+ memberships include a one-time Joiners Fee of $12 (Individual) and $18 (Family).

Family YMCA of Black Hawk Country • 669 South Hackett Road • Waterloo, IA 50701

YMCA mission: To put Christian principles into practice through programs that build healthy spirit, mind, and body for all.

Government grants. Nonprofit organizations are eligible to receive funding from the state and federal government. Such support often enables nonprofit organizations to provide meal functions, program development, and other services.

Corporate gifts. Donations by corporations comprise a substantial portion of the budgets of national youth service organizations. When seeking such gifts, nonprofit organizations must match their interests with the philosophy of the corporations' giving programs—and often submit a prospectus outlining the programs and services to be offered.

Donations and gifts. Individual giving provides an important source of support for nonprofit organizations, which can seek unrestricted contributions from individuals, local businesses, and other groups. Often these donations result from annual gift-giving programs organized by peer groups or community-service organizations. Donations also come in the form of bequests. A bequest is established in a person's will and allows an organization to use the individual's assets after his or her death. Another form of gift is the purchase of a life insurance policy with the death benefits assigned to a nonprofit organization.

Foundation grants. Foundations often supply considerable revenue for nonprofit organizations. Using resources such as the Foundation Grant Index or the Foundation Directory can help identify the vast network of foundation support in the United States and Canada. Foundations provide large restricted-grant support that organizations can use for program development or to focus on targeted populations. Foundations, interested in the ability of organizations to deliver services, need to know what problem is being addressed, the capability of the organization, anticipated evaluation strategies, and the resources required.

Interest and dividends. Nonprofit organizations sometimes have established endowments or trusts. Such financial arrangements enable an organization to earn interest or dividends on the principal that has been invested.

Scholarships. A scholarship may be thought of as aid or funds given to an individual to enable participation in a program. For example, an individual, group, or business could provide scholarships to enable a selected number of individuals to participate in a program such as a day camp. Scholarships often target financially disadvantaged individuals and, as a result, help provide equity.

Sales revenue. Nonprofit organizations can sell equipment, clothing, food, and other items that generate revenue for the enterprise. Over the years, the Girl Scouts of the U.S.A. and Camp Fire Boys and Girls, Inc. have generated great support for their endeavors through the sale of cookies and candy. Such fundraising activities have become institutionalized and are a part of popular culture.

Admissions. Admission fees to areas and facilities, another source of potential revenue, can be assessed for specific programs as well as for the use of facilities and equipment.

Rental fees. Income derived from the short-term, temporary, exclusive use of an area, facility, or piece of equipment is called a rental fee. Individuals and groups often rent facilities for meetings, special events, receptions, and other activities.

These and other miscellaneous sources of revenue provide the revenue base of nonprofit leisure service organizations. Nonprofit organizations work diligently to promote sources of revenue in order to prosper. Often, they organize internal programs directed toward raising their own funds. If they are a part of a national organization, they can participate in national or regional fundraising programs.

Fundraising Nonprofit organizations depend on motivating individuals to provide financial support for their programs. As such, almost all nonprofit organizations have some type of fundraising program in place. Fundraising provides an opportunity for individuals to engage in philanthropic activity, which is the voluntary sharing of wealth. Canadians and U.S. citizens are extremely generous and contribute for various reasons, including out of their sense of moral responsibility to promote community welfare. There is also great personal satisfaction in assisting others by providing support.

Most nonprofit organizations have some type of annual fund campaign. Such campaigns generate funds to support the operation of nonprofit programs and services on a year-to-year basis. Fundraising campaigns are also organized in support of capital developments for new facilities or facility improvements. Among the many ways of soliciting funds from individuals, by far the most preferred means is the direct contact method. This method involves direct personal contact with potential donors. Other forms of fundraising include direct mail, telephone solicitations, special events, and other methods.

Partnerships and Building Collaborative Efforts The twenty-first century will be an age of alliances (Austin, 2000). It will be important for businesses, government agencies, and nonprofit agencies to link together in partnerships to provide quality services and programs. Building collaborative relationships between various entities will be essential. Such collaborations will enable the sharing of organizational resources including areas, facilities, staff, information technology, marketing strategies, and numerous other concerns.

Building partnerships and collaborative efforts will be essential in the years to come for many reasons. Economic factors alone are forcing government agencies to think in new and innovative ways. Businesses seeking to build community goodwill are extending themselves and their resources to assist in the provision of community services. Nonprofit organizations are often underfunded to meet the demands they face and seek to increase their resource base.

There are numerous benefits for businesses, government agencies, and nonprofits to partner with one another. Austin (2000) has suggested the following are benefits for partnering:

- *Cost savings.* By cooperating, organizations can eliminate duplication of cost and also decrease unneeded resources.
- *Economies of scale and scope.* By working together, organizations can build a larger base to serve similar customer populations.
- *Synergies.* Collaborations promote greater thinking, problem solving, and solutions to community concerns.
- *Revenue enhancement.* By combining various organizations' resources, revenue is enhanced.
- *Strategy enrichment.* By collaborating, organizations are viewed as contributing to the welfare of the society.
- *Human resource management.* By combining human resources, organizations can enhance opportunities for leadership, community involvement, culture building, and so on.
- *Culture building.* Community service is a way of life for many individuals within organizations. Collaborative efforts enable this type of culture to thrive.
- *Business generation.* Collaborative relationships may create new markets by linking with potential new customers. Certainly it creates a sense of goodwill, which enhances business opportunities.

Clearly, there are numerous benefits to building collaborative partnerships. In the future this will become a key element in the success of professionals working in nonprofit organizations as well as businesses and government agencies.

Characteristics of Professionals

The nonprofit sector varies in terms of the types of organizations that deliver leisure services. As a result, it is difficult to analyze professionals in the industry with a great deal of precision. Nonetheless, a profile has emerged regarding the nature of employees in this sector, educational levels, salary structure, and job satisfaction. In general, the nonprofit area employs more women than men, particularly in positions focused on the delivery of program activities and/or the management of facilities.

The employees working in this segment of the industry, interestingly, express high job satisfaction. In fact, studies conducted comparing the nonprofit sector with the commercial and public sectors suggest that the level of satisfaction among this group ranks highest. Nonprofit sector workers express a high level of satisfaction with their work. They also note a high degree of satisfaction with the amount of control they have over their work life, with management, career progress, and even pay. Mason (1996) has written that paid staff members in nonprofit organizations:

> . . . enjoy their jobs for the sake of the work itself, and their ideal reward is more work with more responsibility. They enjoy a collegial environment and gain satisfaction from their work. They tend to be better educated than their business counterparts and tend to think of their work as being more important than any material rewards. (p. 33)

It is also interesting to note that individuals in this area indicate a long-term commitment to their profession. Furthermore, individuals stay with their careers and on average spend nine years at one work site, suggesting that this area is very stable.

Range of Personnel   Nonprofit organizations require a full range of individuals who contribute to the success of these types of endeavors. Nonprofit organizations have many different types of stakeholders who share in the success of the endeavor. As stakeholders, they all contribute to the organization, but in different ways. Mason (1996) notes that some of the types of salaried staff and unpaid volunteers often associated with nonprofit organizations include the following:

- *Founders.* These individuals are the originators of the nonprofit organization. Such individuals are often visionary, charismatic, driven, and intensely committed individuals.
- *Chief executive officers/managers.* Individuals occupying the roles of CEO or manager of a nonprofit organization provide overall managerial leadership to the organization, or a component of the organization, on a day-to-day basis. Such individuals have skills in fiscal resource management, human resource management, programming, and providing strategic direction and supervision to the work of an organization.
- *Program personnel.* These individuals are responsible for supervising a program area, facility, or age grouping, or some combination of these. They are responsible for the planning, promotion, implementation, and evaluation of specific programs in their assigned area. Duties may include the creation and implementation of direct services and/or programs that offer opportunities for enabling activities such as providing consultation and/or information.
- *Development personnel (fundraisers).* Nonprofit organizations must raise their own funding. They are dependent upon membership drives, donations, gifts, grants, endowments, trusts, and other forms of fundraising. Often, a nonprofit organization will secure the services of an individual who will, as a part of her/his responsibilities, or as her/his primary role, organize this effort within an organization.

- *Support staff.* As Mason (1996, p. 36) writes, ". . . support staff are those who file, drive, type, keep books, operate computers, clean and attend to other technical or administrative details, much as do their business counterparts. They may or may not exhibit strong commitment, and their pay and work are often quite similar to that in comparable business positions."
- *Volunteers.* As mentioned earlier, nonprofit organizations often rely heavily on the use of volunteers to carry out the work of the organization. There are three types of volunteers. First are individuals who serve as members of a *board of directors.* A board of directors provides oversight governance, helping define ". . . an organization's mission . . . establish its policies, and . . . [determine] . . . the control mechanisms it will use to allocate power, establish decision-making processes and set up procedures for performing specific tasks" (Mason, 1996, p. 36).

   The second type of volunteers are those who assist in providing *direct face-to-face leadership or general supervision* to programs. Such volunteers often serve as coaches, scout leaders, teen specialists, program hosts, teacher aides, and other roles. The third type of volunteers are those who assist with *administrative or support functions.* These individuals aid in the activities of the organization that often involve their annual fundraising campaign, registration activities, clerical activities, or other support functions as mentioned previously.
- *Rank and file members.* Many nonprofit organizations are membership organizations; that is, they are dependent upon and seek a membership base that meet selected criteria. Such criteria may be broad or specific. The membership of an organization may contribute to the governance of the agency, support its financial goals and, in general, contribute to its well-being. Members are instrumental in recruiting new members, recommending program enhancements, paying dues, fundraising, and providing leadership to the nonprofit organizations.
- *Contributors.* Individuals, organizations, or agencies may support the goals of a nonprofit organization with various forms of contributions. As Mason (1996, p. 40) notes ". . . individuals, governments, businesses, foundations and unaffiliated individuals can and do support . . . [nonprofit] organizations." People contribute to nonprofit organizations because they value the work of a group, because it is consistent with their interests, or because they have respect for its efforts. Further, contributors often give simply because they are asked.

Types of Youth and Voluntary Nonprofit Leisure Service Organizations

Many voluntary, charitable, and social welfare organizations exist in the United States and Canada. Hodgkinson and Weitzman (1996, p. 25) have noted that there are "approximately 11.03 million independent sector organizations, including 689,000 charitable 501(c)(3) organizations, and 143,000 social welfare 501(c)(4) organizations reported by the Internal Revenue Service and an estimated 341,000 religious organizations. There are another 396,000 tax-exempt organizations outside of these categories." Many of these organizations are involved in recreation and leisure in a variety of ways. This section of the chapter presents an overview of many specific nonprofit organizations, grouped according to the participants they serve: youth serving organizations (both nonsectarian and religious), religious organizations, organizations serving special populations (including people with disabilities), relief and social service organizations, conservation organizations, and service and fraternal clubs.

TABLE

10.4 NONPROFIT ASSOCIATIONS RELATED TO LEISURE

Type	Number of Associations			
	1985	1990	1995	1997
Cultural	N/A	1,886	1,918	1,918
Social welfare	1,450	1,705	1,885	1,934
Fraternal	462	573	552	541
Religious	953	1,172	1,230	1,230
Patriotic	281	462	686	745
Hobby/avocational	1,311	1,475	1,549	1,548
Athletic sports	787	840	838	836
Fan clubs	N/A	581	460	491

Source: R. Famighetti (ed.), 1996. *World Almanac and Book of Facts*. Mahwah, NJ: Funk and Wagnalls, U.S. Bureau of the Census. 1999. *Statistical Abstracts of the United States: 1999*. 119th ed. Washington, DC: U.S. Government Printing Office.

Table 10.4 presents information regarding nonprofit organizations related to leisure in the United States. As one can see from viewing this table, a diverse number of nonprofit organizations provide leisure or related services. Between 1985 and 1997 the number of nonprofit organizations has grown dramatically.

Youth Serving Organizations

A large and important part of the nonprofit segment of the leisure service industry is dedicated to providing youth services. The Carnegie Corporation (1992) estimates that more than 400 national organizations provide services to youth. Table 10.5 provides information concerning a variety of these types of organizations, ranging from sports groups to fraternal organizations with youth programs.

One of the developments among such organizations involves the movement away from traditional programs which focus exclusively on recreation, to those that consider principles of education and youth development within leisure programs and services. The Carnegie Corporation (1992) also reports ". . . greater emphasis being placed on building specific skills and competencies rather than self-esteem and self-confidence" (p. 44). The characteristics of these organizations depend on the mission and philosophy of the organization. Several unique components of youth serving nonprofit organizations, as reported by the Carnegie Corporation, appear in table 10.6.

While religious organizations sponsor and support many youth organizations, others are nonsectarian. The nonsectarian organizations often have goals connected to social development and good citizenship.

Nonsectarian-Sponsored Organizations The goals and objectives of nonsectarian-sponsored organizations supply an overview of youth development objectives that they would promote. Youth serving organizations that are committed to youth development all have related objectives toward which they focus their efforts. The organizations described include 4–H Clubs, Boy and Girl Scouts, Junior Achievement, Camp Fire Boys and Girls, Inc., Girls, Inc., Boys and Girls Clubs of America, and Big Brothers/Big Sisters of America.

TABLE

YOUTH SERVED BY SELECTED NATIONAL ORGANIZATIONS

Organization	Total Youth Served	Percentage Adolescents	Percentage Female	Percentage Minority
American Camping Assoc.	9,000,000	NA	55	NA
American Red Cross	306,852 volunteers (ages 25 and under)	NA	NA	NA
ASPIRA	25,000	NA	NA	100 Hispanic
Boy Scouts of America	6,621,218 (ages 7–20)	15 (ages 11–17)	NA	NA
Boys and Girls Clubs	3,300,000	50 (ages 11–18)	41	61
Camp Fire Boys and Girls	650,000 (ages 21 and under)	NA	54	NA
Child Welfare League	3,500,000	NA	NA	NA
4-H Clubs	6,512,606 (ages 5–19)	66.7 (ages 4–12)	52	27
Girl Scouts of the U.S.A.	2,748,917 (ages 5–17)	NA	100	21
Girls Incorporated	350,000 (ages 6–18)	NA	NA	61
Junior Achievement	3,583,481	NA	NA	NA
National Runaway Switchboard	250,000	11 (ages 11–13)	74	30
YMCA of the USA	8,521,983 (ages 18 and under)	NA	NA	NA
YWCA of the USA	2,000,000 (including adults)	NA	NA	NA

Source: Information taken from the following websites:
  http://dir.yahoo.com/Recreation/Outdoors/Camping/Organizations/American_Camping_Association
  www.redcross.org
  http://dir.yahoo.com/Recreation
  www.mossbeachhomes.com
  www.bgca.org
  http://dir.yahoo.com/Recreation/Outdoors/Scouting/Boy_Scouts_of_America
  http://dir.yahoo.com/Recreation/Outdoors/Scouting/Camp_Fire_Boys_and_Girls
  www.children.org.tw
  http://dir.yahoo.com/Society_and_Culture/Cultures_and_Groups/Children/Organizations/4_H/United_States
  http://dir.yahoo.com/Recreation/Outdoors/Scouting/Girl_Scouts_of_the_United_States_of_America
  http://dir.yahoo.com/Society_and_Culture/Cultures_and_Groups/Women/Organizations/Girls_Incorporated
  http://dir.yahoo.com/Business_and_Economy/Educaiton/K_12/Organizations/Junior_Achievement
  www.nrscrisisline.org
  www.ymca.net
  www.ywca.org

4-H for Youth of America The national 4–H program is part of the U.S. Department of Agriculture's Cooperative Extension Service program. The four Hs of the 4–H program, which was founded in 1924, stand for *Head, Heart, Hands,* and *Health* and represent the organization's emphasis on education and living a healthy and productive life. Its main goal is to create a learning environment for youth that stimulates the development of particular life skills: (1) competency—developing skills and knowledge; (2) coping—dealing with stress; and (3) contributory—learning to help others. The 4–H program serves young people ages nine to nineteen. The 4–H program operates in more than 3,000 counties in the United States, District of Columbia, Puerto Rico, Virgin Islands, Guam, American Samoa, and Micronesia. Estimates show an enrollment of nearly 6 million boys and girls in 4–H programs. Most live in rural areas, although the program now operates in suburban and urban areas as well.

TABLE

10.6   UNIQUE CHARACTERISTICS OF YOUTH SERVING NONPROFIT ORGANIZATIONS AS REPORTED BY THE CARNEGIE CORPORATION

- Some organizations are facility-based, others are organized around a specific group or troop, and still others rely on a one-to-one match between a young person and an adult mentor. The programs offered by these organizations are often led by volunteers; others (usually the facility-based organizations) rely primarily on paid staff.

- Troop or group-based agencies tend to meet once a week, for an hour or two, while facility-based agencies generally offer services for twenty to thirty hours per week (although the extent to which individual members make use of the entire array of services varies).

- Program content and approaches vary. Some organizations offer a comprehensive "core" program, while others focus on one or two aspects of overall youth development, such as academic enrichment or leadership skills.

- The demographics of service populations can differ in composition in terms of socioeconomic status, race and ethnic background, age, and gender and in total number of youths served.

- Some organizations are well funded (e.g., Boy Scouts of America and Girl Scouts of the U.S.A.) while others struggle. Some national troops rely heavily on affiliate dues and on revenues from the sale of equipment, products, and supplies; others receive the bulk of their support from government or charitable contributions.

- Every organization defines its membership differently—in general, the national organizations try to maximize their membership numbers occasionally by including leaders and others.

- Most organizations try to encourage active youth participation at the local level, but they seldom permit young people to take part in genuine decision making. Only a few national organizations appoint youth members to their boards or commissions. (p. 44)

Source: *A Matter of Time: Risk and Opportunity in the Nonschool Hours,* a report of the Carnegie Council on Adolescent Development. Copyright© December 1992 by Carnegie Corporation of New York.

The 4–H program operates a variety of services including clubs, projects, activities, outreach, and international programs. The 4–H program depends on more than 500,000 volunteer leaders who give an average of 220 hours per year. The 4–H program provides opportunities for youth to work with adult volunteer leaders on one or more projects. The club program forms the backbone of 4–H, and most activities are carried out in this format. 4–H projects are grouped in the areas of animal science, plant science, home economics, natural science, mechanical science, and expressive arts. These programs provide real-life experiences for participants. Activities provided by 4–H include opportunities for individuals to participate in fairs, contests, camps, tours, exchanges, and special events. The 4–H program also operates on extensive outreach effort. 4–H materials are used in schools, seen on television, and used in other formats. International 4–H programs provide opportunities for exchanges for young adults to live and work with families in other countries.

Boy Scouts of America   Scouting, a program that covers the globe, was founded in Britain by Lord Baden Powell. The Boy Scouts of America was founded in the United States by William D. Boyce in 1910. The purpose of Boy Scouts is to build character; foster citizenship; and develop mental, moral, and physical fitness in young people, while endeavoring to meet the needs for fun, adventure, and meaningful learning. In general, the Boy Scouts of America program pursues three purposes: (1) character development, (2) citizenship training, and (3) personal fitness. Scouting units are sponsored by churches, schools, and civic groups. Sponsoring groups form a partnership with local Boy Scout Councils that help train, supervise, and deliver services.

The scouting program is organized into several units: (1) Tiger Cubs, (2) Cub Scouts, (3) Boy Scouts, (4) Explorers, (5) Varsity Scouts, and (6) Learning for Life, a program designed for inner-city and rural youth. Boys in first grade can participate in the Tiger Cub program that features field trips, picnics, and other scouting activities. Cub Scouts offers opportunities for boys in second through fifth grades to develop skills and participate in community activities. The Boy Scout program includes sixth graders through age eighteen. Individuals advancing through Boy Scout ranks have the opportunity to master a broad range of skills and participate in a variety of service projects. The Explorer program, designed for young women and men ages fourteen to twenty, focuses on specialized topics such as conservation, law enforcement, forestry, and others. The Varsity Scouts program promotes high-adventure activities. This program serves individuals who would not normally participate in the scouting program. The Learning for Life program is an in-school program that is targeted for hard-to-reach individuals.

Girl Scouts of the U.S.A. The Girl Scout organization was established in 1912 and founded by Juliette Gordon Lowe, who organized the first group of girls in Savannah, Georgia. This program for girls ages five to seventeen builds on an informal educational foundation. The mission of the Girl Scouts is to inspire girls with the highest ideals of character, conduct, patriotism, and service so that they may become happy and resourceful citizens. A congressional charter was conferred on the Girl Scouts of the U.S.A. in 1950 by a special act of Congress. This charter provides the basic guidelines for the operations of the Girl Scout program, which now serves approximately 2.5 million individuals. Most of the funding for the Girl Scout program comes from two basic income streams: (1) revenue generated from membership dues, uniform sales, books, and other equipment, and (2) local United Way contributions, corporate gifts, foundation grants and gifts, and individual philanthropic efforts.

The program of the Girl Scouts centers in the five following areas: (1) personal well-being and fitness, (2) awareness of other cultures, (3) exploring new technologies, (4) the arts, and (5) the out-of-doors. Most Girl Scout programs operate in the troop/group format. Girl Scout programs include a variety of activities, including opportunities for camping, skill-development activities, trips and tours, and exchanges. The Girl Scout program promotes adventure in learning with activities focused on helping girls address both their current interests and future roles in society. The United States has more than 300 Girl Scout councils. The Girl Scout program is offered in over 100 countries and the Girl Scouts of the U.S.A. are affiliated with the World Association of Girl Guides and Girl Scouts.

Junior Achievement Junior Achievement, established in 1919, assists youth in gaining knowledge about the business world and prepares them for roles as entrepreneurs or professionals in the future. The Junior Achievement program involves more than 3.5 million youth a year in various activities. The Junior Achievement program uses volunteers to provide services to youth and, on a yearly basis, sees 100,000 individuals support the programs and services offered by the organization. The mission of Junior Achievement is ". . . to promote economic literacy and understanding of business and competitive private enterprise among young people through hands-on experience" (Carnegie Corp., 1992, p. 146). Junior Achievement is a nonprofit, tax-exempt organization that is international in scope with programs in every major city in the United States. The program also operates in seven foreign countries.

Junior Achievement operates a number of programs, including the following: (1) applied economics, (2) project business, (3) business basics, and (4) J. A. Company. The applied economics program is a one-semester elective course that may be taken by high school students. Basically, this activity involves establishing a mini-company and marketing a product or service to the community. The project business program, directed toward eighth and ninth graders, is offered as a part of the social studies curriculum in middle or junior high school. The program features activities that deal with business, free enterprise, and economics. Business basics, a program directed at younger children, is provided by high school and college students involved in Junior Achievement. The program introduces basic economic concepts to children in all elementary grades. In this program children learn how people and businesses interact together both economically and socially. The last program, J. A. Company, is directed toward high school students and enables them to develop a mini-business. Youth elect their own officers, sell stock, manufacture and market a product or service, and manage financial activities, including paying shareholders of the organization.

Camp Fire Boys and Girls, Inc.   The Camp Fire program was founded (as Camp Fire Girls) in 1910 by Luther and Charlotte Gulick. During the past decade this national youth serving organization has modified its program structure to make its services available to all young people. The Camp Fire program provides informal education that gives youth an opportunity to realize their potential and to function effectively as caring, self-directed individuals, responsible to themselves and others. As an organization, it seeks to improve conditions in society that affect youth. Membership in the program is open to everyone, regardless of race, creed, religion, national origin, or sex. Camp Fire, like other youth service organizations, depends on adult volunteer leaders. Such individuals provide guidance and support for most programs. Because Camp Fire is coeducational, it offers opportunities for female and male teams to provide leadership to the programs and services of Camp Fire.

The Camp Fire program is organized primarily into a club format. The Camp Fire Sparks program for boys and girls in kindergarten emphasizes creating opportunities for individuals to gain self-confidence, self-image, creativity, sharing, friendship, and joy in participating in activities. Children in grades one, two, and three may join the Camp Fire Blue Bird club program, which helps individuals learn about themselves while sharing a sense of belonging and personal growth. Camp Fire Adventurers for children in grades four and five offers activities such as cooking, computers, sign language, and other skill-oriented activities. Further, the Adventurers program promotes involvement in community service along with good citizenship. The Camp Fire Discovery and Horizon program, directed toward children in grades six through twelve, promotes building a positive self-image, skill development, and values clarification—all aimed at building greater self-confidence.

In addition to the club program, Camp Fire offers camping and environmental education programs, child-care programs, self-reliance programs that promote acquisition of life skills, and leadership development activities that are aimed at empowering youth. The Camp Fire program involves more than 650,000 children each year. The majority of these participants are female (62%), which may reflect the founding mission of the organization.

Girls, Inc.   Girls, Inc., founded in 1945, was initially established as the Girls Clubs of America and offers more than 400 local centers supported by a national headquarters and regional offices. Girls, Inc. works to assist local affiliates in meeting the needs of girls in their communities; to help girls and young women overcome the effects of discrimination; to develop their capacity to be self-sufficient, responsible citizens; and to serve as a vigorous advocate for girls, focusing attention on their special needs. The program serves more than a quarter of a million girls ages six through eighteen years of age. Girls, Inc. employs 2,500 professionals and receives assistance from 8,000 volunteers. The national organization provides management, administrative, communications, and fundraising services, as well as program development.

Girls, Inc. offers several specific programs directed toward helping individuals gain skills, have fun, and meet with friends. Programs, offered in the centers operated by Girls, Inc., include the following: (1) Operation SMART (Science, Math, and Relevant Technology), (2) Preventing Adolescent Pregnancy, (3) Friendly PEERsuasion, (4) Teen Connections, and (5) Sporting Chance. The Operation SMART program helps girls understand and pursue math and science activities. The Preventing Adolescent Pregnancy program, directed toward girls ages nine to eighteen, encourages them to develop attitudes and practice behavior that prevents early pregnancy. Another program, Friendly PEERsuasion, helps girls avoid the hazards of alcohol, tobacco, and other drugs. This program contributes to the development of leadership skills and leads to a greater awareness of health concerns. Teen Connections also deals with community health issues, teaching teens about health through a variety of activities such as skits, speaking, and other forums. The Sporting Chance program focuses on teen physical activities and building a commitment to lifetime fitness.

Boys and Girls Clubs of America The Boys and Girls Clubs of America, founded in 1906 as the Boys Club of America, changed its name in 1990 to reflect a coeducational philosophy. The Boys and Girls Clubs operate in centers and, in that sense, are facility based. The core program emphasizes promoting the physical, emotional, cultural, and social needs and interests of girls and boys while recognizing developmental principles. Boys and Girls Clubs build their program around six core program areas: (1) personal and educational development, (2) citizenship and leadership development, (3) cultural enrichment, (4) health and physical education, (5) social recreation, and (6) outdoor and environmental education. Club programs and services promote a sense of competence, a sense of usefulness, a sense of belonging, and a sense of power or influence. Three basic methods are used by the Boys and Girls Clubs. The first, individual assistance, involves one-to-one interaction with participants. The second is the carrying out of activities in small groups, and the third method promotes activities in large-group, or drop-in, situations.

The varied and numerous programs offered by the Boys and Girls Clubs include the following educational programs and activities: library; tutorial/basic skills assistance; computer skills; environmental education/camping program; dropout prevention; communication skills development, speaking, and reading; specialized education classes; pre-employment skills training; teen pregnancy/suicide prevention; health and hygiene; cooking classes; nutrition education; basic money management; woodshop; field trips; and alcohol/drug abuse prevention and others. Social development programs offered by the Boys and Girls Clubs include activities such as the following: special events (talent shows, carnivals, dances); computer club, photography club, government club, and human relations club; inter/intraclub tournaments; counseling/referral; nutritional feeding program; games room; leadership training; movies; arts and crafts; camping, hiking, and fishing; monthly birthday parties; awards banquets and ceremonies; attitude and motivation development; and field trips. The Boys and Girls Clubs serve nearly 1.7 million participants on a yearly basis.

Big Brothers/Big Sisters of America Big Brothers/Big Sisters of America was founded in 1904 and is designed to match children one-on-one with adults. Originally established for fatherless boys who were facing legal action, it is believed to be one of the earliest prevention programs aimed at reducing juvenile delinquency in the United States. The first Big Sisters program started in 1908 for delinquent girls. Over the years the program has served to help match a child, usually from a single-parent family, with an adult who serves as a support, friend, mentor, and positive role model. The one-to-one friendships established in the Big Brothers/Big Sisters program serve as a highly effective way of supporting children and can curb problems that might later lead to more serious criminal activity.

The program serves children and youth ages seven to thirteen. Adult volunteers in the Big Brothers/Big Sisters program provide guidance, companionship, and emotional support. Volunteers must be at least eighteen years old and evidence a stable lifestyle. They usually commit between three and six hours a week, working with a little brother or little sister aged seven to thirteen. The Big Brother or Big Sister does not act as a substitute parent or child-care provider, but as a friend. Adult volunteers are screened in a stringent application and reference checking process that includes a police check. Volunteers are further oriented through Empower, a child sexual abuse education and prevention program, and Alternatives, a substance abuse education and prevention program.

Religious-Sponsored Organizations   Religious organizations have traditionally cared about the development of children and youth. Some organizations are connected with a specific church or denomination, while others are connected to various religions throughout the world. The larger youth serving organizations with religious affiliation in the United States include the Young Men's Christian Association (YMCA), Young Women's Christian Association (YWCA), the Catholic Youth Organization (CYO), Young Men's Hebrew Association (YMHA), and the Young Women's Hebrew Association (YWHA). Although this list is not inclusive, it does represent a cross section of the types of programs offered by youth serving organizations with religious affiliation.

Young Men's Christian Association   The YMCA movement was established in England in the early 1800s by Sir George Williams. In the United States, the first YMCA was established in 1851 in the city of Boston. From a historical perspective, the YMCA programs were established to meet the spiritual needs of young men. Today, that philosophy, while intact, has broadened considerably in terms of the types of services and programs offered. The mission statement of the YMCA is "to share Christian principles with all, with services building spirit, mind, and body" (Carnegie Corp., 1992, p. 150). Many YMCAs today feature family services; with a broader perspective than just males, they provide opportunities for a cross section of the population and emphasize family considerations.

YMCA programs are facility centered. Individuals or families buy a membership that covers the use of basic services such as a gymnasium, exercise area, swimming pool, locker rooms, game rooms, and lounge. Members also receive reduced fees on other programs. For example, YMCAs run extensive resident and day camp programs for children. In fact, the YMCA was a pioneer in the camping movement, with its first camp established in New York in 1885. Further, YMCA activities for youth include sports clinics, volleyball, health enhancement, karate, gymnastics, swimming programs, dance classes, tennis instruction, fitness and aerobic activities, racquetball, youth and adult sports leagues, and teen programs. The range of services provided by many YMCAs is virtually unlimited. YMCAs also have strong adult education programs offered through a variety of instructional strategies.

Young Women's Christian Association of the United States of America   The YWCA of the U.S.A. was established in 1858. Today the YWCA has more than 4 million members. The program, historically rooted in the Christian religion, focuses on drawing together women and girls of ". . . diverse experiences and faith, that their lives may be open to new understanding and deeper relationships, and that they may join in the struggle for peace and justice, freedom and dignity for all people" (Carnegie Corp., 1992, p. 151). Today the mission of the YWCA seeks to empower women and eliminate racism. The YWCA operates at

4,000 locations throughout the United States, and local YWCAs are supported by a national association that provides support services to each of the units.

The services of a local YWCA, both varied and diverse, depend on the local needs and conditions of various communities. Programs include services for women in crisis, refugee women, single parents, displaced homemakers, homeless women, women in prison, ex-offenders and women coping with substance abuse, as well as others in the general population. The YWCA runs programs for teens directed toward the development of self-reliance, self-esteem, and acquisition of life skills. A strong component works toward supporting programs in the areas of health, physical education, and recreation. Leadership activities promote volunteer training, as well as teen leadership development. Sample programs operated by a midwestern YWCA include a young mother's support group, women in transition, day camp for children, child care, mother's support center, cake decorating, candy making, hiking club, book discussion group, fitness and aquatics, parent/teen communication skill development, teen educational multicultural awareness, and trips and tours.

Catholic Youth Organization The Catholic Youth Organization is the leading Catholic organization concerned with meeting the spiritual, social, and recreational needs of young people in the United States. The CYO, officially established in the early 1950s as a component of the National Council of Catholic Youth, implements its programs on a parish level and relies on the leadership of a local priest as well as volunteers from the parish. Youth are encouraged to become involved in such activities as retreats, sports programs, service programs, religious workshops, and educational classes.

Young Men's and Young Women's Hebrew Association According to Kraus (1991) the YMHA and YWHA do not regard themselves as recreation agencies, but rather as community organizations devoted to social service, with a strong Jewish cultural component. The YM-YWHA identifies social work as its major professional discipline. Staff try to create opportunities for participants to meet their physical, social, and emotional needs while stimulating individual growth, leadership, and responsibility.

Programs offered by the YM-YWHA are facility based and focus on sports, cultural arts, and outdoor activities. The YM-YWHA operate a number of recreation centers and camps primarily concentrated in the northeast portion of the United States.

Religious Organizations

Beyond serving youth, many churches of various denominations and other religious organizations plan, organize, and implement a variety of recreation and leisure services for families, seniors, and other special groups. These programs usually have either one or two broad purposes—to provide activities to promote fellowship with one another and to encourage involvement within the organization. For example, the Church of Jesus Christ of Latter Day Saints has a strong program of organized events for church members of all ages. These activities help church members meet their spiritual, social, cultural, physical, and emotional needs. Activities include such services as competitive sports, scouting, cultural arts, drama, camping, art, hobbies, crafts, music and dance, fitness, home improvement skills, single adult programs, genealogy, and special events.

Recreation activities also provide a means of bringing others into the organization and serve as a means to help others. For example, the Salvation Army is a religious organization committed to promoting a ministry of religious activities combined with social service work, education, training, fellowship, and recreation. The Salvation Army operates most of its center programs in disadvantaged areas and generally targets its services to meet the needs of the disadvantaged population. The Salvation Army serves more than 4 million individuals annually. The greatest participation occurs in camping programs, boys' and girls' clubs, and community centers. Membership fees for participants are nominal, usually under ten dollars. The Salvation Army programs, while usually driven by local needs, sometimes receive support for individual centers and programs from a national headquarters and four regional offices.

While exact purposes differ, these organizations base the philosophy of service on their religious beliefs. For Christian churches and organizations, this means infusing a strong moral ethic based on the Judeo-Christian credo, as well as merging their specific doctrine and beliefs with their recreation and leisure program offerings. An organization based on Islamic principles would integrate teachings of the Koran and Arabic customs with the activities it offered. For example, Christian organizations may structure many activities and events around Easter or the Christmas holidays, Jewish organizations would organize events and activities around Passover or Purim, and Islamic organizations might emphasize a holiday season such as Ramadan.

Organizations Serving Special Populations

Beyond serving youth, a variety of organizations serve other specific groups. Some groups have been created to meet the needs of enlisted personnel in the U.S. Armed Forces (e.g., USO); some organizations work with people with specific disabilities (e.g., Recreation Center for the Handicapped, Inc.); still others work with youth who are adjudicated as delinquent (e.g., Eckerd Foundation). This section profiles several of these types of organizations.

USO   The United Service Organization, Inc. (USO), formed in 1941, provides a broad range of programs for U.S. Armed Forces and their families throughout the world. The USO is a private nonprofit voluntary organization that is congressionally chartered; it receives no funding from the federal government, but rather is supported by private donations, including contributions from the United Way. At 160 locations throughout the world, the USO provides various types of programs through Family and Community Centers, Fleet Centers, Airport Centers, Intercultural Programs, and Celebrity Entertainment. The USO mission is "to provide morale, welfare, and recreation-type services to uniformed military personnel. The original intent of Congress—and enduring style of USO delivery—is to represent the American people by extending a "touch of home" to their military members. Thus, although some USO programs/services are similar to those provided by other agencies, the hallmark of the USO has been and will continue to be *how,* as much as *what* services are provided" (USO-We Deliver America, 2001).

The USO operates a wide variety of human services, including many involving recreation and leisure. For instance, the USO operates Family and Community Centers in fourteen states, as well as Puerto Rico, the Virgin Islands, and the District of Columbia. In addition, the USO operates similar facilities in eight foreign countries. These centers help individuals adjust to new surroundings and provide information and program services concerning employment opportunities, parenting, nutrition, budgeting, and children's recreation programs.

The USO also operates thirteen Fleet Centers serving the United States Naval Fleet worldwide. When the fleet makes a port call, the USO is poised to provide services—maps, directions, currency exchange, language assistance, hotels, travel connections, and family exchange programs. All of these services are available to members of the fleet. Probably the best-known USO activity is the Celebrity Entertainment program—USO shows around the world feature a variety of entertainment, from sports celebrities to musical reviews. Perhaps the most famous celebrity associated with the USO is Bob Hope. Annually, over 5,000,000 patrons are served through USO programs and services.

Recreation Center for the Handicapped, Inc. The Recreation Center for the Handicapped, Inc. established in 1952 in San Francisco, California as a community-based facility, serves individuals of all ages and disabilities. The Center has a threefold purpose. First, it stimulates the development of skills, attitudes, and knowledge necessary for successful participation in community life through recreation, habilitation, education, and socialization experiences. Second, it provides social recreation and leisure skills designed to assist individuals with disabilities to progress to programs that are in the least restrictive environment. Third, it strives to educate participants and community members to act as advocates for the rights of individuals with disabilities, to train new and existing professionals, and to develop innovative programs that meet the ever-changing, leisure-related needs of people with disabilities.

The Center has five departments—adult development, children and teens, community leisure training, leisure outreach, and adult behavior. These five departments work together to provide a variety of direct services to participants, including camping and outdoor education activities; sports programs; arts and crafts projects; special events; and "Theatre Unlimited," the center's famous mainstreamed theater company.

The Center operates on a budget of more than $3.4 million. A large proportion of the operating budget is raised annually by the board of directors through individual solicitation of individuals, service clubs, and fundraising (Kennedy, Smith, and Austin, 1991). Other funding sources include the California State Department of Education and the Department of Developmental Services as well as the San Francisco Department of Social Services and the Commission on Aging.

More than 11.6 million children and youth in the school system have some form of disability; in addition, 16.7 million Americans use some sort of assistive technology device in their homes (U.S. Bureau of Census, 1997). It is estimated that 24% of the population of individuals fifteen years or older have some sort of disability; this represents more than 48 million people (U.S. Bureau of the Census, 1997). Many of these people are not involved with traditional recreation programs for a variety of reasons. Many nonprofit organizations have worked to meet the needs of people with disabilities. For example, Special Olympics, Inc. provides people with mental retardation an opportunity to compete in more than twenty-five different Olympic-type events throughout the year; Camp Confidence in Brainerd, Minnesota, provides year-round camping activities and outdoor education for people who are developmentally disabled.

Eckerd Foundation The Eckerd Foundation, established in 1961, has a commitment to meet the needs of emotionally disturbed children. The Eckerd Wilderness Educational System Camping Program is a part of the Eckerd Foundation—in the late 1960s the Eckerd Foundation opened its first alternative camp in Florida. Since then the program has expanded to develop coeducational facilities in Florida, North Carolina, Vermont, and Rhode Island.

The program provides year-round residential therapy in a nurturing wilderness environment. Groups of ten children and two counselors work together to construct their own shelters, cut their own wood for campfires and cooking, repair their equipment, arrange their own recreation and meal plans, and do all the things necessary to live in the outdoors. Participants stay in the program for nine to twelve months and receive extensive aftercare upon release from the program. Research shows that such opportunities can create a sense of accomplishment, self-worth, and cooperation within the participant.

Many nonprofit organizations provide programs and services for the increasing number of youth involved in some form of socially deviant behavior. Many of these programs have

Treats

Creating magic moments for children is becoming a worldwide endeavor as nonprofit organizations around the world try to brighten a child's day through recreation and play. For example, TREATS, a nonprofit organization based in Hong Kong, strives to integrate children of different backgrounds and abilities in a recreation setting to help promote better understanding of one another and to provide them with enjoyable ways of learning life skills. TREATS' emphasis on inclusion and integration as well as its experience in partnerships and collaboration with other organizations are fine examples of the type of programs that can evolve in response to knowing and understanding the needs of the local community.

Hong Kong, a city of 6.2 million people, can be a scary place to grow up, especially for children from disadvantaged backgrounds. TREATS was established in 1979 when very little was being done to promote recreation and play in Hong Kong and play facilities were scarce. Initially the aim of TREATS was simply to give children a fun and happy day—a treat—a day away from their noisy, crowded urban environment. Trips were organized for children living in institutions, special schools, and crowded settlement estates to overnight camps in the countryside. There were also day trips to the beach and other special locations and events.

In the late 1980s, with greater awareness of the importance of recreation in the overall well-being of children and the development of recreation facilities throughout Hong Kong, TREATS began its own recreation program.

The aim of TREATS is still to provide fun and enjoyment by providing well-organized, well-executed, and caring youth development services, but additional goals have been added to include an emphasis on integrating children with and without disabilities.

TREATS works closely with Hong Kong's Education Department, Social Welfare Department, Youth and Community Centers, and other nongovernmental organizations to reach a wide variety of children including children with special needs, children living in institutions and small group homes, children who have recently immigrated from China, children on public assistance, children with only one parent, and children living in crowded public temporary housing. Within TREATS programs, children from two or more of these diverse targeted groups are brought together in a camp setting and through games and activities encouraged to communicate, understand, respect, and trust one another. In 1995, TREATS programs reached a total of 4,498 children in both day and resident camps as well as cooperative games sessions at schools throughout Hong Kong.

developed outdoor components designed to either prescribe treatment for, reduce, or prevent the socially deviant behavior of youth who are labeled as juvenile delinquents. This often means addressing some of the variables that seem to contribute to juvenile delinquency, such as low self-esteem, emotional problems, inadequate socialization, lack of moral judgment, and consistent failure in school (Laurence and Stuart, 1990). Examples of these types of programs may be found throughout the United States and include long-term residential therapeutic camping, stress/adventure experiences based on a modified Outward Bound model, and school-based programs following the Project Adventure model.

Relief Organizations

Recreation services form a vital part of many relief organizations. In relief organizations such as the Red Cross, programs are offered to make many recreation activities safer, and, because of the voluntary nature of the Red Cross, many volunteers donate their leisure time to provide these programs.

American Red Cross   The mission of the American Red Cross is to "improve the quality of human life; enhance self-reliance and concern for others; and to help people avoid, prepare for, and cope with emergencies. Its services are governed and directed by volunteers consistent with a congressional charter" (Carnegie Corp., 1992, p. 141). The American Red Cross values impartiality, volunteerism, humanitarianism, service excellence, and internationalism.

American Red Cross organizations are community-based voluntary organizations that are governed, supported, and principally staffed by volunteers who work in conjunction with paid staff members. The American Red Cross helps to provide and support the delivery of recreation and leisure services from a number of different perspectives; for example, the Red Cross provides training courses in areas such as boating and water safety. Additionally, the Red Cross provides recreation events to veterans, members of the Armed Forces, and their families. Furthermore, the American Red Cross operates a large youth services program.

Perhaps the most well-known program operated by the American Red Cross has been the Aquatics Safety program. This program, designed to provide individuals with a full range of courses, helps increase aquatic fun while promoting safety. The Red Cross operates standardized courses for individuals of all ages and swimming abilities. Many public parks and recreation agencies, as well as other private voluntary organizations, use the American Red Cross system to provide aquatic programs.

The American Red Cross also operates Boating Safety courses. These courses aim to teach individuals the fundamentals of safe canoeing, kayaking, rowing, sailing, and use of outboard motor boats. The American Red Cross courses provide individuals with lectures, discussions, and hands-on experiences directed toward improving competence in the water.

Another program operated by the American Red Cross is the Leadership Development/ Volunteerism program. The American Red Cross offers many direct-service opportunities for individuals to use their leisure time to volunteer. As indicated in the American Red Cross publication *Youth, a Timeless Resource,* ". . . there is no better way to help young people learn about the value of caring for others than by introducing them to volunteerism through Red Cross service projects." Other Red Cross programs aimed at helping youth gain leadership opportunities include the International Understanding program and Leadership Development program.

Social Service Organizations

Social service organizations have traditionally viewed recreation as a social instrument. Historically the provision of wholesome recreation served as a central part of the settlement-house movement, discussed in chapter 3, established to ease the transition to urban living for thousands of persons immigrating to the cities of America during the Industrial Revolution. Metropolitan Family Services, a local social service organization, has incorporated recreation into its overall program.

Metropolitan Family Services   Metropolitan Family Services offers a variety of social services throughout the metropolitan Chicago area, including a camping program at Camp Algonquin. This year-round camping program enables campers to acquire and/or strengthen skills that will help them to cope more effectively with their life situations in the city. In addition, the program provides campers with a sustained positive experience with people of diverse ethnic groups and generations whereby stereotypes and prejudices can be diminished. The camp setting removes many of the constraints of the city and provides a place where campers of all ages can interact, test new behaviors, and plan future directions. To assist in this process the camp program includes traditional camp activities as well as professional social work interventions such as family assessments, group discussions, and crisis counseling.

Conservation Organizations

Many nonprofit special-interest organizations seek to educate the public and influence governmental policy in the areas of conservation and outdoor recreation. In the areas of conservation, organizations range from radical organizations like the Sea Shepherd Conservation Society to conservative organizations like the Nature Conservancy. The Sea Shepherds advocate sabotage to prevent the killing of dolphins in the tuna industry and to protect whales from the whaling industry. On the other hand, the Nature Conservancy uses a businesslike approach to purchase threatened areas. The Nature Conservancy is a nonprofit organization that was founded in 1951. Through its efforts and mission "to preserve the plants, animals, and natural communities that represent the diversity of life on Earth by protecting the lands and waters they need to survive" the Nature Conservancy has protected nearly 12 million acres and 1400 preserves in the United States, and over 80 million acres internationally (The Nature Conservancy, 2001).

The Appalachian Mountain Club and the National Rifle Association are examples of nonprofit special-interest organizations involved in the promotion of various aspects of outdoor recreation. For example, the Appalachian Mountain Club advocates conservation efforts throughout the northeast and maintains trails and a network of huts and shelters, publishes guides, and promotes programs for developing outdoor leaders. The National Rifle Association carries on extensive lobbying efforts involving gun control and also sponsors firearm instruction, safety training, and shooting tournaments. Many of these conservation organizations combine conservation and outdoor recreation initiatives. For example, the Sierra Club is a well-respected conservation organization as well as being the nation's largest skiing and hiking club.

Sierra Club   The Sierra Club, founded in 1892, resulted from the passion of a small group of people for the mountains of California. Its first president was the famous preservationist, John Muir. The purpose of the club is to explore, enjoy, and protect the wild places of the earth; to practice and promote the responsible use of the earth's ecosystems and resources; to educate and enlist humanity to protect and restore the quality of the natural and human environment; and to use all lawful means to carry out these objectives.

The Sierra Club has more than 648,000 members and an annual revenue of $52 million is generated from memberships, book sales, trip revenues, and fundraising (*Earth Journal,* 1993). In the 1992 centennial celebration, *Sierra Magazine* noted,

> The Sierra Club's first century comes to a close with our view having widened from the mountains of California to all seven continents, and on into the highest reaches of the atmosphere. Our second century may well see that gaze embrace still broader horizons, as all that we learn about the environment—and humanity's niche within it—provides further proof of John Muir's maxim: 'When we try to pick out anything by itself, we find it hitched to everything else in the universe.' (p. 73)

Service Clubs

Service clubs, often made up of various professional and business organizations within a community, have a twofold involvement in recreation and leisure. First, many of these organizations provide recreation, fellowship, and service opportunities for their members. Second, many of these organizations, such as the Kiwanis, Lions, or Junior League, sponsor recreation programs for other groups within the community. They promote diverse programs that include

Engineering Satisfaction Among Constituents

I n the nonprofit sector, marketing is the engineering of *satisfaction* among a variety of groups including users of an organization's services, funders, trustees, regulators, and others who can influence the success of the organization—such as the media and even the general public.

One of the most important aspects of marketing is called *market segmentation.* In the nonprofit sector, market segmentation refers to the various constituencies whose satisfaction must be addressed. In most cases different strategies need to be developed for each group, but many nonprofit organizations do not correctly identify all their constituencies.

This was certainly the case with Abbott Academy, which had stated publicly and quite explicitly that the single constituency to which it needed to address

itself was its students. The . . . catalogue of the school began with the following words: "Abbott Academy was founded with the express intent of providing an outstanding education to young people. It is to our students, therefore, that we devote our attention, our resources, and our energies."

From a marketing point of view, students were not the only constituency whose needs had to be addressed if Abbott was to be successful. Other groups included parents, college representatives, potential applicants/prospective students, minority representatives, faculty, trustees, and other donors. . . . Each of these constituent groups could have been a vital link in helping Abbott Academy solve its problems, achieve its goals, and remain fiscally healthy. Yet, by focusing on only one group—its students—the school's leadership paid a very high price.

Source: Thomas Wolf, *Managing a Nonprofit Organization,* 1990, Fireside, NY.

sports programs, programs for disadvantaged children and youth, programs for the arts and other cultural activities, and camping for children with disabilities.

Challenges for the Future

Nonprofit organizations face many challenges today. Like other leisure service organizations, nonprofit agencies face an increased demand for the services they provide while funding dollars become more difficult to obtain. For example, the Carnegie Corporation (1992) suggests that nonprofit organizations serving youth are being challenged to expand their services to younger children and promote outreach programs while at the same time they must deal with shrinking resources and increasing incidences of litigation. Meanwhile, the changing needs of youth require program expansion, including providing more job training, promoting diversity and tolerance of differences in terms of religion, ethnicity, physical abilities, and sexual orientation, and taking a more holistic approach to youth development.

Other issues affecting nonprofit organizations include effective fundraising; attracting, training, and managing volunteer workers; creating staff development opportunities for paid staff; and developing partnerships with both the public and private sector.

Summary

Nonprofit organizations form an important part of the leisure service industry. They focus their services on a variety of constituents of all ages and of both sexes. Some nonprofit organizations have a commitment to a broad segment of the population, whereas others serve specific groups and promote a specific set of goals, such as the character development of youth. Estimates suggest that the nonprofit sector spends nearly $15 billion a year. Among youth serving organizations, some 400 agencies deliver leisure services to youth either exclusively or as a part of their mission.

In general, nonprofit organizations can be subdivided into three major categories—public benefit, mutual benefit, and private benefit. Public benefit nonprofit organizations have a broad focus and serve the general welfare of the public. Nonprofit organizations that focus on the mutual benefit of their membership are organized to bring together individuals and/or groups with complementary or mutual needs and interests. A private benefit nonprofit organization usually has a more exclusive membership, focuses on an activity, or provides the opportunity for individuals to interact in some type of social environment, such as a swim, tennis, or country club.

Nonprofit organizations have four primary elements. First, a nonprofit organization must operate with a degree of altruism. In other words, nonprofits are not in the business of making money. Second, most nonprofit organizations have at their core a public-service mission—they promote the general public welfare in some way. In addition, nonprofit organizations fall under special tax-exempt considerations for organizational purposes; they do not pay taxes on their assets. The last element of nonprofit organizations relates to the organization of their governance structure. Most have boards of directors that serve to promote the altruistic values reflected in the mission statement.

Discussion Questions

1. What is a nonprofit organization? What are its distinguishing characteristics?
2. Compare and contrast expenditures for nonprofit, government, and commercial leisure service organizations.
3. Identify three basic types of nonprofit organizations.
4. What are some of the ways of financing nonprofit organizations?
5. Locate three nonprofit organizations in your community; identify and detail their fundraising programs. Do they sell a product? Seek donations? Sponsorships? Gifts?
6. Profile a local professional working in a nonprofit organization. How does this individual's characteristics equate with the general information presented in this section of the book?
7. Locate a nonprofit organization in your community and detail its organization, budget, programs, and methods of publicity.
8. The Carnegie Corporation states that youth serving organizations pursue not only recreational ends, but also consider the principles of education and youth development. How might this influence the work of a youth serving organization?
9. Churches, as nonprofit organizations, provide recreation services as a secondary component to their spiritual endeavors. Locate two different churches in your community and compare and contrast their recreation-related program services.
10. Develop a charter for a new nonprofit youth service organization. What would be its mission? Scope of programs? Methods of funding?

References

Austin, J. E. 2000. *The Collaboration Challenge.* San Francisco: Jossey-Bass.
Carnegie Corporation of New York. 1992. *A Matter of Time: Risk and Opportunity in the Non-School Hours.* Woodlawn, MD: Wolk Press.
Drucker, P. F. 1999. *Management Challenges for the 21st Century.* New York: HarperBusiness.
Hodgkinson, V. A., and M. S. Weitzman. 1996. *Nonprofit Almanac 1996–1997.* San Francisco: Jossey-Bass.
Kennedy, D., R. Smith, and D. Austin. 1991. 3d ed. *Special Recreation.* Dubuque, IA: Wm. C. Brown.
Kraus, R. 1991. *Creative Management in Recreation Parks and Leisure.* St. Louis: Mosby.

Laurence, M., and T. Stuart. 1990. The use of adventure in reducing and preventing socially deviant youth behavior. Edited by J. Miles and S. Priest, in *Adventure Education.* State College, PA: Venture.

Mason, D. E. 1996. *Leading and Managing the Expressive Dimension.* San Francisco: Jossey-Bass.

The Nature Conservancy: Saving the Last Great Places. 2001. http://nature.org/aboutus/

Oleck, H. L. 1988. *Non-Profit Corporations, Organizations and Associations.* New York: Prentice Hall.

Steckel, R., and J. Lehman. 1997. *In Search of America's Best Nonprofits.* San Francisco: Jossey-Bass.

Staff. 1993. *1993 Earth Journal.* Boulder, CO: Buzzworm Books.

U.S. Bureau of the Census. 1997. *Statistical Abstract of the United States, 1997.* 117th ed. Washington, DC: U.S. Government Printing Office.

USO-We Deliver America. 2001. www.uso.org/about_uso.htm

Wolf, T. 1990. *Managing a Nonprofit Organization.* New York: Fireside.

C H A P T E R

11

Delivery of Leisure Services: Commercial

Commercial recreation venues provide many opportunities for leisure. Waterslides and water parks are among the most popular commercial leisure facilities.

Introduction

By far, the majority of organizations delivering leisure services in the United States and Canada today are commercial ventures. In fact, nearly 90 percent of all expenditures made for leisure goods and services takes place in the commercial sector (U.S. Bureau of the Census, 1999). Business opportunities in the area of commercial leisure services range from managing retail outlets that distribute leisure apparel to working in large theme or amusement parks. This chapter discusses the delivery of commercial leisure services.

Working in the commercial leisure business sector presents unique challenges and opportunities. The ability to develop and successfully manage a commercial leisure service venture requires knowledge of marketing, management, and finance, as well as a keen understanding of the leisure field. Individuals who are involved in the creation and delivery of commercial leisure services often seek the opportunity to operate in an independent fashion. Professionals in this area care about service and quality, as well as producing a profit for their effort.

This chapter reviews a number of specific topics. First, it defines and describes the distinguishing characteristics of commercial leisure service organizations, followed by a discussion of the three major types of business ownership and the major categories of commercial leisure services. The next section includes a discussion of professional roles and responsibilities in commercial leisure service businesses. The chapter concludes with a review of the current status of commercial leisure services as well as prospects for the future.

Characteristics of Commercial Leisure Services

In spite of the great growth of government and private nonprofit leisure services in the last century, private enterprise in the United States and Canada delivers by far the largest segment of leisure services. The private sector differs from both public and nonprofit organizations in many ways. This section discusses these differences in terms of goals, fiscal base, personnel, orientation to the customer, and other distinguishing characteristics.

Goals and Functions

The primary objective of a commercial leisure service organization is both simple and complex. Most commercial leisure service organizations have, as their primary goal, earning a profit. To earn a profit, however, a commercial leisure service organization must meet the needs of its customers. Figure 11.1 shows the relationship of customer service, profit, and outstanding satisfaction, comparing commercial leisure services with public or nonprofit leisure service organizations.

Successful commercial leisure organizations attempt to build a strong bond between themselves and their customers. This ensures a sense of loyalty on the part of customers. For a commercial leisure service organization to be successful and profitable, it must not only initially attract and serve target customers, but also retain them. So, while the goal of commercial leisure service organizations is to make a profit, serving the needs of customers ensures long-term profitability.

Who benefits from the efforts of a commercial leisure service business? At first glance, it appears that the profit earned by a business primarily benefits its owner(s) by increasing wealth. Profits also assist in the growth and expansion of a business, however, and pay dividends to stockholders. Most commercial leisure service businesses reinvest a portion of their profits in improving their quality of services, thus serving to benefit their customers.

Resource Base

Unlike the public sector that relies heavily on tax dollars to support its operations, commercial leisure service organizations must generate their own funds. When establishing a new commercial leisure service organization, two basic approaches can be taken to acquire the funds (capital) necessary to start the business—*equity* and *debt financing*. Equity financing involves the investment of an individual's own financial resources. Debt financing involves borrowing money from another source, which must eventually be repaid, in order to start a business venture.

According to Bullaro and Edginton (1986), six basic sources of capital can be used in establishing a new commercial leisure service business. These include personal savings; commercial bank loans; trade credit (credit on goods purchased for the business); equipment loans and

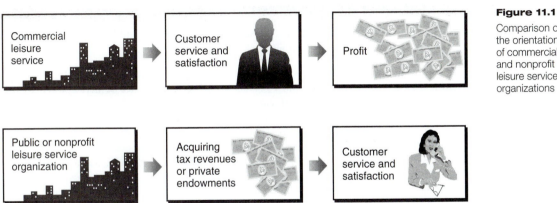

Figure 11.1

Comparison of the orientations of commercial and nonprofit leisure service organizations leases; and funds from friends, relatives, and local investors (often known as venture capitalists). According to Crossley and Jamieson (1993), typical start-up costs for commercial leisure enterprises involve such things as legal and professional consultants, insurance, incorporation expenses, tax deposits, licenses and permits, cost of obtaining loans, land and buildings, equipment, vehicles, machinery, remodeling and decorations, fixtures, displays, signs, salaries, utilities, staff development, supplies and equipment, inventory, maintenance expenses, advertising, and reserves.

The amount of capital necessary to operate a leisure service business varies according to the size, scope, and type of services provided. A key to obtaining capital and building and maintaining a successful business is the development of a *profit plan*. This detailed report about a proposed business venture shows potential sales (revenues) and costs (expenditures). A variety of factors must be taken into consideration when developing such a plan, including types of services to be offered, changing market conditions, customer preferences, the influence of governmental regulations, the cost of labor, estimates of profitability, and other factors (Bullaro and Edginton, 1986; Crossley and Jamieson, 1993).

Not only does the commercial leisure service organization need to generate start-up capital, but it also must generate sufficient income to maintain itself, through the sale of its products or services. In other words, it must carefully calculate the cost and worth of its service or product and affix a price. This price must reflect the cost of production, take into consideration the willingness of people to consume the product or service, and the need to produce a profit.

Characteristics of Professionals/Owners

Although it is difficult to distinguish between professionals working in public, private nonprofit, and commercial leisure service organizations, some unique characteristics generally apply to entrepreneurs in the commercial leisure service sector. In general, these individuals, especially in small businesses, perceive themselves as being goal-oriented, self-reliant, and self-motivated (Pinchot, 1985). They like moderate risk and see themselves as the creator of needs. They also view themselves as being action-oriented and see mistakes and failures as learning experiences. Crossley and Jamieson (1993) write that entrepreneurs ". . . come from a family value system that emphasizes an independent work life, leadership and a strong educational background" (p. 22). Furthermore, they note that goals of accomplishment, self-respect, freedom, family security, honesty, independence, competence, and ambition, as well as the desire to serve others, are a part of the makeup of entrepreneurs in the leisure services area.

Orientation to Customers

Discussing the role of commercial leisure service organizations and their relationship to consumers, Bullaro and Edginton (1986) write,

> Organizations that are wedded to their consumers are, by and large, more successful than those organizations that are not. It is therefore essential that primary importance be placed on serving people. This involves placing consumers first, ensuring that they are greeted with respect, dignity, courtesy, thoughtfulness, and ensuring that their welfare is utmost in the mind of the commercial leisure service professional. . . . This is accomplished by having a philosophy of service to people.
>
> What is the relationship between a commercial leisure service organization's philosophy regarding service to people and its profitability? Basically, people must perceive that a product or service has value to them . . . or they will not purchase it. In other words, they must feel that they will derive some benefit from the service. If the commercial leisure service organization is able to cultivate this type of feeling in its consumers, then with good management profitability will follow. (p. 5)

Obviously, it is in the best interest of the commercial leisure service organization to place customer needs first. Although all types of leisure service organizations now implement some type of marketing information, commercial organizations must use marketing strategies to meet customer needs if they are to survive in a competitive environment.

Marketing concepts suggest organizations must first determine their target markets—discrete clusters of homogeneous customers. In other words, a group of individuals who have a common set of characteristics or needs that can be satisfied by the provision of a particular product or service comprise a target market. For example, teens aged fourteen to nineteen whose parents earn more than $100,000 a year comprise a target market for expensive stereo equipment, trendy clothing, or videotapes. Figure 11.2 presents an example of a vendor not accurately determining his target market—young children like ice cream, not liver and onions.

In using a marketing strategy, commercial leisure service organizations focus on creating, communicating, and delivering a product that satisfies customer needs in a way that also results in profitability for the organization. Numerous psychological and sociological factors influence the needs of customers. Psychological factors include an individual's perceptions of the quality of a specific program, the motivation to participate in certain recreational activities, and the needs and attitudes of specific groups. Sociological influences include cultural factors, social class, and cohort groups. For example, a person's choice of recreation could result from the likes and dislikes of his or her social group.

THE FAR SIDE By GARY LARSON

Figure 11.2

An example of poor marketing strategy by a commercial leisure business

The Far Side cartoon by Gary Larson is reprinted by permission of Chronicle Features, San Francisco, CA. All rights reserved.

Types of Business Ownership

Each of the three basic forms of business ownership—sole proprietorship, partnership, and corporation—has certain merits. Any individual who decides to establish a leisure service business must first consider the relative advantages and disadvantages of each and determine which form best meets the business needs. In addition, as a business grows, the type of business ownership might evolve and change. This portion of the chapter deals with the characteristics of each of these three forms of legal organization (see figure 11.3).

Sole Proprietorship

A sole proprietorship—the simplest and least costly form of business ownership to establish—occurs when one person owns a business and is legally responsible for its debts and legal obligations (Crossley and Jamieson, 1993). In other words, the sole proprietor controls all of the assets of the organization and also is responsible for any of its liabilities. A sole proprietorship is the most common form of business ownership among service industries in the United States, with 82 percent organized as such (U.S. Bureau of Census, 1999). Figure 11.4 shows the relationship of the percentages of types of business organization in the service industries.

Figure 11.3

Types of business ownership

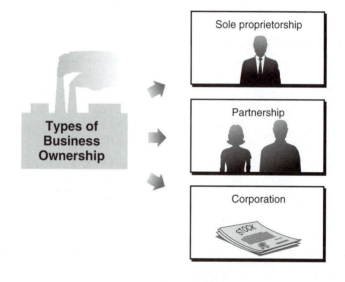

Figure 11.4

Forms of legal organization in service-type industries.

Source: Data from the Statistical Abstract of the United States, 1999 (119th ed.), Washington, D.C.

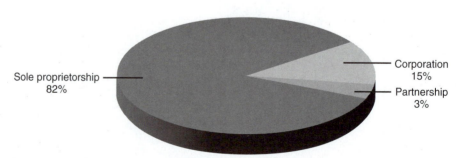

Sole proprietorships provide individuals with a great deal of flexibility and latitude in the management of a business. One person makes the decisions about the types of products or services to be provided and the way in which these are marketed. The sole proprietor takes all of the risks associated with the business venture and also has, as a major advantage, the opportunity to reap the profits that are derived from it. On the other hand, the sole proprietor also faces the risk of personal loss, extending to loss of personal assets, should the business fail.

Advantages of this form of ownership of a commercial leisure service organization include high personal incentive, freedom to act, less cost to establish, private financial statements, opportunity for tax savings, and the ability to be dissolved quickly. Some of the disadvantages of a sole proprietorship result from limited capital, limited talent (due to just one owner), unlimited liability, lack of continuity (if the owner dies or sells the business), and possible heavier taxation (Bullaro and Edginton, 1986).

Partnerships

A business partnership results when two or more people voluntarily decide to pool their funds and abilities and to go into business for profit (Crossley and Jamieson, 1993). The reasons for forming partnerships vary. A partnership allows two or more individuals to couple their skills, talents, and abilities to more effectively manage a commercial enterprise. It also offers a way to provide more capital to establish and maintain the venture. Partnerships are not as widespread as sole proprietorships; as depicted in figure 11.4, only 3 percent of all service-oriented businesses use this method of organization.

What makes a partnership successful? A successful partnership brings together individuals with complementary knowledge and skills that provide value to the enterprise. In the case of a commercial leisure service organization, one person might have a great deal of technical knowledge, while the other partner brings good managerial skills. For example, in a river rafting business one partner might have the technical skills necessary to plan and implement a series of adventure-oriented rafting trips. This person's knowledge of the outdoor environment would be essential to the success of the business. On the other hand, another partner might possess skills in the area of marketing, management, and accounting. This person would collect and receive monies, promote the program, and recruit staff. The combination of the talents of these two individuals would contribute to the success of the business as a whole. Without either of the partners, the business might be in jeopardy.

As is the case with sole proprietorships, partnerships also have advantages and disadvantages. Some of the advantages of a partnership are the possibility of greater capital, improved credit standing, more talent, and few legal restrictions. Some of the disadvantages of a partnership include the potential for management conflict, unlimited liability, constraints on capital, difficulty in withdrawing financial investment, and problems with the continuity of the business (Bullaro and Edginton, 1986).

Corporations

A corporation may be thought of as a separate legal entity. It is, as Chief Justice John Marshall of the United States Supreme Court defined it in 1819, an "artificial being, invisible, intangible, and resting only in the contemplation of the law." This means that a corporation has rights and privileges under the law, similar to those of an individual. A corporation can transact business, buy and sell property, sue and be sued, and engage in other activities as defined in its bylaws.

The corporation itself is responsible for the liabilities that are incurred as a result of its actions, whereas in sole proprietorships and partnerships, the owners are legally responsible for the obligations incurred by the business.

Corporations are owned by stockholders—those individuals who own shares of stock in them. Individuals who own the majority of the shares of a corporation's stock control its direction. Stockholders, rewarded when the business succeeds, earn dividends on their shares based on the profits earned by the corporation. In the United States today, corporations are generally more profitable than sole proprietorships or partnerships. Only 15 percent of service businesses are organized as corporations. As depicted in figure 11.5, however, corporations have receipts that total 72 percent of the total receipts of service-type industries (U.S. Bureau of Census, 1999).

Organizing as a corporation has a number of advantages and disadvantages. The principal advantage of a corporation is the limited liability of its owners (stockholders). In other words, individual investors are only liable for the amount that they have invested in the organization. Some of the other advantages of corporations include their ease in raising capital (through selling shares of stock), the ability to transfer ownership easily (also through the selling of shares of stock), and the fact that corporations enable continuity of operations.

The disadvantages of corporations as a form of organization include the higher costs involved in establishing them (higher than either a sole proprietorship or a partnership), possible double taxation of shareholders, and the fact that corporations must disclose information concerning their financial affairs.

A form of organizing as a corporation, known as the *S Corporation,* presents the stockholder with limited liability and taxes the profits of the corporation as if it were a partnership. This form of organization has a number of legal advantages. As Crossley and Jamieson (1993) note, "This form is very popular among small businesses where the owners desire the legal protection of the corporation but the flexibility and tax treatment of a partnership" (p. 79).

One leisure service organization organized as a corporation is Magic Theater Video. This commercial leisure service business was developed as a result of the expansion of home entertainment and was first conceptualized as a graduate class project. One of the first questions the initiators of this business, Marsha and Tom Johnson, asked, "was what form of legal organization would be most appropriate?" Because they used their personal savings as their primary source of capital, they decided to establish the business as a corporation. This enabled them to limit their personal liability for any losses that the business might incur. It also enabled them to receive capital from investors (two other stockholders) and certain tax benefits.

According to Marsha Johnson, the couple's motivation to develop Magic Theater Video was to become involved in a perceived rapid-growth industry, to control their own destiny (be their own boss), and to enjoy the excitement of making and acting on decisions in a rapidly

Figure 11.5
Percentage of business receipts of service-type industries for sole proprietorships, partnerships and corporations

Source: Data from Statistical Abstract of the United States, 1999 (119th ed.), Washington, D.C.

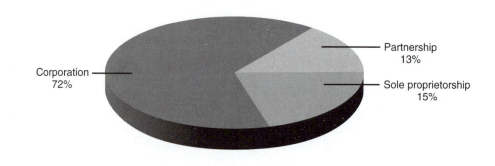

Corporation 72%

Partnership 13%

Sole proprietorship 15%

changing marketplace. In its first two years of business, Magic Theater Video doubled its inventory and quadrupled its sales.

Types of Commercial Leisure Services

With so many commercial leisure services, it becomes difficult to classify all of them. Crossley and Jamieson (1993) propose a classification system that includes the following commercial leisure services: travel/transportation industry, hospitality industry, local commercial recreation industry, and facilitators. Chubb and Chubb (1981) list the following businesses as examples of commercial recreation services: shopping facilities; food and drink services; participatory facilities; amusement parks; museums, gardens, and parks; shows, trips, and tours; stadiums and racetracks; camps, hotels, and resorts; and farms and estates. Kelly (1996) suggests that commercial leisure services may be categorized to include travel, sports, popular culture, the arts, and others. Types of commercial leisure resources identified by Kelly (1996) include destination attractions, travel support, community activity centers, outdoor sports provisions, spectator sports, skill acquisition, outdoor resource sites, mechanized activities, equipment and service retailers, popular culture, high culture, gambling, food and drink provisions, and equipment manufacturing.

The Play Station located in Cedar Rapids, Iowa, provides a playground environment where children can have fun while developing mental, physical, and social skills. This is done with accompanying adults. Figure 11.6 is a flyer outlining group trip opportunities to Play Station Family Fun Center. Still another example of this type of enterprise is the Playfair Discovery Center located in Duluth, Minnesota. Promoting family activities, this operation provides opportunities to explore the similarities and differences between Americans and families who dwell in various countries including Japan, Russia, Canada, and Sweden. Programs include art projects, role playing, cooperative games, storytelling, and live performances.

This section of the book presents major categories or types of commercial leisure services, including travel and tourism, hospitality and food services, manufacture of leisure products, entertainment services, contracting for services, retail outlets, and commercial leisure services in the natural environment. Figure 11.7 graphically represents the categories of commercial leisure services presented in this book.

Travel and Tourism

Tourism ranks as one of the most vital industries in the United States and Canada today. Between 1990 and 1997 the number of foreign visitors admitted for pleasure trips to the United States increased from 39.3 million to 47.7 million (U.S. Bureau of Census, 1999). Likewise, the number of individuals traveling from the United States abroad has also increased. In 1990, 44.6 million individuals traveled abroad compared with 52.7 million in 1997 (U.S. Bureau of Census, 1999). The U.S. Travel Data Center in Washington, D.C., reports that the number of pleasure trips to places of 100 miles or more from an individual's home increased from 301.2 in 1985 to 443.2 in 1997 (U.S. Bureau of Census, 1999). This was a decline from 1990, when individual pleasure trips were at an all-time high of 460.9 million.

The statistics on travel and tourism activities in the United States are staggering. Bullaro and Edginton (1986) report that travel ranks as the second-largest retail industry in the United States and the second-largest private employer. They further note that the highly diversified travel and tourism industry has more than 1 million component companies, ranging from small agencies to large hotel chains. Most, however, can be classified as small business.

The travel and tourism industry exists primarily to provide services to tourists and people traveling for business purposes. A tourist is an individual who moves from one location to

Play Station Information

We welcome you to The Play Station family fun center!

We offer a fun and imaginative 3 level play center specially designed for kids 12 and under. It's a safe place where children and adults can spend quality time together playing, pretending, challenging, and giggling.

The Play Station's purpose is to build physical fitness, enhance imagination and boost self-confidence in a stimulating and fun-filled environment.

Kids will increase their physical fitness and challenge their imagination as they climb, crawl, bounce, and slide through our colorful indoor play land with over 12,000 square feet of excitement! The fun will double when Mom and Dad play along!

The Play Station is open for fun 7 days a week, 360 days of the year. Stop in:
Monday - Thursday 10am - 8pm
Friday - Saturday 10am - 9pm
Sunday 11am - 6pm

ADMISSION RATES:
General Admission...............$5.50 + tax
Children 12 - 36 mths. ....$4.50 + tax
Children under 1 yr.............. FREE
Parents/Adults.................... FREE
Perpetual Player Card..........$44.00 + tax
(10 Admissions for price of 8,good for one year)

*Monday - Friday 10am - 4pm

PLAY STATION GIFT CERTIFICATES MAKE GREAT GIFTS!...........Play Station gift certificates are available all year long at our front desk -- good for one free admission.

We are located at 200 Collins Rd. NE; behind Lindale Mall, west of K-Mart. Call us at 373-1111. All play participants must wear socks!

Best Birthday Parties

Our birthday parties are led by your very own Personal Party Coach who will make your child feel extra special on their big day! Party time includes fun and games in our huge indoor playground and game depot, plus cake and refreshments in a private partyroom. Maximum fun for kids, minimum fuss for parents! We take care of the entertainment, party supplies, tokens, favors, and clean-up!

LOCK - INS

Bring the whole gang for a Play Station overnight! The ultimate in slumber party fun, play from 10pm - 7am! Your group of 40 or more can play till the cows come home for just $14.95 per child. Price includes overnight admission, free pop all night donut and milk in the morning, organized games. Reservations, deposit and chaperones required.
Call for more info!

SPECIAL GROUP RATES

Our field trips make the perfect outing for your class, troop, team, or group. With reservations for your group of 10 or more you can share the fun with special discounted rates. Call for more information! 373-1111

FUNraisers

We offer easy FUNraisers for non-profit organizations with no hassle, tons of fun and great success! The Play Station will sponsor your school or charitable group for a fun-filled weekday evening and donate 25% of the admissions for your cause. Call for more information! 373-1111

FACILITY RENTALS

Searching for a unique activity for your company or large group party? The Play Station can be yours alone for a private party. Just $375 gets your group of 100 guests unlimited soda and 2 hours of fun. $3.00 per additional guest, Pizza buffet available, extended parties and special catering or entertainment options negotiated.

another, primarily for the purpose of experiencing leisure. The dictionary defines a tourist as an individual who "travels for pleasure." Tourism can be defined as the business of serving tourists, and travel is the movement of a person from one place to another. Most definitions of tourists suggest that individuals must be away from home overnight, for a twenty-four-hour period of time. Zabel (1992) notes that the U.S. Travel Data Center defines travel and tourism as synonymous terms—". . . the actions and activities of international and domestic travelers taking trips to places outside their home communities for any purpose except commuting to and from work or attending school" (p. 96).

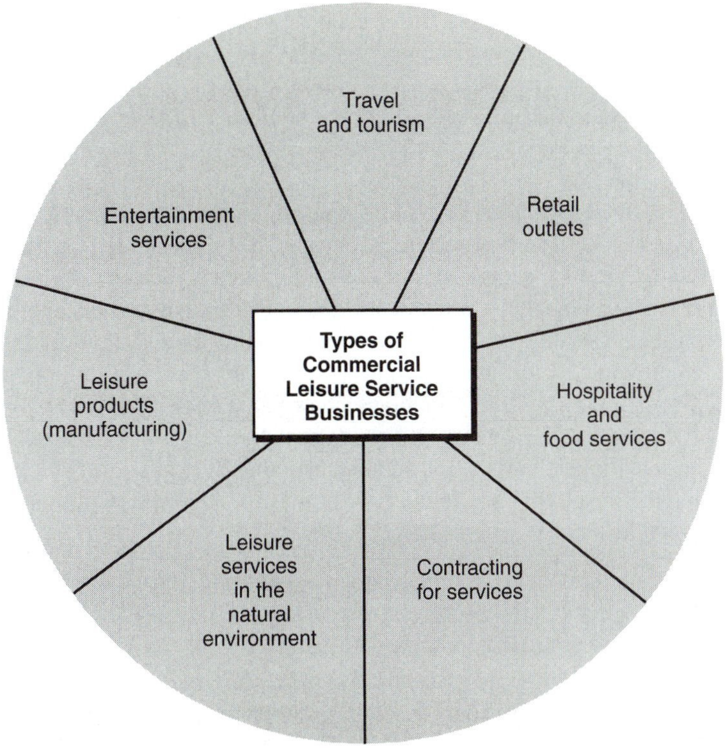

Figure 11.7

Seven types of
commercial
leisure service
businesses

Types of Commercial Leisure Service Businesses

- Travel and tourism
- Retail outlets
- Hospitality and food services
- Contracting for services
- Leisure services in the natural environment
- Leisure products (manufacturing)
- Entertainment services

The travel and tourism industry concerns itself with the movement of people to and from destination areas. Destination areas may be thought of as resources, whether natural or artificial, that attract people to spend time and money in an area. Disneyland and Disney World are examples of artificial structures that attract tourists; Yosemite, Yellowstone, and Crater Lake national parks are natural resources. Destination areas can also refer to events, such as the Rose Bowl and Rose Parade in Pasadena, California, that attract tourists.

Hospitality and Food Services

An industry closely aligned with the travel and tourism industry is the food and hospitality industry, concerned with the lodging and feeding of people. As the tourism industry has grown, so has the hospitality and food industry. Food franchises have become the fastest-growing franchises in the United States today. In 1955, 25 percent of the food dollar spent by each family was spent away from home. By 1985 that figure increased to 40 percent (Gottschalk, 1986). Estimates suggest that this growth continues.

Ritzer (2000) reports that there has been a wholesale movement associated with the fast-food industry that has ". . . reverberations extending far beyond its point-of-origin in the United States." In fact, it has influenced a wide range of undertakings, indeed, the way of life of a significant portion of the world. Of course, the leaders of this movement worldwide have been McDonald's and TRICOM (Pizza Hut, Kentucky Fried Chicken, and Taco Bell), which have 53,800 restaurants between them worldwide. Subway has 13,000 outlets.

The hotel and lodging industry experienced great growth over the last decade. For example, in 1996 there were 47,000 hotels and motels in the United States. The average occupancy rate for these rooms was 65.2 percent. This compares with 1992 where 39,500 hotel and motel rooms were available, reporting an occupancy rate of 61.7 percent. When viewing annual receipts of hotels and motels, they earned $90.7 billion in 1996. This compares with 1985 when hotel and motels earned $45.4 billion (U.S. Bureau of Census, 1999). The length of stay found 46 percent of leisure travelers staying one night, 26 percent two nights, and 29 percent three or more nights.

Between 1980 and 1998, sales for eating and drinking establishments, including restaurants, nightclubs, and other establishments, rose from $90 billion to $247 billion (U.S. Bureau of Census, 1999). Obviously, people are not cooking at home. We also can look at the growth of these types of establishments in terms of the number of establishments, employees, and the amount spent on their payrolls. In 1996, there were 466,000 eating and drinking places in the United States employing 7.4 million individuals with a payroll of $69 billion, compared with 402,000 in 1990, employing 6.4 million individuals with a payroll of $49.6 billion.

The numerous types of hospitality and food businesses each cater to specific target markets. Resorts, hostels, hotels, motels, restaurants, bed-and-breakfast inns, and convention centers all fall within the hospitality and food service industry. A brief description of each of these types of commercial leisure service businesses follows:

> *Resorts.* Resort facilities serve people who go to them primarily to experience leisure. In addition to lodging and food services, resorts also have recreation areas and facilities and, often, leisure programs and services.
>
> *Hostel.* A hostel is a lodging place usually designated for young people. Hostels often cater to individuals who use other than motor transportation, such as bicycles or hiking. Guests are charged a nominal lodging fee and are expected to help with housekeeping chores.
>
> *Hotels.* Hotels supply sleeping accommodations, usually have some type of dining area, and may have recreation areas, pools, and fitness centers.
>
> *Motels.* Motels, like hotels, supply sleeping accommodations and, often, food to tourists and other individuals. Motels can be distinguished from hotels in that their units can usually be entered directly from an outdoor court or parking lot.
>
> *Restaurants.* Restaurants allow people to purchase and consume meals. Many restaurants are designed to facilitate unique leisure experiences. For example, pizza parlors with a gay nineties motif provide both food and a fun leisure atmosphere.
>
> *Bed-and-breakfast inns.* These types of accommodations provide individuals with lodging and breakfast—breakfasts range from light continental fare to several courses of country cooking. Bed-and-breakfast inns are found in renovated houses, barns, and other buildings that evoke an old world or homey atmosphere.
>
> *Convention centers.* Many communities have facilities to accommodate conventions and conferences. Typically, these complexes offer meeting facilities, lodging facilities, and restaurants within close proximity to one another.
>
> *Casino resorts.* Family casino resorts have created a new trend in the leisure service industry. Several areas in the United States—Atlantic City, Reno, Lake Tahoe, Las Vegas, and others—have constructed elaborate family resorts that include gaming facilities, theme parks, entertainment, shopping malls, and special events.

The hospitality and food service business presents many challenges. As the margin of profit in the food and hospitality industry is narrow, these types of businesses must employ careful planning and management techniques.

Leisure Products (Manufacturing)

A myriad of recreation products is manufactured and sold in the United States and Canada today. As Kelly (1996) indicates, no list of all those "things" is possible. Leisure products, so evident in everyday life, have a tremendous impact not only on recreational pursuits, but in other aspects of life as well. Leisure apparel—shorts, tennis shoes, and athletic apparel—influences how people dress and, in a sense, their self-concept.

In 1996, total expenditures for personal consumption for recreation was $431.1 billion. This compares with $281.6 billion in 1990. In 1998, Americans spent over $66 billion on sporting goods. In 1990, this figure was $48 billion (U.S. Bureau of Census, 1999). For example, in 1998 Americans spent $12.4 billion on athletic and sport clothing, $13.6 billion on athletic and sport footwear, $18.2 billion on sport equipment, $10.6 billion on pleasure boats, $7.3 billion on recreational vehicles, and $3.1 billion on bicycles. Between 1990 and 1999, there was nearly a 35 percent increase in expenditures (U.S. Bureau of Census, 1999).

The production of finished leisure goods and products from processed raw materials is a secondary process of manufacturing. Manufacturing involves the planning and controlling of human resources, machines, and materials in such a way as to efficiently and effectively create desired products. In general, individuals who manufacture leisure products are concerned with producing a quality product in the right quantity at the right time. Products that do not meet consumer expectations in terms of quality will be at a disadvantage in the competitive market place. Furthermore, manufacturers must produce enough products to meet consumer demand. Today, people look for quality products of high value at a reasonable cost. Thus, those who produce leisure products must carefully consider costs and the break-even point for each product. Table 11.1 presents a partial listing of leisure products available in the marketplace today.

Kelly (1996) writes that six types of leisure products exist—namely sports, services, arts, technology-based, hobby-based, and market segment-oriented. He also indicates that a new

TABLE

11.1   A PARTIAL LIST OF LEISURE PRODUCTS

Toys	Food preparation equipment
Games	Musical instruments
Sports equipment	Arts and crafts supplies
Leisure apparel	Camping equipment
Computers	Tools
Home entertainment units	Hobby products
Televisions	Gardening supplies
Stereos	Video/audiotapes
Recreation vehicles	Records
Water-based equipment	Cooking supplies
Cars	Fabrics/sewing supplies
Bicycles	Books
Playground apparatus	Magazines
Fitness/exercise equipment	Needlework/knitting supplies
Photography supplies	Electronic equipment

product may be viewed as either an improvement, innovation, or invention (Kelly, 1985). Most newly developed products are actually improvements on existing ones. For example, recreation vehicles improved upon travel trailers. Travel trailers improved upon tents. A product innovation occurs when a substantial change is made to a piece of equipment or other product that significantly influences the leisure experiences. Kelly explains, "The introduction of fiberglass boats not only reduced maintenance and prolonged life, but also increased performance. It made boating quite different and more accessible" (Kelly, 1985, p. 343). A product invention occurs when someone creates a new product that heretofore did not exist—the invention of magnetic tape and its resultant application to home entertainment have revolutionized home-based leisure pursuits.

Entertainment Services

Canadians and U.S. citizens, like other people throughout the world, like to be entertained. In the entertainment industry, professionals actually deliver entertainment or entertainment services, or support individuals providing entertainment. Participation in such services ranges from viewing professional sporting events to attending community festivals. The production of entertainment services may involve live performances and/or the creation of productions that are electronically or technologically reproduced through the media. Entertainment services also encompass the management of such attractions as theme and amusement parks, circuses, gaming establishments, race tracks, and live concerts.

As the entertainment industry is vast, it is difficult to identify discrete categories within it. Some of the more obvious general categories within the entertainment industry, however, include the following:

Professional sports. This involves the management and promotion of a wide variety of professional men's and women's sports activities, including baseball, football, basketball, hockey, figure skating, tennis, golf, and soccer.

Gaming establishments. Many types of gaming establishments exist in the United States, and their impact is enormous. For example, total ticket sales for lotteries increased from $2.3 billion in 1980 to $35.5 billion in 1998 (U.S. Bureau of Census, 1999). The bulk of the proceeds support educational endeavors, although some proceeds in various states support infrastructure development, recreation concerns, and the environment. Casino gambling, pari-mutuel betting, and lotteries—including the nationwide Powerball™— fall in this category.

Horse racing and dog racing. Due to attendance, thoroughbred, harness, and greyhound racing rank among the top ten spectator sports in the United States.

Automobile racing. Automobile racing is the number one spectator sport in the United States, drawing more than 50 million people a year.

Circuses and carnivals. The circus and the carnival have long been standbys in the entertainment industry in the United States and Canada.

Theme and amusement parks. Theme/amusement parks have become one of the dominant forms of entertainment in the United States. Disneyland, Disney World, Six Flags, Great America, and Knott's Berry Farm all serve as examples of this component within the entertainment industry.

Special events and festivals. These activities contribute to community morale. They are built around a variety of different themes, including geographic, historic, and cultural

Disney's New Adventures

The sun never sets on the Disney Empire. But for more than forty-five years, Disneyland—the first house of the Mouse that roared—has had to soldier on while more money and attention were paid to its younger siblings, first Florida's Walt Disney World and later Tokyo Disneyland and Disneyland Paris. Next month, all that changes when the California Disney facility that invented the concept of the modern theme park reinvents itself.

And just two months later, Walt Disney World in Florida debuts perhaps the most innovative resort hotel in the Disney system—Disney's Animal Kingdom Lodge—located near the fourth and newest Walt Disney World theme park, Disney's Animal Kingdom. Many of the guest rooms look out over a thirty-three-acre savanna where more than 200 mammals and birds will be on view, much like an African game preserve. Both the California and Florida constructions signal Disney's intent to continue expansion of its U.S. parks.

On February 8, the doors swing open to Disney's California Adventure, centerpiece of a ten-year, $4 billion effort to revitalize and expand the Disneyland Resort and the surrounding city of Anaheim, coordinated by Disneyland Resort, the city of Anaheim, Orange County, the state of California, and a number of federal agencies. The result will pair the two adjacent parks with a variety of other Anaheim developments to create an extended-stay resort destination expected to attract visitors from around the globe.

The newly expanded Disneyland Resort in Anaheim includes six components: Disney's California Adventure, a new fifty-five-acre, $14 billion theme park adjacent to the original Disneyland celebrating California's culture, spirit, and natural beauty in three distinct themed "lands"; the original Disneyland park, created in 1955 and now sprawling over eighty-five acres; Downtown Disney, a public esplanade of shops, restaurants, and entertainment venues centrally located between the two park entrances and near surrounding hotels; Disney's Grand California Hotel, a 750-room hotel located within California Adventure, the first Disney hotel inside a theme park; Disney's Paradise Pier Hotel (formerly the Disneyland Pacific Hotel), a 502-room hotel that overlooks the Paradise Pier themed area inside Disney's California Adventure; and Disneyland Hotel, the original 990-room hotel that already serves the Disneyland park.

"This is a very different kind of experience, much more pop culture and MTV-like," says Barry Braverman, Disney Imagineering's creative director for the California designs and iconographies. "As visitors approach, they'll feel like they're walking into a postcard of California."

The entrance features massive freestanding letters spelling the state's name, a hand-glazed ceramic wall mural, a sixty-foot mirrored heliostat that continuously tracks and reflects the sun, and gates that open beneath an overarching Golden Gate Bridge. The park itself is composed of three lands that represent various California cultural and natural icons.

First is Hollywood Pictures Backlot, a mock studio that mimics the architecture and film-industry structures of Hollywood while immersing visitors in movie-making attractions, rides, and films. Themed movie sets and interactive animation displays let visitors take part in the creative process. A 2,000-seat, state-of-the art theater will host live shows.

The park's second land is The Golden State, a section that pays tribute to California's natural beauty and microclimates. Visitors can sample California produce and take part in wine tastings next to actual on-site Robert Mondavi vineyards. Dominating the land is Grizzly Peak, a constructed mountain with rock formations at the summit shaped to look like the head of a growling grizzly bear. The most popular ride in the new park is likely to be Soarin' Over California, a mock hang-gliding experience that lifts visitors forty feet up and into the concavity of a huge surrounding projection screen. Visitors will "fly" above twelve different California locales, including Yosemite, Lake Tahoe, and Napa Valley.

Paradise Pier, the third section, is a tribute to California oceanfront amusemant park piers and beach culture. The area will contain classic amusement park rides such as the 150-foot-tall Sun

—continued

Disney's New Adventures—concluded

Wheel ferris wheel and the California Screamin' roller coaster. Rounding out Paradise Pier will be midway games, street musicians, and artists.

Beyond the Disney facilities, the city of Anaheim has completed a $177 million expansion of nearby Anaheim Convention Center, which, with the Disney properties, is part of the 1,100-acre Anaheim Resort District. Citywide construction projects are improving residential areas, parking, mass transit, and retail and commercial areas.

Three thousand miles away, Florida's Walt Disney World is opening Disney's Animal Kingdom Lodge in April. The 1,293-room, six-story hotel features hand-carved furnishings, a semicircular *kraal* African village design, and views of an expansive grassland filled with birds and free-roaming mammals, including giraffes, zebra, Thomson's gazelle, ostrich, and ibis.

The viewing areas and walkways are intended to make guests feel as though they are in Africa. The lodge features three African-inspired restaurants, a thatch-roofed lobby with a massive mud fireplace, and an indoor flowing stream.

Source: Bateman, S. 2001, January. Travel trends: Disney's new adventures. *Hemisphere Magazine,* 42, 44.

Theme Park Attendance at Record Levels in 2000

ORLANDO, Fla. (AP)

A record 175 million people stood in line for rides at North America's top fifty theme parks, a trade magazine reported Friday. Attendance was up 3 percent, matching last year's increase, according to *Amusement Business.*

Florida and California parks, which cater to out-of-town tourists, dominated the top ten spots, with Disney parks occupying the first five, the magazine said. For the fourth year in a row, the Magic Kingdom at Walt Disney World in Orlando was the most visited park in North America, with approximately 15 million visitors, up 1.3 percent from last year. Worldwide, the park was only outdistanced by Tokyo Disneyland, the world's best-attended park, which had an estimated 16.5 million visitors, down more than 5 percent from last year.

The larger theme parks don't release attendance figures, but the Nashville, Tennessee–based trade publication calculates them each year based on inside sources and information provided by visitors and convention bureaus. The figures showed no signs of an economic slowdown, said Tim O'Brien, one of the magazine's editors.

Regional parks in the Midwest and Northeast, which cater to visitors living within 150 miles, were hurt by cool and wet weather in the spring, despite new multimillion-dollar rides at several parks. Cedar Point in Sandusky, Ohio, for example, expected to get a large attendance boost from the debut of its $25 million Millennium Force roller coaster, the first coaster more than 300-feet tall. But cold and rainy weather kept visitors away, the park said.

In Florida, Sea World Orlando and Busch Gardens Tampa Bay saw double-digit attendance gains due largely to a discount program targeting local residents.

Source: *Waterloo-Cedar Falls Courier,* Sunday, December 24, 2000, A-4.

ones. The Rhododendron Festival in Florence, Oregon, illustrates this concept. Festivals generate funds for a community, including many leisure-oriented businesses within it, and impact its economic well-being.

Live, filmed, taped, or broadcasted performances. Plays, operas, concerts, movies, television broadcasts, compact disks (CDs), tapes, and videotapes are all examples of products and services that relate to this component of the entertainment industry to produce a unique blend of entertainment services. When looking at the composite of this area, which could include motion pictures, entertainers, commercial sports, sports clubs, and amusement parks as well as others mentioned, the growth is spectacular. In billions of dollars, these combined areas generated $156.8 billion in receipts in 1997 (U.S. Bureau of Census, 1999). This compares with $52.7 billion in 1985.

Retail Outlets

Retail outlets provide a way of moving leisure products to consumers. Some businesses provide leisure products as one line in their total merchandising effort, whereas other retail outlets specialize exclusively in leisure products. For example, many stores focus exclusively on the provision of sports equipment and apparel. The Sports Line, a retail outlet located in Cedar Falls, Iowa, sells only sports apparel from professional athletic teams and sports hobby cards (e.g., baseball cards). Play It Again Sports in Stillwater, Oklahoma, focuses its retail business on buying and selling both used and new sporting goods. Some of the retail outlets often associated with leisure products include radio, television, and stereo outlets; bicycle shops; athletic equipment stores, including shoes and apparel; outdoor stores; bookstores; toy and hobby stores; photography stores; video rental outlets; and catalog sales (e.g., L. L. Bean and Patagonia).

Retail outlets can generally be categorized into two classifications—store and nonstore outlets. Nonstore outlets, as contrasted with store outlets, bring their products to the customer's home, for example, in the case of catalog sales. Some of the different types of store and nonstore outlets that distribute commercial leisure products and services include the following:

Specialty store. Offering merchandise in a specific area, such as athletics, outdoor recreation, and music or art supplies, specialty stores provide the customer with an opportunity to purchase a particular type of item.

Variety store. These moderately priced retail outlets provide a wide variety of merchandise, usually inexpensively.

Department store. While department stores also provide a wide variety of merchandise, they often target their lines to particular income levels or target markets. Their merchandise is often of a higher quality than the variety store.

Full-line discount store. This type of retail outlet provides merchandise at discount prices. Discount stores focus on price and value, as contrasted with quality and value (as might be the case in a department store).

Retail catalog showroom. This type of store, often self-service, usually offers its products at a discount.

Factory outlet. The purpose of this type of retail outlet is to sell factory seconds and factory overruns.

Flea market. A flea market is a leisure experience in and of itself, with many different products offered for sale in a festive atmosphere.

Video ordering system. Recently there has been a growth in the ordering of merchandise via the use of cable television. Individuals can see products on television and order them over the phone.

Retail outlets fall into a number of ownership categories—independent, corporate, and/or a chain of stores. Most retail trade stores in the United States are organized as sole proprietorships (65.4%), while 3.8 percent are organized as partnerships, and 28.8 percent are organized as corporations (U.S. Bureau of Census, 1999).

Leisure Services in the Natural Environment

Canadians and U.S. citizens enjoy many leisure activities in the natural environment such as swimming, hiking, boating, camping, backpacking, hunting, waterskiing, diving, fishing, and skiing. While many of these activities take place on public land, private entrepreneurs often provide the equipment, instruction, guide services, and so forth to meet the demand for leisure experiences in the natural environment.

The United States has nearly 700,000 private outdoor enterprises in operation. Some of these agencies control their own natural resources in terms of land and water; however, most use public resources. Many outdoor recreation services are seasonally based. This creates a challenge in terms of return on investment and year-round financial planning, staffing, and marketing. Ski resorts, for example, only operate when snow is available. This influences profit, work schedules, and promotional activities.

People who want to work in commercial leisure service organizations in the natural environment have many work opportunities; these include owner, manager, marketing director, instructor, guide, concession operator, ticket seller, clerk, site attendant, and maintenance manager. Direct-service positions (face-to-face) often require a high level of skill, knowledge, and competency in specific areas. For example, outdoor leaders must not only have technical knowledge related to the out-of-doors, but must also know how to interact positively with people.

Commercial leisure service activities and businesses that depend on the natural environment fall into five general categories: land-based, water-based, air-based, historically/culturally-based, and geographically-based. Their descriptions follow:

Land-based. Land-based activities in the natural environment include touring, mountain climbing, rappelling, backpacking, spelunking, skiing, camping (tent, trailer, RV), bird watching, hiking, hunting, and driving off-the-road vehicles. Many types of commercial leisure service businesses support these activities, such as commercial campgrounds (e.g., Thousand Trails and KOA), RV rentals and sales, trail guide businesses, and outdoor schools.

Water-based. Water-based activities in the natural environment range from luxurious cruises to wind surfing. Other water-based activities include canoeing, fishing, rafting, boating, kayaking, snorkeling and diving, swimming, waterskiing, and surfing. Some of the commercial leisure service businesses supporting these activities are cruise lines, commercial fishing boats, river guides, boating equipment and sales, and training schools for diving and snorkeling.

Air-based. Only a few leisure activities occur in the air, such as flying, ballooning, hang gliding, and parachuting. All of these have related commercial leisure service businesses that support them in terms of training and sales of equipment.

Historically and culturally-based. Some commercial leisure service businesses manage, for profit, historical or cultural sites. The exhibition of the Queen Mary in Long Beach,

Dolphin Dive a Peaceful Trip

PORT LUCAYA, Bahamas (AP)

An open hand brings Romballa the dolphin sidling up for a stroke of her silky skin. Holding up a rubber ring will prompt her to scoop it up and take it to the next person.

For those who wish Sea World offered season tickets, or who get excited by reruns of the *Flipper* television show, the Dolphin Experience on Grand Bahamas Island offers a chance to swim with the beloved marine mammals in the open ocean.

Chris Allison, president of the Dolphin Experience, said about 50,000 people a year visit his nine-and-a-half-acre dolphin center in Sanctuary Bay to interact with seventeen trained dolphins, either by just sitting on the dock, swimming with them in shallow water, or scuba diving with them off

the coast. "What we are providing is a safe and controlled interaction with the dolphins, where the dolphins know and understand the interaction," Allison explains.

Allison says the dives offer an opportunity to fulfill a fantasy in a way that protects both the divers and wild dolphins. The United States and the Bahamas have outlawed swimming with wild dolphins, which have been known to attack people who get too close.

"Everyone relates to dolphins," Allison says. "By the time they leave us, everybody realizes not only how important dolphins are, but how important the whole eco-structure is, what great responsibilities we have to take care of the ocean."

Source: *Waterloo-Cedar Falls Courier*, Sunday, April, 2, 2000, E-8.

California, is an example of a historically based commercial leisure service business operating in the natural environment.

Geographically-based. Some commercial leisure service businesses manage natural habitats for profit. Sea Lion Caves in Florence, Oregon, an example of this type of commercial leisure service business, bases its business on the natural environment. These types of businesses often have food, lodging, and souvenir services associated with them.

Entrepreneurship, Opportunities, and Challenges

Working in the commercial leisure service area provides many opportunities and involves risk. Approximately 95 percent of all small businesses fail within the first five years of start-up. Constant shifts in demand for services and products result in great entrepreneurial activity and opportunity, but also involve certain challenges. This section discusses the concept of entrepreneurship and the opportunities and challenges in the commercial leisure service sector.

What Is Entrepreneurship?

This is an age of entrepreneurship. Increasingly, the economies of the United States and Canada rely on the ability of small businesses to flex in response to rapid shifts in the marketplace. Individuals who seek risk and have the desire to operate independently and creatively are often referred to as entrepreneurs. Entrepreneurs make an investment or take a risk to start a new enterprise. If the business succeeds, these people benefit from their activity. Entrepreneurs often create perceived need through effective marketing, and people often view them as decisive and action-oriented.

Peter Drucker, a noted management theorist, writes that entrepreneurship involves systematic innovation. According to Drucker (1985), systematic innovation consists of the purposeful and organized search for changes and a systematic analysis of the opportunities such changes might offer for economic or social innovation. Thus, entrepreneurship deals with change, innovation, and a systematic analysis of conditions. While entrepreneurs do take risks, Drucker points out that entrepreneurs take calculated risks that minimize their exposure to failure and enhance their opportunity for success.

What key entrepreneurial skills do people need to succeed? First, they must have a firm commitment to the free-enterprise system; they believe that each individual has the freedom to use his or her own resources, talent, time, and energy to pursue a vision. Edginton, Carpenter, and Chenery (1987) observe a number of key entrepreneurial skills that enhance success in managing a commercial leisure service organization (see figure 11.8).

Vision. Vision, often thought of as forward thinking, is the ability to move in a new direction with purpose, to see a new reality.

Creativity. Creativity is the ability to be imaginative, inventive, resourceful, or constructive. Creative entrepreneurs generate new ideas and bring them to fruition.

Figure 11.8

Six key entrepreneurial skills

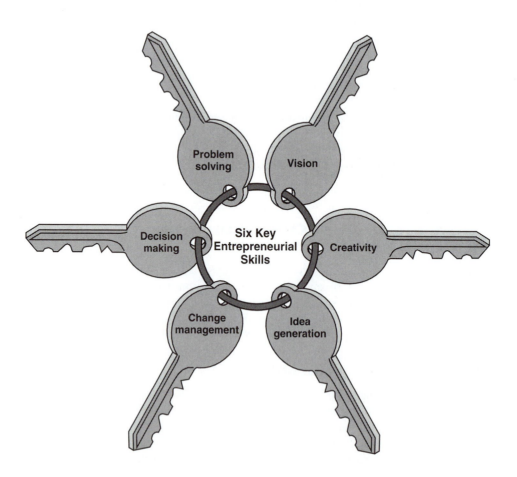

Idea generation. An idea is a mental image, a thought, or an opinion. Generating ideas involves brainstorming, reflecting, reasoning, and imagining. Idea generation is closely related to creativity.

Problem solving. Problem solving involves the ability to overcome barriers and obstacles and create solutions. Problem solvers use creativity, idea generation, and other resources to move forward even in the face of great difficulty.

Decision making. Entrepreneurs tend to be independent decision makers who learn from their mistakes. Because entrepreneurs can see a need that may not exist, decisions often involve risk and must be done in a thoughtful yet decisive manner.

Change management. Change management involves the ability to move into organizations and unfreeze ideas, structures, values, opinions, attitudes, methods, and procedures that influence the way people live and work. This often requires an ability to communicate effectively and persuasively.

A new entrepreneurial spirit has apparently emerged in the United States and Canada, reflected partly by the number of new jobs that have emerged over the past several decades; for example, between 1985 and 1998, jobs showed a net gain of 18.5 million in the United States (U.S. Bureau of Census, 1999). By the year 2005, it is projected that there will be 150.5 million individuals in the workforce, an anticipated gain of 67.7 million jobs when compared with 1970. There are currently 95.5 million individuals in the workforce. These new jobs primarily result from entrepreneurial ventures in the service and information sectors of society, with many in the leisure area. Entrepreneurs serve as pacesetters of opportunity, a challenging and demanding role. Their work is dynamic, diverse, inventive, and creative. Entrepreneurs produce new ways of meeting needs, work to improve existing products and services, and respond to changing demographic conditions.

Opportunities in the Commercial Leisure Services Sector

The size of the commercial leisure service market is staggering when compared with the delivery of public leisure services. As indicated, expenditures for personal consumption for recreation was $431.1 billion in 1997 (U.S. Bureau of Census, 1999). Expenditures for state and local government were $19.1 billion and $2.2 billion at the federal level (U.S. Bureau of Census, 1999). If we add $20 billion to this total figure for expenditures for youth, recreation, and environmental programs, there is a total of approximately $471 billion being spent. We estimate that somewhere between 85 percent and 95 percent is spent in the commercial sector. All indications suggest that this area will continue to grow.

Prospects for Profit The leisure industry is one market area in which profits have grown dramatically. In a study of the top 1,000 businesses in the United States, *Business Week* reports that a composite of the top leisure industries showed a significantly higher change in profits than other businesses. In 1986, profits among the top leisure service industries accounted for $1.7 billion (*Business Week,* 1987). This represented a 28 percent increase over the previous year. By 1992, however, profits for a similar group of the top leisure industries exceeded $5 billion and represented a 32 percent increase over the previous year. In 1999, the composite earnings for all leisure time industries was $6.7 billion in profits on $111.6 billion in sales (*Business Week,* 1999, p. 112). This reflects a 394 percent increase in profits between 1996 and 1999.

According to *Business Week* (1999) the average profit margin was 6.5 percent for 1999 on its top 1,000 companies. In 1992, the average profit margin was 4.7 percent (*Business Week,* 1993). Compared with profit margins earned in the top leisure enterprises, the results are significant. These figures, however, do not reflect the total dimensions of the commercial leisure service area. They do indicate that the commercial leisure market is healthy and viable. The Walt Disney Company illustrates the recent growth of profits in a particular leisure service business. In 1987, its profit margin was $247 million. During the same period, the price of the company's stock grew more than fivefold (Grover, Vamos, and Mason, 1987). In 1992, its profits showed a 22 percent increase from the previous year. In 1987, its profit margin was $247 million, in 1999, $678 million. This is an enormous increase in profits. The Walt Disney Company has engaged in a major program of expansion. It has added an additional theme park in Europe and is adding another in Asia, to be located in Hong Kong. The organization has expanded its television and movie productions and product merchandising. While not every venture achieves the level of anticipated success, the resurgence of the Disney Company has resulted from visionary leadership and new opportunities in the leisure industry. Profits for the Walt Disney Company increased 14 percent from 1994 to 1995 (*Business Week,* 1996).

The Top Leisure Industries   How do the top leisure industries in the United States rank in terms of profit? Table 11.2 presents, in rank order, these large corporations; it does not reflect the many small businesses providing leisure services. Among the companies listed are Walt Disney, McDonald's, Viacom, Eastman Kodak, Carnival, Harley-Davidson, Marriott International, TRICOM Global Restaurants, Mattel, Mirage Resorts, Hasbro, Harrah's Entertainment, Wendy's International, Hilton Hotels, and Darden Restaurants.

These figures include hospitality services, both fast food and lodging, which are considered to be a part of the leisure industry. In 1986, the food and lodging industry earned profits of $1.1 billion. Profits between 1985 and 1986 showed a healthy 14 percent increase (*Business Week,* 1987). In 1992, this same group earned profits of $6.6 billion. The food and lodging industry earned profits of $2.8 billion between 1998 and 1999 for eating places (food) and showed a healthy increase of 16 percent. The group composite for hotels and motels reflected a 5 percent increase (*Business Week,* 1999). The leaders in the food and lodging industry include such corporations as Brinker International, CBRL Group, CKE Restaurants, Darden Restaurants, McDonald's, Outback Steakhouse, TRICOM Global Restaurants, Hilton Hotels, Marriott International, and Meristar Hotels and Resorts. When viewing the entertainment component of leisure time industries, such companies as AMC Entertainment, Blockbuster, Disney, Fox Entertainment Group, Harrah's Entertainment, Loew's Cineplex Entertainment, Mandalay Resort Group, MGM Grand, Mirage Resorts, Park Place Entertainment, SFX Entertainment, Trump Hotels and Casino Resorts, and Viacom earned profits of $1.3 billion on sales of $47.3 billion in the third quarter of 1999 (*Business Week,* 1999).

In the food and lodging industry, franchising has become an important means to deliver goods and services. By the year 2005, franchising will have become a $1 trillion-a-year industry—about double the current level—and will account for half of all retail sales (Pettsinger, 1987). Table 11.3 shows the fastest-growing franchises in the United States. It is interesting to note that in 1995 the fastest-growing franchises dealt with leisure and related areas such as fast-food establishments and hotels and motels. There are still a number of fast-food and other eating establishments identified on the current list. We suspect that list changes very rapidly from year to year depending on demands in the marketplace.

TABLE

11.2 TOP LEISURE INDUSTRIES IN TERMS OF PROFITS EARNED

Rank	Company	Market Value (Millions of Dollars)
1.	Walt Disney	$70,745
2.	McDonald's	$42,820
3.	Viacom	$38,841
4.	Eastman Kodak	$18,088
5.	Carnival	$17,777
6.	Harley-Davidson	$10,309
7.	Marriott International	$6,757
8.	TRICOM Global Restaurants	$4,100
9.	Mattel	$4,052
10.	Mirage Resorts	$3,134
11.	Hasbro	$3,068
12.	Harrah's Entertainment	$2,459
13.	Wendy's International	$1,902
14.	Hilton Hotels	$1,785
15.	Darden Restaurants	$1,690

Source: "The S&P 500 Business Week Industry Rankings," *Business Week,* March 27, 2000, p. 180.

TABLE

11.3 FASTEST GROWING FRANCHISES

Company	Type of Business	Start-up Costs (U.S. Dollars)
McDonald's	Fast foods	$433,800
Subway	Fast foods	$66,200–175,000
Jackson Hewitt Tax Service	Tax services	$49,400–74,900
7-11 Convenience Stores	Convenience stores	$12,500
Jiffy Lube Int'l, Inc.	Auto-oil-change services	$174,000–194,000
Snap-On Tools	Retail-hardware	$121,600–209,000
Mail Boxes Etc.	Postal and business services	$107,500–195,200
Radio Shack	Retail-electronics stores	$59,300
Sonic Drive-In Restaurants	Fast foods	$530,800–672,800
GNC Franchising Inc.	Vitamin store	$102,000–154,800
Dunkin' Donuts	Bakery products donuts	$131,990–880,800
Domino's Pizza Inc.	Fast foods	$8,400–34,800
Jani-King	Commercial cleaning	$103,000–233,000
Blimpie Int'l, Inc.	Fast foods	$434,700–775,100

Source: *Entrepreneur Magazine,* January 2000.

Small Leisure Service Businesses   The United States has more than 15 million small business owners. Of all businesses in the United States, more (perhaps as many as 81%) could be defined as small businesses (U.S. Bureau of the Census, 1995). Bullaro and Edginton (1986), discussing commercial leisure services, suggest that this rate is even higher, noting that 95 percent of all businesses are small businesses. They suggest that small businesses can uniquely respond to the emerging diverse leisure lifestyles and cultural patterns. Since they do not have the same constraints as large businesses or corporations, small businesses can respond more quickly to innovations and fluctuations in the fad-oriented leisure service market. Significant growth has occurred in the number of new entrepreneurial ventures in the last thirty years. According to Naisbitt and Aburdene (1986) approximately 93,000 new businesses started in the 1950s and over 700,000 new businesses started by the mid-1980s. Most of these are small businesses.

In reviewing the state of small business in the United States, The *Wall Street Journal* reported in 1987 that the fastest-growing small businesses dealt with amusement and recreation services, resulting, no doubt, from the growth of leisure in an era of change. A great deal of entrepreneurial activity exists, and much of it focuses on the creation of new ways to meet people's needs, including their leisure needs. Such businesses range from providing play and motor learning opportunities for young children to fantasy camps for adults. The fastest-growing small businesses in the United States appear in table 11.4. What is interesting about this table is that amusement and recreation service as reported in the late 1980s had the greatest percentage of growth among the industries listed. The growth rate is not as significant as it was a decade ago, although certainly comparable with other industries.

TABLE

11.4 FASTEST GROWING INDUSTRIES IN EMPLOYMENT, RANK BY PERCENT CHANGE 1997–1998 (THOUSANDS)

Industry	Annual Emp. 1997	1998	Absolute Change, 1997–1998	Percent Change, 1997–1998	Industry Type
Holding and other investment offices	221.8	242.8	21.0	9.5	Indeterminate
Nondepository institutions	567.2	620.1	52.9	9.3	Large
Security and commodity brokers	596.8	648.5	51.7	8.7	Large
Engineering and management services	3,004.8	3,235.7	230.9	7.7	Small
Amusement and recreation services	1,572.9	1,688.3	115.4	7.3	Small
Business services	7,982.7	8,546.15	563.4	7.1	Indeterminate
General building	1,316.3	1,398.7	82.4	6.3	Small
Contractors' services, nec	49.6	52.4	2.8	5.6	Small
Furniture and home furnishings stores	1,009.0	1,061.8	52.8	5.2	Indeterminate
Special trade contractors	3,574.7	3,742.5	167.8	4.7	Small

nec = Not elsewhere classified.
Note: Small-business-dominated industries are industries in which a minimum of 60 percent of employment is in firms with fewer than 500 employees (as of 1996). Large-business-dominated industries are industries in which a minimum of 60 percent of employment is in firms with 500 or more employees. The remaining industries were classified as indeterminate.

Source: Office of Advocacy, U.S. Small Business Administration from employment data provided by the U.S. Department of Labor, Bureau of Labor Statistics, and employment firm size data provided by the U.S. Department of Commerce, Bureau of the Census.

Challenges to the Entrepreneur

The owner or operator of a commercial leisure service enterprise faces many challenges. Not only must commercial leisure service providers remain responsive to customer needs, they also must carefully price and market their services and products to ensure profitability. Furthermore, ethical considerations come into play when providing leisure services in certain environments, especially the natural environment. Some of the challenges that a commercial leisure service entrepreneur may face include the following:

Responsiveness to changing conditions. Leisure interests are often fad-oriented, changing rapidly. Most leisure service organizations, to remain competitive, must constantly change, upgrade, or enhance their products or services.

Capital. Difficulty can arise when commercial leisure service organizations need capital to start new enterprises. They must be creative and innovative, yet have a practical, well-thought-out profit plan. In addition, cash flow into a leisure business is often irregular and requires a keen sense of fiscal management.

Seasonal factors. Many leisure activities are seasonal in nature. For example, businesses that cater to skiing in the winter, water activities in the summer, or various types of sports all require seasonal adjustments in staff, cash flow, and promotion.

Ethical considerations. The leisure service field has, as core values, the preservation and conservation of the environment and the wise use of leisure. Commercial businesses can meet ethical considerations when they focus on values, quality, and service, as well as fair profit, within the framework of the foundational ethics of the profession.

Risk management. Issues surrounding liability, especially as related to high-adventure recreation programs, are increasing. Businesses need to identify major risks and establish a program to effectively manage risk, either by purchasing insurance, avoiding the high-risk activities, establishing preventive measures, or other means.

Social responsibilities. Owners and managers have a responsibility to invest in their communities—a practice that is also "good business." It often involves contributing to community projects and activities with the resources of the organization, in terms of money, time, personnel, or other resources.

Consumer protection. Successful commercial leisure service organizations provide safe and satisfying leisure experiences for their customers.

Knowledge of consumers. Knowledge of consumers and consumer markets can make the difference between success or failure. To gain this knowledge, the business might engage in market research and acquire information that will help in making decisions.

Lack of personal time. Running a small commercial leisure business can result in a lack of personal or leisure time. The challenge is one of finding a balance between the two.

Inadequate managerial skills. Few small commercial leisure service business professionals have all of the skills necessary to operate an enterprise effectively and efficiently. This challenge can be met by finding ways to augment one's abilities and skills—for example, through business assistance programs, taking on a partner, hiring a consultant, or taking classes.

Overregulation. Governmental regulations can be burdensome. They can put undue constraints on the operation of businesses and may impact on profits.

These challenges need not deter the entrepreneur from succeeding. When faced squarely, they become opportunities for an interesting and stimulating work environment. A key to excellence involves understanding the challenges that exist and then anticipating them with a planned strategy that produces successful results.

Summary

Commercial leisure service ventures make up a large proportion of the entire leisure market. In fact, estimates indicate that over 90 percent of all expenditures for leisure goods and services occur in the commercial leisure service sector. Commercial leisure service organizations have, as their primary objective, earning a profit. They also work, however, to build strong bonds between themselves and their consumers. This loyalty often results in sustained profits over a long period of time.

While there are numerous ways to classify commercial leisure service organizations, this chapter identifies six major classifications: travel and tourism, hospitality and food services, leisure products, entertainment services, retail outlets, and leisure in the natural environment. Each type of service has unique patterns of organization, management, and marketing and can be legally organized as a sole proprietorship, partnership, or corporation.

Most commercial leisure service organizations are organized as small businesses. In fact, the fastest-growing small businesses in the United States deal with amusement and recreation services. The management and organization of small businesses are often conducted by individuals referred to as entrepreneurs. Entrepreneurs, individuals who seek systematic innovation, often perceive themselves as being goal-oriented, self-reliant, and self-motivated. Some entrepreneurial skills include vision, creativity, idea generation, problem solving, decision making, and change management. Individuals who work in the commercial sector show a high degree of job satisfaction related to such variables as pay and control over job environment. As in any business, however, owners and managers of commercial leisure service businesses face a number of challenges. These challenges provide opportunities for forward thinking and planning and impact on the managing, marketing, and pricing of services and products.

The commercial leisure service sector holds many opportunities for success and great promise for individuals wishing to pursue careers in this area. The commercial leisure service sector involves a full range of products and services from amusement/theme parks to leisure apparel. Individuals wishing to pursue professional careers in this area should acquire a foundation in areas such as leisure, marketing, financial management, and entrepreneurship.

Discussion Questions

1. From your perspective, what opportunities are available in the commercial leisure service sector today? List as many as possible.
2. What are the primary motives of commercial leisure service organizations? How do they contrast with those of public and nonprofit leisure service organizations?
3. What are the types of legal ownership of commercial leisure service organizations? What are their advantages and disadvantages?
4. Identify six major categories of commercial leisure service organizations.
5. Choose one leisure service organization and describe it in terms of its products, services, target markets, and form of ownership.
6. What is entrepreneurship? What skills does an entrepreneur need to be successful?
7. Why is entrepreneurship important in the delivery of leisure services?
8. Discuss the current state of the leisure service industry in the United States and Canada.
9. Identify what you think will be the fastest-growing commercial service industries in the United States and Canada in the next decade. Why do you believe this?
10. Identify and describe eleven challenges to individuals working in the commercial leisure service sector.

References

Bullaro, J., and C. Edginton. 1986. *Commercial Leisure Services: Managing for Profit, Service, and Personal Satisfaction.* New York: Macmillan.

Chubb, M., and H. Chubb. 1981. *One Third of Our Time.* New York: Wiley.

Crossley, J. C., and L. M. Jamieson. 1993. *Introduction to Commercial and Entrepreneurial Recreation.* 2d ed. Champaign, IL: Sagamore.

Cutler, B. 1990. Where does the free time go? *American Demographics* (November), 31–32.

Drucker, P. 1985. *Innovation and Entrepreneurship.* New York: Harper & Row.

Edginton, C. R., G. Carpenter, and M. F. Chenery. 1987. Educating for entrepreneurship in leisure services. *SPRE Annual on Education 2,* 30–58.

Gottschalk, E. C., Jr. 1986. Dining out chic to chic. *The Wall Street Journal* (April 21), 2D.

Grover, R., R. Vamos, and T. Mason. 1987. Disney's magic. *Business Week* (March 9), 62.

Kelly, J. 1985. *Recreation Business.* New York: Wiley.

Kelly, J. 1996. *Leisure.* 3d ed. Boston: Allyn & Bacon.

Naisbitt, J., and P. Aburdene. 1986. *Reinventing the Corporation.* New York: Warner Books.

Pettsinger, T. 1987. So you want to get rich. *The Wall Street Journal* (May 15), 2–15.

Pinchot, G. 1985. *Entrepreneuring.* New York: Harper & Row.

Ritzer, G. 2000. *The McDonaldization of Society.* Thousand Oaks, CA: Pine Forge Press.

Staff. 1987. The top U.S. companies ranked by industry. *Business Week* (April 17), 127.

Staff. 1993. The top U.S. companies ranked by industry. *Business Week* (April 7), 182–183.

Staff. 1996. The Business Week 1000. *Business Week* (March 25), 106.

Staff. 2000. The S&P 500 *Business Week* industry rankings. *Business Week* (March 27), 112.

U.S. Bureau of the Census. 1995. *Statistical Abstract of the United States: 1995.* 115th ed. Washington, DC: U.S. Government Printing Office.

U.S. Bureau of the Census. 1999. *Statistical Abstract of the United States: 1999.* 119th ed. Washington, DC: U.S. Government Printing Office.

Zabel, D. 1992. The literature of travel tourism. Edited by N. Herron, in *The Leisure Literature.* Englewood, CO: Libraries Unlimited.

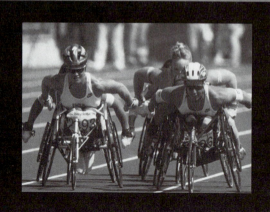

Delivery of Leisure Services: Therapeutic Recreation

Sports offer individuals opportunities to participate in activities and events that promote competition, sportsmanship, and a healthy and vigorous lifestyle.

Introduction

Whereas the other chapters in part 2 of this book classify leisure service delivery systems in terms of the type of funding they receive (public, nonprofit, or commercial), this chapter discusses a program area of leisure services—therapeutic recreation. Therapeutic recreation programs are found in public, private, nonprofit, and commercial organizations. This specialized form of organized recreation programming involves professionals and organizations that either use recreation activities as a means to intervene in people's lives to accomplish desired ends (therapeutic recreation) or provide recreation opportunities for people who are part of special populations (inclusive recreation).

Over the last half of the twentieth century, there was an increased recognition in the potential of recreation as a treatment modality as well as the need to provide inclusive or special recreation programs for people with disabilities. Persons with disabilities are becoming more vocal about their needs and wants, and society is recognizing that meeting this increased demand is the "right thing to do." The emerging field of therapeutic recreation services has contributed significantly to these trends as well as grown as a field of professional service because of these trends (Kraus and Shank, 1992).

This chapter chronicles the development of these fields of practice and provides insights into prevailing goals, the available resource base, characteristics of professionals, and orientation to customers. In addition, it describes various types of programs as well as some of the many challenges for the future that both therapeutic recreation and inclusive special recreation programs may face.

The Emergence of Therapeutic Recreation as a Profession

The use of recreation as a tool to address social problems in the United States can be traced to the late 1800s as social reformers used play and recreation to address the problems and needs that grew out of the Industrial Revolution. For instance, the first playground, the Boston Sand Gardens, was established to meet the play needs of disadvantaged children. Also, many of the first organized camps were designed for and targeted "sickly boys." Further, the settlement house movement used recreation as a means to ease the transition of immigrants to life in large urban American cities. Sessoms and Stevenson (1981) have written that

> Adult education, recreation, and social group work all have a common heritage. Each is a product of the social welfare reforms that occurred in our cities and industries at the turn of the nineteenth century. Their founders shared a belief—they were concerned with the quality of life and believed that through the "proper" use of leisure it could be achieved. (p. 2)

As public recreation departments grew, the philosophy that views recreation as an end in itself was adopted by most public recreation agencies across the country (Gray, 1969). In other words, public recreation drifted away from a social welfare model; a basic gap in the continuum of recreation services emerged. This gap was filled by professionals who were the forerunners to therapeutic recreation specialists today. Thus, the beginning of therapeutic recreation as a profession can be attributed to developments that took shape in the early part of the twentieth century and have continued into today. These developments include the need for specialized services for people with special needs, the influx of wounded soldiers from various wars and military conflicts, the emergence of professional organizations, and the number of landmark legislative bills that became law throughout the twentieth century.

The Need for Specialized Services

During the early history of the United States, those with mental illness and physical disabilities did not pose much of a challenge for communities. Population density was low and most communities were predominately rural and agricultural. The few cases of special needs that did become evident were addressed on a case-by-case basis by the family or the community. For the most part, communities became involved only when an individual seemed to threaten public safety or had no means of support. For example, in 1694 Massachusetts enacted "An Act for the Relief of Idiots and Distracted Persons." Under this provision all persons who had special needs and did not have family to take care of them were aided by the state. In 1699, Connecticut followed Massachusetts' lead; other colonies such as New York and Vermont passed similar laws.

The responsibility of taking care of those with mental illness when family care was unavailable fell to public almshouses. Almshouses typically provided a minimal level of food and shelter to a mixed grouping of able-bodied poor, ill, and disabled persons. An almshouse was in existence in Boston as early as 1662. The physical environs of almshouses were said to have been dungeonlike; the emotional environment was not any more humane. Records show that these places provided bizarre entertainment for the community. Cruel treatment, including the use of chains for restraints, led to the eventual outcry that demanded changes be made in caring for the disabled.

The first documented medical institution in the United States was the Pennsylvania Hospital in Philadelphia, which was established in 1751. The services provided at this hospital included programs for mentally ill persons who had been previously denied treatment. The first U.S. hospital devoted exclusively to the care of the mentally ill was established in Williamsburg, Virginia, in 1773 to make provisions for the "Support and Maintenance of Idiots, Lunatics, and Other Persons of Unsound Minds." As the United States moved into the 1800s, hospitals and custodial care facilities were constructed for the mentally ill, deaf, blind, mentally challenged, and physically disabled. Private voluntary charity blossomed in the late 1800s to take care of the poor, the ill, the elderly, and the disabled. These institutions often became warehouses for individuals who had been shunned by society and contributed to the negative attitudes toward "people who were different." Many of these attitudes were perpetuated late into the twentieth century. The first private school to educate severely retarded individuals opened in Massachusetts in 1848. Many of the early reformers and proponents of the forerunner of modern rehabilitation services are presented in table 12.1.

Many of these early institutions began to offer recreation opportunities in both formal and informal programs. In the case of mental patients, the conviction grew that occupations of various kinds would be helpful in overcoming mental illness and restoring rational functioning. As a result, mental patients in the late 1800s were allowed to dance, take part in outdoor sports, and use "airing courts," rocking horses, and other special equipment (Kraus and Shank, 1992).

Carter, Van Andel, and Robb (1995) have identified a number of developments of the late nineteenth and early twentieth centuries that set the stage for the development of specialized services for a variety of people with special needs. These developments include the following:

- Health care reform that emphasized the dignity of all persons and the therapeutic value of humane treatment that included the social and environmental stimulation of recreation activities;
- Private and public hospital systems that created the structure for health care providers to experiment with programs and services that included recreation activities as a component of care; and
- The playground movement that reemphasized the role that play activities and spaces serve in social and environmental reform. The playground movement also spawned professional associations that supported therapeutic recreation.

The Influx of Wounded Soldiers from the World Wars

Following the Civil War, the importance of recreation for wounded soldiers was acknowledged. Florence Nightingale, in her 1873 text on nursing, "urged nurses to pay attention not only to the patient's body but also to his mind and morale. She urged that music and conversation be encouraged, that beautiful objects be placed in patient wards, that the family be encouraged to visit and that patients keep small pets. Under her leadership, so-called bedside occupations were introduced in military hospitals to cheer up injured soldiers" (Kraus and Shank, 1992, p. 7).

The sudden influx of traumatic and permanent injuries into American society as a result of participation in the World Wars served as a stimulus for the improvement of recreation programs in hospitals and long-term treatment facilities as well as a slow change in attitudes toward special populations (Crawford, 1996). Under the leadership of the American Red Cross, the use of recreational activities to treat those who sustained various injuries in military combat during World War I was expanded.

As a result of the success experienced by the American Red Cross, in the 1920s and 1930s recreation services began to appear in other settings such as state mental hospitals (Carter et al.,

12.1 EARLY REFORMERS IN PUBLIC HEALTH CARE AND THERAPEUTIC RECREATION

Phillippe Pinel (1745–1826)

A French physician who advocated for the humane treatment of persons with mental illness and the economically disadvantaged, Pinel believed these people were capable human beings who deserved to be treated with compassion and dignity. His approach became known as moral treatment and included purposeful recreational activity and work experiences to restore mental and physical health (Carter, Van Andel, and Robb, 1995).

Benjamin Rush (1745–1813)

One early reformer addressing the needs of the mentally ill at the end of the 1700s was Benjamin Rush, an influential physician. Rush was a signer of the Declaration of Independence, member of Continental Congress, Surgeon General to the Continental Army during the Revolution, Treasurer of the United States Mint, passionate reformer, brilliant physician, and the first important American psychiatrist. After joining the staff of the Pennsylvania Hospital in 1783, he became the first American physician to develop a comprehensive course of study in mental disease. Rush wrote the first textbook on mental health in 1812 (Crawford, 1996).

Dorothy Dix (1802–1887)

The most famous and influential psychiatric reformer of the nineteenth century was Dorothy Dix. A woman who dedicated her life to the proper care of the mentally ill, her influence spanned three decades (1840s to the 1870s). By the close of her career she had been responsible for founding or enlarging over thirty mental hospitals in the United States and abroad (Crawford, 1996).

Florence Nightingale (1820–1910)

A British nurse in military hospitals who was a pioneer of modern nursing, Florence Nightingale was a strong advocate for improving the rehabilitation environment of hospitals. She organized classes, reading rooms, and recreation huts to combat the negative side effects of being a wounded soldier. In 1873, she wrote a book that included guidelines for visitor conversation, promoted the psychological benefits of music and pets, and highlighted the need for variety in both the objects and the color of hospital environments (Avedon, 1974).

Howard Rusk (1901–1989)

Physician and international authority on physical rehabilitation who believed that both individual and group recreation had a direct and positive relationship upon recovery, Rusk helped to establish the credibility of recreation as an adjunctive therapy (Crawford, 1996).

Paul Haun (1906–1969)

A physician/advocate in the 1940s and 1950s whose writings and presentations supported recreation as a therapeutic modality able to create a desirable psychological state within the patient, Haun was a respected leader in the field (Crawford, 1996).

Eunice Kennedy Shriver (1921-   )

Founder of the Special Olympics movement under the auspices of the Joseph P. Kennedy, Jr. Foundation in 1968, Shriver helped to spread recreation as formal community movement throughout community-based programs for the mentally retarded and mentally ill (Crawford, 1996).

1995). The Easter Seals Society began providing day and residential camp programs in the 1930s. These types of programs continued to expand, and with the outbreak of World War II therapeutic recreation became an important element in the rehabilitation of wounded soldiers. The increase in therapeutic recreation programs is evident in the over 1,800 recreation leaders the Red Cross trained and employed during World War II (Frye and Peters, 1972). After the war these leaders became the core of young professionals who pushed the field of therapeutic recreation into other community and clinical settings.

Professional Organizations

As the ranks of hospital workers grew in the mid-1940s, several organizations began to emerge. Carter, Van Andel, and Robb (1995) report that the first effort toward professionalization came from the American Recreation Society (ARS) in 1948 when members laid the groundwork for the establishment of the Hospital Recreation Section (HRS) within ARS. Early members of this section represented hospital recreation workers from military, veterans, and public institutions.

In the early 1950s an organization emerged from within the American Alliance for Health, Physical Education, Recreation and Dance—the Recreation Therapy Section (RTS). Members of this organization felt that HRS was too closely aligned with the community recreation movement and did not adequately represent the recreational therapy perspective. The interests of the membership focused on developing recreation and physical education programs in schools, serving students with disabilities, and adapting physical education programs in integrated schools (Carter et al., 1995).

A third organization emerged in 1953 to meet the needs of recreational therapists from state hospitals and schools serving persons with mental illness or mental retardation. The National Association of Recreational Therapists (NART) became involved in the development of standards for professional education, outlining professional qualifications for clinical practice and defining the role of the profession (Carter et al., 1995).

These three organizations (ARS, RTS, and NART) merged in 1966 to form the National Therapeutic Recreation Society (NTRS) within the National Recreation and Park Association (NRPA). The combined resources and energies of these three organizations pushed the field of therapeutic recreation to new heights in the areas of credentialing, accreditation, and personnel and program standards. In the mid-1980s friction concerning the governance of the organization and the development of a definition and philosophical statement for the organization contributed to the formation of a new professional organization—the American Therapeutic Recreation Association (ATRA) (Carter et al., 1995).

Although the goals of ATRA are similar to NTRS, the process of pursuing these goals is different. Today, ATRA advocates recreation as a form of treatment, hence recreation therapy. This philosophy represents the view of professionals who work in health-care settings where "professional services are more likely to be judged by their effectiveness in improving the functional capacity, health status, and/or quality of life of the client" (Carter et al., 1995, p. 58), whereas NTRS has advocated more for community-based recreation services for persons with disabilities. Together, these two perspectives provide a comprehensive continuum of services to serve the total person; they are discussed in more depth later in this chapter.

Legislation

In the latter half of the twentieth century, the concern for the equal rights of all Americans (including those with disabilities) has increased. This concern has been translated into action as legislation pertaining to equal access and rights to educational and recreational services has evolved. Legislation affecting the delivery of recreation services to persons with disabilities is listed in table 12.2. These laws have led to the passing of the most powerful legislation pertaining to persons with disabilities, the Americans with Disabilities Act of 1990 (ADA, PL 101–336). ADA is a civil rights law that extends the same protection against

TABLE

12.2 LEGISLATION AND OTHER EVENTS AFFECTING RECREATION FOR SPECIAL POPULATIONS

1932	**The Bill of Rights for the Handicapped.** Adopted by the White House Conference on Child Health and Protection, it provided an important endorsement of recreation for disabled children.
1936	**The Social Security Act.** A compilation of laws, including numerous amendments over the last several years related specifically to the elderly and disabled, it includes provisions for physical education and recreation through formal procedures for review of professional services, establishes funds to states for self-support services for individuals, and gives grants to states to provide community-based care.
1963	**Vocational Rehabilitation Act.** This Act provided training and research funds for recreation for the ill and handicapped. This was the first recognition by a specific federal agency of the importance of recreation services in rehabilitation.
1963	**National Outdoor Recreation Plan,** PL 88–29. Directing the formulation and maintenance of a comprehensive nationwide outdoor plan, this plan was completed in 1973 and included an emphasis on compliance with PL 90–480 (see below). Concerns for the handicapped were listed as a priority area.
1967	**Education for Handicapped Children Act,** PL 90–170. This law established the unit of physical education and recreation for handicapped children within the Bureau of Education for the Handicapped; it became the largest federal program for training, research, and special projects related to recreation for special populations.
1968	**Architectural Barriers Act,** PL 90–480. Simply stated, this law indicates that "any building or facility, constructed in whole or part by federal funds must be accessible to and usable by the physically handicapped."
1971	**Developmental Disabilities Services and Facilities Construction Act,** PL 91–517. Developmentally disabled persons are specifically defined and recreation is listed as a specific service to be included as a fundable service in this federal law.
1973	**Rehabilitation Act,** PL 93–112. This Rehabilitation Act was a comprehensive revision of the 1963 Vocational Rehabilitation Act that included an emphasis on the "total" rehabilitation of the individual.
1974	**Rehabilitation Act Amendment,** PL 93–516. This law authorized the planning and implementation of the White House Conference on Handicapped Individuals. The final report noted the importance of recreation for individuals with disabilities and called for the expansion of recreation services, as well as an increase in the number of professionally trained individuals employed in the field of recreation.
1975	**Education for All Handicapped Children Act,** PL 94–142. By mandating free and appropriate education for all handicapped children, this law identified physical education as a direct service and recreation as a related service to be offered to those with disabilities. Mainstreaming in the school system is usually viewed as an outgrowth of this Act providing the legislative leverage for disabled children and their families to gain access to often denied educational services.
1978	**Rehabilitation Act,** PL 95–602. As with many federal programs, the 1973 Rehabilitation Act and the programs it authorized expired at the end of five years. In 1978, legislation was introduced to extend and amend the 1973 Act. This renewal called for recreation and leisure services to be a part of the rehabilitation process.
1981	Designated by the United Nations as the **International Year of Disabled Persons,** the theme chosen for 1981 was "the full participation of disabled persons in the life of their society."
1986	**Education of the Handicapped Act Amendment,** PL 99–457. This law emphasized the development of comprehensive statewide programs for early intervention services for handicapped infants, toddlers, and families. A multidisciplinary team to develop an individualized family service plan was advocated. Recreation is cited as a related service in this amendment.
1990	**Americans with Disabilities Act,** PL 101–336. Probably the best known of all the laws protecting those with disabilities, the ADA provides comprehensive guidelines banning discrimination against people with disabilities. It is an omnibus civil rights statute that prohibits discrimination against people with disabilities in sectors of private and public employment, all public sectors (including recreation), public accommodations, transportation, and telecommunications.

From D. R. Austin and M. E. Crawford (eds.), "Organization and Formation of the Profession" in *Therapeutic Recreation: An Introduction,* 2nd edition, 1996. Copyright © 1996 by Allyn and Bacon. Reprinted by permission.

discrimination now provided by other federal civil rights laws to people with disabilities. It is the purpose of the act

- to provide a clear and comprehensive national mandate for the elimination of discrimination against individuals with disabilities;
- to provide clear, strong, consistent, enforceable standards addressing discrimination against individuals with disabilities;
- to ensure that the federal government plays a central role in enforcing the standards established in this act on behalf of individuals with disabilities; and
- to invoke the sweep of congressional authority, including the power to enforce the 14th Amendment and to regulate commerce, in order to address the major areas of discrimination faced daily by people with disabilities.

The ADA has offered certified therapeutic recreation specialists (CTRSs) and others working in recreation settings a powerful tool to advocate for the rights of people with disabilities to receive the services and support they need to improve the quality of their lives. The ADA provides the basis to demand full and equal access by persons with disabilities to all types of government and private facilities and programs (restaurants, theaters, stadiums, museums, parks, amusement centers, or other places of recreation). For example, Casey Martin used the ADA to win his right to use a golf cart in Professional Golf Association (PGA) events due to disability (i.e., congenital circulatory disorder) that prevents him from walking long distances (*Golf Magazine,* March 31, 1998). Despite the many strides that have occurred due to the ADA, many Americans are still unaware of the implications of the ADA. As one poll found, 54 percent of individuals over age sixteen with disabilities who took part in the survey did not know that the ADA existed (Farrell, 1998 as cited in Smith, Austin, and Kennedy, 2000).

The legislative history in the United States is encouraging, but old stereotypes and attitudes do not die easily. All too often, people with disabilities are still marginalized and deprived of equal opportunities due to unnecessary barriers and fears. The legislation discussed in this section is not the end of discrimination but it does serve as the beginning where individuals (such as CTRSs) can work to make the dream of equal opportunities for people with disabilities a reality.

Characteristics of Therapeutic Recreation: People with Disabilities Today

An estimated 19.4 percent of noninstitutionalized citizens in the United States, totaling 48.9 million people, have a disability; almost half of these people (an estimated 24.1 million people) can be considered to have a severe disability (Kraus, Stoddard, and Gilmartin, 1996). A large number of these individuals (37.7 million people) have an activity limitation that confines their ability to fully participate in a wide range of life opportunities ranging from education and employment to marital and family involvement, as well as recreation participation. Although many of these disabilities are apparent, others are not. Disabilities such as HIV, dyslexia, or being subject to seizures are not always apparent. All disabilities (hidden or apparent) are often heightened by society's response to people with disabilities and from their own lack of a positive self-concept and confidence in meeting society's challenges. A description of common disabilities is found in Table 12.3.

Therapeutic recreation programs and services serve a wide range of individuals. Programs can help individuals in numerous ways to develop skills, contribute to self-concept and awareness, and, in general, contribute in a positive way to a higher quality of life through the constructive use of leisure. In discussing the ways in which therapeutic recreation can help people

12.3 DISABLING DISEASES AND CONDITIONS

Alcoholism	A complex, progressive disease in which the use of alcohol interferes with health, social, and economic functioning. It ranks with cancer and heart disease as a major threat to the nation's health (Carter et al., 1995).
Alzheimer's Disease	A progressive, irreversible neurological disorder that results in complete loss of cognitive functioning, followed by loss of physical abilities. Although common in persons over the age of sixty-five, Alzheimer's disease may appear in individuals in their forties (Carter, Van Andel, and Robb, 1995).
Anorexia	A physical and psychological syndrome marked by severe and prolonged inability to eat with marked weight loss. This illness commonly afflicts teenaged girls and can result in death.
Arthritis	A joint condition characterized by inflammation, pain, swelling, and other changes varying with the type. It is common late in the aging process, although it also affects young people (Gunn, 1975).
Autism	This has been characterized as absorption in fantasy to the exclusion of interest in reality. Mental introversion in which the attention or interest is fastened within one's ego; a self-centered mental state from which reality tends to be excluded (Gunn, 1975).
Behavior Disorder	A term used to refer to observable general behavior abnormalities; impaired development of internalized controls so that the individual cannot effectively cope with natural and social demands of his or her environment (Gunn, 1975).
Bulimia	Refers to an insatiable appetite causing excessive eating or bingeing. This is followed by purging, using laxatives, diuretics, strict dieting or fasting, vigorous exercise, and/or self-induced vomiting to prevent weight gain—hence, reference to the disease as the binge-purge syndrome. To be clinically defined as having an eating disorder, a person must have had a minimum of two binge-eating episodes a week for at least three months (Carter et al., 1995).
Cerebral Palsy	A nonprogressive disorder of movement or posture due to malfunction of or injury to the brain. Several types of cerebral palsy (spasticity, athetoisis, rigidity, ataxia, and tremors) are a result of the specific location of the brain injury (Carter et al., 1995).
Cystic Fibrosis	A hereditary disease affecting children involving defective production of enzymes in the pancreas, which leaves disturbances throughout the body and usually involves the heart (Carter et al., 1995).
Developmental Disabilities	Disabilities that become evident in childhood and are expected to continue indefinitely constitute a substantial handicap to the affected individual and are attributed to mental retardation, cerebral palsy, epilepsy, or other neurological conditions requiring treatment (Gunn, 1975).
Down Syndrome	Common form of mental retardation in which the individual has a chromosomal abnormality; characterized by a broad nose, slanting eyes, protruding large tongue, open mouth, square-shaped ears, large muscles, broad, short skull, and often congenital heart disease (Goldman, 1987).
Epilepsy	A central nervous system disorder marked by transient periods of unconsciousness or psychic disturbance, twitching, delirium, or convulsive movements (Carter et al., 1995).
Hemiplegia	A person who is paralyzed on one half of her or his body (right or left side). Often, hemiplegia is a result of a stroke or brain injury.
Hyperactivity	Also known as Attention Deficit Hyperactivity Disorder (ADHD), it is common among school age children who are perceived as extremely active in situations that demand high degrees of composure or compliance (Carter et al., 1995).

—continued

TABLE

12.3 CONCLUDED

Manic-Depression	A major affective disorder characterized by severe mood swings and a tendency to remission and recurrence; sometimes referred to as bi-polar disorder (Gunn, 1975).
Multiple Sclerosis	A neurological disease characterized by periods of exacerbation and remission with progressive degeneration caused by plaques that interrupt transmission of impulses to and from the brain (Carter et al., 1995).
Muscular Dystrophy	A group of progressive disorders evidenced by diffuse weakness of muscle groups. Muscle cells degenerate and are replaced by nonfunctional fat and fibrous tissue (Carter et al., 1995).
Paraplegia	The lesion of the spinal cord at or below the second thoracic vertebra resulting in either complete or incomplete loss of sensation and movement in both legs and the lower trunk (Carter et al., 1995).
Parkinson's Disease	A chronic progressive nervous disease of later life that is marked by tremors and weakness of resting muscles (Gunn, 1975).
Quadraplegia	The condition of all four limbs, both arms and legs, being paralyzed or severely limited in movement (Goldman, 1987).
Spina Bifida	A series of spinal cord defects caused by abnormal fetal development. The major types include myelomeningocele (an outpoaching of the spinal cord through the back of the bony vertebral column that has formed incompletely); meningocele (an outpoaching consisting of only the covering of the spinal cord and not the cord itself); and spina bifida occulta (the failure of the back arch to form—no poaching exists and the bony defect is covered with skin) (Carter et al., 1995).
Stroke	CVA—Cerebral Vascular Accident—refers to the stoppage of circulation to part of the brain either by the blood vessel bursting or being narrowed enough to deprive the area of blood (Gunn, 1975).

of all ages reach their goals, the National Therapeutic Recreation Society (1993) and Carter, Van Andel, and Robb (1995) have identified how programs can help individuals with varying disabilities. The National Therapeutic Recreation Society offers the following:

People with Physical Disabilities. Therapeutic recreation can help people with physical disabilities, sensory impairments, or other health-related disabilities to learn new skills and/or modify old ones to compensate for abilities they have lost; practice self-care skills; get involved in community recreation programs; and feel a sense of accomplishment.

People with Developmental Disabilities. Therapeutic recreation can help people with mental retardation, cerebral palsy, or other developmental disabilities to develop and use their physical and intellectual abilities to the fullest; develop independence; gain confidence in themselves; and interact with others and participate in community recreation activities.

People with Mental Illness. Taking time to "play" is an important part of good mental health. Therapeutic recreation gives people an opportunity to feel good about themselves and their accomplishments; improve relationships with others; relieve tension; develop healthy coping techniques; and express and communicate their needs.

Older Adults with Limitations. Services can help older adults continue to be involved socially; express themselves creatively; maintain independence; and live fully in spite of any limitations they may have.

People Dependent on Alcohol or Other Drugs. Therapeutic recreation can help people who abuse chemical substances to learn new skills that will enhance their self-esteem to find healthy alternatives to substance abuse, and to feel fit and appreciate the value of wellness.

At-Risk Youth, and Juvenile and Adult Offenders. Therapeutic recreation can provide healthy outlets for energy and activity—recreation is a way to release tension that can be destructive if it remains bottled up; teach people to cooperate with others—through group activities, individuals can learn to work and play together; and improve self-esteem—people need to feel good about themselves before they can feel good about others.

Homeless and Destitute. According to Carter, Van Andel, and Robb (1995, pp. 459–460), therapeutic recreation can serve to assist in "assessment of social and functional capacity to behavioral change and acquisition of coping strategies for daily living" for individuals who are homeless and destitute. Autonomy, control, self-esteem, independent functioning, self-awareness, decision making, planning, and participation in socially valued roles can be enhanced through therapeutic recreation (Kunstler, 1991).

Barriers to Success in Leisure

As can be surmised, to be successfully integrated into society, people with disabilities must overcome a number of barriers. Smith, Austin, and Kennedy (2000) have identified three categories of barriers preventing individuals with disabilities from full leisure participation. We have added additional items to their lists. These are found in table 12.4.

Leisure service professionals working with people with disabilities must strive to create an environment whereby many of these barriers can be overcome or negotiated. In the process, it is important for leisure service professionals to work "with" persons with disabilities, empowering them and working together to improve their quality of life. Specifically, leisure service professionals need to create accessible programs and facilities, promote inclusive programs whereby people from different backgrounds and abilities can interact together, and facilitate open communication.

Leisure service programs can offer a valuable experience to people with disabilities. The modifications that are needed to integrate individuals who have special needs is usually very minimal. "These modifications should result in the individualization of the activity and should be taken into account when planning for all peoples. The modifications may require a change in the rules to make the activity more or less challenging. It may require a change in the time allowed for completion. Equipment may need to be modified. The process may need to be stressed instead of the product" (Eller and Mulroy, 1996, p. 6). In the end, being committed to creating integrated programs means

- knocking down the barriers and roadblocks that may exist so that everyone, regardless of ability or background, feels welcome at your program;
- having staff and volunteers who are aware, trained, and ready to facilitate an integrated program;
- promoting a process in which each individual is seen and respected as an individual with strengths and abilities;
- encouraging both physical and social inclusion in all aspects the program; and

- creating a supportive environment where everyone feels both physically and psychologically safe to participate. This means that specific supports are available for individuals with disabilities or medical needs to ensure that they have equitable opportunities for involvement (Blake, 1996).

Goals and Functions

Therapeutic recreation programs serve a variety of different age groups with a wide range of characteristics. As a result, defining therapeutic recreation is often difficult. After a quarter of a

TABLE

12.4   BARRIERS/BEHAVIORS

Attitudinal Barriers

These behaviors are usually intentional and obvious. They clearly inform the individual that he or she has less value than individuals without disabilities. An obvious example would be mocking or ridiculing a person with a visible disability while a more subtle example would be avoiding a person with a disability.

Paternalistic Behaviors

Head patting, giving undue or excessive praise, and providing help when it is not needed are examples of paternalistic behaviors. Unlike negative behaviors, paternalistic behaviors arise out of a desire to show the person with a disability that you care or that you have a favorable view of a person with a disability. Unfortunately, the message conveyed is that people with disabilities lack competence, maturity, and the capacity for independence.

Apathetic Behaviors

People who are apathetic toward individuals with disabilities express no feelings of sympathy, understanding, or caring toward people with disabilities.

Intrinsic Barriers

These barriers result from an individual's own limitations and may be associated with a physical, psychological, or cognitive disability. These barriers may be associated with the disability but may also arise from other factors such as parental overprotection or inadequate educational opportunities. Regardless of their cause, intrinsic barriers are permanent or temporary limitations that reside within the individual. Intrinsic barriers include lack of knowledge, social ineffectiveness, health problems, physical and psychological dependency, and lack of skill.

Environmental Barriers

Barriers that result from many of the external forces that impose limitations on the individual with a disability are considered to be evnironmental. No matter how well a person with a disability copes with intrinsic barriers to recreation participation, he or she is faced with other forces that are out of his or her control. These barriers are often complex and require a great deal of cooperation to solve. As a result, these issues can be frustrating to people with disabilities as they are out of their control. Environmental barriers include attitudinal barriers, architectural barriers, transportation barriers, ecological barriers, economic barriers, rules and regulations, and barriers of omission (i.e., failure to publicize adequately those programs that offer appropriate service to people with disabilities).

Communication Barriers

Those factors that block interaction between the individual and his or her social environment are part of communication barriers. These barriers cannot be thought of as either intrinsic or environmental. Communication barriers result from a reciprocal interaction between individuals with disabilities and their social environment.

century of inquiry and debate, the profession continues to have difficulty defining terms and precisely describing the goals and functions of therapeutic recreation. Evidence of this continued disagreement over philosophy, terms, and definitions is illustrated in the existence of both NTRS and ATRA.

An excerpt of the philosophical statement of NTRS (1996) provides a broad framework for understanding the goals and functions of therapeutic recreation. The purpose of this statement is not to suggest how to practice therapeutic recreation, but rather to articulate a value structure for the profession. The statement includes three broad values:

- *The right to leisure.* The right to leisure is grounded in the notion that the individual is entitled to the opportunity to express unique interests and pursue, develop, and improve talents and abilities because of his/her abilities. The right to leisure is a condition for human dignity and well-being.
- *Self-determination.* Self-determination holds that leisure is an arena of action wherein the individual can express unique abilities and preferences that are encompassed within leisure experiences.
- *Quality of life.* The quality of leisure of persons with disabilities contributes to their quality of life. Leisure should be fun, enjoyable, or satisfying regardless of the participant's abilities. Quality of life also extends beyond the idea of fun. Leisure activities may help prevent illness and secondary disabilities. Within the context of leisure, quality of life also includes prevention of illness within the context of preexisting impairments and promotion of health and functional abilities through leisure.

From this statement, we can see that therapeutic recreation promotes the right of persons with disabilities to have leisure as well as uses leisure to improve individuals overall quality of life. A number of models in therapeutic recreation have been developed to accomplish this purpose. One such model is the Leisure Ability Model, which is based on the concept of identified client need related to leisure involvement (Peterson and Stumbo, 2000). This model is presented in figure 12.1 and includes the elements of treatment, leisure education, and recreation participation.

As can be seen in figure 12.1, these professional services are viewed on a continuum. Therapy is directed toward improvement of functional behavior that may impede leisure involvement or using leisure to help individuals reach other treatment-related goals. Leisure education teaches new recreation and social skills to help expand a person's leisure repertoire or assist in adapting her or his interests and hobbies into a new situation (e.g., a basketball player learning how to play wheelchair basketball after a spinal cord injury). The last component, recreation participation, concerns the provision of self-directed leisure participation for individuals with disabilities.

Smith, Austin, and Kennedy (2000) point out that when closely examined, it becomes apparent that therapy and leisure education components merge as both deal with facilitating change. This results in leaving only two components of the model presented in figure 12.1—treatment and recreation. Within the treatment mode, therapeutic recreation uses recreation as a purposeful intervention designed to help clients relieve or prevent problems and to assist them in personal growth in an effort to achieve the highest level of health possible. This is what ATRA (1987) emphasizes in its philosophical statement that states "the primary purpose of treatment services, which is often referred to as recreation therapy, is to restore, remediate, or rehabilitate in order to improve functioning and independence as well as reduce or eliminate the effects of illness or disability" (Carter et al., 1995, p. 59). Strong proponents of recreation as therapy often feel that the provision of community recreation for people with disabilities should

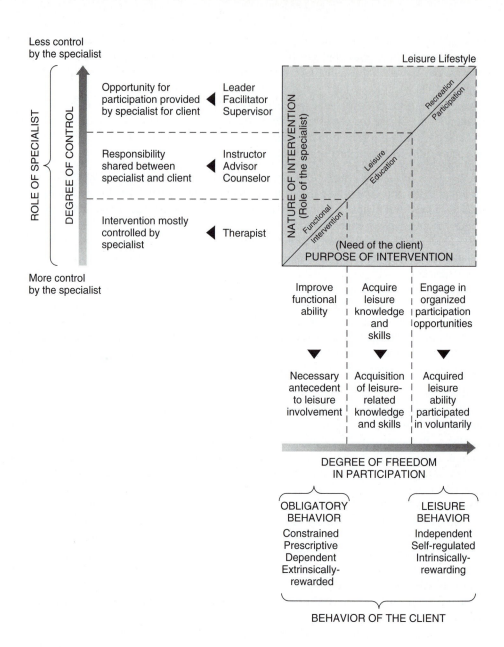

Figure 12.1

Leisure ability model

*Source:
Peterson, C. and
Stumbo, N. 2000.
Therapeutic
Recreation
Program Design:
Principles and
Procedures.
Boston, MA: Allyn
& Bacon, p. 26.*

Less control
by the specialist

Leisure Lifestyle

ROLE OF SPECIALIST

DEGREE OF CONTROL

Opportunity for
participation provided
by specialist for client

Leader
Facilitator
Supervisor

Responsibility
shared between
specialist and client

Instructor
Advisor
Counselor

Intervention mostly
controlled by
specialist

Therapist

More control
by the specialist

NATURE OF INTERVENTION
(Role of the specialist)

Recreation
Participation

Leisure
Education

Functional
Intervention

(Need of the client)
PURPOSE OF INTERVENTION

Improve
functional
ability

Acquire
leisure
knowledge
and
skills

Engage in
organized
participation
opportunities

▼

▼

▼

Necessary
antecedent
to leisure
involvement

Acquisition
of leisure-
related
knowledge
and skills

Acquired
leisure
ability
participated
in voluntarily

DEGREE OF FREEDOM
IN PARTICIPATION

OBLIGATORY
BEHAVIOR

Constrained
Prescriptive
Dependent
Extrinsically-
rewarded

LEISURE
BEHAVIOR

Independent
Self-regulated
Intrinsically-
rewarding

BEHAVIOR OF THE CLIENT

be the responsibility of community recreation and parks personnel, who are trained to assist individuals in adapting these activities to their unique needs.

Viewing therapeutic recreation as purposeful intervention does not diminish the importance of providing recreation opportunities for everyone in society. Such programs referred to as inclusive or special recreation programs are equally important if the continuum of services (presented in figure 12.1) is to be complete. In many ways the term *inclusive recreation* is being used to describe full inclusion of persons with disabilities into the recreation mainstream whereby equal and joint participation of persons with and without disabilities can take place

(Smith et al., 2000). In contrast, *special recreation* programs refer to special or adapted activities, such as Special Olympics and wheelchair sports, through which special needs are met. The emphasis on inclusive and special recreation programs demonstrates the increasing importance for recreation providers in all areas of the economy (public, nonprofit, and commercial operators) to provide recreation services for persons with disabilities. As these types of programs continue to grow, there is a need for therapeutic recreation specialists to help organizations meet the diverse needs of all people in the community.

Resource Base

The resource base or revenue for therapeutic recreation services is diverse. Therapeutic recreation services may be found in public organizations (e.g., federal, state, county, and municipal government), private nonprofit organizations (e.g., group homes, advocacy groups), as well as commercial organizations (e.g., for profit hospitals, nursing homes). In addition, today's competitive health-care environment is encouraging a number of innovative collaborative projects between public, private, and commercial organizations. As a result, funding may be a complex issue for many therapeutic recreation programs.

Insurance payments further compound the issue of funding for therapeutic recreation services. Although third party billing is not a reality for many agencies devoted to therapeutic recreation, insurance companies often pay for related services such as therapeutic recreation in inpatient and outpatient care in medically-based facilities. Within the funding framework, one constant is clear. Therapeutic recreation specialists need to be creative to continue funding programs at the needed level because the rising costs of medical care are shrinking health-care dollars.

To remain competitive, therapeutic recreation specialists are constantly looking for opportunities to document the outcomes of their programs (Coveliers, Milliron, Page, and Rath, 1996). Programs are developed with specific benefits, values, and goals in mind. It is only through an underlying commitment to fostering these benefits that they will be achieved. One of the results of such an analysis is identifying the benefits associated with various programs. In many areas of the parks and recreation field, professionals are embracing such a benefits-based approach to providing services.

Characteristics of Professionals

In 1998, there were approximately 39,000 recreation therapists employed throughout the United States. Almost 40 percent were employed in hospitals, with a little over 25 percent working in nursing and personal care facilities. Others were employed in residential facilities, community mental health centers, adult day-care programs, correctional facilities, substance abuse centers, and community programs for persons with disabilities. About one in three recreation therapists was self-employed, generally contracting with long-term care facilities or community agencies to develop or oversee programs (*Occupational Outlook Handbook,* 2000).

Generally, therapeutic recreation professionals have at least a bachelor's degree in therapeutic recreation, which is essential for hospital and other clinical positions. In addition to a college degree, CTRSs must have completed an internship (of at least 400 hours) under the supervision of a CTRS, passed a certification exam, and maintained a program of continuing education as set forth by the National Council for Therapeutic Recreation Certification (NCTRC).

In addition to these educational and certification requirements, the *Occupational Outlook Handbook* (2000) states that "recreation therapists should be comfortable working with people with disabilities and be patient, tactful, and persuasive. Ingenuity, a sense of humor, and imagination are needed to adapt activities to individual needs" (p. 210).

In an empirical study examining the competencies entry-level recreational professionals should possess to serve people with disabilities, Austin and Powell (as cited in Smith, Austin, & Kennedy, 2000) identified eighty-six different competencies. These competencies were then organized into clusters. The highest-rating cluster related to attitudes (i.e., understands how to promote positive attitudes toward people with disabilities through recreation programs). The second cluster related to areas and facilities (i.e., understands the frustration experienced in an inaccessible environment). The third cluster related to having a philosophical position that advocates for the recreation needs of people with disabilities. The fourth cluster related to leadership issues in which recreational professionals know how to facilitate integrated recreational groups.

In related research connected to the characteristics of leaders who make a difference in the lives of youth, a variety of studies have identified the need for leaders to focus on the potential of youth rather than on their problems, focusing on the needs of clients first, having a passion for one's work, and finding a personalized style in working with youth (DeGraaf, Ramsing, Gassman, and DeGraaf, 2001). Although many of these characteristics relate specifically to youth leaders, they are also transferable to working with other populations, including those with disabilities.

Types of Therapeutic Recreation Programs/Settings

As previously discussed in the goals and functions section, there is a difference between therapeutic recreation and special or inclusive recreation, and each stands alone as an important element in meeting the needs of all members of a community. While distinct, these two entities often overlap. Overlap occurs when a therapeutic recreation program offers a client an accompanying benefit of a recreative experience, or when a special or inclusive recreation program serves as an intervention, bringing about a desired therapeutic benefit (Smith et al., 2000). This overlap may also be seen in the variety of agencies that offer both therapeutic recreation programs as well as special/inclusive recreation. Kraus and Shank (1992) and the NTRS (1993) have identified several types of agencies or settings that provide a variety of programs along the continuum presented in figure 12.1.

> *Outpatient clinics.* Outpatient clinics provide a number of therapeutic recreation services and programs. In general, outpatient programs provide services for individuals who do not stay overnight. Length of treatment can vary, as can the number of hours per day that patients are involved in treatment. For example, outpatient programs may be offered to support and treat individuals with substance abuse problems. Such programs may include counseling, information, small-group discussion, and a variety of leisure activities and services.
>
> *Group homes.* A group home is usually thought of as a residential facility that houses six or more individuals. These types of residential care units provide therapeutic recreation programs and services such as sports, trips and tours, arts and crafts, aquatics, literary self-improvement, and others. In addition, group homes provide leisure education programs that prepare individuals to live more independently and/or improve their leisure skills. A group home is a controlled, strongly supervised environment.
>
> *Home health care agencies.* Such organizations provide in-home care and associated support services for individuals. For example, the hospice concept found in many communities throughout the United States provides in-home health care and other

support services for terminally ill individuals and their families. For example, the Cedar Valley (Iowa) Hospice has as its mission a commitment ". . . to providing quality palliative and support services to help meet the physical, psychological, social and spiritual needs of dying persons and their families, during the patient's illness and throughout bereavement."

Substance abuse facilities. There are several different types of settings in which therapeutic recreation services are offered as a part of a substance abuse program. Some of these include acute care hospital programs, residential care, and outpatient services. Programs include self-help, education, counseling, therapy (e.g., milieu, psychotherapy, group therapy, etc.), and others. The purpose of therapeutic recreation in these types of settings is to help individuals find a ". . . healthy means to satisfy needs previously met through drug-taking . . . TR can facilitate new learning related to social and free-time choices, and provide a natural but supportive environment to practice new skills and pursue positive alternative ways of behaving" (Austin and Crawford, 1996, p. 98).

Halfway houses. This type of facility may be thought of as a treatment site that is located in the community. Halfway houses provide opportunities for reintegration of individuals into community life, while still providing structure and assistance. Therapeutic recreation programs may be offered within the halfway house or may be organized for halfway house residents using community resources.

Vocational training centers. These types of settings provide individuals with training and counseling focused on an individual's work or career goals. For example, Goodwill Industries of America provides career training while offering social skills development, medical management, and leisure education. Vocational training centers are often associated with treatment or rehabilitation programs. Such programs provide opportunities for involvement in action-oriented therapies such as art, dance, music, occupational, and, of course, therapeutic recreation.

Camps. Numerous day and residential camp programs are targeted specifically for individuals with disabilities. Camp Courageous in the state of Iowa provides opportunities for individuals with a full range of disabilities to participate in a wide variety of therapeutic recreation programs including outdoor adventure, camping, sports, arts and crafts, aquatics, and others. This organization is a nonprofit, year-round, recreational, and respite care facility for individuals with disabilities.

Centers for independent living. Usually, facilities for independent living are supervised residential facilities for one or more individuals. These arrangements are clustered in several combined units such as an apartment complex. Centers for independent living provide opportunities for individuals to continue their career training while engaging in activities for social skill development and leisure education. Following a stay in a halfway house, an individual might transition to a center for independent living.

Sheltered workshops. This type of setting provides a protective environment in which individuals engage in meaningful work experiences and learn job skills. Sheltered workshops may provide therapeutic recreation services as a part of their support for participating individuals. An example, Adults, Inc. in Waterloo, Iowa, uses therapeutic recreation to enhance its clients' social and recreational skills.

Community mental health centers. Gallagher (1980) refers to a community mental health center as a program that provides partial (day) hospitalization for individuals with psychiatric disorders. These types of centers may provide inpatient and outpatient services, partial hospitalization, emergency services, consultation, and education. Therapeutic recreation services vary, but usually emphasize community recreational activities such as sports, drama, trips, camping, outdoor pursuits, and others. For example, the Merced (California) County Mental Health program offers all of the previously mentioned services as well as conducts a fully developed therapeutic recreation staff by certified therapeutic recreation specialists and aides.

Adult day-care centers. An adult day-care center ". . . is a community-based group program designed to meet the needs of functionally impaired adults through an individual plan of care. It is a structured, comprehensive program that provides a variety of health, social, and related support services in a protected setting during any part of the day, but less than 24-hours . . ." (Behren, 1986, p. 2).

Senior centers. These types of settings provide opportunities for individuals to pursue leisure activities as a major focal point of their effort. As Austin and Crawford (1996) write, "senior centers provide a place for older adults to come together for socialization, leisure activity and other services" (p. 234). Nearly every community in the United States provides some type of support for such a program. Activities found in these types of programs include current events, literature, trips, genealogy, art, fitness, social recreation, and numerous others. Programs also provide information, referral services, and treatment programs related to the needs of participants.

Psychiatric facilities. Therapeutic recreation programs in psychiatric facilities focus on rehabilitation, education, and participation (Peterson and Gunn, 1984). In these environments, the role of the therapeutic recreation specialist is ". . . to help the individual free himself from the constraints that are limiting his personal growth and healthy choices in behavior . . . typical settings include inpatient, outpatient, partial or day settings, transitional settings, and individualized settings . . ." (Austin and Crawford, 1996, pp. 65–66).

Hospitals. Hospitals are housed under various sponsorship such as the Veterans' Administration, military, public health (federal, state, county, municipal), nonprofit hospitals, sectarian, and proprietary. Many of them offer therapeutic recreation services as a part of patient rehabilitation.

Nursing homes. Nursing homes can be described as long-term care facilities for ill or disabled (and often, senior) citizens who can no longer function in the community or reside with their own families. Nursing homes are increasingly admitting younger patients who may be profoundly mentally retarded or have head injuries, strokes, or other traumas, and who cannot live independently.

Settings serving elderly persons. There are increasing numbers of residential centers for seniors who cannot or choose not to live independently or with their families, do not require intensive nursing or medical care, and meet many of their own needs independently. These types of programs/settings include municipal, county, or state homes for the elderly; residential centers sponsored by sectarian or service organizations; low income housing projects with special units for the aging; and commercially developed retirement centers. In the future, this type of setting may also include senior day-care programs as well as in-home care programs that may be offered to seniors who live in their own homes.

Schools or residential centers for those with specific disabilities. These institutions permanently house people with physical disabilities (e.g., visually impaired, hearing impaired, orthopedically or neurologically impaired), those with mental retardation, or emotionally ill persons. These centers offer "full service programming" with schooling, recreation, religion, and living skills all a part of the services provided.

Penal institutions and other programs for socially deviant persons. These types of institutions include adult penal institutions such as prisons, jails, and other detention centers, as well as work camps, reformatories, therapeutic camps, wilderness programs, and special schools for youth who have been committed by the courts for delinquent behavior. In addition, special schools and shelters for emotionally disturbed children and youth, or for those from broken families or families incapable of providing adequate care, are included here.

Centers for physical medicine and rehabilitation. Often these types of facilities are found in close proximity to hospital complexes, universities, and/or medical schools and serve as treatment centers for a variety of people who have suffered serious physical injury. Such people are no longer under treatment for the acute phase of their illness or injury and are receiving varied forms of physical, psychological, vocational, and social rehabilitation to facilitate their return to their families and community life.

Programs of voluntary agencies. A number of national organizations have been established to promote services for specific groups of people with disabilities such as cerebral palsy, orthopedic or neurological disorders, and mental retardation. Special Olympics International and Easter Seals (which provides special camping programs) are two examples of the growing number of these types of programs. National youth serving organizations are also increasing their programs targeting specific groups of children and adolescents facing specific risks (e.g., gangs, violence, pregnancy, drug abuse).

Public recreation and parks departments. Governmental leisure service agencies on every level—federal, state, and local—have increasingly accepted responsibility for providing recreation for persons with disabilities. In some cases the sponsor may offer segregated activities for customers with severe disabilities while encouraging opportunities for fully integrated participation for others. With the emphasis on integration and mainstreaming, and with the support of legislation such as the Americans with Disabilities Act, more emphasis will be placed on creating inclusive recreation opportunities for all.

Challenges for the Future

The 1990s have been a time of tremendous change in health care. Therapeutic recreation specialists in both clinical and community settings are facing a work environment that is constantly changing. On one hand professionals are being asked to document outcomes, respond to the needs of the customer, and provide quality services, while on the other hand they are being asked to deal with budget cuts and staff reductions. Managers and staff everywhere must meet the challenge of doing more, doing it faster and better, and with fewer resources.

Little, Lankford, DeGraaf, and Tashiro (1995) used a nominal group process technique to identify the issues and trends with which therapeutic recreation professionals were most concerned. Specifically, participants viewed the related issues/trends of budget cuts, health care reform, and reduction of staff as the most important changes related to the field of therapeutic recreation. (See table 12.5 for the shifts in approaches to health care.) "Lack of awareness of therapeutic recreation by political leadership" and "salary equity of therapeutic recreation workers" also ranked high. Other issues identified included transportation and mobility issues for people with disabilities, the need for staff (and volunteer) training, need for services in

12.5 HEALTH SHIFTS—CHANGES IN ALL ASPECTS OF HEALTH CARE

Shifts From	To
Doctor-Care	Self-Care
Treatment	Prevention
Sole Provider	Health Promotion Team
Exercise and Fitness	Wellness
Looking Good	Living Well
The Years in Your Life	The Life in Your Years

Source: Trends Action Group, 1993, National Recreation and Park Association.

developing countries, motivating staff, having less time to assist patients to re-enter the community, fundraising, promotion of community outings for residential patients, lack of qualified personnel, deinstitutionalization, the impact of ADA, need for certification, value of TR in general hospital setting, and the lack of opportunities and funding for continuing education units (cells).

As all agencies deal with the rising costs of health care, it will be increasingly important to document the effectiveness of therapeutic recreation in clinical and community settings and to increase programs and find innovative funding sources and partnerships. For example, home-based recreation services will serve a wide range of populations, especially an increasing number of senior citizens. Home health care in the United States is expanding because it reduces health-care costs while helping individuals to maintain some of their independence.

Dealing with Assistive Technology

Keeping current with technological breakthroughs is a constant challenge for therapeutic recreation professionals today. New technologies to assist individuals with disabilities enhance their quality of life are developed everyday. Simply stated, assistive technologies include all devices that increase independence and enable people with disabilities to enjoy learning, living, working, and playing more fully. "Assistive technology is any device or piece of equipment that can be used by a person with a disability to become less dependent. Examples of assistive technology include the following: computers, seating systems, communication devices, magnifiers, beeper balls, sit skis, assistive listening devices, and many, many more" (Bullock and Mahon, 1997, p. 430). As can be seen from this list, assistive technology does not necessarily mean high-cost, complex technology items. Rather, assistive technology is any item that enhances the lives of people with disabilities.

In dealing with assistive technology, Broach, Datilo, and Deavours (2000) have suggested that CTRSs and other recreation professionals remember the following suggestions:

- Focus on the person rather than on the technology.
- Focus on a person's abilities rather than his or her limitations when using technology.
- Provide technology—assistive technology cannot provide empowerment or access unless it is made available. Many people do not access technology due to a lack of community services and funding. As a result CTRSs and other recreation professionals need to be

strong advocates for the development of inexpensive and versatile technology and providing this technology to the people who need it.

- Encourage independence, as dependence may result when technology does too much for individuals with disabilities, thus discouraging them from reaching their potential.
- Develop competence in assistive technology—one of the barriers to using assistive technology is lack of knowledge and how to select appropriate devices. CTRSs and other recreation professionals who are knowledgeable about new technology and how to use the technology are a tremendous resource to people with disabilities as they attempt to learn about and incorporate assistive technologies into their lives.

Addressing New/Growing Social Problems

CTRSs must continue to serve those outside of the mainstream. It is easy to serve those outside the mainstream in times of affluence, but when resources begin to dwindle, a conflict in values can result. For while good times provide increased options and encourage the free play of individual interests, hard times diminish options and create competition for resources. Professionals in the field of therapeutic recreation must seek out connections with other fields and social service agencies. Professionals need to build bridges between fields, especially in community therapeutic recreation programs. Expanding an agency's role in the community increases political strength for, and public awareness of, the therapeutic recreation profession. Through collaboration and partnerships therapeutic recreation can be involved in addressing a variety of new and/or growing social problems that include the following:

- *AIDS.* AIDS affects three groups: those with clinical cases of AIDS, those with AIDS-related complex, and those who are infected with the AIDS virus but are asymptomatic. CTRSs may work with persons with AIDS in a variety of clinical and community settings including hospitals, long-term care facilities, prisons, substance abuse centers, and hospices. Because there is no cure for AIDS, individuals will need activities that provide immediate gratification as well as those that assist them in coping with the demands and uncertainty of the disease. Persons with AIDS and related illnesses need opportunities to learn coping and leisure skills that are appropriate to their health status and emotional needs.
- *Brain Injured.* Therapeutic recreation professionals need to be sensitive to a new population created due to technology. For example, whereas twenty years ago the majority of brain-injured people died soon after the injury, today 95 percent of people with head injuries survive—technology helps keep people alive. An estimated 15 percent of survivors of brain injury are left with permanent deficits that prevent them from returning to their previous school, job, or relationships. Responding to this group of people means providing programs in all areas of the service continuum: therapy, leisure education, and recreation.
- *Homeless.* According to the Department of Housing and Urban Development, homelessness is "a condition of being without a regular dwelling place whereby a person or family lives outside on the streets, tries to find a public or private shelter at night or sleeps in a makeshift dwelling such as a car or a train station" (Kunstler, 1991, p. 31). CTRSs desire to serve those with a variety of disabilities, including those who have any condition that appreciably impairs their ability to make a minimally successful connection with the labor market, and to form mutually satisfactory relationships with family and friends. By this definition, many homeless people are disabled (Kunstler, 1991).
- *New Poor.* Lahey (1991) has identified three groups that are the hardest hit by today's growing inequity in the health-care system who should be of major concern for all recreation professionals. These groups include children living in poverty, the working poor

(an alarming number are homeless and without medical insurance), and the frail elderly. By strict clinical/medical definitions, these groups would not qualify for services until the difficulty of their situations brings them to the point of hospitalization and short-term intervention. As recreation professionals continue to look for ways to develop preventative approaches rather than reactive programs, those living in poverty should not be overlooked. One example of a organization reaching out to this segment of the population through recreation programs is Degage, a nonprofit organization in Grand Rapids, Michigan, that attempts to reach out to the poor and dispossessed and create a safe harbor where friendships are formed and community begins. Affectionately nicknamed "the living room" of the Heartside community, Degage offers an informal space for leisure, recreation, and connecting with others.

- *Gangs.* Although not a new problem, gang activity has intensified and become more violent in recent years. Homicide is the number one cause of death among African American and Latino fifteen to twenty-four-year-old males, and the third leading killer of Whites in that age group. Approximately 125,000 youth younger than eighteen were arrested for violent crimes in 1994, and although the number of homicides committed by juveniles (ages ten to eighteen) not involving guns has held steady over nearly two decades, the number of gun homicides by juveniles has almost quadrupled since 1984 (Children's Defense Fund, 1996). Many of these violent crimes are related to gangs. One example of a public recreation department reaching out to gangs can be found in the city of Phoenix Parks, Recreation, and Library Department. This department has created an At-Risk Youth Division, which supports, develops, and maintains community resources for partnerships and coordinates direct services for youths (City of Phoenix, 1999). One specific program offered is the X-TATTOO: Tattoo Removal Program, which provides former gang members an opportunity to remove tattoos on their face, neck, and hands that pose a significant barrier to leaving their former life. In partnership with local plastic surgeons, youth can have tattoos removed free of charge in exchange for community service and their attendance in educational classes.

Recreation professionals have much to offer as communities search out multidimensional solutions to gangs. As society moves toward a more holistic youth development model for dealing with young people, recreation professionals must see youth as a resource to be developed rather than as a problem to be fixed. Such an approach to youth development creates programs where youth can acquire a broad range of competencies and demonstrate a full complement of connections to self, others, and the larger communities.

This list is not all-inclusive of the new and emerging problems facing our communities but it does demonstrate the need for CTRSs to continue to look for ways to extend our services. The possibilities are everywhere; using cooperative arrangements with other social service agencies, we can continue to meet the changing needs of everyone, including people with disabilities.

As therapeutic recreation professionals look to the future, the challenges can seem overwhelming. There is opportunity in change, however, and the profession must move forward. In the words of Broida (1996), "Now is the time for us to mobilize our creativity and meet our professional challenges in positive, proactive ways. We need to communicate our ideas with others so that we all benefit from the expertise of our colleagues. This probably means losing some ego, letting up on the protection of our 'turf' and having everyone in the field commit to move the professional toward the unified goal of better services for our customers" (p. 37).

Summary

Oliver Wendall Holmes once said, "The great thing in this world is not so much where we are, but in what direction we are moving." This chapter has documented the movement of society in providing recreation opportunities for everyone. Much still needs to be done, but the field of therapeutic recreation is moving forward in the right direction. With the increased recognition of the potential of recreation as a treatment modality as well as the increasing need to provide inclusive or special recreation programs for persons with disabilities, the field of therapeutic recreation has grown tremendously.

Therapeutic recreation emerged over the last century as a result of a number of different factors including the influx of wounded soldiers from both World War I and World War II, the emergence of professional organizations, and a variety of federal legislation. Despite the growth of services for people with disabilities, a number of barriers still exist in truly integrating them back into society. This chapter discusses two types of barriers—physical and attitudinal. Professionals in the field of therapeutic recreation are constantly advocating for their clients and assisting them in overcoming these barriers.

Within the field of therapeutic recreation, two distinct aspects of the profession remain. The first is often referred to as therapeutic recreation, which is a purposeful intervention designed to help clients grow and to assist them to relieve or prevent problems through recreation. A second aspect of the profession, often referred to as inclusive or special recreation programs, provides recreation services for people with disabilities. With the growth of legislation (like ADA), it is becoming increasingly important for all recreation providers (public, private, nonprofit, and commercial) to provide recreation services for people with disabilities.

The growth in services for people with disabilities and increased awareness of society to meet the needs of people with disabilities translate to a bright future for those interested in both therapeutic recreation and inclusive recreation. Yet many challenges exist, ranging from financing and assuring quality in program development to meeting the program needs for new disability groups and growing social problems. As therapeutic recreation professionals look to the future, the challenges can seem overwhelming; yet, if one looks how far the profession has come, one realizes that anything is possible.

Discussion Questions

1. Define therapeutic recreation and inclusive recreation. Why is there a need for both types of services?
2. How do the philosophical statements of NTRS and ATRA differ?
3. What are the barriers people with disabilities face in participating in leisure and recreation? What are three specific things that could be done to make community recreation programs more inclusive?
4. Identify several of the major types of sponsors of therapeutic recreation service (e.g., nursing homes) and clarify the role recreation can play in the lives of the population they serve.
5. How did the U.S. Armed Forces assist in the development of therapeutic recreation programs?
6. As people move more to a wellness approach to medical care, how will the role of therapeutic recreation change?
7. In your own words, explain the impact of the ADA on the provision of recreation services.
8. Identify five or more disabling conditions and discuss how therapeutic recreation services can assist individuals to improve their quality of life.
9. Discuss the emergence of therapeutic recreation as a profession.
10. Identify and discuss successful leadership strategies and characteristics of leaders who work with people who have disabilities.

References

Austin, D. R. 1996. The therapeutic recreation process. Edited by D. R. Austin and M. E. Crawford, in *Therapeutic Recreation: An Introduction*. Boston, MA: Allyn & Bacon.

Austin, D. R., and M. E. Crawford, eds. 1996. *Therapeutic Recreation: An Introduction*. Boston, MA: Allyn & Bacon.

Avedon, E. M. 1974. *Therapeutic Recreation Service: An Applied Behavior Science Approach.* Englewood Cliffs, NJ: Prentice Hall.

Behren, R. V. 1986. *Adult Day Care in America: Summary of a National Survey.* Washington, DC: The National Council on Aging and National Institute on Adult Day Care.

Blake, J. 1996. Opening doors: Integration of persons with a disability in organized children's camping in Canada. *Leisurability 23*(2), 3–9.

Broach, E., J. Datilo, and M. Deavours. 2000. Assistive technologies. Edited by J. Datilo, in *Facilitation Techniques in Therapeutic Recreation.* 99–132. State College, PA: Venture.

Broida, J. K. 1996. Innovation in therapeutic recreation. *Parks and Recreation 31*(5), 37+.

Bullock, C., and M. Mahon. 1997. *Introduction to Recreation Services for People with Disabilities: A People Centered Approach.* Champaign, IL: Sagamore.

Carter, M. J., G. E. Van Andel, and G. M. Robb. 1995. *Therapeutic Recreation: A Practical Approach.* Prospect Heights, IL: Waveland Press.

Children's Defense Fund. 1996. *The State of America's Children.* Washington, DC: Children's Defense Fund.

City of Phoenix. 1999. *Making a Difference in Phoenix.* Phoenix, AZ: Phoenix Parks, Recreation, and Library Department.

Coveliers, L., T. Milliron, G. Page, and K. Rath. 1996. Advancement of therapeutic recreation through "creative administration." *Parks and Recreation 31*(5), 54–57.

Crawford, M. E. 1996. Organization and formation of the profession. Edited by D. R. Austin and M. E. Crawford, in *Therapeutic Recreation: An Introduction.* Boston, MA: Allyn & Bacon.

DeGraaf, D., R. Ramsing, J. Gassman, and K. DeGraaf. 2001. *Camp Leadership: A Staff Development Approach.* Dubuque, IA: Eddie Bowers.

Eller, C. L., and M. T. Mulroy. 1996. *Developmentally Appropriate Programming for School-Age Children.* Available at www.exnet.iastate.edu/pages/nncc/SACC/dev.approp.sac.html.

Frye, V., and M. Peters. 1972. *Therapeutic Recreation: Its Theory, Philosophy and Practice.* Harrisburg, PA: Stackpole Books.

Gallagher, B. J. 1980. *The Sociology of Mental Illness.* Englewood Cliffs, NJ: Prentice Hall.

Goldman, C. 1987. *Disability Rights Guide: Practical Solutions to Problems Affecting People with Disabilities.* Lincoln, NE: Media Publications.

Gray, D. E. 1969. The case for compensatory recreation. *Parks and Recreation 4*(4), 23–24.

Kraus, R., and J. Shank. 1992. *Therapeutic Recreation Service: Principles and Practices.* Dubuque, IA: Wm. C. Brown.

Kraus, L., S. Stoddard, and D. Gilmartin. 1996. *Chartbook on Disability.* Washington DC: National Institute on Disability and Rehabilitation Research.

Kunstler, R. 1991. There but for a fortune: A therapeutic recreation perspective on the homeless in America. *Therapeutic Recreation Journal 25*(2), 31–38.

Lahey, M. P. 1991. Serving the new poor: Therapeutic recreation values in hard times. *Therapeutic Recreation Journal 25*(2), 9–19.

Little, J., S. Lankford, D. DeGraaf, and A. Tashiro. 1995. An exploratory study of issues and trends in therapeutic recreation: A recreation perspective. *Journal of Applied Recreation Research 20*(4), 269–282.

National Therapeutic Recreation Society. 1993. *About Therapeutic Recreation.* South Deerfield, MA: Channing L. Bete Co.

National Therapeutic Recreation Society. 1996. *Philosophical Position Statement of the National Therapeutic Recreation Society.*

Peterson, C. A., and S. L. Gunn. 1984. *Therapeutic Recreation Program Design: Principles and Procedures.* Englewood Cliffs, NJ: Prentice Hall.

Peterson, C., and N. Stumbo. 2000. *Therapeutic Recreation Program Design: Principles and Procedures.* Boston, MA: Allyn & Bacon.

Sessoms, H. G., and J. L. Stevenson. 1981. *Leadership and Group Dynamics in Recreation Services.* Boston, MA: Allyn & Bacon.

Smith, R., D. Austin, and D. Kennedy. 2000. *Inclusive and Special Recreation: Opportunities for Persons with Disabilities.* Boston, MA: McGraw-Hill.

Staff. March 31, 1998. Martin to use cart for U.S. Open qualifier. *Golf Magazine* online found at: www.golfonline.com/tours/caseymartin/usopencart0331.html.

Staff. 2000. *Occupational Outlook Handbook.* Washington, DC: U.S. Government Printing Office, U.S. Department of Labor.

Trends Action Group (TAG). 1993. *Trends being Tracked.* Presented at the National Recreation and Park Association national conference, San Jose, CA.

PART THREE

Issues, Trends, and Professional Practice

Leisure service professionals manage a wide array of programs and activities that require continuous learning and development to respond to the ever-changing needs of individuals.

Leisure Programming: Promoting Quality Services

Here, a father and son enjoy the exhilaration of a quality play experience.

Introduction

Leisure programming, creating leisure experiences and benefits, is central to the work of the profession. It has become a primary focus of professionals because of increased emphasis on accountability and a desire to provide more relevant, meaningful programs and services to customers. The key to successfully meeting customer needs is to provide services of quality and value. All individuals involved in leisure service organizations touch the customer, either directly or indirectly. Those who are involved in the area of programming work *directly* with customers and plan, organize, implement, and evaluate services. Speaking to the importance of programming, Stenger, Ryan, and Jordan (1999, pp. 28, 39) have written:

> Programming is often perceived as the heart of the field of leisure services. At the very least, we could probably all agree that programming is a common denominator of leisure entities, no matter the setting, philosophy, or funding sources. . . . Programming serves as the common denominator among all parks, recreation and leisure service delivery programs.

As Johnson-Tew, Havitz, and McCarville (1999, p. 2) have noted, ". . . leisure programming is dynamic. It is characterized by ongoing planning, implementation, and refinement."

Programs, the products produced by programmers, enable individuals to receive the outcomes and benefits of leisure participation. Knowledge of programming and its relationship to the leisure experience is important to the leisure service professional. Furthermore, a keen awareness of the importance of quality in leisure programming forms an essential building block of professional success.

This chapter, divided into four major sections, first discusses information about the importance of providing quality services. The next section focuses on strategies used in developing a customer service orientation. The third portion of this chapter defines the various types of programs and suggests a cyclical program planning process. The last section discusses different types of direct-service leadership roles found in public, private, nonprofit, and commercial leisure service organizations.

Promoting Quality and Value

Quality and value have become important elements of the work of leisure service professionals, as well as the yardstick by which customers measure the success of their involvement in terms of time, money, and commitment. Quality—a perception of excellence—is the extent to which the services received by the customer equal or exceed expectations. The term *quality services* suggests that individuals have engaged in thorough planning, have attempted to anticipate the needs of consumers, and have brought the sum of their resources to bear as effectively as possible on meeting those needs.

Value can be thought of as the extent to which the return on one's investment in leisure services and programs—as measured in time, money, or other factors—equals or exceeds the investment made. Value involves providing people with an effective return on their investment so that their monetary investment equals the services received. Leisure service organizations may also increase value by providing customers with a return on investment that is perceived to be greater than expected. This builds consumer commitment and loyalty as customers make comparisons with other competitive providers. Quality and value are hallmarks of successful organizations.

To be successful, leisure programmers must understand the expectations of their customers (McCarville, 1993). They must understand the characteristics that influence the perceptions of customers concerning issues related to quality in the delivery of leisure services. Zeithaml, Parasuraman, and Berry (1988) have identified the five following distinct characteristics or dimensions to evaluate service programs in terms of quality:

- *Tangibility*—physical cues provided by staff, other users, facilities, and equipment;
- *Reliability*—consistently providing the promised service;
- *Empathy*—caring and individualized attention;
- *Assurance*—knowledgeable staff able to convey trust and confidence; and
- *Responsiveness*—willingness to provide prompt attention.

In the leisure services field, Crompton and McKay (1989) studied these dimensions and their relationship to program satisfaction. These researchers found that reliability—the ability to consistently deliver a service with great quality—consistently ranked as the most important characteristic desired by individuals. For example, at a well-organized, clean, welcoming, contemporary theme park such as Disney World, customers can depend on the delivery of high-quality services in a consistent fashion each time they visit the park environment.

Another important dimension in the delivery of quality leisure services is the management of leader-customer interfaces—where the leader communicates and interacts with customers in person or on the telephone. According to Swell and Brown (1990), appropriate training must be provided to professionals and others who manage these key encounters. The ability of leaders to respond with empathy and relevance in a timely fashion often contributes greatly to the perception of quality.

Commitment to quality requires the leisure service programmer to find better ways to serve customers. It involves a commitment to creating better leisure services by working in a way that leads to innovation, reduction of mistakes, a positive attitude, attention to detail, and other factors. Commitment to quality requires leaders to develop their expertise and knowledge through continuous development.

The leisure services programmer who uses principles of quality and value produces technically and developmentally sound programs and creates programs that *exceed minimum requirements,* that is, programs that create a special intangible quality that inspires customers, provides heightened insight, introspection, development, and is meaningful (Edginton and Edginton, 1993a). A quality program produces positive experiences that will be locked into the minds and emotions of customers and serve as a beacon for future positive leisure behaviors.

Building a Commitment to Quality

The leisure services professional has a responsibility to build staff training and program efforts around the idea of commitment to quality. This focus on quality must permeate the organization thoroughly. Leisure service professionals must work toward eliminating poorly organized services, poor attitudes toward customers, use of poor equipment/materials, and willingness to live with mediocrity.

A philosophy of excellence focuses on high-quality programs and services; it should be applied vigorously in the area of leisure services. The hallmarks or guidelines that are used by organizations and leaders with a strong commitment to quality follow (Edginton and Edginton, 1993b):

Innovation. Success in programming stems from a commitment to innovation. No program should be the same from one year to the next; rather, programs should constantly evolve to meet the needs of customers. Innovative organizations are constantly looking for new and different services, equipment, areas, and facilities that improve the quality of services to customers.

Future orientation. Leisure service professionals who address quality issues not only of today but also of tomorrow will be successful. Leisure service organizations that invest in the future invest some of their resources in ensuring that their programs and services are successful and vibrant in months and years to come.

Getting things right the first time. Perhaps the most efficient way to promote quality within an organization is to do things right the first time. Sloppiness and a "seat of the pants," last-minute approach to planning often lead to having to redo activities or services. This is not only costly, but often results in poor performance. Some activities and programs cannot be corrected if they are not planned effectively, and the opportunity they presented is lost.

Continuous improvement. The best way to achieve quality is to improve the processes associated with creating leisure services. The job of any leisure service programmer should be to find ways to continuously improve programs and services. Programmers constantly search out new ways of doing things better, more cost-efficiently, and/or in a way that is more meaningful to customers. In addition, quality recreation programmers often establish a goal of making one small change in every program every week to improve the quality. This is a never-ending dynamic process; it should not be thought of as a one-time event.

Continuous education. The continuous development of the leader's knowledge and skills is essential to achieving quality. Good people make good programs, but the needs of customers are dynamic and changing, requiring continuous education and development. Recreation leaders should seek ways to improve their knowledge base.

Attention to detail. Success in programs is painted in small steps as well as broad strokes. The little things make a program of high quality and make the difference between superior services and mediocre ones.

Pride. Belief in what you are doing is contagious. Pride is having a high opinion of yourself and your work. Pride comes from doing a job competently as well as having ownership in the effort.

Anticipatory planning. Do not merely respond to the needs of customers as they are expressed from moment to moment. Learn how to anticipate needs in advance and meet them before they are requested. Anticipatory planning requires the leader to think in advance (days, weeks, months) and to visualize services as they will likely unfold, and to anticipate actions that may be needed.

Performance measurements. Find ways to record progress toward achieving quality by creating performance measurements. Determine how to chart progress toward the achievement of quality. Graphs and charts provide opportunities for discussion and focus on opportunities for change, and they may lead to the development of new programs and/or better methods and procedures. Participant numbers, customer outcomes related to performance measures, program costs, participant use hours, and participant survey results are all sources of data for charts to measure performance. Measuring achievement over a period of time enables the leisure services programmer to see the gains in quality and performance and possibly to justify future program developments.

Elimination of mistakes. Mistakes are costly to an organization both in terms of funds and image. Mistakes made in program planning are costly to participants in terms of opportunity for development. If play/leisure is powerful enough to help customers, it is powerful enough to hurt them. When mistakes in program planning impact the quality of services, they also impact customers. Eliminating mistakes helps improve quality, morale, cost-effectiveness, and other critical factors.

Elimination of negativeness. Positive attitudes are important in the delivery of leisure services. Programmers should strive to be enthusiastic, energetic, and zestful. If you enjoy what you are doing, that quality will rub off on others; the reverse is also true. Positiveness is a "can do" attitude that promotes a willingness to find ways to effectively serve customers with quality programs.

Assume personal responsibility for quality. The old way to get quality was to supervise and inspect services and manage change from the top down, or from without. The new way of promoting quality is to build it from within. The best way to promote quality from within is to ensure that each individual assumes personal responsibility and accountability for making sure that services are provided in an excellent, high-quality manner.

Teaming: Doing what it takes to get the job done. The leisure services programmer as well as other staff must be willing to do what it takes to get the job done, and to get it done right. The "quality" approach depends upon teamwork, cooperation, and supportive behavior. It is not "your job" or "my job" but, rather, "our job." All staff should be focused and have their eyes and efforts directed toward the primary goal, that is, providing the very highest quality service for customers, and they should be willing to do what it takes to make that happen.

The leisure services professional who is committed to excellence and who follows the guidelines that are discussed in the preceding section will outperform those who are not committed to excellence. The committed leisure service professional's programs will likely have a greater impact on customers.

Developing a Service Orientation

Leisure service professionals operate within an occupational area known as a service area. As indicated in chapter 4 dealing with historical concepts, service-related industries have seen great growth since society has progressed from the industrial era to the technological/information era. One of the important distinguishing characteristics of a service industry is that it does not deal in the manufacturing of products, but rather delivers experiences to customers.

Today, the golden arches of McDonald's may more accurately symbolize America than does the industrial heartland. As a society that is immediate- and convenience-oriented, Americans require the delivery of products and services in ways that match the nature of their lifestyles—fast-paced, efficient, dynamic, changing, and immediate. For example, we may not have time to cook our own foods, to maintain our own gardens, to clean our own homes, or to organize our own leisure. DINKS (double income, no kids), FLYERS (fun loving youth en-route to success), YUPPIES (young, upwardly mobile professionals), DENKS (dual employed, no kids), and DEWKS (dual employed, with kids) often require other individuals to provide basic services, which in other eras were achieved through self-sufficiency.

What Is a Service? A Product?

The fast-growing service sector includes a vast array of business services and a wide variety of personal services, including the provision of leisure experiences. What is the difference between a service and a product? A service is a process whereby arrangements are made to provide something desired, useful, or necessary, often an experience. A product is a tangible item. For example, to participate in skiing, individuals must have proper equipment and clothing. They also need skills, lodging, food, transportation, a ski run, and other support services in order to participate. The equipment and clothing constitute products, whereas the organization and management of the support services that enable the leisure experience come within the service domain. Interestingly, the actual sales process of equipment and clothing (the products) also falls within the service sector.

Service is the primary focus of any leisure service organization. Since service is not a single-dimension item, however, it can be difficult to define. Most products that customers purchase may be categorized as single-item commodities. A service, on the other hand, may have many dimensions. Someone may sell the service, another person may deliver it, and still another person may evaluate its effectiveness.

Services are less tangible than products. Whereas products usually are evaluated in terms of concrete quality and production standards, the quality, caliber, and effectiveness of a service can be more difficult to measure. Services often involve transmittal and exchange of knowledge, information, or the creation of an emotional state (e.g., excitement within an experience). Many variables are difficult to control and predict in producing a leisure experience. For example, each individual comes to a leisure experience with a unique set of expectations, experiences, values, and attitudes; this makes it difficult to produce and/or replicate a leisure experience consistently across all types of participants.

Albrecht and Zemke (1985), writing in a book entitled *Service America!,* suggest that a service can be thought of as "any incident of doing for others for a fee" (p. 36). The fee for services does not necessarily have to be paid by the individual; it can be offset by taxes, donations, gifts, or in-kind contributions. Following are characteristics of services:

1. A service is produced at the instant of delivery; it *cannot be created in advance* or held in readiness.
2. A service cannot be centrally produced, inspected, stockpiled, or warehoused. It is usually *delivered wherever the customer is* by people who are beyond the immediate influence of management.
3. The "product" *cannot be demonstrated,* nor can a sample be sent for customer approval in advance of the service; the provider can show various examples, but the customer's own haircut, for example, does not yet exist and cannot be shown.
4. The person receiving the service *has nothing tangible;* the value of the service depends on his or her personal experience.
5. The experience *cannot be sold or passed on to a third party.*
6. If improperly performed, a service *cannot be "recalled."* If it cannot be repeated, then reparations or apologies are the only means of recourse for customer satisfaction.
7. *Quality assurance must take place before production* rather than after production, as would be the case in a manufacturing situation.
8. Delivery of the service usually *requires human interaction* to some degree; buyer and seller come into contact in some relatively personal way to create the service.
9. The receiver's expectations of the service are integral to his or her satisfaction with the outcome. Quality of service is largely a *subjective* matter.
10. The more people the customer must *encounter during the delivery of the service,* the less likely it is that he or she will be satisfied with the service (Albrecht and Zemke, 1985, pp. 36–37).

Albrecht and Zemke (1985) note that not all of these characteristics necessarily appear in all services. Their assumptions have not been tested in leisure service organizations, but can help to clarify the differences between products and services. Leisure service professionals must recognize the challenges and opportunities that providing quality leisure services presents.

Organizing a Strategy to Provide Services

Outstanding leisure service organizations do not just happen. Successful organizations have a strong vision or direction for their actions. In other words, they develop a strategy that guides the work of the organization in terms of the quality of its services.

What necessary elements will ensure effective service delivery and profitability? Three quality factors are essential in the successful provision of services. The first is the organization's definition of what is unique or different about its services, called *value-added service delivery.* The second factor involves the *promotion of positive customer relations.* The third area includes *organizational policies and procedures* that create an attitude that the organization exists to meet customers' needs rather than the reverse.

Value-Added Services Individuals have certain expectations for the level of service they expect prior to engaging the service. The value-added concept involves adding a dimension or quality of service that goes beyond the customer's basic expectation. In other words, the organization attempts to give customers or clients a better service than they expected. This

Characteristics of Servant Leaders

Listening — Traditionally, leaders have been valued for their communication and decision-making skills. Servant leaders must reinforce these important skills by making a deep commitment to listening intently to others. Listening, coupled with regular periods of reflection, are essential to the growth of the servant leader.

Empathy — Servant leaders strive to understand and empathize with others. People need to be accepted and recognized for their special and unique spirits. The most successful servant leaders are those who have become skilled empathetic listeners.

Healing — Learning to heal is a powerful force for transformation and integration. Many people have broken spirits and suffered from a variety of emotional hurts. Although this is a part of being human, servant leaders recognize that they have an opportunity to help make whole those with whom they come in contact.

Awareness — General awareness, and especially self-awareness, strengthens the servant leader. Awareness also aids in understanding issues involving ethics and values. It enables one to view most situations from a more integrated position.

Persuasion — Servant leaders rely on persuasion rather than positional authority in making decisions. Servant leaders seek to convince others rather than coerce compliance. The servant leader is effective at building consensus within groups.

Conceptualization — Servant leaders seek to nurture their abilities to dream great dreams. Servant leaders must seek a delicate balance between conceptualization and day-to-day focus.

Foresight — Foresight is a characteristic that enables servant leaders to understand lessons from the past, the realities of the present, and the likely consequence of a decision for the future.

Stewardship — Stewardship is defined as holding something in trust for another. Servant leadership, like stewardship, assumes first and foremost a commitment to serving the needs of others. It also emphasizes the use of openness and persuasion, rather than control.

Commitment to the growth of people — Servant leaders believe that people have intrinsic value and must be included in decisions affecting their lives.

Building community — Servant leaders are aware of the need to build community and actively seek to involve people in the process.

Source: Spears, L. 1995. Servant leadership and the Greenleaf legacy. In L. Spear (ed.), *Reflections on Leadership: How Robert K. Greenleaf's Theory of Servant Leadership Influenced Today's Top Management Thinkers*, 1–16. New York: Wiley.

strategy effectively ensures long-term customer loyalty. By adding to a service and improving its quality, efficiency, attractiveness, convenience, format, and intensity, an organization focuses clearly on the needs of the customers to be served. This approach to providing leisure services creates unique market niches and is the hallmark of any successful public, private, nonprofit, or commercial organization.

Examples of the value-added concept in successful organizations abound. Tom Peters (1987), speaking to managers at the Hult Center in Eugene, Oregon, relates the story of a gas station in the San Francisco Bay area that employs the value-added concept and whose sales are thirteen times higher than the average gas station in the United States. As Peters relates this story, he says that he sent an associate to investigate this phenomenon. Upon returning, the associate declared that having a vehicle serviced while purchasing gas at this particular service station is as close as one could come to being in a pit stop at the Indianapolis 500. The gas station attendants not only pumped the gas (self-service stations predominate in California), washed the windows in the front and back and on the inside and on the outside but also vacuumed the inside of the car in the front and back and topped it off by giving him a cup of coffee and a newspaper. As Peters notes, the gas being sold in this station is no different from the gas being pumped in any other gas station. The major difference, resulting in increased sales and consumer loyalty, is the "value-add-ons" to the basic commodity.

How do organizations create value-added leisure services? The process requires continuous work, with constant improvement, innovation, and evaluation of the ways in which services are delivered. Peters (1987) notes that every organization should "add at least value-increasing 'differentiators' to each service every ninety days" (p. 50). He suggests that no matter how mundane a product or service, it can become a highly value-added product or service. Using the illustration of the gas station, pumping gas is usually perceived as a mundane activity; however, the Bay area gas station made it a highly unique, visible, dynamic, and differentiated service.

Which value-added items can be added to services within leisure service organizations? The following areas within leisure service agencies could benefit from the value-added concept:

1. *Features.* Every service can be augmented or enhanced by adding specialized, unique features that cannot be obtained elsewhere. The Louisville Redbirds minor league Triple A baseball team augments its basic entertainment service, the baseball game, by providing other unique entertainment and food-service features. Bands, family picnic areas, infant care areas, fireworks, and daily steam-cleaned stadium seats all contribute to an environment that results in this organization's annually attracting over 1 million participants.

2. *Customer-leader interaction.* No other area offers a greater opportunity to add value than in the customer-leader interaction. On a day-to-day basis, the way frontline service providers interact with customers greatly impacts their perception of the organization. Acts of courtesy, helpfulness, sincerity, generosity, as well as inspired instruction, direction, and supervision—all these areas of value influence the delivery of services within a leisure service organization. Leisure service organizations must focus constant attention and effort toward improving these interpersonal relations.

3. *Image.* Organizations can add value to a service in several ways by enhancing or improving the image of an activity or event. First, and perhaps the simplest and most inexpensive, is using contemporary and up-to-date terms to define activities. In describing the work of a textile manufacturer, the Millikin Company, Peters (1987) notes that it does not make "rags," but rather is in the "shop towels" business. The simple change in terms adds distinction and value to the perceptions of customers with regard to this commodity.

Another way to enhance the image of services involves paying close attention to pricing strategies since individuals often equate quality with price. Leisure services are often underpriced, especially those offered by public service agencies.

4. *Order and cleanliness.* An impressive hallmark of Disney theme parks—Disneyland, Disney World, Tokyo Disneyland, Disneyland Paris—is the cleanliness maintained at these facilities. People far more prefer a clean, orderly leisure environment to one that is cluttered, dirty, and disorganized. Organizations can quickly add value to any service by ensuring that standards for orderliness and cleanliness are upgraded and maintained. This applies to the maintenance of areas and facilities, and even more to the grooming and dress of employees. Interestingly, this results in a cost-effective approach over the long term; individual behavior regarding cleanliness tends to support or correspond to the status quo—in other words, if consumers sense that cleanliness and orderliness are a priority, they will respond in kind and help to keep things clean.

Positive Customer Relations Leisure service professionals must remember that their business emphasizes service and relies on the goodwill generated between customers and providers. There is no secret to providing positive customer relations; it simply means operating so that the customers' "current situation, frame of mind, and needs are addressed" (Albrecht and Zemke, 1985, p. 39). A customer-oriented professional operates with a high degree of "responsiveness, attentiveness and willingness to help others" (Albrecht and Zemke, 1985, p. 39). Being customer-oriented means being attentive to the details that make leisure activities enjoyable and leisure facilities and areas hospitable and attractive. As Siegenthaler (2000, p. 101) has written, "Leisure service providers are in a competitive market to attract and retain customers; therefore, customer service must be a priority."

Miller (2000, p. 61) notes that in delivering quality customer services, leisure service professionals must "continually examine and evaluate existing policies, procedures, signage, staff training, mission and goal statements, and how to turn negative situations into a 'win-win,' customer friendly" one. He notes that customer service is a two-way street and that we must seek out both positive and negative feedback in order to learn about ourselves and our image.

L e i s u r e   L i n e

Anshin: **Understanding the Customer**

Anshin is the Japanese word for . . . security and comfort. Increasing the comfort level of your associates and customers in Japan goes far beyond providing quality products delivered on time and at the right price. Japanese want to feel comfortable and "in touch" with their suppliers and business partners. There is a human dimension to this desire along with the business side.

Japanese want to know you can be trusted and are as interested in their success as you are in your own. The first order of *anshin* is to understand the customer's needs: response to customer demands is an obligation. This takes time and close relations. Two-way obligations between customers and suppliers are built over many years, and go far beyond traditional American expectations.

Source: Jim and Jeffrey Morgan, *Cracking the Japanese Market.*

An organization should not assume that its employees will be positively oriented toward customers. It must teach, encourage, and reinforce its values and reward employee behavior that leads to positive customer relations.

Key employee behaviors that produce positive customer relations include the following (see figure 13.1):

1. *Exceeding expectations.* People like to feel that when they communicate their needs the provider is attentive. People hate to be ignored or made to feel that their needs are not important. Being responsive means listening carefully and attending to people's needs in a timely fashion and in a way that exceeds their expectations.
2. *Anticipating needs.* It is not enough to merely respond to customers' needs; one must anticipate those needs and meet them as they occur. Anticipatory behavior is central to producing a satisfied customer.
3. *Effective performance.* A service, effectively performed, greatly enhances positive customer relations. In fact, there is no substitute—effective performance is the bottom line,

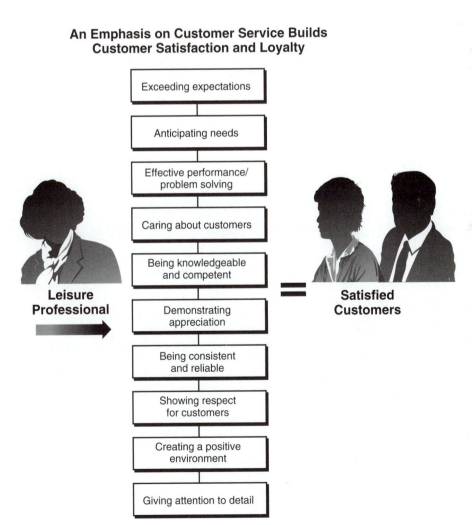

An Emphasis on Customer Service Builds Customer Satisfaction and Loyalty

Exceeding expectations

Anticipating needs

Effective performance/ problem solving

Caring about customers

Being knowledgeable and competent

Demonstrating appreciation

Being consistent and reliable

Showing respect for customers

Creating a positive environment

Giving attention to detail

Leisure Professional

Satisfied Customers

Figure 13.1
Employee behaviors that result in positive customer service

and people will often forgo some of the other elements mentioned if the service is delivered in an effective, reliable, and consistent manner.

4. *Caring about customers.* Responding to individuals with polite and thoughtful behavior is essential. Courtesy also includes kindness, generosity, and supportive behavior.

5. *Being knowledgeable and competent.* The way an organization provides information about services impacts customers. People should be set at ease about asking questions that require direction and interpretation. Accuracy and thoughtfulness in providing such information can influence the success of a leisure experience. The initial contact a customer may make with a leisure service organization often involves requests for information or clarification. First impressions are lasting ones.

6. *Demonstrating appreciation.* People like to feel that their business is valued and that they are appreciated. Thanking a person is good business. Sometimes organizations place an ad in the paper or mail holiday cards, but even more important is the day-to-day interaction between the customer and the provider.

7. *Being consistent and reliable.* Cooperating with customers in a positive, reliable, and consistent manner is vital to customer satisfaction. Customers should be able to count on the same excellent service every time they interact with the organization.

8. *Showing respect for customers.* Enthusiasm, energy and zestfulness are important elements in successful leisure experiences. No matter how many times a professional has successfully implemented a given service, he or she should approach each new customer and each new situation with the same level of respect, intensity, and positiveness— qualities that will rub off on the customer.

9. *Creating a positive ambiance and environment.* Creating a positive feeling or mood greatly influences perceptions of quality. This mood may be one of warmth and relaxation or one

L e i s u r e   L i n e

FISH: An Approach to Customer Service

The combination of fish and chlorinated pool water may sound like a deadly one, but the Roseville (Calif.) Parks and Recreation Department aquatics division's FISH approach to customer service is alive and swimming. There was the stuffed fish pillow being thrown out the concessions service window at a customer. If the lucky customer caught the fish pillow, he or she was treated to a gummy worm, a favorite snack of fish-catchers. There was the fish decoupage megaphone awarded to the day's best lifeguard. There were the fish key chains given to staff who were caught displaying above-and-beyond-the-call-of-duty customer service. There were fish stickers, fish squirters, and fish decorations. It was a fishy summer.

The FISH philosophy to customer service contains four basic concepts: (1) *Play*—It's about having fun, enjoying yourself for your customers and co-workers. Make it a day to remember; (2) *Make their day*—It's about doing something special for your customers and coworkers. Make it a day to remember; (3) *Be there*—It's about being totally focused on the moment and on the person or task with which you are engaged. When we are fully present with our customers and with each other, we are listening deeply and important opportunities do not escape us; and (4) *Choose your attitude*—It's about accepting full responsibility for all of our choices, even our attitudes at work. A positive attitude is a decision we make moment to moment.

Source: Pritchard, A. 2000, February. Go fish. *Parks & Recreation 35*(2), 64–67.

of excitement and risk. Whatever the intent, the achievement of a mood needs to be carried out through careful planning and organization.

10. *Giving attention to detail.* The little things make a difference between superior organizational effort and mediocre performance. Attention to detail requires thought, planning, and a creative nature. A wrapped piece of chocolate on a pillow at a resort is a thoughtful act that represents attention to detail.

McChesney (1999, p. 6) has suggested that a focus on customer service is an important element in the effective management of leisure service organizations. He has indicated that "customer loyalty can be promoted and nurtured via customer service, resulting in added value to the business exchange, reduced cost of doing business, and customer acceptance of less than perfect program delivery." According to this author (McChesney, 1999), important characteristics required to promote customer service include the following:

1. Assisting customers takes precedence over all tasks.
2. Customers are satisfied when they perceive value—give it to them.
3. Complaining customers are an opportunity for us to learn about our company.
4. Always look at situations through the eyes of the customer.
5. The purpose of your job is to satisfy the customer!
6. Realize you don't have a job without customers!
7. "I don't know" should never be said without "I'll find out."
8. If a customer is dissatisfied, it's not enough to just give them what you should have provided in the first place. Give them something extra.
9. Be positive when you interact with customers—smile!
10. Follow up!

The Disney Company has made thoughtful, attentive behavior toward consumers a hallmark of the services it provides. At Disneyland, customers are treated as guests—hospitably, courteously placing the needs of these guests first. This action results in services of a superior nature, a model for the leisure service industry.

Organizational Policies and Procedures   To promote positive consumer relations, values must be backed with organizational policies and procedures. In other words, an organization must have a system in place to ensure compliance with its vision. Policies and procedures can deal with a variety of topics, including how to approach customers, how to handle complaints, how facilities are to be used and maintained, safety regulations, and others. McChesney (1999) has suggested that there are five important customer service strategies that are important and can be applied to any leisure service organization. These strategies are (1) hiring practices, (2) customer service training, (3) frontline responsiveness, (4) customer response networks, and (5) management by walking around. The first strategy suggests that you have to get the right people in place, people who enjoy working with others. The second element suggests that the training of employees should be done from the prospective of the employees or the organization. Frontline responsiveness is about ensuring that individuals at the frontline are empowered to make important decisions influencing customer satisfaction. A customer response network refers to the way a leisure organization communicates with its customers. How are complaints handled? How are customers shown appreciation for their participation? The last strategy, management by wandering around, suggests that leisure service professionals should be hands-on, listening to customers, employees, and others who influence the work of the organization.

Camp Adventure™ Youth Services, a contracted youth developement service between the University of Northern Iowa and the U.S. Armed Forces, provides guidelines for staff working in resident and day camp situations. These guidelines govern the day-to-day interactions and behaviors that are expected between the providers and the customers. For example, staff are expected to use positive reinforcement, serve as positive role models, teach new skills, work as a part of a team, provide effective communications, be prepared and organized, make a genuine commitment to youth, establish a warm and caring atmosphere, anticipate and thereby prevent problems, provide a structure in which children can be successful, provide an atmosphere for learning, and treat each child as an individual. Individuals who participate in leading this program are reminded that *Camp Adventure*™ Youth Services is a business and that its primary reason for engaging in the activity is the success of the business enterprise. Policies and procedures for *Camp Adventure*™ Youth Services are documented in written form in the *Camp Adventure*™ Staff Handbook. In addition, the policies and procedures are systematically taught and reinforced to service providers. By understanding and adhering to the expectations concerning consumer relations, students participating in this program have made it an outstanding success and a model for this type of contractual effort.

Programs: The Services of Leisure Service Organizations

Programs may be thought of as the raison d'etre of any leisure service organization. Programs are created to deliver something of value—a benefit or the expectation of a benefit—to a customer or group of customers. Edginton and Rossman (1988) write that "by organizing, promoting, and delivering programs, leisure managers help their constituents experience leisure" (p. viii).

L e i s u r e   L i n e

The Customer Game

The customer game is ultimately won or lost on the front lines—where the customer comes in contact with *any* member of the firm. The frontline team *is* the firm in the customer's eyes. Therefore, the frontline team must be treated as the heroes they genuinely are—and supported with tools . . . that allow them to regularly serve the customer heroically.

. . . Regional vice president Betsy Sanders of Nordstrom captured [this] spirit in a talk to a group of technology executives.

"How many of you know Nordstrom?"
All hands go up.

"How many of you have a positive image of Nordstrom?"
Once more, all hands go up.
"How many of you know me?"
No hands go up.
"How many of you know Jim or Bruce Nordstrom?"
No hands.
"How many of you know our store manager in Palo Alto, or wherever you might have visited us?"
Still no hands.

"You see, Nordstrom is the *salesperson* to you. It's not me, not Bruce Nordstrom . . . It is that one person you are in contact with when you are in the department you want."

Source: Tom Peters, *Thriving on Chaos*, 1987.

Programming involves arranging social, physical, and natural environments in such a way as to produce leisure experiences. For example, leisure programmers may create situations where social interaction between individuals is arranged, heightened, or encouraged. Programmers also build facilities and make natural areas accessible in order to support the leisure experience. All of these actions help individuals to engage in positive leisure opportunities. Bullaro and Edginton (1986) suggest that the work of programmers "may involve planning and organizing, assembling materials and supplies, providing leadership and other actions that create opportunities for leisure" (p. 12).

Programmers may create highly structured activities or they may enable individuals to experience leisure opportunities. The programmer's intervention can range from nearly total control of all of the elements of planning, organizing, and implementing the chosen event or activity to teaching or enabling participants to assume control of the experience. From an organizational perspective, planned intervention results in agency control. On the other hand, enabling services place a great degree of control and responsibility with the participant.

Types of Programs

Leisure service organizations provide many types of programs. Edginton and Rossman (1988) write that "programming involves the creation and distribution of activities, areas and facilities, information and leadership opportunities" (p. viii). In other words, programming involves more than the creation of activities or events (see figure 13.2). Programs can be far-reaching and involve a high level of sophistication, depending on the nature of the event to be produced or the facility to be developed. Listed here are four general categories of programs that can be offered by a leisure service organization:

1. *Activities.* Activities or events include those services that occur primarily in social settings. Activities often involve assisting individuals to acquire new knowledge or skill or arranging social situations to promote fun, enjoyment, and/or companionship. Activities may also include testing or demonstration of skills. Some examples include festivals, tournaments, leagues, lessons, drop-in programs, dances, clubs, parties, carnivals, and other special events.
2. *Areas and facilities.* An area is an open space that provides opportunities for individuals to experience leisure. A park, a ball diamond, picnic area, soccer field, playground, hiking trail, bicycle path, jogging trail, lakes and ponds, and other areas suitable for recreational use fall within this category. Facilities are artificial structures used for leisure, not necessarily confined to indoor usage. Gymnasiums, recreation centers, skateboard parks,

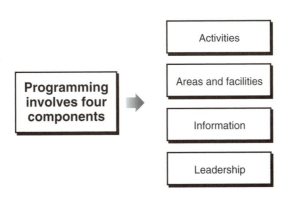

Figure 13.2

Types of programs provided by leisure service organizations

ice rinks, tennis courts, racquetball centers, roller skating rinks, bowling centers, and theaters are all examples of leisure facilities.

3. *Information.* Leisure service organizations provide individuals with information about their own services, as well as other services that may contribute to the consumer's general satisfaction and well-being. Public agencies and private, nonprofit organizations often build customer awareness about various leisure opportunities. Leisure service organizations also develop and disperse interpretive material such as information regarding historical and cultural events or sites and information about the natural environment. Face-to-face interpretation, often presented by volunteer tour guides, requires great skill in bringing alive past history or the uniqueness of an environment area.

4. *Leadership.* Some leisure service organizations focus on the development of individuals as leaders. Youth serving voluntary organizations, in particular, engage in leadership development of youth participants and adult volunteer leaders. A number of program formats also require leaders to emerge from the participating group itself. Athletic teams and leagues require captains to exhibit leadership. Leisure-oriented clubs also require self-generated leadership.

Not all leisure service organizations provide a full range of programs and services. Often they specialize in one particular area or a combination of areas. For example, McKay and Crompton (1988) write, ". . . no longer do public recreation agencies aim to deliver a full range of recreation programs. Rather, they realize increasingly that they are only one small component of the total recreation system" (p. 53). They suggest a different system of categorizing leisure programs that focuses primarily on identifying and meeting the needs of participants. These categories include (1) the nature of the service, (2) the relationship between the programmer and the customer, (3) potential for customization, (4) the nature of the demand for a program, (5) attributes of the program, and (6) program beneficiaries. The major benefit of this classification system results from more succinctly differentiating or defining the target market.

Factors Influencing Leisure Program Planning

A number of variables should be considered by leisure program planners. In an effort to help individuals grow and develop, leisure professionals must understand these factors and how they impact leisure pursuits. Some of these variables include generation, environmental factors, level of education, and cultural background. This section briefly discusses each of these factors as well as the program planning process.

Generation   Each person belongs to an *age cohort or generation,* and as a cohort, individuals face different circumstances and events that shape their perceptions. Thus, one generation of teenagers may gain a perspective of the world differently from teenagers of a different generation as they grow up in different "worlds." Today's newest generation or cohort faces a world of technology that earlier generations could only dream about. Advances in computers, electronics, transportation, and communication have created many new opportunities for young people, as well as problems and issues with which to cope.

One's age cohort provides a frame of reference from which to view the world. Someone who was born and lived through the Great Depression of the 1930s has a vastly different outlook on life than someone who grew up in the more liberal 1960s. For example, those born in the 1930s might have difficulty feeling comfortable buying on credit and spending money that has not yet been earned, while children of the 1960s use credit readily. In many respects, these changing frames of reference cause the generation gaps between older and younger people.

Seniors Travel the Information Superhighway

For years, senior centers have been seen as places where older adults can gather to play Bingo or cards. This image, however, is continually changing. Older adults are not moving slowly and cautiously but are racing into the computer age.

Ten years ago, seniors were interested in the computer; they were curious. They wanted to be informed and desired to be able to understand computer terminology. The ability to carry on an informed conversation with their children and grandchildren was important. However, the hands-on experience was intimidating at times.

The Park Ridge Senior Center in Park Ridge, Illinois, got its start when a computer company called and offered free introductory lessons to any interested senior. We coordinated the onslaught of registrations. Twelve sessions with ten students apiece made the center's staff and the computer company realize that this was only the beginning.

Many participants went on to purchase their own computers, while some inherited older models from their children. They were enthusiastic and aggressive in learning the skills necessary to use the computers for practical matters and also wanted to have some fun with them. They were using their computers primarily for word processing, record keeping, and paying bills.

Years later, the center approached with an idea for further computer classroom experience. A center member came forward with the idea of a computer discussion group. It was to be an information-sharing group for those who had some computer expertise. Once again, there was tremendous response. However, the members found the format too limiting. It was only for people who knew something about computers, and there was no opportunity for hands-on experience. Left out were those who had no idea how to turn on the computer and those who knew the basics but needed some practical instruction.

Source: Pritchard, A. 1998, June. Seniors travel the Information Superhighway. *Parks & Recreation 33*(6), 70–74.

The older generation was born before 1940. For the most part this generation lived through the Great Depression and World War II. Many are immigrants or first-generation Americans and Canadians who grew up in rural areas. This generation views leisure as a way to re-create themselves for more work. They played so they could work better.

The middle generation was born between 1940 and 1960. This generation entered adulthood during a period of affluence and optimism about the future. Such events as Vietnam and Watergate changed this generation, however, making it skeptical of big government. This generation viewed leisure as a central aspect of life and worked only to get to the weekend. Leisure was viewed as an end in itself rather than as a reward for working hard.

The younger generation was born after 1960. This generation was born into an affluent society that now struggles with what is next. This is the first generation where individuals may not be better off than their parents. It faces global environmental problems as well as the role of America in a post–cold war period. In many cases, leisure has become a major form of self-expression. This group works hard, plays hard, and tries to have it all, while wondering what the future holds.

America's newest generation has a number of interesting characteristics. It has high-tech literacy, is diverse, has high discretionary income, seeks independence, is action-oriented, and wants to return to traditional family values.

Environmental Factors   Environmental factors include such things as place of residence and financial resources. For example, a person living in Florida often participates in different leisure pursuits than does someone living in Canada. While influenced largely by climate, these differences also result from topography and leisure opportunities. People living in Florida participate in many year-round water-based leisure activities (e.g., fishing, boating, waterskiing, windsurfing, scuba diving), whereas individuals living in the Canadian Rockies participate in more winter sports (e.g., snow skiing, hockey, skating).

Likewise, people living in rural areas and small towns have different day-to-day leisure patterns than people living in large metropolitan areas. Rural residents often travel farther to participate in organized recreation. Urban residents often try to escape the city and participate in such outdoor recreation as bicycling, swimming, and waterskiing, whereas people who live and work outdoors on a daily basis may seek other forms of leisure and recreation.

A second environmental factor affects leisure participation: income. Leisure does not have to cost money—the old adage says, "The best things in life are free." Yet, in an increasingly materialistic society, money has great impact on leisure patterns. The *Third Nationwide Outdoor Recreation Plan* (Department of the Interior, 1979) reported a positive association between increased leisure participation and rising incomes. Howard and Crompton (1984) identified the factor "it cost too much" as an obstacle to participation by respondents in three large metropolitan areas in the United States. Lankford (1990) found that money was one of the top five barriers to leisure participation in Oregon and Washington. Jackson (1994) identifies cost of participating as one of the constraints to leisure participation, including the cost of transportation, cost of equipment, lack of transportation, and admission fees/other charges.

Income affects a person's leisure in a variety of ways: neighborhood and type of housing, the purchase of leisure equipment, and the type and affordability of leisure activities. Those of low income do not constitute a viable market for many leisure programs or provisions. Hence, lower-income individuals must rely on public and quasi-public leisure facilities and programs.

Level of Education   According to Godbey (1985), education stimulates interest in many forms of leisure activities. Individuals with higher levels of education often experience more leisure variety and are encouraged to try a variety of leisure activities. Specifically, studies show that individuals with higher levels of education participate in more outdoor recreation, sports, high-culture activities (e.g., the arts), and tourism. An educated person, often due to higher income, is able to follow through on leisure wishes and desires. Yet, even when the effects of age and income are taken into account, education itself often has a distinct bearing on leisure participation.

Within specific types of leisure activities, such as sports and outdoor recreation, certain activities are strongly associated with low or high education groups (Godbey, 1985). For example, hunting and fishing are associated more with individuals with lower education levels (*Nationwide Outdoor Recreation Survey,* 1984), whereas activities such as backpacking, nature study, kayaking, and adventure recreation are associated more with individuals with higher levels of education.

Cultural Background   Culture—defined as the attitudes, beliefs, values, ideas, and assumptions that a group passes on from generation to generation—is influenced by environment and history. People absorb their culture at an early age; they learn the habits and rules of behaving and how to do things, along with standards of right and wrong, beautiful and ugly, valuable or unimportant. For example, an open and friendly attitude toward new people may result from a history of moving frequently and constantly needing to make new friends to survive. These habits become so much a part of a person that he or she considers them natural or "just the way things are." As Godbey (1985) notes, leisure is a product of culture, and to some extent, culture is a product of leisure.

Another cultural difference centers around how people view time. Most Americans and Canadians come from a large land mass situated in a temperate zone with four seasons. The four seasons have caused the cultures to develop the notion of future-mindedness, planting, harvesting, and storing. In addition, the transportation system, beginning with the railroad, placed punctuality high in the spectrum of cultural values. People from island countries, such as the Philippines, do not have four seasons. Many Filipinos see no need to slice their time into distinct periods and do not place punctuality high in their value spectrum. In the past, when a canoe sailed from one island to another, the sailors had a general idea of how long the trip would take but the specific time depended on the wind and waves. Therefore, the notion of general time still prevails today.

People often judge different cultures by their own value system, which can result in ethnocentrism—an attitude that one's culture is superior to others. In today's multicultural world (by the year 2000 California had no majority ethnic group), leisure professionals must learn to understand the cultural values of those they serve.

> Cultural pluralism emphasizes the role of leisure as anything the individual chooses to do for pleasure. The limits of such behavior are defined only by laws, with activity representing an expression of personal interest, or lifestyle, rather than one's culture. Fads and created leisure needs may cause more innovation, a speeding up of the consumption of leisure experience with a corresponding questioning of what is worth doing. One resolution to this uncertainty is to try to do nothing, but a more prevalent reaction is to try to do everything. (Godbey, 1985, p. 115)

A pluralistic society must develop programs and experiences that help people to value their own unique culture while celebrating and respecting the cultures of others.

The Process of Program Planning

Current literature dealing with leisure programming suggests that planning occurs in a cyclical fashion. Leisure service professionals engage in a step-by-step process to produce services. Most program models suggest that program planning involves the following processes: (1) development of program goals, (2) needs assessment, (3) program planning, and (4) program evaluation.

Development of Program Goals Organizations have broad goals and their programs and services reflect that broad mission. In addition, leisure service organizations often develop particular goals and objectives to guide the development and implementation of specific programs and services. Such goals and objectives help to identify specific behavioral outcomes by participants engaging in specific programs and services. These types of statements are referred to as *performance* or *behavioral objectives.*

The development of performance or behavioral objectives plays an important role in measuring the impact of program services and is usually stated in quantifiable (measurable) terms. For example, an individual working with physically challenged individuals in a learn-to-swim program may develop a behavioral objective that describes specifically the outcomes that should result from participation in the activity—"The participant will demonstrate success in swimming by treading water for three minutes without needing assistance."

Needs Assessment   Most cyclical models of programming recommend the use of a needs assessment, either preceding or following the development of program objectives. Discussing needs assessment, Russell (1982) suggests that the "*identification of needs, interest and problems* of the program constituency is a logical place to start the planning process" (p. 68). She further notes that needs assessment helps in "[establishing] program form and content" (p. 68).

Needs assessment involves discovering information about participants' leisure needs, interests, value states, behaviors, and attitudes. Such information helps to determine the most appropriate programs and services. Howe and Qui (1988) suggest that leisure service professionals can approach needs assessment in two ways. First, public service providers primarily use a process of systematic inquiry. Second, the problem-solving approach involves identifying problems and barriers that prevent individuals from having successful leisure experiences. Edginton and Edginton (1993a) suggest that the programmer should consider some of the broad issues presented in figure 13.3 when engaged in needs assessment and program planning for youth. The model refers to some of the underlying needs of youth for leadership and achievement, youth involvement, family involvement, achieving youth development competencies, meeting the needs of the whole person (within the context of school, health issues, and other factors), clarifying values, and others.

Figure 13.3

Youth-centered programming

Issues to Be Considered
When Planning Programs for Youth

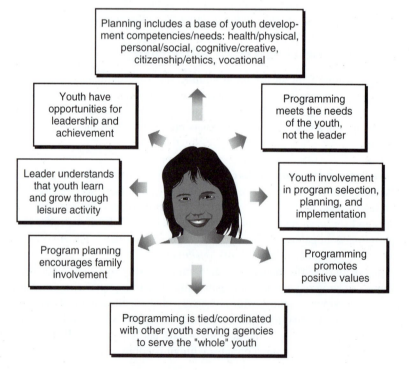

Program Planning Once needs and objectives are determined, the next step involves planning for the program's implementation and includes locating the site for the service, arranging for leadership, promoting the activity, and developing the program content. A vast array of potential program areas can be provided to meet the leisure needs of individuals. Some of these program areas include the following:

1. *Visual arts.* Visual arts refer to decorative objects that are created for their own sake (fine art) or for some utilitarian purpose (a craft).
2. *Performing arts.* The performing arts include music, drama, and dance. The human being is the creative mode of expression.
3. *New arts.* New arts involve the use of contemporary technology to create art, such as photography, computer, synthesizers, and so forth.
4. *Hobbies.* Hobbies, activities pursued in an intense way over an extended period of time, include four types—collecting, creative, educational, and performing.
5. *Sports, games, and athletics.* Sports, games, and athletics are activities that involve the use of fine and gross motor skills. Sports, more sophisticated than games, require a higher degree of organization, skill, and endurance. Athletics are often characterized by their competitive nature.
6. *Outdoor recreation.* Outdoor recreation activities depend on the natural environment. Mountaineering, spelunking, hiking, windsurfing, and others serve as examples.
7. *Social recreation.* The primary function of social recreation is to promote social interaction among people. Parties, carnivals, festivals, social gatherings, and picnics are examples of social recreation.
8. *Volunteer services.* Volunteering during one's leisure can be a creative, fulfilling, and valuable experience. As a program area, volunteering involves work in leadership roles, such as coaching, and as activity leaders, hosts, and guides.
9. *Literary and self-improvement programs.* Popular programs that contribute to the development of individuals intellectually, socially, or spiritually fall within this program area. Book discussion groups, parent groups, toastmasters, and others serve to illustrate this area.
10. *Travel and tourism.* Leisure service organizations often manage destination points (featured attractions). In addition, leisure service organizations often manage travel and tour activities.

Several different program formats or forms can be used to organize services for delivery. It is extremely important to use an appropriate format. For example, in contemporary society individuals increasingly require programs with convenient, intense formats. People trying to pack more and more into less and less time are challenging leisure service organizations to provide more accessible and efficient formats for their services. Some potential program formats include the following:

1. *Leagues, tournaments, and contests.* This program format emphasizes competition. There are basically three types of leagues, tournaments, or contests—self-perpetuating, round robin, and elimination.
2. *Drop-in programs.* Drop-in activities provide areas, facilities, and equipment with little structured leadership so that participants can engage in self-directed activities.
3. *Instructional classes.* Classes help people acquire specific leisure competencies, skills, or knowledge. There are two approaches—the humanistic and the systems approach—to instruction. The humanistic approach focuses on growth and development of each individual, whereas the systems approach measures minimal standards of competence.

4. *Clubs.* Clubs provide an opportunity for self-directed leadership to flourish. Clubs are often built around special themes, age groups, hobby interests, education endeavors, and political activities.

5. *Special events.* Special events, programs organized in a unique manner deviating from the routine, can take months of planning but can be implemented in a matter of hours or even minutes.

6. *Seminars, workshops, and conferences.* These involve short, intense instructional efforts aimed at providing concise information. Such formats are gaining in popularity due to the desire for convenient and efficient services of short duration.

7. *Outreach programs.* These programs are taken to customers in their own locale. This type of program format may involve mobile recreation equipment and roving leaders and often occurs in densely populated urban areas where entire programs can be organized and implemented on site.

Two of the greatest barriers to participating in leisure are lack of convenience and time commitments. A program's format has a direct bearing on its attractiveness and accessibility to its intended audience.

Program Evaluation Program evaluation refers to the measurement of the effectiveness and efficiency of program services. Leisure service organizations usually attempt to measure or evaluate two specific areas—impact and process. The first type of evaluation attempts to assess the impact—behaviorally, socially, and economically—of the program on its participants. The second evaluation or measurement concerns the process that is used to produce the program. In other words, evaluation focuses on the step-by-step procedures used in constructing and implementing the program. For example, it addresses such questions as "Are the promotional materials communicating the intended message?" and "Was the format the right length?"

L e i s u r e   L i n e

Working Out

For decades, local park and recreation departments have cultivated community involvement in activities that promote health and well-being. Spurred by the fitness boom that exploded within mainstream America three decades ago, today's parks and recreation programs are more varied, and the facilities are better equipped to assist local residents in achieving their exercise goals.

But as parks and recreation offerings expand across the nation, directors are faced with the challenge of providing quality programs that benefit not only the participants but the districts and facilities that serve them.

"We've come a long way as a nation in terms of addressing the value of and need for daily exercise," states fitness expert Judi Sheppard Missett. Jazzercise, Missett's international fitness program, offers more than 2,100 dance exercise classes weekly at 430 parks and recreation facilities across the United States.

"The 1996 U.S. Surgeon General's groundbreaking report on the dangers of physical inactivity is a prime example of this," she continues, "and there are so many more fitness programs and community recreation activities available to satisfy a variety of interests, ages, and abilities. But we still face the challenge of transforming knowledge into participation."

Source: Pritchard, A. 1999, August. Working out. *Parks & Recreation* 34(8), 53–55.

Generally speaking, two methods are used in measurement and evaluation—formative evaluation and summative evaluation. *Formative evaluation* takes place on a continuous basis throughout the life of the program. All programs require constant, ongoing monitoring, and such evaluation often results in midcourse corrections in the program. *Summative evaluation* takes place at the conclusion of the program. It provides a final assessment and "sums up" the impact and process of the program effort.

Management Approaches to Programming

A number of management systems have been applied to the leisure programming process in the last several years. More specifically, the concepts of *Total Quality Program Planning (TQP), Just-In-Time Programming (JIT), Agile Leisure Programming,* and *Benefits-Based Programming (BBP)* have been discussed in the literature as ways of integrating the program planning process into a management system.

- *Total Quality Program Planning (TQP).* Total Quality Program Planning is built on the assumptions of W. Edward Deming. It infuses concern for innovation, focus on quality, and use of benchmarks to measure improvement. It is also known as Total Quality Management (TQM) or Total Quality Leadership (TQL). Edginton and Edginton (1993c) have applied this concept to the management of leisure services, in particular school-age care. The focus of their work is one of promoting leader/participant interactions that result in high-quality, high-impact services.
- *Just-In-Time Programming (JIT).* This concept, initially applied to the manufacturing process, has been successfully adapted to leisure programming from a theoretical standpoint by Glancy, Coles, Detzel, Luck, and Rupe (1994) and Edginton, Little, and DeGraaf (1992). Basically, this management concept involves employing only the required effort or investment to produce a program offering. It is an effort at linking resources of an organization in such a way as to bring them in line precisely with customer needs, emphasizing efficiency. Just-In-Time Programming requires careful planning and the ability to accurately forecast or predict leisure needs.
- *Agile Leisure Programming.* This concept was first introduced into the literature by Edginton and Edginton (1993a). The focus of Agile Leisure Programming is one of being responsive to customer needs and ensuring that the organization is organic, flexible, and capable of shifting its resources rapidly to meet emerging customer needs. Many leisure programs have short life cycles. As a result, leisure service organizations must be flexible enough to reconfigure their resources and organizational framework quickly and efficiently to meet newly emerging interests and trends.
- *Benefits-Based Programming (BBP).* This concept was introduced by the National Recreation and Park Association as a way of assisting leisure service professionals with the issue of identifying the values and benefits of their services. The BBP's strategy is based on four basic principles: (1) outcome-oriented goals that address social issues and concerns that society views as significant must be articulated; (2) recreation opportunities need to be structured to directly address stated goals; (3) comprehensive monitoring and evaluation procedures that document goal achievement and the ensuing benefits to the individual and beyond must be established; and (4) a comprehensive information system that effectively communicates the significance of programs and services is required. (Edginton and O'Neil, 1999, pp. 198–199)

Roles of Leisure Programmers

Generally speaking, professionals in leisure service organizations perform three roles—management, supervisory, and direct service. Although organizing the program effort involves all of these roles to one degree or another, the supervisory and especially the direct-service levels carry out the actual organization and implementation of program services. Professionals occupying *direct-service* roles actually meet face-to-face with customers to provide activities, manage facilities, provide information, and train leaders. *Supervisory* responsibilities regarding programming involve identifying needs, establishing program goals, and, often, hiring, training, and supervising direct-service staff to implement services. This discussion focuses on the direct-service provider roles.

Direct-Service Roles

Literally thousands of different types of direct-service roles are carried out by professionals and others. Coaches, ride operators, tour directors, ballet instructors, camp counselors, teen leaders, convention hosts, lifeguards, leisure counselors, interpretive naturalists, park rangers, referees, drama directors, playground leaders, therapeutic recreation specialists, and craft instructors are but a few of the direct-service roles that can be found in leisure service organizations. These direct leadership roles all help bring about the leisure experience. Leisure service organizations also have other support roles, such as receptionists, cashiers, concession attendants, and others who back up the work of those actually delivering the service.

Direct-service program roles fall into a number of categories. Edginton and Ford (1985) suggest six types of direct face-to-face leadership roles—direct program leadership, team leadership, instructional leadership, counselor, outreach worker, and host/guide. Niepoth (1983) writes that the responsibilities of direct face-to-face leaders include a number of tasks such as (1) providing opportunities for people to engage in recreation behavior, (2) promoting interpersonal relationships between people, (3) leading, (4) teaching, and (5) referral and advocacy. Leaders perform diverse functions and carry out a wide variety of tasks.

What special skills or competencies do direct-service personnel need on an entry-level basis to perform effectively? Niepoth (1974) suggests fifteen core processes that enhance the effectiveness of direct-service personnel. The following criteria describe the skills necessary to perform effectively in the direct-service personnel role:

1. *Communication.* Entry-level direct-service personnel should be able to communicate effectively, both orally and in writing.
2. *Leadership.* Knowledge of leadership skills and the ability to use them appropriately and effectively is a key skill that should be possessed by direct-service personnel.
3. *Planning.* Direct-service personnel engage in effective program planning, as well as long-range and short-range organizational planning.
4. *Teaching.* Teaching is an important function carried out, either directly or indirectly, within most direct-service personnel roles. This type of leader should have knowledge of various teaching strategies and should know which strategies are most effective in different types of teaching situations.
5. *Organization.* Entry-level direct-service personnel should be able to organize available resources, as well as their own time and energies, in an effective and efficient manner.
6. *Evaluation.* The ability to effectively evaluate programs (operations) and staff is a skill that should be possessed by direct-service personnel.
7. *Management.* The entry-level direct-service provider should possess the skills necessary to manage organizational resources effectively and efficiently, including fiscal resources, personnel, facilities, and supplies.
8. *Group dynamics.* Direct-service personnel should possess knowledge of group dynamics. It is vital that this type of leader work well with different types of groups.
9. *Problem solving.* The ability to use independent problem-solving techniques is another skill that is important for the direct-service provider to have.
10. *Information gathering.* The entry-level direct-service provider should have skills in the area of information or data gathering. In other words, this type of leader should be able to assimilate relevant information about the population and community served that has potential for influencing service.
11. *Interpersonal skills.* The ability to interact positively and effectively with professional and community groups is an important skill that direct-service personnel should possess.
12. *Relevant legal knowledge.* Entry-level direct-service personnel should have sufficient knowledge of the law as it pertains to their professional area to ensure that they are able to operate well within legal and safety regulations.
13. *Professional philosophy.* The direct-service provider should have a personal and professional philosophy on which to base professional practice.
14. *Professional vernacular.* The entry-level direct-service provider should have a working knowledge of the "special language" or vernacular associated with the profession.
15. *Professional skills.* The entry-level direct-service provider should possess a variety of technical skills. (Niepoth, 1974)

To effectively serve in the direct-service program role requires a wide variety of skills and knowledge.

Types of Direct-Service Leadership

A number of types of direct-service leadership roles exist and can be categorized into nine general areas expanding upon Edginton and Ford's (1985) six direct-service roles. These include direct program leadership, team leadership, instructional, official/referee, host/guide/interpreter, counselor, outreach worker, facility operator, and sales personnel. Some leisure service organizations employ all of these different types of leaders; others employ one or a combination of several. A short discussion of each of these nine types of direct-service leadership roles follows.

Direct Program Leadership   The direct program leadership role involves helping individuals participate successfully in some type of activity. Direct program leadership, often general in nature, can require many skills, including serving as a teacher, coach, counselor, and/or group organizer. Direct leaders usually develop skills in scheduling, organizing special events, and promotion, and they often exhibit enthusiastic, energetic qualities.

Direct program leaders often plan programs and then lead the activities associated with these programs. Thus, they usually have specific technical knowledge related to the program. Leaders must guide and direct participants, maintain group cohesion, and at the same time create a leisure environment that is consistent with the goals of the program and organization. Direct leaders in this role often handle and inventory supplies, materials, and equipment.

Team Leadership   Team leadership involves working with a group of individuals, usually in some type of competitive format. Team leadership, often associated with athletics and the team coach or captain, is not necessarily confined to this area. Individuals occupying these roles often exert a great deal of influence, either positively or negatively, over team members.

What do team leaders do? What do coaches do? The coaching function is one of teaching, clarifying values, and inspiring individuals to their highest levels of performance. The coach teaches basic skills to team members by organizing practice sessions, meetings, and study guides. The motivation and direction activities usually take place daily in practice sessions and also help the team develop a strategy to successfully compete with its opponents. This strategy becomes apparent when specific plays are implemented during a game.

Instructional Leadership   This type of leadership involves organizing a learning environment that helps individuals acquire specific skills, knowledge, or competencies. The leader serves as a teacher. Instruction is a process of communicating with individuals so that learning occurs.

The learning process can be organized in both a formal and an informal manner. Teachers use a variety of instructional strategies, including lectures, demonstrations, role playing, problem solving, guided readings, and experiential activities. Teachers often develop lesson plans that identify course objectives, the course content, and instructional strategies.

Official/Referee   Leaders often officiate or serve as referees in leisure service programs. The official/referee helps maintain the integrity of the event. In other words, the official or referee enforces the rules and regulations of the event or game. Officials or referees must be well schooled in the technical aspects of the activity they oversee. In addition, they must have good human relations skills because of the potential conflicts between individuals during the course of an event.

What types of skills do officials need? They must know much more than the rules of the game. An official or referee should maintain a calm and confident demeanor. Officiating also often requires a great deal of physical exertion. Furthermore, good officiating involves the use of common sense; different game situations require judgments based on commonsense application of the rules and regulations. Last, the official/referee must be consistent and fair in both judgments and behavior.

Host/Guide/Interpreter This direct-service role provides information to participants regarding a particular site, event, or thing and helps participants feel comfortable about their involvement in a particular activity or facility. As a host or guide, the leader must be courteous and anticipate participants' needs. As an interpreter, the leader should convey information in a lively, enthusiastic, and interesting manner. Interpreters often bring the subject matter to life—whether it is natural history or cultural or historical events.

The host/guide/interpreter must have a pleasant personality, have specialized knowledge, and understand the work of the organization in general. These individuals must genuinely love people and desire to make the participant's activity or stay at a facility more enjoyable and hospitable. This role requires highly organized individuals who research the topic or site prior to engaging with participants, anticipate contingencies, and plan for them.

Counselor Counseling takes place in a variety of leisure service settings. Although the camp counselor may predominate in this area, persons in the positions of leisure counselors and leisure educators (as well as other leaders) also engage in the counseling process. The leisure service counselor helps people understand, discover, or define their leisure interests and potential. Counseling not only involves the act of exchanging of ideas and values, but it also may involve providing advice to people.

Most counseling activities involve either values-clarification or values-development exercises or the planning and designing of programs to help individuals. A leisure service counselor works with individuals to help them define their values as related to leisure. In addition, these counselors help people learn to make decisions and to discover and examine alternative leisure choices independently. They help individuals act and behave in accordance with the choices they make in life. A camp counselor serves as a parent, teacher, friend, and confidant to campers (Edginton and Ford, 1985).

Outreach Worker Outreach workers extend themselves into neighborhoods, communities, or situations in order to provide leisure services. An outreach worker reaches out and assists individuals who are unreceptive, have been excluded, or lack information about a leisure service organization's program. Outreach workers operate in a variety of settings and use a variety of strategies to provide services. Mobile swimming pools, libraries, and playgrounds are a few of the services that might be extended through an outreach program. Outreach workers often work with groups of disadvantaged individuals and/or those who exhibit delinquent behavior.

The outreach worker's role closely resembles the roles of other activity leaders and counselors—it involves direct, face-to-face leadership. The major differences are the setting and the population being served. These factors make the work of the outreach worker intense, requiring specialized skills in interacting with hard-to-reach individuals whose problems may require specialized, creative solutions and program strategies. Outreach workers also sometimes undertake the role of advocate for the needs of disadvantaged groups.

Facility Operator   Leisure service organizations often manage areas and facilities. Facility operators differ from activity leaders in that they focus on the operation and maintenance of a particular facility rather than activity organization. The facility is the "program" in this case. For example, a person who manages a marina does little in terms of activity management; however, this individual keeps the boat docks and support services in excellent running condition in order to maintain a high-caliber leisure environment.

Facility operators, like other leaders, must work well with people and have technical knowledge related to their particular facility. The swimming pool operator, for instance, must understand the fundamentals of pool sanitation, filtration, and so forth. Facility operators also support staff such as cashiers, clerks, and maintenance personnel.

Sales Personnel   In commercial leisure service organizations, sales personnel serve as direct-service providers. They help customers make choices about leisure products or services. For example, an individual working as a convention or event planner at a hotel or resort assists the customer in making decisions about types of facilities, activities, and perhaps food services required for an event. This person might also be involved in the selection of entertainment. A tour or travel agent also works as a salesperson. The individual in this role helps identify points of interest and options in transportation, lodging, and food.

Good sales personnel have a thorough knowledge of their products or services. They must enthusiastically support or endorse the products and be flexible enough to customize services to meet individual needs. Like other leaders, a salesperson must learn to anticipate the needs of the customer, demonstrating a genuine interest in his or her welfare. Effective salespersons are friendly, courteous, effective, and efficient.

Summary

This chapter focused on the development of leisure programs and services. Leisure programs are vehicles that help individuals experience leisure. Those involved in programming work directly with customers and engage in the planning, organizing, and implementation of services. Leisure service organizations fall within the service industry.

An important process in the operation of any leisure service organization, the development of a service orientation or strategy, requires the consideration of three factors: value-added service delivery, positive customer relations, and supportive policies and procedures. Value-added service delivery advocates adding an additional dimension of quality to a program to enhance the attractiveness of the service. Organizations build positive customer relations by having professional staff members who anticipate customers' needs, are courteous, pay attention to detail, are responsive, create a positive environment, demonstrate appreciation, cooperate, demonstrate pride, perform effectively, give out reliable and timely information, and maintain a positive attitude. Building supportive policies and procedures helps reinforce the basic service strategy.

Leisure service organizations provide a number of programs that fall into four general categories: activities, areas and facilities, information, and leadership. The creation of such programs occurs in a cyclical fashion initiated by the development of program goals, followed by needs assessment, program planning, and program evaluation.

Programmers engage in a number of roles. This chapter identifies nine specific direct-service program roles that are common in public, private, nonprofit, and/or commercial leisure service organizations. These include direct program leadership, team leadership, instructional leadership, official/referee, host/guide/interpreter, counselor, outreach worker, facility operator, and sales personnel. Some general requirements of these roles include the ability to work successfully with people, technical competence in the program area assigned, and program-planning and organizational skills.

Discussion Questions

1. Why are leisure services considered a part of the service industry?
2. Explain what is meant by *service.*
3. Define the term *value-added services.* What can a leisure service organization do to add value to its programs and services?
4. What key behaviors produce positive customer relationships?
5. How can such behaviors be taught, reinforced, and maintained in a leisure service organization?
6. What is a leisure service program? What are the different types of leisure service programs?
7. Discuss the cyclical process of program planning. Outline the steps in this procedure.
8. Identify ten program areas. Identify seven program formats.
9. What is the difference between formative and summative evaluation?
10. Identify and describe nine key direct-service roles operating in leisure service organizations.

References

Albrecht, K., and R. Zemke. 1985. *Service America!* Homewood, IL: Dow Jones-Irwin.

Bullaro, J., and C. Edginton. 1986. *Commercial Leisure Services.* New York: Macmillan.

Crompton, J., and K. McKay. 1989. Users' perceptions of the relative importance of service quality dimensions in selected public recreation programs. *Leisure Sciences 11,* 367–375.

Department of the Interior. 1979. *Third Nationwide Outdoor Recreation Plan.* Washington, DC: U.S. Government Printing Office.

Edginton, C. R., and J. P. O'Neil. 1999. Program, services, and event management. Edited by B. van der Smissen, M. Moiseichik, V. J. Hartenburg, and L. F. Twardzik, in *Management of Park and Recreation Agencies.* Ashburn, VA: National Recreation of Park Association.

Edginton, C. R., and S. R. Edginton. 1993a. Agile leisure programming. *Management Strategy 17*(3), 1.

Edginton, C. R., and S. R. Edginton. 1993b. Total quality programming planning. *Journal of Physical Education, Recreation and Dance 64*(8), 40–43.

Edginton, C. R., and S. R. Edginton. 1993c. Total quality program planning. *Journal of Physical Education, Recreation and Dance 64*(9), 41–42.

Edginton, C. R., and P. Ford. 1985. *Leadership in Recreation and Leisure-Service Organizations.* New York: Wiley.

Edginton, C. R., S. L. Little, and D. G. DeGraaf. 1992. Just-in-Time programming: Just for you. *Parks & Recreation 27*(11), 68–72.

Edginton, C. R., and R. Rossman. 1988. Leisure programming: Building a theoretical base. *Journal of Park and Recreation Administration 6*(4), viii.

Glancy, M., J. E. Coles, D. Detzel, L. B. Luck, and S. Rupe. 1994. Lessons for manager: Thinking lean with just-in-time management principles. *Journal of Park and Recreation Administration 2*(2), 1–13.

Godbey, G. 1985. Nonuse of public leisure services: A model. *Journal of Park and Recreation Administration 3*(2), 1–12.

Howard, D., and J. Crompton. 1984. Who are the consumers of public recreation services? An analysis of the users and non-users of three municipal leisure service organizations. *Journal of Parks and Recreation Administration 2,* 38–42.

Howe, C., and Y. Qui. 1988. The programming process revisited: Assumptions underlying the needs-based models. *Journal of Park and Recreation Administration 6*(4), 14–27.

Jackson, E. L. 1994. Activity-specific constraints on leisure participation. *Journal of Park and Recreation Administration 12*(2), 33–49.

Johnson-Tew, C. P., M. E. Havitz, and R. E. McCarville. 1999, Spring. The role of marketing in municipal recreation programming decisions: A challenge to conventional wisdom. *Journal of Park and Recreation Administration 17*(1), 1–20.

Lankford, S. V. 1990, November 5. *Barriers to leisure participation—a future problem.* Presentation to the 1990 Oregon Parks and Recreation Society Annual Conference. Springfield, OR.

McCarville, R. E. 1993. Keys to quality leisure programming. *Journal of Physical Education, Recreation and Dance 64*(9), 34–37.

McChesney, J. C. 1999, October. Strategies for improving customer service in leisure organizations. *NIRSA Journal 23*(2), 6–13.

McKay, K., and J. Crompton. 1988. Alternative typologies of leisure programs. *Journal of Park and Recreation Administration* 6(4), 53.

Miller, R. D. 2000. Customer service for the new millennium. *NIRSA Journal* 24(1), 61–67.

Morgan, J., and J. J. Morgan, (1991). *Cracking the Japanese Market: Strategies for Success in the New Global Economy.* New York: The Free Press.

Nationwide Outdoor Recreation Survey. 1984. Washington, DC: Heritage Conservation and Recreation Service. U.S. Department of the Interior.

Niepoth, W. 1974. *Competency Assessment Processes in Curricula, 1973–74.* Long Beach, CA: Office of the Chancellor, California State University.

Niepoth, W. 1983. *Leisure Leadership.* Englewood Cliffs, NJ: Prentice Hall.

Peters, T. 1987. *Thriving on Chaos.* New York: Knopf.

Russell, R. 1982. *Planning Programs in Recreation.* St. Louis: Mosby.

Siegenthaler, K. L. 2000, April. Hello operator: Front-line staff performance reflects the entire organization. *Parks & Recreation* 35(4), 100–103.

Stenger, T., B. Ryan, and D. Jordan. 1999, November. Positive programming: The common denominator. *Parks & Recreation* 34(11), 28–40.

Swell, C., and P. Brown. 1990. *Customers for Life.* Toronto: Pocketbooks.

Zeithaml, V., A. Parasuraman, and L. Berry. 1988. *Delivering Quality Service: Balancing Customer Perceptions and Expectations.* New York: The Free Press.

CHAPTER 14

Professional Career Development

Professionals bind together in associations and other forums to advocate and promote quality-of-life issues.

Introduction

The leisure services field is exciting and dynamic. A professional career in the leisure services field can provide meaningful, challenging, and valuable work and life experiences. However, the process of professional career development requires forethought and planning; it does not "just happen."

A leisure services professional has mastered a body of knowledge and, as a result, can provide a unique and valuable service to society. Leisure services professionals possess knowledge related to the behavior of people during leisure, management techniques, and strategies used to provide leisure services. They have a value structure or philosophy that promotes such ends as the wise use of leisure, preservation and conservation of resources, and the promotion of human dignity. Possessing such knowledge, leisure services professionals are, in fact, uniquely equipped to plan, organize, provide, and evaluate the impact of leisure experiences.

Success in pursuing a professional career requires consideration of a number of key factors related to professional practice. A person acquires some professional knowledge and competencies through formal and informal educational programs and gains others from valuable on-the-job experience. In addition, one's professional career can be enhanced by endorsements through programs of certification. This chapter examines information concerning the common elements of a profession along with information about membership and association with professional organizations. It also presents the key elements in pursuing a professional career.

Common Elements of a Profession

The first step in becoming a part of the leisure services field is to understand the common elements of any profession and the specific traits that make the leisure services profession unique.

All professions possess four common elements: an organized body of knowledge, organizations and institutions that exist to transmit professional knowledge, creation of professional authority as a result of public sanction, and a code of ethics and standards to guide professional practice.

An Organized Body of Knowledge

One of a profession's primary requisites is that it serve society in some specific way. In order to perform a unique function, a profession must have a distinct body of knowledge. The leisure services field tends to be eclectic in that it draws from a number of different disciplines in providing services. Edginton, Hanson, Edginton, and Hudson (1998) identify three components of the professional knowledge needed in the leisure service field: *information drawn from the scientific disciplines, appropriate values,* and *applied or engineered skills.*

Information drawn from the scientific disciplines includes such areas as sociology, psychology, anthropology, business, biology, and botany. Information from biology and botany assists leisure professionals in understanding the environment and how to interact with it. Information from sociology, psychology, and anthropology assists leisure services professionals to examine and understand the human experience. The information we gain from business impacts parks and recreation professionals in terms of economics and management issues.

The values leisure professionals profess include enriching the quality of human life, advocating for the rights of all people to have access to leisure experiences, assisting people in the wise use of leisure, and working for the conservation and preservation of natural resources. These values give professionals a strong ethical framework through which to filter empirical information and advance the profession.

Applied or engineered skills are the practical skills that leisure services professionals must have to perform their jobs. Examples of these skills include knowing how to lead and program activities, understanding the budgeting process, managing park resources, and knowing how to use public media to promote leisure programs. These skills also are referred to as technical skills.

The uniqueness of the profession's body of knowledge results from application of this knowledge to planning, implementing, and evaluating leisure services. As Edginton and colleagues (1998, p. 59) note, "The relationship between general scientific knowledge and professional practice is a linear one. As new bodies of knowledge are produced, the applicable or useful knowledge is incorporated into a professional framework (sometimes with modification due to professional values). This process results in the development of *quasi*-theories of professional knowledge." Leisure service professionals can find these theories and other new knowledge in a variety of sources, including books, magazines, journals, manuals, technical and research reports, conferences, and statements by professional associations, agencies, and individuals.

Organizations and Institutions that Exist to Transmit Professional Knowledge

Organizations and institutions play an important role in organizing and transmitting the leisure service profession's body of knowledge in a systematic way. In the late 1930s and 1940s, colleges and universities developed formalized curricula focused on in parks and recreation. By the early 1990s, more than 300 baccalaureate programs and more than 280 associate degree programs in parks, recreation, leisure, tourism, and natural resource management had developed in the United States. These numbers have held steady since that time. The National Recreation and Park Association (NRPA), in cooperation with the American Association for Leisure and Recreation (AALR), developed standards of accreditation for the four-year programs. Approximately 100 of these four-year programs are currently accredited. An additional 100 graduate degree programs are in place in the field of parks and recreation (NRPA, 2000). Professional organizations also play a major role in the advancement of a profession. The role of professional organizations is discussed later in this chapter along with profiles of specific organizations within the leisure field.

Creation of Professional Authority as a Result of Public Sanction

Public sanction implies that an occupation is given authority to operate as a profession. According to Edginton and colleagues (1998), one may view professional authority from two perspectives. First, the public at large may grant authority for an occupation to intervene on behalf of or in concert with the customer without assuming full responsibility for its actions. Second, as an occupation achieves full professional status, it monopolizes services. Thus, the profession gains considerable authority, since it is the only occupational group with acknowledged ability in a given area of demand. The professional authority of leisure professionals does not appear to be widely recognized in the United States and Canada at the current time. Leisure services professionals have not monopolized services, nor has the work of the leisure practitioner been sanctioned to any great extent. Yet this is changing as the profession has established procedures to certify professionals in a variety of areas—exams are now in place for both certified therapeutic recreation specialists (CTRSs) as well as certified parks and recreation professionals (CPRPs). In addition, depending on their area of specialization, leisure services professionals may be certified as certified recreational sports specialists (CRSSs) and certified commercial recreation professionals (CCRPs).

Ethics and the Leisure Services Profession

Every profession has a set of ethics. Those who practice the profession make ongoing attempts to maintain a professional identity supported by those ethics. Ethics involve the study and practice of an intellectual endeavor, which leisure service professionals believe must include attitudes and behaviors that add dignity to life. A professional, as one who lives the ethics of the field, knows that a moral action is greater than one without moral foundation (Fain, 1985).

Ethics are an integral part of all human services professions; members of the profession deal with political climates, the well-being of many individuals, and social issues, all of which involve ethics. Professional and ethical behaviors go hand in hand—professional actions uphold a certain level of ethics, and ethical actions uphold professionalism (Stumbo, 1985). Issues such as privacy, privilege, autonomy, and other values of leisure dictate a moral position.

The parks, recreation, and leisure services profession believes that all people have the right to personal autonomy, to be self-governing, and to be morally free to make the choices that direct their lives (Sylvester, 1985). The dignity of self-determination should be preserved. Leisure professionals particularly value autonomy because it is fundamental to the free choices associated with play, recreation, and leisure (Shank, 1985). Most leisure philosophies also hold that people benefit from play and recreation opportunities, with an underlying belief structure that leisure and recreation contribute to the quality of life of participants.

Code of Ethics

A code of ethics develops from the key values of the leisure profession. Some of these key values include: enriching the quality of human life, advocating for the rights of all individuals to have access to leisure experiences, assisting people in the wise use of leisure, and working for the conservation and preservation of natural resources. A set of ethics or standards develops from these values and governs the relationship between the professional and those he or she serves.

The leisure services field has been lethargic in the development and enforcement of behavioral standards. Not until 1960 did the American Recreation Society (a forerunner to the NRPA) establish a code of ethics. It was updated and rearticulated in 1995 and reaffirmed in 2000 by NRPA (see table 14.1). Professionals are becoming aware of the document and investigating how the code might be used as a mechanism for self-control. While many leisure services organizations have developed specific statements for use within their organizations, the development of ethics and standards requires further work in the leisure services field. Specific branches of the field (e.g., parks and recreation, therapeutic recreation, campus recreation, commercial recreation) must continue their work on developing codes that reflect their uniqueness. It is not enough simply to have a code of ethics; leisure services professionals must commit to the ideals presented in the code.

Commitment to Professional Ideals

What professional ideals does the leisure services profession hold? Does it promote a commitment to the natural environment, diversity, dignity of life, program quality, or self-expression? Should it? These questions reach the heart of the leisure services profession. Professionals must respond to these questions from their own source of personal and professional ethics. Furthermore, professional standards affect every aspect of the profession—programming, leadership, the provision of facilities, and administrative practices.

TABLE

14.1   NRPA PROFESSIONAL CODE OF ETHICS

The National Recreation and Park Association has provided leadership to the nation in fostering the expansion of recreation and parks. NRPA has stressed the value of recreation, both active and passive, for individual growth and development. Its members are dedicated to the common cause of assuring that people of all ages and abilities have the opportunity to find the most satisfying use of their leisure time and enjoy an improved quality of life.

The Association has consistently affirmed the importance of well informed and professionally trained personnel to continually improve the administration of recreation and park programs. Members of NRPA are encouraged to support the efforts of the Association and profession by supporting state affiliate and national activities and participating in continuing education opportunities, certification, and accreditation.

Membership in NRPA carries with it special responsibilities to the public at large, and to the specific communities and agencies in which recreation and park services are offered. As a member of the National Recreation and Park Association I accept and agree to abide by this Code of Ethics and pledge myself to:

- Adhere to the highest standards of integrity and honesty in all public and personal activities to inspire public confidence and trust.
- Strive for personal and professional excellence and encourage the professional development of associates and students.
- Strive for the highest standards of professional competence, fairness, impartiality, efficiency, effectiveness, and fiscal responsibility.
- Avoid any interest or activity that is in conflict with the performance of job responsibilities.
- Promote the public interest and avoid personal gain or profit from the performance of job duties and responsibilities.
- Support equal employment opportunities.

From D. Clark, "A New Code of Ethics for NRPA" in *Parks & Recreation Magazine 30*(8), pp. 38–43, 1995. Reprinted by permission of National Recreation and Park Association, Ashborn, VA.

Disney's Centers of Excellence

The Disney Company recognizes the need for ongoing education of its employees. At the Disney University, located at Disney World in Orlando, cast members (employees) can access various Centers of Excellence and enroll in a wide variety of learning activities. These self-paced programs are designed to enhance cast members' personal skills, creativity, communication, leadership, Disney heritage, and environmental issues. With recognition of the need for balance in one's life, many learning activities cover topics such as personal goal setting, time management, paying for eldercare, healthy lifestyles, managing personal change, and goal setting for success.

Professional Associations

Professional associations play an important role in the work of professionals. They advocate on behalf of the interests of a group, the members of which share some common interest. Membership in such organizations provides a means to network with others, gather new information, and promote the interests of the organization. Some professional organizations have a narrow focus or are limited to a region or state; others represent the leisure services movement on a nationwide or international basis. For example, the NRPA strongly advocates conservation, preservation, and leisure concerns to a national and international audience.

Holding a membership in one or more professional associations is important to one's professional life. Often, a person first asks, "What benefits or services does membership bring to me personally?" However, another perspective about whether or not to join a professional organization deserves consideration. Membership in a professional association offers opportunities to serve, as well as to promote and further one's own professional interests. In other words, many people give talent, time, and energy to the work of a professional organization in order to promote important ideals.

Professional associations serve as vehicles to advance the interests of their membership. In that context, a professional should seek membership in an appropriate organization, one within which to advocate, to promote ideals, and to serve other professionals. In short, membership in a professional associations provides an opportunity for individuals to give to their profession and at the same time receive various benefits. Professional associations serve multiple ends, with the following among them (see figure 14.1):

Advocacy. Professional associations work to promote their ideals and to convince their constituency of the worthiness and value of their activities. Advocacy activities often include providing testimony, information, and lobbying for important pieces of legislation that can impact on the work of the profession. Most professional associations provide a platform for their membership to promote common interests through advocacy activities. Such activities help to establish and maintain the value and worth of a profession to society.

Educational opportunities. Professional associations provide educational opportunities for their members, often in the form of conferences, workshops, institutes, and seminars. Large national associations provide conferences that feature educational presentations and sessions and also display and demonstrate the latest and most innovative equipment, supplies, programs, and services.

Figure 14.1

Benefits of
membership in
professional
associations

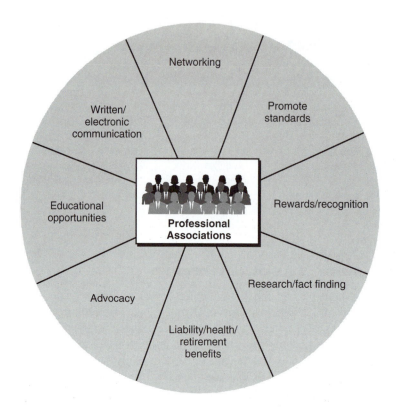

Written and electronic communication. Most professionals agree that the most important benefit of association membership is the professional magazine, newsletter, or other written and electronic communication. Such communication provides information concerning the activities of the association, job opportunities, information about current trends and issues, and new knowledge as reflected in articles, research briefs, and legislative notes.

Networking. Membership in professional associations allows individuals to meet and interact with other professionals. Networking with people who have common interests provides a means to learn about new and improved ways of delivering services, identification of common problems and potential solutions, and, perhaps most important, an opportunity for individuals to reaffirm their commitment to a set of similarly held ideals and values. With the rise in access to computer technology, networking opportunities exist in two formats: directly through face-to-face contact and indirectly through Internet listserves.

Promote standards. Professional associations often work to promote higher standards of practice, as reflected in the creation of programs of voluntary registration, certification, and licensing. Professional associations often create codes of ethics that serve as standards of practice to guide individual action, and they influence the quality of educational institutions by establishing and administering programs of accreditation.

Rewards and recognition. Professional associations provide a means for recognizing the outstanding work of individuals, associations, and groups. Not only do professional associations reward and acknowledge the work of their own membership, they often acknowledge other individuals and groups that have contributed toward common values. Some national associations regularly acknowledge a legislator whose work has positively influenced their professional area of interest. Professional associations often provide scholarships to outstanding students to help defray costs associated with attending a college or university, or to attend a professional meeting or conference.

Research and fact finding. Many professional associations conduct research and fact-finding surveys, and some study the status of the profession on a yearly basis. Such studies provide valuable baseline information that is used to compare the growth or progress of the profession from one year to the next. Further, professional associations often devote resources toward solving emerging issues and specific problems. Such activities may involve the creation of task forces or special study groups that focus on specific issues and recommend courses of action.

Liability, health, or retirement benefits. Professional associations often serve their membership by providing benefits such as individual and group insurance—retirement, liability, health, and others. A professional association can often purchase services at a reduced cost on a group basis and then make these services available to individual members. These association packages provide financial savings and also meet the specific needs of the professional membership.

The value of these benefits and services to an individual depends on his or her position within the profession. Individuals in entry-level positions often find that conferences and workshops provide valuable information and opportunities to network for the purposes of socializing, job hunting, and meeting others in the profession. More seasoned professionals view the same conferences as an opportunity to pursue legislative initiatives, plan for future professional endeavors, and promote the interests of their profession.

Again, professional associations provide an opportunity for individuals to serve as well as to derive meaning from their work. Joining one or more professional associations or societies offers numerous benefits to members. Individuals should carefully consider which professional association(s) best serves their interests and ideals.

Types of Professional Associations

Since the leisure services field is so diverse, a large number of professional societies and associations exist to represent the varying nature and character of the profession. Many associations are referred to by their initials. For example, the American Camping Association is often called the ACA. While it is not possible to include all professional associations related to the field of leisure services here, some of the more common professional associations that employ individuals in the leisure services field include those mentioned in the following section. World Wide Web addresses have been provided for those associations that have Web pages. Readers should be aware that street and Web addresses change over time—it is good policy to double-check information before attempting to contact a professional association.

American Alliance for Health, Physical Education, Recreation and Dance (AAHPERD)
1900 Association Drive
Reston, VA 22091
www.aahperd.org

AAHPERD is dedicated to promoting professional activities for those who have interests in health and safety education, intramurals, aging, fitness research, physical education, athletics, sport, dance, outdoor education, and recreation. The organization, founded in the late 1800s, provides publications, research, and special projects consistent with the needs of its membership. While AAHPERD publishes several magazines and journals, its major publication is the *Journal of Physical Education, Recreation and Dance*. It also offers a job bulletin to both members and nonmembers, as well as other resources related to the profession.

The organization operates by promoting the work of a number of affiliate associations, including the American Association for Leisure and Recreation (AALR); the National Association for Sport and Physical Education (NASPE); National Association for Girls and Women in Sport (NAGWS); Association for the Advancement of Health Education (AAHE); National Dance Association (NDA); and American Association for Active Lifestyles and Fitness (AAALF).

American Association for Leisure and Recreation (AALR)

1900 Association Drive

Reston, VA 22091

www.aahperd.org/aalr.html

AALR, an affiliate of AAHPERD, promotes the improvement of the quality of life of Americans through the creative and meaningful use of leisure and recreation experiences. AALR, established in 1938, provides an important vehicle for professionals to promote the leisure services field. It also produces a newsletter, the *AALR Reporter*. The association serves as a forum to exchange information, ideas, and concepts related to leisure and provides excellent publications and other professional services. Its major publication is *Leisure Today*. In conjunction with NRPA, AALR accredits university curricula and certifies individuals as certified parks and recreation professionals.

American Camping Association (ACA)

Bradford Woods

5000 State Road 67N

Martinsville, IN 46151

www.aca-camps.org

The ACA works primarily to increase the quality of the organized camping movement. Membership in ACA is open to individuals and organized camps that promote camping activities, including those involved in providing camping programs at private, youth serving, church, and in agency/nonprofit organizations. As an organization, ACA accredits camps and conference centers. In addition, ACA holds an annual convention and produces *Camping Magazine* as its primary publication. Another important publication of the ACA is the *ACA Guide to Accredited Camps*. This guide includes information about camps all over North America, describing programs, fees, staffing structures, and the like. ACA also offers an extensive bookstore with a wide variety of professional publications.

American Therapeutic Recreation Association (ATRA)

1414 Prince Street, Suite 204

Alexandria, VA 22314

www.atra-tr.org

The ATRA, one of the newest professional organizations related to our field, was founded in 1984. As a nonprofit organization, its primary purpose is to promote the needs of therapeutic recreation professionals in health care and human services. Among other things, ATRA is very active in legislative lobbying efforts to advance the therapeutic recreation profession. Professional education efforts include an annual and midyear conference, and the ATRA Academy, which offers training opportunities on a regional basis. Publications include a newsletter, job bulletin, *Treatment Networks* where professionals can share treatment ideas for a particular population, and other resources that address professional ethics issues such as reimbursment, and concerns related to professional practice. ATRA's primary publication is the *Therapeutic Recreation Annual.*

Association for Experiential Education (AEE)

2305 Canyon Boulevard, Suite 100

Boulder, CO 80302-5651

www.aee.org

The AEE was formed in 1972 as a nonprofit, international association. Today the association has a membership of some 1,600 individual and organizational members committed to furthering experience-based teaching and learning. AEE members include people involved in adventure programming, ropes courses, schools, recreation programs, human service providers, correctional and mental health institutions, youth servicing agencies, programs for people with disabilities, environmental centers, outdoor adventure organizations, and universities. Each year AEE hosts an international conference as well as regional conferences across the country. Membership benefits include receiving the *Journal of Experiential Education,* newsletters, a job bulletin, and discounts on AEE publications and conferences.

Canadian Parks/Recreation Association (CPRA)

216-1600 James Naismith Drive

Gloucester, Ontario K1B 5N4

www.cdnsport.ca/activeliving/cpra.html

The CPRA, a national, independent, voluntary service and education organization, perceives its primary mission as promoting enhanced quality of life for Canadians through the development, organization, and promotion of parks, recreation, and leisure services in Canada. CPRA publishes a magazine entitled *Recreation Canada.* The organization hosts an annual national conference and several other specialized educational services. Its educational services include a professional development program, international study tours, and services to special interests such as the disabled, seniors, and students.

International Ecotourism Society (IES)

P.O. Box 668

Burlington, VT 05402

www.ecotourism.org

This nonprofit organization was founded in 1990. It serves tour operators, conservation professionals, park managers, government officials, lodge owners, guides, and other professionals who promote eco-tourism worldwide. Eco-tourism, a growing phenomenon, finds individuals traveling to remote and unspoiled areas without the luxuries associated with most vacation travel. The Ecotourism Society provides publications, workshops, training programs, and an evaluation program for areas and facilities to its membership.

International Festivals and Events Association (IFEA)

P.O. Box 2950

Port Angeles, WA 98362

www.ifea.com

The IFEA is a membership organization for special events; its Web site reports over 2,400 members. IFEA assists festival and event professionals with fundraising as well as the production and delivery of festivals, civic celebrations, and special events. The IFEA shares information with its members related to event sponsorship, marketing, operations, working with volunteers, and management. It also provides a variety of services to its membership, including regional seminars, an annual convention and trade show, publications, travel discounts, internship placement, and a resource center. The primary magazine is *The How-To of Festivals & Events*. In addition, the IFEA offers a certification for festival administrators called the Certified Festival Executive (CFE).

Employee Services Management Association (ESMA)

2211 York Road, Suite 207

Oak Brook, IL 60523-2371

www.nesra.org

ESMA primarily serves corporate recreation and fitness directors, personnel managers, and human resource development specialists. It sees its primary role as one of disseminating information about current trends and industry developments to its membership. Primary vehicles for dissemination of information include national and regional conferences, a monthly magazine entitled *Employee Services Management Magazine*, newsletters, and research data. ESMA works to promote the interests of its membership and has more than 4,000 individuals and organizations on its roster.

National Intramural-Recreation Sports Association (NIRSA)

4185 SW Research Parkway

Corvallis, OR 97333-1067

www.nirsa.org

NIRSA is a nonprofit organization devoted to the promotion of quality recreation sports programs and services. This organization provides up-to-date information and resource materials for colleges, universities, and other institutions that are involved in providing intramural sports, campus recreation, and community recreation services. Through national and regional conferences, NIRSA seeks to be a strong advocate, resource, and professional network for this area, and publishes the *NIRSA Journal*. In addition, NIRSA provides standards and professional ethics as guides for its members. One element of this is the Certified Recreational Sports Specialist (CRSS) certification.

National Recreation and Park Association (NRPA)

22377 Belmont Ridge Road

Ashburn, VA 20148

www.activeparks.org

State Park and Recreation Societies & Associations

Alabama Recreation and Parks Association	Mississippi Recreation and Park Association
Alaska Recreation and Park Association	Missouri Park and Recreation Association
Arizona Parks and Recreation Association	Montana Recreation and Park Association
Arkansas Recreation and Park Association	Nebraska Recreation and Park Association
California Park and Recreation Society	Nevada Recreation and Park Society
California Association of Park and Recreation Commissioners and Board Members	New Hampshire Recreation and Park Association
	New Jersey Recreation and Park Association
Colorado Parks and Recreation Association	New Mexico Recreation and Park Association
Connecticut Recreation and Parks Association	New York State Recreation and Park Society
Delaware Recreation and Park Society	North Carolina Recreation and Park Society
District of Columbia Recreation and Park Society	North Dakota Parks and Recreation Association
Florida Recreation and Park Association	Ohio Parks and Recreation Association
Georgia Recreation and Park Association, Inc.	Oklahoma Recreation and Parks Society
Hawaii Recreation and Park Association	Oregon Recreation and Park Association
Idaho Recreation and Park Association	Pennsylvania Recreation and Park Society
Illinois Association of Park Districts	Rhode Island Park and Recreation Society
Illinois Park and Recreation Association	South Carolina Recreation and Park Society
Indiana Park and Recreation Association	South Dakota Park and Recreation Association
Iowa Park and Recreation Association	Tennessee Recreation and Park Society
Kansas Recreation and Park Association	Texas Recreation and Park Society
Kentucky Recreation and Park Society	Utah Recreation and Park Association
Louisiana Recreation and Park Association	Vermont Recreation and Park Association
Maine Recreation and Park Association	Virginia Recreation and Park Society
Maryland Recreation and Park Association	Washington Recreation and Park Association
Massachusetts Recreation and Parks Association	West Virginia Park and Recreation Association
Michigan Recreation and Park Association	Wisconsin Recreation and Park Association
Minnesota Recreation and Park Association	Wyoming Recreation and Park Association

For many, the NRPA is the major professional association of the parks and recreation profession. It traces its heritage to the late 1800s. This amalgamation of professional associations merged in 1965 to form a nonprofit service, research, and educational organization. Its membership consists of professionals, volunteers (lay citizens), students, and organizations. NRPA holds an annual congress and provides a variety of services and publications consistent with the needs of branch members, including a job bulletin. Its major publication is *Parks and Recreation,* although it also publishes *Trends, Therapeutic Recreation Journal,* and others.

Currently, NRPA conducts many of its activities through a number of branch affiliates including: National Student Recreation and Park Society (NSRPS), National Therapeutic Recreation Society (NTRS), Society of Park and Recreation Educators (SPRE), American Park and Recreation Society (APRS), National Society for Park Resources (NSPR), Armed Forces Recreation Society (AFRS), Citizen Board Member (CBM), National Aquatics Section (NAS), and Leisure and Aging Section (LAS). In conjunction with AALR, NRPA accredits university curricula and certifies individuals as Certified Parks and Recreation Professionals.

Resort & Commercial Recreation Association (RCRA)

P.O. Box 1998

Tarpon Springs, FL 34688-1998

www.r-c-r-a.org

One of the newest professional associations, RCRA, promotes the interests of the resort and commercial recreation area. RCRA holds regional and national conferences, a Program Leadership Workshop, and provides a number of services to its members, including a job-placement service, job fair, internship placement opportunities, and a newsletter. The RCRA publishes recreation program standards for commercial and resort recreation programs, as well as books related to this specialty area of the leisure services field. In addition, RCRA conducts and disseminates research information and offers a Certified Commercial Recreation Professional (CCRP) certification.

World Leisure and Recreation Association (WLRA)

Site 81C, Comp 0

Okanogan Falls, British Columbia V0H 1R0

www.worldleisure.org

WLRA, a nonprofit, nongovernmental worldwide agency, promotes leisure and recreation around the globe. The organization was founded in 1956 and has been in the forefront of efforts to promote awareness of recreation and leisure as a basic human need in all countries and regions of the world. The organization publishes its magazine, *World Leisure,* six times a year. Its conference attracts professionals, educators, and interested individuals from throughout the world. WLRA has a consultative status with the United Nations—it is considered a nongovernmental organization (NGO). In this capacity, the WLRA performs its services in cooperation with other international organizations, specialized agencies of the United Nations, affiliated national associations, and organizations in more than 100 countries.

In addition to these organizations, nearly every state and/or province has its own professional organization. For example, the British Columbia Recreation Association serves the interests of individuals involved in the delivery of recreation services in the province. It publishes a magazine entitled *Recreation Reporter* and offers an annual conference, an awards program, and other services. In conjunction with the Canadian Parks and Recreation Association, it offers a discounted joint membership. Another example, the Arizona Parks and Recreation Association (APRA), views itself as a service organization supported by membership dues and voluntary contributions. It publishes a quarterly magazine entitled *Arizona Parks and Recreation.* The organization offers an annual conference, awards program, merchandise program, a certification program, and other services and opportunities to network. APRA provides both an individual and group membership.

Other examples of state organizations include the Illinois Park and Recreation Association (IPRA), the California Park and Recreation Society (CPRS), and the Florida Recreation and Park Association (FRPA). IPRA provides a full range of benefits to its membership, including an annual conference, educational seminars, video library, technical assistance library, leadership opportunities, government and media representation, annual salary survey, statewide marketing campaign, cooperative purchase program, packaged tours, discount tickets, investment fund, and multiple publications, including *Illinois Parks and Recreation, Leisure Review, Management Strategy, Get the Message,* and *Membership Directory.* IPRA operates several special-interest sections to meet membership needs, including those dealing with administration and finance, facility management, parks and natural resource management, recreation programming, therapeutic recreation, and a student section.

The CPRS also provides a full range of services to members, including an awards program, annual conference, publications such as *California Parks and Recreation, Leisure Lines, Job Line, CPRS Directory Service,* and other services. CPRS has nine special interest sections that offer training, publications, and network opportunities, including administrators, aging, armed forces, commercial, educators, park operations, recreation supervisors, students, and therapeutic recreation.

The FPRA also provides a broad range of services, including conferences, workshops, legislative representation, voluntary certification, liaison services, networking opportunities, scholarships, employment opportunities, special discounts and programs, and publications, including *Florida Recreation and Park News.* Special-interest groups include aquatics, athletics, commercial/exhibitors, community centers, ethnic minorities, leisure arts, parks and natural resources, and resort/commercial and therapeutic recreation. Special committees and categories represent retirees, students, and military personnel.

In addition to state parks and recreation associations, many recreation and leisure services departments in colleges and universities have student recreation clubs. These clubs offer students opportunities to get involved with their chosen profession while they are still in school. Other benefits of such organizations include opportunities to gain experience, network, and learn more about the profession. For example, Club QOLLA (Quality of Life, Leisure Administrators) at the University of Northern Iowa provides an awareness of the human and leisure services profession by promoting growth opportunities through community service, education, and social experiences.

Three other types of leisure service professional organizations provide services and serve as a forum for advocacy activities. They include special-interest groups, trade associations, and futurist groups.

Special-Interest Groups Organizations such as the Sierra Club, National Audubon Society, Izaac Walton League, World Wildlife Fund, Earthwatch, and the Nature Conservancy—all special-interest groups—provide opportunities for individuals to participate in an organization with a specific focus. Such organizations do not perceive themselves as professional societies or associations, but rather as advocacy, information, and support groups. There are as many national and international special-interest groups as there are people with interests. One can find special-interest groups that relate to serving the needs of people with disabilities, the environment, special activities such as hot air ballooning, and the like.

Trade Associations Another type of organization, the trade association, provides information and services related to a specific element of an industry. These organizations often do not have members, but interested individuals and/or organizations purchase their services as products. For example, Athletic Business Publications, Inc., a trade association, publishes a magazine, *Athletic Business*™, on a monthly basis and distributes it without charge to athletic, recreation, and fitness professionals. Its annual conference features in-depth, well-developed presentations and exhibits. This group provides up-to-date information about athletic, fitness, and recreation areas by providing a professional directory and identifying the most current and contemporary concepts related to products, equipment, and professional services.

Futurist Groups Futurist groups are organized in different ways, depending on their orientation. Some provide services on a consulting basis, such as Rethink, a highly respected

Canadian consulting group. Others provide cutting-edge information about the future of the leisure service industry. *Leisure Watch,* a quarterly publication of *Future Focus,* provides information about the leisure service industry that reflects innovations and issues that will dramatically affect the future of leisure in America. Another publication, *Leisure Industry Digest,* provides information on "futures" activities.

The decision to participate in professional organizations or activities is an important one. Such associations provide an invaluable opportunity for individuals to contribute to their profession, as they receive the benefits of membership. Professional involvement in activities offers stimulation and excitement; attendance at an exciting national conference can shape one's professional future in a dramatic way.

Obviously, an individual must select an appropriate professional association in which to become a member. Guidelines to follow in pursuing membership include:

1. *Be selective.* Write to different professional associations and ask for their literature. Investigate their services and the avenues for participation through your library and connections on the Internet.
2. *Start locally.* Perhaps the best way to begin participation in a professional association is to seek membership in your local university's professional leisure club or society; membership in state associations also can be helpful.
3. *Look for opportunities for membership involvement.* Look for associations that actively promote membership involvement—many encourage high levels of involvement in their affairs. Committee assignments, conference presentations, and legislative activities offer opportunities for new members. By becoming involved, one can better understand the needs of the profession and his or her role in it.
4. *Align interests.* Align your interests with professional associations that are consistent with your focus and reflect your career path. In this way, you can network with appropriate individuals and understand the underpinnings of your particular interest area.
5. *Be aware of discount memberships.* A number of professional associations provide discount memberships for students or organizations. Such membership fees provide access to the services of an organization at a reduced cost with no reduction in services.

Membership in a professional organization forms an essential part of one's professional career. Potential employers look for evidence of professional involvement on an individual's portfolio or resume. In part, professional involvement indicates a commitment to the profession as well as one's own professional development. Furthermore, joining a professional organization provides rewarding and worthwhile opportunities to serve one's profession in a positive and meaningful way and provides many useful benefits to the individual.

Pursuing a Professional Career: Key Elements

When considering a professional career, many individuals wonder where to begin. "How do I find the right position in a professional setting that will meet my needs and interests? What challenges will I find in the job market?" These complex questions require careful examination.

As seen in earlier chapters of this text, the leisure services field is highly diverse, with a number of different career pathways available. An individual must carefully assess his or her interests, desires, and career aspirations in order to establish an appropriate plan. Parts of the leisure services industry are competitive, with many seeking employment for similar jobs. Without proper planning and preparation, it may be difficult to achieve a position with the most

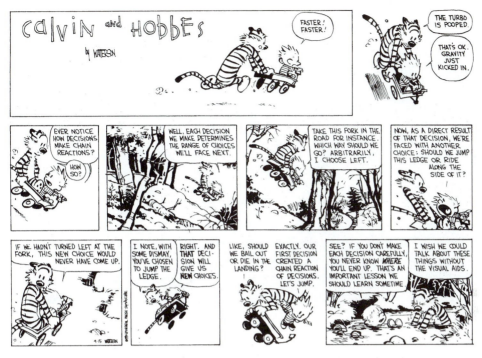

Figure 14.2

Making life decisions

CALVIN AND HOBBES copyright 1990 Watterson. Reprinted with permission of UNIVERSAL PRESS SYNDICATE. All rights reserved.

desirable agencies. On the other hand, opportunities always exist for individuals who have prepared themselves and who have planned effectively for the future. Figure 14.2 humorously illustrates the results of failing to plan carefully.

This portion of the chapter discusses the process of career assessment and exploration. In addition, it presents information concerning education, professional experiences, and certifications. Lastly, the chapter emphasizes the importance of lifelong education and continuous professional development. All of these are essential elements in pursuing a professional career (see figure 14.3).

Career Assessment and Exploration

Each person considering a career as a leisure services professional must ask, "Where shall I focus my professional career endeavors? How do I know what professional direction to take?" Individuals must find a professional focus to assist them in decision making. First, one needs to determine whether or not to seek employment in the leisure services field. The next step is to hone in on the area of greatest interest. The leisure services field presents a number of opportunities, with many potential career ladders. It is impossible to climb all of them simultaneously. Rather, a person should concentrate on particular career options and strive to do well in them.

Previous chapters discussed professional opportunities available: working in government (local, state, federal), nonprofit organizations (youth serving organizations, voluntary agencies, clubs), the private commercial sector (resorts, theme parks, hospitality industry, travel, and tourism) and/or therapeutic recreation arena (clinical- or community-based). Each of these sectors requires a specific strategy for career development—a unique set of educational competencies or a combination of professional work experiences. Certain sectors of the profession

Figure 14.3

Essential elements in pursuing a professional career

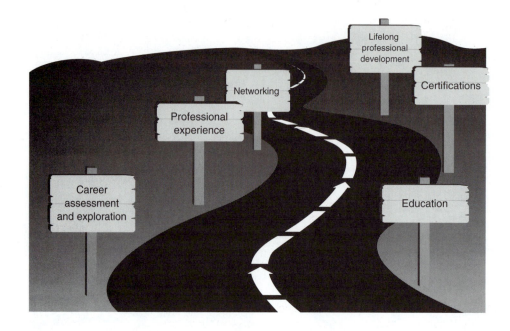

require detailed certification procedures. Different sectors of the profession conduct their professional business through their own professional associations. Knowledge of and membership in a particular association are important.

It is important to plan ahead in career development. Some students graduate from college or university and say, "OK, I've graduated, now what do I do?" This lack of planning puts the person at a professional disadvantage. Rather, an individual should establish options and then choose between desirable alternatives. Wise students lay the appropriate groundwork so that multiple options are available upon graduation. They have answered these questions: Will I choose a full-time job in the commercial sector? In a community park and recreation department? In a hospital as a therapeutic recreation specialist? Or should I go to graduate school, and, if so, what specialization should I pursue?

Education

Perhaps the most important element in developing a professional career in leisure services area is to study at a college or university that offers an appropriate degree in parks, recreation, or leisure services, preferably one accredited by the National Recreation and Park Association/American Association for Leisure and Recreation's Council on Accreditation. One can obtain a list of accredited programs by writing to either of these two professional associations or accessing the NRPA Web site at www.activeparks.com.

What makes higher education so important? A career in the leisure services area requires unique foundational knowledge best acquired by enrolling in an undergraduate program that offers the appropriate degree. Usually, the Bachelor of Arts or Bachelor of Science degree serves as the key entry-level requirement for employment. One's educational experience blends theoretical knowledge, applied or engineered skills, and professional values. The information presented in an undergraduate degree program enables a student to develop the basic knowledge, competencies, and skills required for entry-level positions.

Many colleges and universities provide specialized courses and degree offerings that have a particular focus, such as therapeutic recreation, travel and tourism, community recreation, sports management, natural resource management, and others. An advanced degree—Master of Arts or Master of Science—provides additional opportunities for specialization and focused study.

Professional Experience

Another essential element—experience—gives an aspiring leisure services professional a great advantage. The leisure services field has numerous opportunities available for part-time or seasonal professional work experiences. For example, nearly every community parks and recreation department offers extensive summer employment. Commercial resorts, theme parks, camps, and other settings provide similar opportunities. In addition, volunteer opportunities are widely available in a wide variety of human service settings. For example, working as a volunteer in organizations such as the Big Brothers/Big Sisters program and Boys and Girls Clubs of America can provide invaluable insight into dealing with children who are at risk.

Preprofessional experiences, which are often part-time or voluntary in nature, provide the foundation for one's professional values, strategies, and interests. *Camp Adventure*™ Youth Services Program, operated by the University of Northern Iowa. It provides contracted youth services to U.S. military installations worldwide. In addition to providing high-quality, high-impact youth services, the program dedicates itself to providing students with a hands-on orientation to the profession. *Camp Adventure*™, a value-driven program, strongly emphasizes quality in all that it does. This value structure translates into students who are highly motivated, as they participate in a model program of excellence. Such foundational experiences guide the professional endeavors of participating students as they pursue careers.

When leisure agencies, businesses, and organizations seek individuals to employ they will, invariably, look for relevant experience with all aspects of a job. For instance, in many organizations, computer skills (knowledge of word processing, spreadsheets, graphics) are a must. Almost all organizations will also look for previous experience in the field where a student has had practice in direct leadership or programming settings. Many college and university curricula require organized field study programs, practicums, and internships as a part of their degree offerings. Participation in such activities provides the minimum requirements for entry-level professional positions. Individuals should enhance their backgrounds by actively seeking these and similar opportunities. Part-time summer jobs, volunteer activities, and other experiences provide necessary real-life opportunities to increase relevant professional experience.

Networking

Meeting and interacting positively with other professionals also comprises a key element in developing a professional career. The networking process starts immediately upon entering an academic program, since professors are usually the first important contacts with the profession. These individuals should know their students and have the ability to analyze their strengths and weaknesses effectively. They prepare and will promote students' initial entry into the profession. Also, supervisors of part-time, voluntary, and seasonal positions become important contacts. These people can provide an analysis of opportunities and often have other professional contacts who may help in professional career development. Certainly, such individuals can provide a perspective on the quality of professional work.

Involvement in professional associations also creates important opportunities to network. Attending conferences, meetings, greeting professionals, and serving as an advocate for professional interests are important elements of professional career development. The Oregon

What Are Your Goals?

No one expects you to say with absolute resoluteness what you plan to be doing five, ten, or twenty years from the time you enter the job market. However, many employers will ask this question. Their purpose is to see if you have thought about where your entry-level job may take you and where, at this time, you would like it to take you.

It is important for you to realize that you are being hired, not only for what you can contribute today, but for the potential you are exhibiting tomorrow. Today is a developmental stage bringing about change, growth, and future direction. . . . Thinking about goals *now* helps you stay on target as you develop, learn, and implement skills.

Source: University of Oregon Career Planning and Placement *Job Search.*

Women in Leisure, an affiliate of the Oregon Park and Recreation Society, has developed a student program known as PROFILE. This program enables students and others to meet and interview professionals. The PROFILE program helps students learn about the work of a professional in their environment and, in this way, gain valuable insight and knowledge about a potential career opportunity. In addition, at NRPA congresses, formal mechanisms are established for a practitioner to take a student to lunch and engage in mentoring and networking.

Individuals should consider joining one or more professional associations. Such organizations provide opportunities to better understand the profession, stay abreast of professional developments, and for networking by helping to identify job opportunities and other useful services.

Certifications

Certification, licensure, and registration often are viewed as hallmarks of a profession. As such, they attest to the fact that the holder is committed to the profession and has achieved certain levels of knowledge and skill. Certification is the chosen method of attesting to one's knowledge or skill that is being used by leisure services professional organizations. As the field of leisure services continues to evolve, certification is becoming increasingly important to those employed in the profession. In addition, it is a statement about one's commitment to the development of the leisure services profession, and of one's concern for a baseline of competence.

After receiving a degree from an accredited university, persons in the field of leisure services are eligible to become certified as a certified parks and recreation professional (CPRP). Those in the area of therapeutic recreation are eligible to be certified as both a CPRP and as a CTRS, a certified therapeutic recreation specialist. The CTRS, similar to the CPRP, affirms that the holder possesses certain standards of knowledge necessary to effectively and safely conduct job functions. The CTRS certification is administered by the National Council for Therapeutic Recreation Certification. To maintain professional certifications, one must continue to seek out educational experiences (Continuing Education Units—CEUs) to perpetuate the addition of knowledge, and thus, the profession.

Technical Certification Other common certifications sought and gained by those committed to the delivery of leisure services include some form of advanced first aid, cardiopulmonary resuscitation (CPR), mandatory child abuse reporting certification, certification in the handling of blood-borne pathogens, ropes course facilitation, wilderness first aid, and certification as a aquatic facility operator (AFO). Once gained, maintaining these certifications through recertification courses and CEUs is desirable.

Lifelong Education and Professional Development

The half-life of knowledge in the area of management is seven years; in physics, four. In the leisure services field, the half-life of knowledge is perceived to be ten years. What does this mean? Basically, it means that half of the knowledge that one learns becomes obsolete in a short time. Society is constantly challenged by change, with new products, new processes, and new methods of delivering services. All of these require the constant attention of the successful professional. Therefore, all professionals should dedicate themselves to lifelong education and professional development.

Lifelong education and continuous professional development means constant involvement with and commitment to learning throughout life. Professional success requires attendance at professional conferences, intensive seminars, workshops, and institutes. Enrolling in college and university courses also upgrades a professional's development, knowledge, and skills. For example, the NRPA provides extensive, in-depth management and program institutes for parks and recreation professionals in the areas of risk management, playground safety, public golf course management, park maintenance, finance and revenue, aquatics, therapeutic recreation and inclusion, and administration.

Continuous review of electronic and written communications also serves as a valuable source of new information. A leisure services professional not only should read from within the leisure services field but also should review materials outside the profession; for example, management literature, human resources, current events, and philosophy. An organization can promote its staff's professional development by organizing preservice, in-service, and development programs. Such staff development initiatives may draw on internal resources, external consultants, colleagues, and others.

The Use of a Professional Portfolio

The importance of lifelong education and professional development cannot be overstated. Professionals must constantly be looking to improve and become better in everything they do. It is also important to document individual professional growth and development. One specific way to document these experiences is by utilizing a resource file and portfolio system. A resource file and subsequent portfolios will assist students in developing the needed skills to interpret an individual student's experiences to a specific person, group, or agency (DeGraaf and Jordan, 1996).

A portfolio development system is designed to assist students in the ongoing process of compiling and organizing the resources needed to interpret their preprofessional and professional experiences (academic and experiential) to others both inside and outside the profession. This process takes place throughout one's academic and professional career.

There are two elements within a portfolio development system—a resource file and a portfolio. A resource file is a collection of documents, papers, pictures, certificates, letters, work samples, references, recommendations, professional involvement logs, course descriptions, creative endeavors, and other pertinent materials that relate to the educational and career goals established by the student or professional. Students would be wise to begin collecting these items early in their academic, volunteer, and work careers.

A portfolio is a smaller collection of materials purposely drawn from the resource file to meet a particular purpose (e.g., to apply for a position as a programmer in a municipal recreation organization or to provide documentation in a specific skill area). Viewed as a professional self-portrait, a portfolio should illustrate an individual's proficiency in areas deemed important to being a professional in leisure services. The portfolio is an authentic measurement or assessment strategy that allows individuals to document their unique skills and abilities related to lifelong learning (DeGraaf and Jordan, 1996). In other words, a portfolio is an evolving tool that helps individuals to exhibit their talents and experiences. Using a portfolio enables one to document the technical skills, human resource skills, and conceptual skills needed to succeed in a specific career. In addition, a portfolio could be used to reflect on past experiences to develop a philosophy of delivering services to customers, as discussed in chapter four.

A portfolio can be organized in any number of ways. One consideration to bear in mind as it is developed is the intended reader or reviewer. Keep the presentation and layout simple and easy to follow (indexed in some fashion). Wisely utilize graphics and monitor the amount, type, and style of language. A professional appearance is important—remember, the reviewer is gaining an impression of the type of person you are and the type of employee you might be. Attention to detail is a hallmark of people who care about their work. One way to organize a portfolio would be to highlight various types of work experience. For instance, one might have direct leadership, programming, supervisory, and administrative skills or work experience. Within each of those categories one might choose to highlight his or her technical, interpersonal, and conceptual skills. A wise preprofessional is one who begins development of his or her portfolio materials early and continually reviews and updates those materials.

It is never too early to begin this documentation process. Undergraduate students should pay particular attention to beginning a documentation system that assists them in identifying strategies to meet specific professional goals as well as interpret experiential learning to potential employers. Such a system could be adapted to document lifelong education and professional development through one's professional career.

Summary

The leisure services field provides many diverse and challenging work opportunities. Preparing for one's career involves a process of planning and decision making in order to successfully locate an entry-level professional position. In developing a career path, individuals should focus their efforts in a specific direction. The leisure service field has many career ladders; the best employment opportunities require focused attention on only a few.

The first step in becoming a part of the leisure service field involves understanding the characteristics of the profession, the common elements of any profession, and the specifics that make leisure services unique. Four common elements all professions possess include: an organized body of knowledge, organizations and institutions that exist to transmit professional knowledge, creation of professional authority as a result of public sanction, and a code of ethics and standards to guide professional practice.

In crafting a professional career in the leisure services field, one must acquire foundational knowledge. This can be most effectively achieved by enrolling in a college or university in an accredited degree program. Part-time, seasonal, or voluntary work experiences often provide a long-standing foundation for one's career. Networking with practicing professionals, joining professional associations, and interacting with professionals in the field also play an important role. Professionals should seek appropriate certifications and credentials that attest to their competence, capability, and knowledge.

Professionals have a responsibility to be involved in professional organizations. Such organizations serve multiple ends, including providing opportunities for advocacy, education, communications, networking, promotion of standards, rewards and recognition, research and fact finding, and others.

Membership in professional associations should be selective; it may be better initially to join a state or regional group. Membership in professional associations also provides opportunities for individuals to give back to their profession.

Discussion Questions

1. Identify the key elements in pursuing a professional career in the leisure services area.
2. What benefits result from attending a college or university whose program is accredited by the NRPA/AALR Council on Accreditation?
3. Discuss the importance of lifelong education as a part of the process of one's professional career development.
4. What are the common elements of all professions?
5. After reading some of the core values of the leisure field, what five standards would you like to see become a part of a code of ethics for the profession?
6. Identify the types of experiences (volunteer and paid) you think you need in the next three years to enhance your ability to get a job when you graduate.
7. Identify the courses you should take within your institution to graduate with a degree in recreation or leisure services.
8. What common functions do professional associations share?
9. Identify four or more professional associations. Write, or call them up on the Internet, and ask for pertinent information concerning membership services, fees, and other activities.
10. What is the difference between a professional association, special-interest group, trade association, and/or futurist group? Of what value is it to belong to these types of groups?

References

Clark D. 1995. A new code of ethics for NRPA. *Parks & Recreation 30*(8), 38–43.

DeGraaf, D., and D. Jordan. 1996. The use of a portfolio system as a pedagogical tool. *SCHOLE 11,* 37–45.

Edginton, C., C. Hanson, S. Edginton, and S. Hudson. 1998. *Leisure Programming: A Service-Centered and Benefits Approach.* 3d ed. Dubuque, IA: McGraw-Hill.

Fain, S. M. 1985. The art of teaching professional ethics. *Therapeutic Recreation Journal 19*(4), 68–74.

NRPA. 2000. Data available on-line at www.activeparks.org.

Shank, J. W. 1985. Bioethical principles and the practice of therapeutic recreation in clinical settings. *Therapeutic Recreation Journal 19*(4), 31–39.

Stumbo, N. J. 1985. Knowledge of professional and ethical behavior in therapeutic recreation services. *Therapeutic Recreation Journal 19*(4), 59–67.

Sylvester, C. D. 1985. An analysis of selected ethical issues in therapeutic recreation. *Therapeutic Recreation Journal 19*(4), 8–21.

CHAPTER

15

Leisure and Cultural Diversity

These youth learn the value of diversity while enjoying an outdoor celebration.

Introduction

As society increasingly becomes multicultural, it is important that leisure services professionals understand and value pluralism or diversity. By understanding the dynamics of differences and the processes used to develop perceptions and assumptions, one can examine and analyze the accuracy and validity of such assumptions. The concept of diversity presented in this chapter implies sensitivity to differences of physical qualities and abilities, race and ethnicity, gender, age, and sexual orientation—*unity without uniformity.* People also differ on socioeconomic status, religion, educational levels, and others. A positive focus on the multicultural populations of the United States and Canada highlights the benefits of a multicultural population.

The leisure services professional has a responsibility to create a climate that advocates diversity, gains accurate information about differences, and evaluates those differences in a context of mutual respect. Leisure services professionals have an opportunity to celebrate diversity, personally and professionally. Customers, colleagues, and employers need to keep in touch with the issues of a rapidly changing world. Leisure services professionals must move from a point of merely acknowledging differences to a place of assigning merit and worth to these differences.

In a diverse culture, the nature of leisure draws upon the richness offered by many influences. North American leisure lifestyles, a mosaic of many cultures, exhibit the influences of Native peoples, Hispanics, Mexicans, Latinos, Asians, and African Americans as well as those of Norwegian, Irish, Scottish, German, Slovakian, and other cultural groups in games, sports, festivals, arts, music, and other leisure forms. This chapter examines a variety of aspects of leisure related to diversity, beginning with a short discussion of trends followed by a foundation of working definitions and terms. Dimensions of diversity and direct implications for the leisure services profession are discussed.

Future Trends: A Dramatic Increase in Diversity

The third millennium, punctuated with rapid social, economic, political, and cultural change, will present opportunities and challenges to leisure services professionals. The increasing diversity of the population will greatly impact leisure services organizations. To be effective as a leisure services professional, one must have knowledge in the area of diversity, as well as skills to manage diversity in terms of customers, staff, and the community at-large.

Trends for the twenty-first century show an increasingly multicultural population and labor force, an increase in women in the workforce, a trend toward a more mature workforce, and opportunities for previously underused segments of the workforce. All of these trends have implications for issues of diversity. Chapter 16 presents a summary of statistics related to these trends; however, this chapter briefly mentions these trends to provide a foundation for this topic and to underscore the importance of this issue.

Ethnic minorities. In late 2000, California reached a milestone where no one ethnic group is in the majority (more than 50% of the population). This trend will continue across the United States and in Canada.

Women. In the next decade two out of three new workers will be women, and women will constitute approximately 48 percent of the workforce in the year 2008 (Ameristat, 2000).

Individuals with physical disabilities. Computer-aided technologies will allow individuals with physical disabilities to compete more effectively for employment within leisure services organizations. In addition, the Americans with Disabilities Act will continue to impact this group in a positive fashion.

Older individuals. The number of people sixty-five and older who will remain in their jobs is predicted to increase in the next decade, partially due to the fact that U.S. Congress banned forced retirement in 1986.

People who are gay or lesbian. In 2000, Vermont became the first state to officially recognize same-sex civil unions, which carry the same legal benefits as marriage. Canada and some European countries have similar legal benefits for gays and lesbians.

These trends will impact all leisure services organizations. Some of the emerging organizational considerations related to these trends include equal opportunity, child care, flexible work schedules, staff development in the area of diversity, and others. Following is a brief outline of potential organizational outcomes if the trend toward increased diversity continues as anticipated.

- To remain competitive and retain employees, leisure services professionals must be increasingly sensitive and responsive to issues related to diversity, including age, gender, ethnicity, disability, and sexual orientation.
- As the workforce becomes almost half female, there will be pressure on leisure services professionals to respond to the increased need for adequate child-care programs, parental leave, flexible hours, and innovative child-care options. Equity issues also will be important.
- Leisure services professionals must respond to the values, needs, and desires of a diverse constituency. Cultural competence will be demanded of staff at all levels.

Women Do Not Speak with One Voice

Women do not speak with one voice. Each voice represents her own unique experiences of culture, religion, race, class, family, environment, and sexuality. Circumstances of birth contribute to who she is and who she will become. Women are as distinctive as the stripes of zebras. When viewing a herd of zebra, each zebra's unique markings are not seen. In much the same way, women are often seen as similar when looking at them as a group.

Each woman sings uniquely—soprano, alto, or contralto. When blended together in harmony, the collective choir of sopranos, altos, and contraltos provides sounds which are quite different from men's voices in harmony. Each woman speaks uniquely and in a way that is different from a man's. . . . [There are] . . . distinctive differences between women's and men's values as they relate to morality. Choices made as a result of these differences in value orientation represent many of the differences in our voices.

Source: Pritchard, A. 1997, Fall. Challenges for women in sport in the new millennium. *The Journal of the International Council for Health, Physical Education, Recreation, Sport and Dance 33*(1), 15–18.

- Equal opportunity issues will persist for people of color as they seek promotion within organizational hierarchies and own their own businesses.
- In terms of both customers and staff, the leisure services professional must deal with issues of discrimination regarding HIV infection and AIDS, rights to privacy, and rights of noninfected customers and staff.
- Staff development will continue to play a key role in responding to issues related to the broad spectrum of diversity.

Issues related to increasing diversity continue to challenge leisure services organizations and leisure service professionals to develop policies and procedures to guide the direction of their organizations in a positive and responsive manner. This begins with a personal understanding of diversity by each leisure services professional, as well as the organizations in which we work.

This discussion of trends has laid the groundwork for the realization that diversity is an important issue in the leisure services field. The next section of the chapter, which deals with foundational perspectives, attempts to determine what diversity is—the dimensions, definitions, and terms that describe diversity and contribute to a greater understanding of the topic.

Diversity: Foundational Perspectives

The term *diversity* suggests a variety of topics—affirmative action, racial or ethnic issues, and sometimes simply difference. A discussion about diversity requires a conceptual framework and working definitions in order to operate from a common starting point.

Words can have a tremendous impact on self-esteem, the way one views the world, and the perspectives of others. Language is not static; it changes constantly. Common meanings for terms change and become acceptable or not as the culture evolves and grows. Even the language in this book will become outdated and require revision to maintain original meanings.

Women: A Critical Mass

. . . Women have reached a critical mass in the professions. No longer are they a token minority. . . . Since 1972, the percentage of women physicians has doubled. In 1966, fewer than 7 percent of MDs were granted to women. By 1987 it had reached 32.3 percent, nearly one third. In 1966 women were awarded an even tinier proportion of law degrees . . . a mere 3.5 percent. But by 1987, women were taking home 40 percent of all law degrees. . . .

Women have achieved, if not a majority, a substantial proportion of the previously male-dominated careers in the information and service industries. . . . Women hold some 39.3 percent of the 14.2 million executive, administrative and management jobs, according to the Bureau of Labor Statistics . . . nearly one third of computer scientists are women. . . . Male or female, the effective leader wins commitment by setting an example of excellence: being ethical, open, empowering and inspiring.

From John Naisbitt and Patricia Aburdene, *Megatrends for Women,* Copyright © 1990 by Megatrends Ltd., reprinted by permission of William Morrow and Company.

However, the definitions provided in this section help establish a framework for communication. We discuss terminology related to culture, discrimination, and prejudice and look at the role of power in the formation of "isms" (e.g., racism, ageism, and other forms of discrimination) in order to set the framework for understanding.

Culture

Culture permeates everything that people do, think, and feel. The concept of culture includes the values, traditions, norms, customs, rituals, and ways of viewing the world of a group of people who are tied together by common factors. These factors may include a common history, geographic location, language, food, music, social class, and/or religion (Schwartz and Conley, 2000). In addition, leisure as a construct (what it means to different people) and as an activity also forms a component of culture.

We know that culture consists of at least two levels: surface culture and deep culture. *Surface culture* consists of those elements of culture that are visible to others—food, dress, appearance, music, use of gestures, and so on. We tend to draw conclusions about people based on what we see and think we know about them. *Deep culture* includes the elements of an individual that are not necessarily visible to others, yet are incredibly important in terms of self-identity. Examples of these are worldviews, social systems, beliefs, values, and unstated norms (Guirdham, 1999).

It is common for most people to belong to one primary culture and one or more subcultures. For instance, a typical college student might belong to the Panhellenic subculture (a sorority/fraternity), be considered middle class, and be of African American descent. Each subculture influences the individual's attitudes, thoughts, and actions. Leisure activities both produce subcultures and are the products of subcultures within society. Golfers, fantasy football team owners, country western line dancers, collectors of baseball cards, curlers, and quilting groups are all subcultures associated with leisure.

Disabled Outdoor Sports

AccessAdventure is a service that designs outdoor adventure challenge programs that challenge existing notions of what is achievable; designs programs with people with disabilities, rather than for people with disabilities; ensures the program is "tailor made" and that the challenges are proportional to the skills of the individuals; offers people with disabilities the opportunity to learn and develop skills that will help enhance quality of life; and facilitates outdoor adventure challenge activities in an atmosphere of care, support, and fun. HEAD OFFICE: Physical Difference, PO Box 216, Kurrajong NSW 2758.

Quad Rugby, or wheelchair rugby as it is also called, is a sport with roots going back to wheelchair basketball and ice hockey, which is not surprising, since it was developed by three Canadians from Winnipeg, Manitoba, as a quadriplegic equivalent to wheelchair basketball. The sport was originally called murderball due to the aggressive nature of the game. It was introduced in the United States in 1981 by Brad Mikkelson, who with the aid of the University of North Dakota's Disabled Student Services, formed the first team, the Wallbangers, and changed the game's name from murderball to quad rugby.

In 1979, a team from Winnipeg organized an exhibition at the regional track meet held at Southwest State University in Minnesota. Canada went on to play their first national championship that same year. The first quad rugby match in the United States was between North Dakota and Minnesota, as an exhibition game at the 1982 National Wheelchair games, also held at Southwest State University. This same year, the University of South Dakota hosted the first international tournament, with participating teams from Manitoba, Saskatchewan, North Dakota, and Minnesota.

In 1988, the United States Quad Rugby Association (USQRA) was formed to help regulate and promote the sport on both a national and international level. Since its introduction Quad Rugby has grown to become a truly international sport, with teams now competing from around the globe. There are now more than forty-five organized teams in the United States with many others in the developmental stage. In addition to the teams in the United States, there is estimated to be at least twenty international teams from as far away as Australia in addition to those in Canada. Without question, quad rugby is the fastest-growing wheelchair sport in the world today.

Who Can Play?

Players may have various disabilities that preclude their play in able-bodied sport competition. Players must have a combination of upper and lower extremity impairment to be considered as eligible to participate. Most of the players have sustained cervical-level spinal injuries and have some type of quadriplegia as a result. Players are given a classification number from one of seven classifications ranging from 0.5 to 3.5. The 0.5 player has the greatest impairment and is comparable to a C5 quadriplegic. Of those eligible to participate, the 3.5 player has the least impairment and is similar to a C7-8 incomplete quadriplegic. Both males and females are encouraged to play, and because of the classification process gender advantages don't exist.

The Game

Four players from each team are allowed on the court at a time. Classifications of the four players on the court must total no more than 8.0 points at one time. The action occurs on a regulation-sized basketball court with some minor changes. During the games team players pass a volleyball back and forth while advancing into the opponent's half court and then crossing over the goal line with the ball in one player's possession. While the offense is trying to advance the ball, the defense is trying to take it away and keep the opposing team from scoring. Certain restrictions apply in the key area. One restriction is that only three defensive players are allowed in the key, and if a fourth enters, a penalty can be assessed or a goal awarded. Another restriction is that an offensive player can only stay in the key area for ten seconds. Otherwise a turnover will be assessed.

Some groups have been *marginalized* by society—pushed by the dominant culture to the *margins* or fringes of society in terms of social and economic resources (power). As Healey (1997) notes, minority status has more to do with the distribution of resources and power than with simple numbers. He suggests five characteristics that are part of the definition of a minority: (1) the members of the group experience a pattern of disadvantage or inequality; (2) group members share invisible traits or characteristics that differentiate them from other groups; (3) the minority group is a self-conscious social unit; (4) membership in the group is usually determined at birth; and (5) members tend to marry within the group.

Thus, marginalized or minority groups generally consist of individuals from outside the dominant, or most common, culture. Leisure programs and events can promote certain leisure outcomes that enable marginalized or minority individuals to maintain their cultural integrity and take advantage of opportunities for self-expression. This is important, because people are more likely to adjust to a new culture (i.e., immigrants) when they have contact with compatriots; people who share a culture affirm one another's cultural identity and validate the everyday realities of the acculturation process (Kurtz-Costes and Pungello, 2000). For example, celebrations such as Cinco de Mayo, a festival that is part of the Hispanic culture, offer opportunities to celebrate diversity and maintain traditions. While anyone might attend Cinco de Mayo and learn something about the Hispanic culture, the festival helps to maintain the Hispanic cultural identity. Marginalized groups often use leisure to affirm their cultural identity and values, and to promote their traditions and heritage.

Prejudice

Prejudice is an attitude or opinion that indicates a preconceived judgment, made before all information has been gathered. It is irrational and based on myth, fiction, and misinformation rather than fact. This negative bias against a person or group limits understanding of individuality and may constrain an individual from reaching his or her potential. Humans all have prejudices and prejudices interfere with the ability to perceive reality accurately. Table 15.1 offers a case in

TABLE

15.1 UNDERSTANDING PREJUDICE

Prejudice: A Case in Point

Many of our prejudices about others are unfounded; that is, they are not based in fact. Society, media, and culture have programmed us to accept stereotypes of others. Thus, it is important to acknowledge our prejudices and the danger of faulty stereotypes. The following two scenarios illustrate this point:

Scenario One: It is 3:00 A.M. and a white college student is walking down a dark street alone; there are no other people in the vicinity. He/she sees a group of five black youths coming from the opposite direction. They are talking loudly. What do you think the initial reaction of the white college student will be?

Scenario Two: It is 3:00 A.M. and a black college student is walking down a dark street alone; there are no other people in the vicinity. He/she sees a group of five white youths coming from the opposite direction. They are talking loudly. What do you think the initial reaction of the black college student will be?

We all have been programmed in a way that encourages us to react emotionally to situations like the one above, without foundation of fact. Based on societal stereotypes the two college students in the scenarios above will likely experience feelings of concern, possibly panic, and physical symptoms that usually accompany danger. Have either of the individuals, however, had time to make a logical or rational assessment of the situation? Isn't it possible that the two groups of five individuals are simply having a good time and are individuals of good character and values?

point regarding prejudice and illustrates the way people can react, physically and emotionally, and sometimes stereotype individuals who are "different."

Contact Conditions for Reducing Prejudice Many leisure services and programs contain elements, identified by Amir (1976) and presented by Hayles (1989), that meet criteria for reducing prejudice. By facilitating positive interaction, these factors reduce many of the barriers that may interfere with meaningful communication. These factors, depicted in table 15.2, contribute to reducing prejudice. Conditions such as equal status (e.g., individuals dressed similarly), intergroup cooperation (e.g., dramatic play, games), interdependence or superordinate goals (e.g., sports), intimate contact, service to others, and pleasant/rewarding contact all exist within a number of leisure programs and activities. Leisure programs and services offer an effective vehicle for promoting values related to diversity. Virtually all of the criteria cited may be easily and consistently applied within the leisure service setting.

TABLE

15.2 MANY LEISURE PROGRAMS/ACTIVITIES MEET CRITERIA FOR REDUCING PREJUDICE

Contact Conditions for Reducing Prejudice

1. *Equal status.* Creating conditions to make all people feel equal may reduce prejudice; for example, individuals wear similar clothing, casual clothing, uniforms (e.g., sports). Individuals leave their rank, status, level of authority outside. Group use of identity markers, such as logos, uniforms, and other items that publicly attest to membership may also be effective.

2. *Positive perceptions of other group occurs.* Positive, successful images of all types of people, including women, people of color, and older people, are shown.

3. *Other majority group members are involved.* Majority group members offer support and indicate by their behavior and actions that valuing diversity is the right thing to do. Strong role models are important.

4. *Activities require intergroup cooperation.* To achieve goals, individuals must cooperate (e.g., organizational projects, sports, games). A sense of belonging is reinforced through rituals such as ceremonies, songs, and group cheers, as well as public commitment to vision and mission statements, codes of conduct, values, and other expressions of unity and loyalty.

5. *Situations entail interdependence of superordinate goals.* Individuals have a common goal or purpose as a group, for example, in the military or on sports teams. Goals tied to a base of moral action may be effective in binding people together.

6. *Contact is more intimate than casual.* Contact is more than just "Hello, how are you?" Individuals experience meaningful interaction that may involve goals, sharing, developing new strengths, clarifying values.

7. *Social climate promotes intergroup contact.* A social climate is created that promotes the ideal that diversity is an asset and that it enriches the effort.

8. *Contact is pleasant or rewarding.* When contact is fun, exciting, stimulating, and meaningful, these feelings contribute to the reduction of prejudice.

9. *Engaging in service to others.* As a group, serving prosocial ends and demonstrating altruistic behaviors can break down barriers and create common bonds. These types of behaviors are seen in Camp Fire, scouting, 4-H, Rotary, and other groups for adults and youth. Service learning programs for youth provide this opportunity.

Source: Adapted from Yehuda Amir. 1976. The role of intergroup contact in change of prejudice and ethnic relations. Edited by Phyllis A. Katz (ed.), in *Towards the Elimination of Racism,* Chapter 8, pp. 245–308. New York: Pergamon Press.

Discrimination

Discrimination describes the action(s) that accompany prejudice—the actions that hinder equal access to economic resources, educational systems, and leisure opportunities. Unfounded discrimination leads to the various "isms" in society (e.g., racism, ageism, heterosexism, ableism, classism, sexism). The lack of access to power is a recurring theme of discrimination.

The Role of Power   Power has several definitions depending on its context. In discussions about discrimination, power refers to an individual's ability to influence and enforce decisions in the community. Power comes in many forms: economic power, social power, personal power, political power, and spiritual power (Kraus, 1994; Loden and Rosener, 1991; Nieto, 1992).

Those with access to the various forms of power can "use" or neglect those without that access. In a social system built on stratification, such as is found in both Canada and the United States, power differentials exist. Some people and/or groups of people have power, others have less, and others essentially have none. As may be seen in various states and provinces, minority groups have made some strides in the area of political influence. There are larger numbers of minority elected officials now than there have been in previous times in history.

Discrimination cannot exist in the absence of power (Loden and Rosener, 1991). While one can try to act in a discriminatory way, the lack of power to support that discrimination renders it simply prejudice. However, both prejudice and discrimination damage society because they impact the way people view themselves and others. The most damaging aspect of discrimination and prejudice appears at an institutional level, where prejudice and discrimination are so pervasive that discriminatory policies and actions become "acceptable" business operations. Institutionalized discrimination creates social policies that perpetuate the inequities while appearing to be "good."

Status   Status crosses the boundaries of society and influences the lives of every person. All people have a concept of their own status or place in society, and they usually recognize the relative status of others. In a stratified society (every society has different "layers" of people based on some aspect—economic status, family connections, level of education, and so on), society as a whole attributes varying degrees of worth, esteem, respect, and prestige to different groups of people (Kraus, 1994; Nieto, 1992). Status is the amount of esteem and prestige that one can elicit from others in society. That status might be based on any of the primary and secondary characteristics that form the dimensions of diversity.

Dimensions of Diversity

To ensure fair treatment of the topic of diversity, the leisure services professional must examine its many dimensions. Diversity consists of much more than simply race or ethnicity—within-group differences are as important as between-group differences. For instance, as a group, Hispanic people differ from Asians; however, within the Hispanic culture some identify with a Mexican heritage, others with a Latin heritage, and still others with a Cuban tradition. These all represent distinct cultures with differences in beliefs, values, customs, and social patterns.

Discussion in this section focuses on two major categories of characteristics of individuals—*primary characteristics* and *secondary characteristics* (Loden and Rosener, 1991). Figure 15.1 depicts these characteristics. Primary characteristics (such as ethnicity, sex, age) may appear obvious upon meeting an individual, and secondary characteristics (such as education, religion, economic status) are revealed later. Each characteristic has a related "ism"—actions and

Figure 15.1

Examples of dimensions of diversity

Source: Data from M. Loden and J. Rosener, 1991. Workforce America: Managing Employee Diversity as a Vital Resource, Professional Book Group. Burr Ridge, IL.

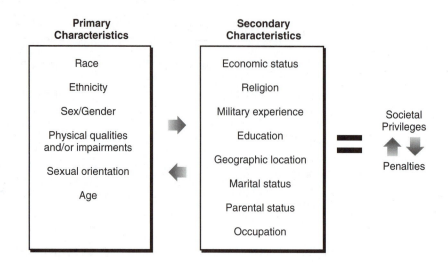

Primary Characteristics	Secondary Characteristics	
Race	Economic status	Societal Privileges
Ethnicity	Religion	
Sex/Gender	Military experience	
Physical qualities and/or impairments	Education	
Sexual orientation	Geographic location	Penalties
Age	Marital status	
	Parental status	
	Occupation	

attitudes that express the interrelationship of status and attributions of value or worth, and the discriminating characteristic. These actions and attitudes imply worth, normalcy, and a sense of rightness in society.

Isms are perpetuated in and through every aspect of society—television commercials and shows, magazine advertisements and articles, sports (types of people who play certain positions or sports), religious leadership, and education (students being tracked into certain fields of study). While those who receive advantages from discrimination may believe it to be morally wrong, they often do not want to give up the benefits of being "on top."

Five characteristics, identified as the primary dimensions of diversity, generally are obvious when meeting others, and they tend to generate the strongest emotional response. People tend to refine their judgments of others based on secondary characteristics that become apparent with further personal interaction.

Primary Characteristics

Primary characteristics generate first impressions and are things, generally, over which people have no control. They include race and ethnicity, sex and gender, physical and mental qualities and/or impairments, sexual orientation, and age (Loden and Rosener, 1991). Primary characteristics have a tremendous impact on how an individual is socialized from birth. These primary dimensions, found throughout every culture, generally have varying levels of status associated with them. Differing status attributions lead to discrimination and acts of prejudice solely based on that trait. The discrimination might manifest itself in negative actions (people of color being denied housing) or positive actions (treating the elderly with more respect than younger people).

Race and Ethnicity   Although used interchangeably by many, race and ethnicity have been perceived as different, yet related constructs. Race has implied the biological differences of a group of people that are transmissible by descent (skin pigment, eye folds). Ethnicity, on the other hand, is typically used to define the common qualities, language, history, customs, and traditions of a people. Ethnic groups cross racial boundaries (Kraus, 1994; Loden and Rosener, 1991; Nieto, 1992). Scientists are now beginning to believe that race is a sociological construct, rather than a biological one; therefore, ethnicity is the more accurate term to connote differences between cultural groups.

Racism basically involves the manifestation of a system of penalty and privilege based on race or ethnicity. It is based on the belief that one race or ethnic group is inherently superior (are born superior), and it presumes that other races or ethnic groups are inherently inferior (Loden and Rosener, 1991). The belief is that it is "only natural" for the better (smarter, richer, stronger, etc.) ethnic group to have access to more and better resources (Naylor, 1998).

One of the difficulties in addressing racism (and all isms) results from this system of penalty and privilege—one group is penalized for its assumed inferiority; another is privileged for its assumed superiority. This system of social comparison perpetuates feelings of self-esteem at the expense of others (Pelled, Eisenhardt, and Xin, 1999). Due to the institutionalized nature of racism, however, most of those in the privileged group and many of those in the penalized group do not recognize the privileges and penalties. Examples of privileges of being White include being able to

- obtain housing in a reasonably priced and well-maintained neighborhood,
- go to the mall without fear of being followed by security or asked to leave stores if nothing is purchased,
- go into almost any salon for a haircut or style, and
- swim in a public pool without fear of "chasing" others out (adapted from McIntosh, 1991).

Sex and Gender People also make immediate judgments based on sex and gender. Like race, the word *sex* is one that refers to biological differences between individuals—in this case, female and male individuals. Gender is the psychological construct a society forms to describe and explain masculinity and femininity (those traits that are more commonly ascribed to males and those ascribed more commonly to females). Gender is what informs us that a truck is a "boy's toy" while a doll is a "girl's toy." As can be imagined, gender differentiation affects every aspect of life: work, play, education, religion, politics, and family.

Discrimination or prejudice against a person based on sex or gender is defined as *sexism* or *gender discrimination.* As power is an integral part of any ism, many instances of sexism negatively impact women. In most societies with a European influence, being a white male is considered the "norm"; females rank lower in status. Over the years women have been considered less physically capable and less intelligent than men; too emotional and, therefore, unsuitable for certain situations; and more sexual than is good for them (Henderson, Bialeschki, Shaw, and Freysinger, 1996). Men are also negatively impacted by sexism (men should not cry, men should earn money, men should be physically strong). Examples of sexism include:

- use of language that denigrates or puts down women (e.g., calling adult women "girls" or the purportedly generic "guys");
- a lack of paid parental leave for men;
- peer and social pressure that keeps girls and women from participating in activities such as rugby, boxing, and rebuilding cars;
- peer and social pressure that inhibits boys and men from participating in activities such as sewing, cooking, ceramics, and ballet; and
- a lack of available child care in leisure facilities and centers.

Mental and Physical Impairment and Qualities Those with mental and physical impairments include a variety of people with varying degrees of inconvenience and challenge. Some use wheelchairs, some use canes, some walkers. Some people wear thick corrective eyeglasses, others use a dog to help them see. Others live in a group home and work at a sheltered workshop. Some have less visible disabilities such as mild mental retardation, epilepsy, or learning disabilities. People with disabilities differ from one another just as any other people do.

Ableism is the act of discrimination or prejudice against those who are physically or mentally impaired (Nieto, 1992). As with racism, ableism implies a superior worth to able-bodied individuals. It extends the system of penalty and privilege to one's physical and mental abilities. Examples of ableism include:

- a refusal to remodel stairs into ramps because of the cost,
- a lack of signage in Braille in public and private facilities,
- a restaurant refusing service to a double-arm amputee who must eat with his feet, and
- refusing to hire an obese person as a front desk worker based strictly on appearance.

Individuals also differ in physical qualities: Some are tall, others short, some are thin, others obese. People tend to respond more favorably to those whom they consider attractive than to those who do not meet the societal or cultural standards of beauty. This inequity can be considered a form of prejudice.

Sexual Orientation While not necessarily visible upon an initial meeting, sexual orientation generates strong reactions and has enormous socializing implications for a person, no matter his or her race, ethnicity, sex, or physical qualities/abilities (Loden and Rosener, 1991). Sexual orientation is an element of personal identity that differs from one's sexual behaviors and his or her sex. One's sexual orientation is typically labeled as heterosexual, homosexual, or bisexual.

Heterosexism involves discrimination or prejudice based on one's sexual orientation. It includes the belief that heterosexuality is superior to either homosexuality or bisexuality and can manifest itself in penalties toward assumed or avowed gay, lesbian, or bisexual persons. The privileges and penalties of sexual orientation include:

- negative public reaction to two men dancing together on a public dance floor,
- tax breaks for legally married couples, yet only heterosexuals can be legally married,
- a lack of civil rights protection against discrimination based on sexual orientation, and
- the assumption that all gay men are HIV positive or have AIDS.

Age Although many people overlook the influence of age on the treatment of people and the expectations placed on them, age comprises an important dimension of diversity. Western cultures tend to glorify youth and disparage age. Reactions to age change with culture as well as the age of the group. Children, adolescents, young adults, mature adults, and seniors all command different levels and degrees of respect based on culture and situation.

Ageism includes acts of prejudice and discrimination against people based on their age. Western societies tend to discriminate against both ends of the age continuum perhaps because of the tremendous value placed on success and achievement in the workforce. An ongoing struggle for the rights of children works to ensure that although legally minors, they are considered worthwhile and viable beings. On the other end, the elderly are also discriminated against. Examples of ageism include:

- calling or referring to elderly leisure participants as "cute,"
- ignoring the concerns of children in planning and developing leisure facilities for youth,
- not hiring or promoting older workers strictly due to their age, and
- assuming that all adolescents prefer to hang out on street corners rather than participate in structured activities.

Secondary Characteristics

Secondary characteristics of diversity impact judgments about people as further interaction takes place. These traits can often change, yet they still influence judgments and affect socialization. People ascertain these traits after getting to know someone and adjust their thoughts and biases accordingly. Secondary traits play an extremely important role in the way that they interact with primary characteristics to result in both overt and covert forms of discrimination (Loden and Rosener, 1991). Secondary traits include economic status, religion, military experience, education, geographic location, marital status, parental status, occupation, and other demographic characteristics.

Economic Status   One's access to material wealth and family history combine to influence social status. As economic wealth tends to translate directly into better health, education, and political influence, it affects other dimensions of diversity as well.

Classism is discrimination or prejudice against a person based on socal and economic status (Nieto, 1992; Schwartz and Conley, 2000). As power forms an integral part of any ism, most instances of classism focus on those who are at or below the poverty line. Therefore, members of the working class or the poor experience the negative effects of classism from some individuals who have economic power.

Religion   Societies differ in the religions they value. In most societies, the dominant culture establishes its religion as the norm. Individuals who participate in religions outside the cultural norm may experience a high degree of prejudice and persecution (e.g., Hasidic Jews in the United States, Christians in Saudi Arabia).

Military Experience   The impact of military experience on one's social situation tends to change with the atmosphere of culture. In the United States, veterans of World War II and the Gulf War received a hero's welcome while many Vietnam War veterans were ostracized and denigrated.

Education   One's level of education and where it is received affect social status. Attendance at elite schools generates prestige, and the lack of a high school education has a detrimental impact on one's social status.

Geographic Location   Both the current residence and a person's place of origin impact social status—from the side of town where one lives to the part of the country or world one considers home. Geographic location influences speech (e.g., accent, word usage, intonation), dress, attitudes, thoughts, and behaviors. Society as a whole makes judgments based on geographic location.

Marital Status   Societies attribute different values of merit and worth to people based on their marital status—single, married, divorced, widowed, or domestic partnership whether it be gay or straight. The age at which one married, number of marriages, and other factors also influence social judgments.

Parental Status   Many aspects of parental status impact individuals—whether one has children or not; the number of children; the age of the parents; whether it was a traditional birth, through artificial insemination, a surrogate mother or adoption; and parental status combined with marital status.

Occupation Reflected in levels of education and economic status, a person's job influences societal status. Whether one is a blue-collar worker, unskilled laborer, professional, or volunteer may all have an impact on how one is perceived by others. Even the days of the week, the hours of work, and insurance coverage affect social ranking.

Interaction of Primary/Secondary Characteristics

No one falls within just one primary or secondary dimension of diversity; people are composites with many different characteristics. Each trait or dimension of diversity carries with it its own social penalties and privileges. An individual's combined characteristics affect penalties and privileges and may serve to either mitigate negative sanctions and increase privilege, or increase negative sanctions and lessen the effects of privilege (Loden and Rosener, 1991).

At different times in one's life and in society some dimensions of diversity have greater effects than others. For instance, an African American female may experience discrimination because of her ethnicity; at other times her sex could prevent her from access to resources, even within her own ethnic group. The combined action of dimensions lessens the impact of some; for instance, a Hispanic person might receive negative social reactions based on ethnicity alone. However, economic success and a Harvard education usually generates a positive response. A sixty-two-year-old Native American with a twelfth-grade education and who is a retired construction worker will probably experience accumulated sanctions: racism, ageism, and classism.

Cultural Sensitivity: Valuing Differences

Becoming culturally sensitive involves the awareness of one's own ethnicity and differences and acknowledging and respecting differences in others. While tolerating differences may mean enduring or putting up with them, it does not imply a positive approach to cultural diversity. Leisure service professionals should understand the way in which individuals reach a point of valuing all cultures and ethnic groups.

A Process for Valuing Differences

Some individuals do not want anything to do with "different" people. Others think that all people are really just like them. Yet others strive to learn about a wide variety of differences. These individuals are developing skills to enhance their cultural competence and are at the beginning stages of the process of valuing diversity. This process leads one through many phases progressing toward the belief that all cultures and ethnic groups have value.

Figure 15.2 offers a model of these processes. The model represents a continuum of behavior in terms of awareness and valuing diversity—progressing from an ethnocentric stage (other groups/cultures are inferior) to an ethnorelative stage (all cultures/ethnic groups have equal value). At the bottom of the figure, an individual in a *denial state,* or stage, does not want to have anything to do with those who are different. In the next step (*defense*), the individual struggles with differences, although on the surface he or she appears to value diversity.

On the next level, the individual engages in *minimization,* mistakenly believing that "different people are *really* just like me." Although often intended as a gesture of goodwill, this attitude values others, but denies their diversity. An underlying foundation of affirmative action characterizes the *acceptance* stage. As the *adaptation* stage is reached, the individual attempts to create win/win situations and to be flexible, perhaps, for example, by supporting an em-

A Process for Valuing Differences
Moving from a monocultural, ethnocentric mind-set to
one of understanding, awareness, integration/inclusion

Ethnorelative Stages
(all cultures or ethnic groups
have equal value; no culture
is superior to another)

Ethnocentric Stages
(other cultures/ethnic groups
are inferior to your culture)

Integration/inclusion
(taking the best of a variety of ways)

Adaptation
(flexibility, synergy occurs)

Acceptance
(foundation of affirmative action)

Minimization
(belief that people are really alike;
ignoring part of the person)

Defense
(putting up positive appearances;
reality is negative)

Denial
(not wanting to have anything to
do with people who are different)

Figure 15.2

How we respond
and relate to
differences

*Source: Data from
Milton J. Bennett,
"A Developmential
Approach to
Training for
Intercultural
Sensitivity" in
International*
Journal of
Intercultural
Relations, *Vol. 10,
No. 2,
pp. 179–196.*

ployee's time off for a significant cultural event. *Integration/inclusion* is reached when the individual acknowledges that all cultures/ethnic groups have value, and results in actions based on selecting the best from diverse cultures.

Implications of Diversity for Leisure Services Professionals

Issues of diversity impact all levels and aspects of leisure services organizations and the profession as a whole. Administrators can establish management systems that effectively recruit and hire people of color, women, people with disabilities, and other individuals from underrepresented groups. Leisure services professionals in program and leadership roles who see leisure as basic to life should provide leisure services that are culturally relevant to all people.

The leisure services professional can no longer assume that everyone has similar leisure needs and desires or pretend not to be an active member of a system that perpetuates racism, classism, sexism, and other forms of oppression. Practitioners must journey back to the roots of the leisure services profession and again serve those who need opportunities and encouragement to reach their full potential. We must remind ourselves that every individual has a right to an ethnic identity and respect for that ethnic identity regardless of the cultural traits associated with that identity. This viewpoint can aid parks and recreation professionals in their growth toward cultural competence (Goldberg, 2000). Cultural competence refers to the ability to provide professional services in a way that is congruent with behavior and expectations that are normative for a given community (Green, 1995 as cited in Goldberg, 2000).

Although many view valuing diversity as a moral/ethical issue, other compelling forces provide motivation to support diversity. The following section discusses such factors as enrichment, demographic trends, external forces, and internal forces that speak strongly to the need for continued growth and development in multiculturalism and diversity within leisure service organizations.

Enrichment of the organization. Diverse individuals bring with them experiences and add viewpoints that enrich the organization. For example, it has been suggested that male-female work teams operate more effectively than all-male or all-female work teams, because the synergy of both sexes strengthens the team (Hayles, 1996). In addition, diverse work groups tend to develop more creative ideas and have increased work efficiency (Knouse and Dansby, 1999).

Response to demographic trends. The population from which the leisure services organization will recruit applicants continues to show sharp increases in diverse groups. Increases in minority populations due to immigration as well as birthrates will continue to significantly change the potential workforce as well as constituent groups.

Acknowledgment of external forces. Leisure services organizations are accountable to the larger community, which is increasingly more diverse. The needs of constituent groups in the community must be addressed.

Response to internal forces. Individuals within leisure services organizations seek respect, equity, and opportunities for promotion and advancement.

Diversity also applies to administration, leadership, programming, and facilities design. Tools can be used in staff development, communication, guidelines for interactions, and other activities to support diversity.

Administrative Practices

Much can be done "at the top" to ensure cultural equity in the administration and provision of leisure services. Administration and management have a tremendous impact on the organizational culture and conduct. Effective administration and management of diversity includes a statement of beliefs, adherence to affirmative action and Equal Employment Opportunity (EEO) guidelines, appropriate staff development, and policies and practices that have impact.

Mission   An agency's mission, philosophy, and vision statements set the stage for its activity. These statements serve as the foundation for all other administrative and programmatic functions and initially express the commitment to diversity. Consider the following component of the mission statement from the Leisure Services Division at the University of Northern Iowa:

The Leisure Services Division envisions a world where people are accepted and valued for their strengths and abilities rather than the way they look, speak, think, or live their lives. To that end the Leisure Services Division strives to prepare students to meet the challenges of a diverse world through empowerment and diversity. In a rapidly changing world, it is critical that each individual be empowered to take charge of their lives and assist others; this philosophy is based on the concept of fully valuing selves and others . . . and is committed to studying and learning about differences . . .

Rules and Regulations   The rules, regulations, policies, and procedures within an agency or organization serve as its agents of action. Some regulations and rules are mandated by law, and agencies should actively promote the ideals of affirmative action.

Equal Employment Opportunity (EEO) regulations. Equal employment regulations require that leisure service organizations eliminate all existing discriminatory conditions whether purposeful or inadvertent. The regulations further require the examination of employment and other policies to make sure that they do not operate to the detriment of persons in terms of ". . . race, color, gender, national origin, religion, age, marital status, disability or handicap status, veteran status, sexual orientation, or any other extraneous consideration not directly related to performance."

Affirmative Action. Affirmative action refers to proactive efforts to achieve a diverse workforce. It often makes use of goals to increase participation of underrepresented groups. It also requires the leisure services organization to do more than ensure employment neutrality—it must attempt to recruit, hire, and advance qualified group members who were previously excluded.

Title IX. In the United States in 1972, Title IX of the Educational Amendments Act was passed to ensure equal rights for girls in sports at any agency or program that received federal support. Shortly after that time, girls' involvement with physical activity skyrocketed. Leisure services organizations should promote the ideals of Title IX, ensuring that both girls and boys may engage in activities as they wish.

Americans with Disabilities Act (ADA). The Americans with Disabilities Act (ADA) "establishes a clear and comprehensive federal prohibition of discrimination against persons with disabilities in private sector employment and ensures equal access for persons with disabilities to public accommodations, public services, transportation and telecommunications" (Stein, 1993).

The ADA has a broad scope and impacts building contractors, service providers, employers, and others. Individuals within leisure services organizations must plan accordingly in terms of building modifications, programming, employment, and other relevant factors. Of interest and importance to those in the leisure services profession are the edicts that state and local governments shall not

- deny a qualified person with a disability the opportunity to participate or benefit from services (every opportunity) available to people without disabilities;
- provide opportunity for a qualified person with a disability that does not equal the opportunity for those without disabilities;
- offer less effective opportunities to the disabled;
- provide different or separate aids, benefits, or services for people with disabilities, unless such are necessary to make services available and enjoyable;
- aid or perpetuate discrimination;
- deny a person the opportunity to serve on a board or committee;
- select sites that result in the exclusion of people with disabilities;
- administer testing, licensing, or certifications that discriminate, or
- charge a higher fee or surcharge to a person with a disability for the cost of delivering services in compliance with the ADA.

The ADA also states that state and local governments shall

- make reasonable accommodations for a qualified person with a disability to enable the full enjoyable use of services, programs, and facilities; and
- administer services, programs, and activities with the most interaction possible.

As mentioned, those providing public access and accommodations (most leisure services agencies and organizations fall into this category) may need to change rules, policies, and practices to enable persons with disabilities equal access to services. Transportation and architectural barriers may require adaptation, and the program delivery may require alteration.

Policies, Procedures, and Practices Administrative policies and leisure service practices require periodic scrutiny to determine their relative impact on issues of diversity. This is sometimes referred to as a *cultural audit* and is one way to conduct an internal review of policies, procedures, and norms to determine their impact on perceptions of diversity acceptance (Dreachslin, 1999; Jordan, 2001). These issues affect such elements as:

- personnel recruitment, employment, and promotion;
- program development, implementation, and evaluation;
- facility use;
- registration for programs;
- promotional techniques, materials, and avenues;
- accessibility, both considering the buildings themselves as well as accessibility related to location of facilities;
- the times that programs are offered;
- fee structures; and
- in-service and ongoing educational opportunities for staff.

Methods of Communication Individuals from different cultures and different ethnic groups have unique methods and styles of communication. For example, many Anglo-Americans are frank, direct, and look other people in the eye. Individuals from some other cultures may find this disconcerting. For example, in Japan it is rude to begin talking business immediately. It is more appropriate to speak to one another first about personal matters, such as family, establishing personal contact, and then move on to business topics. Different cultures also have different personal space needs and other communication considerations. Table 15.3 presents information regarding a number of communication patterns to help the leisure services administrator or manager communicate more effectively with diverse constituents and employees.

Staff Development Model The administrator or manager can arrange for a number of staff development activities to support diversity. Effective orientation programs, ongoing staff-development programs, release time to attend off-site diversity training, and other types of staff development serve as appropriate tools. Table 15.4 presents a model for staff training based on a review by Edginton (1991) of the diversity training programs of several top U.S. corporations and PAC 10 universities.

The model offers a comprehensive list of topics; the leisure services administrator may select those relevant to the organization's needs. The topics include: benefits and challenges of diversity, affirmative action and EEO, trends, cultural awareness, managing diversity, maximizing benefits, and minimizing challenges of diversity. Leisure services organizations should have a consistent, ongoing program of diversity training in order to (1) continually reinforce commitment to and support of diversity; (2) ensure continuity of training, expectations, and goals across the entire organization; and (3) ensure that all employees have access to informed supervisors and managers.

Actions Related to Diversity in "Best" Organizations In addition to adhering to defined rules, regulations, policies, and procedures and engaging in staff development, other actions can be taken to promote diversity. Hayles (1989, 1996), consultant to a num-

TABLE

15.3 COMMUNICATION PATTERNS: A POTENTIAL SOURCE OF MISCOMMUNICATION

The way in which individuals use words, the way they interact physically in terms of touch, their attire, and other factors can influence communication—they can even be a source of communication problems between individuals. Effective intercultural communication depends on knowledge and awareness of the factors that underlie communication within different cultural groups. Some of the factors that may cause communication problems follow:

Use of words. Cultures differ in how they use words. For example, some cultures do not like to use the word "no" or to say "I don't know." In some Asian cultures, an individual would not want to say "I don't know" if asked for directions by a passerby and might attempt to circumvent the original question, rather than just saying "I don't know." In addition, some words may have more than one meaning, opening up the possibility of miscommunication. Some cultures use many emotional phrases, and others make great use of adjectives. Some cultures consider it rude if a conversation does not start out with an exchange of personal information and questions before business is discussed.

Tone of voice. The tone of voice used for communication may vary from culture to culture. Some cultures speak loudly, some softly, some in a monotone. In some cultures it is appropriate to speak very softly to those in authority; in other cultures this appears as a sign of weakness. For example, some Chinese dialects, have a wide range of tones from high to low, with the meaning of words changing as the tone of voice changes.

Type of attire. Different cultures place greater or less emphasis on formality of attire, modesty of dress, and other factors. Americans are fairly casual in much of their attire. In some cultures, immodest dress serves as grounds for abusive verbal or physical action by passersby.

Degree of physical contact and personal space. Different cultures are comfortable with varying degrees of touching and amount of personal space. Some cultures are very comfortable with touching, and women or men hold hands in public. Some cultures like to be in close proximity to others, with little distance between them while talking; others feel more comfortable if a speaker is at least a few feet away.

Facial gestures. The meanings of facial gestures may change from culture to culture. In particular, eye contact has different impact in different cultures. For example, direct eye contact may mean interest and attention to one culture, but may be a sign of disrespect or a direct challenge in another culture. For some cultures it is not appropriate to make eye contact in public. The degree of animation of the face when communicating may vary greatly between cultures.

Body gestures. Different cultures vary in types of body movements—slow and deliberate, tense and highly directed, fast-paced, or relaxed and social. Certain gestures may also be expected. For example, removing one's shoes in Japan or bowing at an appropriate level to show respect are two such expected gestures.

Characteristics of speech. Different cultures may communicate differently in terms of the speed of speech, the degree of feedback to communication, the degree of directness and frankness of communication, and use of silence. Whereas in the American culture, silence may be perceived to be an insult, in other cultures, silence may be a form of individual privacy or may indicate a feeling of well-being and fullness of life. In addition, in American culture laughter usually indicates happiness; however, in some cultures it may be a sign of embarrassment or loss.

Differences in communication between cultures requires consideration of the impact such factors have on the communication process. Within the leisure services workplace, as different cultures attempt to communicate with one another, individuals must realize that these differences exist and will affect the communication process. An effective organization offers informational vehicles that address communication patterns within the workplace so that communication can be enhanced.

---

ber of major United States corporations, presents a list of actions that are being carried out by what he terms the "best" organizations. These actions range from events celebrating diversity, to outreach, pay for performance regarding diversity (e.g., pay for attending diversity training), organization-supported networks, diversity councils, and others. Table 15.5 presents this list of actions that leisure services professionals can apply throughout their agencies.

15.4 SUGGESTED STAFF DEVELOPMENT TOPICS CURRICULUM MODEL: MANAGING FOR DIVERSITY

I. Benefits and challenges of diversity

Valuing diversity. How does diversity enhance the leisure services organization's synergy, productivity, and impact?

Benefits and challenges of diversity. What does the leisure services manager need to know to effectively meet the challenges and reap the benefits of a diverse workforce?

Manager's role. How is the leisure services manager's role different when managing diversity as compared with implementing Affirmative Action and EEO?

II. Affirmative Action and EEO

Compliance issues. Management problems and issues associated with compliance/lack of compliance with affirmative action and EEO laws that impact upon the workplace: Guidelines for the leisure services manager, definition of terms, legal framework.

Policies and practices. How does diversity relate to organizational policies and practices?

III. Trends analysis: Workforce 2000

Workforce 2000. The emergence of demographic trends that will offer opportunities/challenges to the leisure services manager.

Diversity issues in the workplace. New management methods and approaches that can be used to respond to Workforce 2000 issues in a way that enhances the leisure services organization.

IV. Cultural awareness

Perceptions and worldview. Helping the leisure services manager solve problems related to employees' different perceptions and worldview, based on age, ethnicity, background, religion, gender, and other variables.

Increasing cultural awareness. Strategies that the leisure services manager can use to increase cultural awareness among employees—values, communication styles, stereotyping, accommodation styles.

Critical issues. Helping the leisure services manager become informed about critical issues related to different groups—gender, race, disability, age, religion, and others.

V. Managing diversity

Applications. What the leisure services manager can learn and apply from other organizations, models of multicultural development and cross-cultural management.

Tools. Available tools to help the leisure manager assess needs related to diversity: Employee/management surveys that assess needs, interests, attitudes.

Supporting diversity. What the leisure services manager can do to promote the values of diversity within the organization: Supporting diversity through mentoring, merit structure, management of the formal and informal organization, cross-cultural skills and communication.

VI. Maximizing benefits and minimizing challenges of diversity

Setting goals and objectives. Helping the leisure services manager set program goals and objectives to maximize benefits and minimize challenges related to diversity.

Source: S. Edginton, "PAC 10 Higher Education Institutions: Training for Managers in the Area of Diversity," 1991, University of Oregon.

Leveraging Pluralism for Competitive Advantage Pluralism or diversity can be leveraged in a way that benefits the organization in terms of competitive advantage (Hayles, 1996). This author notes that the advantages of supporting pluralism or diversity work occur on two levels:

> The goal of pluralism work at a *personal level* is to create an environment in which everyone feels included and valued—just as they would if they were among people they considered to be like themselves. The goal of pluralism work at the organizational or *systems level* is to leverage diversity to achieve exceptional performance. The work recognizes similarities and differences while focusing on unity without uniformity.

TABLE

15.5 SUGGESTED ACTIONS TO PROMOTE DIVERSITY

Diversity: What Are the Best Organizations Doing?

- Pay for performance regarding diversity
- Strong affirmative action
- Organization-supported networks
- Mandatory diversity training at all levels
- Line leadership
- Diversity councils, boards, and task forces
- Outreach, interns, scholarships
- Events celebrating diversity
- Address more than protected classes
- Address both organizational climate and numbers
- Develop internal talent to do lead work

From Robert Hayles, 1989, Arizona Affirmative Action Association 14th Annual Conference. Phoenix, AZ. Reprinted by permission of Robert Hayles.

A list of six advantages of pluralism or diversity work within organizations, as adapted from Hayles (1996), includes the following: personal effectiveness, responsiveness to social and demographic changes, promotion of fairness and equity, avoidance of related litigation, productivity, and profitability. These advantages are described in more detail in table 15.6.

An organization that has implemented many recommended actions for organizations employing "best" practice is the Digital Equipment Corporation. Practices of this business related to diversity within its Finance organization may be applicable to other types of organizations, including leisure services organizations. Within its Finance organization, Digital Equipment Corporation has achieved 50 percent hiring goal for the past three years, has an active People of Color Leadership Forum, and a mentoring program. The company has also organized and implemented a worldwide diversity conference attended by company employees (see table 15.7). In addition, Digital Equipment Corporation has an award program to recognize employees' efforts related to pluralism or diversity work within the company.

Diversity and Leadership

Leadership and programming, the most visible functions of leisure services organizations, exhibit the important commitment to diversity and celebration of differences. Program design, leadership, marketing practices, and other aspects of leisure services make continual statements to the public about values and belief structures.

Leadership Considerations for Diverse Groups Face-to-face leadership holds many opportunities to directly impact the lives of leisure services customers. Leisure services professionals must examine verbal and nonverbal customer treatment, ways of showing respect, and the inadvertent perpetuation of stereotypes through behaviors and programs.

If leisure services professionals promote only basketball to African American youth because "that is all they want," discourage girls from participating in football because they might

TABLE

15.6 ADVANTAGES OF PLURALISM WITHIN ORGANIZATIONS

Personal effectiveness. People who learn to live and/or work in integrated settings develop stronger interpersonal, communication, and negotiation skills. Employees become more effective inside and outside of the workplace.

Response to social and demographic changes. Social and demographic changes when ignored lead to reduced effectiveness in social and government services and mixed opportunities for business growth. Organizations that become more multilingual and multicultural will be the most successful in the global marketplace; those that accurately predict change and embrace it will outperform their competitors.

Fairness and equity. When individuals or groups perceive that they have been treated unfairly or inequitably, they seek justice. Peaceful means are used when people feel that they will be listened to; more disturbing approaches are taken when people feel they are not being heard. Pluralism creates a climate of fairness and equity for all.

Litigation avoidance. Lawsuits are painful as well as expensive. Fear of litigation is a powerful but unhealthy motivation for promoting workforce pluralism. It is reluctantly included here only because it reflects reality.

Productivity. Well-managed, diverse teams typically outperform homogeneous teams in terms of quantity, creativity, and quality of results. Diverse teams see more aspects of each issue and make fewer mistakes. For example, the team with a Spanish-speaking member would not try to market a car called "Nova" in Spanish-speaking countries where "no va" translates to "no go." Complex problems are best solved by multidisciplinary or cross-functional teams.

Profitability. The profitability case for pluralism has become increasingly clear. Investment clubs of women and men significantly outperform clubs composed only of men. When the five-year, ten-year, fifteen-year, and twenty-year financial performance of companies engaged in pluralism and related progressive human resource work is compared with the performance of those that are not doing such work or are doing it poorly, the former companies significantly outperform the latter in terms of sales growth, profit growth, and performance in a downturning economy.

Source: Hayles, 1996

---

get hurt, discourage boys from entering a ballet class because the other children might tease them, have user fees so high that many cannot afford the cost, or allow children to call each other derogatory names, then they are not meeting professional obligations. Examples of how professionals can respond to the dimensions of diversity follow:

- Use pictures of people who are old, young, in wheelchairs, girls, boys, and of a variety of racial and ethnic backgrounds in literature.
- Structure user fees to meet the needs of people from different economic backgrounds.
- Assist with community celebrations of religious and cultural holidays (e.g., Martin Luther King Day, Kwanzaa, Rosh Hashanah, Cinco de Mayo, see figure 15.3).
- In skill-development programs, particularly sport programs for youth, use equipment that equalizes ability levels (e.g., t-ball instead of baseball, bowling ramps).
- Monitor behaviors that perpetuate sexism (or any type of ism). For example, when a young girl gets hurt we tend to nurture her, bandage her, and give her a hug before sending her back to play. When a young boy gets hurt, we tell him to "stop crying, it's not that bad," pat him on the back, and send him out. All hurt children need nurturing.
- Watch language when leading groups (e.g., when asking that people sit cross-legged on the floor, ask for people to sit cross-legged on the floor, not "Indian style").

These examples show how cultural sensitivity among leisure services customers and staff can be increased. Professional obligations require the provision of a sense of safety—physical,

15.7 SUPPORTING PLURALISM AND DIVERSITY WORK: A PARTNERSHIP BETWEEN LINE AND STAFF

Patricia Adams, Human Resources Manager supporting the Finance organization at Digital Equipment Corporation (Maynard, MA), describes the efforts of the company in the area of diversity from the perspective of the Corporate Controller's organization:

We have a strong and sustained hiring effort in our Financial Development Program that supports diversity with a fifty percent hiring goal set and achieved for the past three years. There are five female vice presidents in Finance, two of whom are officers of the Corporation.

The Finance function has an active People of Color Leadership Forum, a U.S.-based organization which meets with the CFO quarterly and advocates for senior people of color in the Company when senior level positions become available. A mentoring program is in place where senior managers are matched with junior staff to ensure that people of color have access to informal rules and other information that helps them operate successfully. Finance also sponsors Digital's participation in the National Black MBA Association Convention, this year in New Orleans.

On a broader note, Ron Glover, Director of Corporate Employee Relations at Digital, recently organized a worldwide diversity conference, attended by Company line, staff, supervisors and administrators from sites in the U.S., Europe, and Asia Pacific. The conference had the effect of building a unified vision in the area of diversity by helping to clarify definitions and re-energizing and re-focusing the efforts of the Company towards its diversity goals.

Successful action in the area of diversity at Digital takes a *champion,* and Human Resources has been that champion. It also takes *supporters,* and line people in Digital's Finance function support diversity in their groups. We engage active and sustained support for diversity in Finance.

Clearly, many of the methods and concepts used by this company can be applied in other settings to offer effective institutionalized support for diversity.

In recognition of heritage

A celebration to recognize and strengthen contributions to the unity, preservation and development of the African family, community and culture, will take place on the Northern Iowa campus for the first time this Thursday.

Kwanzaa—Swahili for "first fruits"—is an African-American holiday conceptualized 26 years ago by Dr. Maulana Karenga of Los Angeles. The idea was to develop a non-religious holiday for African-Americans which did not center around a "hero," but did honor and commemorate the heritage.

Although Kwanzaa is scheduled as a one-day event at UNI, the holiday is traditionally celebrated December 26th to January 1st. Through the week, each day focuses on one of Kwanzaa's Seven Principles: umoja (unity), kujichagulia (self-determination), ujima (collective work and responsibility), ujamaa (cooperative economics), nia (purpose), kuumba (creativity), and imani (faith).

Symbolic items, such as candles of different colors, fruit, and a unity cup, are usually placed at the family meal table to represent the struggles and achievements within the heritage and to foster family discussion in this area.

Jim Johnson, director of the Ethnic Minorities Cultural and Educational Center, notes that while Kwanzaa symbols and rituals are rooted in African tradition, at the same time, they are meant to address the concerns of urban-based black people living in 20th century America.

KWANZAA

A CELEBRATION OF FAMILY, COMMUNITY AND CULTURE

Thursday, December 3
7:00 p.m.
Maucker Union Expansion
Food, Music, Entertainment

Kwanzaa is free
and open to the public.

Sponsored in part by:
Ethnic Minorities Cultural
and Educational Center,
Union Policy Board,
UNI Entertainment Committee,
Ethnic Student Senate,
and the Office of the
Vice-President of Academic
Affairs.

**Funded in part by
Student Activity Fees.**

Figure 15.3

Kwanzaa: An event celebrating diversity

emotional, and psychological—to all potential constituents. The professional must also facilitate programs and environments that encourage all customers to freely choose their leisure experiences.

Impact of Leader Expectations   In addition to examining how people are addressed and how their needs are met at the direct-service level, recreation and leisure leaders will want to examine their own expectations of others. According to Scales (1991), "Large and small scale data alike show that African American, Latino, Native American and Alaska Native youth believe that their teachers and [leaders] do not expect much of them." These low expectations often translate into low performance. Bannon (1973, p. 53) notes:

> In every successful . . . program with youth, a major reason for success was that the . . . [leaders] . . . *expected* the youth to do well, involved them in the planning and implementation of the program, learned as much about the youths as possible, and held him [her]self responsible if the program[s] failed.

This comment about leader expectations of youth may be extrapolated to leader expectations of all participants. As the leisure services professional works with diverse groups, he or she should examine how "leader expectations" might affect the quality and character of the interface between leader and participant. The degree to which the leader has high expectations and standards for *all* people will influence the success of programs and services.

Equity Issues: Actions Speak Louder Than Words   A number of important equity issues involve the role of the leader and his or her impact on diversity. A leader imparts values, either intentionally or unintentionally. No situation is value-free. Therefore, the leader must carefully consider his or her values and their impact on others. Five leadership issues follow:

Customer composition. The leadership of programs and activities should resemble as closely as possible the composition of the organization's constituency. Customers, particularly youth, need leaders who resemble them as role models.

Dialogue. The way in which the leader speaks to participants impacts the comfort level of the interaction. Leaders should interact with youth in a variety of ways, using different types of dialogue—not just the traditional Anglo-Saxon forms of greeting.

Leader tone and body language. Estimates suggest that an individual's words have an impact of just 7 percent on the listener while the other 93 percent of communication results from body language, tone of voice, and other factors.

Consistency. The leisure services leader must be consistent with rewards and negative consequences. Participants pick up on inequitable treatment based on race or other factors.

Program choices. The leader's choices in terms of programs, activities, and events that promote diversity have great impact.

These and other factors demonstrate the leader's influence in providing a creative climate that benefits all individuals. Table 15.8 presents additional guidelines for the leisure services leader in terms of respecting the cultural differences of participating youth. (Note: These same guidelines can be adapted and used to facilitate interaction between leisure services managers and their employees.)

TABLE
15.8 LEADERSHIP GUIDELINES FOR THE LEISURE SERVICES YOUTH LEADER RESPECTING CULTURAL DIFFERENCES

1. Get to know youth.
2. Take the time to learn about the culture(s) of youth.
3. With sensitivity to cultural values, get to know youth as *individuals* who may or may not fit the norms of their culture. Do not make assumptions or judgments based on stereotypes or cultural generalizations about their group.
4. Adapt policies and practices to allow for cultural differences. Make room for treating youth fairly and equitably while respecting their different motivations, values, styles, and traditions.
5. Help youth communicate with one another to understand their cultural differences and to work more productively together.
6. Understand your own culture and the assumptions that result from your upbringing. Learn about your cultural influences, your assumptions of others, as well as the assumptions others have of you.
7. Build on individual and cultural differences to enrich the creativity and productivity of your youth center.

Source: Originally developed by the University of California at Los Angeles: Office of Affirmative Action and Diversity Education, *Understanding and Managing a Diverse Workforce,* October, 1990. Adapted by S. Edginton, University of Northern Iowa, 1993.

Use of Language Language—whether verbal, symbolic, or written—affects people. Professing belief in equal rights for everyone, but taking no action when racial or other slurs are used by others sends a contradictory message. If "silence is complicity," then ignoring injustice makes one an accomplice to it—and as guilty as the offender. Verbal language includes terms used to describe people (guys, gimp, hick), their titles (Ms., Mr., Mrs., ma'am, sir), and general references to people by position or job title (the director as he, the secretary as she, fireman, policeman). Terms can perpetuate the system of inequities; helping others reach their full potential requires care in naming and identifying others.

The leisure services profession also uses symbolic language—logos on team T-shirts, graphics on promotional literature, and photographs in annual reports. Do those logos, graphics, and photographs represent society at-large in a positive fashion? Do they promote a feeling of inclusion? Do they help to break stereotypes and the attendant biases and prejudices? How are the graphics and logos we use perceived by those in the general public?

Leisure services professionals use the written word extensively in annual reports, fliers, staff manuals, and newspaper announcements. Rules posted in facilities and posters help motivate people in the healthy use of leisure. Does the language invite all segments of society? Does it encourage participation by everyone? Is it exclusionary by omission? Continual examination of language helps to promote an atmosphere of inclusion and welcome.

Diversity Programming: Building Self-Esteem

A number of programs and activities can be selected by the leader to promote and support diversity. These activities contribute to fun and enjoyment, and they help build self-esteem and respect for others. A well-developed program of activities related to diversity involves all constituent groups. Cultural celebrations, special events, arts and crafts, food, music, dance, and books can all be used by the leisure services programmer to support diversity.

Esteem-Building Activities Feelings of prejudice toward others often occur in persons who do not feel good about themselves. *Camp Adventure*™ Youth Services has developed materials that offer instruction for self-esteem-building programs and activities that support positive interaction. Table 15.9 presents several small-group activities that support diversity and promote the building of self-esteem. A good programmer engages in research and uses a variety of sources to build a repertoire of culturally and ethnically relevant activities within all programs.

Program Design for Individuals with Disabilities

Schleien and Green (1992) suggest a continuum of leisure services options for persons with disabilities. This framework can be adapted for the primary characteristics of diversity. Noninvolvement serves as the first aspect, followed by segregation, integration, and accessibility.

Noninvolvement In noninvolvement, individuals feel barriers of omission (people simply don't think to include them), negative attitudes from others (e.g., "old people shouldn't be here"), and a community or organizational stigma ("gay people are less than whole beings").

Segregation At the segregation level, people may participate in "special recreation" (a somewhat patronizing approach), stay in homogeneous groups (segregated to be with their

TABLE

15.9 ACTIVITIES THAT BUILD SELF-ESTEEM

I Spy, FBI. Youth set up an FBI adventure lab using an ink pad and paper and then conduct a fingerprint investigation. Each youth makes a set of his/her fingerprints. Youth are then encouraged to examine the different fingerprints to see how each person is individual and unique and no two sets of prints are the same (a magnifying glass is useful). The point can also be made that each person not only has unique fingerprints, but that each individual has unique talents and abilities that he/she can bring up to the group. Youth can also use fingerprint art to create individual or group creations or collages.

You Are the Star! Take a picture of each child and then have each child make a poster about him/herself that includes his/her picture within a large star in the middle of the poster. Have the child leave room on the poster for each of the other children to write a positive comment about the rising "star."

Hollywood Minute. Have youth write and produce a video in which each youth has an opportunity to express him/herself. Youth can tell about themselves, their hopes and goals; they can sing or dance or bring items from home that are important to them to tell about and other things that they want to share.

Time Capsule. An extension of Hollywood Minute, Time Capsule has youth reviewing the video that they made about themselves six months later, a year later, or even at a later time. Youth discuss how they have changed, how their goals have changed, and what is important to them both in terms of themselves and others.

You Are Special. Each member of the group, in turn, tells the person who is "it" why he or she is special and what attribute they most admire.

"Me" Baggie. Each youth is given a large, gallon size Zip-lock® bag with his/her name on it in magic marker. They take the baggies home and fill them with things that tell about who they are as people. The bags might include things they collect, treasures, things they have made, their favorite book, a poem. When baggies are brought back to the youth program, youth can share what they have brought. Or baggies can be put on a table, name side down, and youth can guess whose baggie is whose. This activity helps address issues of individual and cultural awareness.

own kind), must have a prerequisite skill development (can be in Special Olympics if a basic skill level exists), utilize segregation as a stepping-stone for personal advancement, and view leisure as therapeutic intervention (people's value improves as they engage in activity).

Integration   Integration has mixed-ability groups (able-bodied and disabled) participating together, a focus on the participating individual, leisure experience as an ongoing process, and views leisure as activity participation.

Accessibility   Accessibility provides for all people to have multiple opportunities and freedom of choice and to interact in an interdependent manner. It allows individuals to experience a self-satisfying leisure lifestyle and views leisure as a state of mind.

Leisure services professionals must examine the leadership and programming functions of their services. Can all skill levels participate to their fullest potential? Do programs, activities, and events reflect the cultural aspects of diversity? Do the activities perpetuate or help to break down stereotypes? In some communities, dwarf tossing is still an acceptable leisure activity. Pseudo-Sumo, a fad in the United States, mocks the religiously based Sumo wrestling. Leisure services professionals must respect their customers—people from all walks of life.

Marketing Practices

Every leisure services organization must market its programs and services in order to survive financially and meet its mission. Many decisions must be made about marketing and promotions; serving all potential constituents requires open and sensitive marketing endeavors. Leisure services professionals must carefully consider marketing to ensure diversity throughout all promotional efforts. Do needs assessments reach all possible constituents? Does newspaper advertising reach both sexes, all ages, ethnic, and different socioeconomic groups? Do the wording, graphics, and photographs used in promotional materials reflect society? Does the professional promote an air of inclusion, of accessibility?

Other Considerations

Other aspects of leisure services can be designed to enhance commitment to diversity. Leisure services professionals must consider the various constraints to leisure and attempt to mitigate them. For instance, adequate, inexpensive, and convenient or on-site child care eliminates one barrier to full and free participation in leisure for women with children, or single parents. Similarly, leisure programs and facilities should consider the scheduling needs of both nine-to-five workers and those employed with shift work. Those who work nontraditional hours and days tend to be working-class people with limited economic resources for leisure experiences.

Summary

Leisure services professionals have an opportunity and responsibility to promote diversity. Leisure serves as an excellent vehicle to promote and encourage diversity as it touches the lives of everyone. Leisure, a universal human experience, is perceived as a fundamental human right. The topic of diversity requires a definition of such terms as culture, prejudice, discrimination, and status. Wide diversity exists among cultures and people that encompasses both primary and secondary characteristics. Every society has dominant cultures and subcultures, and leisure provides opportunities to participate in the activities of many cultures while also pursuing activities of various subcultures.

Leisure services professionals must deal with a variety of issues related to diversity. Discrimination issues affect the way people are perceived in society and how they experience leisure. Forms of discrimination—sexism, ageism, ableism, heterosexism, racism, and classism—all ascribe penalties and privileges to individuals. These isms create barriers that prevent individuals from experiencing the freedoms associated with leisure. An organization can counter discriminatory activities by crafting an appropriate mission statement, following sensitive administrative practices and policies, staff development related to diversity, marketing, leadership, and programming.

The celebration of diversity is more than a social responsibility. It encourages proactive response to individual needs and facilitates leisure experiences through careful planning. Interestingly, the discovery of our differences also reveals common ground—activities differ, but people find similar benefits such as joy, freedom, and happiness.

Discussion Questions

1. Why is the pursuit of diversity important to leisure services professionals today?
2. Define the concept of culture and identify leisure values, norms, or attitudes that influence it.
3. Identify three individuals who are members of three distinct subcultures and profile their unique leisure characteristics.
4. Identify forms of leisure in which you have personally experienced some form of discrimination in terms of racism, ageism, sexism, heterosexism, ableism, or classism. Describe the situation.
5. Identify the primary and secondary dimensions of diversity that most directly impact your life. How has your leisure been affected by these traits?
6. Locate a community leisure services agency and profile any programs that promote the concept of cultural diversity. How are those programs determined? How do they impact the community? How do they affect the subcultures they are intended to serve?
7. Select a leisure services agency and ask the director how s/he keeps its programs free of the many forms of discrimination.
8. Develop a mission statement for a leisure services organization that promotes cultural diversity.
9. List fifty leisure activities or events that promote the celebration of diversity within Canadian and U.S. culture.
10. Using the model presented by Schleien, discuss how to implement leisure services options for a person with disabilities.

References

Ameristat. 2000. Minority statistics in the U.S. [available on-line at http://www.ameristat.org].

Amir, Y. 1976. The role of intergroup contact in change of prejudice and ethnic relations. Edited by Phyllis A. Katz, in *Towards the Elimination of Racism,* New York: Pergamon Press.

Bannon, J. 1973. *Outreach: Extending Community Service in Urban Areas.* Springfield, IL: Charles C. Thomas.

Digital Equipment Corporation. n.d. Corporate Finance Newsletter.

Dreachslin, J., and J. Saunders. 1999. Diversity leadership and organization performance. *Journal of Healthcare Management* 44(6), 427–439.

Edginton, S. R. 1991. *PAC 10 Higher Education Institutions: Training for Managers in the Area of Diversity.* University of Oregon, Eugene, OR.

Goldberg, M. 2000. Conflicting principles in multicultural social work. *Families in Society* 81(1), 12–21.

Guirdham, M. 1999. *Communicating Across Cultures.* West Lafayette, IN: Ichor Business Books.

Hayles, V. R. 1989. Arizona Affirmative Action Association 14th Annual Conference. Phoenix, AZ.

Hayles, V. R. 1996. *Leveraging Pluralism for Global Competitive Advantage,* December 9, 1996, Effectiveness/Diversity. Arden Hills, MN.

Healey, 1997. *Race, Ethnicity and Gender in the United States.* Thousand Oaks, CA: Pine Forge Press.

Henderson, K. A., M. D. Bialeschki, S. M. Shaw, and V. J. Freysinger. 1996. *Both Gains and Gaps: Feminist Perspectives on Women's Leisure.* State College, PA: Venture.

Jordan, D. 2001. *Leadership in Leisure Services: Making a Difference.* 2d. ed. State College, PA: Venture.

Knouse, S., and M. Dansby. 1999. Percentage of work-group diversity and work-group effectiveness. *The Journal of Psychology 135*(5), 486–494.

Kurtz-Costes, B., and E. Pungello. 2000. Acculturation and immigrant children: Implications for educators. *Social Education 64*(2), 121–125.

Kraus, R. 1994. *Leisure in a Changing America.* New York: Macmillan.

Loden, M., and J. Rosener. 1991. *Workforce America!: Managing Employee Diversity as a Vital Resource.* Homewood, IL: Business One Irwin.

McIntosh, P. 1991. White privilege: Unpacking the invisible knapsack. *Matrix,* 5–6.

Naylor, L. 1998. *American culture: Myth and reality of a culture of diversity.* Westport, CN: Bergin & Garvey.

Nieto, S. 1992. *Affirming Diversity: The Sociopolitical Context of Multicultural Education.* New York: Longman.

Pelled, L., K. Eisenhardt, and K. Xin. 1999. Exploring the black box: An analysis of work group diversity, conflict, and performance. *Administrative Science Quarterly 44*(1), 1–28.

Scales, P. 1991. *A Portrait of Youth Adolescents in the 1900s.* Carborro, NC: Center for Early Adolescents.

Schleien, S., and F. Green. 1992. Three approaches for integrating persons with disabilities into community recreation. *Journal of Park and Recreation Administration 10*(2), 51–66.

Stein, J. U. 1993. The Americans with Disabilities Act: Implications for recreation and leisure. Edited by S. J. Grosse & D. Thompson, in *Leisure Opportunities for Individuals with Disabilities: Legal Issues,* 1. Reston, VA: AAHPERD.

CHAPTER  16

Future Trends

Leisure experiences often involve inter-generational activities. A grandfather shares his wisdom with his grandson who reflects his hope for the future.

Introduction

Forecasters study present movements and trends to make projections into the future. Examining current issues and attempting to forecast their impact has great value to leisure services professionals. Current issues in the United States and Canada influence the local provision of services, agency missions, and understanding of participant life satisfaction as it relates to leisure services.

Information and projections about future trends enable leisure services professionals to rethink and reexamine many aspects of their organizations—business practices, program offerings, scheduling, promotional strategies, and facilities maintenance. Similar to weather forecasting, a knowledge of trends offers practitioners information about new opportunities, pitfalls to avoid, potential problems regarding consumers, new twists to the provision of services, and environmental concerns. In addition, trends can redefine the nature of leisure services, helping to determine whether leisure services should operate from a social service perspective, an entrepreneurial approach, have a youth or adult focus, or simply provide leisure opportunities.

Milani (2000, p. 59) offers a perspective of the potentials that may be available in post-industrial societies. As one can see viewing these scenarios the opportunities for improving life satisfaction in knowledge-based economies is evident. The opportunity to expand the potential of individuals through additional opportunities for learning, democracy as well as continued development of the human culture all would be available in this future scenario.

- A new role for human creativity in production
- Mass production for "higher" or non-material needs
- The potential for information to displace both cog-labor and physical capital from direct production
- The new importance of quality in production

420

- The centrality of consumption and end-use in economic planning
- The technological extension of our minds and nervous systems through new electronic hypermedia
- The new centrality of learning to work and life
- The strategic role of organizational factors in economic life
- The emergence of more culturally defined social movements with more qualitative concerns
- Growing mass pressure for an end of all forms of domination, that is, an end to all restrictions on human-potential development; class, sexism, racism, and so on
- Growing potential—pressures—for direct democracy and popular participation
- The reemergence of aesthetic, nurturing, and intuitive/mythic sensibilities into the mainstream of human cultural development
- The birth of an unprecedented global culture and human species-consciousness, which paradoxically emphasizes the importance of cultural roots and diversity
- The emergence of new forms of individuality—particularly holistic, non-dependent identities—based on equality, cooperation, and self-development
- The new importance of biological science, and of biological/ecological organization as a metaphor to model social and economic activity

As one can see, these tendencies create opportunities for greater enhancement of life through leisure experiences. They also call for the reorganization of our economy from an industrial one to one that is built on concerns of our professions related to ecological and environmental issues. In other words, they represent a call for a "green economy"; a merging of cultural concerns related to the human condition and integrated with ecologically sensitive practices.

This chapter examines trends within society, including social trends, health trends, environmental concerns, educational issues, technological influences, and economic trends. We discuss environmental issues, such as resource depletion, overuse of outdoor recreation areas, and ongoing conflicts between the economy and the environment. The educational arena also holds new trends in the public educational system, effects of desegregation and open enrollment, and the impact of varying levels of education on the future of leisure and life satisfaction. Consumer-friendly technological changes greatly impact society in both positive and negative ways. Globally, as well as locally, evolving political situations affect leisure services. Economics also affect every aspect of leisure services and life satisfaction.

Social Trends and Leisure

A host of social influences will impact leisure in the future. Social conditions in society influence the lives of individuals—relationships with others, the use and perceptions of leisure, the relationship of leisure to work, spatial arrangements in living conditions, and the way people live and interact with each other and with the environment. A number of social trends influence leisure, including shifts in population patterns, changes in family composition, changing social roles, greater equality for women, the blurring of public and private involvement in leisure, and increased diversity.

Population Shifts

The world population, continuing to expand rapidly, will dramatically impact society—including leisure patterns and opportunities—for decades to come. The world population was 6.1 billion in 2001 and is projected to grow to 7.8 billion by 2025. Further, projections suggest the world

A Visit in the Future

The year is 2035, and you look marvelous for someone your age. How old are you now, anyway? Watching your diet and exercise have really paid off. Even so, it's easy to look good—considering the company you keep. Your apartment complex is full of elderly baby boomers.

Still you like it here. People look out for one another. Many residents live alone, so you make a point of checking up on your older and more fragile neighbors. The apartments are comfortable and easily accessible, even for the oldest tenants. Outdoor safety lighting illuminates the ramps that lead to sheltered entrances. Levered handles make it easy for both elderly and younger people to open doors when their hands are full of packages. Of course, these are modest apartments. In more upscale neighborhoods, retired boomers have voice-activated entry systems.

Inside ample skylights let in the sun during the day and the stars at night. Good lighting is increasingly important to you, because your eyesight began weakening sometime after your fortieth birthday. Your apartment has floor lighting that automatically turns on whenever you get out of bed in the middle of the night. But this feature is now common in many homes, especially those with young children.

Like many older Americans, you are living with a chronic health condition that impairs your strength and mobility. Fortunately, your home is stocked with hair brushes, back brushes, wash cloth holders, and other grooming products that have long, angled adjustable handles. Your clothing has easy-to-manipulate fasteners, such as ring-pull zippers and self-adhesive fasteners.

Comfortable clothing has become more fashionable, so you don't feel conspicuous in your easy-care smock. After all, it is 2035—there are 130 million Americans aged fifty and older and 45 million Americans under age ten who wear these things. Millions of pregnant women, younger adults with disabilities, and people temporarily disabled by accidents or illnesses also find these clothing features desirable. Still, you're old-fashioned. It annoys you that many children grow up without ever learning how to tie a shoelace.

You started this morning with a refreshing bath in a tub designed for safety and easy access. Those old-fashioned tubs—the kind that helped make the bathroom one of the most dangerous rooms of the house back in 1994—have been outlawed. Special electronic outlets, slip-resistant flooring, and water sources that cannot run too hot or too cold have minimized risks in all homes built after 2010. An electric-powered, adjustable height toilet makes the bathroom comfortable for you and your younger guests. And even though your commode-mounted minishower and blow dryer were designed back in the 1990s for people who have difficulty with personal hygiene after toileting, the system is now common in most homes.

Your kitchen is filled with the latest appliances. There's a smooth-top range with burner lights that indicate when burners have not yet cooled down, even after being turned off. Everything is the right height and designed for easy maintenance. But you don't cook much. Why bother, when microwaveable dinners are so good and nutritious? Besides, you're too busy. Those computer skills you learned at work are still an important part of your life in retirement. You even do a little consulting work. With all your years of experience, why not?

You never did stop learning. Telecommunications make it easy for you to attend classes on anything you like, shop from the convenience of your kitchen, and regularly consult your doctor or nurse practitioner in the privacy of your own home.

It's ironic that most technology that helps make your life so comfortable in 2035 was available way back in the 1990s. However, few marketers saw the potential of these products. Some said that older people would never use advanced technology. But then came entrepreneurs who redesigned the technology to suit the older consumer, and made billions. Hearing aids are a good example. Models of the 1990s helped people hear better but they were never meant for people with arthritic hands or visual problems. They were hard to insert, clean, and replace batteries, so a lot of people never wore them.

Now that boomers are older, most assistive technology isn't stigmatized by the label "handicapped." Instead it is used by people of all ages to make their lives safer and easier.

population will reach 9.0 billion by 2050. This can be compared with 1970, when the world population was 3.9 billion.

As of 2001, there were 31 million Canadians with more than 75 percent living within two hours of the Canadian/American border. The population of Canada is expected to rise to 36 million by 2025 and 40.2 million by 2050. In the United States, the population stood at 283 million in 2001; this exceeded estimates which suggested that by 2000 the U.S. population would reach 268.3 million. The annual growth rate in the last decade was 1 percent. Although the populations continue to rise, both the Canadian and the U.S. rates of population growth diminish slightly each year (Famighetti, 1995; Law, 1995). This section of the book discusses some of the factors related to population patterns—an aging society, changing leisure needs, rising immigration, and others.

Middle-Aging of America   One prominent trend related to social structure is changes in population patterns. The rising median age of the population in the United States shows an increase in the proportion of Americans over the age of seventy-five, an increase in the proportion of middle-aged Americans, and a decline in the proportion of children and young adults (Law, 1995). Figure 16.1 illustrates the middle-aging of the United States. As the population bulge increases in age, leisure service professionals must respond to changing needs. People from the baby boom generation have entered middle age with expectations for leisure and life satisfaction that may differ from traditional models of leisure services (Kelly and Godbey, 1992). Traditional services focus on youth and have a social service perspective; baby boomers remain active, have different needs than youth, and demand greater accountability from service providers. Canada also shares many of these concerns.

Changing Leisure Needs   Enculturation is the impact of social and cultural influences—including parents, peers, religion, school, and other institutions—on the interests and desires of a people. Baby boomers have been enculturated to expect a variety of both work and leisure experiences. They expect experiences that involve risk, solitude, large groups, personal satisfaction, the out-of-doors, and technology (Godbey, 1989; Kelly and Godbey, 1992; Kraus, 1994). People continue to seek these diverse stimuli even as they age. Leisure services

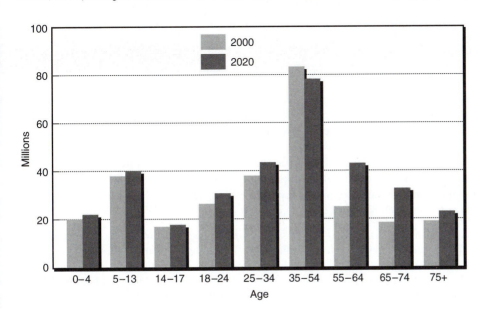

Figure 16.1

America Entering "Middle Age" —a surge in the number of people aged 35 to 45: 2000 to 2020

professionals face increasing challenges to provide for these interests. In addition, participants of all ages demand quality experiences customized to their individual needs; this expectation will grow for the baby boom generation, particularly in retirement years.

Dramatic Increase of Older Population   Proportionately, older Americans will show the most dramatic population increases (see figure 16.2). Between 1960 and 1990 there was a tremendous shift in the population. This shift will continue as the "baby boom bulge" (that is, individuals born between 1946 and 1964) moves through their life span. Currently, these baby boomers represent one-third of America's population. In 2011, the baby boom generation will turn sixty-five. At that point, there will be a tremendous surge in the number of individuals, with growth for the population aged sixty-five to seventy growing by 74 percent between 1990 and 2020. This can be contrasted with the population under the age of sixty-five, which will increase only by 24 percent (U.S. Bureau of the Census, 1999). Overall, individuals are living longer, birthrates are declining, and people are waiting longer to have children. Those within the aging population generally experience better health than earlier counterparts, remain active longer, and have more discretionary income than ever before. These trends show a need for leisure practitioners to serve this growing population in a relevant manner. As most people age, participation in some activities declines while participation rates in other activities increase. Active participation in some sports may decrease, as may involvement in high-risk outdoor activities (Kelly and Godbey, 1992). Travel, television watching, and involvement in less active outdoor activities tend to increase with age.

In addition, as people age, they may lose physical strength and often live alone due to loss of spouse or partner. Therefore, older people tend to have greater concerns about safety, social interaction, and predictability in their lives, including their leisure, than younger consumers. This has implications for leisure providers in terms of staffing, programming, and facilities. For example, avoiding late evening programs, providing transportation to and from recreation facilities, providing well-planned programs, and involving participants in preparations will help to accommodate the growing older population.

Shifts in Population Distribution   Another population issue or trend involves the distribution of people across the United States and Canada. In the continuing flight from the effects of poverty, lack of health care, violence, and other social problems, the population continues to shift away from urban to suburban areas. More than 75 percent of U.S. citizens now live in urban areas; only 24 percent of Americans live in rural areas (U.S. Bureau of the Census, 1999). The continuing influx of immigrants into the United States and Canada also results in changing cultural influences and impacts leisure, health concerns, and social needs. Language, employment, education, health, and other social issues must be addressed, as well as the provision of relevant, accessible leisure services to these individuals.

Overpopulation   Increased life expectancy, lower infant mortality rates, increases in immigration, and other factors underlay a continuing rise in population. This dilemma impacts the environment, the economy, education, and life satisfaction of people everywhere. The following excerpt from Davidson (1993) discusses world population trends:

> From the beginning of creation to 1850 A.D., world population grew to one billion. It grew to two billion by 1930, three billion by 1960, four billion by 1979 and five billion by 1987, with six billion en route. Every 33 months, the current population of America, 256 million people, is added to the planet. . . . The present is crowded and becoming more so. . . . When John Kennedy was elected president, domestic population was 180 million. It grew by 70 million in one generation. Our

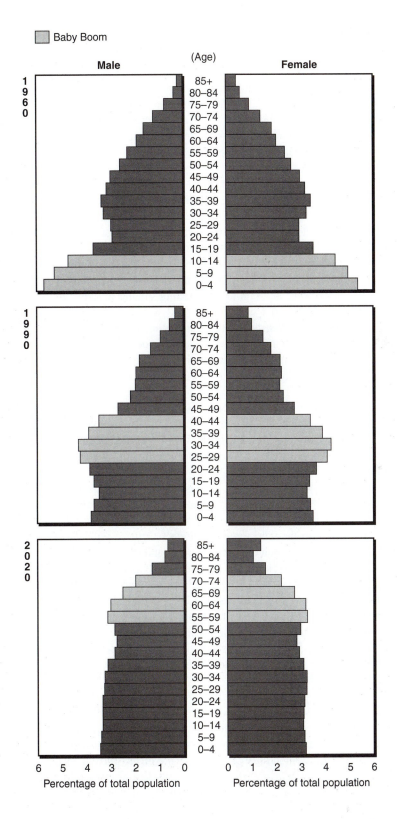

Figure 16.2

Population age structure: 1960 to 2020

Source: U.S. Bureau of the Census.

growing population has not dispersed over the nation's 5.4 million square miles. About 97 percent of the U.S. population resides on 3 percent of its land mass. Half of our population resides within 50 miles of the Atlantic or Pacific Ocean. (p. 8)

Many countries are making excellent progress toward zero population growth, yet increased longevity and declining infant mortality rates offset some of these achievements. Many attribute contemporary social ills—rising health problems, increasing violence, poverty, and starvation—to overpopulation. Leisure professionals in urban and suburban areas are challenged to respond in new ways to the needs of people in these areas.

Changes in Family Composition/Family Concerns Many issues affect life satisfaction, including economic status, personal health, and family status. The nature of the family has changed over the years and continues to evolve (Kraus, 1994). Once believed to consist of a homemaker (mother), breadwinner (father), 2.3 children, a pet, and ready access to an extended family, "family" is now recognized to mean different things to many different people. Families may consist of one parent, two parents, two parents of the same sex, stepparents, older parents, grandparent heads of households, and adoptive and natural children. Single person households are on the rise, and families are getting smaller in size, with an increase in step-families and blended families.

The evolution of the family structure has tremendous implications for leisure services professionals. Children often are unattended during nonschool hours; the latch-key child has become the norm. The changes in family structure have altered the design and implementation of family programming. Child care has become a necessity for people from all walks of life.

Increased Numbers of Latch-Key Children It is predicted that nearly all children in the six- to twelve-year-old age group in the United States will need out-of-school care within the decade. Currently, it is estimated that 1.3 million latch-key children, in the five- to fourteen-year-old age group, care for themselves during nonschool hours (United Way Strategic Institute, 1992).

Availability of quality child care is an increasingly important issue. In 1996 it was reported that over 7 million children of working parents receive child care each month. In addition, 60 percent of women with children younger than six, and 57 percent of women with children younger than three, were in the workforce (Children's Defense Fund, 1996). At the same time studies noted that only one in seven child-care centers and one in ten family care homes were of good enough quality to enhance children's development (Children's Defense Fund, 1996).

Low-cost supervised after-school programs have become critical to the functioning of the family unit. Without such programs children are left unattended to watch television, play video games, and perhaps engage in other less-than-healthy leisure-time alternatives. Leisure services organizations should carefully examine the escalating need for these programs as well as the provision of wholesome, safe, and supervised before- and after-school leisure services. There is also a need for programs for youth that teach them life skills to help them operate independently and make healthy decisions.

Changes in the Extended Family Twenty or thirty years ago one could count on the support and nurture of extended family members. Many family units lived in fairly close proximity to relatives, making child care and family leisure more broadly defined. In the nineties and beyond, the tremendous capacity for travel has moved many out of immediate reach of other family members. In earlier decades families often sought one another for support, love, and leisure; people now turn to themselves and their immediate family and community for such support. Often, grandparents, aunts, uncles, and cousins are no longer available for family-based leisure (Kelly and Godbey, 1992; Kraus, 1994). Provision of leisure programs that facilitate social interaction, including interaction among different generations, is increasingly important to the social health of individuals.

Reevaluation of Family Structure   Evidence reveals that people are beginning to reevaluate and appreciate the importance of the family (Aburdene and Naisbitt, 1992). It is suggested that despite the changes and apparent upheaval in family structure, children of working mothers do not suffer (Aburdene and Naisbitt, 1992). In fact, according to Aburdene and Naisbitt, these children hold less sex-stereotyped views of the world, have fewer behavior problems, and are healthier than children of stay-at-home mothers.

Changing Household Composition   The composition of households/families continues to change and evolve. Married-couple families represented 56 percent of all households in 1990 and decreased to 53 percent in 1998 (U.S. Bureau of the Census, 1999). The traditional family households with children remained relatively constant between 1990 and 1997 with 71 percent of family households with children in 1990 and 69 percent in 1998 (U.S. Bureau of the Census, 1999). The average size of households continues to decline; in 1970, the average size was 3.14, and it was 2.62 in 1998 (U.S. Bureau of the Census, 1999). Although married-couple families still represent the largest units, nonfamily households and single-parent families have increased. Between 1990 and 1998 the percentage of nonfamily households only increased by 2 percent, from 29 percent to 31 percent. There is a continued need for leisure services that respond to the needs of families as well as the needs of single-parent and nonfamily households. In 1998, 26.3 million people lived alone. This was an increase of over 8.1 million people when compared with 1980. Leisure services programs that promote interaction with others may be a way to meet the needs of this portion of the population.

Changes in Social Roles

Social roles include behavior patterns defined by expectations, norms, customs, and rituals of society. Society in the United States and Canada continues to evolve as people and institutions come to new understandings of the world. Social roles, currently being rewritten across the globe, suggest that people will not necessarily embrace the social roles of the past.

A great example of changing social roles is the infusion of women into the political arena. Canada, for the first time, elected a female prime minister. While still low, in overall numbers the United States now has more women in the Senate and more female state governors than ever before. This trend is projected to continue (Aburdene and Naisbitt, 1992).

Shifts in Gender Roles   Significant changes have taken place in the definitions of social roles for women and men. Women have entered the paid workforce in great numbers and will stay there. As depicted in figure 16.3, the workforce will be divided almost equally between men and women. In 1988, 45 percent of the workforce were women, and 55 percent were men. By 1998, the percentage of women had increased to 46 percent, and it is projected that by the year 2008, 48 percent of the workforce will be women and 52 percent will be men. Today, most women work out of economic necessity, although some work to retain a sense of self and individuation. The shift in gender roles also has resulted in increased leisure opportunities for women. Both women and men recognize the place of leisure in helping to define one's sense of self and adding richness to life.

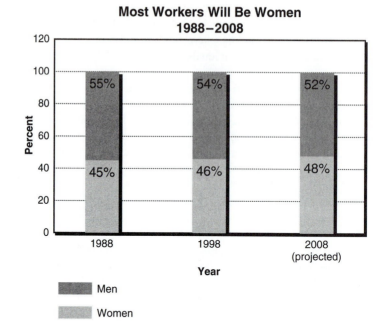

Figure 16.3

Percentages of women and men in the workforce

Source: Data from The Bureau of Labor Statistics, the U.S. Department of Labor.

Most Workers Will Be Women
1988–2008

Year

Men

Women

Men also have new avenues for self-identification. Stay-at-home dads, "men of the 90s" who share in domestic life, and fathers who equally value work and family life are on the rise. Men and boys are finding it increasingly socially acceptable to engage in a variety of leisure experiences without the worry of gender-role appropriateness.

Elder Issues   With the graying of the population and the loosening of gender role restrictions, the issue of family care becomes increasingly complex. Elder care now joins child care on the list of family needs. With two working parents, longer expected life spans, and decreased mortality of those with severe physical and mental impairments, care issues can become complicated (Henderson, Bialeschki, Shaw, and Freysinger, 1996). Rising health-care costs may make it commonplace for an elderly parent to receive care in the home of adult children. The leisure needs of the care-giver and the care-receiver will require consideration by leisure services professionals.

Linear Life Pattern   In the past most people lived a rather linear life pattern and experienced a similar sequence: childhood, part-time work, full-time work (at the same job for years), family, and retirement. In previous generations most people followed a specific, predictable pattern. One graduated from high school, went to college, took a job, got married, bought a house, had children, continued to work (often in the same work environment with the same company), and then retired (to Florida or Arizona). Today people tend to drop in and out of school, change careers three or four times, postpone childbearing until later in life, have several partners (some in marriage, some as significant others), and retire into new jobs (Kelly and Godbey, 1992).

As job definitions change, family structures fluctuate, and as the economy necessitates, more people will enter and leave the workforce many times, change jobs in the search for self-fulfillment, and raise separate families. The entering and leaving of the workforce exposes individuals to a variety of experiences and people. Leisure interests and opportunities also change during the different stages of life (Kelly and Godbey, 1992). The intensity with which a person pursues leisure interests varies, depending on the ebb and flow of life patterns.

Greater Equality in Sports and Athletics for Women

The general desire for equality for all continues to drive changes in the nature of leisure experiences. In the past decade, girls have grown up with relatively equitable opportunities in sports and athletics in public school. More women are demanding equal access to collegiate athletic teams than ever before. As women become involved and successful in sports, athletics, and other activities, the image of women as strong, capable individuals able to compete may help to open doors for women and girls in areas such as business, personal relationships, politics, and leisure.

Title IX   Aburdene and Naisbitt (1992) report that in the 1990s women made up the majority of new participants in weight training, cycling, and basketball. Nearly one-half of new golfers each year are women. Although Title IX, the law forbidding sex discrimination in schools that receive federal funding in the United States, was passed in 1972, only recently has its enforcement taken place. Women and girls will reap the benefits of Title IX in coming years. The exposure to skill development and training in school years opens many leisure opportunities for girls and women.

College Athletics   Women now participate in college athletics in record numbers (Aburdene and Naisbitt, 1992). The top ten sports for women in college include basketball, volleyball, tennis, cross-country, softball, track, swimming/diving, soccer, field hockey, and golf. Women also seek out nontraditional sports and activities. The first women's ice hockey tournament was held in 1990; weight lifting is becoming the choice of recreational activities for many women, as are rugby and boxing.

Adventure travel for women has positive repercussions in other areas of women's lives. Women now engage in coed and all-women's trips. The support experienced on all-women trips may empower female adventurers to expand their leisure activities to new traditional and nontraditional leisure roles.

As women's leisure experiences impact and influence other aspects of their lives (e.g., career, family), society will experience further change. As women seek careers for experience, rather than jobs to fill time, they gain increased economic parity with men. More discretionary income can result in more spending for leisure activities (Aburdene and Naisbitt, 1992; Henderson et al., 1996).

Blurring of Public/Private Involvement in Leisure

The blurring of public and private sectors in the provision of many human services (Kelly and Godbey, 1992) results from increased private involvement in social issues and an increased state involvement in private issues. Currently, a shift from institutional responsibility to individual responsibility is taking place.

Cooperation between Public and Private Sectors   Changes will occur in the roles of the public and private sectors in the provision of leisure services. More private agencies will become involved in what is now considered the responsibility of public agencies—services for those below the poverty line, at-risk youth, those with long-term health-care needs, and the like. Several examples of cooperative ventures in leisure services follow:

> The City of Portland (Oregon) Park Bureau entered into negotiations with Sea World to lease land in support of the development of a theme attraction—Sea World would build the amusement park on undeveloped public park land. A portion of the funds generated from the revenues would return to the city, which would, in turn, use these funds to develop and maintain the park land adjoining the Sea World facility. While this public-private venture did not come to fruition, it serves as an example of the potential opportunities that exist when government and business collaborate.

> The *Camp Adventure*™ Youth Services program provides an example of an entrepreneurial program operated within a public institution, the University of Northern Iowa. *Camp Adventure*™ Youth Services program, run much like a business, receives no tax subsidies and must generate its own revenues to sustain its operations. Its major partners include other public agencies, particularly the U.S. Armed Forces. This model of cooperation between two different types of government agencies has resulted in many mutually beneficial program services and relationships.

> AquaArena, a theme park located adjacent to Southwest Texas State University and purchased by the university with state funds, continues to be operated as a revenue-producing venture. In addition, it serves as a laboratory for the biology, archaeology, and recreation management departments. Similarly, the city of Santa Clara, California, in order to preserve open space from industrial development, purchased the Great America theme park when its sale to developers was imminent. These two examples show how private organizations and public bodies can work together to meet both the needs of the community and the natural environment. In both cases, the private organizations recouped their investment.

As these examples indicate, individuals and organizations now accept greater responsibility for social actions, becoming active where they once had little impact.

Increase in Diversity

The increased diversity in U.S. and Canadian populations carries over into the workplace, with more people of color, women, older persons, and person with disabilities entering this arena. This phenomenon accentuates the need for culturally sensitive leisure organizations. Recent years have seen an increase in hate crimes and overt prejudice, while a resurgence in pride related to ethnic and racial identity has also taken place. Leisure services professionals must anticipate the needs and expectations of people from a variety of cultural backgrounds. Standard mechanisms for the provision of programs, customary games and activities, and underlying assumptions must change.

Increase in Number of People of Color   The race composition of the United States is changing dramatically. In 2000, 72.3 percent of the population were White. The Black population represented 12.7 percent and the Hispanic population, 10.2 percent. American Indians, Eskimo, and/or Aleut made up 0.87 percent of the population. Asian or Pacific Islanders represented 3.8 percent of the population. It is estimated by year 2015 that one-third of Americans will be from a minority group (see figure 16.4). Sometime around the year 2050, all of the so-called minorities will together surpass in numbers the current Anglo majority. Indeed, the term *minority* will essentially lose its meaning. Our children or grandchildren will live in a society where, in today's terms, everyone will be a minority (Yzaguirre, 1998). Further, by 2050 it is projected that the proportion of the White population will decrease by 60 percent, the Black community will increase slightly, the number of Asians will increase tenfold, and Hispanics will almost triple their numbers (Nieto, 1992). Diversity has been significantly influenced by immigration; within the last decades of this century, immigration has played the

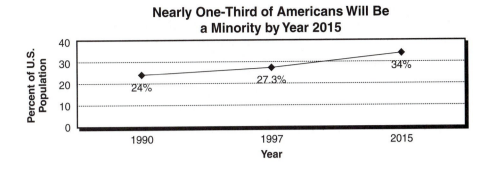

Figure 16.4

Projected minority percentages

Source: Population Reference Bureau. 1999. United States Population Data Sheet.

largest role in the growth of our population since the beginning of the twentieth century (U.S. Bureau of the Census, 1999).

Leisure services organizations will have both a more diverse constituency and a more diverse staff. Obviously, leisure services delivery systems must prepare to respond to changing population patterns. The future calls for a responsive delivery system, with effective programming, personnel, administrative practices, and facility-usage policies.

Increase in Women in the Workplace Currently women represent 59 percent of all *new* workers entering the workforce (Law, 1995). As indicated, it is projected that women will constitute 48 percent of the workforce by the year 2008. This influx of women will contribute to the projected increase of diversity within organizations. As more women enter the workplace, their leisure needs will change. Additional issues regarding child care, latch-key programs, and other support services will require action by leisure services organizations.

Increase in the Proportion of Older Individuals The dramatic increase in the proportion of older individuals has implications for leisure programs and services, as well as staffing. The number of people sixty-five and older who will opt to remain in their jobs should increase in the next decade, partially due to the fact that Congress banned forced retirement in 1986.

Opportunities for Individuals with Physical Disabilities As the Information Age shifts the national perspective from an industrial to a service economy, society places greater emphasis on knowledge than on physical ability. Computer-aided technologies allow individuals with physical disabilities to compete more effectively for employment within organizations, including leisure services organizations. In addition, the Americans with Disabilities Act will continue to have significant implications for this group, both in terms of work and leisure opportunities.

Progress for Those Who Live Alternative Lifestyles Steps have been taken to ensure equal rights for individuals who live alternative lifestyles. While controversial dialogue continues, equal rights deals with issues related to these groups of individuals (i.e., gay, lesbian, and bisexual youth and adults) so that they may reach their potential in terms of work, service, family, and leisure.

To meet the needs of an expanding constituency, leisure services professionals must understand diversity. Differences in religion, education, socioeconomic status, sexual orientation, race/ethnicity, ablebodiedness, and the like have become more widely accepted. As leisure services professionals address diversity in administration, programming, leadership, staffing, and facility use, the field of leisure services will begin to provide appropriate services for people with special needs such as the homeless, recovering substance abusers, gang members, survivors of sexual assault, the unemployed, and youth of various sexual orientations.

Health Trends and Issues

Health issues concern the continent as the gap between the haves and have-nots increases. Fewer people can afford health-care costs, and health-care reform has become the issue of the decade. People turn to leisure and physical activity as a way of maintaining personal health and fitness. Increasing numbers of insurance companies provide rate reductions to organizations that have a no-smoking policy, random drug testing, and employee-provided recreation and fitness programs.

With no cure nor successful long-term treatment yet found, HIV infection and AIDS continue to be at the forefront of health concerns, placing increased burdens on the public health-care system and stretching the imagination of leisure services providers. Leisure services providers may react to the increasing numbers of home-bound ill by providing services in homes. Despite concerns about substance abuse, addictions to drugs and alcohol will probably rise. Job stress, recognized as a detriment to health, will call for leisure in the management of stress. This section of the chapter discusses a number of health issues in relationship to leisure, particularly trends related to physical and social health. Many of these topics have an extensive impact on youth and society at large.

Changes in Physical Health

Both positive and negative changes have taken place in the physical health of U.S. citizens and Canadians. Issues related to physical health include a rising incidence of substance abuse and consequent costs to society, fitness concerns, the increasing problem of AIDS and HIV infection, a decline in youth fitness, health-care issues, and the rising stress level of all people.

Increase in Cardiovascular Fitness Leisure services organizations can offer programs and services that improve people's health and physical quality of life. The development and availability of new treatment methods, along with a commitment to a healthier way of life, have cut the deaths of Americans from heart disease by more than a third, and from stroke by one-half (Wilkinson, 1989). Clearly, greater awareness and increased leisure values related to fitness and well-being have influenced this phenomenon.

The U.S. Surgeon General's report *Physical Activity and Health* suggests the importance of vigorous physical activity for all Americans. Despite common knowledge that exercise is healthful, more than 60 percent of American adults are not regularly active, and 25 percent of the adult population are not active at all (Surgeon General, 1996).

Increase in Costs of Substance Abuse Leisure services professionals often deal with substance abuse by providing information and supervision. Substance abuse, including drug abuse, alcohol abuse, and abuse of tobacco, continues to plague Canadians and U.S. citizens. Newspapers have estimated that substance abuse in the workplace costs taxpayers over $100 billion a year.

Continued Interest in Wellness　Leisure services organizations serve as important vehicles for improving people's health and wellness through diet, information, and exercise. Studies indicate that most U.S. citizens are overweight, and show a clear link between poor diet and lack of exercise and heart disease and other ailments. As a result, Americans now recognize that proper diet and exercise contribute to better health. Many individuals eat healthier foods and participate in physical activities—often offered by leisure service organizations—that contribute to their fitness and well-being, including jogging, aerobics, water aerobics, fitness clubs, swimming, and various sports activities.

Increase in AIDS　Some leisure professionals have begun to disperse information to young people about AIDS within youth centers and youth programs. Statistics regarding AIDS and HIV already cause great concern and will become even more alarming in the decades to come. AIDS-related issues, such as discrimination, the rights of non-infected individuals and other issues, will impact leisure services. Worldwide, 34.3 million people are living with HIV/AIDS. Since the beginning of the AIDS epidemic 18.8 million individuals have died. In the United States at the end of 1999, 733,374 AIDS cases have been reported to the Centers for Disease Control and Prevention. Although the majority of these individuals were White (43%), since 1996, when calculated in absolute numbers, Blacks have outnumbered Whites in diagnoses and deaths. It has been reported that as many as 4 million Americans may carry the human immunodeficiency virus that causes AIDS.

Dramatic Decline in Youth Fitness　A 1990 national commission report states that "for the first time in the history of this country, young people are less healthy and less prepared to take their places in society than were their parents" (p. 6). This has obvious implications for leisure services organizations and their role in helping youth improve the state of their physical health (National Commission on the Role of the School and the Community in Improving Adolescent Health, 1990). Again, the Surgeon General's report notes that 65 percent of American adults are not regularly active, and 25 percent, not at all. The report suggests that sustained periods of vigorous periods of activities for at least twenty minutes, three or four days a week is desirable. To build support for healthy exercise and vigorous lifestyles, the report calls on schools, community agencies, parks, recreational facilities, and health clubs to be involved in the effort.

Rising Health-Care Costs　Although not directly linked, rising health-care costs will impact leisure services organizations. Between 1980 and 1997 health-care costs increased from $247.3 billion to $1.0 trillion. In recent years the annual percentage of change has declined for health-care costs. For example, between 1985 and 1990, the change was 11 percent. On the other hand, the change between 1996 and 1997 was 3.7 percent. The percentage of federal public expenditures has increased from 68.7 percent in 1980 to 72.4 percent in 1997 (U.S. Bureau of the Census, 1999).

Increased Stress/Increase in Employee Assistance Programs (EAPs)　Increased stress, a symptom of the 1990s, will continue as an issue that requires attention in people's work and leisure experiences into the twenty-first century. Most of the nation's

500 largest companies had instituted some type of Employee Assistance Program (EAP) to assist employees with stress and other health-related matters (Wilkinson, 1989). Some attribute rising stress to the unstable economy, gender shifts in the workplace, the changing nature of work, and other factors. The changing nature of families, with more women juggling home and work responsibilities, also contributes to higher stress levels for both men and women.

Changes in Social Health

Both positive and negative changes have occurred in the social health of U.S. citizens and Canadians. Issues related to quality of life, social health of youth and adolescents, materialism, and random violence stand at the forefront of discussion.

Increased Interest in Quality of Life/Balance   Positive actions toward better social health increase along with concern for the quality of life. People will make decisions about work, family, and leisure based on quality of life issues—a balance of work, family, a healthy lifestyle, and time for self. Many corporate workers now opt for more family or self-time instead of an increase in salary. As Robinson notes, ". . . quality time will become a status symbol and a luxury item" (1991, p. 23). In this study, Robinson (1991) also found that respondents take salary reductions in order to get more time off, and the findings cut across all segments of the workforce. Most individuals agreed that having free time is as important as making money.

Leveling Off or Continued Increase of Teen Pregnancy   Teen pregnancy rates go through cycles of leveling off and rising. Teen pregnancy rates increase as young people search for excitement, instant gratification, and something to fill the love-and-belonging void. In 1998, the birthrate was 48.0 for every 1,000 teenage girls in the fifteen- to nineteen-year-old age group. This is a decrease in the number of births per thousand for teens in this age grouping. In 1993, the figure stood at 56.5 for every 1,000 teenaged girls in the same category. For example, birthrates for White teenagers declined from 52.8 in 1991 to 46.8 in 1997 (U.S. Bureau of the Census, 1999) and for Black teenagers from 115.5 in 1991 to 89.5 in 1997. Children giving birth to children leads to increased needs for child care for young mothers, and adapted leisure opportunities. The leisure lives of young parents are severely disrupted. Leisure education and services that provide meaningful programs will help these youth. Leisure professionals must determine their view of leisure—as an instrument of social change or experience for its own sake.

Youth At Risk: A Dramatic Decline in Social Health   The social health of youth has deteriorated dramatically, and projections anticipate continued decline into the twenty-first century. Social health of youth includes such factors as success in school, being substance free, and other behaviors that are in accordance with social mores.

At least 25 percent of American adolescents in the ten- to seventeen-year-old age group are at "serious risk" of not becoming successful, productive adults, and 25 percent are at "moderate risk" for this outcome (Dryfoos, 1990). According to this source,

> *Youth at-risk* are those youth that exhibit behaviors that are associated with such factors as delinquency, substance abuse, adolescent pregnancy and dropping out of school/school failure. These types of *high-risk behaviors* are related to low achievement motivation, poor school performance, antisocial behaviors and conduct disorders, lack of parental supervision and support and living in areas of economic deprivation (p. 25).

A recent study found that the number of twelve- to seventeen-year olds using marijuana nearly doubled between 1992 and 1994; 28 percent of 1994 high school seniors said they had binged on alcohol recently (Children's Defense Fund, 1996). According to a study by the Fordham Institute, the social health of youth in the United States dropped almost 50 percent within the last twenty years (Jennings, 1989). This has strong implications for leisure service organizations, which have traditionally played an important role in improving the social health of constituent youth.

It is important that leisure services professionals be aware of the factors that put youth at risk, as well as strategies that can be used to help youth *build assets and reduce deficits* to increase the likelihood that they will engage in healthy, positive behaviors. There is a need for all agencies and organizations within each community to improve systems of service delivery, coordinate services, improve public policies, and enhance the climate of public support.

Continued Concern Regarding Violence and Drug Use   According to the Bureau of Justice Statistics, crime is high, but it remains steady. It will continue to be a problem of concern and high priority as the generation of those born between 1961 and 1982 ("Generation X") reaches maturity. Domestic violence, and violence among children and against the elderly will continue to be issues of importance. According to the Children's Defense Fund (1996), homicide is the number one cause of death among Black and Latino fifteen- to twenty-four-year-olds, and the third-leading killer of Whites in that age group. In addition, approximately 99,342 juveniles were arrested for violent crimes in 1997. This represents a slight increase from 1990 when the figure stood at 97,103 (U.S. Bureau of the Census, 1999). However, total crime between 1990 and 1997 in all areas among juveniles has increased from 196,526 arrests in 1990 to 292,883 in 1997 (U.S. Bureau of the Census, 1999). Most alarming is the increase in arrests among juveniles for drug abuse. Where in 1990 the arrest record was 66,300, in 1997, there were 154,540 arrests among juveniles for either the sale or manufacture of drugs. Arrests for possession of drugs among juveniles has increased from 41,725 in 1990 to 116,225 in 1997 (U.S. Bureau of the Census, 1999). Those engaged in away-from-home leisure activities in high-risk areas will see safety as a primary concern. Leisure services professionals offering evening and nighttime activities must address growing concerns about personal safety. Hate crimes are also increasing. Leisure services may "return to its roots" and help manage the social ills of the time. Leisure services, such as tourism, will continue to be negatively affected by violence in the area.

Increase of Materialism   The Roper Organization (1987) notes that materialism has achieved a new high. The organization indicates that "The 'good life' now requires 'a lot of money' (according to more than six in ten Americans, up from four in ten in 1975), as well as a job that pays more than the average" (p. 20). Whereas people preferred an interesting job over a high-paying one in the 1970s through the mid-1980s, both now rank as equally important, and things that money can buy now rank higher in importance than they did in 1981. As people recognize that the world has finite resources, however, the "good life" may be redefined to come from a balanced life rather than the accumulation of goods.

Return to a More Relaxed Lifestyle   According to a Time/CNN poll (1999), seven in ten people surveyed said that they would like to "slow down and live a more relaxed life." In addition a number of respondents, six in ten, indicated that "earning a living today requires so much effort that it is difficult to find time to enjoy life." Many individuals today want to focus less on work and more on time with their families (see figure 16.5).

Figure 16.5

The traditional work-life pattern has evolved into a pattern of flexibility, reflecting current lifestyles.

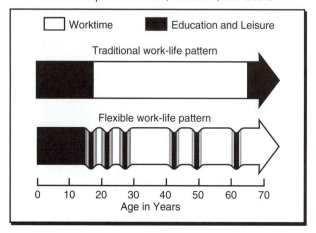

Work-Life Patterns Changing
Traditional work-life path evolving to intermittent periods of work, education, and leisure

☐ Worktime   ■ Education and Leisure

Traditional work-life pattern

Flexible work-life pattern

0 10 20 30 40 50 60 70
Age in Years

Environmental Concerns

Environmental concerns and causes will continue to besiege the United States and Canada. Global warming, acid rain, losses related to biodiversity, and abandoned nuclear waste products will be health and environmental concerns of the decade. Participation in outdoor leisure pursuits will increase (Ibraham and Cordes, 1993). Individuals seeking a return to nature and their roots will place an increased load on the natural world. Designated recreation areas, in particular, may see this factor impact resource quality. Parks will continue to move toward closing their entrance gates once a preestablished visitor capacity has been met. User and entrance fees to outdoor areas will increase and the concern about the rights of all users will mount. Many environmental issues and concerns will continue to be linked to leisure. Political, social, and natural environments are inescapably intertwined. Governmental policies and regulations (or lack thereof) will heavily impact the availability of the out-of-doors for leisure pursuits. Continued logging and mining, particularly in the western states and provinces, may affect outdoor recreation areas.

The essence of the American ethos is subduing or conquering the frontier (Sax, 1980). When the United States was first settled by Europeans, conquering the wilderness drove people to points farther west. Cutting great forests, burning the prairies, and damming rivers and waterways were integral to survival of the culture. Even now, Canadians and U.S. citizens seem to buy into the philosophy of beating back nature and controlling the environment. It increasingly becomes apparent that this philosophy is no longer a viable belief structure. People now know, although they do not always act in conjunction with that knowledge, that subduing the environment results in the decimation of plant and animal species. Leisure services will continue to be severely impacted by human intervention within the natural environment.

Consider these facts that relate to issues of leisure and the environment both now and in the future:

- Canada is bounded by the longest coastline of any nation (150,000 miles).
- As of 2001, there were 364 species identified as at risk in Canada. This is an increase from 193 reported in 1991.

- The United States is the world's largest consumer of energy, consuming 94.2 percent of the world's primary energy (U.S. Bureau of the Census, 1999). Interestingly, the United States only produces 23 percent of the natural gas, 10 percent of crude petroleum, and 21 percent of the coal of the world's production.
- The demand for energy is met primarily by fossil fuels oil, natural gas, and coal. Fossil fuels will supply almost 90 percent of the world's energy by 2015.
- Twenty-four countries in the world rank above the United States in terms of the percentage of land area set aside as protected. However, the actual landmass is the highest in the world with Canada and the United States representing 40 percent of the total protected land area (World Resources Institute, 2000)
- Canada and the United States have 139 and 381, respectively, marine protected areas (World Resources Institute, 2000).
- There are forty-four biosphere reserves in the United States and eight in Canada which are a part of global agreements.
- Canada and the United States have twenty world heritage sites (eight in Canada and twelve in the United States) and operate fifty-three wetlands of international importance (seventeen in United States and thirty-six in Canada).
- Almost 4 million children die each year of acute respiratory infections, linked with indoor air pollution (especially smoky cooking fuels) and outdoor air pollution (especially from industrialization (World Resources Institute, 2001).
- In developing nations, there may be as many as 3.5 million to 5 million acute pesticide poisonings per year due to lack of protection during application, with millions more exposed to lower but still dangerous levels (World Resources Institute, 2001).
- More than 100 million people in Europe and North America are still exposed to unsafe air, and some air pollutants are proving more recalcitrant to control than expected (World Resources Institute, 2001).

Several environmental issues and trends will have an impact on the provision and nature of leisure service outdoor pursuits long into the future. This section of the chapter focuses on the ongoing battles between developers, the preservation of entire ecosystems, the depletion of resources, and the degradation of natural resources.

Development Versus Ecosystems

Ongoing battles will take place between environmentalists and developers who want to use the remaining virgin land and open space for different purposes. People will begin to realize that saving an ecosystem, not just a species, is the key to solving problems of overuse and destruction.

User Conflicts   User conflicts will continue to mount between consumptive (e.g., hunters) and nonconsumptive (e.g., bird watchers) users (Kuzmic, 1992). Consumers will demand environmentally friendly leisure, yet be enticed by high-tech leisure opportunities (e.g., Mall of America). Those who engage in motorized recreation (e.g., motor boats, snowmobiles) will become increasingly at odds with purists (e.g., canoeists, hikers). Resource managers will face more ethical decision-making situations related to rights of use and environmental preservation. Some common examples of this conflict include (1) the draining of wetlands for construction of highways; (2) the near extinction of populations of alligators and crocodiles in Florida to create safe waterparks; (3) the ten-year-long battle to protect an endangered songbird outside of Austin, Texas, where a developer wants to build a housing complex; (4) the destruction of old-growth forests to develop a condominium complex with an ocean view; and (5) the damming of Hetch-Hetchy to develop a recreational water area and adjacent housing and rental units.

Although development versus preservation conflicts have increased, so has the environmental education of Canadians and U.S. citizens. Young people will continue to be educated in issues impacting the environment; one can hope that younger generations will make more earth-friendly choices than previous generations.

Resource Depletion

The continuing patterns of resource depletion (such as the clear-cutting of the virgin old growth forests in the Pacific Northwest) pose a problem when humans continue to take from the environment, but do not put back. This will soon catch the attention of mainstream users—bird watchers, hikers, and picnickers. To preserve resources, people must realize that resources are finite and should be managed rather than collected and used. As trees are cut for timber and paper, new trees must be planted. Slowly, people will understand that using coal and petroleum-based energy sources will result in the eventual disappearance of those resources.

Continued Movement Toward Nonconsumptive Energy Sources

Nonconsumptive energy sources—those resources that do not get used up, such as wind and sun—will be increasingly studied and made available to the general public. People will consume energy and resource-based products but will look for "green" appeal. Use of postconsumer recycled goods will become increasingly mainstream (Zeiger and Caneday, 1991), and ecological harmony will become a major goal. Tourism will increase, by both national and international visitors, with genuine concern that the integrity of the resources be maintained.

Further Examination of Multiple-Use Areas

Conflicts between those who want to recreate in wilderness settings and those who want to explore for natural minerals and gas will rise. While not always the best policy, multiple use—where people can mine for minerals, graze animals, cut timber, and engage in outdoor leisure pursuits—will remain the watchword for outdoor areas (LaPage and Ranney, 1988). Mining in wilderness and backcountry areas will continue to affect those seeking leisure opportunities.

As consumers become more aware of government-subsidized practices harmful to the environment, such as logging on federally owned lands, demands to stop will be made. People will become better educated about the out-of-doors and will understand that clear-cutting (the practice of cutting every tree in an area) also harms wildlife in the area. In British Columbia and Vancouver, bald eagles have nearly been destroyed because of habitat destruction. General awareness will also lead to a reduction in many consumptive forms of recreation.

Environmental Degradation

Continued attention will focus on the degradation of the natural world. For example, climbers used to climb the Himalayan Mountains in clear and pristine conditions. Climbers must now face huge mounds of trash left by other climbers, smell the odors of piles of human waste, and hike through barely recognizable mountain meadows. For several years to come people will continue to love the parks and natural areas to death; then there will be a resurgence in eco- and environmentally sound recreation and tour packages (Caneday, 1991).

New Perspective on Eco-Vacations Eco-vacations, where people volunteer their labor to work in the out-of-doors (trail maintenance, research related to botany or animal life), will soon become "in" forms of leisure experience. Meeting multiple goals for service, socialization, and leisure, these opportunities will expand.

Continued Progress Toward Environmental Responsibility As technology increases, so will the need for outdoor activity. People desire to relate to the natural environment on a personal level. Issues related to recycling, reusing, and reducing will become the norm in most communities across the United States and Canada. The cost of environmental cleanup will continue to be high, and environmental ethics will become an increasingly important topic of discussion (DeGraaf and DeGraaf, 1993). The National Audubon Society has developed travel ethics for the environmentally responsible traveler (World Resources Institute, 1993, p. 151):

1. Wildlife and their habitats must not be disturbed.
2. Tourism to natural areas will be sustainable.
3. Waste disposal must have neither environmental nor aesthetic impacts.
4. The experience a tourist gains in traveling with Audubon must enrich his or her appreciation of nature, conservation, and the environment.
5. Audubon tours must strengthen the conservation effort and enhance the natural integrity of the place visited.
6. Traffic in products that threaten wildlife and plant populations must not occur.
7. The sensibilities of other cultures must be respected.

In addition to developing similar ethics, those in the leisure services profession must properly deal with the use and disposal of commodities and durable goods used in the provision of leisure services. The layout and design of new facilities, maintenance and refurbishing of existing structures, and the impact of programs and services on the environment will become integral to the provision of leisure services.

Ongoing Focus on Global Issues The greenhouse effect and ozone depletion serve as two global examples of environmental degradation. Some scientists indicate that the greenhouse effect, an increase in the average temperature of the earth, comprises the most crucial environmental threat facing the world as it moves into the twenty-first century. Ozone depletion will create an increasing health hazard for human beings. The amount of CO_2 concentrated in the earth's atmosphere has increased significantly—25 percent since the Industrial Revolution. Within the next fifty years, the concentration of CO_2 may again double (United Way Strategic Planning Institute, 1992). This phenomenon may have implications for the provision of outdoor leisure services. Scientists continue to develop less environmentally damaging materials for energy and other needs. For example, fusion is a promising yet remote alternative for future energy needs.

Educational Issues

Changes occurring in educational systems across the continent include a rise in the raw numbers of people receiving postsecondary education. The more education people receive, the higher the likelihood of securing a good paying job and settling in with a career. This results in higher discretionary income to be spent on leisure. In addition, the higher one's level of education, the more exposed he or she may be to different forms of leisure; hence, the greater the potential for diversity in their leisure choices. In the future, people will stay in school longer and will tend to look to leisure as more than just a diversion (Godbey, 1989). An increased concern for ecologically safe leisure will correspond with a rise in education.

People will continue to seek leisure experiences for socialization, excitement, escape, and furthering educational and skill development. Some of the important educational issues to be presented in this portion of the chapter include desegregation and open enrollment, the reduction of school services and alternative uses for school facilities, lifelong education and development, and increased emphasis on higher education.

Desegregation and Open Enrollment

Continued efforts to ensure that public school systems are equitable between areas of high property tax bases and low tax bases will occur. Financial resources of school systems will change as parents and children decide which school to attend. Inner-city schools with diminished human and economic resources will be heavily impacted (Godbey, 1989; Kelly and Godbey, 1992). Shifting teachers and other resources may lead to an unstable educational system, which could affect the quality of education.

Decreased Support for Extracurricular Programs

A lack of adequate resources for schools often results in the elimination of extracurricular activities, many of which are leisure-based (Seefeldt, 1996). In school districts across the United States, battles over funding have led to the reduction or elimination of music programs, art classes, and after-school sport and athletic programs. Classroom activities may be affected as well. If this trend continues, some leisure experiences for young people will require funding through sources other than schools, creating a need for more private and public nonschool-based programs. Several examples that speak to the issue of support and lack of support for extracurricular programs and activities follow:

> In the Department of Defense Dependents Schools System (DoDDS), the school system no longer supports extracurricular sporting activities. For example, Seoul American High School, a secondary school providing educational services to family members of military personnel in Seoul, Korea, dropped its competitive sports program. The Morale, Welfare, and Recreation Services department, the community-based leisure service provider, now operates these programs. In the City of Chicago, the entire high school sports program was eliminated, only to be reinstated after massive fundraising brought in more than one million dollars.
>
> A counter example shows a school that has promoted and, in fact, internalized the importance and value of leisure and after-school activities and committed funds to that end. In the state of Indiana, any youth who tries out for any after-school program makes the team—cheerleading, band, football, and so on. This strategy toward participation and mass involvement promotes the idea that everyone can have a successful leisure experience.

The scaling back or dropping of after-school programs may also result in an increase in the number of at-risk youth—youth with little direction and time on their hands.

According to Wilkinson (1989), the work-life patterns of individuals are changing. Individuals traditionally engaged in education and leisure early in life, work in midlife, and education and leisure again during old age. This pattern, however, is changing (Kelly and Godbey, 1992). Individuals will increasingly have within their life span recurring intermittent periods of education and leisure interspersed with their work life.

Increased Emphasis on Higher Education

Most new jobs will occur in the service sector, so people will need a higher level of education to compete effectively. Estimates project that 75 percent of all new jobs will require some college education.

Educational Reform Educational reform in America will continue to be a high priority. The nature of this reform will be hotly debated. Reform issues that will be on the table throughout the twenty-first century include national education goals, national examinations, school-based or site-based management, school choice, vouchers, magnet schools, charter schools, year-round schools, and others. To initiate an effective interface between school and nonschool programs, leisure service professionals must be informed regarding current educational issues and reforms.

Technological Influences

Technology will have a tremendous impact on the future of leisure services. New and improved equipment, the changing nature of job-related duties, and the creation of new leisure opportunities will result from continued technological development. Of the workforce, 2 percent are involved in agricultural jobs, 16 percent in manufacturing, and the remaining 82 percent in managerial and professional specialties, sales, administrative, and/or service occupations. This is a significant change from 1980 when 75 percent of the workforce were involved in nonagricultural or manufacturing-type positions.

Over the past fifteen years, leisure services professionals have seen the influences of technology on desires, needs, and expectations of leisure consumers. Computer, video, and electronic games have become readily available to the masses. Leisure activities made possible by improvements in technology include in-line skating, karaoke, and virtual reality games/software. Technological advances also have resulted in higher expectations of quality and the ability to respond quickly to changes, needs, and desires of leisure customers.

This section of the chapter discusses the impact of technology on the changing nature of time, systems and innovations/services and equipment, and transportation. As information systems continue to outdistance themselves, and the technological revolution results in increased information access for customers, leisure service providers will need to be responsive and on the cutting edge.

Changes in Time Use

People from western cultures believe that an increase in technology effectively releases additional time from the "time bank," which, in essence, becomes free time. This means that with technological advances, people expect more free time to engage in leisure experiences. Mere advances in technology and information systems, however, do not automatically free up additional time from work and subsistence needs (Kelly and Godbey, 1992). Contrary to popular belief, even with the invention of time-saving devices such as the microwave oven and the desktop computer, people actually have about the same or just slightly more free time than people had twenty years ago.

Changes in Amount of Leisure Time Robinson and Godbey (1997) note that America's leisure (averaged for both men and women) has increased from thirty-five to forty

From Baseball to Ballet?

ometime in the millennial 1990s the arts will replace sports as society's dominant leisure activity. By one measure it already has. A landmark 1988 report by the National Endowment for the Arts calculated Americans now spend $3.7 billion attending arts events, compared with $2.8 billion for sports events. . . . Just twenty years ago people spent twice as much on sports as on the arts. *In less than a generation Americans have reversed their leisure spending habits.*

. . . This dramatic change parallels the shift from an industrial to an informational society and has been accelerated by the coming of age of the baby boomers, a well-educated and . . . arts-loving generation. . . . In Boston, home of the Celtics, Red Sox, and Bruins, *twice* as many people went to the theater, museums, or art shows as attended sports events. . . . Sports still dominate the media, but with increased corporate support during the 1990s, consumers will be able to watch ballet as well as baseball.

Figure 16.6

Changes in leisure and work hours

Source: Data from University of Maryland, 1989.

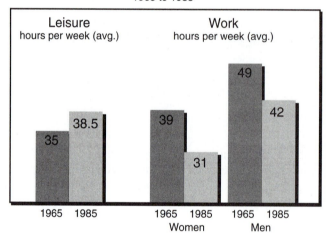

Average Changes in Leisure and Work Hours
1965 to 1985

hours per week. In 1989 America's leisure (averaged for both men and women) increased from thirty-five to thirty-eight and one-half hours per week and the work week for both men and women declined (Robinson, 1989) (see figure 16.6). In further examination of these figures, however, Robinson (1989, p. 34) states, "Men ages eighteen to sixty-four report that they had forty hours of free time twenty years ago," and that they have the same amount today. Women in the same age bracket, however, report an increase in leisure from thirty-four to thirty-nine hours per week. Robinson also reports ". . . that Americans are facing a time famine and that an increasing proportion of Americans say they always feel rushed" (p. 35).

As indicated in chapter 5, Schor suggests that less leisure is available to individuals. Many Americans are driven and unhappy despite the fact that they have achieved success in their work and perhaps even in gains in leisure (Schor, 1993). Further, Junin (2000, p. 71) suggests,

"The pressure of today's life, reinforced by the workplace, economic, social, and political climate, has reduced our quality of life. We live to work and don't work to live." This author suggests that perhaps we need to downshift, simplify our lives, and create a slower pace of life in order to promote greater happiness.

A study of work hours conducted in five countries in 1990 by the Leisure Development Center (Japan), however, reports that the workweek in Japan, the United States, and Great Britain has increased since 1975 and the workweek has decreased in France and the Federal Republic of Germany (1991). Definitions of work, leisure, and other factors may impact on the interpretation of results of the two studies. Most Americans and Canadians, however, feel a sense of time squeeze or time famine. Robinson (1989) notes that quality time will become a status symbol or luxury item as Americans continue to feel overworked and overwhelmed. Also, new standards or lack of resources often push people to do more in less actual clock time.

Fluctuations in Time Availability to Participate in Leisure   The time available to engage in leisure activities continues to change. Once leisure time occurred primarily during evenings after work, on weekends, and during holidays when people took vacations. Now leisure time tends to fall in less predictable time periods (Godbey, 1989; Kelly and Godbey, 1992; Robinson and Godbey, 1997). Work no longer connotes a 9:00 A.M. to 5:00 P.M. availability. People will continue to work varying hours. Weekends will no longer always be one unit of time. More people will have staggered days off from work, thus breaking up the forty-eight- to seventy-two-hour block of time often used for leisure.

The nature of vacations has also changed. In past years, a U.S. or Canadian worker typically started the first year of employment with one week of vacation and, with continued employment, worked up to three to four weeks off. People took these vacation days as integrated packages of time from one- to two-week periods. In the future, the trend for taking a day here and a day there will continue. People will have available more, but shorter periods of time in which to engage in leisure.

Systems and Innovations/Services and Equipment

New technology has resulted in the development of systems and innovations that make services and equipment extremely accessible and user-friendly. Almost anyone can set a DVD player, cook dinner, and teach a child grammar in the privacy of one's home. Children receive exposure to computers in preschool and elementary school and are often computer literate by the time they reach junior high school. The craving for increased sophistication in home toys and educational items is on the rise.

While advancements in technology have positive results, leisure service providers must also consider marginal impacts. These include more "couch potatoes" who sit in front of the television for hours, an increase in sedentary leisure activities, and a potential rise in thrill-seeking leisure. This section considers the increase in use of and access to home-based computers and electronics, improvements in leisure equipment, and improved safety in leisure experiences, and includes the following:

Lifestyle Coaching   There is a growing trend focused on lifestyle coaching. Much of the literature and information available is found in the popular press. An example of this is Martin Kimeldorf's work, *Serious Play: A Leisure Wellness Workbook* (1994). From a historical perspective, Chet McDowell's books, *Leisure Counseling: Selected Lifestyle Processes*

(1976) and *Leisure Wellness: Concepts on Helping Strategies* (1983), provide a foundational basis for this type of work.

Home Electronics   Home electronic entertainment will become less costly and easier to use for the general population (Kelly and Godbey, 1992). The ease with which telecommunications enters the family home will impact leisure and leisure concepts. Many people will opt for the comfort of home-based versions of sporting events and computer simulations. Interactive television and movies will become standard in U.S. and Canadian households. More passive leisure may result in increased needs to experience other sensory activities more fully or to achieve a balance between passive and physically active pursuits.

Improved High-Tech Leisure Equipment   An increase in technology has always had a corresponding increase in new and improved leisure equipment. This trend will continue and these changes will revolutionize the leisure industry. Jet-skis, fiberglass-bottom boats, in-line skates, high-definition television sets, and computer activities all provide new, high-tech, faster, more exciting forms of leisure activity.

New Roles for Commercial Enterprises   Stores have become skill teachers and leisure providers, as well as vendors of leisure equipment and toys. Oshmans Sporting Goods Company has several "super stores" in the west and southwest. Consumers entering the store not only receive assistance from store clerks but can try out a variety of equipment on true-to-size courts. Customers can try on a pair of basketball shoes and then play a pickup game of three-on-three on the in-store basketball court; potential racquetball or tennis players test new racquets in one of the in-store tennis or racquetball courts; a bow hunter can experiment with a new bow or hunting accessories in the target range; and those who want to purchase skis can try them out on the indoor ski slope. Shopping has become a leisure experience in and of itself.

Improved Safety   Increased technology also impacts safety and early skill development in some leisure activities. Alpine skiing, tennis, and golf can now be learned from the safety of an indoor facility with one-on-one instruction, indoor comfort, and cushioned slopes and courts. New materials receive constant experimentation in relation to favorite leisure pastimes. Fiberglass boats, tent poles that are impossible to break, the plastic composites used in lightweight bicycle helmets, and safety ropes and nets devised for safe gymnastics all serve as examples of the benefits of technology on the safety of leisure activities.

Simulated Outdoor Natural Phenomena   With new inroads in commercial reproduction of activities usually found only in nature, some service providers can make them available in any desired location. Wave-tech swimming pools and life-size functional indoor and outdoor ski slopes with snow can now operate in areas and climates that were once incompatible with these activities. These commercially available leisure activities can bring opportunities for instruction and enjoyment to those who could not otherwise participate in them.

Virtual Reality: A New Medium for Leisure   Virtual reality is a technological form that is interactive, visual, auditory, and kinetic. How would an individual like to meet with Susan B. Anthony and have her respond to questions? Or practice baseball pitching, watch the effort on the computer screen, and receive immediate feedback on style and accuracy?

Virtual reality has great implications for leisure, entertainment, self-development, and education. In the future, youth centers may have virtual reality stations rather than video games.

On-Line with Networks An increasingly popular form of leisure activity involves participation in the expanding array of computer network services. Hobby clubs, special-interest groups, investment groups, correspondence between friends, and other types of network opportunities are available to individuals who have a modem, a computer, and who subscribe to one of the network systems. As more individuals purchase computers for personal use, this type of leisure activity will increase. Fiber optics allows for easy and convenient in-home setup.

Organizational Impacts of Technology New strategies and concepts for managing Technological/Information Era organizations are emerging. As we move from the Agricultural Era through the Industrial Era to the Technological/Learning Era, it is necessary to rethink the way that organizations and employees operate, basing systems on new assumptions and rapidly changing technology. A number of new concepts have emerged that relate specifically to the Technological/Learning Era of management.

Just as scientific management theory was formulated to systematize and offer structure to industrial technology, the "learning organization" concept has evolved to provide a foundation for organizations operating within the Technological/Information Era. "Forget your old, tired ideas about leadership. The most successful corporation of the future will be something called a learning organization" (*Fortune Magazine*). Within the Technological/Information Era, it is necessary to put into place organizational systems that facilitate a state of accelerated, independent, and collective learning on the part of individuals within the organization, that is, teaching individuals how to teach themselves.

Information from the sciences—*chaos theory, complexity theory,* and others—is increasingly being applied to management of individuals and complex organizations. A major theme of chaotic and complex systems is that components that may not look related may interact and influence each other (Gleick, 1987). It encourages managers to seek out and incorporate the complexity that exists in organizations. Chaos theory suggests that there are patterns of order that exist beneath the surface of chaos. Seeking the order that is found in these underlying structures and methods of interaction can assist in drawing energy from within any organization.

Transportation

Transportation has a tremendous impact on leisure and related factors; it offers access to leisure opportunities and serves as a leisure experience in itself. Transportation involves water-based transport (boats, jet-skis), ground-based transport (cars, buses, trains, bicycles), and airborne transportation (airplanes, gliders). New technologies will continue to transform transportation (Naisbitt Trends Newsletter, April 30, 1992). In fact, in 1996 the Lockheed Corporation received a multibillion dollar government contract to develop a new space shuttle that will have the capacity to take tourists into space for a few orbits around the earth. The first space tourist travelled to the International Space Station in a Russian spacecraft in 2001. He paid millions of dollars for the adventure. Some transportation issues include the following.

Mass Transportation as a Future Necessity Mass transportation will become more affordable, convenient, and fast. More citizens will use mass transit as gasoline prices increase, commuting times get longer, and mass transportation becomes safer and more accessible. High-speed trains will enhance distant travel, and travel to major attractions will increase.

Transportation-Centered Destination Points   Major transportation hubs (e.g., airports, bus terminals) will become leisure service centers in themselves. Entrepreneurs have designed unique destination points located at transportation hubs. Many larger airports already sport tanning booths, relaxation centers, and athletic courts (racquetball), as well as work stations complete with fax and Internet access. Shopping will continue as a high-tech leisure service activity for travelers. New and improved access to large shopping centers, discount shopping malls, and mall-amusement centers will occur.

The Mall of America (Minneapolis, Minnesota) and the East Edmonton Mall (Edmonton, Alberta) have become a new type of destination point, designed to be a vacation experience (complete with theme park) as well as a shopping destination. Amusement parks, leisure sports facilities, dining establishments, and other tourist activities have seen tremendous commercial success. The Mall of America, located near the Minneapolis airport, depends on this vehicle of transportation to provide a steady stream of shoppers and tourists.

Economic Trends

Economic changes will continue to influence the leisure habits of the general populace. Slow growth will continue, and it will be some time before the country will see the affluence of the 1990s again. People feel insecure about their jobs and may continue to have less trust in government; saving money may become increasingly difficult with greater government involvement in state finances; and people will spend cautiously. While leisure spending has varied little over the years, the demand for quality services and products, and people getting "their money's worth" has increased.

The economy tends to be cyclical. As we enter the twenty-first century the economy seems to be sliding backwards after the robust years of the 1990s. Due to the fact that the economy has shifted from a product-oriented economy to an information economy, changes in spending habits, consumer decision making, and other variables impacting on leisure practices may change quite rapidly. The half-life of knowledge and information continues to shorten, and leisure service providers must respond rapidly. The move from an industrialized to an information-based economy has resulted in a shift from valuing products to valuing ideas.

Changing Nature of Work

The nature of work has changed over the years; it will continue to evolve. Society has moved from being product-driven to information-based. People continue to work both out of necessity and in the search for self-identity. In the move toward an improved quality of life, people will find identity outside of work. Women in the workforce and jobs for teens will grow in importance.

Flexible work schedules, working during commuting hours, satellite offices, contingent workforce, telecommuting, and compressed workweeks will become more prevalent. "More than 93 percent of America's largest corporations offer a flexible workplace to accommodate workers for whom a daily 9-to-5 on-site work schedule causes difficulty" (Lynch, 1992, p. 58). People will continue to change jobs several times throughout their careers, entering and leaving the workforce as personal needs dictate. The work ethic will remain strong, yet will mesh with other aspects of peoples' lives. Time off for self and family will become increasingly important.

Flex Time   Flex time provides an individual with blocks of time for work and leisure outside of a conventional 8:00 A.M. to 5:00 P.M. workday. Although flex time could mean going to work at 7:00 A.M. and leaving at 4:00 P.M., some workers have complete discretion to organize their work in blocks of time that meet personal as well as work goals. In many creative situations, work is accomplished around personal bursts of inspiration, insight, and effort. These highly personal bursts capture an individual's focus at peak times of energy and intellectual vigor. For example, higher education offers opportunities for flex time; professors can structure their schedules around class times, personal needs, and meetings. Any one of these activities might occur in the morning, afternoon, or evening.

Flex Place The physical location for people's work and play may become irrelevant in the future. People will work at home, in the car, on the train, in the air, or at a local coffee shop with multiple activities occurring at once. For instance, people now grocery shop, work, walk down the street, or drive cars while talking on a cellular phone. Laptop computers, fax machines, public access to the Internet, and other equipment enable work to occur in various locations. Many businesses such as coffee shops, hotels, and athletic clubs offer access to technology that will enable flex place activity.

Flex Schedule Rearranging the work schedule can facilitate larger or different blocks of time for work or leisure. A common form of this is the four-day workweek where people work ten hours a day and have three-day weekends. Such forms of organizing work time have not diminished worker productivity, and, in fact, have led to gains in employee morale and work functions. Selected occupations, such as airline pilots, flight attendants, fire fighters, oil riggers, and emergency-crew personnel, work a certain number of days on the job and have a similar number of days off. For example, an oil rigger might work twenty-eight days on the job away from home at an isolated off-shore oil platform and then have twenty-eight days to spend at home or on another job. Individuals in this type of situation often seek additional employment or serious leisure opportunities to fill those days.

Job Sharing Currently occurring in some work settings, job sharing will become an increasingly important vehicle to accomplish work tasks while accommodating the needs of individuals. Job sharing consists of two related people sharing one job (at home or at a separate worksite), or two unrelated people who work in environments that are conveniently organized to meet their current focuses in life. One worker might work mornings, another afternoons; one might work the first two days of the week, the other the next three. Job sharing greatly benefits a participating organization. Two different sets of skills and expertise become a part of the organization, employees tend to be highly committed, and benefits may be divided among the workers in a variety of configurations.

The portability of technology and the rise of telecommunications dramatically support flex time, flex place, flex scheduling, and job sharing. People from across the globe will continue to work together on tasks in two different time zones. For example, a person can interact, day or night, via computer, fax machine, telephone, and satellite dish. These forms of communication allow for instantaneous access to others; their computers or fax machines can receive and store the data or information until such time as they are ready to receive such communications.

Continued Growth of the Service Sector of Employment

The service sector of employment will experience continued growth. As the United States and Canada moved from industrial societies to the information age, corresponding increases in jobs in the service area have resulted. As most leisure service organizations fall within the service category, projections anticipate growth in the number of future jobs, particularly in the commercial sector. As we look forward, many growth opportunities for employment in leisure services exist, especially dealing with child care, food service, lodging, and amusement and recreation (U.S. Bureau of the Census, 1999). These categories are projected as ones with the greatest number and/or percentage of change among occupations as we compare employment between 1996 and 2006.

Summary

Many changes face the leisure service profession in the next few decades. It has been said, "There are two rules about change: change is inevitable, and people hate change." To be responsive, to remain on the cutting edge and in the forefront of the leisure service profession, one must both accept and embrace change. These changes suggest several policy issues:

- Leisure opportunities will continue to evolve and be redefined by society for women, men, and children.
- Family-based leisure services will be eclectic.
- People in their forties, fifties, and sixties will demand active leisure services.
- Cultural diversity and sensitivity will become hallmarks of quality leisure service programs.
- Accessibility for all people, and the delivery of services to all people, will continue to challenge the field.
- Parks, recreation, and leisure service programs will be in high demand due to the increased need for nonschool programs and the problem of unattended hours among youth.
- The ADA will alter access to facilities and programs and the way leisure services providers think about the delivery of services.
- The general population will demand a change in service provision, both in hours of operation and increased diversity in program offerings.
- The provision of services will meet an increased need for nonviolence education and an increased concern in dealing with violence.
- Service providers must address AIDS education and increased concern about issues related to AIDS.
- Environmental awareness will become integrated into all levels of leisure services organizations: administration, maintenance, program delivery, staffing, and facilities.
- The shifting work hours of users will require flexible programming hours.
- The increased interest in time off to spend with family will alter traditional ways of viewing family leisure.

Peters (1993) writes that society is currently in the midst of the largest change that has occurred in the last two centuries. In part, this results from a massive change in technology and the tools available to individuals and organizations to store and process information and communicate with one another. As Peters notes, ". . . the technical impact of new tools will largely be settled in the next 25 years." He goes on to point out, however, that the "social shakeout will linger for another century," (p. 2D).

Peters recommends the following: (1) with no certain answers, a tolerance for ambiguity will be the number one success tool; (2) there is no insulation from change; (3) reinvent yourself—people, businesses, and government must be transformed, and success will go to the curious with a passion for learning; and (4) remind yourself that you are a part of an exciting transformation that occurs infrequently and provides great opportunities for self-renewal.

Discussion Questions

1. What does the statement "change is constant" mean as applied to the concept of leisure and the delivery of leisure services?

2. Identify five key population trends and their potential impacts on leisure.
3. How have changing social roles affected your life? How have they affected your leisure choices and opportunities?
4. Discuss the effect of the women's movement on the leisure experiences of men; of women.
5. Select one ongoing environmental concern (such as acid rain) and describe its effects on the leisure profession.
6. Identify three technological advances and describe their potential impact on leisure.
7. Talk with your parents and grandparents or other older people and ask them to identify the number of hours they typically worked per week and the number of hours that were available for leisure when they were in their thirties and forties. What did they do during their leisure between the ages of nineteen and twenty-four? Compare their responses with yours and present the information in the following chart.

	Work hours	Leisure hours	Activities
You			
Parents			
Grandparents			

8. Define the following: flex time, flex place, job sharing, and flex schedule.
9. As Peters notes, we live in a period of great technological change. What implications can be drawn from the statement, "social shakeout will linger for another century"?
10. What do you think will be the role of leisure and leisure professionals in future society?

References

Aburdene, P., and J. Naisbitt. 1992. *Megatrends for Women.* New York: Random House.
Bureau of Justice Statistics. 1989. Edited by George W. Wilkinson, in *What Lies Ahead.* Alexandria, VA: United Way Strategic Planning Institute.
Caneday, L. 1991. Parks, recreation, and the environment: Allies or adversaries. *Parks and Recreation* (September), 88–93+.
Children's Defense Fund. 1996. *The State of America's Children Yearbook 1996.* Washington, DC: Children's Defense Fund.
Davidson, J. W. 1993. Overworked Americans or overwhelmed Americans. *Public Management* (May), 8.
DeGraaf, K., and D. DeGraaf. 1993. Environmentally hot or not. *Camping Magazine* (May–June), 24–27, 30.
Dryfoos, J. 1990. *Adolescents at Risk: Prevalence and Prevention.* New York: Oxford University Press.
Famighetti, R., ed. 1995. *The World Almanac & Book of Facts 1996.* Mahwah, NJ: Funk & Wagnalls Corp.
Gleick, J. 1987. *Chaos making a new science.* New York: Penguin Books.
Godbey, G. 1989. *The Future of Leisure Services: Thriving on Change.* State College, PA: Venture.
Goodale, T. L., and P. A. Witt. 1985. *Recreation and Leisure Issues in an Era of Change.* State College, PA: Venture.
Henderson, K. A., M. D. Bialeschki, S. M. Shaw, and V. J. Freysinger. 1996. *Both Gains and Gaps: Feminist Perspectives on Women's Leisure.* State College, PA: Venture.
Ibrahim, H., and K. Cordes. 1993. *Outdoor Recreation.* Dubuque, IA: Brown & Benchmark.
Jennings, L. 1989. Fordham Institute's index documents steep decline in children's and youth's social health since 1970. *Education Week 9*(9), 7.
Junin, S. 2000. Downshifting: Regaining the essence of leisure. *Journal of Leisure and Research 32*(1), 69–73.
Kelly, J., and G. Godbey. 1992. *The Sociology of Leisure.* State College, PA: Venture.
Kimeldorf, M. 1994. *Serious Play: A Leisure Wellness Workbook.* Berkeley, CA: Ten Speed Press.
Kraus, R. 1994. *Leisure in a Changing America.* New York: Macmillan.
Kuzmic, T. 1992. Islands of wilderness in a sea of civilization. *Parks and Recreation* (August), 34+.
LaPage, W., and S. Ranney. 1988. America's wilderness: The heart and soul of culture. *Parks and Recreation* (July), 24–31+.
Law, B., ed. 1995. *1996 Corpus Almanac & Canadian Sourcebook.* Ontario: Southam, Inc.
The Leisure Development Center. 1991. *Leisure and Recreational Activities in Japan,* 7.
Lynch, A.F., ed. 1992. *What Lies Ahead: A Decade of Decision.* Alexandria, VA: United Way Strategic Institute.
McDowell, C. F. 1976. *Leisure Counseling: Selected Lifestyle Processes.* Eugene, OR: Center for Leisure Studies.

McDowell, C. F. 1983. *Leisure Wellness: Concepts on Helping Strategies.* Eugene, OR: Sun Moon Press.

Milani, B. 2000. *Designing the Green Economy: The Postindustrial Alternative to Corporate Globalization.* Lanham, MD: Rowman & Littlefield Publishers, Inc.

Naisbitt Trends Newsletter. 1992. *11*(9): (April 30).

National Commission on the Role of the School and the Community in Improving Adolescent Health. 1990. *Code Blue: Uniting for Healthier Youth.* Alexandria, VA: National Association of State Boards of Education.

Nieto, S. 1992. *Affirming Diversity: The Sociopolitical Context of Multicultural Education.* New York: Longman.

Peters, T. 1993. How do you cope with changes ahead? Reinvent yourself, go nuts. *San Jose Mercury News* (September 13), 2D.

Robinson, J. P. 1989. Time's up. *American Demographics* (July), 33.

Robinson, J. P. 1991. Your money or your time. *American Demographics* (November), 23.

Robinson, J. P., and G. Godbey. 1997. *Time for Life: The Surprising Ways Americans Use Their Time.* University Park, PA: The Pennsylvania State University Press.

The Roper Organization. 1987. *The American Dream.* New York: The Roper Organization.

Sax, J. 1980. *Mountains without Handrails, Reflections on the National Parks.* Ann Arbor, MI: University of Michigan Press.

Schor, J. B. 1993, February. *Overworked Americans: The Unexpected Decline of Leisure.* New York Basic Books.

Seefeldt, V. 1996. F. Smoll and R. Smith, eds. The future of youth sports in America. *Children and Youth in Sport: A Biopsychosocial Perspective.* Dubuque, IA: Brown & Benchmark.

Surgeon General. 1996. *Physical Activity and Health.*

Time/CNN, 1999. As appeared in *What Lies Ahead: A Decade of Decision,* from the United Way of America, 1992, United Way Strategic Institute, Alexandria, VA.

University of Maryland. 1989. Edited by George Wilkinson, in *What Lies Ahead.* Alexandria, VA: United Way Strategic Institute.

U.S. Bureau of the Census. 1999. *Statistical Abstract of the United States: 1999.* 119th ed. Washington, DC: U.S. Government Printing Office.

Wilkinson, G.W., ed. 1989. *What Lies Ahead.* Alexandria, VA: United Way Strategic Planning Institute.

World Resources Institute. 1993. *Environmental Almanac.* Boston: Houghton Mifflin.

World Resources Institute. 2000. *World Resources: A Guide to the Global Environment, 1998–99.* London: Oxford University Press.

World Resources Institute. 2001, February 21. *New Report on Global Health Warns Environmental Degradation is Contributing to Preventable Health Threats Worldwide.* www.wri.org/wri/press/wr98nr01.htm.

Yzaguirre, R. 1998. The new American identity. Edited by F. Hesselbein, M. Goldsmith, R. Beckhard, and R. Schubert, in *The Community of the Future.* San Francisco: Jossey-Bass.

Zeiger, J., and L. Caneday. 1991. Aldo Leopold's plea: A study of preservation. *Parks and Recreation* (September), 80–82.

CREDITS

CREDITS

Text and Line Art

Chapter 1

Excerpt, pp. 7-8: Seven Elements of Enjoyment from *Flow: The Psychology of Optimal Experience,* by Mihaly Csikszentmihalyi. Reprinted by permission of HarperCollins Publishers, Inc.

Leisure Line, p. 21: From *Liberation Management,* by Tom Peters. Copyright © 1992 by Excel, a California Limited Partnership. Reprinted by permission of Alfred A. Knopf, Inc.

Chapter 3

Figures 3.12 and 3.13: Reprinted by permission of The Civilian Conservation Corps in Iowa, Iowa Department of Natural Resources, Dundee, Iowa.

Chapter 4

Leisure Line, p. 97: Excerpt as submitted from *Finding Joy: 101 Ways to Free Your Spirit and Dance with Life* by Charlotte Davis Kasl. Copyright © 1995 by Charlotte Davis Kasl. Reprinted by permission of HarperCollins Publishers, Inc.

Leisure Line, p. 100: From the *Kitchener-Waterloo Record,* June 19, 1976. Reprinted by permission.

Figures 4.3, 4.4, and 4.7: From Willamalane Park and Recreation District, Springfield, OR. Reprinted by permission.

Chapter 5

Leisure Line, p. 125: From John Naisbitt and Patricia Aburdene, *Megatrends 2000.* Copyright © 1990 by Megatrends Ltd. By permission of Wm. Morrow & Company, Inc.

Chapter 6

Leisure Line, p. 144: From "Americans' Active Lifestyles Often an Illusion." April 8, 1996, as appeared in *Des Moines Register.* Copyright © 1996 by Associated Press. Reprinted by permission.

Figures 6.1 and 6.2: From Seppo E. Iso-Ahola, *The Social Psychology of Leisure and Recreation.* Copyright © 1980 McGraw-Hill Companies: Dubuque, Iowa. All Rights Reserved. Reprinted by permission.

Figure 6.3 text and excerpt, pp. 153-154: *From A Portrait of Young Adolescents in the 1990s: Implications for Promoting Healthy Growth and Development,* by Peter C. Scales, 1991. Center for Early Adolescence, University of North Carolina at Chapel Hill, Carrboro, NC.

Leisure Line, p. 165: From Paula Kephart, "Retiring Where the Mariachis Play" in *American Demographics,* 1994. Reprinted by permission of American Demographics, Inc., Ithaca, NY.

Chapter 7

Figure 7.5: City of Albany Park and Recreation Department, Albany, OR. Reprinted by permission.

Figure 7.6: Reprinted by permission of Lane County Parks Division, Eugene, OR.

Figure 7.7: From Willamalane Park and Recreation District, Springfield, OR. Reprinted by permission.

Figure 7.8: Printed by permission of the National Program for Playground Safety, University of Northern Iowa, Cedar Falls, IA.

Figure 7.9: From the City of Calgary Parks and Recreation Department, Calgary, Alberta, Canada. Reprinted by permission.

Chapter 8

Leisure Line, p. 223: Osborn, D. and Goebler, T. *Reinventing government: How the entrepreneurial spirit is transforming the public sector.* 1993.

Chapter 10

Leisure Line, pp. 268–269: From *A Portrait of Young Adolescents in the 1990s: Implications for Promoting Healthy Growth and Development,* by Peter C. Scales, 1991. Center

for Early Adolescence, University of North Carolina at Chapel Hill, Carrboro, NC.

Figure 10.2: From Black Hawk County YMCA, Waterloo, IA. Reprinted by permission.

Chapter 11

Figure 11.6: Used with permission of Play Station, Cedar Rapids, IA.

Chapter 13

Figures 13.1 and 13.3: © C. Edginton and S. Edginton, 1993.

Leisure Line, p. 363: Excerpted from "A Matter of Time: Risk and Opportunity in the Nonschool Hours," a report of the Carnegie Council on Adolescent Development. Copyright © December 1992 by Carnegie Corporation of New York.

Chapter 15

Leisure Lines, p. 395: From John Naisbitt and Patricia Aburdene, *Megatrends 2000.* Copyright © 1990 by Megatrends Ltd. By permission of Wm. Morrow & Company, Inc.

Figure 15.3: From Campus News Network (Newsletter), Office of Public Relations, University of Northern Iowa. Reprinted by permission.

Chapter 16

Leisure Line, p. 422: From J. Waldrop, "A Visit to the Old Hippies' Home" in *American Demographics,* August, 1994. Reprinted by permission of American Demographics, Inc., Ithaca, NY.

Figure 16.5: From Fred Best, "Recycling-People: Work-Sharing Through the Flexible Life Scheduling" in *The Futurist,* February 1978. World Future Society, 7910 Woodmont Ave., Suite 450, Bethesda, MD, 20814.

Leisure Line, p. 442: From John Naisbitt and Patricia Aburdene, *Megatrends 2000.* Copyright © 1990 by Megatrends Ltd. By permission of Wm. Morrow & Company, Inc.

NAME INDEX

NAME INDEX

A

AARP, 143, 167
Aburdene, P., 102, 115, 128, 141, 171, 203, 314, 317, 395, 427, 429, 430, 449
Addams, J., 86, 90
Adler, J., 134, 140
Administration on Aging, 162, 164, 167
Albrecht, K., 346, 349, 368
Albright, H., 242, 262
Allen, L. R., 12, 22, 27
American Camping Association, 85, 90
American Motion Picture Assocation, 138, 140
Ameristat, 418
Amir, Y., 398, 418
Atkinson, J. W., 47, 49
ATRA, 329
Austin, D. R., 285, 290, 323, 324, 327, 329, 331, 332–334, 339, 340
Austin, J. E., 273, 290
Avedon, E. M., 321, 340

B

Baker, J., 199, 202
Baltic, T., 114
Bammel, G., 11, 27, 118, 140, 148, 164, 167
Bammel, L., 118, 140, 148, 164, 167
Bandalos, D. L., 22, 29
Bannon, J., 414, 418
Barker, E., 31, 49
Beard, 125
Beattie, R., 12, 27
Beggs, B., 224, 226
Behren, R. V., 334, 340
Bell, B., 249, 262
Bell, D., 54, 90
Bergemaier, R., 27
Bergin, D. A., 23, 27
Bergstrom, L., 262
Berry, L., 342, 369
Berstein, C., 82, 83, 90
Bialeschki, D., 91, 114

Bialeschki, M. D., 23, 25, 28, 401, 418, 428, 449
Bishop, D. W., 47, 50
Blake, J., 328, 340
Book Industry Supply Group, 138, 140
Borg, I., 11, 27
Bowen, L. K., 67, 91
Brayley, R. E., 93, 113, 115, 122, 141, 173–175, 202, 250, 251, 253, 256, 259, 262
Brightbill, C., 114, 135, 140, 205, 206, 227
Brill, N., 145, 167
Broach, E., 336, 340
Broida, J. K., 338, 340
Brown, K. A., 11, 27
Brown, P., 18–20, 27, 173, 202, 342, 369
Brown, R., 121, 140
Brown, W., 164, 167
Bullaro, J., 86, 91, 293, 294, 297, 299, 314, 317, 354, 368
Bullock, C., 336, 340
Burch, W. R., 20, 22, 27
Bureau of Justice Statistics, 449
Bureau of Land Management, 262
Bureau of Reclamation, 248, 262
Burke, W., 189, 202
Burris-Bammel, L., 11, 27
Business Week, 90, 311, 312
Busser, J., 176, 202

C

Caldwell, L., 200, 202
Campbell, S., 149, 151, 168
Caneday, L., 438, 449, 450
Carlson, C., 152, 167
Carlson, R., 131, 140
Carnegie Corporation of New York, 151, 167, 276, 278, 279, 282, 287, 290
Carnegie Foundation, 156
Carpenter, G., 310, 317
Carr, H. H., 46, 49
Carter, M. J., 320–322, 325–327, 329, 340

Cashel, C., 11, 27
Champoux, J., 11, 27
Chavez, D., 224, 226
Cheek, N. H., 20, 22, 27
Chenery, M. F., 310, 317
Children's Defense Fund, 338, 340, 426, 435, 449
Chubb, H., 72, 91, 299, 317
Chubb, M., 72, 91, 299, 317
City of Phoenix, 338, 340
Claparede, E., 46, 49
Clark, D., 373, 390
Clough, P. J., 23, 27
Coe, W., 31, 49
Cohen, A., 134, 140
Colb, S., 18, 29
Coles, J. E., 362, 368
Conley, 395, 403
Cooper, E., 6, 29
Cooper, W., 94, 114
Cordell, H., 262
Cordes, K., 19, 28, 208, 211, 212, 218, 226, 241, 262, 436, 449
Coveliers, L., 331, 340
Cranz, 166
Crawford, D. W., 25, 27, 28
Crawford, M. E., 320, 321, 323, 333, 334, 339, 340
Crompton, J., 194, 202, 342, 355, 357, 368, 369
Crompton, J. L., 36, 50
Crossley, J. C., 294, 296–299, 317
Csikszentmihalyi, M., 7, 8, 27, 31, 33, 45, 47, 49, 50, 134–136, 141
Culp, R., 152, 167
Curtis, H., 43, 49, 80, 91
Curtis, J., 178, 179, 188, 202
Cutler, B., 117, 140, 317
Cutler, S., 11, 27

D

Dansby, M., 419
Dare, B., 31, 49

Datilo, J., 336, 340
Davidson, J. W., 15, 424, 449
de Grazia, S., 94, 114, 118, 140
Deavours, M., 336, 340
DeGraaf, D. G., 35, 49, 70, 91, 162, 167, 177, 199, 202, 332, 335, 340, 362, 368, 388–390, 449
DeGraaf, K., 35, 49, 177, 199, 202, 332, 340, 449
Department of the Army, 250, 262
Department of the Interior, 357, 368
Deppe, T., 111, 112, 114, 173, 202
Detzel, D., 362, 368
Dickenson, R., 242, 262
Dickinson, R., 198, 202
Diener, E., 6, 9, 27
DiFiori, 150, 151, 167
Digital Equipment Corporation, 418
Disney, 133, 140
Dottavio, A., 164, 167
Dreachslin, 408, 418
Driver, B. L., 18–20, 27, 114, 173, 202
Drucker, P. F., 263, 269, 290, 310, 317
Dryfoos, J., 87, 91, 434, 449
DuBois, P., 178, 203
Dulles, F., 65, 91, 138, 140
Dumazedier, J., 35, 49
Dunn, D., 193, 202
Durant, W., 56–59, 91
Dustin, D., 22, 88–89, 91, 114, 261, 262

E

Earth Journal, 134, 140, 288
Ebberson, A., 219, 226
Edginton, C. R., 13, 14, 17, 18, 27, 30, 35, 49, 86, 91, 96, 98, 112, 114, 125, 140, 171–173, 202, 293, 294, 297, 299, 310, 314, 317, 343, 353, 354, 359, 362, 363, 365, 366, 368, 371, 390
Edginton, S. R., 35, 49, 98, 114, 125, 140, 343, 359, 362, 368, 371, 390, 408, 410, 418
Edwards, R. H., 66, 91
Eells, E., 85, 91
Eisenhardt, K., 419
Eller, C. L., 327, 340
Ellis, G., 23, 27
Ellis, M. J., 13, 14, 27, 31, 45, 47, 49
Elsner, G., 114
English, D., 262
Erikson, E. H., 46, 49, 142, 145, 146, 148, 152, 153, 158, 162, 167
Ewert, A., 23, 27, 131, 140
Ewing, M., 150, 167

F

Fabos, J., 75, 91
Fain, G., 95, 114
Fain, S. M., 372, 390
Famighetti, R., 140, 276, 423, 449
Farrell, 324
Fetto, J., 133, 140
Flegal, K., 149, 151, 168
Ford, P., 96, 114, 363, 365, 366, 368
Forest Service. *See* U.S. Forest Service
Fortune Magazine, 445
Forum on Child and Family Statistics, 148, 150, 167
Foss, P., 226
Freysinger, V. J., 23, 28, 35, 50, 91, 114, 401, 418, 428, 449
Frye, V., 66, 91, 322, 340

G

Gaitz, C., 11, 28, 161, 167
Gallagher, B. J., 333, 340
Gardyn, R., 133, 140
Gass, M., 131, 141
Gassman, J., 199, 202, 340
Gibbs, N., 117, 140
Gilmartin, D., 324, 340
Glancy, M., 362, 368
Gleick, J., 449
Glick, D., 134, 140
Godbey, G., 3, 4, 9, 11, 12, 24, 25, 27, 28, 38, 40, 42, 43, 48–50, 55, 86–89, 91, 93, 95, 102, 114–117, 120–122, 124, 126, 134, 140, 141, 145, 164, 166, 167, 176, 177, 202, 357, 358, 368, 423, 424, 427–429, 440, 441, 443, 444, 449, 450
Goldberg, M., 405, 418
Goldman, C., 325, 340
Golf Magazine, 324
Goodale, T. L., 25, 27, 93, 96, 102, 114, 449
Gorden, C., 161, 167
Gorden, J., 134, 140
Gordon, C., 11, 28
Gottschalk, E. C., Jr., 301, 317
Gray, D. E., 194, 202, 319, 340
Greben, S., 108, 114, 142, 167
Green, F., 405, 416, 419
Greenleaf, R., 177, 202
Grey, D., 108, 114, 142, 167
Griffee, T., 11, 28
Groos, K., 45, 49
Grover, R., 312, 317
Guirdham, M., 395, 418
Gunn, C., 123, 141

Gunn, S. L., 325, 334, 340
Gunter, B. G., 31, 49

H

Hall, G. S., 46, 49
Hansel, T., 148, 167
Hanson, C., 35, 49, 125, 140, 371, 390
Harper, W., 4, 28
Hartmenn, L., 262
Hartsoe, C., 200, 202
Hastings, M., 171, 202
Haun, P., 16, 28, 42, 49
Haurwitz, R., 189, 202
Havitz, M. E., 341, 368
Hayles, R., 411
Hayles, V. R., 398, 406, 408–411, 418
Healey, 397, 418
Hemphill, S., 173, 202
Hemphill, S. A., 174
Henderson, K. A., 23, 25, 28, 66, 91, 114, 401, 418, 428, 449
Hendricks, J., 11, 27
Henneman, H. G., 40, 49
Hitt, W., 98, 101, 111, 114
Hodgkinson, V. A., 265, 275, 290
Hopkins, H., 106, 114
Howard, D. R., 13, 14, 27, 357, 368
Howat, G., 171, 202
Howe, C., 359, 368
Hudson, S., 35, 49, 125, 140, 371, 390
Huizinga, J., 114, 148, 167
Hull, R. B., 9, 14, 28
Hultsman, J., 4, 28
Hultsman, W., 24, 25, 28
Hunnicutt, B. K., 95, 114
Hurd, A., 224, 226

I

Ibrahim, H., 19, 28, 30, 43, 49, 138, 141, 208, 211, 212, 218, 226, 241, 262, 436, 449
Inglehart, R., 9, 28
Iso-Ahola, S., 9, 28, 31, 33, 35, 50

J

Jackson, E. L., 24–26, 27, 28, 29, 162, 167, 357, 368
Jackson, G., 23, 28
Jaffe, M., 153, 156, 167
Jamieson, L. M., 294, 296–299, 317
Jarvi, C., 173, 202
Jekubovich, N. J., 26, 29
Jennings, L., 435, 449
Jensen, C., 211, 213–216, 218, 226, 238, 246, 262
Johnson, C., 149, 151, 168

Johnson, M. A., 84, 91
Johnson-Tew, C. P., 341, 368
Jones, 214
Jordan, D., 35, 49, 102, 114, 150, 167, 177,
    191, 202, 341, 369, 388–390,
    408, 418
Junin, S., 442, 449
Juniu, S., 35, 37, 50

K

Kando, T. M., 47, 50, 116, 120, 121, 127,
    128, 141
Katz, 200, 202
Kay, T., 23, 28
Kelly, J. R., 4, 9–12, 24, 28, 31, 35, 36,
    38, 39, 40, 42, 43, 45, 48, 50,
    55, 91, 114, 120, 122, 124,
    126, 127, 141, 153, 158, 161,
    167, 299, 303, 304, 317, 423,
    424, 427–429, 440, 441, 443,
    444, 449
Kennedy, D., 324, 327, 329, 331, 332, 340
Kennedy, R., 285, 290
Kimeldorf, M., 114, 443, 449
King, P., 134, 140
Kleiber, D., 31, 33, 44, 50, 158, 159,
    161, 167
Knouse, S., 406, 419
Knudson, D., 210, 226
Knustler, R., 340
Kraus, R., 12, 18, 28, 35, 38–40, 42, 44,
    48, 50, 56–58, 61, 91, 178,
    179, 188, 198, 202, 204,
    206, 226, 229, 232, 262,
    283, 290, 318, 320, 324, 332,
    340, 399, 400, 419, 423, 426,
    427, 449
Krause, D., 198, 202
Kreck, C., 171, 203
Kreisberg, L., 219, 226
Kubey, R., 134–136, 141
Kuczmarski, R., 149, 151, 168
Kunstler, R., 327, 337, 340
Kurtz-Costes, B., 397, 419
Kuzmic, T., 437, 449

L

Lahey, M. P., 337, 340
Land Letter, 262
Lankford, S. V., 70, 91, 162, 167, 335, 340,
    357, 368
LaPage, W., 438, 449
Lappe, F., 178, 203
Larson, R., 31, 50
Laurence, M., 286, 291
Law, B., 423, 431, 449

Lazarus, M., 46, 50
Lee, J., 38, 43, 50, 75, 81, 91
Lee, R., 242, 262
Lehman, J., 264, 291
Leisure Development Center, 449
Leitner, M. J., 9–10, 28, 37, 38, 50, 115
Leitner, S. F., 28, 37, 38, 50, 115
Lemke, J., 11, 28
Levinson, D., 146, 159, 167
Levy, J., 45, 47, 50
Little, C., 262
Little, J., 335, 340
Little, S. L., 362, 368
Loden, M., 399–404, 419
Lothian, W., 76, 91, 253, 262
Luck, L. B., 362, 368
Lynch, A. F., 446, 449

M

McAvoy, L., 88–89, 91, 114
McCarville, R. E., 341, 342, 368
McChesney, J. C., 352, 368
McDowell, C. F., 443, 449, 450
McFarland, E., 81, 91
McGregor, B., 194, 202
McGuire, F. A., 25, 28, 164, 167
McIntosh, P., 401, 419
McKay, K., 342, 355, 368, 369
MacKay, K. J., 36, 50
McLean, D. D., 173–175, 202, 224, 226
MacLean, J., 55, 56, 91
Mahon, M., 336, 340
Mannell, R., 31, 33, 40, 44, 50
Martin, D., 55, 56, 91
Mason, D. E., 266, 274, 275, 291
Mason, T., 312, 317
Mattson, L., 85, 91
Maughan, R., 23, 27
May, H., 116, 141
Mertesdorf, J., 102, 114
Meyer, H., 205, 206, 227
Milani, B., 420, 450
Milde, G., 75, 91
Miller, R. D., 349, 369
Milliron, T., 331, 340
Mobily, K., 11, 28
Mobley, T., 195, 203
Molitor, G. T., 119, 126, 131–133, 141
Montgomery, S., 156, 168
Moore, R. L., 217
Morgan, J. J., 349, 369
Mott, W., 242, 262
Mulroy, M. T., 327, 340
Munson, W., 26, 29
Murphy, D., 194, 203
Murphy, J. F., 37–39, 50, 95, 108, 115
Muuss, R., 146, 167

Myers, D. G., 6, 8, 9, 28
Myers, P., 224, 227

N

Naisbitt, J., 54, 91, 102, 115, 128, 139, 141,
    171, 203, 314, 317, 395, 427,
    429, 430, 449
Naisbitt Trends Newsletter, 445, 450
Nash, J. B., 104, 113, 115
Nash, R., 130, 141
NASPD. See National Association of State
    Park Directors
National Alliance for Youth Sports, 151
National Association of State Park Directors
    (NASPD), 210, 212, 227
National Commission on the Role of the
    School and the Community in
    Improving Adolescent
    Health, 433, 450
National Recreation and Park Association
    (NRPA), 142, 167, 177, 199,
    203, 372, 390
National Sporting Goods Association, 122,
    129, 141, 151, 167
National Therapeutic Recreation Society,
    326, 329, 332, 340
Nationwide Outdoor Recreation Survey,
    357, 369
Nature Conservancy, 288, 291
Naylor, L., 401, 419
Neal, L., 162, 167, 171, 202
Nelson, P., 164, 167
Neulinger, J., 31, 38, 40, 41, 50
Newman, T., 156, 168
Newton, N., 77, 91
Niepoth, W., 363, 364, 369
Nieto, S., 399, 400, 402, 403, 419, 430, 450
NRPA. See National Recreation and Park
    Association

O

Occupational Outlook Handbook, 175,
    193, 331
O'Dell, I., 11, 29
O'Leary, J. T., 25, 28, 164, 167
Oleck, H. L., 263, 264, 266, 291
Olmsted, Frederick Law, 74–75, 91
O'Neil, J. P., 362, 368
O'Neill, J., 173, 202
Ostiguy, L., 11, 28
Outdoor Recreation Resources Review
    Commission, 206, 227

P

Page, G., 331, 340
Parasuraman, A., 342, 369

Pate, R., 150, 153, 168
Patrick, G. T. W., 46, 50
Patterson, M. E., 4, 28
Patterson, P., 164, 167
PCAO. *See* President's Commission on
    American Outdoors
Peene, L., 220, 227
Pelled, L., 401, 419
Peller, L. E., 46, 50
Peters, M., 322, 340
Peters, T., 54, 91, 348, 353, 369, 448, 450
Peterson, C. A., 329, 334, 340
Peterson, G., 114, 173, 202
Peterson, J., 55, 56, 91
Petgin, D., 116, 141
Pettsinger, T., 312, 317
Peyser, 4
Phillips, S. F., 26, 28
Piaget, J., 47, 50
Pickens, C., 11, 28
Pieper, J., 36, 50, 115
Pierce, R., 11, 28
Pinchot, G., 234, 237, 244, 294, 317
Pittman, K. J., 153, 156, 167, 168
President's Commission on American
        Outdoors (PCAO), 209, 227,
        231, 260, 262
Priest, S., 131, 141
Pritchard, A., 351, 356, 361, 394
Prosser, E., 152, 167
Pungello, E., 419
Purpel, D., 99, 115
Putnam, R., 123, 124, 141, 199, 200, 203

Q

Qui, Y., 359, 368

R

Rademacher, C., 23, 27
Ragheb, 125
Rails to Trails Conservancy, 188, 203
Ramsin, R., 199, 202
Ramsing, R., 332, 340
Ranney, S., 438, 449
Rath, K., 331, 340
Raymond, J., 130, 141
Reaney, M. J., 46, 50
Recording Industry Association, 141
Reich, C., 50
Reich, J., 8, 28
Reid, D., 40, 50
Riddick, C., 11, 28
Rifkin, J., 95, 115
Ritzer, G., 301, 317
Robb, G. M., 320–322, 325–327, 329, 340
Roberts, J., 47, 50

Robinson, E. S., 46, 50
Robinson, J. P., 95, 115, 117, 119, 121, 134,
        141, 434, 441–443, 450
Rodney, L., 181, 203
Rolston, H., 20, 22, 28
Roper Organization, 435, 450
Rosener, J., 399–404, 419
Ross, D. T., 217
Ross, J., 150, 153, 168
Rossman, J. R., 30, 33, 49, 50
Rossman, R., 353, 354, 368
Rucks, V. C., 26, 28
Runte, A., 91
Rupe, S., 362, 368
Russell, R. V., 6, 28, 36, 41, 50, 115,
        359, 369
Ryan, B., 341, 369
Ryan, F., 99, 115
Ryken, L., 65, 91

S

Salkind, N., 146, 168
Samdahl, D. M., 26, 29, 31, 50, 125, 141
Sax, J., 77, 91, 436, 450
Scales, P., 153, 168, 414, 419
Schiller, F. V., 45, 50
Schleien, S., 416, 419
Schor, J. B., 95, 115, 118, 119, 141, 442, 450
Schreyer, R., 18, 29
Schultz, J., 88–89, 91, 114
Schwartz, 395, 403
Scott, D., 25, 26, 28, 29, 162, 167
Scott, J., 11, 28
Searle, M. S., 25, 29, 93, 113, 115, 122, 141,
        250, 251, 253, 256, 259, 262
Second Annual Oregonian's Outdoor
        Conference, 225
Seefeldt, V., 150, 151, 167, 168, 440, 450
Sessoms, H. D., 143, 145, 168
Sessoms, H. G., 319, 340
Seuss, Dr., 86, 91
Shanahan, J., 220, 227
Shank, J. W., 318, 320, 332, 340, 390
Shaw, S. M., 23, 28, 31, 50, 91, 114, 401,
        418, 428, 449
Shepherd, J., 23, 27
Shichman, S., 6, 29
Siegenthaler, K. L., 11, 29, 349, 369
Simon, T., 156, 168
Smith, R., 285, 290, 324, 327, 329, 331,
        332, 340
Sneegas, J., 11, 29
Spears, B., 65, 91
Spears, L., 177, 203, 347
Spencer, H., 45, 50
Spring, J., 117, 134, 141
Staff, 91, 118, 203, 232, 262, 291, 317, 340

Statistics Canada, 253, 262
Stebbins, R., 39, 50
Steckel, R., 264, 291
Stein, J. U., 407, 419
Stein Wellner, A., 119, 141
Steinkamp, M., 10, 28
Stenger, R., 341, 369
Stevenson, J. L., 319, 340
Stewart, W. P., 9, 28
Stoddard, S., 324, 340
Stodolska, M., 26, 29
Stuart, T., 286, 291
Stumbo, N. J., 329, 340, 372, 390
Summers, W. C., 47, 50
Surgeon General, 432, 450
Sutton-Smith, B., 47, 50
Swanson, R., 65, 91
Swell, C., 342, 369
Sylvester, C. D., 93, 94, 97, 106, 115,
        372, 390

T

TAG. *See* Trends Action Group
Talbot, W. T., 85, 91
Tashiro, A., 335, 340
Teaff, J., 18, 29
Time/CNN, 9, 10, 435, 450
Tinsley, H., 18, 29
Toalson, R., 181, 195, 203
Toffler, A., 54, 91, 121
Trends Action Group (TAG), 340
Troiano, R., 149, 151, 168

U

Unger, J., 156, 168
Unger, L. S., 31, 50
United Way of America, 9, 10, 29
United Way Strategic Institute, 426, 439
University of Maryland, 442, 450
Uppal, S., 152, 167
U.S. Bureau of Economic Analysis,
        134, 141
U.S. Bureau of the Census, 129, 130, 141,
        208, 209, 211, 214, 216, 218,
        220, 227, 232, 233, 235, 238,
        239, 250, 262, 285, 291, 292,
        296, 298, 299, 302–304, 307,
        308, 311, 314, 317, 424, 427,
        431, 433–435, 437, 448, 450
U.S. Census Bureau, 175, 184–186, 203
U.S. Corps of Engineers, 246, 262
U.S. Department of Health and Human
        Services, 150, 153, 168
U.S. Forest Service, 234, 237–240, 262
U.S. National Endowment for the
        Arts, 221

U.S. National Endowment for the
Humanities, 221
USA Weekend, 34
USO-We Deliver America, 284, 291

Vamos, R., 312, 317
Van Andel, G. E., 320–322, 325–327,
329, 340
Van den Haag, E., 120, 141
Veblen, T. B., 36, 50

Waedler, R., 46, 50
Walters, W., 195, 203
Weinmayr, V., 75, 91
Weisse, C. S., 6, 29
Weissinger, E., 22, 29, 194, 203

Weitzman, M. S., 265, 275, 290
Welton, G., 31, 49
West Suburban Special Recreation
Association (WSSRA),
186, 203
Westfall, R., 200, 203, 224, 227
Whyte, D., 197, 203
Wilkinson, G. W., 432, 440, 450
Williams, A., 70, 91
Wilson, M., 85, 91
Wilson, W., 29
Witt, P. A., 25, 27, 47, 50, 114, 199,
202, 449
Wolf, T., 264, 266, 289, 291
Woodard, R., 11, 28
World Resources Institute, 437, 439, 450
Wright, M., 168
WSSRA. *See* West Suburban Special
Recreation Association

Xin, K., 419

Yi, Y. K., 9, 28
Yoder, D., 40, 50
Yzaguirre, R., 430, 450

Z

Zabel, D., 300, 317
Zautra, A., 8, 28
Zeiger, J., 438, 450
Zeithaml, V., 342, 369
Zemke, R., 346, 349, 368
Zigler, E., 106, 107, 115

SUBJECT INDEX

A

AAHE. *See* Association for the Advancement of Health Education

AAHPERD. *See* American Alliance for Health, Physical Education, Recreation and Dance

AALR. *See* American Association for Leisure and Recreation

AARP. *See* American Association of Retired Persons

Abbott Academy, 289

Ableism, 402

ACA. *See* American Camping Association

Accessibility, 417
  issues, 261

Achievement, feeling/sense, 155

Achievement-motivation theory, 47

ACL. *See* Active Living Canada

Act for the Relief of Idiots and Distracted Persons, 319

Action, awareness (merging), 7

Action-oriented therapies, 333

Actions/words, usage, 414

Active Living Canada (ACL), 257–258

Activities, 354. *See also* Cultural activities; Leisure; Mass leisure; Outdoors; Recreation; Social activities; Tourism
  centers. *See* Care/activity centers
  challenge, 7
  integration/segregation, contrast, 166
  need. *See* Physical activity
  participation. *See* Sports
  record, 51

ADA. *See* Americans with Disabilities Act

Addams, Jane, 67, 82–83, 86

Adirondack Forest Preserve, 210

Administration on Aging, 232

Administrative practices, 406–411
  policies/procedures/practices, 408

Administrative roles, 191, 193

Admissions, 272

Adolescence, 147
  developmental characteristics, 154
  leisure, relationship, 153–158

Adult daycare centers, 334

Adult offenders, 327

Adulthood, 147. *See also* Older adulthood
  characteristics. *See* Early adulthood; Late adulthood; Middle adulthood
  leisure, relationship, 158–162

Adults
  characteristics. *See* Older adults
  leisure (relationship). *See* Older adults

Adventure-oriented rafting trips, 297

Adventures. *See* Eco-conscious outdoor adventures
  recreation, 34
  tourism, 133, 134

Advisory assistance, 230

Advisory boards, 180

Advocacy, 374
  activities, 382
  groups, 331

AEE. *See* Association for Experiential Education

Affirmative action, 407

AFO. *See* Aquatic facility operator

AFRS. *See* Armed Forces Recreation Society

After-school programs, 426

After-school sport/athletic programs, 440

Age, 9, 402
  leisure, relationship, 10–11
  life satisfaction, relationship, 10–11

Ageism, 402

Agencies
  mission, 406
  rules/regulations, 406–411
  types. *See* Federal agencies

Agile Leisure Programming, 362

Aging. *See* Middle aging

Agricultural era, 55, 445
  leisure, 57–66

AIDS, 72, 337, 394, 402
  epidemic, 433
  increase, 432, 433

Air-based activities, 308

Alaska National Interest Lands Conservation Act, 88

Alcohol
  abuse, 432
  usage, 126

Alcoholics, 327

Alternative lifestyles, progress, 431–432

Altruism, 266

American Academy for Park and Recreation Administration and Academy of Leisure Services, 194

American Alliance for Health, Physical Education, Recreation and Dance (AAHPERD), 376–377

American Association for Leisure and Recreation (AALR), 371, 377, 380
  Council on Accreditation, 385

American Association of Retired Persons (AARP), 143, 164

American Camping Association (ACA), 376, 377

American League (baseball), 127

American Park and Recreation Society (APRS), 380

American Recreation Society (ARS), 322, 373

American Red Cross, 89, 287, 320

American Therapeutic Recreation Association (ATRA), 322, 329, 377–378

American Youth Hostels, 224. *See also* Hosteling International—American Youth Hostels

American Youth Soccer Organization, 150

Americans, leisure philosophy, 113

Americans with Disabilities Act (ADA), 89, 232, 323–324, 335–336, 407

Amusement parks, 304
Anaheim Convention Center, 306
Ancient Greece, leisure, 58
    legacy, 59
Ancient Rome, leisure, 58–61
Anshin, 349
Antecedent constraints, 24
Anticipatory planning, 344
Anti-utilitarian concept. *See* Leisure
Anxious (people), 143
Appalachian Mountain Club, 288
Appreciation, demonstration, 351
APRA. *See* Arizona Parks and Recreation
        Association
APRS. *See* American Park and Recreation
        Society
AquaArena, 430
Aquatic facilities, 188
Aquatic facility operator (AFO), 388
Aravaipa Creek Wilderness Area, 241
Areas/facilities, 188–189, 354–355
Aristotle, 58
Arizona Parks and Recreation Association
        (APRA), 381
Arkansas Hot Springs, 211
Armed Forces Recreation Society
        (AFRS), 380
ARS. *See* American Recreation Society
Arts, 442. *See also* New arts; Performing
                arts; Visual arts
    institutions, management, 222
    involvement, increase, 129
    state agencies, involvement, 219–222
Assets, building, 435
Assistive techology, 336–337
Association for Experiential Education
        (AEE), 378
Association for the Advancement of Health
        Education (AAHE), 377
Association of Junior Leagues, Teen
        Outreach Program, 269
Associative behaviors, 42
Assurance, 342
Athlete Business Publications, Inc., 382
Athletics. *See* College athletics
    equality, increase. *See* Women
ATRA. *See* American Therapeutic
        Recreation Association
At-risk youth, 327, 434
At-Risk Youth Division, 338
Attitude, 16
Attribution theory, 47
Atwell, Ernest, 67
Automobile racing, 304
Autonomy, need, 155
Autotelic (flow) experience, 33, 47–48

Awareness
    building, 15
    lack, 335
    merging. *See* Action

B

Baby boom generation, 143
Balance, increased interest, 434
Ballet, 442
Banff National Park, 76
Baseball, 442
BBP. *See* Benefits-Based Programming
Bed-and-breakfast inns, 302
Beecher, Henry Ward, 200
Behavior. *See* Work-oriented behavior
        form, 48
Behavioral conditions, 13
Behavioral objectives, 358
Bellini, 63
Benefits. *See* Mutual benefit; Private
                benefit; Public benefit
        documentation. *See* Professionals
Benefits-Based Programming (BBP),
        173, 362
BIA. *See* Bureau of Indian Affairs
Bible, 106
Big Brothers/Big Sisters, 270, 386
Big Brothers/Big Sisters of America,
        281–282
BLM. *See* Bureau of Land Management
Blue-collar workers, 87
Board of directors, 275
Boy Scouts of America, 44, 83, 85, 150,
        278–279
Boyce, William D., 67, 84, 278
Boys and Girls Clubs of America, 44, 85,
        92, 150, 281
Boys Club, 84
Brain injury, 337
British Columbia Recreation
        Association, 381
Bryant, William Cullen, 72
Buddha, 106
Budget cuts, opportunities, 223
Build a Bear workshop, 151
Bureau of Indian Affairs (BIA), 245
Bureau of Land Management (BLM), 229,
        235, 240–242
Bureau of Outdoor Recreation, 88
Bureau of Reclamation, 236, 248
Business
    generation, 273
    ownership, types, 296–299

C

California Park and Recreation Society
        (CPRS), 381, 382
Calvin, John, 61, 62
Camp Adventure, 353, 386, 416, 430
Camp Fire Boys and Girls, Inc., 44, 84, 109,
        272, 280
Camp Snoopy, 133
Camps, 333, 386
Can do attitude, 344
Canada. *See* Active Living Canada; Health
                Canada; Parks Canada;
                Sports Canada
Canadian federal agencies, types, 252–258
Canadian Heritage River System
        (CHRS), 256
Canadian Outdoor Recreation Demands
        Study (CORDS), 88
Canadian Pacific Railway, 253
Canadian Parks/Recreation Association
        (CPRA), 378
Canadian Tourism Commission (CTC), 259
Capital, 294. *See also* Human capital;
                Physical capital; Social
                capital
Capitalism, excesses, 95
Cardiopulmonary resuscitation (CPR), 388
Cardiovascular fitness, increase, 432
Care ethic, value (effect), 100–101
Care/activity centers, 223
Career
    assessment/exploration, 384–385
    development. *See* Professional career,
                development
    finding, 39
    opportunities. *See* Public parks;
                Recreation
Carnival, 21
Carnivals, 304
Carter, Jimmy, 88
Casino resorts, 302
Catharsis theory, 46
Catholic Youth Organization (CYO),
        282, 283
Catlin, Georg, 77
Cato the Elder, 58
CBM. *See* Citizen and/or Board Member
CCC. *See* Civilian Conservation Corps
CCRP. *See* Certified commercial recreation
                professional
Centers for independent living. *See*
                Independent living centers
Certification, 387–388. *See also* Technical
                certification
        creation. *See* State leisure services

Certified commercial recreation professional (CCRP), 372, 381
Certified festival executive (CFE), 379
Certified parks and recreation professional (CPRP), 372, 387
Certified recreational sports specialist (CRSS), 372, 379
Certified therapeutic recreation specialist (CTRS), 324, 331, 336–337, 372, 387
    need, 338
CEU. *See* Continuing Education Unit
CFE. *See* Certified festival executive
Challenge, 23
Challenger Middle School, 268
Change management, 311
Character formation, 16
Characteristics. *See* Primary characteristics; Secondary characteristics
Charles Bank Outdoor Gymnasium, 81
Chemical-dependency rehabilitation programs, 223
Chief executive officers/managers, 274
Child care, 198
    options, 393
    programs, 393
Child development, play (relationship), 80
Child, Julia, 144
Childbearing, postponement, 428
Childhood, 147
    leisure, relationship, 148–153
Children, 149
    development characteristics. *See* Younger children
    increase. *See* Latch-key children
    outdoor play. *See* Young children
Children's Museum (Boston), 269
Choice, 165
Christianity, leisure, 61–62
Christians, 403
CHRS. *See* Canadian Heritage River System
Church of Jesus Christ of Latter Day Saints, 283
Cinco de Mayo, 87, 397, 412
Circus maximus, 60
Circuses, 304
Citizen and/or Board Member (CBM), 380
Citizenship
    competencies, 157
    freedom of choice, relationship. *See* Democracy
City life, enriching, 172
Civilian Conservation Corps (CCC), 71, 78, 213
Class. *See* Leisure; Working class
    clown, 153
    distinctions, 62, 66

Cleanliness. *See* Value-added services
Clear-cutting, 438
Clients, relationships (clarification), 102–104
Climbing walls, 188
Clubs, 361
Coaching. *See* Lifestyles
Coalition for Active Living, 257
Cog-labor, 420
Cognitive/creative competence, 157
Cold War. *See* Post–Cold War period
Coliseum (Rome), 60
College athletics, 429
College-educated workers, 193
Colonial America, leisure, 65–66
Commercial enterprises, role, 444
Commercial leisure services, 89–90
    characteristics, 292–293
    goals/functions, 293
    resource base, 293–294
    sector, opportunities, 311–314
    types, 299–302
Commercial recreation venues
    discussion questions, 316
    introduction, 292
Commercial resorts, 386
Commission on Children, 268
Commitment, 23
Commodities. *See* Single-item commodities
Communication, 364. *See also* Electronic communication; Sophisticated communications; Written communication
    methods, 408
    patterns, 409
    source. *See* Miscommunication
Community
    belonging/involvement, 154
    festivals, 304
    values, examination. *See* Local community
    well-being, relationship. *See* Leisure
Community mental health centers, 333–334
Companionship, 18
Compensation, 18
    theory, 46
Competence, 23. *See also* Citizenship; Cognitive/creative competence; Health, physical competence; Perceived competence; Personal/social competence; Vocational competence
    feeling/sense, 155
Competitive advantage, 410–411

Competitive behaviors, 42
Compulsory resources, 173–174
Computer games, 138
Concentration. *See* Total concentration
Conceptual themes, 92
    discussion questions, 114
    introduction, 92–93
Concessions, sales revenue, 207
Conferences, 361
Conflict-enculturation theory, 47
Confucius, 106
Congressional Declaration of Purpose, 219
Conservation, 230
    organizations, 288
Consistency, 414
Constraints, 24. *See also* Antecedent constraints; Intervening constraints
    dimensions, 25
Consumers, relationships (clarification), 102–104
Consumption, centrality, 421
Consumptive recreation, nonconsumptive recreation (contrast), 261
Contests. *See* Leagues/tournaments/contests
Continuing Education Unit (CEU), 387, 388
    opportunities, 336
Continuous education, 343
Continuous improvement, 343
Contracting services, 198
Contractual receipts, 175
Contributors, 275
Control
    need, 155
    paradox, 8
    sense, 18
Convention centers, 302
Coolidge, Calvin, 230
Cooper, James Fenimore, 77
Cooperative Extension Service program. *See* U.S. Department of Agriculture
Coping skills, 157
CORDS. *See* Canadian Outdoor Recreation Demands Study
Core values, 112
Corporate gifts, 272
Corporations, 297–299
Corps of Engineers. *See* U.S. Corps of Engineers
Correctional institutions, 222
Couch potatoes, 443
Counselor, 366
County government, 180–184
CPR. *See* Cardiopulmonary resuscitation
CPRA. *See* Canadian Parks/Recreation Association

CPRP. *See* Certified parks and recreation professional
CPRS. *See* California Park and Recreation Society
Crate Lake National Park, 301
Creative competence. *See* Cognitive/creative competence
Creative expression, 157
    need, 154
Creativity, 9, 310
    promotion, 16–17
CRSS. *See* Certified recreational sports specialist
Cruise lines, 34
CTC. *See* Canadian Tourism Commission
CTRS. *See* Certified therapeutic recreation specialist
Cultural activities, 123
    mass leisure, relationship, 128
Cultural background, 357–358
Cultural celebrations, 415
Cultural competence, 393
Cultural differences, 358, 415
Cultural diversity
    discussion questions, 418
    introduction, 392
Cultural heritage, transmission, 16
Cultural parity, 132
Cultural pluralism, 87
Cultural programs/facilities, 223
Cultural sensitivity, 404–405
Culturally based activities, 308–309
Culture, 357, 395–397
    building, 273
Curtis, Henry, 67
Customerizing, 21
Customer-leader interaction, 348
Customer-oriented professional, 349
Customers
    assistance, 352
    caring, 351
    composition, 414
    game, 353
    orientation, 178, 234–235, 294–295
    relations. *See* Positive customer relations
    respect, 351
    response networks, 352
    service
        approach, 351
        delivery, 346
        training, 352
    understanding, 349
CYO. *See* Catholic Youth Organization

D

da Vinci, Leonardo, 63
Dating games, 158

Daycare centers. *See* Adult daycare centers
Day-to-day interactions, 353
Debt financing, 293
Decision making, 311
Deficits, reduction, 435
Degage, 338
Democracy, citizenship/freedom of choice (relationship), 97
Demographic trends, response, 406
Demographic variables, 9
Demographics, change, 87
DENKS. *See* Dual employed no kids
Department of Agriculture. *See* U.S. Department of Agriculture
Department of Conservation. *See* Illinois Department of Conservation
Department of Natural Resources, 213
Department of the Interior, 235, 240, 245
Department store, 307
Depression. *See* Great Depression
Desegregation, open enrollment (relationship), 440
Destination points. *See* Transportation-centered destination points
Destitute (people), 327
Development
    competencies. *See* Youth
    contrast. *See* Ecosystems
    personnel, 274
    theory, 47
Developmental disabilities. *See* People with developmental disabilities
Dewey, John, 107
Dialogue, 414
Differences, valuing, 404–405
    process, 404–405
Digital Equipment Corporation, 411
DINKS. *See* Double income no kids
Direct face-to-face leadership, 275
Direct program leadership, 365
Direct recreation resources/services, types. *See* State-provided direct recreation resources/services
Direct service
    leadership, types, 365–367
    levels, 363
    personnel role, characteristics, 364
    professional roles, 191, 192
    provider, 364
    roles, 363–364
Disabilities. *See* People with disabilities
    schools/residential centers, 334–335
Disabled outdoor sports, 396
Disabling diseases, 325–326
Discount memberships, 383
Discount store. *See* Full-line discount store
Discretionary income, increase, 120, 217

Discrimination, 394, 399. *See also* Gender; Sex discrimination
Disengagement, theory, 164
Disney. *See* Walt Disney Company
Disney World, 301, 304, 305, 349
Disneyland, 89, 301, 304, 349. *See also* Tokyo Disneyland
    vacation, 36
Disneyland Paris, 305, 349
District laws. *See* Special districts
Diverse groups, leadership considerations, 411–414
Diversity, 198. *See also* Cultural diversity
    dimensions, 399–400
    foundational perspectives, 394–399
    implications. *See* Leisure service
    increase, 393–394, 430–432
    leadership, interaction, 411–415
    management, 410
    performance, 409
    programming, 415–416
    promotion, suggested actions, 411
    related actions, 408–411
    support, 408, 413
    valuing, 404, 406
    work, 411
Dividends. *See* Interest/dividends
Divine contemplation, 94
Divine ends, 94
Dog racing, 304
Dolphin Dive, 309
Dominance, 14
Donations/gifts, 272
Double income no kids (DINKS), 345
Downing, Andrew, 72
Drop-in programs, 360
Dropouts, 156
Drucker, Peter, 310
Drugs, 72, 156
    abuse, 432
    usage, 126
        concern, 435
    users, 327
Dual employed no kids (DENKS), 345
Dyslexia, 324

E

Eagle Creek State Park, 224
EAPs. *See* Employee Assistance Programs
Early Adolescent Helper Program, 268
Early adulthood, characteristics, 159
Earned income, 174–175
Earth-friendly choices, 438
Easter Seals Society, 322
Eckerd Camps, 284
Eckerd Foundation, 285–286
Eco-conscious outdoor adventures, 34

Ecological recovery sites, 189
Economic development, 220
Economic planning, end-use, 421
Economic status, 403
Economic trends, 446
Economies of scale/scope, 273
Ecosystems, development (contrast),
          437–438
Eco-tourism, 378
     markets, 133
Eco-vacations, perspective, 439
Education, 9, 249, 385–386, 403. *See also*
          Continuous education;
          Lifelong education
     emphasis. *See* Higher education
     level, 357
Education for All Handicapped Children
          Act, 89
Educational Amendments Act, 407
Educational issues, 439–440
Educational opportunities, 374–375
Educational reform, 441
EEO. *See* Equal Employment Opportunity
Effective performance, 350–351
Elder issues, 428
Elderly persons, 393
     settings, 334
Electronic communication, 375
Electronics. *See* Home electronics
Emerson, Ralph Waldo, 77
Empathy, 342
Employee Assistance Programs (EAPs),
          increase, 433–434
Employee behaviors, 350–352
Employee Services Management
          Association (ESMA), 379
Employment, 9. *See also* Underemployment
     service sector, growth, 447–448
Enabling laws, 180
Enculturation theory. *See* Conflict-
          enculturation theory
Endowments/trusts, 207
Energy sources. *See* Nonconsumptive
          energy sources
Entertainment, 137
     services, 304–307
Enthusiasts, 143
Entrepreneur, 177
     challenges, 315
Entrepreneurial skills, 310
Entrepreneurship
     definition, 309–311
     opportunities/challenges, 309–314
Environment, mass leisure (relationship),
          130–131
Environmental battleground, 244
Environmental concerns, 436–439
Environmental conditions, 13

Environmental degradation, 438–439
Environmental ethics, 439
Environmental factors, 357
Environmental responsibility, progress, 439
Environmental sources, 88–89
Equal Employment Opportunity (EEO),
          406–408
Equality, increase. *See* Women
Equipment. *See* High-tech leisure equipment
     usage, 443–445
Equity
     financing, 293
     issues, 414
Erikson, Erik H., 146
ESMA. *See* Employee Services
          Management Association
Esteem, building. *See* Self-esteem
Esteem-building activities, 416
Ethics, 96. *See also* Environmental ethics;
          Judeo-Christian ethic;
          Leisure service
     code, 372–373. *See also* National
          Recreation and Park
          Association
     value, effect. *See* Care ethic
Ethnic minorities, 393, 405
Ethnicity. *See* Race/ethnicity
     outdoors, relationship, 232
Ethos, 39
Evaluation, 364
Events. *See* Special events
Excursion boats, 67
Exercise (working out), 361
Existentialism, leisure (relationship), 105,
          107–108
Expectations, exceeding, 350
Experience. *See* Military experience;
          Professional experience
Experimentalism, leisure (relationship),
          105, 107
Exploratory behaviors, 42
Expressive dimension, 266
Expressive-instrumental dimension, 266
Extended family, changes, 426–427
External forces, acknowledgment, 406
External relationships, 104
External/normative criteria, 6–7
Extracurricular programs, decreased
          support, 440

F

Face-to-face contact, 375
Face-to-face leadership, 366. *See also* Direct
          face-to-face leadership
Facility operator, 367
Facility usage policies, 431
Fact finding. *See* Research

Factory outlet, 307
Fad-oriented leisure service market, 314
Fairgrounds, 223
Family
     belonging/involvement, 154
     changes. *See* Extended family
     composition, changes, 426
     concerns, changes, 426
     structure, reevaluation, 427
Fast food, faxing, 41
Federal agencies, types, 235–236. *See also*
          Canadian federal agencies
Federal funds, 207
Federal government
     achievements, 237
     challenges, 260–261
     coordination. *See* State leisure services
     discussion questions, 261–262
     introduction, 228
     regulatory activities, 232
     resource base, 233
Federal Job Information Center, 234
Federal Land Policy and Management Act,
          241
Federal leisure service agencies
     characteristics, 229
     goals/functions, 229–232
Federal Water Projects Recreation Act, 248
Feedback, clarity, 8
Fees/charges. *See* Public parks; Recreation;
          State leisure services
Fees/tuition. *See* Programs
Fern Ridge Reservoir, 246
Festivals. *See* Special festivals
Financial assistance, 175, 230
Financial crises, 224
FISH, philosophy, 351
Fish/wildlife agencies. *See* State
          fish/wildlife agencies; U.S.
          Fish and Wildlife Service
Fitness
     centers, 188
     decline. *See* Youth
     increase. *See* Cardiovascular fitness
Flea market, 307
Fleet Centers, 284
Flex place, 447
Flex schedule, 447
Flex time, 446–447
Flexibility, 178
Florida Park and Recreation Association
          (FPRA), 381, 382
Flow experience. *See* Autotelic experience
FLYERS. *See* Fun Loving Youth En Route
          to Success
FONUTAR, 165
Food services, 301–302
Forced retirement, 393

Forces
    acknowledgment. *See* External forces
    response. *See* Internal forces
Forest Service. *See* U.S. Forest Service
Forestry projects. *See* Urban forestry
        projects
Forests. *See* State forests
    management/protection/usage. *See*
        National forest system
Foundation Grant Index, 272
Foundation grants, 272
Founders, 274
4-H for Youth of America. *See* Head Heart
        Hands and Health
FPRA. *See* Florida Park and Recreation
        Association
Franchises, 313
Franklin, Benjamin, 32
Free time, 37, 42, 119
Freedom, 24, 31–32. *See also* Perceived
        freedom
    independence, 20
Freedom of choice, relationship. *See*
        Democracy
Fresh Air camps, 85
Friends, making, 151
Frontline responsiveness, 352
Fulfillment. *See* Personal fulfillment
Full-line discount store, 307
Fun, 16
Fun Loving Youth En Route to Success
        (FLYERS), 345
Funding, decrease, 260
Fundraisers, 274
Fundraising, 273
Future orientation, 343
Future trends. *See* Leisure
Futurist groups, 382–383

G

Gaming establishments, 304
Gangs, 338
Gay/lesbian people, 393
Gender, 9. *See also* Sex/gender
    discrimination, 401
    roles
        acceptance, 24
        shifts, 427–428
General supervision, 275
Generalization theory, 47
Generation, 355–356
Generation X, 435
Geographic location, 403
Geographical location, 51
Geographically based activity, 309
Gifts. *See* Donations/gifts

Gila Box Riparian Natural Conservation
        Area, 241
Gila Wilderness, 238
Girl Scouts of the U.S.A., 44, 109, 272, 279
Girls, Incorporated, 150, 269, 270,
        280–281
Global issues, focus, 439
Global leisure, 125
Goals, 98, 171. *See also* Outcome-oriented
        goals
    clarity, 8
    defining, 387
    interdependence, 102
Golden Age, 94
Good life, 99
Gotcha Glacier, 133–134
Governance, 266
Government. *See* County government; Local
        government; Municipal
        government
    grants, 272
Government Service (GS) ranking, 234
Grandchildren, play, 5
Grants. *See* Foundation grants; Government
Great America, 304
Great Depression, 71, 355, 356
Green appeal, 438
Group dynamics, 364
Group homes, 331, 332
Group therapy, 333
Groups, leadership considerations. *See*
        Diverse groups
Growth. *See* Personal growth
GS. *See* Government Service
Guide. *See* Host/guide/interpreter
Gulick, Charlotte, 84, 280
Gulick, Luther H., 67, 84, 85, 280

H

Halfway houses, 333
Happiness, 6, 94. *See also* Human
        happiness
    definition, 6–7
Hasidic Jews, 403
Head Heart Hands and Health (4-H) for
        Youth of America, 85, 109,
        154, 277–278
Health
    benefits, 376
    care
        costs, increase, 433
        reform, 320
    changes. *See* Physical health; Social
        health
    physical competence, 156
    trends/issues, 432–436

Health Canada, 256–258
Health-care services, 165
Help Us Grow through Service and Smiles
        (HUGSS), 268
Herodotus, 2, 57
Hertzberg, Frederick, 17
Hetch Hetchy Valley, 244
Heterosexism, 402
HI-AYH. *See* Hosteling International—
        American Youth Hostels
Hierarchy of leisure pursuits. *See* Leisure
Higher education, emphasis, 441
High-impact services, 362
High-performance athletes/coaches, 252
High-tech leisure equipment, 444
Hiring practices, 352
Historic American Building Survey, 245
Historic American Engineering
        Record, 245
Historical events/places, knowledge,
        53–54
Historical philosophical foundations,
        examination, 108
Historically based activities, 308–309
History. *See* Leisure
    involved people, understanding, 53
    studying (reasons), 52
    understanding, 54
HIV, 324, 402
    concern, 432
    infection, 394, 432
Hobbies, 360
Hoffer, Eric, 20
Holistic concept. *See* Leisure
Holmes, Oliver Wendell, 52
Home electronics, 444
Home health care agencies, 332–333
Home rule legislation, 180
Homeless, 327, 337
Homelessness, 72
Homeplace, 247
Horse racing, 304
Hospital Recreation Section (HRS), 322
Hospitality services, 301–302
Hospitals, 334. *See also* State hospitals/
        institutions
Hosteling International, 198
Hosteling International—American Youth
        Hostels (HI-AYH), 132
Hostelling, 132
Hostels, 302
Host/guide/interpreter, 366
Hotels, 302
Household composition, changes, 427
HRS. *See* Hospital Recreation Section
HUGSS. *See* Help Us Grow through Service
        and Smiles

Hull House, 82
Human capital, 124
Human development, stages, 145–147
Human dignity, protection/promotion, 97
Human doings, 15
Human happiness, 97
Human resources, 87
    management, 273
Human skills, 208
Humanism, leisure (relationship), 105, 108

I

Idea generation, 311
Idealism, leisure (relationship), 105, 106
Ideals, commitment. *See* Professional ideals
Identity, sense, 155
IES. *See* International Ecotourism Society
IFEA. *See* International Festivals and Events
        Association
Illinois Department of Conservation, 224
Illinois Park and Recreation Association
        (IPRA), 381
Illinois Park District Code, 186
Image, 348–349
Immersion. *See* Total immersion
Improvement. *See* Continuous
        improvement
Inclusion, 198
Inclusive recreation, 330
Inclusivity, 86
Income, 9. *See also* Earned income
    increase. *See* Discretionary income
Independence. *See* Freedom
    need, 155
Independent living centers, 333
Indian Black Expo, Inc., 269
Individualism, sense, 155
Individuality, forms emergence, 421
Individuals with disabilities. *See* People with
        disabilities
Individuals with physical disabilities. *See*
        People with physical
        disabilities
Indoor leisure pursuits, 19
Industrial era, 55, 445
    leisure, 66–86
Industrial Revolution, 35, 94, 319, 439
Industrialization, 437
Information, 355
    era, 55, 86–90
    gathering, 364
    superhighway, seniors (usage), 356
    usage, 189–190
Information-based societies, 87
Innovation, 166, 343
    services, usage, 443–445

Institutional help/self-help, change, 87–88
Institutionalized movement, 70
Institutions, 51. *See also* Penal institutions;
        State hospitals/institutions
    movements, 67–72
    relationships, clarification, 104–105
Institutions, involvement. *See* Knowledge
Instructional classes, 360
Instructional leadership, 365
Instrumental dimension, 266
Instrumental-expressive dimension, 266
Integration, 417
Interest/dividends, 272
Interests, alignment, 383
Internal forces, response, 406
Internal Revenue Service, 266
Internal/emotional state, 7
Internal/subjective criteria, 7
International Ecotourism Society (IES),
        378–379
International Festivals and Events
        Association (IFEA), 379
Internet listservs, 375
Interpersonal skills, 157, 208, 364
Interpreter. *See* Host/guide/interpreter
Intervening constraints, 24
Intrapersonal skills, 157
Intrinsic motivation, 32–33
IPRA. *See* Illinois Park and Recreation
        Association
Izaac Walton League, 382

J

James, William, 107
Jensen, Jans, 74
JIT. *See* Just-In-Time Programming
Job. *See* Pure job
    relationship. *See* Leisure
    sharing, 447
    stress, 432
    type, 404
Joy, promotion, 16
Judeo-Christian credo, 284
Judeo-Christian ethic, 111
Junior Achievement, 279–280
Just-In-Time Programming (JIT), 362
Juveniles, 327

K

Kasl, Charlotte Davis, 97
Kennedy, John F., 230
KidsPlaces, 269
Kierkegaard, Soren, 107
Knott's Berry Farm, 304
Knowledge, 16. *See also* Legal knowledge
    organized body, 371

transmitting, organizations/institutions
        (involvement), 371–372
    usefulness, 54
KOA, 308
Koppel, Ted, 125
Koran, 106
Kwanzaa, 87, 412

L

Land and Water Conservation Fund, 127, 244
    continuation, 260
Land and Water Conservation Fund Act, 88,
        206, 213, 230
Land Between the Lakes Program, 247, 248
Land-based activities, 308
Landowners, 57
    assistance, 215
Lane County Park and Recreation
        Department, 184
Langford, Nathaniel P., 75
Language, usage, 415
LAS. *See* Leisure and Aging Section
Latch-key children, increase, 426
Late adulthood, characteristics, 161
Leaders. *See* Youth
    body language, 414
    expectations, 414
        impact, 414
    tone, 414
Leadership, 190–191, 355, 364. *See also*
        Direct face-to-face
        leadership; Direct program
        leadership; Face-to-face
        leadership; Instructional
        leadership; Team leadership
    considerations. *See* Diverse groups
    development, 98
    guidelines, 415
    interaction. *See* Diversity
    types. *See* Direct service
Leagues/tournaments/contests, 360
Learning
    centrality, 421
    era, 445
    opportunities, seeking, 177
Lee, Joseph, 67
Legal knowledge, 364
Legislation, 322–323. *See also* Home rule
        legislation; State leisure
        services
    types, 179–180
Lego Land, 133
Leisure. *See* Agricultural era; Ancient
        Greece; Ancient Rome;
        Christianity; Colonial
        America; Global leisure;

Leisure—*Cont.*
　　Middle Ages; Non-leisure;
　　Preliterate society; Pure
　　leisure; Renaissance; Serious
　　leisure; Virtual leisure
　activity, 35–36, 158, 180, 357, 441
　　young children, participation
　　　location, 150
　agencies, 386
　anti-utilitarian concept, 38
　awareness, 98
　balancing. *See* Work
　children, viewpoint, 4–5
　class, 57
　commercialization, 67
　community well-being, relationship, 12
　competencies, 360
　concepts, knowledge, 52
　constraints, 23–26
　culture, 32
　definition, 31
　discussion questions, 27, 49, 90,
　　　166–167, 201–202
　enjoyment
　　facilities/structures, providing, 17
　　space, providing, 17
　equipment. *See* High-tech leisure
　　　equipment
　experience, 351
　　satisfaction, factors, 31–33
　future trends, 422
　　discussion questions, 448–449
　　introduction, 420–421
　grandparents, viewpoint, 3–5
　historical perspective, 51
　history, 54–55
　holistic concept, 38–39
　industries, ranking, 312–313
　introduction, 2, 30–31, 51–52, 142, 170
　job, relationship, 41
　life cycle, 142–143
　managers, 124
　motives, 18–23
　needs, change, 423–424
　organizations, 15–17
　　relationship. *See* Life satisfaction
　perceptions, changes, 88
　philosophy, 92. *See also* Americans
　　construction, reasons, 101
　products, 303–304
　program planning, influencing factors,
　　　355–358
　programmers, roles, 363
　programming, 341
　public/private involvement, blurring,
　　　429–430
　pursuing, motivation, 17–18

　pursuits, 97. *See also* Indoor leisure
　　　pursuits
　　hierarchy, 104
　relationship. *See* Age; Childhood;
　　　Existentialism;
　　　Experimentalism;
　　　Humanism; Idealism; Life
　　　satisfaction; Lifestyles; Mass
　　　media; Perennialism;
　　　Pragmatism; Realism;
　　　Technology; Work
　right, 329
　role, 161
　satisfaction, relationship, 12
　social capital, construction, 123–124
　social instrument, 37
　social status symbol, 36–37
　state of mind, 36
　success, barriers, 327–328
　symbolic nature, 37
　time, 34–35
　　alternatives, 426
　　amount, changes, 441–443
　　participation availability,
　　　fluctuations, 443
　21st century, 3–6
　use, 96–97
　viewing, 33–39
　work, relationship, 41
Leisure Ability Model, 329
Leisure and Aging Section (LAS), 380
Leisure service. *See* Commercial leisure
　　　services; State leisure
　　　services
　agencies, characteristics. *See* Federal
　　　leisure service agencies;
　　　Local service agencies
　business. *See* Small leisure service
　　　businesses
　delivery, 109, 170, 204, 228, 263–264,
　　　292, 318
　market. *See* Fad-oriented leisure service
　　　market
　organizations, 150
　　characteristics. *See* Private
　　　nonprofit leisure service
　　　organizations
　　philosophy, 101
　　philosophy, meaning, 111–113
　　services, 353–358
　　types. *See* Voluntary nonprofit
　　　leisure service organizations;
　　　Youth nonprofit leisure
　　　service organizations
　pioneers, 68–70
　profession
　　ethics, 372

　　foundations, appreciation, 53
　　professionals, diversity implications,
　　　405–411
Leonardo da Vinci. *See* da Vinci
Lesbian people. *See* Gay/lesbian people
Liability, benefits, 376
Licenses, issuance, 215
Life. *See* Good life
　cycle, 145. *See also* Leisure
　enriching. *See* City life
　force, 14
　pattern. *See* Linear life pattern
　quality, 6, 98, 327
　　increased interest, 434
　social capital, construction, 123–124
　stages, 145, 146
　values, effect, 98
Life, quality, 329
Life satisfaction, 2, 6–9
　discussion questions, 27
　introduction, 2
　leisure
　　organizations, relationship, 15–17
　　relationship, 9–10
　relationship. *See* Age; Work
Lifelong education, 388
Life-maintenance activities, 35
Lifestyles, 143–145. *See also* Optimal
　　　lifestyle
　balancing, 15
　coaching, 443–444
　leisure, relationship, 12–13
　management, 13–15
　pace, increase, 209
　progress. *See* Alternative lifestyles
　return. *See* Relaxed lifestyle
Limits, need, 153
Linear life pattern, 428–429
Line/staff, partnership, 413
Literary programs, 360
Little League baseball, 150
Living History Program, 247
Local community, values (examination), 109
Local government, 170
　coordination. *See* State leisure services
　discussion questions, 201–202
　introduction, 170
　recreation/park administration,
　　　trends/issues, 196–197
　types, 178–184
Local leisure service agencies,
　　　characteristics, 171
Local parks
　agencies, goals/functions, 171–173
　services, 170
Lockheed Corporation, 445
Lord of Misrule, 62

Love/worship, combination. *See* Work
Lowe, Juliette, 67, 84
LSD, usage, 126
Luther, Martin, 61
Lutheran Brotherhood, 268

M

Magic Me program, 268
Mall of America, 133, 437, 446
Management, 352, 364
Manufacturing products, 303–304
Marital status, 403
Marketing
    concepts, 295
    orientation. *See* Public parks; Recreation
    practices, 417
Married-couple families, 427
Marshall, John, 297
Martin Luther King Day, 412
Mass leisure, 116, 125. *See also* Movies;
        Television
    common elements, 120–122
    discussion questions, 140
    forms, 138–139
    introduction, 116
    people, interaction, 122–123
    relationship. *See* Cultural activities;
            Environment; Sports;
            Tourism
    social activities, 123–127
    time, allotment, 116–119
Mass media, 120, 123
    amount, increase, 122
    leisure, relationship, 134–139
Mass production, 420
Mass society, emergence, 120
Mass transportation, 445–446
Massachusetts Bay Company, 65
Massachusetts Emergency and Hygiene
        Association, 81
Massachusetts Great Ponds Act, 66
Materialism, 120
    increase, 435
Mather, Stephen T., 67, 76–77, 212
Matriarchs, 165
Media. *See* Mass media
    de-massification, 121
    forms, 138–139
Medicare, 144
Megamovies, 138
Members. *See* Rank and file members
Membership. *See* Discount memberships
    fees, 270
    guidelines, 383
    involvement, opportunities, 383
Mental illness. *See* People with mental illness

Mental impairment/qualities, 401–402
Merced County Mental Health program, 334
Metaphors, quest, 21
Michelangelo, 63
Microeconomy, 21
Middle adulthood, characteristics, 160
Middle Ages, leisure, 62–63
Middle aging, 423
Military experience, 403
Military recreation departments, 109
Millikin Company, 348
Minorities. *See* Ethnic minorities
Miscommunication, source, 409
Mission. *See* Agencies
Mistakes, elimination, 344
Mobility, 88
Money, value, 117
Mood, 9
    three-dimensional representation, 14
Moral character development, 98
Morale, 249–250
Morale Welfare and Recreation (MWR),
        249–250
Morality, 96
Motels, 302
Mothers. *See* Stay-at-home mothers
Motion Picture Association of America, 138
Motivation. *See* Intrinsic motivation
    theory, 17. *See also* Achievement-
            motivation theory
Motor skill development, 151
Movies, mass leisure, 136–138
Moving target, 21
MTV. *See* Music Television
Muir, John, 67, 79
Multiculturalism, 406
Multidimensionality, 11
Multi-entrepreneurial atmosphere, 21
Multiple-use areas, examination, 438
Municipal government, 180–181
Municipal parks, 72–76
    resource base, 173–175
Museums, 223
Music Television (MTV), 98, 136, 305
    Hong Kong, 136
Mutual benefit, 267
MWR. *See* Morale Welfare and Recreation

N

NAFTA treaty, 165
NAGWS. *See* National Association for Girls
        and Women in Sport
NAS. *See* National Aquatics Section
Nash, J.B., 104
NASPD. *See* National Association of State
        Park Directors

NASPE. *See* National Association for Sport
        and Physical Education
National Advisory Council on Fitness and
        Amateur Sport, 256
National Aquatics Section (NAS), 380
National Association for Girls and Women
        in Sport (NAGWS), 377
National Association for Sport and Physical
        Education (NASPE), 377
National Association for Stock Car
        Racing, 127
National Association of State Foresters, 214
National Association of State Park Directors
        (NASPD), 210
National Audubon Society, 382
National Capital Commission, 256
National Children and Youth Fitness Study,
        149, 153
National Council for Therapeutic Recreation
        Certification (NCTRC),
        331, 387
National Council of Women, 81
National Dance Association (NDA), 377
National Endowment for the Arts (NEA),
        219, 232, 236, 250–251
National Endowment for the Humanities,
        236, 251–252
National forest system, management/
        protection/use, 238
National Intramural-Recreation Sports
        Association (NIRSA), 379
National League of Cities, 171
National League of Professional Baseball
        Clubs, 127
National Park Service, 95, 130, 212,
        228–230, 235, 242–245, 260
National Park System, 76, 88, 244
National parks, 76–77
    creation, 76
National Program for Playground
        Safety, 189
National Recreation and Park Association
        (NRPA), 173, 362, 371, 374,
        379–380, 385
    congresses, 387
    ethics code, 176, 373
    National Certification Board, 176
    support, 388
    Urban Youth Initiative, 199
National Register of Historic Places, 245
National Rifle Association, 288
National Society for Park Resources
        (NSPR), 380
National Student Recreation and Park
        Society (NSRPS), 380
National Taxonomy of Exempt Entities
        (NTEE), 264–265

National Therapeutic Recreation Society (NTRS), 322, 326, 329
National Trails System, 245
National Wild and Scenic River System, 245
National Wilderness Preservation System, 244
Nationwide Outdoor Recreation Plan, 244–245
Natural environment, leisure services, 308–309
Natural resources
conservation, 96
degradation, 437
improved infrastructure, 121
preservation, 96
Nature Conservancy, 288
NCTRC. *See* National Council for Therapeutic Recreation Certification
NDA. *See* National Dance Association
NEA. *See* National Endowment for the Arts
Needs
anticipation, 350
assessment, 359
Negativeness, elimination, 344
Networking, 198, 386–387
Networks, on-line connection, 445
New arts, 360
New poor, 337–338
New technology, 87
New Urbanism, 200, 201
NGO. *See* Nongovernmental organization
Nietzsche, Frederic, 107
Nintendo, 138
NIRSA. *See* National Intramural-Recreation Sports Association
Nonappropriated funds, 233
Nonconsumptive energy sources, 438
Nonconsumptive recreation, contrast. *See* Consumptive recreation
Nongovernmental organization (NGO), 381
Noninfected customers/staff, rights, 394
Noninvolvement, 416
Non-leisure, 40
Non-material needs, 420
Nonprofit leisure service, 263
organizations
characteristics. *See* Private nonprofit leisure service organizations
types. *See* Voluntary nonprofit leisure service organizations; Youth nonprofit leisure service organizations
Nonprofit organizations, 384
challenge, 289
characteristics, 266
discussion questions, 290
employer, 269

goals, 267
introduction, 263–264
resource base, 270–273
Nonsectarian organizations, 276
Nonsectarian-sponsored organizations, 276–282
Nontraditional wilderness, 244
No-relationship model, 11
Northern Yukon National Park, 253
Nostalgia, 20
NRPA. *See* National Recreation and Park Association
NSPR. *See* National Society for Park Resources
NSRPS. *See* National Student Recreation and Park Society
NTEE. *See* National Taxonomy of Exempt Entities
NTRS. *See* National Therapeutic Recreation Society
Nursing homes, 334

O

Offenders. *See* Adult offenders
Official/referee, 365–366
Older adulthood, 147
Older adults
characteristics, 163
leisure, relationship, 162–166
Older children, developmental characteristics, 152
Older individuals (proportion), increase, 431
Older population, increase, 424
Olmsted, Sr., Frederick Law, 67, 72, 74–75, 77
Open enrollment, relationship. *See* Desegregation
Open space, 200
programs, assistance, 230
Optimal arousal theory, 47
Optimal lifestyle, 12
Order. *See* Value-added services
Oregon Park and Recreation Society, 387
Organization, 364, 408–411
enrichment, 406
impact. *See* Technology
involvement. *See* Knowledge
pluralism, advantages, 412
Organizational policies/procedures, 346, 352–353
Organizations. *See* Professional organizations
knowledge, 102
relationships. *See* Life satisfaction clarification, 104
service. *See* Special populations
values, examinations, 109
Orientation. *See* Future orientation
ORRRC. *See* Outdoor Recreation Resource Review Commission

Oshmans Sporting Goods Company, 444
Outcome-oriented goals, 362
Outdoor recreation, 360
definition, 131
resources, 210–217
direct management, 229
Outdoor Recreation Resource Review Commission (ORRRC), 88, 230
Outdoors
activities, 123
adventures. *See* Eco-conscious outdoor adventures
natural phenomena, simulation, 444
play. *See* Young children
relationship. *See* Ethnicity
sports. *See* Disabled outdoor sports
Outpatient clinics, 332
Outreach programs, 361
Outreach worker, 366
Overhead, 21
Overpopulation, 424–426
Owners, characteristics, 294
Ownership, types. *See* Business

P

PAC 10 universities, 408
Panhellenic subculture, 395
Parental status, 403
Parks. *See* Amusement parks; Municipal parks; National parks; State parks; Theme parks
administration, trends/issues. *See* Local government
boards, 180
departments, 335
development, assistance, 230
laws. *See* Special park/recreation laws
services, providing, 178–184
Parks Canada, 253–256
Parks Commission, 198
Participant numbers, 344
Participants, involvement, 165
Partnering, benefits, 273
Partnerships, 297. *See also* Line/staff
building, 195–199
collaborative efforts, 273
Parts/wholes, 21
Passion, power, 85–86
PBS. *See* Public Broadcasting System
PCAO. *See* President's Commission on Americans Outdoors
Peer pressure, 401
PEERsuasion, 280, 281
Penal institutions, 335
People of color, 394
number, increase, 430–431

People of Color Leadership Forum, 411
People with developmental disabilities, 326
People with disabilities, 324–327
    program design, 416–417
    services, 89
People with mental illness, 326
People with physical disabilities, 326, 393
    opportunities, 431
Perceived competence, 32
Perceived freedom, 31, 41
Perennialism, leisure (relationship),
    105, 106
Performance. *See* Effective performance
    measurements, 344
    objectives, 358
Performing arts, 360
Perserverance, 39
Personal development, 19–20
Personal effort, 39
Personal fulfillment, 88
Personal growth, 97
Personal levels, 410
Personal values, examination, 108
Personality, 9
Personal/social competence, 157
Personnel. *See* Development; Programs;
    Sales
    range, 274–275
Peters, Mabel, 67
PGA. *See* Professional Golf Association
Philadelphia Hostel, 198
Philosophical attitude, construction, 93–96
Philosophical books/articles, 110
Philosophical themes, 92
    discussion questions, 114
    introduction, 92–93
Philosophy. *See* Leisure service;
    Professional philosophy
    categories, 105–108
    circumstances, 93
    construction, 105–108
        reasons. *See* Leisure
        steps, 108–111
    definition, 93
    development, 96
    discussion. *See* Professionals
    meaning. *See* Leisure
    relationship. *See* Value
Physical abilities, 12
Physical activity, 20
    need, 155
Physical capital, 124, 420
Physical competence. *See* Health
Physical conditions, 13
Physical culture, 31
Physical disabilities. *See* People with
    physical disabilities
Physical expression, 42

Physical fitness, 95
Physical health, changes, 432–434
Physical impairment/qualities, 401–402
Physical inclusion, 327
Physical injury, 335
Physical medicine centers, 335
Physical resources, improved
    infrastructure, 121
Physical strength, loss, 424
Physical well-being, 20
Pierce, Charles, 107
Pilgrims, 65
Pinchot, Gifford, 67
Planning, 364
    efforts, 206
Play, 94. *See also* Grandchildren; Young
    children
    definition, 44–45
    dimensions, 45–48
    discussion questions, 49
    institutionalized forms, 43
    introduction, 30–31
    love/worship, combination. *See* Work
    movement, 80–83
    reduction, 118
    relationship. *See* Child development
    spaces, 80
    spirit, 81
    time, 326
Play Congress, 53
Play Station Family Fun Center, 299
Playground Association of America, 53
Playground movement, 320
Playing, 52
Pleasuring grounds, 242
Pluralism. *See* Cultural pluralism
    advantages, 411. *See also* Organization
    leveraging, 410–411
    related actions, 408–411
    support, 413
Policy-making boards, 180
Political environment, consistency, 260
Political leadership, 335
Poor. *See* New poor
Pop Warner football, 150
Population. *See* Overpopulation
    distribution, shifts, 424
    increase. *See* Older population
    shifts, 421–427
Portfolio, usage. *See* Professional portfolio
Positive affect, 32
Positive ambiance/environment, 351–352
Positive customer relations, promotion, 346,
    349–352
Positive social interaction, 153
Post–Cold War period, 356
Post–World War II, 120, 143
Powell, Lord Baden, 278

Power
    role, 399
    sense, 18
Powerball, 304
Pragmatism, leisure (relationship), 105, 107
Preexercise theory, 45
Pregnancy, leveling/increase. *See* Teen
    pregnancy
Prejudice, 397–398
    reduction
        contact conditions, 398
        leisure programs/activities, 398
    understanding, 397
Preliterate society, 55
    leisure, 56–57
President's Commission on Americans
    Outdoors (PCAO), 131,
    230, 260
    findings/suggestions, 231
Pride, 344
Primary characteristics, 399–402
    secondary characteristics, interaction, 404
Privacy, rights, 394
Private benefit, 267
Private hospital systems, 320
Private involvement, blurring. *See* Leisure
Private nonprofit leisure service
    organizations
    characteristics, 264–267
    goals/functions, 267–270
Private sectors, cooperation. *See*
    Public/private sectors
Problem solving, 311, 364
Problem-solving process, 178
Production, quality importance, 420
Product-oriented economy, 446
Products, definition, 345–346
Profession, elements, 370–371
Professional associations, 374–376
Professional authority, creation, 372
Professional career
    development, 371
        discussion questions, 390
        introduction, 370
    pursuit, elements, 383–389
Professional development, 388
Professional experience, 386
Professional Golf Association (PGA), 324
Professional ideals, commitment, 373
Professional organizations, 322
    types, 376–383
Professional philosophy, 364
Professional portfolio, usage, 388–389
Professional skills, 364
Professional sports, 304
Professional vernacular, 364
Professionals
    benefits, documentation, 201

Professionals—*Cont.*
    characteristics, 208–209, 274–275, 294, 331–332
    future, challenges, 194–201
    philosophy/values, discussion, 108–109
    roles/opportunities, 191–193
PROFILE, 387
Profit
    plan, 294
    prospects, 311–312
Programmers, role. *See* Leisure
Programming. *See* Agile Leisure Programming; Benefits-Based Programming; Diversity; Just-In-Time Programming
    involvement, 354
    management approaches, 361
Programs, 353–362
    choices, 414
    evaluation, 361–362
    evolving nature, 86
    fees/tuition, 270
    goals, development, 358
    leadership. *See* Direct program leadership
    personnel, 274
    planning, 360–361
        influencing factors. *See* Leisure
    process, 358–362
    types, 354–355
Proprietorship. *See* Sole proprietorship
Protestant work ethic, 61
Psychiatric facilities, 334
Psychoanalytic theory, 46–47
Psychological dimensions, 9
Psychological well-being, 98
    promotion, 16
Psychotherapy, 333
Public baths, 53, 58
Public benefit, 267
Public Broadcasting System (PBS), 98
Public hospital systems, 320
Public involvement, blurring. *See* Leisure
Public parks
    advocating, 177
    career opportunities, 193–194
    fees/charges, 194
    issues/trends, 195
    marketing orientation, 194
Public recreation, 80–81, 335
Public service mission, 266
Public/private sectors, cooperation, 429–430
Pure job, 41
Pure leisure, 41
Pure work, 41
Puritans, 65
    work ethic, 61
Pursuits, identification, 39

Q

QOLLA. *See* Quality of Life Leisure Administrators
Quad Rugby, 396
Quality
    commitment, 342
        building, 343–345
    importance. *See* Production
    personal responsibility, assumption, 344
    promotion, 342–343
Quality of life. *See* Life
    amenities, 220
Quality of Life Leisure Administrators (QOLLA), 382
Quality services, 194
    discussion questions, 368
    promotion, 341–342
Queen Mary exhibition, 308

R

Race/ethnicity, 9, 400–401
Racing. *See* Automobile racing; Dog racing; Horse racing
Racism, 401
Rails to Trails Conservancy (RTC), 217
Rails-to-trails corridors, 188
Rank and file members, 275
Raphael, 63
Rather, Dan, 125
RCRA. *See* Resort & Commercial Recreation Association
R.E.A.L. *See* Recreation Education Activities Leader
Realism, leisure (relationship), 105–107
Reality. *See* Virtual reality
Rebuild Iowa Infrastructure Fund, 216
Recapitulation theory, 46
Recognition. *See* Rewards/recognition
Recovery sites. *See* Ecological recovery sites
Recreation. *See* Adventures; Inclusive recreation; Outdoor recreation; Public recreation; Therapeutic recreation
    activities, 23–24, 187
    advocating, 177
    agencies, goals/functions, 171–173
    areas, 182, 183, 436
    boards, 180
    career opportunities, 193–194
    center, 84
    definition, 42
    departments. *See* Military recreation departments
    discussion questions, 49
    economic function, 232
    fees/charges, 194
    golden/zenith ages, comparison, 73
    introduction, 30–31
    issues/trends, 195
    laws. *See* Special park/recreation laws
    marketing orientation, 194
    participation, direct programs, 230
    professionals, 336
    program, 332
        services, 183
    promotion, 232
    regulations/standards, 232
    research, 232
    resources, direct management. *See* Outdoor recreation resources
    services, 170, 249–250. *See also* Schools
        providing, 178–184
        resource base, 173–175
    social instrument, 43–44
    societies/associations, 380
    systems, 207
    technical assistance, 232
    theory, 46
    trends/issues. *See* Local government
    young children, participation location, 150
Recreation and Public Purposes Act, 213
Recreation Center for the Handicapped, Inc., 285
Recreation Education Activities Leader (R.E.A.L.) Program, 199
Recreation Therapy Section (NART), 322
Recreation Therapy Section (RTS), 322
Recreational activities, 116
Recycled goods, 438
Red Cross, 286, 322. *See also* American Red Cross
Reese (coach), 363
Referee. *See* Official/referee
Regional park areas, 182
Regulations. *See* Agencies; Recreation
Regulatory laws, 180
Rehabilitation, 249
    centers, 335
    programs. *See* Chemical-dependency rehabilitation programs; Substance abuse
Reich, Charles, 38
Relationships, closeness, 155
Relaxation theory, 46
Relaxed lifestyle, return, 435–436
Relief organizations, 286–287
Religion, 403
Religious organizations, 283–284
Religious-sponsored organizations, 282–283
Renaissance, leisure, 63–64
Rental fees, 272
Research. *See* Recreation; U.S. Forest Service
    fact finding, 376

Residential centers. *See* Disabilities

Resort & Commercial Recreation Association (RCRA), 381

Resorts, 302. *See also* Casino resorts

Resource depletion, 438

Resources. *See* Commercial leisure services; Federal government; Human resources; Outdoor recreation/resources

base. *See* Municipal parks; Nonprofit organizations; Recreation; State leisure services; Therapeutic recreation

decrease, 216

direct management. *See* Outdoor recreation resources

improved infrastructure. *See* Natural resources; Physical resources

overuse, 260

reclamation, 230

types. *See* State-provided direct recreation resources/services

usage, competition, 260

Responsiveness, 342. *See also* Frontline responsiveness

Restaurants, 302

Retail catalog showroom, 307

Retail outlets, 307–308

sales revenue, 207

Rethink, 382

Retirement benefits, 376

Retiring, 165

Revenue. *See* State government classification/types, 174

enhancement, 273

Revolutionary War, 215

Rewards/recognition, 376

Rhododendron Festival, 307

Riis, Jacob, 67

Risk, right, 22

Risk-taking behaviors, 42

ROM. *See* Royal Ontario Museum

Roosevelt, Theodore, 67

Rosh Hashanah, 412

Royal Ontario Museum (ROM), 223

RTC. *See* Rails to Trails Conservancy

RTS. *See* Recreation Therapy Section

Rules. *See* Agencies

Rural society, contrast. *See* Urban society

S

S Corporation, 298

Safety

increase, 444

need, 153

Sales

personnel, 367

revenue, 272. *See also* Concessions; Retail outlets

Same/different, aspects, 21

San Pedro Riparian Natural Conservation Area, 241

Satisfaction, relationship. *See* Leisure

Scholarships, 272

Schools. *See* Disabilities

belonging/involvement, 154

failure, 156

recreation services, 187

Science Math and Relevant Technology (SMART), 280, 281

Sea Lion Caves, 309

Sea World, 309

Secondary characteristics, 399, 403–404

interaction. *See* Primary characteristics

Security, 18

Segregation, 416–417

Seizures, 324

Self-actualization, 94

Self-confidence, 16

Self-consciousness, loss, 8

Self-definition, 155

Self-determination, 23, 329

Self-directed activities, 360

Self-directed leisure behavior, 162

Self-discipline, 65, 157

Self-esteem, 16, 158

building, 415–416

activities, 416

Self-expression, 18, 161

Self-forgetfulness, 47

Self-fulfillment, 97

Self-gratification, 97

Self-help, change. *See* Institutional help/self-help

Self-identification, 428

Self-improvement programs, 360

Self-knowledge, 102

Self-realization, 108

Self-reliants, 143–144

Self-worth, feeling, 154–155

Semi-independent boards, 180

Seminars, 361

Senior centers, 334

Seniors, usage. *See* Information

Sensitivity, 166

Sensory stimulation, 42

reduction, 16

Separatists, 65

Serious leisure, 39–40

Servant leaders, characteristics, 347

Service, 18, 177. *See also* Contracting services; Direct service; People with disabilities; Quality services; Value-added services

clubs, 288–289

definition, 345–346

orientation, development, 345

programs, evaluation, 342

providing, organizing strategy, 346–353

sector, growth. *See* Employment

types, 187–191. *See also* State-provided direct recreation resources/services

Service-type industries, 298

Seton, Ernest Thompson, 84

Settling-down period, 159

Sex discrimination, 429

Sex/gender, 401

Sexism, 401

Sex-stereotyped views, 427

Sexual activity, 126

Sexual orientation, 392, 402

Sexuality, 158

Sheltered workshops, 333

Shopping, 52

Sierra Club, 288, 382

Single-item commodities, 345

Six Flags, 304

Skill-development programs, 412

Skills. *See* Human skills; Interpersonal skills; Intrapersonal skills; Professional skills; Technical skills

acquisition, 16

Small leisure service businesses, 314

SMART. *See* Science Math and Relevant Technology

Snowmobiling, halting, 243

Social activities, 122, 124–125. *See also* Mass leisure

Social bonding, 20

Social capital, 123, 124

construction. *See* Leisure; Life

development, 199–200

Social competence. *See* Personal/social competence

Social conditions, 13

Social contact, 9

Social development, 156

Social health

changes, 434–436

decline. *See* Youth

Social inclusion, 327

Social instrument. *See* Leisure; Recreation

Social interaction. *See* Positive social interaction

Social leisure. *See* Value-free social leisure; Value-laden social leisure

activities, 125

Social pressure, 401

Social programs, addressing, 337–338

Social roles, changes, 427–429
Social Security, 144
Social service organizations, 287–288
Social skills/interaction, promotion, 16
Social status, symbol. *See* Leisure
Social trends, 421–427
Socializing, 52
  behaviors, 42
Socially deviant persons, programs, 335
Society
  margins/fringes, 397
  values, examination, 111
Society of Park and Recreation Educators
    (SPRE), 380
Socioeconomic groups, 417
Soldiers, influx. *See* World War soldiers
Sole proprietorship, 296–297
Solitude, 18
Sophisticated communications, 88
Southern hospitality, 219
Southwest State University, 396
Southwest Texas State University, 430
Special districts, 184–186
  laws, 180
Special events, 304, 307, 361
Special festivals, 304, 307
Special interest groups, 382
Special Olympics, 109, 331, 335, 417
Special park/recreation laws, 179
Special populations, organizations (service),
    284–286
Specialized services, need, 319–320
Specialty stores, 307
Spectator sports, attendance, 128
Spillover theory, 11
Spiritual attitude, 36
Spiritual development, 95
Spiritual fulfillment, 88
Spiritual needs, 22
Spiritual themes, 94
Sport system development, 252
Sporting goods, sales, 129
Sports, 122, 162, 360. *See also* Disabled
    outdoor sports; Professional
    sports
  activities, participation, 129
  attendance. *See* Spectator sports
  equality, increase. *See* Women
  mass leisure, relationship, 127–128
  participation, 128
Sports Canada, 252–253
Sports Line, 307
Sports-related violence, 150
SPRE. *See* Society of Park and Recreation
    Educators
Staff development topics, curriculum
    model, 410

Stages. *See* Life
  concept, 145
Standard Metropolitan Statistical Areas, 246
Standards. *See* Recreation
  creation. *See* State leisure services
  promotion, 375
Stanford Research Institute, 89
State agencies, involvement. *See* Arts
State fish/wildlife agencies, 215–216
State forests, 214–215
State government
  discussion questions, 226
  fees, 207
  introduction, 204
  revenues, 207
State hospitals/institutions, 222–223
State leisure services
  challenges, 224–225
  characteristics, 205
  federal/local governments, coordination,
    206–207
  fees/charges, 207
  goals/functions, 205–206
  legislation, 205–206
  resource base, 207–208
  standards/certifications, creation, 206
  taxes, 207
State of mind. *See* Leisure
State parks, 77–80, 211–214
  societies/associations, 380
State services, 222–224
State-provided direct recreation
    resources/services, types,
    209–210
Status, 399. *See also* Economic status;
    Marital status; Parental status
Stay-at-home dads, 428
Stay-at-home mothers, 427
Stewart, Martha, 144
Stimulation, 18, 20
Strategy enrichment, 273
Stress, increase, 433–434
Structure, need, 153
Strugglers, 143
Subject variables, 9
Substance abuse, 156
  costs, increase, 432–433
  facilities, 333
  rehabilitation programs, 223
Summer Citizenship School, 268
Supervisory roles, 191, 192
Support staff, 275
Surface culture, 395
Surgeon General. *See* U.S. Surgeon General
Surplus energy theory, 45
Surplus Property Act, 213
Survival skills, acquisition, 56

Syndicates, 60
Synergies, 273
Systems
  level, 410
  usage, 443–445

T

Task, concentration, 8
Taxes. *See* State leisure services
  exemption, 266
Taxpayer-subsidized access, 207
Teaching, 364
Team leadership, 365
Teaming, 344
Technical assistance. *See* Recreation
Technical certification, 387–388
Technical skills, 208
Technological change, 55
Technological era, 55, 86–90, 445
Technological extension, 421
Technology. *See* New technology
  improvement, 121–122
  influences, 441
  leisure, relationship, 139
  organizational impacts, 445
Teen Outreach Program. *See* Association of
    Junior Leagues
Teen pregnancy, leveling/increase, 434
Telephone Pioneers of America, 189
Television, 122
  effect, 136
  viewing, mass leisure, 134–136
Tennessee Valley Authority (TVA), 229,
    236, 246–248
Texas Travel Information Center, 219
Theme parks, 304, 386
  attendance (2000), 306
Therapeutic healing, 20
Therapeutic recreation (TR)
  challenges, 335–338
  characteristics, 324–327
  discussion questions, 339
  goals/functions, 328–331
  introduction, 318
  profession, emergence, 319–324
  programs/settings, types, 332–335
  resource base, 331
Thoreau, Henry David, 77
Thousand Trails, 308
Time. *See* Flex time; Free time; Leisure; Play
  bank, 441
  crunch, 117
  famine, 118
  society viewpoint, 119
  transformation, 8
  use, changes, 441–443

Tipi living, 190
Titian, 63
Title IX, 407, 429
    legislation, 150
Tobacco
    abuse, 432
    usage, 126
Tokyo Disneyland, 305, 306, 349
Total concentration, 148
Total immersion, 148
Total Quality Leadership (TQL), 362
Total Quality Management (TQM), 100,
        178, 362
Total Quality Program Planning (TQP), 362
Tourism, 360. *See also* Adventures; Travel
    activities, 123
    market. *See* Eco-tourism
    mass leisure, relationship, 131–134
    promotion, 217–219
Tournaments. *See* Leagues/tournaments/
        contests
TQL. *See* Total Quality Leadership
TQM. *See* Total Quality Management
TQP. *See* Total Quality Program Planning
TR. *See* Therapeutic recreation
Trade associations, 382
Traditionalists, 144–145
Trail systems, 216–217
Transportation, 445–446. *See also* Mass
        transportation
    network, 188
Transportation-centered destination points, 446
Travel, 360
    characteristics, 133
    promise, 132
    tourism, 89, 299–301
TREATS, 286
Tree City USA, 189
TRICOM, 301, 312
Trust for Public Land, analysis, 182
Trusts. *See* Endowments/trusts
Tuition. *See* Programs
TVA. *See* Tennessee Valley Authority
Twelve Together, 268

U

Underemployment, 72
Underpark, 21
UNESCO. *See* United Nations Educational
        Scientific and Cultural
        Organization
United Charities of Chicago, 287–288
United Nations Educational Scientific and
        Cultural Organization
        (UNESCO), 248
United Service Organization, Inc. (USO), 284

United States Auto Club, 127
Unity/uniformity, 392
University of Maryland, 117
University of Northern Iowa, 353, 382, 386
    Leisure Services Division, 406
Urban Council, Leisure Service Branch, 172
Urban forestry projects, 189
Urban society, rural society (contrast), 87
Urban Youth Initiative. *See* National
        Recreation and Park
        Association
Urbanism. *See* New Urbanism
U.S. Air Force, 249
U.S. Armed Forces, 228, 230, 236,
        249–250, 353
U.S. Army, 249, 250
U.S. Corps of Engineers, 229, 236, 246
U.S. Department of Agriculture, 235, 236
    Cooperative Extension Service
        program, 277
U.S. Fish and Wildlife Service, 229,
        235, 245
U.S. Forest Service (USFS), 121, 130, 228,
        229, 234–240
    cooperation, 239
    National Recreation Strategy, 241
    research, 239
U.S. Geological Survey, 248
U.S. Ice Hockey Association, 150
U.S. Marine Corps, 249
U.S. Navy, 249
U.S. Surgeon General, 432, 433
U.S. Travel Data Center, 299, 300
User conflicts, 437–438
    increase, 216
USFS. *See* U.S. Forest Service
USO. *See* United Service Organization, Inc.
Utopia, 94

V

VA. *See* Veterans' Administration
Vacations. *See* Disneyland
    nature, 443
    perspective. *See* Eco-vacations
Value
    change, 120–121
    clarity, need, 98–99
    discussion. *See* Professionals
    effect. *See* Life
    ethics, relationship, 98–99
    examination. *See* Local community;
            Personal values; Society
    perception, 352
    philosophy, relationship, 96–98
    promotion, 342–343
    underlying structures, 99

Value add-ons, 348
Value-added items, 348
Value-added services, 346–349
    features, 348
    order/cleanliness, 349
Value-free social leisure, 126–127
Value-laden social leisure, 126–127
Values clarification, 366
Values-free environment, 98
Variety store, 307
Vernacular. *See* Professional vernacular
Veterans' Administration (VA), 230,
        248–249
Vicarious experiences, 42
Video ordering system, 308
Videocassettes, production, 187
Vietnam War, 403
Violence, 156. *See also* Sports-related
        violence
    concern, 435
Virginia Company of London, 65
Virtual leisure, 144
Virtual reality (VR), 139, 444–445
    games/software, 441
Vision, 310
Visual arts, 360
Vocational competence, 157
Vocational training centers, 333
Voluntary agencies, programs, 335
Voluntary nonprofit leisure service
            organizations, types,
            275–276
Voluntary organizations, 44, 83–85
Volunteer services, 360
Volunteering, 360
Volunteers, 275
VR. *See* Virtual reality

W

Walt Disney Company, 312, 352
    adventures, 305–306
War Department, 245
Water pollution, 189
Water-based activities, 308
Welfare, 249–250
Well-being. *See* Physical well-being
    definition, 6–7
    promotion. *See* Psychological well-being
    relationship. *See* Leisure
    sense, 6
Wellness, continued interest, 433
West Suburban Special Recreation
            Association (WSSRA), 186
White-collar workers, 86
Wild and Scenic Rivers and National Trail
            System Act, 88

Wilderness. *See* Nontraditional wilderness
    allocation, 244
      cooperation/coordination, 244
      funding/training/education, 244
Wilderness Act, 243
Wilderness Preservation Act, 88
Wilderness Preservation System, 244
Wildlife agencies. *See* State fish/wildlife
    agencies
Wildlife areas, management, 215
Wildlife Refuge System, 245
Willamalane Park and Recreation
    Department, 188
Willamalane Park and Recreation District,
    102–103, 111–112, 185
Williams, George, 83
WLRA. *See* World Leisure and Recreation
    Association
Women, 393
    athletics equality, increase, 429
    critical mass, 395
    increase. *See* Workplace
    sports equality, increase, 429
    voice, 394
Woodcraft Indians, 84
Work. *See* Pure work
    alignment, 102
    definition, 40
    ethic. *See* Protestant work ethic; Puritans
    increase, 118
    leisure
      balancing, 43
      relationship, 11–12, 40–41
    life satisfaction, relationship, 11–12
    nature, changes, 446–447
    play/love/worship, combination, 94
    relationship. *See* Leisure
    schedules, 446
Work Project Administration (WPA), 71
Working class, 57, 417
Work-oriented activities, 35

Work-oriented behavior, 20
Workplace, women (increase), 431
Workshops, 361
World Leisure and Recreation Association
    (WLRA), 381–382
World Series, 127
World Tourism Organization, 218
World War I, 320
World War II, 71, 214, 320, 322, 356. *See*
    also Post–World War II
    veterans, 403
World War soldiers, influx, 320–322
World Wide Web, 89
WPA. *See* Work Project Administration
Written communication, 375
WSSRA. *See* West Suburban Special
    Recreation Association
Wyoming parks, 243

X-TATTOO, 338

Yellowstone National Park, 76, 301
Yellowstone Park, legacy, 75
YMCA. *See* Young Men's Christian
    Association
YMHA. *See* Young Men's Hebrew
    Association
Yosemite National Park, 301
Young children
    outdoor play, 80
    participation location. *See* Leisure;
      Recreation
Young Men's Christian Association
    (YMCA), 44, 83, 85, 106,
    150, 270, 282
Young Men's Hebrew Association
    (YMHA), 44, 84, 283

Young Upwardly mobile Professionals
    (YUPPIES), 345
Young Women's Christian Association of
    the United States of America
    (YWCA), 44, 83–84, 150,
    282–283
Young Women's Hebrew Association
    (YWHA), 44, 283
Younger children, developmental
    characteristics, 149
Youth
    basic needs, 153–156
    development, 198–199
      competencies, 156–158
      program framework, 156
    fitness, decline, 433
    leaders, 415
    social health, decline, 434–435
Youth at-risk. *See* At-risk youth
Youth nonprofit leisure service
    organizations, types, 275–276
Youth of America. *See* 4-H for Youth of
    America
Youth service opportunities, increase,
    268–269
Youth Services Program, 386
Youth serving organizations, 83–85,
    276–283
Youth-serving organizations, 44
YUPPIES. *See* Young Upwardly mobile
    Professionals
YWCA. *See* Young Women's Christian
    Association of the United
    States of America
YWHA. *See* Young Women's Hebrew
    Association

Zacharuski, Dr. Maria, 81
Zenith Era, 72